BY LARRY CARLEY AND THE
AUTO EDITORS OF CONSUMER GUIDE

DO-IT-YOURSELF
AUTO
REPAIR

CONTENTS

Louis Weber, President
Publications International, Ltd.
3841 W. Oakton Street
Skokie, Illinois 60076

Permission is never granted for commercial purposes.
ISBN 0-88176-295-4

Principal Author: Larry Carley
Illustrations: C. A. Moberg

Publications International, Ltd., has made every
effort to ensure the accuracy and reliability of the
information, instructions, and directions in this
book; however, it is in no way to be construed as a
guarantee, and Publications International, Ltd.,
is not liable in case of misinterpretation of the
directions, human error, or typographical mistakes.

Manufactured in the United States of America
1 2 3 4 5 6 7 8 9 10

DIAGNOSING CAR TROUBLE
79

THE STARTING SYSTEM
92

THE CHARGING SYSTEM
117

THE COOLING SYSTEM
127

THE FUEL SYSTEM
169

CONTENTS

CONTENTS

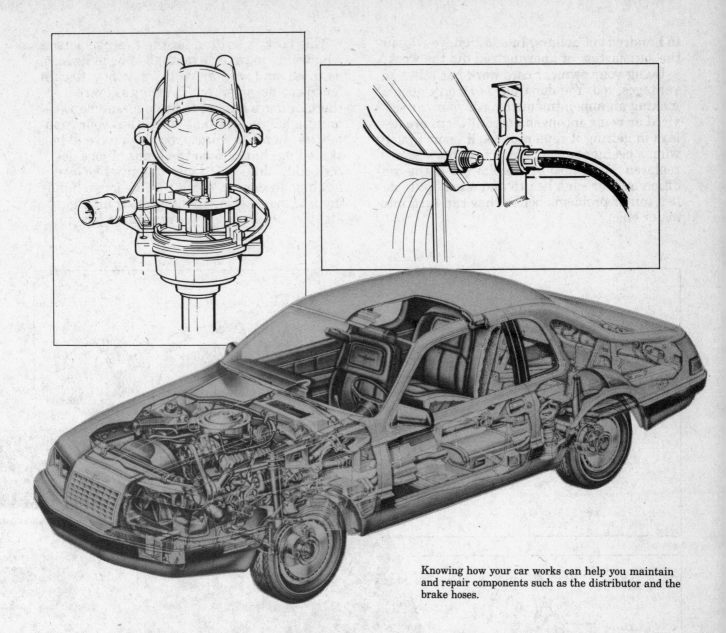

Knowing how your car works can help you maintain and repair components such as the distributor and the brake hoses.

INTRODUCTION

IF YOU'RE a typical car owner, you're probably spending close to $400 per year on maintenance and repairs if you're paying someone else to do all the work for you. Rising labor costs and high parts prices have more than offset the reduced maintenance requirements of most late model cars. The result is many car owners have turned to do-it-yourself maintenance and repairs as a means of saving money. Upwards of 75 percent of all car owners today perform at least some of their own service work, and that includes many women who have discovered do-it-yourself car care isn't limited to men only.

Doing your own work saves you 100 percent on labor and up to 40 percent or more on parts depending on where you buy them. Over the life of your car, these savings can add up to hundreds of dollars. In addition, you'll gain the satisfaction of knowing you did the work.

Doing your own car care work has other advantages, too. You don't have to worry about making an appointment to have your car serviced or being inconvenienced if there are delays in getting it repaired. You'll know exactly what's been done and what parts have been replaced. You'll also be more aware of the condition of your car's health and more apt to detect minor problems before they can turn into major ones.

This book is written for the average person who wants to take advantage of benefits such as these, and who wants to know how to care for his or her own car. The topics covered, therefore, are limited to basic maintenance and "light" repairs that are within your capabilities. In other words, you don't have to be a skilled mechanic to do the kinds of jobs described in this book. Major repairs like overhauling an engine, doing a valve job, rebuilding a transmission, aligning the front end, etc., are not included because these jobs re-

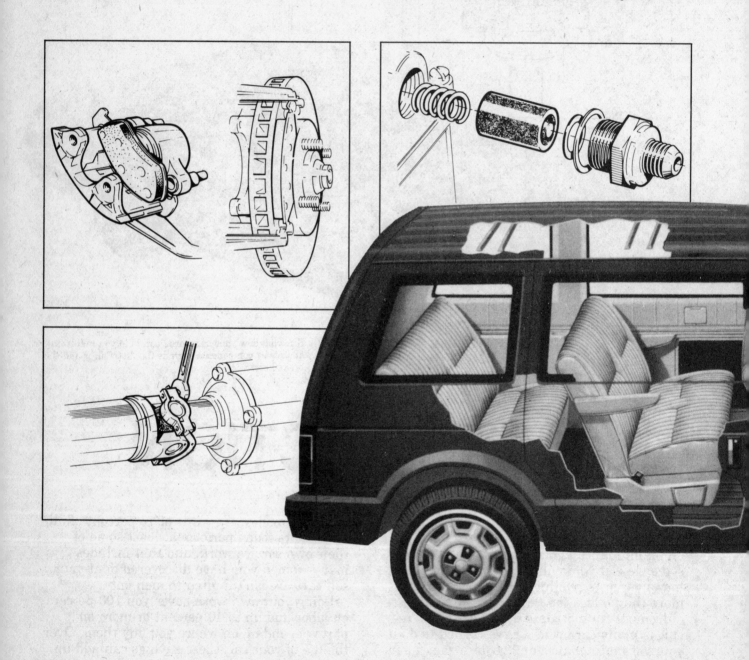

quire considerable expertise along with special tools and equipment. Such jobs are best performed by a professional mechanic.

This book is arranged in an easy-to-follow format with chapters covering car care basics and each of your car's major systems. Sections within each chapter give simple step-by-step instructions on how to do the job, tips on how to make the job easier, what tools and materials are required, any service precautions you should know about, and in some instances suggestions as to when you should leave the work to a professional.

Even if you can't do a job yourself (or choose not to do so) understanding the nature of the problem will enable you to discuss it intelligently with a mechanic. Knowing what's wrong and what needs to be done can prevent unnecessary and often costly repairs from being made.

It pays to take care of your car, and it pays to be an informed consumer. This book can help you accomplish both by taking the mystery out of car care.

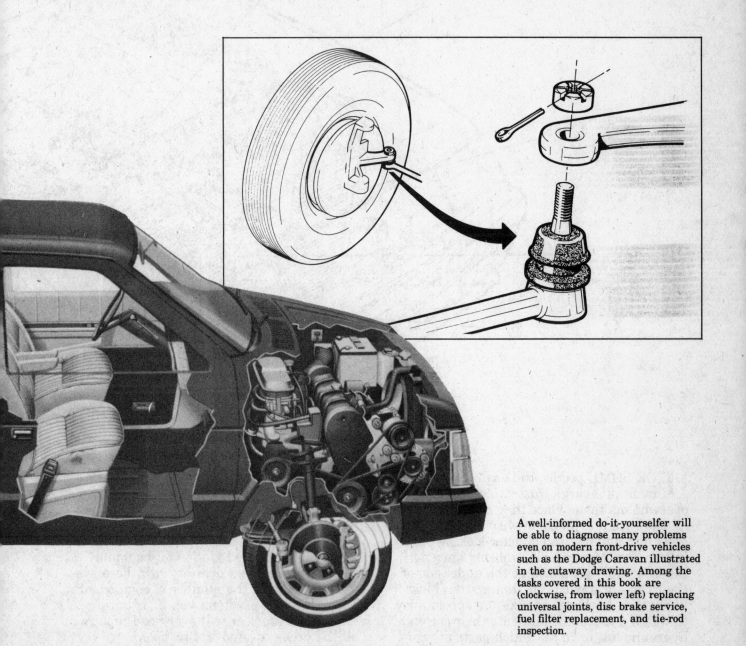

A well-informed do-it-yourselfer will be able to diagnose many problems even on modern front-drive vehicles such as the Dodge Caravan illustrated in the cutaway drawing. Among the tasks covered in this book are (clockwise, from lower left) replacing universal joints, disc brake service, fuel filter replacement, and tie-rod inspection.

GUIDE TO COMPONENTS

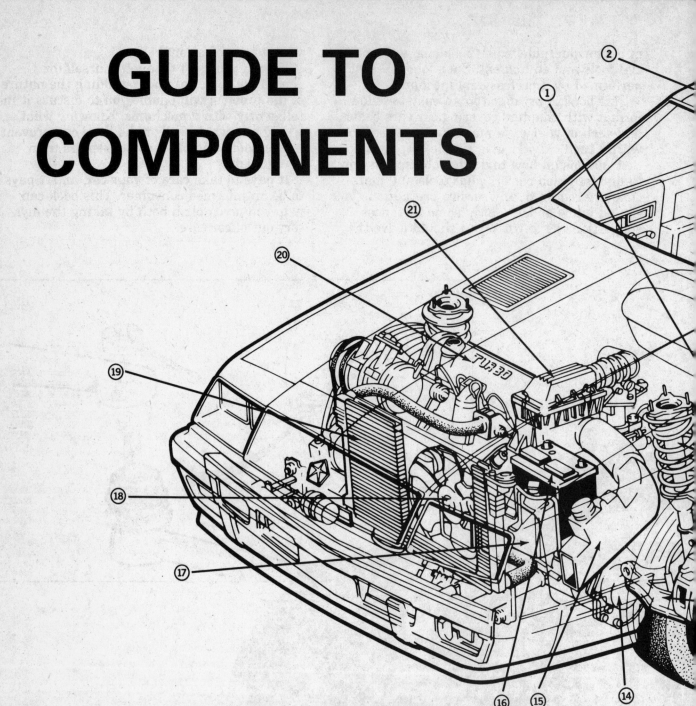

FOR SOME people, the engine compartment of a car is frustrating. It simply overwhelms them. Once they raise the hood, all they see is a jungle of wiring, a maze of belts and pulleys, and sinister-looking parts in between. Most people probably have not taken a really good look at the underside of their car—or any car for that matter. Most likely they neglected to take the opportunity to watch a mechanic lubricate their car on a hydraulic lift, or to see which parts are concealed behind a brake drum.

Now you have an opportunity to get to know your car intimately. Across these pages is a "Guide to Components" that pinpoints many of the parts of a typical car's major systems. More detailed views will be found within the chapters dealing with these systems. Do not let the number of components and systems overwhelm you. It is hardly likely that your car will ever need repairs in all the areas covered in this book.

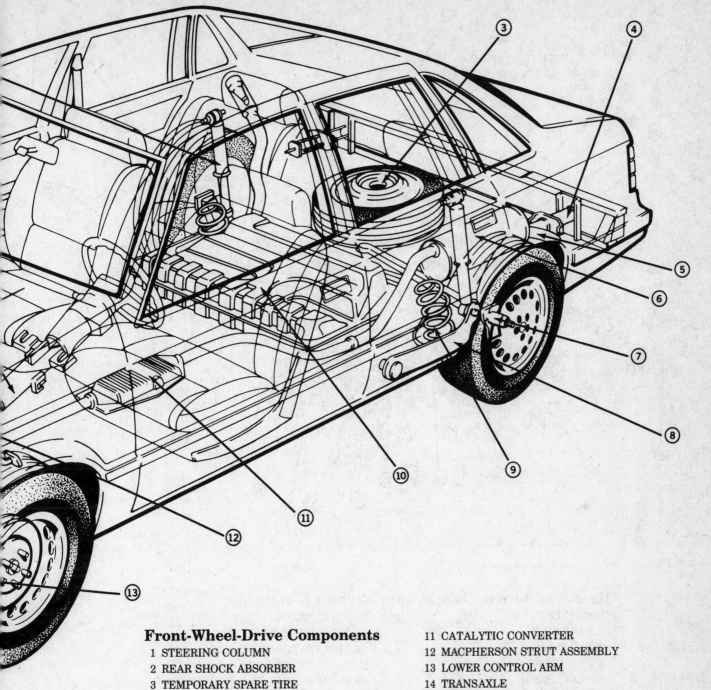

Front-Wheel-Drive Components

1 STEERING COLUMN
2 REAR SHOCK ABSORBER
3 TEMPORARY SPARE TIRE
4 BUMPER ENERGY ABSORBER
5 TAILPIPE
6 MUFFLER
7 REAR WHEEL SPINDLE AND BEARINGS
8 REAR SUSPENSION TRAILING ARM
9 COIL SPRING
10 GAS TANK

11 CATALYTIC CONVERTER
12 MACPHERSON STRUT ASSEMBLY
13 LOWER CONTROL ARM
14 TRANSAXLE
15 SPARK CONTROL COMPUTER
16 BATTERY
17 COOLANT RESERVOIR
18 ELECTRIC RADIATOR FAN
19 RADIATOR
20 TRANSVERSE-MOUNTED ENGINE
21 AIR FILTER HOUSING

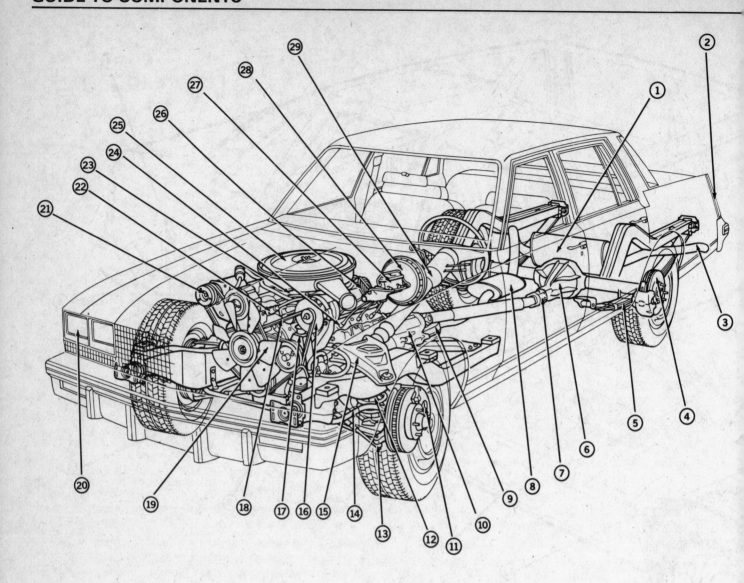

Rear-Wheel-Drive Components

1 MUFFLER
2 TAILLIGHT
3 TAILPIPE
4 DISC BRAKE
5 LEAF SPRING
6 DIFFERENTIAL
7 UNIVERSAL JOINT
8 RESONATOR
9 CATALYTIC CONVERTER
10 TRANSMISSION
11 DISC BRAKE CALIPER
12 SHOCK ABSORBER
13 TIE-ROD END
14 STABILIZER
15 UPPER CONTROL ARM
16 ALTERNATOR
17 POWER STEERING PUMP
18 ALTERNATOR DRIVE BELT
19 FAN
20 HEADLIGHT
21 AIR CONDITIONING COMPRESSOR
22 FUEL LINE FILTER
23 CARBURETOR
24 SPARK PLUG
25 AIR FILTER HOUSING
26 DISTRIBUTOR
27 MASTER CYLINDER
28 BRAKE VACUUM BOOSTER
29 STEERING COLUMN

DO-IT-YOURSELF AUTO REPAIRS

WHAT TYPE of maintenance and repairs can you realistically expect to do yourself? It depends on your abilities, knowledge and determination. The accompanying chart lists some common jobs, and rates them according to their degree of difficulty. If you're contemplating a job that's listed in a category beyond your current abilities, you'd be well advised to wait until you've gained more experience on some easier jobs before attempting to tackle the more difficult projects.

Although this book contains everything you need to know to complete the repairs listed in the table of contents, you may feel more comfortable attending an adult education class on basic car care at a local high school or community college before starting work on your own car—especially if you've never done such work before. Getting acquainted with the basics in a classroom/shop situation can help you feel more confident about what you're doing, and help you overcome the apprehension many newcomers often feel about tackling do-it-yourself car repairs.

Remember, for most maintenance and light repairs you don't need a great deal of mechanical skill or knowledge. But you do have to be willing to roll up your sleeves and get your hands dirty. That's part of the job, and sometimes you may find yourself having to crawl under the car or straining to reach a component buried in a cramped engine compartment. The job itself may not be very complicated, but the physical effort needed to do it may be more than you're up to doing. So know your limits, and if a job seems like more than you can handle, turn it over to a professional.

Service and Repairs You Can Do

THE FOLLOWING do-it-yourself repair guide to 100 common repairs divides the skill levels into three categories: beginner, intermediate, and advanced. Beginners are those with little or no previous experience. Using the instructions in this book, a beginner should be able to perform any of the jobs listed under that category. When you read down the list, you'll be amazed at the things beginners can do. The intermediate level is for those who have gained some mechanical experience and have a better understanding of how the various systems operate. The types of jobs listed under this category require a higher level of knowledge and competence to perform correctly. Again, anyone with intermediate skills should be able to handle the jobs listed with the help of this book. The advanced or professional level is just what the name implies. The jobs listed here require considerable knowledge and experience, and are beyond the scope of this book.

Under tool requirements, there are five categories: none, hand tools only, jack or ramps may be needed, special tools or equipment needed, and professional equipment. Some jobs such as checking the oil level require no tools. Others such as replacing a water pump require only ordinary hand tools such as wrenches, pliers and a screwdriver. A jack or ramps may come in handy for jobs that involve undercar repairs such as replacing the muffler or changing the oil. The category of special tools and equipment would include such items as an oil filter wrench for changing oil, a grease gun for lubricating the chassis, a spring compressor for changing a spring or MacPherson strut, a timing light for adjusting ignition timing, etc. The final category, professional equipment, would include such things as an alignment rack for wheel alignment.

This list is certainly not the final word on auto repairs. The degree of difficulty and the type of equipment required to perform any of the jobs listed can vary considerably from one vehicle to another. Rebuilding a one-barrel carburetor on an older pre-emissions-era vehicle is probably within the ability of most weekend mechanics, yet the majority of late model carburetors are so complicated that even professional mechanics sometimes have difficulty rebuilding them.

	Skill level				Tool/eqpt requirements			
	Beginner	Intermediate	Advanced or pro	None	Hand tools only	Jack or ramps may be needed	Special tools or eqpt needed	Professional eqpt
Check engine oil level	●			●				
Check automatic transmission fluid level	●			●				
Check manual transmission oil level	●				●	●		
Check differential oil level	●				●	●		
Check coolant level	●			●				
Check brake fluid level	●			●				
Check battery water level	●			●				
Change engine oil and filter	●				●	●	●	
Lubricate chassis	●					●	●	
Repack wheel bearings		●			●	●		
Test battery	●						●	
Recharge battery	●						●	
Replace battery	●				●			
Clean or replace battery cables	●				●			
Replace starter or solenoid	●				●	●		
Replace engine drive belt	●				●			
Test alternator or regulator		●					●	
Replace alternator or regulator	●				●			
Pressure test cooling system	●						●	
Check antifreeze strength	●						●	
Flush and refill cooling system	●				●			
Check electric cooling fan	●			●				
Check fan clutch	●			●				
Replace radiator or heater hose	●				●			

	Skill level				Tool/eqpt requirements			
	Beginner	Intermediate	Advanced or pro	None	Hand tools only	Jack or ramps may be needed	Special tools or eqpt needed	Professional eqpt
Replace thermostat	•				•			
Replace water pump	•				•			
Replace freeze plug	•				•			
Replace radiator	•				•			
Recharge air conditioner		•					•	
Replace A/C compressor			•		•		•	
Replace air filter	•			•				
Replace fuel filter	•				•			
Test fuel pump	•						•	
Replace fuel pump	•				•	•		
Adjust carburetor idle speed	•				•		•	
Adjust carburetor idle mixture		•			•		•	
Adjust carburetor choke		•			•			
Rebuild carburetor			•		•			
Replace carburetor	•				•			
Replace fuel injector	•				•			
Adjust diesel pump timing		•			•		•	
Test diesel injector			•		•			•
Replace diesel injector	•				•			
Replace turbocharger	•				•			
Test engine sensors			•				•	•
Replace engine sensors	•				•			
Test PCV valve	•			•				
Replace PCV valve	•			•				
Replace charcoal canister	•				•			
Replace EGR valve	•				•			
Replace air injection pump	•				•			
Replace catalytic converter	•				•	•		
Check vehicle emissions			•					•
Replace ignition points	•				•		•	
Replace distributor cap and rotor	•				•			
Replace electronic ignition pickup	•				•			
Replace electronic ignition module	•				•			
Replace ignition coil	•				•			
Replace spark plug wires	•				•			
Replace spark plugs	•				•			
Check and adjust ignition timing		•			•		•	

	Skill level			Tool/eqpt requirements				
	Beginner	Intermediate	Advanced or pro	None	Hand tools only	Jack or ramps may be needed	Special tools or eqpt needed	Professional eqpt
Replace ignition switch		•			•		•	
Replace diesel glow plugs	•				•			
Check engine compression		•			•		•	
Check engine vacuum		•					•	
Perform power balance test		•					•	
Repair leaky gasket	•				•			
Perform a valve job			•		•			•
Overhaul engine			•		•			•
Adjust engine valves		•			•		•	
Replace timing belt or chain		•			•		•	
Replace muffler or tailpipe	•				•	•		
Change automatic transmission fluid and filter	•				•	•		
Adjust clutch linkage		•			•	•		
Replace clutch			•		•	•		
Replace U-joint or CV-joint		•			•	•	•	
Replace axle or halfshaft		•			•	•	•	
Replace engine mount	•				•	•		
Replace transmission/transaxle			•		•	•		
Overhaul transmission/transaxle			•		•	•	•	•
Replace rack & pinion steering gear		•			•	•	•	
Replace tie-rod end	•				•	•	•	
Replace ball joint		•			•	•	•	
Replace coil spring		•			•	•	•	
Replace shock absorber	•				•	•		
Replace MacPherson strut		•			•	•	•	
Align front and/or rear wheels			•		•	•	•	•
Balance wheels and tires	•						•	•
Reline disc brakes		•			•	•		
Reline drum brakes		•			•	•		
Adjust brakes		•			•	•		
Replace brake caliper		•			•	•		
Overhaul brake caliper		•			•	•	•	
Replace wheel cylinder		•			•	•		
Overhaul wheel cylinder		•			•	•	•	
Replace master cylinder		•			•			
Overhaul master cylinder		•			•		•	
Bleed brakes		•			•	•		
Rotate tires	•				•	•		
Replace fuse	•			•				

Automotive Tools

THE FACT that you have made it this far indicates that you intend to tackle some service or repair jobs on your car. The degree of success and enjoyment you will derive depends on whether you are suitably equipped and working with the right facilities.

Give yourself every chance by having the proper tools for even the smallest job; a clean, well-lighted working area; plenty of time; and adequate instructions. Above all, be sure that whatever you do is done with safety in mind.

Most home mechanics do not have the benefit of a large, heated, and well-illuminated garage in which to work. If you happen to be one of the luckier ones, you are over the first hurdle. If not, try to borrow or rent the best facilities you can. If weather conditions are right, many jobs can be performed in your driveway during daylight hours.

If you do not have a workbench, you can make a makeshift work area near your car with a picnic table or even a sturdy panel of plywood supported by two trash cans. You will need something on which to keep your parts and tools in order. When working outside, you will need someplace to plug in a trouble light if the job continues into dark. Also, be prepared to protect your parts and tools in case of a sudden rain.

If there is a "fix-it" shop in your area where you can rent space and/or tools, you can have the benefit of adequate space, light, and tools, plus in rare cases, trained supervisory personnel to help you for a nominal rental fee.

Some backyard mechanics enjoy this avocation mainly for the satisfaction they get from working with good tools. Others like to see how much they can get done with as little help as possible. In either case, no one will deny that it can be frustrating not to have a tool when you need it. Or worse, to have an inferior tool that just chews up nuts, bolts, and screws.

Some of the tools you will need you may already have. Take an inventory before you start investing. And, take a good look at them to decide whether or not they are adequate.

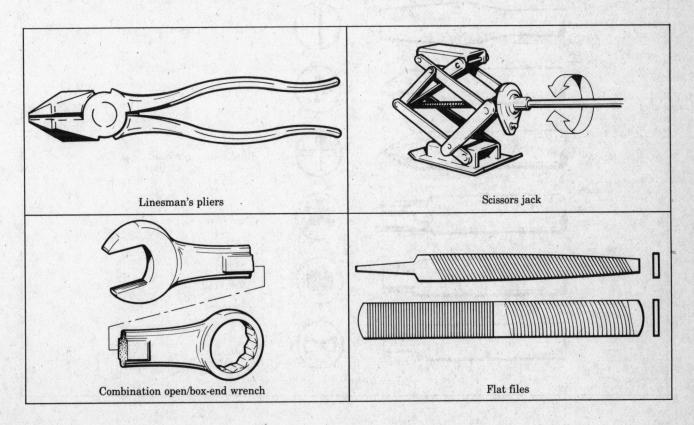

Linesman's pliers

Scissors jack

Combination open/box-end wrench

Flat files

As you begin to build your stock of tools and equipment, use the following list to determine your requirements. Then watch for sales in auto supply stores or for garage sales, and even study the classified section in your local newspaper. You may be able to accumulate a good set of tools and equipment for a modest investment.

Screwdrivers

Your basic tool kit should include several screwdrivers, both of the standard blade and the Phillips, or crosshead, types.

Standard screwdrivers are sometimes called "slot" or "flat" type screwdrivers. Unfortunately, they sometimes become identified with chisels, pry bars, scrapers, and other such items. Anyone who insists on using a screwdriver for these purposes should plan to increase the supply and reserve a few for the job for which they were intended.

Your ideal tool kit should have at least three standard screwdrivers in shaft lengths from 1½ to 8 inches. Remember, just because the blade is flat does not necessarily mean it will fit the screw slot properly. There are varying widths of screw slots and varying thicknesses of screwdriver blades. So, if you are starting out to buy a good set of screwdrivers, invest in a set that will give you at least a few blade thicknesses as well as several shaft lengths.

When considering price, remember this: The harder the blade, the better the tool. Such a tool will take more punishment and the handle will be of better quality.

Crosshead screwdrivers are sometimes known as Phillips or Reed and Prince screwdrivers. At first glance, both Phillips and Prince screwdrivers look alike. The difference is that the Phillips blade has a more blunted point than the Prince. Both types are named after the manufacturers of the screw for which they were designed.

The X-slot in a Phillips-head screw provides a socket for the screwdriver, permitting a stronger twist. The crosshead screwdriver is less likely to slip out of its screw than the standard type. Because there are varying ta-

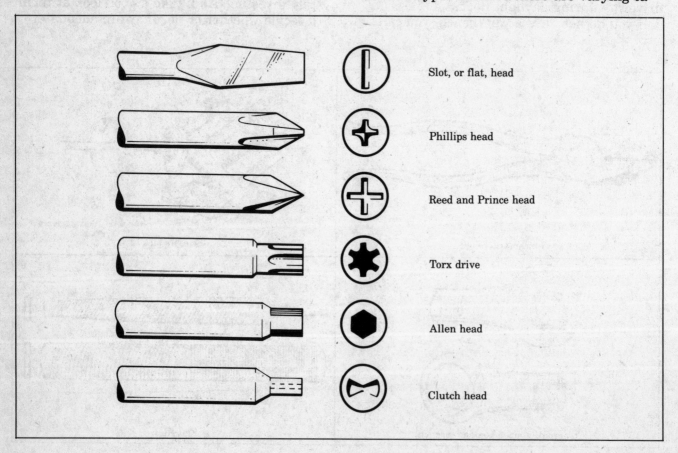

Slot, or flat, head

Phillips head

Reed and Prince head

Torx drive

Allen head

Clutch head

pers and depths of crosshead screw designs, you will minimize the danger of damaging a screw if you have an adequate selection of screwdrivers to accommodate most of them.

There are a number of screwdrivers for special applications. For example, your car may have some screws, especially trim screws, with an odd (hourglass) shape. These must be handled with a clutch-head screwdriver. On many late model cars, you'll also find both Torx-drive and Allen-head fasteners on trim panels, access panels and headlight covers. Again, you'll need special Torx-head screwdrivers or Allen-head wrenches to remove these fasteners. There are also offset screwdrivers, both crosshead and flat-blade, for use in tight places; ratchet offset screwdrivers to speed the job; and screw-holding screwdrivers to start or remove most sizes of standard slotted screws in tight places. Some screwdrivers have larger handles for extra twisting power.

You will find there is always "just one more" screwdriver that would make an ideal addition to your tool collection. Buy good ones—you will live with them for a long time.

Pliers

Virtually every tool drawer has pliers, usually the old faithful household type. That is a good start for any tool kit, but only the beginning.

Added to this, you might want interlocking or water-pump pliers, sometimes known as mechanic's pliers, which have as many as a dozen positions to accommodate the big jobs as well as the small ones.

Linesman's pliers have a beveled nose with a side-cutting jaw for trimming wire and cotter pins.

Long-nose or needle-nose pliers, as the name implies, have a pointed nose for getting into tight places and forming loops of wire.

Bent long-nose pliers are handy for retrieving small parts or doing other things where the straight long-nose pliers cannot fit.

Locking-jaw pliers can do the work of a pipe wrench as well as pliers. They are a valuable part of any tool kit, and are the most versatile pliers you can buy.

Snap ring pliers are another handy addition to your tool collection. This type of pliers is needed to remove snap rings on such parts as brake cylinders, U-joints, and starting drives.

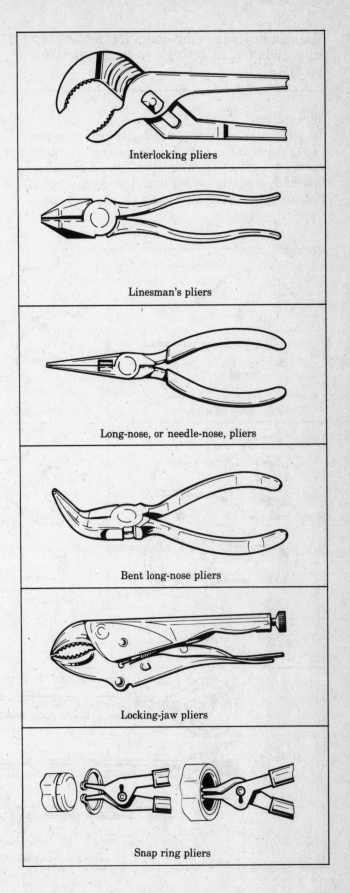

Interlocking pliers

Linesman's pliers

Long-nose, or needle-nose, pliers

Bent long-nose pliers

Locking-jaw pliers

Snap ring pliers

You can buy snap ring pliers for inside snap rings, outside snap rings, or ones that can handle both.

Wrenches
To turn a ½-inch nut, you could use any one of six different types of wrenches: a standard open-end, an adjustable open-end, a standard box-end, a combination box/open-end, a combination open-end/socket, or a ratcheting box-end. Among these are combinations of various size drives for the sockets, offsets for the box wrenches, and various handles and extensions.

It is nice to reach into a neatly organized toolbox and select the wrench that pleases you most, but such a variety is not necessary for most home mechanics. Instead, we suggest that you invest in a good set of combination wrenches, two good-quality adjustable wrenches, plus a set of ⅜-inch-drive ratchet-

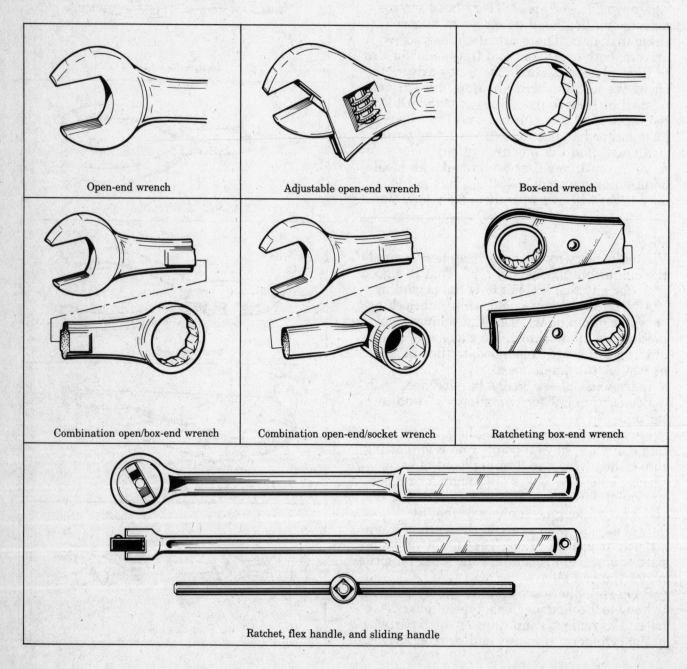

Open-end wrench

Adjustable open-end wrench

Box-end wrench

Combination open/box-end wrench

Combination open-end/socket wrench

Ratcheting box-end wrench

Ratchet, flex handle, and sliding handle

sockets. Consider, too, a set of ratcheting box-end wrenches.

If your car has a conventional ignition system rather than an electronic one, invest in an ignition tool set, which includes small ignition wrenches, screwdrivers, and, possibly, feeler gauges.

A torque wrench is another type of wrench you should consider buying, especially if you plan to tackle repairs beyond simple maintenance. A torque wrench is essential for many types of repairs because it allows you to tighten fasteners exactly to factory specifications. Using a torque wrench helps prevent over-tightening which can break off fasteners—and not getting a fastener tight enough, so that it might work loose later on. This is very important when it comes to brake and suspension work. All torque wrenches today are calibrated in both English (lbs./ft.) and metric (Newton meters or N.m). The least expensive variety is the beam type. The dial

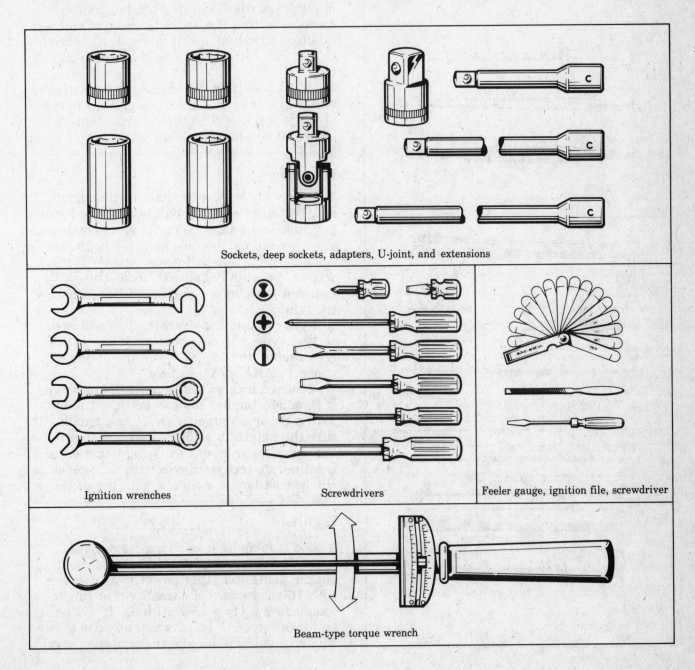

Sockets, deep sockets, adapters, U-joint, and extensions

Ignition wrenches

Screwdrivers

Feeler gauge, ignition file, screwdriver

Beam-type torque wrench

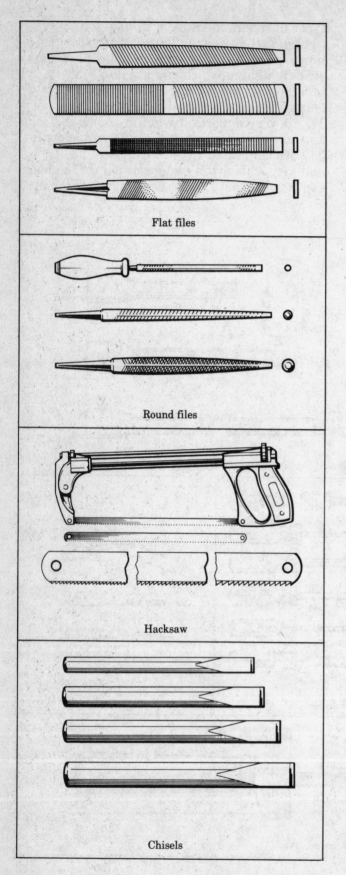

Flat files

Round files

Hacksaw

Chisels

type and adjustable torque wrenches are intended more for professional mechanics.

Files, Chisels, and Cutters

You could virtually fill your toolbox with a selection of files, chisels, punches, hacksaws, cutters, snips, and other metalworking tools. For most car maintenance other than body repairs, this is unnecessary. But it is advisable to have a few basic items—including a flat file and a round file (these can serve a variety of purposes when working around your car); a hacksaw with a few spare blades (get the best quality you can afford, it is worth it); a flat chisel; and cutters, tin snips, and wire cutters.

All of these items are handy to have around and, while they may not be necessary in most of the jobs you will be undertaking, sooner or later you will have a need for them.

Hammers

You probably have a hammer or two right now. Whether or not it will be suitable for automotive work depends on its size and shape. The carpenter's, or claw, hammer is fine for some jobs, but the ball-peen hammer is what you are eventually going to need. This has a rounded peen on one end and a flat face on the other.

If you get into body repairs, you will need several types of soft hammers or one with a replaceable tip that gives you the option of a rubber, plastic, or other face.

Seasoned hickory is the most common type of hammer handle. You can get into trouble with a cheap hammer with a weak handle. Be sure the handle is well secured and that it has no splits or cracks. A flying hammerhead is lethal. Protect your eyes with safety glasses whenever there is a chance of flying metal.

Lights

A good trouble light is a long-term investment. Most have a grounded outlet for plugging in drills and other power tools. Get one with 16-gauge wire of a quality that can accommodate up to a 75-watt bulb. If you need an extension cord, be sure you buy one of sufficient capacity to handle the load that may

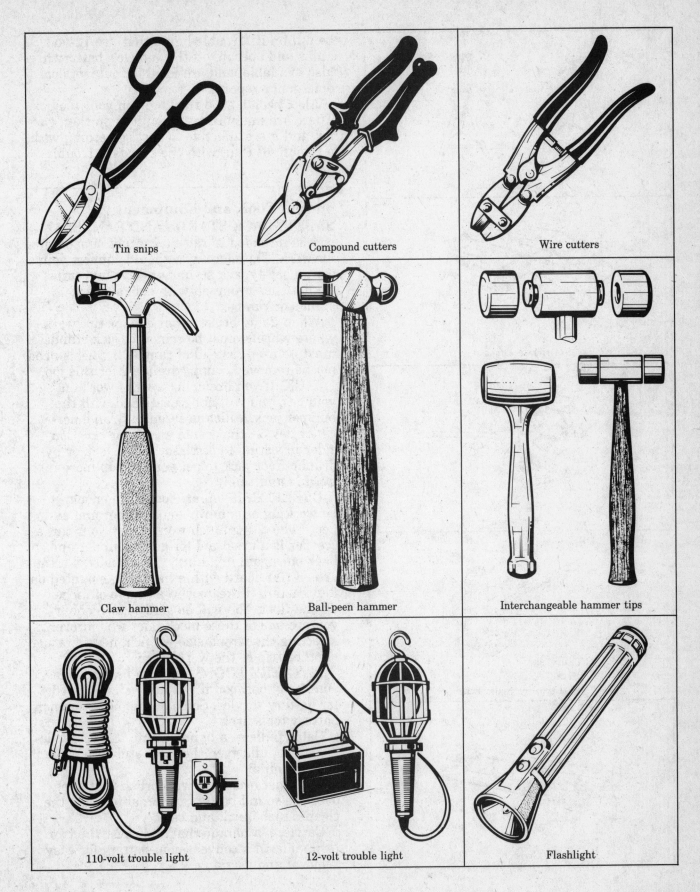

Tin snips

Compound cutters

Wire cutters

Claw hammer

Ball-peen hammer

Interchangeable hammer tips

110-volt trouble light

12-volt trouble light

Flashlight

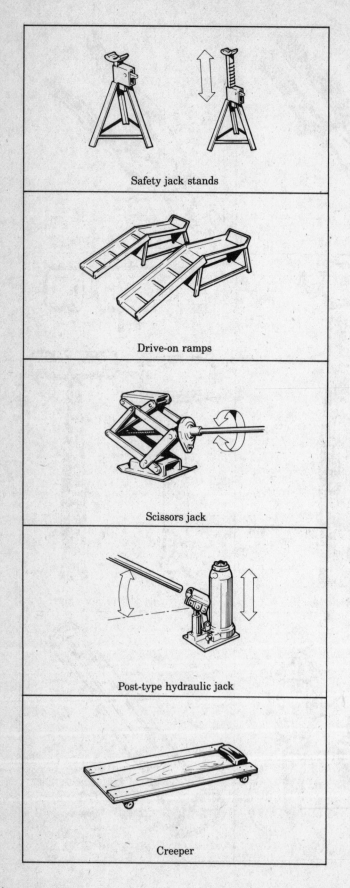

Safety jack stands

Drive-on ramps

Scissors jack

Post-type hydraulic jack

Creeper

be put on it. Trouble lights that use 12-volt bulbs and operate off the vehicle's battery are also available, and are ideal for outdoors or emergency repairs.

Also, keep a good flashlight in your toolbox. There are many times when it is quicker, easier, and more effective to spot something with a flashlight than with the standard trouble light.

Special Tools and Equipment

SAFETY JACK STANDS AND RAMPS. A jack is intended to raise a car, not support it for work. Therefore, you should support your car on safety jack stands or drive-on ramps. Do not cheat yourself with cut-rate jack stands or ramps.

When doing brake, front end, or tire work where wheels must be removed, jack stands must be used instead of ramps. If wheels need not be removed, ramps are ideal for this job.

JACK. If you are doing a lot of work on your car, you will not be satisfied with the bumper jack, which is essentially an emergency device, that came with your car. Consider investing in a scissor tripod jack or hydraulic floor jack to get your car up more quickly and safely.

CREEPER. If you are fortunate enough to be working on a hard, smooth floor and expect to be doing much work under your car, a creeper is a great aid for getting under and back out again in a hurry. Essentially, a creeper is a flat board with a headrest, mounted on four casters. It keeps you a couple of inches off the floor. You will be glad to own one if you are one of those mechanics who forever is selecting the wrong size wrench, necessitating another trip to the workbench.

BATTERY TOOLS. You can be a hero in your neighborhood if you are well equipped for battery service. Some of the more common battery tools are:

Cable puller—a handy clamp and screw device that pulls even the most stubborn cable off a terminal.

Terminal brush—a wire brush that slips over the round battery terminal to make the cleaning job quick and easy.

Carrier—a handle that slips over the two terminals on a conventional battery for easy removal and carrying.

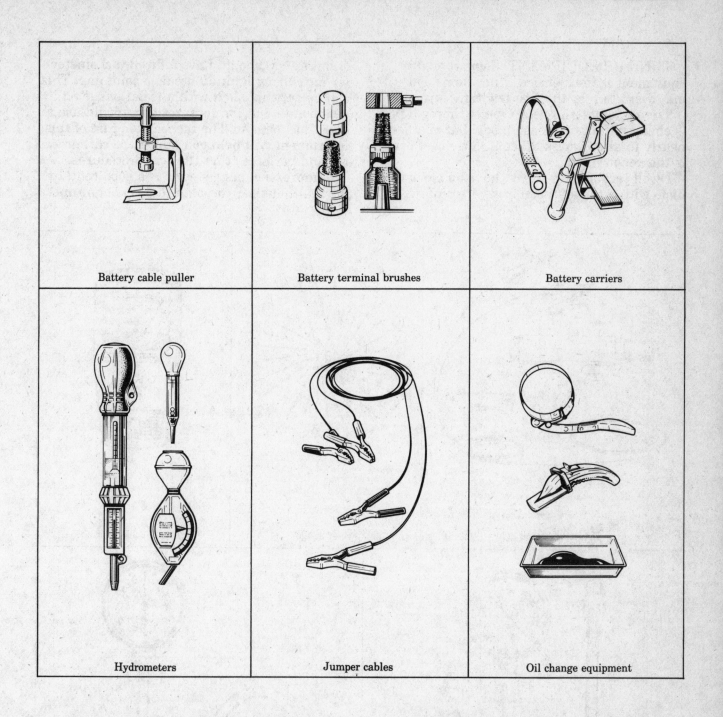

Battery cable puller   Battery terminal brushes   Battery carriers

Hydrometers   Jumper cables   Oil change equipment

Hydrometer—a syringe that measures the specific gravity of your battery fluid to determine its state of charge.

Jumper cables—you already may have jumper cables in your car. Take a look and make sure they are of adequate quality to do the job. They should have sufficient strands of wire, offering the least resistance to deliver the maximum current from the "jumper" to the "jumpee." Handles and wire should be well insulated and properly secured.

OIL CHANGE EQUIPMENT. An oil filter wrench is a simple strap wrench that eases the job of filter removal and installation. It will pay for itself the first time you use it. For an oil drain pan, an old metal dishpan will do the job if it has sufficient capacity. Or, you can buy an inexpensive galvanized or plastic pan that becomes a carry-away container for drained oil.

TUNE-UP EQUIPMENT. Some tune-up equipment is inexpensive; other items you may want to rent the first few times around.

Timing light—the neon type of timing light is cheaper than the xenon model but you need nearly total darkness to see it. Your best bet is the xenon light.

Dwell-tachometer—if you have an older vehicle with a conventional breaker-point dis-tributor, you should have a dwell-tachometer for measuring ignition breaker-point gap. This can be accomplished with a feeler gauge on new points, but for accuracy you should use a dwell-tachometer. The tachometer part of this instrument will help you adjust the carbure-tor and perform other tune-up procedures.

Compression gauge—this is a good rental item, although if you plan to do enough tune-

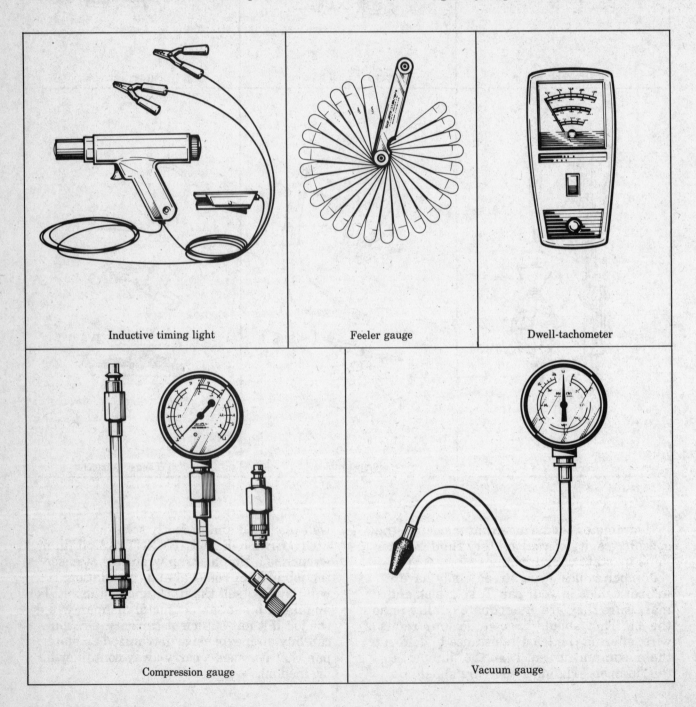

Inductive timing light

Feeler gauge

Dwell-tachometer

Compression gauge

Vacuum gauge

up work, you may want to make the investment. This gauge, which checks compression pressure in each cylinder, can alert you to valve problems or piston ring trouble. A compression test is important, especially on older cars.

Vacuum gauge—this is a valuable and inexpensive gauge that should be a part of any tune-up kit. Properly used, it can inform you about your ignition timing; manifold leaks; carburetor, valve, or head gasket problems; and even a clogged muffler.

Feeler gauge—there are two types of feeler gauges, both of which may be included in a single tool. The round wire type is used for checking and adjusting the spark plug gap. The flat type is for ignition breaker-point spacing and for adjusting valves on cars that have adjustable valve tappets.

TIRE AIR PRESSURE GAUGE. This tool can save its price in a short time. Because improperly inflated tires wear out fast, it is a good idea to carry a tire gauge in your car's glove compartment and check the inflation pressure at least once a month and before every long trip.

LUG WRENCH. The lug wrench that came with your car's jack, like the bumper jack, is an emergency tool. If you are going to be doing considerable wheel removal, buy a cross-shaft wrench, which has four different socket sizes and provides you with much more leverage than you get with the standard lug wrench. It also provides a straighter, more even twist to prevent possible damage to the wheel nuts.

GREASE GUN. Whether or not you should invest in a grease gun depends on the age of your car and how many other pieces of equipment with lube fittings you own. A small grease gun is inexpensive, and it is certainly easy enough to pump a little extra grease into the fittings when you are doing chores under your car.

MISCELLANEOUS ITEMS. On some jobs, when you are handling a number of small parts, it is a good idea to have a couple of egg cartons in which to keep everything clean and orderly.

Start out right by having a professional-type hand cleaner (available from auto supply stores) and plenty of clean rags. You also may

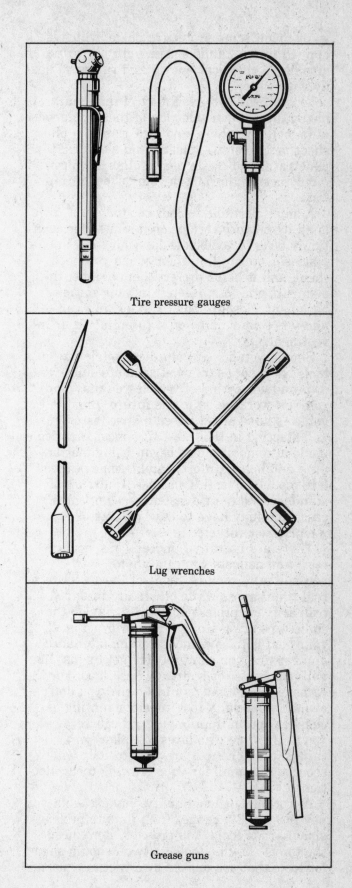

Tire pressure gauges

Lug wrenches

Grease guns

want to get some protective paste, which is applied to the hands before work is started. It acts like a chemical "glove" and rinses off easily with water.

You can save yourself a lot of time and trouble by including a selection of the popular-size nuts, bolts, washers, and lock washers, plus sheet metal screws, plastic and electrical tape, penetrating oil, sealers, and other such commonly used materials in your "shop" inventory.

A small portable toolbox to store your tools is an item every serious do-it-yourselfer eventually buys. A toolbox keeps your tools in one place so you can find them when you need them, and it helps protect them against the elements and loss. Keep it in your garage, basement, closet, or the trunk of your car—and write your name on it to protect your investment.

Should you buy standard or metric size tools? It depends on what kind of vehicle you own and what kind of vehicle you may find yourself working on in the future. Imported vehicles have always used metric fasteners, and starting in the late 1970s most American-made automobiles also began using metric nuts and bolts. Unfortunately, some of these late model domestics also use a mixture of standard and metric fasteners, so in some cases you may have to buy two sets of wrenches or sockets.

There are literally hundreds of specialty tools and gadgets you can buy for do-it-yourself auto repairs. Some of these tools are real time-savers while others are intended primarily for professionals who may do the same type of repair over and over again. If your goal is to save money on maintenance and repairs, you can probably get by just fine with the basic tools already described. For the occasional job that requires a tool you don't own or a specialty tool, consider renting as a cheaper option than buying. Of course, if you're the type who loves to tinker with things, then chances are your toolbox will soon be too small for your growing tool collection.

A word about tool quality: you get what you pay for. Quality ranges from junk to professional-grade tools. You probably don't need the top-of-the-line tools, but you should shop for tools that are backed by a lifetime guaran-

tee and are made from quality materials. Most of the bargain tool sets that sell for incredibly cheap prices are not worth buying unless you plan to use them only once.

You can save up to 50 percent or more on your tool purchases by buying your tools in sets. Sets of wrenches, screwdrivers, sockets, or even complete tool sets with a toolbox are usually priced far less than what it would cost to buy each tool separately. Waiting for seasonal sales can save even more.

Safety Precautions

NO BOOK about do-it-yourself auto repair would be complete without a section covering repair safety. Most of the suggestions we're about to make are common sense precautions that should always be observed when working on, under, or around an automobile. Other warnings you probably don't know about if you're new to working on cars. So please read the list carefully and remember to follow these rules for your own personal safety.

● Remove all jewelry such as rings, watches, and bracelets before starting work. Don't wear loose-fitting clothing, ties, scarves, or coats that might get tangled up in a pulley or drive belt. Keep fingers, hands, hair, clothing, and tools away from moving parts such as the fan, belts, pulleys, and driveshaft.

● Never crawl under a car that isn't adequately supported and never rely on the jack alone to hold it up. The car should be on level ground, with the transmission in gear (manual) or park (automatic), the emergency brake engaged, and one or more wheels blocked with a brick or piece of wood to prevent it from rolling. After raising the car, you should place a jack stand (preferably a pair of jack stands) underneath to support the vehicle's weight. The jack stands should be positioned under a strong part of the chassis—such as the frame rails, control arms, rear axle, or bumper supports—and the jack lowered so that the weight is supported by the jack stands, not the jack. If you don't have jack stands, use something that can safely support several thousand pounds, such as concrete blocks or wood four-by-fours. Don't use milk cartons, footstools, garbage cans, or boxes.

- Don't smoke when working on the fuel system or battery. Gasoline vapors from the fuel tank, fuel lines, carburetor, or fuel injectors are extremely flammable. Hydrogen gas inside the battery is explosive and can be set off by any small spark. It's a good idea to refrain from smoking any time you're working on a car.

- If jump-starting a battery, don't make the final jumper cable connection to the battery itself. Make the final connection to a good ground such as the engine block, frame, or chassis, well away from the battery. The final connection often produces a spark, so keeping the spark away from the battery eliminates the danger of any hydrogen gas exploding. If charging a battery, make the battery connections first and then turn on the charger. This, too, will prevent sparks near the battery.

- Don't do anything that would produce a spark or flame near a leaky gas tank or fuel line. This includes using electric power tools, grinding, welding, or using a propane torch to loosen rusted fasteners. Fix the leak first, then do the other repair work.

- Wear protective eye gear when working under the car, when using a chisel and hammer, when drilling or grinding, and when working on the air conditioning system. The Freon refrigerant inside the air conditioning system can cause frostbite if it comes in contact with exposed skin.

- Avoid breathing the dust from brake linings and clutches. It may contain asbestos dust, a possible carcinogen. Use a liquid cleaner, a vacuum cleaner, or an old paintbrush to remove dust from brake parts.

- Never run an engine inside a closed garage. The buildup of carbon monoxide fumes, which are odorless and colorless, can be lethal. If you must run the engine, open the garage door or vent the fumes outside with a length of tubing.

- Don't open the radiator cap while the engine is hot. Pressure can spray hot water out of the radiator. Also, do not leave antifreeze sitting around in open containers where children or pets may try to drink it. Antifreeze is poisonous if taken internally. The same goes for brake fluid, gasoline, crankcase oil, transmission fluid, power steering fluid, and windshield washer solvent. If antifreeze is splashed on your car's finish, wash it off immediately because it can damage the paint.

- Be careful to avoid touching spark plug wires or the ignition coil high voltage lead while the engine is running. The ignition system carries 20,000 to 40,000 volts of electricity—not enough to kill you but certainly enough to give you a nasty shock if you're careless.

- When doing any kind of electrical work such as replacing a starter, ignition switch, alternator, voltage regulator, radio, etc., it's wise to disconnect the battery ground cable first. This eliminates the possibility of accidentally grounding the circuit and starting a fire or damaging some component in the electrical system.

- On late model vehicles with computerized engine controls, the vehicle computer is very sensitive to voltage overloads. The battery should always be disconnected before charging. Jump-starting should only be done with another 12-volt battery, never a 24-volt generator as some tow trucks use. Before disconnecting any electrical connector in the wiring harness, the key should be off. Above all, if you don't know what you're doing, don't try to jump or test any engine systems or wiring connections or you may ruin an expensive computer or sensor.

• Batteries contain sulfuric acid, so treat them with respect when handling them. Be careful not to upset the battery or to spill acid on the car's finish when installing or removing a battery. Protect your hands with rubber gloves and your eyes with goggles. Corrosion on the outside of the battery can leave an acid residue that will eat holes through clothing, so don't wear your Sunday best when doing battery work.

• Never use gasoline as a cleaning solvent. The vapors are explosive and can be ignited by the pilot light from a nearby furnace or hot water heater. Use kerosene or a cleaning solvent designed especially for this purpose. Put solvent rags into an airtight metal container.

• When disposing of old antifreeze, crankcase oil, or cleaning solvents, don't pour them down the drain or into a storm sewer. Instead, pour them into a sealable container and take them to your local oil recycling center for disposal.

Shopping For Parts

ANOTHER important element of do-it-yourself car care is buying filters, fluids, and replacement parts for your car. Obviously, you want the best price, but you also have to be careful about the quality of the products you buy. As with tools, the product's quality is often reflected in its price. This isn't to say a lower price means lesser quality—often it doesn't. But be wary of really cheap merchandise. Bargain filters use cheap paper that doesn't adequately filter the air. Cheap gaskets made from recycled materials can begin to deteriorate and leak within a few miles. Low-quality ignition parts such as distributor caps, rotors, and plug wires will not last as long as parts manufactured from higher-grade materials. Cheap mufflers with thin metal shells and little or no corrosion protection will not last like the original equipment quality-level replacements that are coated inside and

out to prevent rust.

The consumer's best advice here is to shop for products that are sold under a well-known or recognized brand name, and are backed by a manufacturer's guarantee.

To add to the confusion of shopping for parts, some unscrupulous merchandisers have resorted to using look-alike packaging, or trademarks that are nearly identical to quality brands. Read the packaging label carefully, and if you see words like "replaces original equipment part number so-and-so" and you don't recognize the manufacturer or brand name, it may be an inferior product.

Where you shop for your parts can determine how much money you save. At a new-car dealership, you'll pay full list price for original equipment parts. By shopping around, you can save up to 40 percent or more. Your best buys will be found in "discount" auto parts stores and retailers.

On some types of parts, you're faced with another option: new versus rebuilt (or remanufactured). On parts such as carburetors, master cylinders, and distributors, you can save 40 percent to 60 percent by purchasing a rebuilt replacement instead of a brand new one. A quality rebuilt part is just as good as new, and in some cases actually better. But not all rebuilt parts are a good buy. In some cases, the rebuilder has skimped on quality to maintain a very low price. Again, shop for the product that is sold under a recognized brand name and is backed by a written guarantee.

There is yet a third alternative when it comes to buying replacement parts, and that is buying used parts from a salvage yard (they don't call them junkyards anymore). You can find some real bargains here. Many salvage yards will guarantee the parts they sell as being in good working condition—which doesn't mean they're as good as new but they may be a more economical alternative to buying new or remanufactured parts. Some salvage yards will sell you a pre-tested part off the shelf, while others require you to take it off a wreck yourself. The salvage yard is a good choice for body parts and major components such as engines, transmissions, and rear ends. But for high-wear parts such as alternators, starters, water pumps, ignition parts, etc., you're better off buying new or rebuilt.

MAINTAINING YOUR CAR

IN SPITE of all the talk about today's new cars being nearly maintenance-free, remember that low maintenance doesn't mean no maintenance. True, cars today don't require as much care as those of a decade ago, but they still need a certain amount of attention to keep them in good running condition.

Maintenance neglect is a serious problem. Self-serve gasoline has eliminated the mechanic who used to check your oil for you, and who was apt to spot a potential problem such as a leaky hose, clogged air filter, or frayed fan belt before it failed. Today, too many motorists have become "gas-and-go" drivers completely unaware of the deteriorating condition of their car—until something breaks and causes a problem.

Maintaining your car means preventing premature wear, and the problems wear can cause, through regular periodic inspections and replacement of wear-prone components. This includes such things as the motor oil, automatic transmission fluid, coolant, filters, and various engine, suspension, and brake components that are subjected to rubbing, sliding, turning, pounding, heat, corrosion, or extreme pressure.

Your car's maintenance items should be checked and/or replaced according to the mileage and time recommendations in your owner's manual, or according to the schedule we've suggested in this section. Many professional mechanics believe the service interval recommendations in new-car owner's manuals are overly optimistic for the average driver, and instead suggest intervals that are more frequent. Some car manufacturers recommend 50,000-mile replacement intervals on air filters, PCV valves, and engine coolant in their

owner's manuals—an interval that may only be appropriate for the high-mileage driver who covers a lot of miles in a short period of time. Factory recommended oil change intervals of 7500 to 10,000 miles, with filter changes suggested at only every other oil drain, likewise are probably much too far apart for most short-trip, stop-and-go drivers.

Motor oil should be changed regularly, not because it wears out or because it becomes dirty, but primarily because the protective additives in it are mostly depleted after 3000 to 4000 miles of driving. Once they're gone, wear accelerates quickly. As for the oil filter, most mechanics think it is false economy to run clean oil through a dirty filter. Therefore, they recommend a new filter at every oil change.

Maintaining your car is a way of protecting your investment and it can save you money for several reasons.

(1) It can prevent small problems from becoming big expensive ones.

(2) It keeps your vehicle in good running condition, and that means easier starting, smoother running, peak performance, and fuel economy. This saves gas and reduces the possibility of an unexpected breakdown and the service call and towing charges that usually result.

(3) It helps your vehicle retain greater value so you'll do better when it's time to sell or trade your car for another.

(4) For those who live in areas that require periodic vehicle emissions tests, keeping your car properly tuned lessens the chance of failing the test—and that contributes to clean air.

(5) There's also the satisfaction of knowing you can depend on your car when you need it.

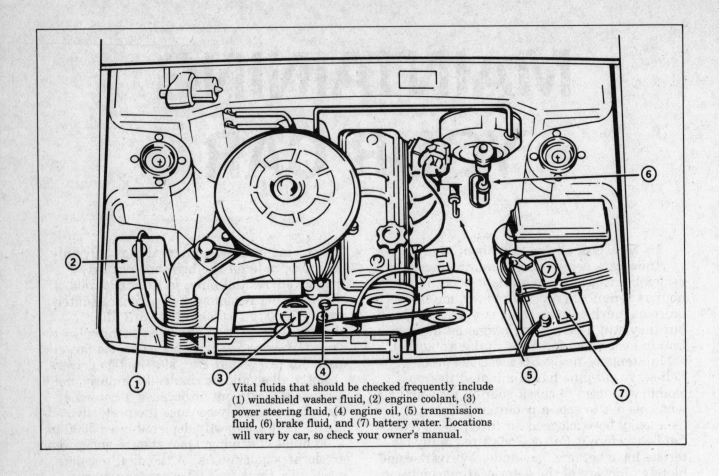

Vital fluids that should be checked frequently include (1) windshield washer fluid, (2) engine coolant, (3) power steering fluid, (4) engine oil, (5) transmission fluid, (6) brake fluid, and (7) battery water. Locations will vary by car, so check your owner's manual.

Maintenance and Safety Inspection Checklist

The accompanying checklist can be used to determine the overall condition of your vehicle. Check each item listed in the chart, and note whether the item is okay or if it needs service. Basically, you look for anything that appears loose, worn, cracked, leaking, or non-functioning.

A brief explanation of each item follows.

Steering play. Steering play should be less than one half inch when the steering wheel is rocked back and forth. Looseness indicates worn tie-rod ends or excessive play in the steering gear.

Brake pedal. The brake pedal should feel firm and travel no more than a few inches. A low pedal indicates worn brake linings or low fluid. A spongy pedal may mean a worn master cylinder or air in the brake lines.

Emergency brake. The emergency brake should lock the rear wheels and be able to hold the car on a slight incline or prevent it from moving when the transmission is put into gear. The rear wheels should turn freely once the brake is released.

Horn. A safety item that should be checked frequently.

Windshield wipers. The wipers should work at all speeds and should clean windows without leaving streaks. Replace blades if rotted, cracked, or pitted.

Windshield washers. The washers should squirt both sides of the windshield when activated.

Mirrors. Inside and outside mirrors should be clear and unobstructed. Check mountings for tightness.

Defroster. Warm air should blow onto the windshield when the defrosters are turned on. Rear window electric defoggers should make the glass feel warm to the touch.

Spare tire and jack. A spare tire and complete jack should be in the trunk. Check the condition and tire pressure of the spare. **(Note:** Some temporary spares are stored uninflated—make sure there is a pressure can to inflate it.) Check to see that all the pieces for the jack are there, and that the jack works. There should also be a lug wrench for the wheels. Better to discover a problem now than after a blowout or flat.

Fluid levels. Fluid levels should be maintained between the "full" and "add" marks. Engine oil should be checked with the engine off, after waiting several minutes for the oil to drain back into the crankcase. Automatic transmission fluid should be checked hot with the engine idling in park or neutral. Coolant level should be checked when the engine is cold and off.

Air filter. The air filter should not restrict airflow. A clogged or damaged filter should be replaced immediately.

V-belts. Check drive belts for looseness, fraying, broken strands, serious cracks, or glazing. Drive belts should be tight enough to prevent slippage but not so tight as to put undue strain on the belt or pulley bearings.

Radiator hoses. Inspect hoses for cracks or age hardening by squeezing them. Hoses should feel soft and pliable, not hard and brittle. Also check hose connections and clamps for looseness or leaks.

Heater hoses. Same as radiator hoses. Also check for rubbing against sharp objects or hot exhaust manifolds. Replace any damaged hoses.

PCV valve and hose. Check the PCV valve and hose with the engine running, by pulling the valve out of its housing and holding your thumb over the open end. You should feel a strong vacuum. Also, the valve should rattle when shaken (turn the engine off first).

Vacuum hoses. Vacuum hoses should be tight and free from cracks, kinks, or burn spots. Hose routing can be checked against the emissions decal under the hood.

Distributor cap. The cap should be free from cracks or other signs of electrical arcing or deterioration. Inside, it should be clean and dry, and the terminal contacts in good condition.

Spark plug wires. Terminals should fit into the distributor cap tightly, and boots should fit around the spark plugs snugly. The wires must be free of visible damage, chafing or burn spots. Arcing is most easily detected by observing the plug wires while the engine is running outdoors after dark.

Battery terminals. The terminals and cables should be tight and free from corrosion.

Headlights. Check both high and low beams. Aiming can be checked by parking about 20 feet from a wall or garage door and noting the light pattern. Both headlights should be aimed level and straight ahead.

Taillights. Check to see that all taillights work when the lights are on.

Brake lights. The brake lights should operate when the brake pedal is depressed.

Turn signals. Check both left and right, front and rear turn signals by working the turn signal switch with the ignition on.

License plate light. An often overlooked item that should come on with the headlights.

Backup lights. They should come on when the transmission is put into reverse.

Tire inflation. Check tire pressures when the tires are cold. Both front tires should have equal pressure, as should both rear tires.

Tire conditions. Look at the tread and note if there is uneven wear or cupping that may indicate misalignment or worn suspension parts. Check the sidewalls for bulges, cracking, or other damage.

Fluid leaks. Check underneath for any fluids that may be leaking from the vehicle. Damp, smelly spots under the rear of the vehicle may indicate a gas leak from the fuel tank or fuel line. Dark brown or black oily spots near the back could be differential oil leaking from the rear axle on rear-wheel-drive cars. Yellow, brown, or black oily spots under the front of your car point to engine oil leaks, or possibly transaxle oil leaks on front-wheel-drive cars. Red oily spots under the middle of rear-wheel-drive cars may be automatic transmission fluid. The same in the front for front-wheel drive would mean a leaky transaxle. Green, blue, or clear wet spots may be due to coolant leaking from the radiator, a bad hose connection, the water pump, or a freeze plug on the engine.

Shock absorbers/struts. The condition of the shocks/struts can be checked by doing a bounce test. Rock either corner of the car several times and then let go. A good shock/strut should stop the bouncing after one or two rebounds. Fluid leaks on shocks indicate replacement is in order; a small amount of seepage is normal on some types of struts. The mounts should be checked for wear.

Tie-rod ends. Tie-rods should have no visible looseness. If rocking the steering wheel or tire causes the joint to wobble, the tie-rod end should be replaced. On rack & pinion steering, the inner tie-rods are enclosed in protective rubber boots. The boots must be replaced if they're cracked or split to protect the steering gear against dirt and moisture. You can feel for looseness in the inner tie-rod sockets by squeezing the boots while someone rocks the steering wheel or tire for you. Again, there should be no looseness. **Note:** If you feel fluid inside the boots, it means your power steering system is leaking and the steering gear may soon need replacement.

Ball joints. Check for looseness with the front wheels raised off the ground and the load off the ball joints. A large screwdriver or pry bar can be used to check for vertical free-play. Some ball joints have a wear indicator as part of the grease fitting. If the wear

shoulder is showing, the joint is worn.

Steering linkage. Check for looseness in the linkage by rocking the steering wheel back and forth.

Brake hoses. All rubber brake hoses must be leak free and in good condition. Replace any found to be leaking, cracked, or damaged. Likewise, any steel brake hoses found to be leaking or damaged should be replaced.

Exhaust system/muffler. The exhaust system must be tight and leak-free. Check for rusted-out pipes, loose hangers, or cracked muffler connections.

Emergency brake cables. The cables should not be frayed or rubbing against sharp objects under the car.

CV-joints or U-joints. The CV-joint boots must be in good condition and tight to protect the joint. A clicking sound when turning indicates a bad CV-joint. U-joints on rear-wheel-drive cars must not have any visible free-play. A "clunk" when shifting into gear may indicate a bad U-joint.

Differential lube. The differential oil level should be up on the full point. Use only the recommended oil when adding lube. On most rear-drive vehicles this would be 80-90W gear oil, but on vehicles equipped with locking differentials, gear oil with special additives is required. Some front-drive cars use transmission fluid to lubricate the differential.

Maintenance and Lubrication Recommendations

Weekly

Check engine oil level
Check coolant level
Check tire pressure
Check washer fluid

MAINTENANCE AND SAFETY
INSPECTION CHECKLIST

INSIDE VEHICLE
OK Needs service
- ☐ ☐ Steering play
- ☐ ☐ Brake pedal
- ☐ ☐ Emergency brake
- ☐ ☐ Horn
- ☐ ☐ Windshield wipers
- ☐ ☐ Windshield washers
- ☐ ☐ Mirrors
- ☐ ☐ Defroster
- ☐ ☐ Spare tire & jack

OUTSIDE VEHICLE
- ☐ ☐ Headlights
- ☐ ☐ Taillights
- ☐ ☐ Brake lights
- ☐ ☐ Turn signals
- ☐ ☐ Backup lights
- ☐ ☐ License plate light
- ☐ ☐ Wiper blades
- ☐ ☐ Tire inflation
- ☐ ☐ Tire condition

UNDERHOOD
Fluid levels:
- ☐ ☐ Engine oil
- ☐ ☐ Coolant
- ☐ ☐ Brakes
- ☐ ☐ Automatic transmission
- ☐ ☐ Battery
- ☐ ☐ Power steering
- ☐ ☐ Windshield washer
- ☐ Air filter
- ☐ V-belts
- ☐ Radiator hoses
- ☐ Heater hoses
- ☐ PCV valve & hose
- ☐ Vacuum hoses
- ☐ Distributor cap
- ☐ Spark plug wires
- ☐ Battery terminals

UNDERNEATH
Fluid leaks:
- ☐ ☐ Engine oil
- ☐ ☐ Cooling system
- ☐ ☐ Brakes
- ☐ ☐ Transmission
- ☐ ☐ Differential
- ☐ ☐ Power steering
- ☐ ☐ Fuel tank & lines
- ☐ Shock absorbers/ struts
- ☐ Tie-rod ends
- ☐ Ball joints
- ☐ Steering linkage
- ☐ Brake hoses
- ☐ Exhaust system/ muffler
- ☐ Emergency brake cables
- ☐ CV-joints & U-joints
- ☐ Differential lube

Monthly

Check automatic transmission fluid level
Check brake fluid level
Check power steering fluid level
Check battery water level (or charge indicator on maintenance-free batteries)
Inspect drive belts
Inspect radiator hoses and heater hoses
Check headlights, taillights, turn signals, brake lights, and other running lights

Twice a year

Change engine oil and filter (every 6 months or 3000 miles, whichever comes first)

Lubricate chassis
Lubricate door hinges, locks, and hood and trunk latches
Inspect suspension (ball joints, tie-rod ends, control arm bushings, etc.)
Check differential and manual transmission/ transaxle fluid levels
Inspect U-joints or CV-joints
Inspect exhaust system
Check coolant concentration and appearance
Check air pressure in spare tire
Check operation of emergency brake
Check emergency flashers
Touch up paint nicks and minor rust damage, and wax car body

Yearly

Replace air filter
Replace fuel filter
Check air conditioner charge
Check PCV valve
Inspect ignition system (distributor cap, rotor, and wires)
Inspect carburetor linkage and operation of choke
Inspect vacuum hoses

Every 2 years

Replace spark plugs (30,000 miles average recommendation for unleaded gas)
Replace automatic transmission fluid and filter
Replace coolant
Replace PCV breather filter
Check engine compression
Check ignition timing
Repack wheel bearings
Inspect brake linings

Every 3 years

Replace drive belts
Replace radiator and heater hoses
Replace distributor cap and rotor

Checking Vital Fluids

YOUR VEHICLE has several "vital fluids" that must be checked periodically so they are maintained at the proper level for safe and trouble-free driving. Checking these fluids regularly is probably the single most important thing you can do to care for your car, and this section will explain where to check each level and how to do it correctly.

Your car's vital fluids include engine oil, transmission/transaxle oil, differential lube (which in most front-wheel-drive cars is the same as the transaxle oil or automatic transmission fluid), coolant, brake fluid, power steering fluid, battery water, and windshield washer fluid.

The previous section on "Maintenance and Lubrication Recommendations" provides some guidelines as to how often you should check your car's fluid levels. The guidelines are "averages" and should be adequate for most situations. However, it should also be obvious that frequency depends on how many miles a vehicle is driven during a given time interval and whether it has any mechanical problems or fluid leaks that may cause it to consume or lose one or more of its vital fluids. Therefore, checking the fluid levels more frequently may be necessary to assure that the levels are properly maintained.

If you're on vacation and are putting a lot of miles on the odometer daily, then checking the engine oil daily may be a wise thing to do—especially if the engine uses or leaks oil. The same would apply to the automatic transmission, coolant level, and tire pressure. Use your judgment and do what seems prudent depending on the circumstances. It's better to check a fluid level more often than is really necessary than to neglect it a little too long and end up with an expensive repair bill or breakdown.

Checking the Engine Oil Level

Oil is the lifeblood of your car's engine, so it should be checked frequently: once a week or perhaps every time you fill the gas tank or open the hood. To check the oil, follow these steps.

1. The best time to check the oil level is in the morning after the car has been sitting overnight. The car should be parked on a level surface so the dipstick reading will be accurate. If the car has been driven, shut the engine off and wait several minutes before checking the level so the oil can drain back into the crankcase. Trying to check the oil level while the engine is running or immediately after shutting it off will give you a false low reading, because some of the oil will still be circulating in the engine.
2. Raise the hood and locate the dipstick. You'll find it on one side of the engine. On front-wheel-drive cars, it is usually

located on the front side of the engine. Refer to your owner's manual if you're not sure where to look.

3. Pull the dipstick out and wipe off the end with a clean rag.

4. Insert the dipstick back into its hole and push it all the way down. Then pull it back out.

5. If the crankcase is full, the oil level will be up to the full mark on the dipstick. The add line is usually one quart below the full mark. Although you don't have to add oil until the level drops to the add line, many professional mechanics recommend adding just enough oil to maintain the level at the full mark. Waiting until the level reaches the add line means your engine is running a quart low; on an engine with a four quart capacity crankcase (which is what most engines have today), driving a quart low can increase oil temperatures, reduce lubrication, and possibly cause damage through oil starvation during hot weather, high-speed driving, or towing.

Note: Don't overfill the crankcase with oil. This can force oil past seals resulting in leaks and smoking. It can also cause oil foaming if the level is high enough to be whipped into foam by the crankshaft. Since air bubbles interfere with lubrication, foaming can reduce the flow of oil to vital engine parts.

Should you find no oil on the dipstick when you check it, first make sure you've pushed it all the way back into its hole or tube. If you've done it right, then add enough oil to bring the crankcase back up to the full level and then check the engine for oil leaks. An engine in good running condition should use less than half a quart between oil changes (3000 mile intervals). Some engines may use more, but if oil consumption is as high as a quart every few hundred miles, it indicates either a severe oil leak or mechanical problems such as worn valve guides, valve seals, and/or piston rings. Blue smoke in the exhaust means the engine is burning oil due to one or more of those problems.

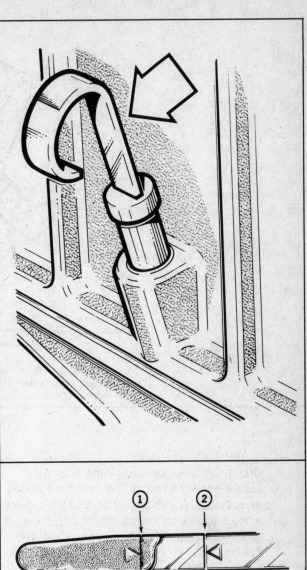

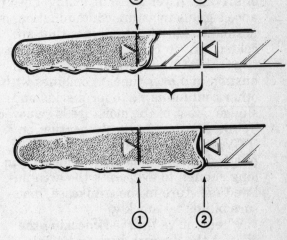

The engine oil dipstick is usually located on the side of the engine (see your owner's manual for the location on your car). To check the oil level, remove the dipstick, wipe it clean with a rag, and insert it back into its hole, pushing it all the way in. Remove it again and check the level against the "add" (1) and "full" (2) marks on the dipstick. Add enough oil to bring it to the "full" mark.

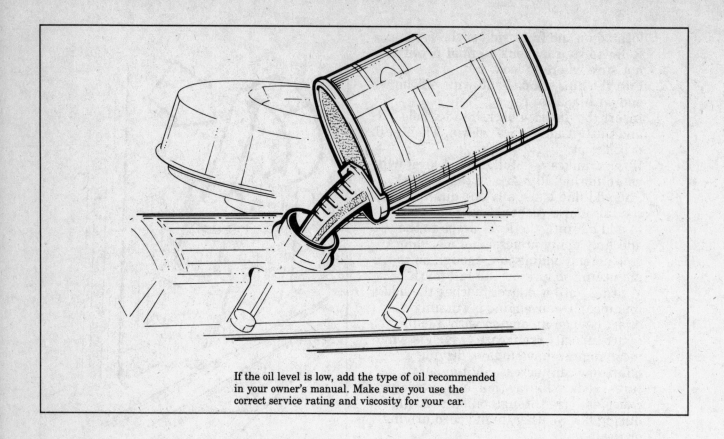

If the oil level is low, add the type of oil recommended in your owner's manual. Make sure you use the correct service rating and viscosity for your car.

You can't tell a lot about the oil's condition by appearance alone, since oil turns brown after a few hundred miles of driving. A yellowish or foamy appearance signals moisture contamination, a normal condition for engines that are seldom driven or used mostly for short trips. Moisture is a by-product of combustion and over time it combines with other contaminants to form acids and sludge. Most of the moisture is removed by the positive crankcase ventilation (PCV) system, but if the PCV valve is plugged and/or the engine is never run long enough to evaporate the accumulated moisture in the crankcase, moisture builds up quickly.

When you've finished checking the oil, put the dipstick back in its hole. Painting the handle of the dipstick a bright color can make it easier to find in a dark engine compartment.

6. To add oil, remove the oil filler cap located on the top engine or valve cover. Some caps twist off and most rubber ones pull out.

7. Add only enough oil to bring the level up to the full mark on the dipstick. Use the type of oil recommended in your owner's manual. It should be the same viscosity and brand as the oil already in the engine. Don't forget to replace the filler cap and recheck the dipstick after adding oil.

Checking Automatic Transmission/ Transaxle Fluid

Just as motor oil is the lifeblood of the engine, automatic transmission fluid (ATF) is essential for proper operation of the transmission, as well as for lubrication. A low fluid level here can allow slipping, shifting hesitation, and accelerated wear. To check the fluid level and condition, follow these steps.

1. The automatic transmission fluid level is checked with the engine idling, the transmission in park (or neutral in some cases) and the fluid at normal operating temperature. If the car has just

been started, it should be driven for 10 to 15 minutes to warm the transmission fluid prior to checking. The reason is that ATF expands as it heats up and checking the level cold would give a false low reading.

   Note: Some cars have transmission dipsticks that are calibrated to read the fluid level either hot or cold. But unless your dipstick has such marks, make sure the fluid is warm before you check it.

2. Park the car on a level surface, set the emergency brake and momentarily place the transmission gear selector in each gear. This circulates ATF through all the passages in the transmission. Then place the gear selector in park (engine idling).

3. Raise the hood and locate the transmission dipstick. On rear-wheel-drive cars, it can usually be found near the rear of the engine compartment on the passenger's side. On front-wheel-drive transverse-mounted engines, look for it on the transaxle housing, to the right of the engine on the driver's side of the engine compartment. If you're not sure where it is, refer to your owner's manual.

4. Remove the dipstick and wipe the end clean with a lint-free cloth.

5. Reinsert the dipstick completely and remove it a second time.

6. Check the fluid level on the dipstick markings. The correct fluid level is between the add and full marks. If the ATF level is below the add line, insert a funnel into the dipstick filler hole or pipe and add a pint of ATF.

DO NOT overfill the transmission, as doing so can cause fluid foaming and leaks. Also, be sure you add the type of ATF specified in your owner's manual. There are two main types of ATF: Dexron II and Type F. The fluids have different friction and viscosity characteristics, so it is important to add the correct type of ATF to your transmission. In some cases, the type of ATF to use will be specified on the dipstick itself, on the dipstick handle, or on a tag attached to the dipstick filler pipe. It also will be listed in the owner's

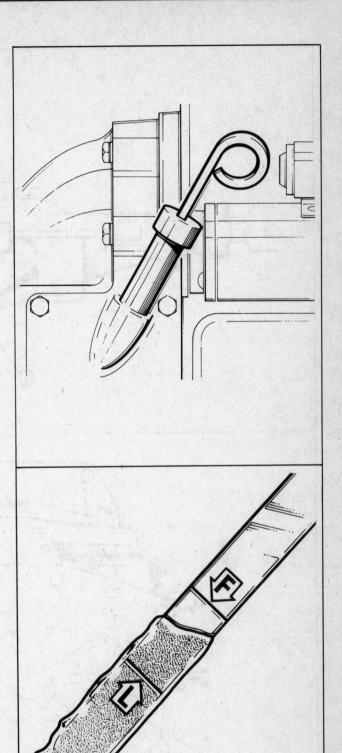

The automatic transmission dipstick is usually located near the rear of the engine. Consult your owner's manual to find the location in your car. Most dipsticks have "L" (low) and "F" (full) marks for checking fluid level.

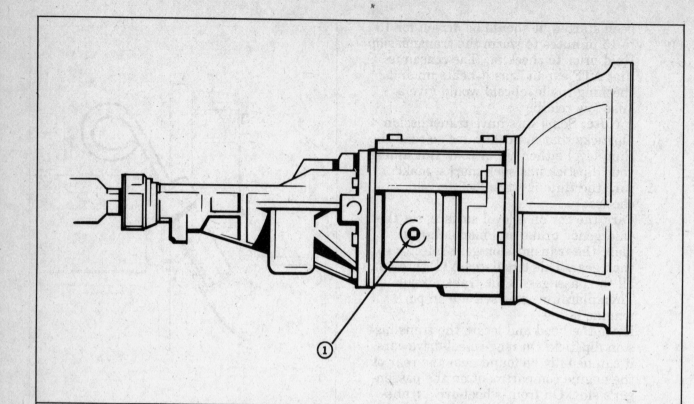

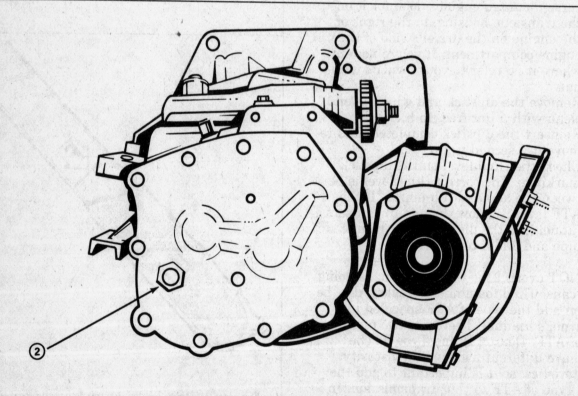

On most rear-drive cars' (top) manual transmissions,
the filler plug (1) is located on the passenger's side.
On most front-drive cars (bottom), the filler plug (2) is
on the end of the manual transaxle.

manual. Recheck the fluid level after adding ATF (leave the engine idling).

7. You should also observe the condition of the transmission fluid. Unlike motor oil, you can tell a lot about transmission fluid by its color and odor. Healthy fluid should be red to pink in appearance. Fluid that has deteriorated with age and heat will be brown in color and have a burned odor. If your fluid doesn't appear or smell healthy, it should be changed to protect your transmission.

8. Replace the dipstick, close the hood, and shut off the engine.

Checking Manual Transmission/Transaxle Fluid Level

The above list of tools is primarily for rear-wheel-drive cars, since most front-wheel-drive transaxles can be checked without having to raise the car. Unlike automatic transmissions and transaxles, manual transmissions and transaxles do not require periodic fluid changes, because the fluid is not subjected to the same operating conditions as those found inside an automatic. However, the fluid level should be checked occasionally to make sure fluid has not been lost through leaks.

To check the manual transmission fluid level in a rear-wheel-drive car, follow these steps.

1. Park the car on a level surface and set the emergency brake. Leave the transmission in gear.
2. Because raising only one end or one side of the car will upset the fluid level inside the transmission, the only way to get an accurate reading is to raise the entire car off the ground. Raise both the front and rear of the car equal amounts until there is enough clearance for you to crawl underneath or reach the transmission. Make sure the car is adequately supported by jack stands before getting underneath.
3. Most manual transmissions have the filler plug located on the passenger's side of the transmission. You'll find it somewhere along the side of the transmission case, up about one third to one fourth of the distance from top to bot-

Tools and Materials

- Jack and Safety Jack Stands
- Adjustable Wrench or ½-inch-Drive Ratchet or Allen-Head Wrench
- Funnel

tom. The filler plug may have a hex head, resemble a pipe plug (four-sided head), or have a concave square fitting for a ½-inch-drive ratchet or large Allen-head wrench.

4. Remove the filler plug and insert your finger into the filler hole. If the transmission is filled to the correct capacity, the fluid level will be within ½-inch of the bottom of the filler hole.
5. If the transmission fluid level is low, add the type of lubricant specified in your owner's manual until fluid just starts to dribble back out of the hole. Most manual transmissions in rear-wheel-drive cars take 80 or 90 weight gear oil. Adding fluid will be difficult because there may not be enough clearance to use a long-neck funnel. Some containers of gear oil come with a spout tip that will fit tight spaces, or an alternative would be to use an old plastic catsup bottle to squirt the fluid into the transmission.
6. After refilling the transmission to the proper level, replace the filler plug and lower the car.

To check the manual transaxle fluid level in a front-wheel-drive car, follow these steps.

1. Park the car on a level surface.
2. Most front-wheel-drive cars do not have to be raised to check the manual transaxle lubricant level because the filler plug is located on the end of the transaxle. On some cars, the plug may be located on the front or back of the transaxle, and on others a dipstick may be provided. In most instances, though, the filler plug is fairly accessible, so jacking is not necessary.
3. Remove the filler plug and insert your finger into the filler hole. The fluid

level should be within ½-inch of the bottom of the filler hole.

4. If the transmission is low, add the type of lubricant specified in your owner's manual until fluid just starts to dribble back out of the hole. **Note:** Some manual transaxles use 80 or 90 weight gear oil while others require automatic transmission fluid (usually Dexron II).
5. Replace the filler plug.

Checking Differential Lubricant Level

The above list of tools is required for rear-wheel-drive cars. With the exception of a couple of cars, most front-wheel-drive transaxles use the same fluid for the transmission gears and differential, so checking the differential separately is not required.

To check the differential lubricant level on rear-wheel-drive cars, follow these steps.

1. To obtain an accurate reading, the rear axle must be level. This means the entire car must be raised off the ground if

Tools and Materials

- Jack and Safety Jack Stands
- Adjustable Wrench or ½-inch-Drive Ratchet or Allen-Head Wrench
- Funnel

you can't reach the axle filler plug with the car on the ground. The car should be parked on a level surface, then both front and rear raised an equal amount to provide enough clearance for you to crawl underneath. Make sure the car is adequately supported by jack stands before you crawl under it.

2. Locate the differential filler plug. You'll find it either on the rear cover plate or on either side of the differential housing. The plug may have a hex-head, square pipe head or inset square, or Allen-head drive.
3. Remove the plug and insert your finger into the filler hole. The lubricant level

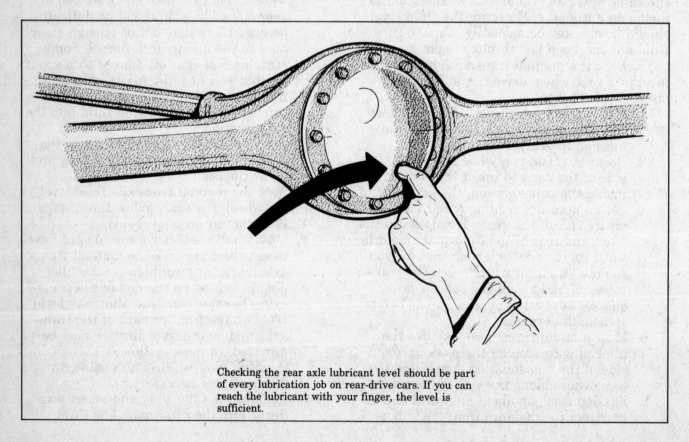

Checking the rear axle lubricant level should be part of every lubrication job on rear-drive cars. If you can reach the lubricant with your finger, the level is sufficient.

should be within ½ inch of the bottom of the hole.

4. If low, add the type of lubricant specified in your owner's manual to bring the level up to the bottom of the hole. Most vehicles take 80 or 90 weight gear oil but those with locking differentials (Positraction) require a lubricant with special friction additives.

5. Replace the filler plug and lower the car.

Checking Coolant Level

Most vehicles today have a coolant recovery system with a reserve tank that allows the radiator to maintain the proper coolant level. The plastic reserve tank is usually located in the vicinity of the radiator, and is marked to indicate the minimum and maximum (or cold full and hot full) coolant levels. In most instances you can read the coolant level through the plastic tank, and antifreeze and water can be added to the reserve tank if the level is low.

To check the coolant level inside the radiator, follow these steps.

1. *Caution: Never remove the radiator cap on a hot engine. The cooling system is under pressure and boiling coolant can spray out. The best advice is to check the coolant inside the radiator when the engine is cold, or wait at least 15 to 20 minutes after shutting the engine off before opening the radiator cap. Use several thicknesses of towels or rags to protect your hands. The radiator cap is removed by pushing down and turning (like a child-proof cap).*

2. The coolant level inside the radiator will vary with the design of the cooling system. On most vehicles with reserve tanks, the coolant will be right up to the top of the radiator. On cooling systems that do not use a reserve tank (although it may have a recovery tank to catch any overflow) the level should be one to three inches below the top of the radiator filler neck. This is to allow room for expansion as the coolant becomes hot. You may find markings on

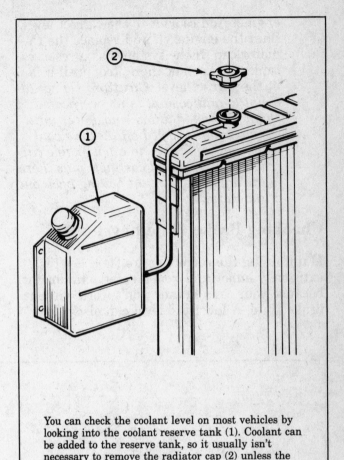

You can check the coolant level on most vehicles by looking into the coolant reserve tank (1). Coolant can be added to the reserve tank, so it usually isn't necessary to remove the radiator cap (2) unless the coolant level is very low.

the outside of the radiator indicating the correct cold and hot full levels for such systems.

3. If the coolant is low, add a 50/50 mixture of water and ethylene glycol antifreeze. For cars with aluminum radiators, engines, or cooling system components, make sure the antifreeze container says "aluminum safe." Never add straight water because it offers no corrosion resistance and no freezing or boilover protection. Nor does straight antifreeze work as well as a mixture of antifreeze and water. If the radiator is almost empty or extremely low, it may be necessary to start the engine to refill the system completely. Allow the engine to idle until the upper radiator hose becomes hot to the touch. This indicates that the thermostat has opened and coolant is now circulating through the

engine. Add coolant to the correct level. Shut the engine off and replace the radiator cap. If the system has a reserve tank, add coolant there, too, until it is at the correct level. *Caution: Do not attempt to add coolant to an overheated engine or one that has boiled over until the engine has cooled off. Adding cold water and antifreeze to a hot engine can crack or warp metal castings, plus there is the danger of coolant boiling back out of the radiator.*

Checking Brake Fluid Level

Maintaining the correct brake fluid level is extremely important from a safety standpoint, because your car's brakes won't work without brake fluid. A low fluid level can also allow air into the system, which can create a spongy-feeling pedal and poor brake performance. To check the level of the brake fluid, follow these steps.

1. Open the hood and locate the master brake cylinder. On nearly all cars it is located on the driver's side of the engine compartment near the firewall. The fluid reservoir is on top of the master cylinder. On some vehicles, the reservoir is part of the casting and is sealed by a metal cover and spring clip. On other vehicles, the reservoir is made of plastic with removable filler caps or a snap-off cap.

2. On vehicles with plastic reservoirs, you can usually check the fluid level inside without having to open the filler caps. On those with metal covers, carefully

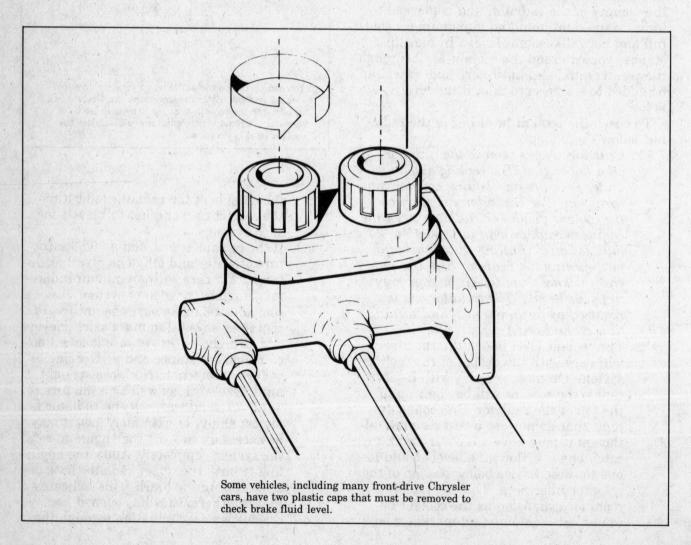

Some vehicles, including many front-drive Chrysler cars, have two plastic caps that must be removed to check brake fluid level.

wipe away any grease or dirt from around the cover, then pry the spring clip to one side with a screwdriver and lift off the cover. The fluid level should be within ½ inch of the top of the fluid reservoir.

3. If low, add the correct brake fluid from a sealed container. Most cars use DOT 3 brake fluid; check your owner's manual for the correct type for your car. Never add used brake fluid or fluid from a container that has been left open for any length of time. Brake fluid is hydroscopic, which means it absorbs water from the air. Moisture-contaminated fluid has a lower boiling point than new fluid, which can result in boiling and brake failure under hard use. Moisture will also contribute to in-ternal corrosion of the master cylinder, brake lines, wheel cylinders, and brake calipers. Never pour oil or any other fluid other than brake fluid into the reservoir, because petroleum-based lubricants can ruin the seals in the master and wheel cylinders. Be careful not to splash brake fluid on your car's finish because it can damage paint.

4. Replace the filler cap or cover and make sure the spring clip is centered, if so equipped.

Checking Power Steering Fluid Level

The power steering fluid level must be maintained at the proper level to keep air out of the system and for the pump to generate adequate steering pressure. To check the fluid level, follow these steps.

1. On some vehicles, the fluid level must be checked hot, while others allow you to check it hot or cold. In either case, the fluid level should be checked after shutting the engine off.

2. Raise the hood and locate the power steering fluid reservoir. Power steering is a belt driven accessory, so it will be mounted to one side of the engine and driven off the crankshaft pulley. On front-wheel-drive vehicles with transverse-mounted engines, the reservoir may be buried behind the engine on the passenger's side of the engine compartment. After you've found the reservoir, wipe any grease or dirt off the filler cap.

3. Open the filler cap and note the fluid level inside. On some vehicles, a dipstick is attached to the underside of the filler cap showing hot and cold full marks. On other vehicles, there is no dipstick and the reservoir may have markings indicating hot or cold full levels. If only hot full marks are provided, the engine should be run for 10 to 15 minutes prior to checking the fluid level, or you'll get a false low reading.

4. If the pump reservoir is low, add only enough power steering fluid to bring it up to the appropriate full mark (hot or

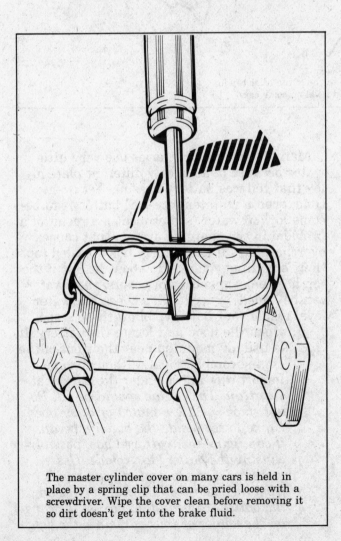

The master cylinder cover on many cars is held in place by a spring clip that can be pried loose with a screwdriver. Wipe the cover clean before removing it so dirt doesn't get into the brake fluid.

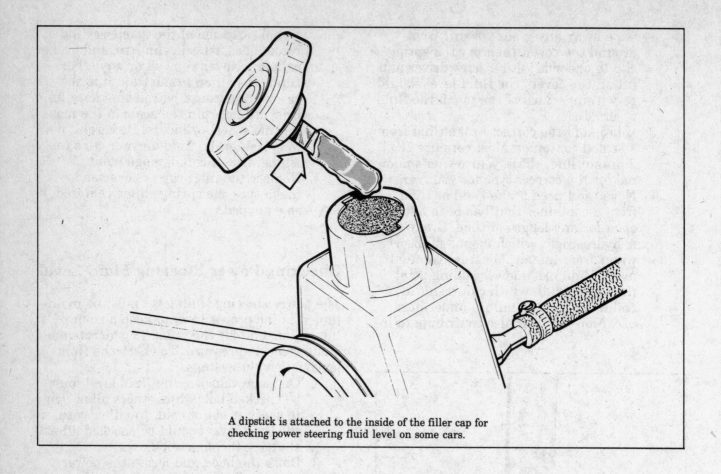

A dipstick is attached to the inside of the filler cap for checking power steering fluid level on some cars.

cold depending on the circumstances). Do not use automatic transmission fluid unless your owner's manual says to do so. Never add engine oil or any other lubricant, as this can damage power steering pump seals and hoses.

5. Replace the filler cap and close the hood.

Checking Battery Water Level

Water is the vital fluid of your car's battery. It contains sulfuric acid, which reacts with the lead plates inside the battery to produce voltage and maintain the battery's charge. During charging, some of the water boils off (actually it's converted to hydrogen and oxygen gas, which then vents out of the battery). Eventually this lowers the water level inside, exposing the lead plates to air, causing them to dry out. To keep the battery in good working condition, therefore, it is necessary to check the water level of your battery periodically.

Maintenance-free batteries use very little water because of a slightly different plate alloy that reduces battery gassing. Yet over time, even a maintenance-free battery can become low on water (sometimes as a result of a problem in the charging system that causes overcharging). If the battery has a sealed top, there's nothing you can do about it. But if the top has removable caps or covers, then water can be added as needed. To check the water level inside your battery, follow these steps.

1. Open the hood and locate the battery. It is usually mounted near the front of the engine compartment, although some import cars put it under the back seat.

2. *Caution: The engine should be off. Do not smoke or use a match or other open flame to see inside the battery, because it can ignite the hydrogen gas, possibly causing the battery to explode. Use gloves or a rag to protect your hands from any acid residue that may be on the battery caps and do not set the caps on the fender of your car, since the acid*

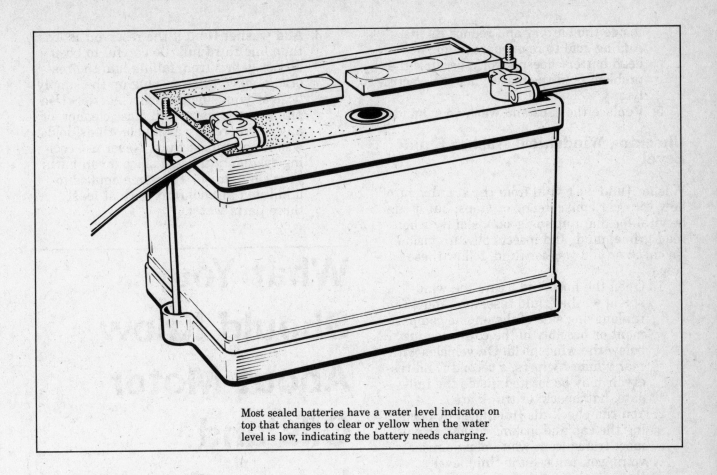

Most sealed batteries have a water level indicator on top that changes to clear or yellow when the water level is low, indicating the battery needs charging.

can damage the paint.

3. The water level inside can be checked one of several ways. On batteries with translucent plastic cases, you can often see the water level through the sides of

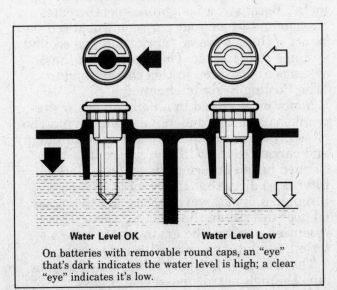

Water Level OK   **Water Level Low**

On batteries with removable round caps, an "eye" that's dark indicates the water level is high; a clear "eye" indicates it's low.

the battery. It should be within one inch of the top. Most sealed batteries have a sight glass or charge indicator on top that can also be used to determine the water level inside. If the indicator appears clear or yellowish, it means the water level inside has dropped below the bottom of the indicator and is too low for charging or continued use. On batteries with removable round caps, one of the caps may have a clear plastic "eye" that appears dark when the water level inside is full, or light when it is low. On batteries without such indicators, you have to unscrew the caps or pry open the covers and look inside. The water level should be up to the bottom of the filler openings (which may be cast with split rings or triangles to help you determine the full mark).

4. Add only distilled water to a battery. Ordinary tap water contains dissolved minerals that will react with the acid

inside the battery and reduce its life. Adding acid to rejuvenate an old or dead battery doesn't work, because the problem is in the plates, not the electrolyte.

5. Replace the caps and wash your hands.

Checking Windshield Washer Fluid Level

Washer fluid isn't vital from the standpoint of how your car runs, steers, or stops, but it can be vital for maintaining good visibility when road grime, mud, and insects obscure vision. To check or add washer fluid, follow these steps.

1. Open the hood and locate the windshield washer fluid reservoir. You'll find it along one side of the engine compartment or possibly in the cowl area just below the windshield. On vehicles with rear window wipers, a second fluid reservoir may be located inside the tailgate, hatchback, or trunk area.

2. You can check the fluid level by opening the cap and looking inside, or with most translucent white plastic reservoirs, you can see the fluid level through the sides of the container.

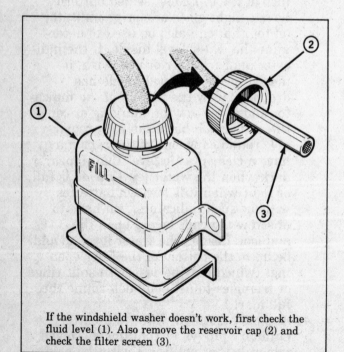

If the windshield washer doesn't work, first check the fluid level (1). Also remove the reservoir cap (2) and check the filter screen (3).

3. Add washer fluid if the reservoir is less than one third full. Be careful to keep dirt or debris from falling into the reservoir, since this can plug up the supply hose or windshield washer nozzles. Use plain water, water and glass cleaner, or any commercially available windshield washer premixed fluid. Never use cooling system antifreeze since it can harm your car's finish. The same applies to undiluted alcohol (mix with at least three parts water).

What You Should Know About Motor Oils and Lubrication

BELIEVE IT OR not, your car is made up of about 15,000 parts, most of which are metal. Because metal-against-metal creates friction and wear, your car soon would self destruct if there were no lubrication and cooling systems to protect it. The functions of these systems are covered in this chapter and in "The Cooling System" chapter.

Motor oil is stored in an oil pan below the crankshaft on the underside of the engine. The oil is drawn out of the oil pan by the oil pump and carried to the oil filter, where it is cleaned before entering the engine. If an oil filter is so dirty that motor oil cannot pass through, a bypass valve opens and the motor oil goes directly to the working parts. This is essential, because the engine must have motor oil, even dirty motor oil if necessary.

The motor oil is forced to the top of the engine through narrow passages. It goes

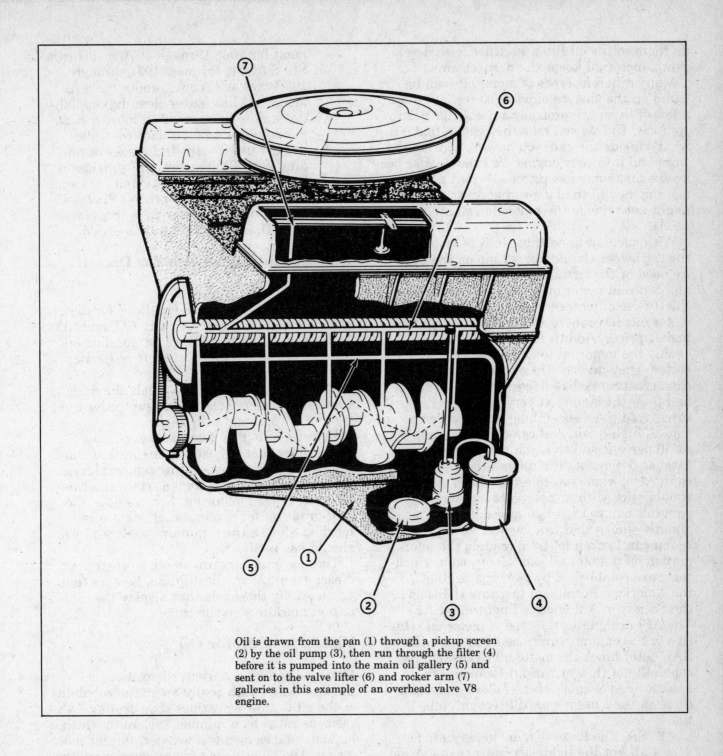

Oil is drawn from the pan (1) through a pickup screen (2) by the oil pump (3), then run through the filter (4) before it is pumped into the main oil gallery (5) and sent on to the valve lifter (6) and rocker arm (7) galleries in this example of an overhead valve V8 engine.

through the camshaft, up to lubricate the valve lifters and rocker arms, then down to the crankshaft, the pistons, and down the walls of the cylinders. Gravity brings the motor oil eventually to the oil pan, where the process begins again. In this way, the motor oil lubricates all engine parts, cooling the surfaces and reducing wear. The motor oil also acts as a liquid washer around the pistons so none of the air/fuel mixture that is compressed for combustion can escape; this boosts cylinder compression, which increases power and maintains a far more efficient engine than would otherwise be possible.

Motor oil carries the dirt, soot, acid, and debris away from the working parts and deposits them in the oil filter. Fortified with detergents, motor oil keeps the parts clean.

Many different types of motor oils can be found on the shelves of parts stores, but only a few of them are probably suitable for use in your car. Unless you take the time to find out what's inside the can, you may be pouring the wrong oil into your engine. You should also be aware that some low-priced oils may cost you more money in the long run because they might not provide the protection your engine needs.

With such an important fluid as motor oil, the car owner should not scrimp on the quality used or the frequency of replacement. The difference in motor oil quality and price is chiefly the difference in additives. Top-quality motor oils have more additives, and usually higher prices. Additives are chemicals that enable the motor oil to do a number of jobs better. They prevent the oil from foaming, from creating tarlike deposits when oxidized, and from thickening at very low temperatures. Additives also inhibit rust and corrosion. A high-quality oil can contain as much as 30 percent additives, an inexpensive oil as little as 5 percent. The difference is significant. Also, when you select a type of oil, you should stick with it: detergent and non-detergent oils can react, when mixed, to form a gummy sludge that can damage an engine.

You can learn a lot from reading the information on a motor oil can. Motor oil specifications are established by two organizations, the American Petroleum Institute (API) and the Society of Automotive Engineers (SAE). The API designates the type of motor oil relative to the engine requirements and use. The SAE determines the motor oil's viscosity, its capability of flow at various temperatures. Look for one or more of the following designations on the can for the API recommendations.

1. SA. The lowest grade, inadequate for all but the lightest requirements. Avoid using it.
2. SB. Not much better than SA.
3. SC. The minimum requirement for 1964 through 1967 cars and trucks. It might not hold up under severe loads in late model cars. Again, move up a grade or two.
4. SD. Designated as minimum requirement for 1968 through 1970 model cars.
5. SE. Suitable for most 1971 through 1979 cars and trucks, and some later models. It has better cleaning capabilities and reduces wear on moving parts in engines with emissions controls.
6. SF. For use in cars and trucks beginning with 1980 models. SF provides better oxidation stability and anti-wear performance over all other API classifications and may be used where classes SE, SD, and SC are recommended.

Service Ratings of Oils for Diesel Engines

There are four service designations for diesel engine lubricating oils: CA, CB, CC, and CD. Like the five service ratings for gasoline engine oil, these oils differ in their properties and additives.

The quality of the oils parallels the designation—A represents the lowest protective quality and D represents the highest.

Because of higher compression (almost three times that of gasoline engines) and accompanying higher operating temperatures, the automotive diesel engine requires a *combination* type of motor oil. For example, the best-grade oil for use in diesel engines is marked SF/CD; the minimum quality oil you should use is SC/CC.

There are no bargains in oil, so treat your diesel engine to the best grade. Be sure that you use *only* those oils that display the *combination* markings on the can.

Viscosity of Motor Oil

Motor oil comes in various viscosities (or thicknesses), which really mean the capability of the oil to flow at various temperatures. Viscosity is rated by a number system in which a higher number means a heavier, thicker motor oil. The older your car and more worn the engine, the more likely a lightweight motor oil will seep past the piston rings and burn off. On the other hand, too heavy a motor oil will provide inadequate lubrication when cold. To some extent, the decision on the correct type of motor oil to select is a matter of trial and error if you are driving an older car. If you are using straight 20W oil on a tired engine

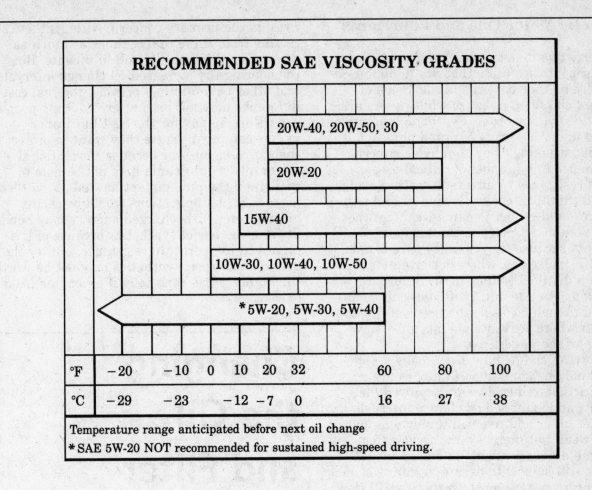

RECOMMENDED SAE VISCOSITY GRADES

20W-40, 20W-50, 30

20W-20

15W-40

10W-30, 10W-40, 10W-50

*5W-20, 5W-30, 5W-40

°F	−20		−10		0	10	20	32		60	80	100
°C	−29		−23			−12	−7	0		16	27	38

Temperature range anticipated before next oil change
*SAE 5W-20 NOT recommended for sustained high-speed driving.

Charts such as this one are provided in most owner's manuals to help owners choose the right oil viscosity for different temperature ranges. The recommendations vary among cars.

in hot weather, you are likely to hear some bearing noise and notice low oil pressure (if you have an oil pressure gauge) plus smoke coming out the exhaust pipe. That engine will require a heavier grade (such as 30W) or possibly a multi-viscosity motor oil.

A multi-viscosity motor oil contains additives that generally provide year-round capabilities. For example, 10W-30 motor oil has the capability of performing in winter as a 10W motor oil and in summer as a 30W motor oil. Multi-viscosity motor oils such as 10W-40, 10W-50, and 20W-50 have wider viscosity ranges. If your engine is fairly new and in good condition, the best oil to use is a good grade of 10W-30. Although 10W-40 is very

popular, some new car manufacturers now say 10W-40 oil may be too thick and lead to piston ring problems. General Motors, for example, says it will not honor warranty claims on late model engines found to be filled with 10W-40 oil if piston sealing problems develop. Therefore, always follow the oil recommendations in your owner's manual.

Stick with one type and grade of motor oil. Avoid pouring a quart of one type of motor oil to top off a crankcase full of another type. There is always the possibility of additives not being compatible, with the result being formation of deposits that may not be good for your engine. You should carry a spare quart of motor oil in the trunk for topping off.

Synthetic Motor Oils and Lubricants

An alternative to petroleum-based motor oils and lubricants are those that are "manufactured" from other base chemicals. Some of these are classified as *esters* while others are *man-made hydrocarbons*. Synthetic lubricants are sold under a variety of brand names, but generally speaking, they do provide superior performance in a number of critical areas such as resistance to high temperature oxidation and thinning, easier flowing in cold temperatures, and reduced engine wear. Synthetics are able to out-perform conventional lubricants because they're fairly pure blends of specific molecules, whereas conventional oils are a distilled soup of many different hydrocarbons. As a result, synthetics can be formulated to match closely the needs of the application where conventional oils must rely more heavily on additives.

All sorts of claims have been made for synthetics, but the most important ones are reduced friction, reduced wear, improved fuel economy, and extended oil change intervals. No motor oil or additive will totally eliminate engine wear, but many synthetics do offer measurable improvements in engine life. How much is still subject to debate. In terms of flow characteristics, most synthetics still flow smoothly at 40 degrees below zero when conventional oils turn to a near-solid gel. At the upper end of the spectrum, synthetics continue to lubricate well beyond 500° F where conventional oils rapidly oxidize and turn to coke. This wide temperature range can improve cold weather starting as well as offer much greater protection under hard use and hot weather driving. As for fuel economy improvements, savings of one to three percent are realistic expectations.

How far you can safely extend oil change intervals depends on the type of driving you do. Some synthetic oil manufacturers claim you can go as far as 24,000 miles between oil changes, provided the filter is changed at 6000-mile intervals and the vehicle is used primarily for open road driving. Short trip stop-and-go driving produces a lot of moisture contamination in the crankcase, so synthetics would not be much help in extending change intervals.

What are the drawbacks of synthetics?

Price is the primary concern, with synthetics costing from three to five times as much as conventional motor oils and lubricants. But considering the increased oil change intervals and other benefits they provide, the real cost difference may not be that great. Some people are willing to pay for the best lubricant money can buy because they want to protect their investment—or because conventional motor oils or lubricants may not be able to withstand the punishment as well as synthetics can. Such applications would be racing, aircraft, etc. Turbocharged engines may benefit from the use of synthetics because of the improved temperature resistance, but for the average motorist, synthetics may not be worth the higher price, especially if an engine leaks or uses oil.

Changing the Oil and Filter

Tools and Materials

- Oil Filter Wrench
- Oil Filter
- Oil Filler Spout or Can Opener and Funnel
- Motor Oil
- Jack and Safety Jack Stands or Auto Ramps
- Wheel Chocks
- Oil Drain Pan
- Wrenches

THERE IS PROBABLY nothing you can do on your car that can save you more dollars per hour than a simple oil and oil filter change. It is a job that, once you have become accustomed to it, can be done in about

15 minutes. If you have had a professional oil and oil filter change performed on your car recently, you know that the tab usually runs between $15 and $20, even more in some cases. By shopping for good oil and oil filters at sale prices, you can save about $7 by doing it yourself.

Furthermore, you can significantly extend the life of your car by changing the oil and oil filter regularly, even more frequently than is recommended by the manufacturer, and by being sure that all grease fittings are properly lubricated. Greasing your car's chassis is covered in the section on "Chassis Lubrication."

Because changing your oil and oil filter is one of the most frequent jobs you will be undertaking on your car, it is a good idea to have tools and supplies neatly stored in an area where they will be readily accessible. Here is how to change your oil and oil filter.

1. Start the car and bring the engine up to its normal operating temperature by letting it run for 15 to 20 minutes. This gets all the contaminants suspended in the oil.

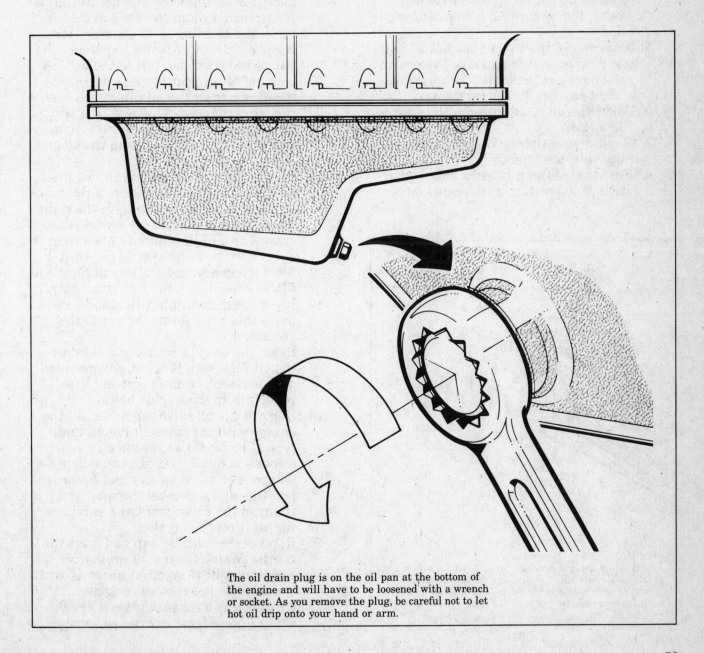

The oil drain plug is on the oil pan at the bottom of the engine and will have to be loosened with a wrench or socket. As you remove the plug, be careful not to let hot oil drip onto your hand or arm.

2. Elevate your car. It is best to use a good jack and firm safety jack stands or a pair of ramps. Use the jack only to put the front of the car on the jack stands. Set your hand brake and block the rear wheels so the car will not roll. Or you can use a pair of auto ramps and block the rear wheels.

3. Slide an oil drain pan under the oil pan drain plug. The plug is located in the oil pan, which is directly under the engine block.

4. With the proper-size box wrench, loosen—do not remove—the oil pan drain plug by turning it counterclockwise.

5. Move out of the way so the hot oil will not drop on you or run down your arm as the plug is removed. Then, remove the oil pan drain plug all the way.

6. Allow the oil to drain completely out of the oil pan.

7. Replace and tighten the oil pan drain plug with the wrench.

8. Find the oil filter. It looks like a quart-sized canister. It can be located on either side of the engine, depending on the type of car you have. On four- or six-cylinder engines, the oil filter is often accessible from the top. But on most American-made V8s, you will have to remove it from underneath the car.

9. If your oil filter must be removed from underneath the car, slide the oil drain pan under the oil filter.

10. To loosen the filter, you will need an oil filter wrench. Filters in use on today's cars are the spin-on type—that is, they go on and come off just like a nut. Remove the oil filter by slipping the oil filter wrench around the body of the oil filter and twisting it off counterclockwise. Be careful to drain its oil into the pan. **Note:** Because this is the dirtiest quart of oil in your system, we recommend replacing the oil filter each time the oil is changed. This way, you will have clean oil throughout the system and a fresh oil filter to keep the oil clean.

11. Place a light coating of clean motor oil on the rubber gasket on top of the new oil filter. Make sure you have the right filter for your specific car model. Then screw the oil filter onto its mounting. It should not be necessary to use the oil filter wrench to tighten the oil filter. Oil filters should be hand-tightened only.

12. If you used ramps or jack stands, remove them and lower the car to the ground.

13. Raise the hood of your car and locate the oil filler cap. It is usually mounted on a valve cover or on a round tube coming from the engine block.

14. Remove the oil filler cap and refill the engine with the correct amount and type of motor oil as specified in your owner's manual. You can use either an oil spout or a can opener and funnel to add the oil. Remember, because you changed the filter, you have to replace the oil it contained also.

15. Replace the oil filler cap and start the engine. Watch for the oil pressure warning light to go off in about 10 or 15 seconds. Do not race the engine. *Caution: If the light does not go off, shut off the engine and make sure you*

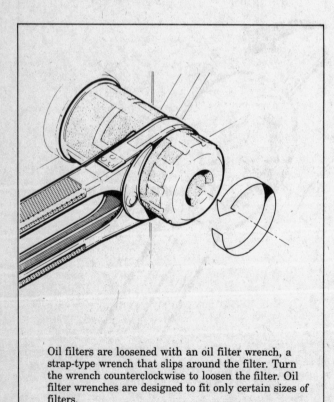

Oil filters are loosened with an oil filter wrench, a strap-type wrench that slips around the filter. Turn the wrench counterclockwise to loosen the filter. Oil filter wrenches are designed to fit only certain sizes of filters.

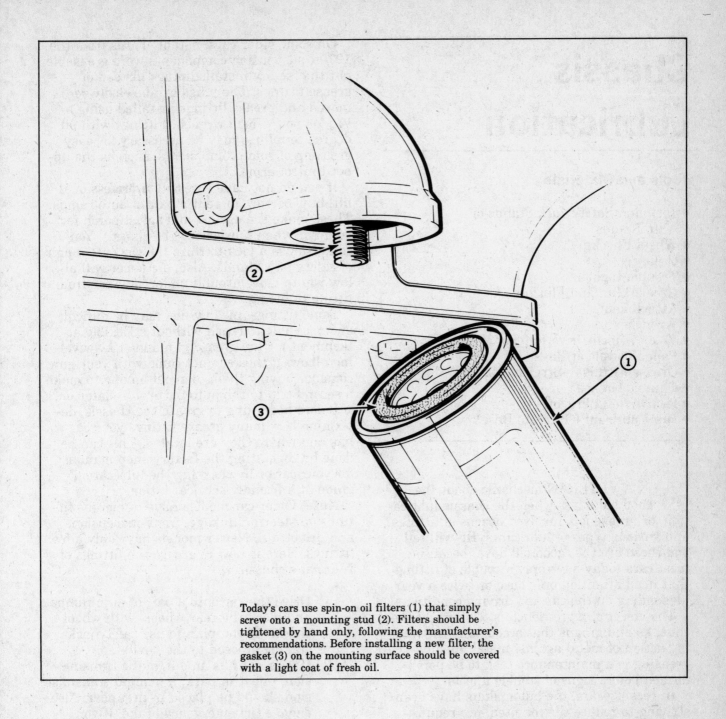

Today's cars use spin-on oil filters (1) that simply screw onto a mounting stud (2). Filters should be tightened by hand only, following the manufacturer's recommendations. Before installing a new filter, the gasket (3) on the mounting surface should be covered with a light coat of fresh oil.

have remembered to put the oil pan drain plug, oil, and oil filter back in the engine!

16. Look under the car for signs of leakage from the oil pan drain plug and oil filter. Retighten if necessary.

17. After the engine has run for a few minutes, shut it off. After 5 minutes, check the oil level on your dipstick. **Note:** Do not overfill. Using more oil than is recommended can cause just as much damage as not having enough oil.

18. Dispose of the used crankcase oil in a sealable container by taking it to a recycling center, service station, or quick lube center. Do not pour it down the drain or into a storm sewer since used motor oil can seep into ground water supplies and contaminate drinking water.

Chassis Lubrication

Tools and Materials

- Jack and Safety Jack Stands or Auto Ramps
- Wheel Chocks
- Creeper
- Trouble Light
- Grease Gun and Flexible Attachments
- Wrenches
- ⅜- or ½-inch-Drive Ratchet Wrench
- Paper Towels or Rags
- Grease Fittings—Straight, 45°, 90°
- Chassis Grease
- Rear Axle Lubricant
- Dry Lubricant (Graphite Base)

ASK A VETERAN mechanic about the "good old days" when the chassis lubrication, or grease job, involved dozens of fittings and various types of lubricants. He will tell you these are the "good old days" because most cars today have only a couple of fittings that need attention only once or twice a year (depending on the car and driving conditions).

The object of a grease job is to stave off the squeaks and groans that accompany the wearing action of metal against metal. Ideally, greasing is a maintenance task to be performed before signs of trouble appear.

In recent years, the automakers have been striving to reduce the maintenance requirements of new cars. Consequently, most now use "lubed for life" suspension components that do not require periodic lubrication. Such components use lubricant-impregnated sintered linings or low-friction plastics such as Teflon and nylon to eliminate the need for grease. The only suspension components where you'll still find grease fittings are the ball joints, and an increasing number of those are now factory sealed.

On some older cars, notably Fords from the 1970s, suspension components were greasable, but the factory installed plugs instead of grease fittings. The plugs can be easily removed and grease fittings installed using a ¼-, ⁵⁄₁₆-, or ⅜-inch wrench. Fittings with 90 degree couplings may be necessary for easy greasing of some components, such as the upper control arms.

If you do not have access to a professional lift, buy, borrow, or rent a pair of auto ramps. These make the easiest and safest perch for your car when lubricating the chassis. You can also use a jack to raise the car onto a pair of safety jack stands. Also, a creeper will allow you to move around under your car from fitting to fitting.

Some fittings, meanwhile, may be difficult or impossible to reach without a flexible attachment for the grease gun and/or a swiveling elbow. If these do not come with your gun, consider buying them to avoid having to make a second trip to the auto parts store later on.

Before beginning to grease the chassis, determine how many grease fittings your car has and where they are located. This can be done by consulting the factory shop manual for your car or by checking the lubrication guide at a friendly service station.

Note: Older car models have numerous fittings on steering linkage, front suspension, and drivetrain. Newer models have only a few fittings. Here is how to grease the fittings of your car's chassis.

1. Drive the car onto a pair of auto ramps and block the rear wheels with wheel chocks. If you plan to use safety jack stands, proceed to the next step.
2. If your car has an automatic transmission, put it in park; a manual transmission should be placed in first gear. Also engage the emergency brake. If you have not done so, block the rear wheels with wheel chocks.
3. Jack the car's front end up and rest the vehicle solidly on a pair of safety jack stands. **Note:** When lubricating ball joints, it is advisable to take the weight off the load-carrying joint by raising the front wheels off the ground. This allows the chassis grease to get into places that would otherwise have been inac-

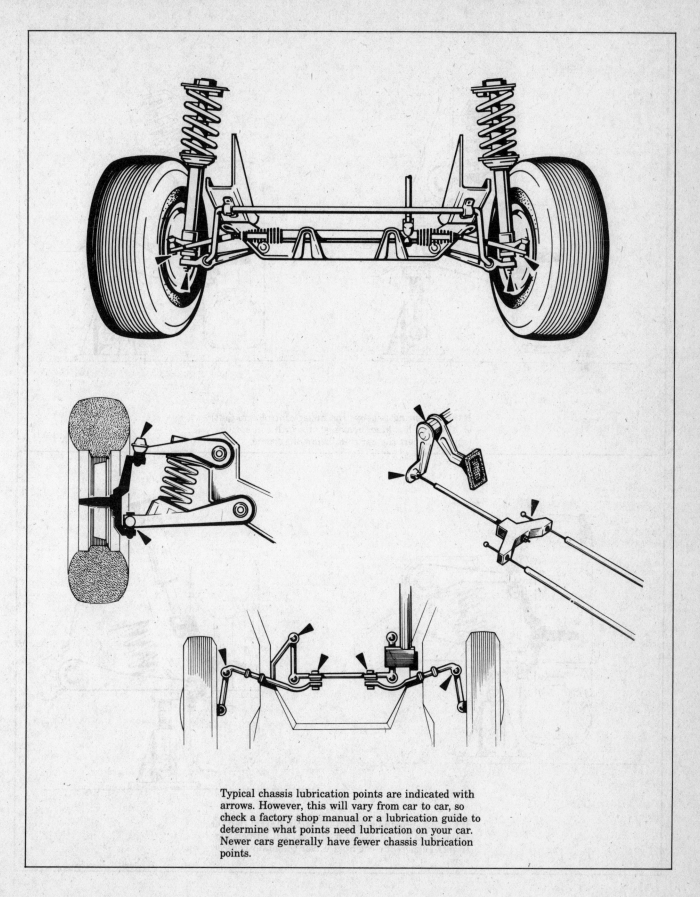

Typical chassis lubrication points are indicated with arrows. However, this will vary from car to car, so check a factory shop manual or a lubrication guide to determine what points need lubrication on your car. Newer cars generally have fewer chassis lubrication points.

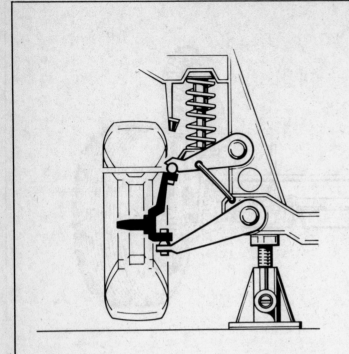
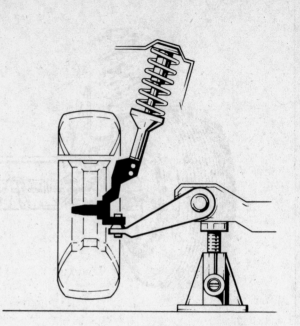

If the coil spring is above the upper control arm (left) or if the car has MacPherson struts with coil springs (right), support the car from below the frame.

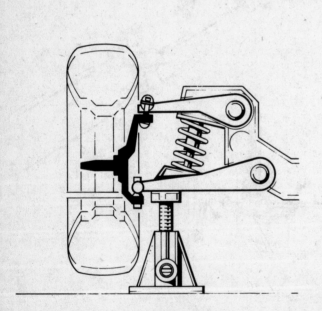
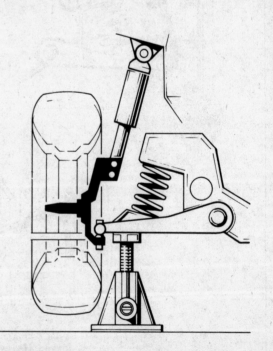

If the coil spring is between the control arms (left) or if the car is a Ford with a modified strut suspension (right), support the car from under the lower control arm.

cessible because of the pressure of one surface against the other. To determine how to jack it up, note the location of the coil spring. If it is above the upper control arm or if the front suspension has MacPherson struts with coil springs, lift from below the frame. If it is above the lower control arm, jack from under the lower control arm.

4. Slide under the car with the grease gun, trouble light, and paper towels or rags.

5. Wipe off the grit and dirt from each of the grease fittings. **Note:** Some late model cars with extended service intervals have nylon plugs where the grease fittings normally would go. If this is the first grease job your car has had, it will be necessary to remove these plugs with a wrench and replace them with standard grease fittings. These are available with straight, 45°, or 90° angle ends. The angled ends allow for easy accessibility in confined areas of the chassis.

6. Place the nozzle of the grease gun over each fitting and apply pressure to the gun's handle. If grease squirts out around the tip of the gun, it may not be properly engaged. Remove the nozzle, wipe the fitting clean, and try again. If the problem persists, the fitting may be blocked. Unscrew it with a wrench and replace it with a new fitting.

Pump grease into ball joints and steering linkage until the joints are full. *Stop pumping when the boot around the joint begins to swell.*

Note: Some universal joints are sealed and cannot be greased. For those that have fittings, leave the front of the car supported by jack stands, jack up the rear, and use two more safety jack stands to support the car. Then release the emergency brake and put the transmission in neutral. Rotate the driveshaft by hand to spot the fittings, and pump in grease until it begins to ooze from the joint. Wipe excess grease from the fittings and bearing surface. Lower the rear of the car. On front-wheel-drive vehicles, the CV-joints are sealed inside

To lubricate a grease fitting, place the gun's nozzle on the fitting and apply pressure to the handle (top). Standard grease fittings (left) can be installed or removed by hand. A grease fitting with an angled end (right) can be easier to reach in confined areas under the car.

a protective boot. The joints do not require greasing unless the boot is being replaced—and then only with special CV-joint grease.

7. Lower the car by reversing steps 1 through 3.

Repacking Wheel Bearings

Tools and Materials

- Large Screwdriver
- Jack and Safety Jack Stands
- Wheel Chocks
- Water-Pump Pliers
- Wrenches
- Brake Spoon or Long, Thin Screwdriver
- Vacuum Cleaner
- Hammer
- Wooden Stick or Brass Drift
- Wooden Block
- Ruler
- Torque Wrench
- Pliers
- Rag
- Face Mask or Respirator
- Nonflammable Cleaning Solution
- Inner and Outer Wheel Bearings
- Wheel Bearing Grease
- Grease Seals
- Cotter Pins

BECAUSE WHEEL BEARINGS are generally ignored until it is time for brake service, they are one of the most badly neglected parts on an automobile. All four wheels of a car have bearings, but the ones that must be maintained periodically are in the front wheels of rear-wheel-drive cars. Rear-wheel bearings are either permanently lubricated at the factory during assembly or are lubricated by rear-axle gear oil. Thus, they need no periodic service. On front-wheel-drive cars, meanwhile, the bearings that must be maintained are in the rear wheels. **Note:** Although the following procedures specifically refer to re-packing front wheel bearings of rear-wheel-drive cars, they are essentially the same procedures used for repacking the rear wheel bearings on front-wheel-drive cars. One obvious difference is that the rear of the car—not the front—must be raised on jack stands.

The need for periodic maintenance on wheel bearings cannot be over-emphasized. One of the functions of front-wheel bearings, when correctly adjusted and serviced, is to allow the tire and wheel to rotate smoothly, quietly, and with minimum friction. The bearings are designed to withstand tremendous load forces over a wide range of road and speed conditions—which would include side thrust when cornering as well as the severe shocks encountered when the vehicle hits chuck holes, curbs, or other obstructions. General dependability of the vehicle, braking, steering, and handling would all be affected if the wheel bearings should fail.

Wheel bearings should be serviced once every 2 years, every 24,000 miles, or as specified by the manufacturer. Servicing once a year or every 12,000 to 15,000 miles is not an uncommon practice if the vehicle is used in heavy-duty applications or is subjected to extreme climatic changes. Proper servicing of the bearings would include disassembly, cleaning and inspection, repacking, and correct wheel bearing adjustment.

On rear-wheel-drive cars, each front wheel is supported by an inner and an outer wheel bearing assembly. The front wheel bearings must be tight enough to retain proper wheel alignment but loose enough to permit free rotation of the wheel. It is a big assignment for a small bearing. On most front-wheel-drive cars, the front bearings are factory sealed and can't be lubricated.

Drum Brakes

Here is how to repack front wheel bearings on cars equipped with drum brakes, or the rear wheel bearings on front-wheel-drive cars with rear drum brakes.

1. Engage the parking gear (except front-wheel-drive).
2. Remove the wheel covers from the wheels, using a large screwdriver or the pointed end of the car's jack handle.

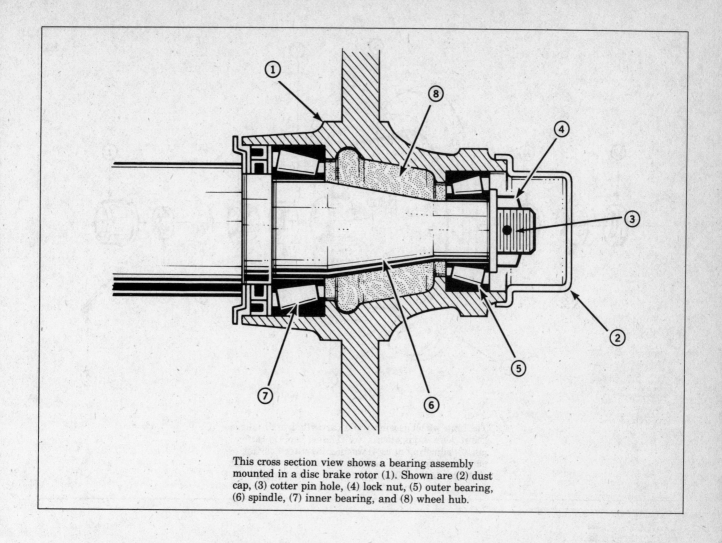

This cross section view shows a bearing assembly mounted in a disc brake rotor (1). Shown are (2) dust cap, (3) cotter pin hole, (4) lock nut, (5) outer bearing, (6) spindle, (7) inner bearing, and (8) wheel hub.

3. Using the wrench end of the jack handle or a socket wrench of the proper size, loosen the lug nuts on both front wheels about one turn.

4. Place wheel chocks behind the front or rear wheels to prevent the car from rolling.

5. Using the car jack, raise the front (or rear) of the car until the wheels are off the ground.

6. Place safety jack stands under the car to support it solidly.

7. Remove the lug nuts of both wheels, placing the nuts for each wheel into their respective wheel covers for safekeeping. Most lug nuts can be removed by turning them counterclockwise. A few cars, however, may have a left-hand thread on the lug nuts. In such a case, the lugs may be marked with the letter

"L." If your car has left-hand threaded lugs, turn the nuts clockwise to loosen them.

8. Remove the wheel and tire assembly from one side of the car. This will allow for easier removal of the drum and hub assembly and reduce the possibility of damage to the brakes and bearing parts.

9. Remove the dust cap, or grease cap. Use large water-pump pliers in combination with a screwdriver. Grip the dust cap with the pliers and pry it off with the screwdriver.

10. Remove the cotter pin. **Note:** The wheel bearing assembly is held in place by one or two nuts. If there are two nuts, the outer nut, or lock nut, is a castellated nut that is held in position by a cotter pin; the inner nut is the adjust-

61

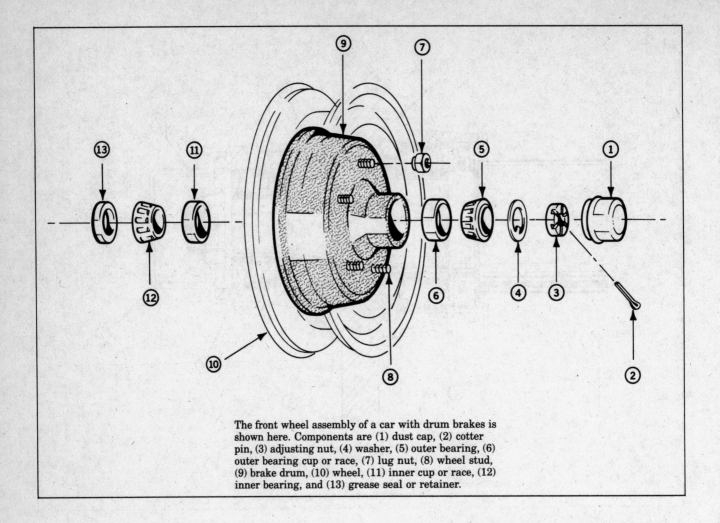

The front wheel assembly of a car with drum brakes is shown here. Components are (1) dust cap, (2) cotter pin, (3) adjusting nut, (4) washer, (5) outer bearing, (6) outer bearing cup or race, (7) lug nut, (8) wheel stud, (9) brake drum, (10) wheel, (11) inner cup or race, (12) inner bearing, and (13) grease seal or retainer.

ing nut. If there is only one nut, it is the adjusting nut, and it is held in place by a cotter pin.

11. Use a wrench to remove the nut or nuts and washer. If the nut or nuts cannot be removed by turning them counter-clockwise, try turning them clockwise.

12. Rock the drum and hub assembly to work the outer bearing loose. Use care to avoid having the bearing fall out on the floor. Have your hand ready to catch it. Place the outer bearing, washer, and adjusting nut on a clean rag.

13. Slide the drum and hub assembly off. Be careful not to allow the inner bearing to drag on the spindle. If resistance is encountered during the removal, it may be necessary to back off the brake adjusting star by using a brake spoon. On late model cars that are equipped with self-adjusting brakes, a long, thin screwdriver will be needed to push the self-adjusting lever away from the star wheel. *Caution: While the drum and hub assembly is off the car, be careful not to allow grease or dirt to contact the drum surface or brake linings. Dirt or grease on these surfaces could cause brake drag or loss of braking ability.*

14. Set the drum and hub assembly aside and prepare to do a little cleaning. *Caution: As brake linings wear, they create dust that contains asbestos. This can get into your skin, or worse, into your lungs if you are not careful. Do not blow this dust from the mechanism. The ideal method is to wear a face mask or respirator while cleaning off the brake mechanism and drums, and to remove the dust with a vacuum cleaner or liquid solvent. Avoid breathing the dust!*

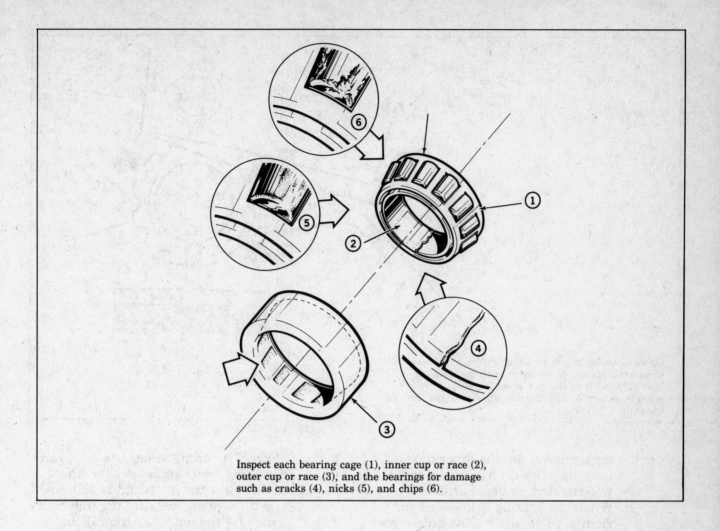

Inspect each bearing cage (1), inner cup or race (2), outer cup or race (3), and the bearings for damage such as cracks (4), nicks (5), and chips (6).

15. Using a nonflammable cleaning solution, available at an auto supply store, wash the bearing free of all grease. This is just a matter of sloshing it up and down in the solution until all the grease has dissolved.

16. Place the bearing on a clean surface and let it air dry.

17. Inspect the bearing for wear conditions such as cracks, chipping, nicks, scratches, flaking of the bearing surface, or corrosion (which should not happen except in the driest of situations). If it is bad, it should be replaced. New bearings will have to be repacked before installation.

18. Assuming your bearing is in good condition, you are ready to repack it. You will need special wheel bearing grease for this, available at auto parts stores. Place a gob of grease in your hand and work it into the bearing. Also coat the inside of the hub and spindle lightly with grease.

19. Set the bearing aside on a clean surface and remove the inner bearing. This is done as follows.

A. With the inside of the brake drum

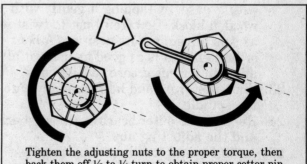

Tighten the adjusting nuts to the proper torque, then back them off ⅙ to ¼ turn to obtain proper cotter pin alignment.

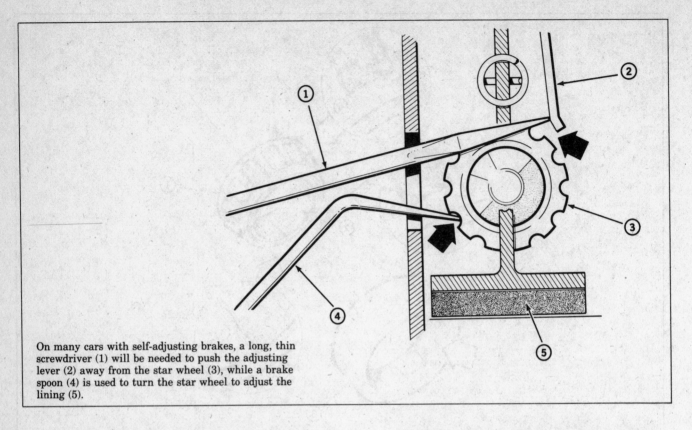

On many cars with self-adjusting brakes, a long, thin screwdriver (1) will be needed to push the adjusting lever (2) away from the star wheel (3), while a brake spoon (4) is used to turn the star wheel to adjust the lining (5).

facing down, tap the inner cone, or race, lightly with a hammer and a wooden stick or brass drift.

B. When the bearing is loosened sufficiently, remove it and its grease seal by hand.

20. Follow the same cleaning, inspection, and packing procedure for the inner bearing as outlined for the outer bearing in Steps 15 through 18.

21. Replace the repacked inner bearing into its place in the hub.

22. Obtain a new inner bearing grease seal from an auto supply store. Install the new inner seal, inner side lightly coated with grease, by tapping it gently with a wooden block. Be careful not to twist it as it is forced into its position. A bent or broken seal is as good as none at all and will permit grease to leak out.

23. Slide the drum and hub assembly onto the spindle.

24. Replace the outer bearing, the washer, and the adjusting nut.

25. At this point, it is necessary to adjust the wheel bearing. **Note:** A manufacturer's specifications should always be followed. If specifications are not available, these basic guidelines for wheel bearing adjustment should be followed.

A. With a ruler, measure the hub bore size for the outer bearing. If the bore size is 1¾ inches or more, tighten the adjusting nut using a torque wrench to 17 foot-pounds while rotating the wheel by hand. If the bore size is less than 1¾ inches, tighten the adjusting nut using a torque wrench to 8 foot-pounds while rotating the wheel by hand.

B. After tightening the adjusting nut to the specified torque, back off the nut ⅙ to ¼ turn to obtain proper cotter pin alignment between the cotter pin hole in the spindle nut and the cotter pin hole in the spindle. **Note:** If there is a lock nut, replace it and align it so its cotter pin hole lines up with the hole in the spindle.

Note: If drum brake adjustment was altered during the repacking procedure, proper brake adjustment will be necessary. This is covered in "The Brake System" chapter.

26. Install a new cotter pin through the adjusting nut or lock nut and spindle. Bend the ends of the pin around the nut with pliers so that it will not come out.

27. Reinstall the dust cap and tire and wheel assembly, reversing Steps 7 through 9.

   Note: Some cars come equipped with spring static suppressors in the dust cap. Be sure that the ends of the cotter pin do not contact the suppressor.

28. Follow Steps 8 through 27 for repacking the bearings on the other front wheel.

29. After both front wheel bearings have been repacked, lower the car, reversing Steps 1 through 6.

Disc Brakes

The procedure for repacking and inspecting front wheel bearings on disc-type brake-equipped vehicles is basically the same as for drum-type brakes, with one exception: the disc brake caliper must be removed before the rotor and hub assembly can be removed.

   Each manufacturer has a different type of caliper mounting system. Generally, it is a

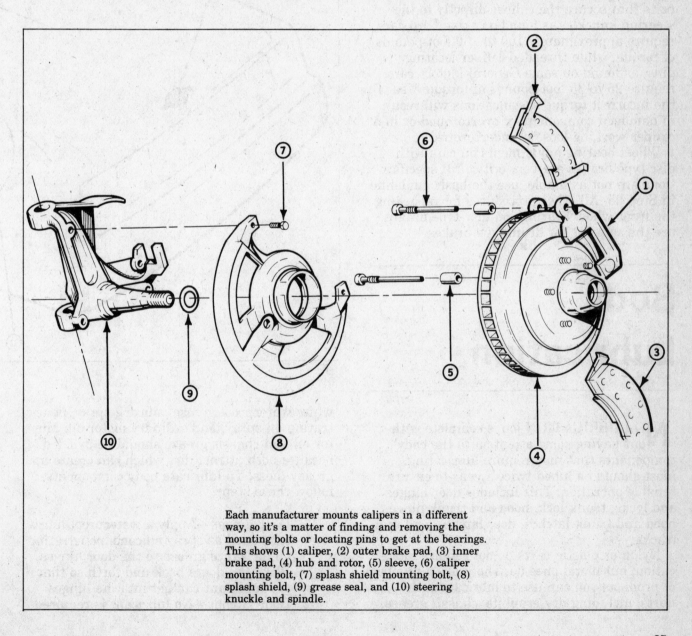

Each manufacturer mounts calipers in a different way, so it's a matter of finding and removing the mounting bolts or locating pins to get at the bearings. This shows (1) caliper, (2) outer brake pad, (3) inner brake pad, (4) hub and rotor, (5) sleeve, (6) caliper mounting bolt, (7) splash shield mounting bolt, (8) splash shield, (9) grease seal, and (10) steering knuckle and spindle.

matter of locating and removing the caliper mounting bolts or threaded caliper guide locating pins that attach the caliper to the steering knuckle or mounting bracket. During the removal of the caliper, it is not usually recommended that the hydraulic brake line be disconnected from the caliper. Doing so will make it necessary to bleed the front brake system. Do not, however, allow the caliper to hang from the brake line. Support the weight of the caliper with a piece of wire.

Note: When installing the caliper after repacking the bearings, be sure to use a torque wrench. Be aware of which bolts you are tightening. For instance, the caliper mounting bolts that secure the caliper directly to the steering knuckle, as found on some Ford cars, require approximately 100 to 130 foot-pounds of torque, while threaded caliper locating pins, as found on some General Motors cars, require 25 to 35 foot-pounds of torque. Use of the incorrect torque specifications will result in damaged components if overtorqued or in a caliper working loose if undertorqued.

Wheel bearing adjustments on cars with disc-type brakes are very critical. If specifications are not available, use the basic guideline in Step 25. All other procedures for repacking the front wheel bearings on disc-type brakes are the same as for drum-type brakes.

Body Lubrication

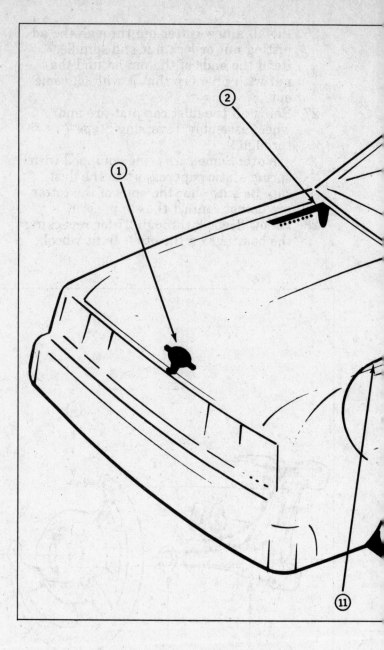

NO LUBRICATION job is complete without paying some attention to the body components that may require lubricating. Most should be lubed twice a year to ensure reliable operation. This includes door hinges and locks, trunk lock, hood and trunk hinges, hood and trunk latches, door latches, and seat tracks.

Nylon or plastic parts do not require lubrication, but metal ones do. There are a number of products you can use to lubricate such parts, including dry graphite, chassis grease, white waterproof grease, silicone spray, penetrating oil spray, and ordinary motor oil. Motor oil and chassis grease should be avoided because both attract dirt which can create a greasy mess. To lubricate body components, follow these steps.

1. Door hinges—Apply a waterproof lubricant such as spray silicone, penetrating oil, or white grease to the door hinges. Work the doors back and forth so that the lubricant can get into the hinges.
2. Door latches—No lubricant is required

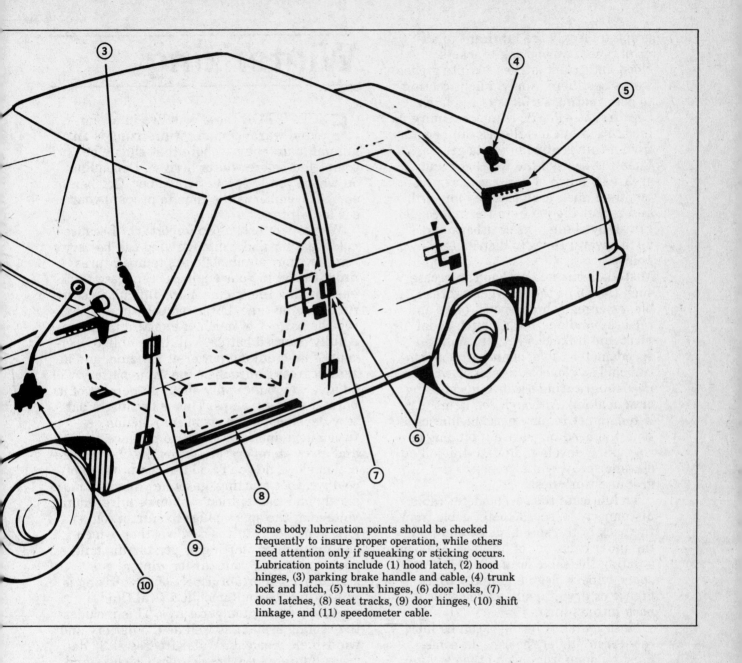

Some body lubrication points should be checked frequently to insure proper operation, while others need attention only if squeaking or sticking occurs. Lubrication points include (1) hood latch, (2) hood hinges, (3) parking brake handle and cable, (4) trunk lock and latch, (5) trunk hinges, (6) door locks, (7) door latches, (8) seat tracks, (9) door hinges, (10) shift linkage, and (11) speedometer cable.

on plastic latches but metal ones can benefit from a waterproof lubricant or dry graphite powder. Apply a thin coating on the latch surface and on the latch mechanism in the door. Some vehicles have lubrication access holes in the door panel that allow you to apply oil or other liquid lubricants to the door latch mechanism. A few drops are all that's necessary.

3. Door locks—Use silicone spray or dry graphite powder. Do not use oil since it can make the lock tumblers sticky. Af-

ter applying the lubricant into the lock, push the key in and out several times and turn the lock to thoroughly distribute the lubricant. Products are available with special applicator tips that apply the lubricant directly into the lock.

4. Trunk lock and glovebox lock—Use the same treatment as you did for the door locks.

5. Hood and trunk hinges—Use a waterproof lubricant such as silicone spray, penetrating oil, white grease, or dry

graphite. Apply the lubricant to all pivot points and spring brackets.

6. Hood and trunk latches—White grease works best here. Apply a light coating to both mating surfaces of the latch.

7. Seat tracks—Plastic runners require no lubrication but metal ones can benefit from a thin coating of white grease. Push the seat all the way back and grease as much of the tracks as possible, then push it all the way forward and repeat the job from the other side. Finish by sliding the seat back and forth several times to distribute the grease.

8. Miscellaneous items—You can grease such things as the emergency brake cable, emergency brake pedal pivot and release handle or lever, clutch pedal pivot and linkage, gearshift linkage, speedometer cable, heater or vent control cables, glovebox hinges or whatever needs lubricating because it's sticking or squeaking. Although the items just listed do not require periodic lubrication, the need may arise if binding or squeaking develops. Penetrating oil or silicone spray, white grease or dry graphite work best.

To lubricate the speedometer cable, disconnect the speedometer cable from the back of the speedometer and pull the inner cable out of its liner. After inspecting the cable for damage or frayed spots, wipe it clean and apply white grease or dry graphite as you slide it back into its liner.

Most gearshift linkages can be lubricated from under the car, but some must be done from inside the car after removing the dust cover or boot from the base of the shifter. White grease works best for this application.

9. A final step in the body lubrication process is to clear the drain holes or channels in the bottom of the doors. The drain holes prevent water from collecting inside the doors and causing rust. Mud, leaves, and insects can clog these holes so periodic cleaning may be necessary. Simply push a narrow screwdriver into the drain hole and work it up and down until the hole is clear.

Winterizing

EXCEPT FOR those who live in a year-round warm climate, winterizing is an annual maintenance chore that should be completed before winter arrives. Depending on where you live, late September, October, or early November is the time to prepare your car for winter.

Why is winterizing so important? Because cold weather and winter driving can be very hard on your automobile. As temperatures drop, the oil in your engine's crankcase thickens, making the engine more difficult to start. At the same time, lower temperatures also rob the battery of much of its cranking power. A fully charged battery will have only 65 percent of its cranking power at freezing, and at zero degrees Fahrenheit the same battery will be able to produce only about 40 percent of its normal starting amps. This is because a battery depends on the chemical reaction between acid and lead plates to produce power, and as the temperature drops the chemical reaction slows down. To add to the problem of cold weather starting, gasoline vaporizes more slowly and the ignition system requires more voltage at the spark plugs to start a cold engine. The net result is cold weather, which can mean hard starting or no starting unless you've prepared your car for winter.

Another important aspect of winterizing is protecting your automobile's vital fluids against freezing temperatures. This includes the cooling system as well as the battery and windshield washers. Water freezes at 32 degrees Fahrenheit (zero degrees Celsius), and when that happens, its volume expands about 10 percent as it turns to ice. If the cooling system is not protected by sufficient antifreeze, freezing can split the radiator or crack the engine block. A rundown battery is also in danger of freezing because the concentration of acid isn't as great as that inside a fully charged battery. And if the battery freezes, it won't produce any voltage because the chemical reaction will be stopped cold. Ice can also crack the battery case, allowing the acid to leak out. As for windshield washers, ice here will usually crack the fluid reservoir or damage the electric pump. To avoid such problems, therefore, you should check the strength of the antifreeze in the cooling system and the battery's state of charge, and add windshield washer antifreeze or pre-mixed solution to the fluid reservoir well in advance of freezing weather.

There are a number of things you can do to minimize the problems brought on by cold weather and to insure that your car will start and run in spite of severe weather. Use the accompanying checklist as a guide to winterizing your car.

WINTERIZING CHECKLIST

☐ **Cooling system.** Check the strength of the antifreeze with a hydrometer and add antifreeze as needed to provide freezing protection to the lowest anticipated temperature—or drain and refill the cooling system with a 50/50 mixture of antifreeze and water (this will provide freezing protection down to minus 34 degrees Fahrenheit).

☐ **Battery.** The battery must be fully charged and in good condition. The battery cables and terminals should be cleaned and tightened. If the battery is more than four years old, you may want to consider investing in a new one of equal or greater capacity. As a rule of thumb, your battery should have a minimum rated amp capacity at least equal to your engine's displacement in cubic inches. If your car sits outside in extremely cold weather, buy the highest rated amp capacity battery that will physically fit in your car.

☐ **Engine.** For cold weather starting, you should have a multi-viscosity oil such as 10W-30 or 10W-40 in your engine's crankcase. Lower viscosity oils such as 5W-20 and 5W-30 can be especially valuable for reducing cranking effort during extremely cold weather. If it's been awhile since you've changed oil, an oil and filter change would be a wise addition to your winterizing "to do" list since fresh oil cranks easier than dirty oil.

☐ **Tune-up.** An engine in proper tune starts much easier than one that is out of tune, warm weather or cold. If your engine has been experiencing any drivability problems such as hard starting, hesitation, stumbling, rough running, stalling, etc., during warm weather, you can bet it will only get worse once the temperatures start to drop. Cleaning and regapping the spark plugs or installing new ones can greatly reduce the starting voltage requirements on the ignition system. Check the rotor, distributor cap, and plug wires, and replace any parts found to be defective. Spraying the ignition wires and distributor cap with a water-repellent spray can help starting, too. Other items to check include ignition timing, idle speed, and operation of the choke on carbureted vehicles.

☐ **Heater and defroster.** The best time to check the operation of the heater and defrosters is before you really need them. Heater output can be increased by installing a hotter thermostat. If the heater and/or defrosters don't seem to be blowing out as much air as they should be, check the operation of the control cables and air control doors. A door that fails to open or only opens partially can block the flow of air. Don't forget to check the rear window defroster if your car has one.

☐ **Exhaust system.** You should carefully inspect the exhaust system for damage or leaks, since carbon monoxide poisoning is one of the major hazards of winter driving. When your car's windows are rolled up, a leaking exhaust pipe or muffler can allow carbon monoxide to get inside the car and build up to dangerous levels. If you find any problems, fix them now.

☐ **Body and chassis lubrication.** Lubricate the suspension to protect the chassis parts. To prevent frozen locks, lubricate the door and trunk locks with silicone, graphite, or another waterproof lubricant. Emergency brake cables and linkage should also be lubed to protect against freezing.

☐ **Windshield washers and wipers.** Make sure the wipers are in good condition (you may wish to consider installing "winter blades" that are wrapped in rubber to prevent ice buildup and streaking), and add antifreeze concentrate or pre-mixed washer fluid to the fluid reservoir.

☐ **Tires.** Mount snow tires on the drive

wheels of your car (front-wheel drive would have the snow tires on the front, not the back).

☐ **Fuel tank.** Add a can of fuel system deicer once a month during cold weather to keep moisture from freezing and blocking the fuel lines. For diesels, switch to the lighter winter grade fuel or a blended fuel to prevent waxing.

☐ **Body protection.** Road salt is great for clearing icy highways but it is also extremely hard on your car's finish, trim, and wheels. Aluminum components such as cast wheels, bumpers, trim strips, and suspension components are very vulnerable to salt corrosion. To protect your car, wax the body, trim, and wheels with a long-lasting sealer such as one of the many different poly- or silicone-based waxes now on the market. If your vehicle has not been undercoated and/or rustproofed, perhaps you should consider doing so before it's too late.

☐ **Survival gear.** You should carry the following "survival gear" in your trunk to help you cope with the emergencies of winter driving: jumper cables, a shovel, a bag of sand (an old milk jug filled with sand works great), a blanket (in case you're stranded), perhaps a pair of boots, gloves, and other winter clothing.

☐ **Cold starting aids.** An engine block heater is one of the best cold weather starting aids you can buy. The type that are installed in the engine block or connect to the heater hoses are best because they keep the coolant in the engine warm. This makes the engine easier to crank and helps the fuel vaporize faster. The heaters plug into an ordinary 110 volt outlet and will use several hundred watts of electricity. Using a timer to turn the heater on several hours before you're ready to start the car can save on your electric bill. Battery heaters are also available, as are dipstick oil heaters, to improve cold weather cranking. On diesel engines, a fuel preheater can prevent waxing and insure trouble-free driving during cold weather. If your vehicle is not already equipped with such a device, you should seriously consider adding one.

Rustproofing

Tools and Materials

- Wire Brush
- Electric Drill and Drill Bits
- Jack and Safety Jack Stands
- Safety Goggles
- Rustproofing Kit
- Kerosene or Mineral Solvent
- Rags

RUSTING of cars has been a problem since the first ones were built. The ferrous metals used in their manufacture, weather conditions where they are driven, and the amount of exposure to the elements all contribute to the development of rust.

Rust not only detracts from the cosmetic appearance of your car, but ultimately can cause serious structural damage. Today, more cars go to the junkyard because of rust than because of mechanical failures.

Cars rust from the inside out, so a small sign of rust on the finish of a car can mean that a much larger area underneath is being ravaged by rust.

There are two methods of deterring the development of rust on your car: undercoating applied by the manufacturer and rustproofing usually applied only at the discretion of the buyer. The standard factory undercoating is applied to only some surfaces on all cars. Usually, it is inadequate. Rustproofing coats the unfinished metal surfaces of your car with a protective layer of a petroleum-based compound.

If you do not trade-in cars frequently, rustproofing is a good investment. One study reported that it can add a full year to the life of your car. However, to be most practical, it should be done before your car has been driven for 3 months or 3,000 miles. Only during this approximate period can you expect to prevent rust from getting started. After that, it would be virtually impossible to find and re-

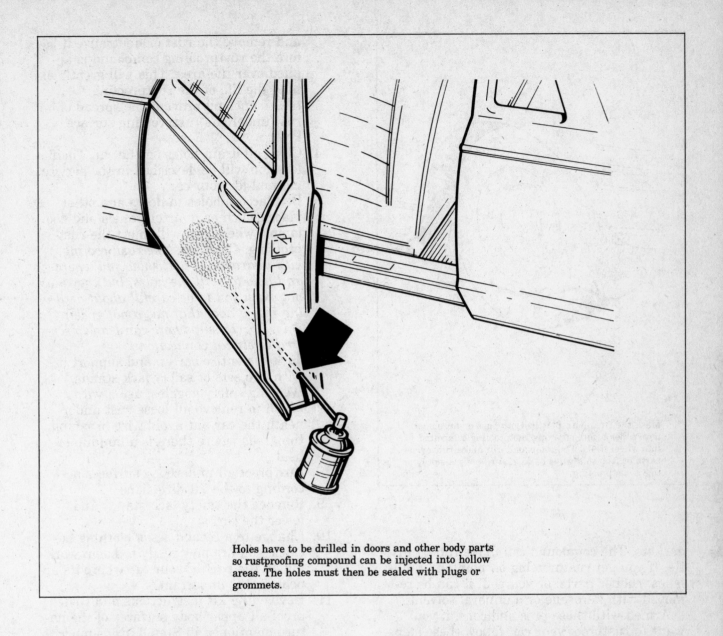

Holes have to be drilled in doors and other body parts so rustproofing compound can be injected into hollow areas. The holes must then be sealed with plugs or grommets.

move all the water-retaining dirt and grime that will have accumulated. Because rustproofing compound can seal in moisture, rust that has already started and is not removed will continue its development. Rustproofing is less advisable after your car has been exposed to a season of road or marine salt.

Rustproofing can be done by your car dealer, a specialty shop, or by yourself. Professionals are likely to do a more thorough job and often guarantee their work. But if you wish to do the job yourself, you can buy a rustproofing kit for about one fifth the amount most professionals charge.

A rustproofing kit usually contains enough material for a full-size car and detailed instructions for the process. After your car is clean and dry, you should be able to finish the procedure in about 4 or 5 hours. Provide at least two changes of old clothing that you can dispose of if necessary when you have finished the job.

Do not begin rustproofing when the humidity is high and metal surfaces are naturally damp. Do not apply rustproofing to any component where there is a buildup of heat, such as the engine, radiator core, transmission, driveshaft, differential, manifold, exhaust pipes, or catalytic converter. And avoid getting the compound on rubber seals, tubes, and

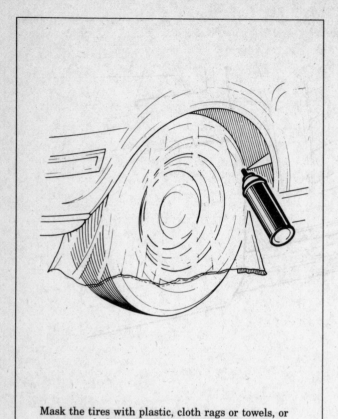

Mask the tires with plastic, cloth rags or towels, or newspaper before spraying rustproofing compound into wheel wells. The compound can make rubber parts brittle, so always be careful where you spray or inject rustproofing.

gaskets. The compound can make rubber brittle. If you get rustproofing on painted finishes, rubber parts, or yourself, it can be removed with kerosene or a mineral solvent.

Armed with these pros and cons, if you want to rustproof your car, follow these steps.

1. Have the engine and engine compartment of your car professionally steam-cleaned.
2. Completely wash your car, following the procedure outlined in the "Appearance Care" section in this chapter.
3. Use a wire brush to remove all loose rust from the body of the car such as under the hood, firewall, wheel cover panels, mounting brackets, battery mount, and inside the trunk. Pay attention to hidden areas. **Note:** Severely rusted areas should be pretreated with chemical products that either dissolve

and remove the rust or neutralize it before the rustproofing compound is applied over the area. This will greatly extend the life of the rustproofing treatment and prevent the spread of rust under the rustproofing surface layer.

4. Clear all drain holes on the car. Their location will be described in the service manual for your car.
5. Drill access holes in doors and other places, such as quarter panels and door jambs, where you will inject the rustproofing. ***Caution:*** *The rustproofing kit's instructions will show you where and how to drill the holes, but they may not warn you to be careful about drilling into a door that has a power window. Carelessness here can lead to severed electrical connections.*
6. Jack the entire car up and support it with two sets of safety jack stands.
7. Wearing safety goggles, use a wire brush to remove all loose rust underneath the car but avoid wire-brushing the areas where there is a buildup of heat.
8. Rustproof all underbody surfaces according to the kit directions.
9. Remove the safety jack stands and lower the car.
10. Change to a second set of clothing because you are now ready to begin working on the part of your car where its appearance is important.
11. Review the kit instructions and rustproof all upper body surfaces of the nature mentioned in Step 3. Remember to avoid rubber components; mask the tires before spraying wheel wells.
12. Remove all removable trim on the car's exterior, rustproof trim and mounting holes and clips, and replace the trim.
13. Install the extension on the rustproofing applicator and, following instructions carefully, inject rustproofing compound into hollow body parts through access holes drilled in Step 5.
14. Install grommets from the kit into the drilled holes to seal them.
15. Remove excess compound from your car and yourself with kerosene or mineral solvent.

Appearance

Tools and Materials

- Garden Hose
- Pail
- Sponge
- Towels
- Rags
- Chamois
- Scrub Brush
- Soft-Bristled Brush
- Lightweight Cardboard
- Vacuum Cleaner
- Water
- Mild Detergent or Car Washing Compound
- Vinyl Top Cleaner
- Cooking Oil
- Vinyl Top Dressing
- Car Polish or Pre-Wax Cleaner
- Tar Remover
- Car Wax
- Cornstarch
- Chrome Cleaner
- Baking Soda
- Clear Spray Acrylic
- Trisodium Phosphate or Abrasive Household Cleaner
- Tire Dressing
- Vinyl or Fabric Cleaner
- Carpet Shampoo
- Glass Cleaner
- Paper Towels

IF YOU maintain the original appearance of your car—inside and out—you can expect to obtain at least several hundred dollars more at trade-in time or when you sell the car to a private individual than you would from a car that has been neglected. So, you would be wise to spend a little time, money, and energy on the appearance of your large investment.

Aside from the mechanical aspects, most used-car appraisers or buyers are looking for rust, dents, and the condition of upholstery and carpeting. To keep your car looking as new as possible, your main concerns should be regular wash jobs, seasonal waxing, repair of minor or major body damage, interior maintenance, and rustproofing.

Washing the Car

Many drivers claim a clean car runs better. Obviously, it does not have any effect, but it certainly seems to be a psychological benefit. It also is said that drivers of clean cars have fewer accidents. Certainly, there is more satisfaction in owning and driving a clean car. And a regular plan of weekly washing is the first step, especially in winter if you live in an area where roads are chemically treated. Follow these steps to wash the car.

1. Park the car in the shade.
2. Using a garden hose and plenty of cold water, rinse the entire surface of the car. If you do not have access to a hose, use pails of water and a sponge. Be sure to hose or wipe along the edges of trim moldings and the undersides of fenders, wheel wells, and bumpers.
3. Wash the car. **Note:** If your car has a vinyl-covered roof, proceed to "Vinyl Roof Care" *before* washing the car. Unless the car is very grimy, do not use a washing compound. Soaps or harsh detergents should not be used. If it is necessary to use anything more than water, use a mild liquid dishwashing detergent or a mild auto washing compound. Do not mix too much detergent or compound. Often, a capful of detergent in a gallon of water will be sufficient. **Note:** Chemically treated cloths sold for cleaning cars are not recommended.

   Wash the car with the hose or pails of clean water, using large pieces of toweling. Start at the top of the car and work downward; wash the top and then one panel or section at a time. **Note:** Bird droppings, insects, and tar marks may be easier to remove if you hold a cloth saturated with cooking oil on the area until the material will lift off.
4. Rinse the car. If you are using detergent to wash the car, use the hose or pails of clean water and clean towels to rinse each panel or section as you go along. By the time you have finished

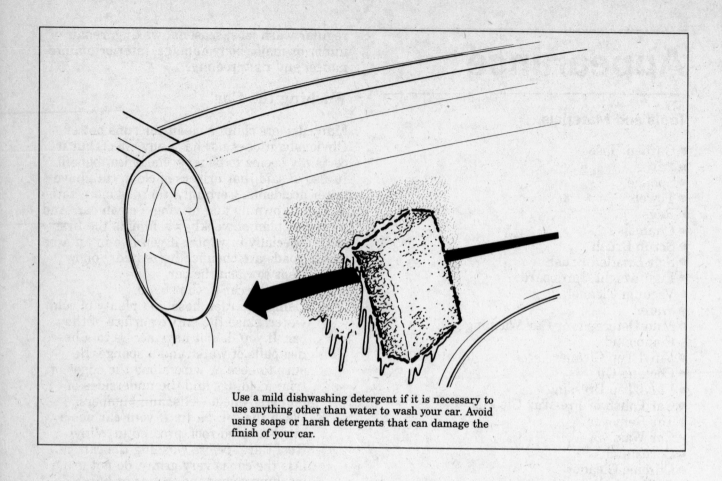

Use a mild dishwashing detergent if it is necessary to use anything other than water to wash your car. Avoid using soaps or harsh detergents that can damage the finish of your car.

washing and rinsing all sections of the car, most areas will have dried and will be somewhat water-spotted. Wet the entire car again. By drying the car while it is still wet, you can avoid water-spotting.

5. Dry car with a damp, clean chamois or towel.

Vinyl Roof Care

The vinyl covering used on the tops of cars is subject to drying and fading. Keeping it clean and protected will lengthen its life. Cleaning a vinyl-covered top is no more difficult than washing the rest of the car. Most vinyl roof materials have a textured surface that resembles embossed leather. A scrub brush with nylon bristles does a good job of cleaning this kind of surface. Vinyl dressings can keep the material soft and pliable, and prevent it from drying out and cracking. In addition, such dressings help retain the original color and texture of the vinyl. To clean a vinyl-covered

top, follow these steps.

1. Before washing the car apply a vinyl top cleaner or a suds solution made with a mild dishwashing liquid and water. Apply and remove the cleaner according to the manufacturer's directions. Apply the suds with a scrub brush, using a circular motion.
2. Rinse the suds off using a garden hose or pails of clean, cold water.
3. Allow the vinyl top to dry.
4. Apply a dressing formulated for vinyl tops. Such dressings are available at auto supply stores. Apply the dressing in the shade according to the manufacturer's directions. Usually, a small, clean cloth is saturated with dressing, and a thin, smooth coating is applied, using a smearing, circular motion. Apply only enough vinyl dressing for the treated area to take on a slight luster.
5. Allow the vinyl dressing to dry for at least 30 minutes.
6. Buff the surface with a clean cloth.

Note: There also are vinyl top dressings that are formulated to restore the color of vinyl tops. However, they should only be used on tops that have been neglected for a long time. These dressings are designed to be sprayed or brushed on. If it is necessary for you to apply such a pigmented vinyl dressing, be sure to follow the manufacturer's directions carefully, because these dressings penetrate the vinyl material and, once applied, they are impossible to remove.

Polishing the Car

Regular washing is not enough to keep a car looking new. No matter what kind of finish is on your car, regular polishing is necessary to keep it clean and bright.

The easiest way to polish a car is to use a liquid cream polish or pre-wax cleaner. Liquid polishes contain agents that pick up surface dirt as the polish is applied and hold it suspended as the polish dries. These one-step polishes do not require hard rubbing for a good shine. When the polish has dried, you need only to wipe off the residue with a cloth.

It is important to wash your car before applying polish. Any dirt particles left on the surface can scratch the paint when you apply the polish.

1. Park the car in the shade; otherwise, heat from the metal surface will interfere with the cleaning action.
2. Apply the polish with a dampened cloth. Large flat surfaces should be polished first, using a circular motion with overlapping strokes. The polish will dry rapidly so it is best to do one panel or section at a time.
3. As each section dries, rub off the dried residue with a clean, dry cloth. A soft-bristled brush is handy for removing dried polish around body trim. Tar remover is useful for removing bits of tar and other gummy substances that will probably be stuck to the lower sides of the car body.
4. Check to make sure that you have treated all surfaces. Any dried polish in cracks and crevices can be buffed out with the soft-bristled brush. Do not forget to buff the edges of the trunk lid, hood, and doors.

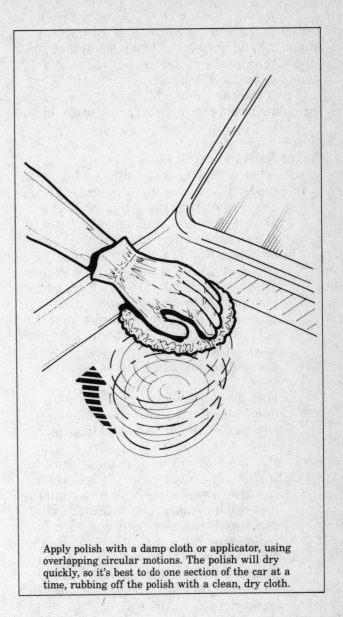

Apply polish with a damp cloth or applicator, using overlapping circular motions. The polish will dry quickly, so it's best to do one section of the car at a time, rubbing off the polish with a clean, dry cloth.

Waxing the Car

The best overall protection you can give the finish of your car is a good coat of wax. The products available today will produce a hard finish that will withstand the ravages of weather, air pollution, and strong detergents. And they have been designed to eliminate much of the labor that used to be associated with waxing.

There are two basic types of waxes. One is carnauba, a true vegetable wax, and the other includes various chemical compounds made of silicone polymers. Both types are available in either liquid or paste form, and both will withstand about 6 months of hard punishment. Liquid wax takes less time and effort to apply than paste wax does, but paste wax tends to be more durable.

Wash the car thoroughly just before waxing it. A fairly cool day with a temperature in the low 70s is best for waxing. To wax your car, follow these steps.

1. Park the car in the shade.
2. After washing, apply either a liquid or paste wax according to the manufacturer's directions. Dampen a soft, clean cloth with water and apply the wax to the cloth. It is important to apply a complete film of wax and to do only one panel at a time. Also, get the wax into all crevices in the car body. Wax will prevent water from getting under trim pieces and other hidden areas that are subject to rusting. A soft-bristled brush works well. **Note:** Do not wax a vinyl-covered roof or black matte painted trim.
3. Wax dries quickly so wipe off the residue immediately with clean cloths. If the wax is applied too thickly or allowed to set for too long after drying, this residue will be difficult to remove. If this happens, cornstarch will absorb the dried residue without removing the wax finish. Apply a light dusting of cornstarch to a dry cloth and wipe the residue away.
4. After you have removed the wax residue, use a soft, clean cloth to buff the surface lightly. Insufficient buffing may leave streaks in the wax.

The proof of a good wax job is when water beads on the surface. Areas that have not been waxed will become unevenly wet and will stay that way until evaporation takes place.

Chrome Care

Now, more than ever, care and precaution are needed to keep "chrome" looking new, because some of your car's bright trimwork is no longer made of metal. Colored plastics, such as Mylar, are being used in place of plated metal. Plastics can be made to resemble metal trim, but they are not as durable. It is sometimes difficult to determine whether the bright work on your car is metal or one of the plastic substitutes.

Whether the trim on your car is metal or plastic, using a commercial chrome cleaner, followed by a protective coating, will keep it looking new. On heavily stained areas, a paste made from water and baking soda will do a better job than most cleaners, because the paste is mildly abrasive. Engine exhaust, for example, contains oily substances that stick to bright work and are difficult to remove with mild cleaners. The best procedure is to go over all the bright trim with a commercial cleaner and then go back to remove any remaining stains with the solution of baking soda and water.

If you do not protect the chrome after it has been cleaned, the stain will return. Large areas of bright work such as the bumpers and side trim can be protected with a coat of durable clear acrylic. Acrylic is extremely tough and fast-drying, and it is best to cover as much of the bright work as possible with it. Surfaces that are protected will not stain and are safe from most weather damage.

Clear acrylic is available in spray cans at most auto supply stores. When applying, use an 8-by-12-inch piece of lightweight cardboard to protect adjacent painted areas from the spray. Hold the cardboard against the surface to be protected as you carefully spray a thin coat of clear acrylic on the bright work.

Tire Care

Improving the appearance of a car must include attention to the tires. Keeping tires clean, however, can be a problem. Various restrictions on the use of phosphates in commercial cleaners have resulted in some products that do not do a very good job. Trisodium phosphate, for example, will remove any whitewall stain from a tire. If phosphates are banned in your area, you will have to substitute one of the abrasive household cleaners. Apply it with a damp cloth and use a scrub brush to work it into discolored areas of the whitewall. Rinse with clean water.

Repeated scuffing against curbs blemishes the whitewall area of a tire, and there is nothing you can do to restore it. Paints that claim to renew the appearance of whitewall tires are available, but they are only stopgap measures. When these coatings are first applied, they have a glossy white look, but soon yellow and fade.

Tires are also subject to attack by pollutants that cause discoloration and the formation of minute checks or cracks in the sidewalls of tires. Keeping the tires clean will slow this process. Applying a commercial tire dressing will slow it even more. Usually, two applications of tire dressing annually are enough to keep your tires looking good. Follow the manufacturer's recommendations about the frequency of application.

Cleaning the Interior

A good vacuum cleaner is the number one tool in keeping your car's interior clean. Auto upholstery and carpeting take a terrific beating and the abrasive action of accumulated dirt and grit help accelerate wear and tear on the carpeting.

The interior of the car should be vacuumed at least once a month. If you do not have floor mats, consider purchasing a set. They make cleaning easier and quicker, and they protect the most vulnerable areas of your car's floor.

There are three types of materials you will need for interior cleaning: vinyl or fabric cleaner, depending on the type of upholstery you have; carpet shampoo, which sometimes is the same product as upholstery cleaner; and glass cleaner, one that leaves no film.

The use of such products will be explained on their containers. The real challenge is to develop the habit of using them as required.

Cleaning the Engine

THERE ARE a number of good reasons for keeping your automobile engine clean of accumulations of grease and oil. You reduce the hazard of fire, and a clean engine has a better appearance and runs cooler. In addition, it's easier to inspect, service, and repair underhood components.

Tools and Materials

- Paintbrush
- Garden Hose
- Putty Knife or Scraper
- Plastic Wrapping Material
- Tape, Rubber Bands, or String
- Engine Degreaser
- Rags

There are several ways to clean your car's engine. If you have access to a steam cleaner, this is the best method to use. Some service stations and auto garages will perform this service. Another alternative is the self-service, coin-operated, high-pressure hose available at car washing facilities.

You can, however, clean your engine yourself with an engine degreaser. In general, engine degreasers have a fairly strong odor, but this type of chemical cleaner is usually nonflammable and will do an adequate job.

Caution: Degreasing products sold as engine or parts cleaners contain chemicals that may damage the painted finish of your car. Some of these undesirable chemicals are trisodium phosphate (TSP), acetone, caustic soda, and lacquer thinner (a petroleum distillate). To be sure that your car is protected from possible paint damage, be sure to cover the cowl (at the bottom of the windshield) and front fenders. If a spill or overspray should touch the painted finish, flush the area with water and wipe it dry.

If you decide to use a commercially available engine degreaser, here is how to do it.

1. Wearing old clothes, start the engine. Run it for about 15 to 20 minutes, until it reaches normal operating temperature. This will speed the removal of grime.
2. Turn the engine off, raise the hood and remove the air filter housing. Instructions are given in the section on "Air Filter Service" in the "Fuel System" chapter.
3. Wrap with plastic (sections of plastic trash bags can be used) all components that might be affected if doused with

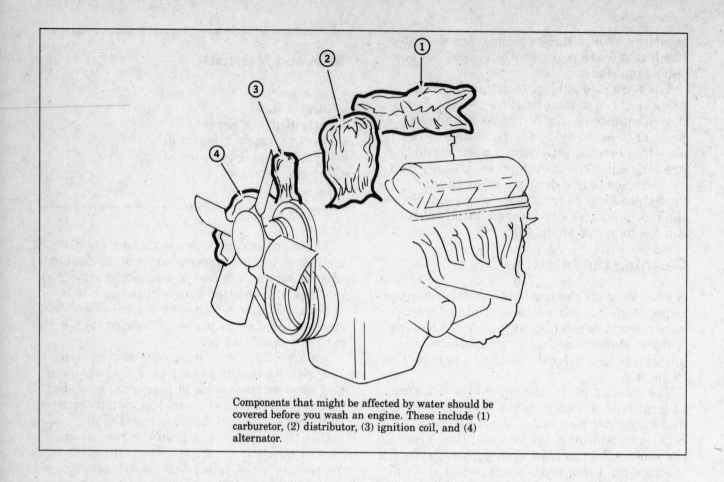

Components that might be affected by water should be covered before you wash an engine. These include (1) carburetor, (2) distributor, (3) ignition coil, and (4) alternator.

water, especially the distributor and the carburetor. Other components to cover include the ignition coil and the alternator. On diesel engines, cover the alternator and intake manifold air inlet.

After covering these components, secure the plastic with tape, rubber bands, or string to prevent it from being dislodged by the water pressure of the hose.

4. Coat the entire engine with the engine degreaser according to the manufacturer's directions. *Caution: Do not smoke. Some degreasers are flammable.* If a product with a squirt-type can is used, you may have to use an old paintbrush to coat inaccessible areas. Some engine degreasers are available in spray cans, which—although more expensive—do a good job of covering the engine.

5. Allow the degreaser to work for the time directed.

6. Wash the engine with water from a garden hose. *Caution: On diesel engines, don't spray the injection pump unless it is cold. Spraying cold water on a hot pump can damage the pump.* (If your engine is quite dirty, you may have to repeat Steps 4, 5, and 6 several times on certain portions of the engine. In addition, you may have to chip some of the heavier accumulations away with a putty knife or other scraper.)

7. After the engine cleaning job is completed, remove the plastic wrapping from the carburetor and other components.

8. Replace the air filter housing and close the hood.

9. Start the engine. **Note:** If you have difficulty getting the engine started, the spark plug wires may be wet. Usually, wiping them off with a clean cloth will solve the problem. If this does not make starting easier, look for excessive moisture at the ignition coil or at the distributor. Wipe these components dry with a clean rag.

DIAGNOSING CAR TROUBLE

ONE OF THE most gratifying experiences for a do-it-yourself mechanic is diagnosing car trouble, especially if he also can correct the problem. Diagnosis, however, can be quite difficult, even for the experienced mechanic. This is particularly true when working on late model cars with more sophisticated electrical, ignition, and fuel systems.

To help you determine the probable causes of some of the most common symptoms, we have provided a series of diagnostic charts. Even if you do not plan to tackle the corrective measures yourself, these charts will help you deal more confidently with a professional mechanic.

Because there may be several areas of the car in which to search for the source of your difficulties (starting trouble, for example, can be related to the ignition, fuel, electrical, or emission-control systems—or a combination of these), we have provided a guide to assist you in pinpointing the specific trouble.

Most troubles, such as brake, steering, or lighting malfunctions, fit into obvious categories. Drivetrain trouble, however, can be more difficult to diagnose because there are so many interrelated components.

Take time to study the charts and you may be ahead of the game when, if ever, you find it necessary to become your own diagnostician.

SYMPTOMS	REFER TO THESE CHARTS
Car performs poorly, runs rough, or uses too much gas	A, C, G, H, or I
Engine stalls	C, H, or I
Engine is difficult to start	A, C, or I
Engine uses excessive motor oil	A or H
Engine overheats	E or G
Car smokes	A, C, or H
Car shifts gears erratically	D
Car makes unusual noises	A, B, C, D, G, H, I, or J
Car handles poorly, vibrates, or is difficult to steer	J
Abnormal braking action	B
Lights, turn signals, or windshield wipers malfunctioning	F
Heater or air conditioner not working properly	E

CHART A
The Engine

SYMPTOMS	PROBABLE CAUSES →	Burned or worn valves	Worn piston rings	Worn valve guides	Motor oil leaks	Valves need adjustment	Faulty valve lifters	Valve sticking	Valve spring broken	Broken timing gear, chain, or belt	Broken distributor drive	Broken engine mounts	Damaged main bearing	Damaged connecting rod bearing	Worn piston pins
Engine lacks power		•	•						•						
Poor gas mileage		•	•												
Excessive motor oil use			•	•	•										
Fumes from engine			•												
Light clicking noise						•	•	•	•						
Rough operation							•	•	•						
Engine will not run										•	•				
Engine shakes												•			
Heavy thudding													•		
Sharp metallic knock														•	•

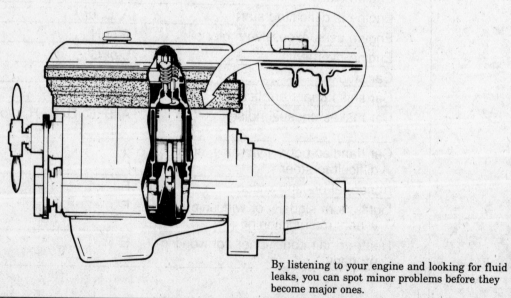

By listening to your engine and looking for fluid leaks, you can spot minor problems before they become major ones.

CHART B
The Brake System

SYMPTOMS	Low fluid level	Air in hydraulic system	Brakes need adjustment	Brake fade due to overheating	Grease or fluid on brake linings	Brake linings glazed	Brakes wet	Faulty vacuum booster	Brake linkage binding	Weak flexible hoses	Loose or worn wheel bearings	Loose or worn front end parts	Front wheels out of alignment	Loose disc brake caliper	Warped brake disc	Eccentric brake drum	Faulty wheel cylinder	Faulty master cylinder	Weak or broken retracting springs	Scored brake drums	Dirt in brake mechanism	Clogged or kinked brake lines	Disc brake caliper piston frozen
Excessive play in pedal	•	•	•							•							•	•					
Hard pedal				•	•	•	•	•	•								•	•				•	•
Spongy pedal	•	•								•													
Pedal sinks to floor	•																•	•					
Pedal vibrates		•									•	•			•	•							
Brakes grab					•															•			
Brakes drag			•						•								•	•				•	•
Brakes pull			•		•		•				•	•	•	•			•					•	•
Erratic braking			•								•	•		•	•	•				•			
Squeal or chatter			•			•									•	•					•		

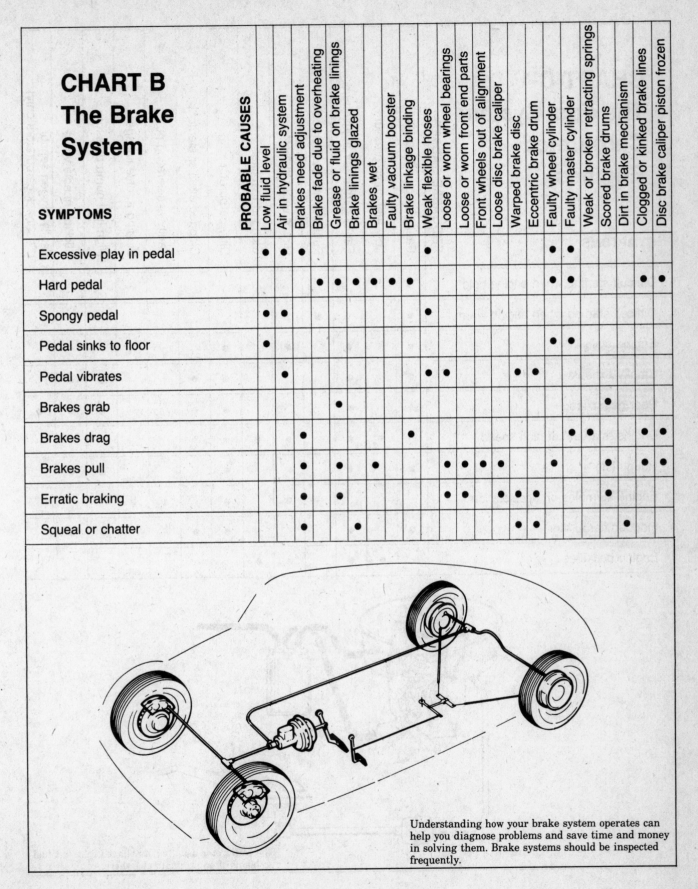

Understanding how your brake system operates can help you diagnose problems and save time and money in solving them. Brake systems should be inspected frequently.

CHART C-1
The Fuel System Carbureted Engines

SYMPTOMS	Faulty automatic choke	Low fuel pump pressure	Faulty carburetor adjustment	Fuel line hot—vapor lock	Dirt or water in fuel	Clogged fuel filter	Dirty carburetor	Clogged air filter element	Faulty accelerating pump	Binding throttle linkage	High fuel pump pressure	Sticking needle valve	Faulty oxygen sensor (Feedback carburetors only)
Difficult starting when engine cold	•												
Difficult starting when engine warm	•			•									
Engine stalls	•		•		•		•						
Smoky exhaust	•	•					•	•			•	•	
Poor gas mileage	•	•					•	•			•	•	•
Engine "starves" at high speed		•	•		•	•	•						
Rough idle	•		•		•		•				•	•	
Engine stumbles on acceleration					•		•		•	•			
Flooded carburetor	•		•				•				•	•	
Engine backfires		•	•		•	•							

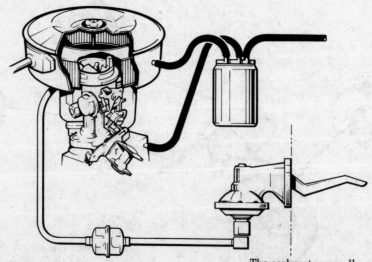

The carburetor usually gets blamed first, but fuel problems often originate elsewhere.

CHART C-2
The Fuel System
Fuel Injected Gasoline Engines

SYMPTOMS	PROBABLE CAUSES	Wrong starting procedure	Leaky fuel injector(s)	Inoperative fuel injector(s)	Vacuum leaks	Misadjusted air flow sensor	Incorrect idle air adjustment	Clogged fuel filter	Defective fuel pump	Low fuel pressure	Restricted fuel line	Restricted air filter
Engine won't start		•		•				•	•	•	•	
Engine hard to start		•		•	•	•		•		•	•	
Engine stalls					•	•	•	•		•	•	
Rough idle			•	•	•	•	•					
Poor gas mileage			•		•	•						•
Engine stumbles on acceleration					•	•	•			•	•	
Engine lacks power				•	•					•	•	•
Smoky exhaust			•			•						•

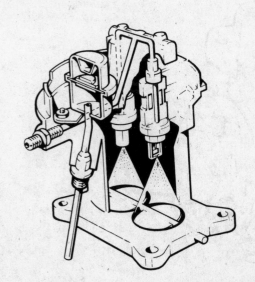
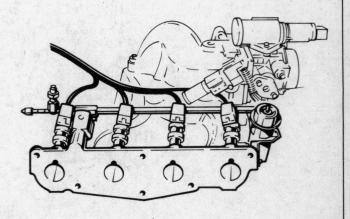

The two kinds of gas fuel injection are the throttle-body type (left), shown with two injectors, and the port, or multi-point, type (right) with an injector for each cylinder.

CHART C-3
The Fuel System
Diesel Engines

SYMPTOMS	PROBABLE CAUSES	Faulty injection pump	Leaky injector(s)	Inoperative injector(s)	Incorrect injection timing	Defective glow plug(s)	Clogged or waxed fuel filter	Contaminated or wrong fuel	Restricted fuel line	Restricted air filter
Engine won't start		•			•	•	•	•	•	
Engine hard to start				•	•	•	•	•	•	
Engine stalls							•	•	•	
Rough idle			•	•						
Smoky exhaust			•		•					•
Poor fuel mileage			•		•			•		•
Engine lacks power		•	•	•	•		•	•		•

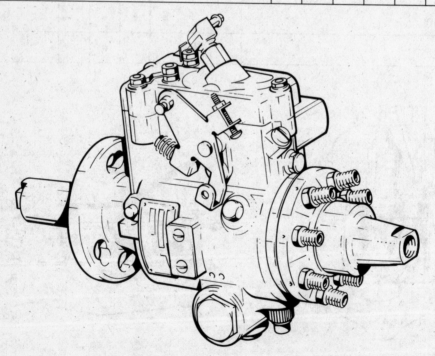

A diesel fuel pump has to deliver fuel to each cylinder at precise intervals, since there is no ignition system on diesels.

CHART D
The Transmission and Driveline

SYMPTOMS	Clutch needs adjustment	Clutch disc worn	Transmission low on lubricant	Incorrect grade of lubricant	Shift linkage out of adjustment	Low fluid level	Bands need adjustment or replacement	Control valve sticking	Throttle linkage needs adjustment	Leaking seals or gaskets	Worn universal joints (RWD)	Worn axle gears	Worn axle bearings	Tire noise	Worn CV-joints (FWD)
Clutch slips	●	●													
Gear shifting difficult	●		●	●	●										
Gears clash	●		●	●	●										
Automatic transmission slips						●	●	●							
Automatic transmission does not shift properly						●	●	●	●						
Transmission low on fluid										●					
Rough engagement of drive or reverse gears								●							
Heavy "clunk" at low speed											●				●
Whine from under car												●	●	●	
Clicking noise when turning															●

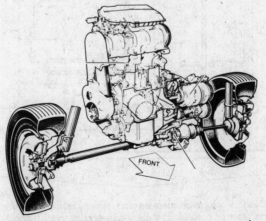

The compact design of front-drive systems can make service access more difficult.

CHART E
The
Cooling
System

SYMPTOMS	Low coolant level	Cooling system clogged	Loose or broken fan belt	Thermostat stuck closed	Thermostat stuck open	Debris on radiator	Faulty water pump	Collapsed radiator hose	Leaking cylinder head gasket	Late ignition timing	Heater core clogged	Faulty temperature control	Low refrigerant charge	Loose or broken drive belt	Faulty compressor clutch	Debris on condenser
PROBABLE CAUSES																
Engine overheats	●	●	●	●		●	●	●	●	●						
Engine warms up slowly					●											
Insufficient heat					●						●	●				
Insufficient air conditioning												●	●	●		●
No air conditioning													●	●	●	

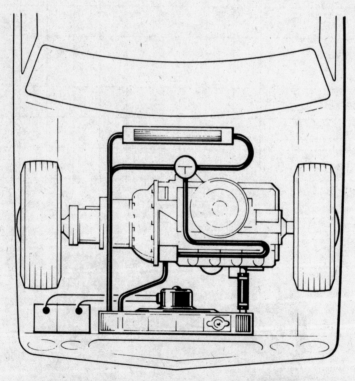

Cooling system problems aren't always related to the radiator or coolant. Problems can originate with the thermostat, heater core, water pump, fan belt, or even ignition timing.

CHART F
Lights and
Safety Devices

SYMPTOMS	Battery discharged	Bulb burned out	Faulty wiring	Fuse blown	Faulty flasher unit	Faulty wiper motor	Faulty wiper linkage	Fluid low in reservoir	Tubing disconnected	Clogged washer jet nozzle	Faulty washer pump	Faulty brake light switch	Short circuit in wiring
Lights dim	●												
One light does not operate		●	●	●									
Turn signals flash on only one side		●	●										
Turn signals do not flash			●	●	●								
Windshield wipers do not operate			●	●		●	●						
Windshield washers do not operate								●	●	●	●		
Brake lights do not operate		●	●	●								●	
Brake lights stay on			●									●	
Headlights flash on and off													●

If an electrical component fails, the fuse block is one of the first things to check. Always carry spare fuses.

CHART G The Exhaust System

SYMPTOMS	Hole in muffler or exhaust pipe	Tailpipe bent or clogged	Exhaust pipe or muffler clogged	Leaking tailpipe	Loose pipe or muffler	Pipe touching frame or body	Loose tubes inside muffler
Loud exhaust	●						
Hissing exhaust		●					
Fumes under car	●			●			
Rattling noise					●		●
Vibration						●	
Engine lacks power		●	●				
Engine overheats		●	●				

(column group heading: PROBABLE CAUSES)

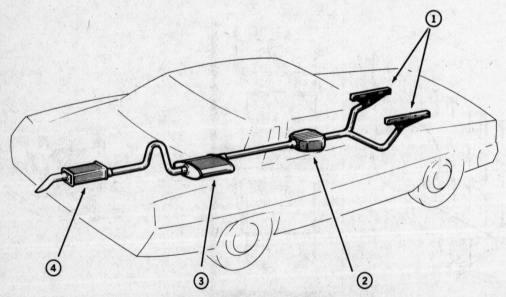

Main components of the exhaust system. (1) exhaust manifolds, (2) catalytic converter, (3) muffler, and on some cars, (4) resonator connected by pipes.

CHART H
The Emission Control System

SYMPTOMS	PROBABLE CAUSES	Clogged or sticking PCV valve	Clogged PCV hoses	Leaking PCV hoses	Vacuum leaks	Faulty air pump	Air pump belt slipping	Faulty spark control	Clogged catalytic converter	EGR valve stuck open	EGR valve not opening	No air intake preheating	Defective engine sensor(s)
Rough idle		•	•	•	•					•			
Oil fumes from engine		•	•	•									
Oil on outside of engine		•	•	•									
Squeal or knock						•	•						
Stalling		•	•	•	•				•	•			•
Engine lacks power					•			•	•				•
Poor gas mileage		•	•	•	•			•	•			•	•
Engine hesitates on acceleration					•							•	•
Engine pings on acceleration											•		•
"Check engine" light on								•					•

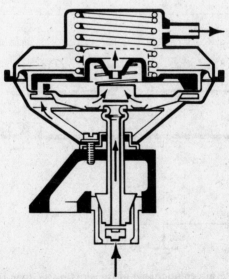

The EGR valve uses vacuum to draw some of the exhaust gases from the exhaust manifold into the intake manifold.

CHART I
The Electrical and Ignition Systems

SYMPTOMS / **PROBABLE CAUSES**

SYMPTOMS	Battery discharged	Loose or broken wires	Faulty starter or solenoid	Faulty ignition switch	Faulty distributor points	Faulty neutral safety switch	Spark plugs fouled	Improper spark plug gap	Faulty ignition coil	Faulty condenser	Damaged distributor cap or rotor	Damaged ignition wires	Incorrect spark timing	Alternator drive belt slipping	Faulty voltage regulator	Low regulator setting	Faulty alternator	Battery worn out	Faulty engine computer
Starter will not operate	•	•	•	•		•													
Starter turns, engine will not start				•	•		•	•	•	•	•	•	•						•
Engine stalls					•		•	•				•							
Engine misfires					•		•	•	•	•	•	•							
Engine cuts out at high speed					•		•	•	•		•	•							
Engine knocks or pings													•						
Engine lacks power					•		•	•	•	•	•	•	•						•
Engine idles roughly					•		•	•				•							
Battery frequently discharged														•	•	•	•	•	
Alternator does not charge														•	•		•		

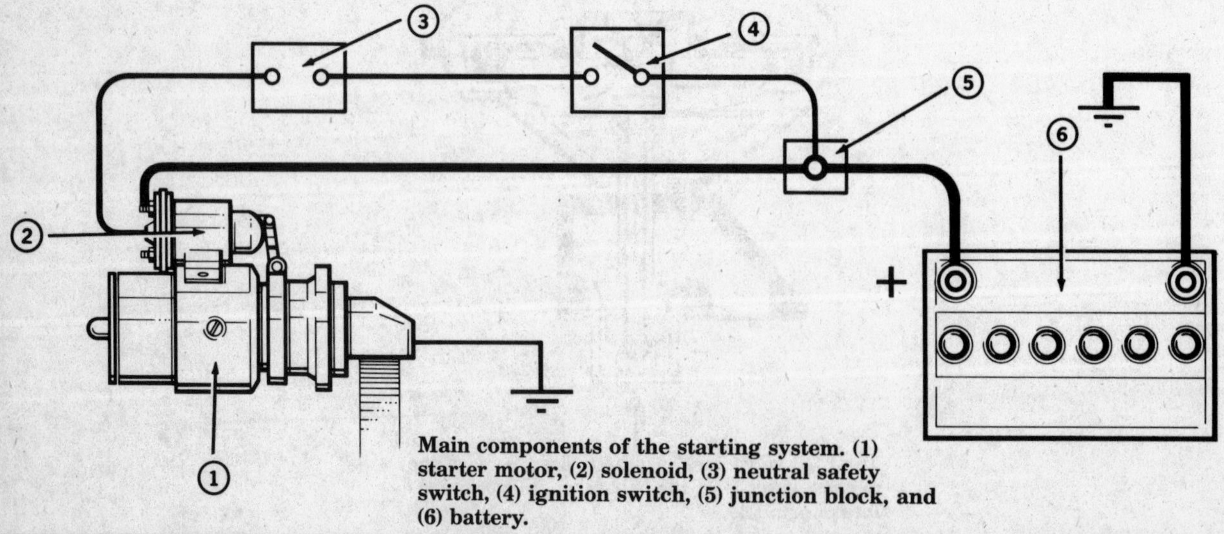

Main components of the starting system. (1) starter motor, (2) solenoid, (3) neutral safety switch, (4) ignition switch, (5) junction block, and (6) battery.

CHART J
The Steering and Suspension Systems

SYMPTOMS	PROBABLE CAUSES → Low or uneven tire pressure	Steering linkage dry	Front end out of alignment	Suspension arms damaged	Ball joints binding	Sagging springs	Power steering belt slipping	Power steering fluid low	Loose wheel bearings	Worn ball joints	Loose steering linkage	Maladjusted steering gear	Worn shock absorbers	Wheels and tires out of balance
Difficult steering	●	●	●	●	●	●	●	●				●		
Car pulls to one side	●		●	●		●			●	●	●	●		
Car wanders from side to side	●		●			●			●	●	●	●	●	
Uneven tire wear	●		●	●					●	●	●		●	●
Front-wheel shimmy									●	●	●			
High-speed vibration													●	●
Car not level				●		●								
Heavy thumps on rough roads				●		●				●			●	
Play or looseness in steering									●	●	●	●		
Rattle in steering gear												●		
Thump from front end				●						●				

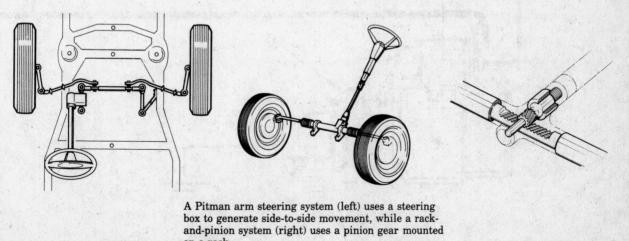

A Pitman arm steering system (left) uses a steering box to generate side-to-side movement, while a rack-and-pinion system (right) uses a pinion gear mounted on a rack.

THE STARTING SYSTEM

PICTURE YOURSELF on a cold morning some 60 years ago, walking out to your car. You climb inside, flip a couple of switches, move a few levers, and then stroll to the front bumper where you grab a big crank handle. With all your strength, you start cranking the engine. If you are lucky, the engine—instead of kicking the crank backwards to break your arm—starts chugging and continues to run.

For most of us today, this is hard to imagine. There is not even a hole through which to insert a crank handle. Even if there were, most engines are too big and have too much compression to be turned over by hand.

Thanks to a big starter motor and a strong battery to power it, we get it all done with a twist of an ignition key.

Indeed, the electric starter is credited with having put women (and many men, too, for that matter) behind the wheel.

The Starting System

The components of a car's starting system are: battery, neutral safety switch, ignition switch, solenoid, starter motor, and wiring.

Basically, the starting system operates as follows. When the ignition key is turned to

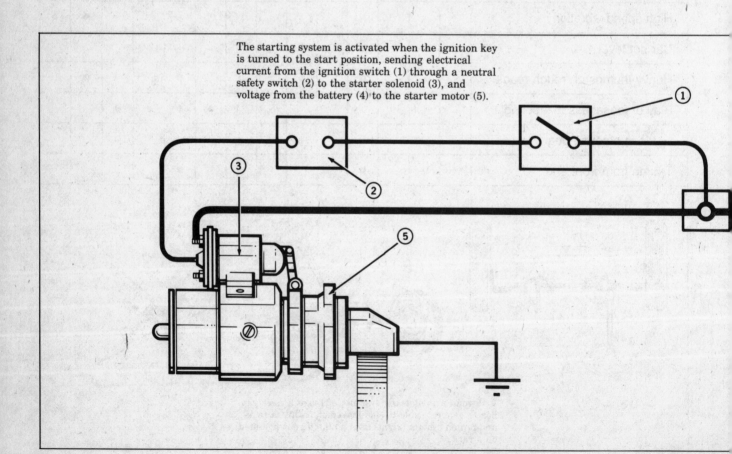

The starting system is activated when the ignition key is turned to the start position, sending electrical current from the ignition switch (1) through a neutral safety switch (2) to the starter solenoid (3), and voltage from the battery (4) to the starter motor (5).

the start position, electrical current is sent to the solenoid and battery voltage is supplied to the starter motor. The starter motor then turns a flywheel mounted on the rear of the crankshaft that starts all engine parts in motion. The ignition system provides a spark to the spark plugs that ignites the air/fuel mixture from the carburetor. If all components are in good working condition, the engine should start immediately. Here are the essential parts of the starting system.

1. THE BATTERY. The heart of the electrical system is the battery. If you were to narrow the functions of the battery down to one, it would be to provide the electrical energy to operate the starter motor and ignition system to start the car. Today, it is also called on to power a few dozen lamp bulbs, the windshield wipers, windshield washer, taillight switch, heater and defroster—and possibly, radio, tape deck, CB radio, electric windows, electric seats, electric

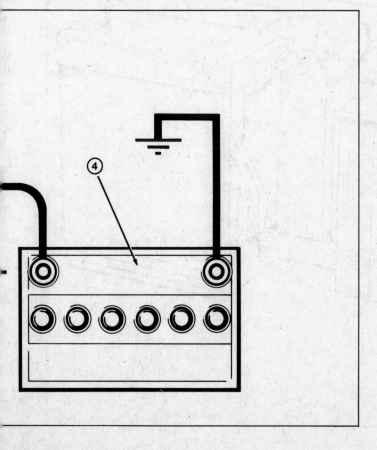

door locks, and engine control computer.

The battery does not store electricity; it stores chemicals and metals that interact to produce electricity on demand. The colder the weather or the lower the charge of the battery, the less capability the battery will have to do its job. A fully charged battery at 80°F will deliver only about 65 percent of its power at 32°F and only 40 percent at 0°F. Unfortunately, the time when the battery is in its weakest condition, in extreme cold, is the time when it is confronted with its heaviest burden—cranking a stiff engine. For this reason, it is advisable to pay special attention to your car's battery during cold weather.

When your battery lets you down, it is probably due to one of four reasons: you have problems in the charging system; it is getting old; it is not powerful enough for your car; or you have some bad connections. The battery should not always be blamed for starting system trouble, however. It could be that your terminal connections are corroded, you might have a bad ground, or your engine might need a tune-up. Be sure that the battery is the culprit before investing in a new one.

2. THE NEUTRAL SAFETY SWITCH. This switch allows the starting system to be operated only when the transmission gearshift lever is in the neutral or park position. This switch is also called a starting safety switch.

3. THE IGNITION SWITCH. The ignition switch has five positions: accessories, lock, off, on, and start. The first four positions of the ignition switch will automatically stay in position when the key is turned there. The start position, however, is like a momentary contact switch; it has to be held there to crank the engine.

4. THE SOLENOID. The solenoid connects the battery to the starter by principles of magnetism. Electrical windings are wrapped around a hollow core and an iron plunger is placed partially in the area. When the key is turned to the start position, a magnetic field is created that pulls the plunger into the

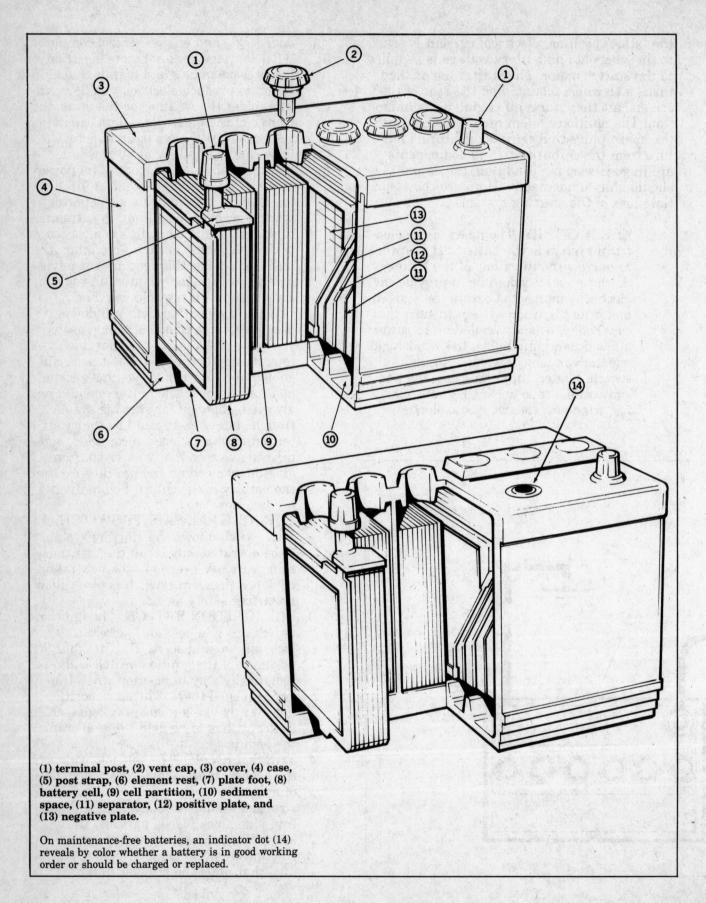

(1) terminal post, (2) vent cap, (3) cover, (4) case,
(5) post strap, (6) element rest, (7) plate foot, (8)
battery cell, (9) cell partition, (10) sediment
space, (11) separator, (12) positive plate, and
(13) negative plate.

On maintenance-free batteries, an indicator dot (14)
reveals by color whether a battery is in good working
order or should be charged or replaced.

core. When the plunger touches two contacts, it connects the circuit between the battery and starter. Some solenoids, such as those used on General Motors, Chrysler, and some late model Ford products, are also used to engage the drive mechanism. The plunger is connected to a shift lever that engages the starter drive gear with the flywheel.

5. THE STARTER MOTOR. The starter motor is a direct-current motor that develops high torque for short periods of time. A starter may draw several hundred amperes of current when it is in operation. For this reason, the wiring in the starter must be in good condition.

6. THE ELECTRICAL WIRING. The wiring in a car is of different types and gauges and is designed to do specific jobs. When replacing a piece of wire on your car, use a wire of the same type, length, and gauge. If the new wire is longer or of too small a gauge, it will increase the resistance or give you poor conductivity, which can have a detrimental effect on some of the system.

Using the wrong gauge of wire is like putting the wrong kind of replacement wire on a toaster. The manufacturer of the toaster originally installed a particular length of heavy-duty gauge wire to provide a given amount of current into the toaster so it can do its job. If you shorten it or if you connect it to a lightweight extension cord, you could run into problems ranging from untoasted bread to an electrical fire.

Your best bet when replacing a wire on your car is to take a piece of the wire you are replacing to an auto parts store and ask for an identical replacement. Be sure the insulation of the wire you are buying is at least as good as the wire you are replacing.

Good connections in your wiring circuit are essential. Whenever possible, you should have soldered connections or good, secure solderless connections. When tightening a nut-type connection, always use a lock washer or an internal tooth lock washer. A loose electrical connection in your car can cause hard starting and undue wear on the battery.

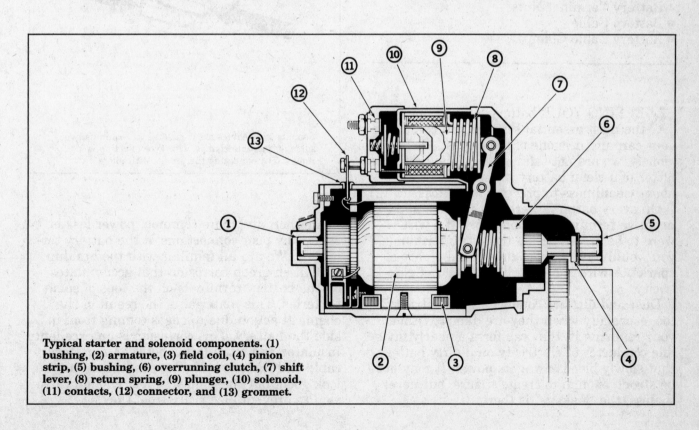

Typical starter and solenoid components. (1) bushing, (2) armature, (3) field coil, (4) pinion strip, (5) bushing, (6) overrunning clutch, (7) shift lever, (8) return spring, (9) plunger, (10) solenoid, (11) contacts, (12) connector, and (13) grommet.

Battery Maintenance

Tools and Materials

- Wrenches
- Battery Pliers
- Battery Terminal Puller
- Penknife
- Battery Terminal-and-Clamp Cleaning Tool
- Wire Brush
- Battery Cable Cutter or Hacksaw
- Masking Tape
- Penetrating Oil
- Steel Wool
- Sandpaper
- Baking Soda
- Water
- Container
- Rags
- Petroleum Jelly or Grease
- Battery Terminal Nuts
- Battery Cable
- Battery Cable Clamps

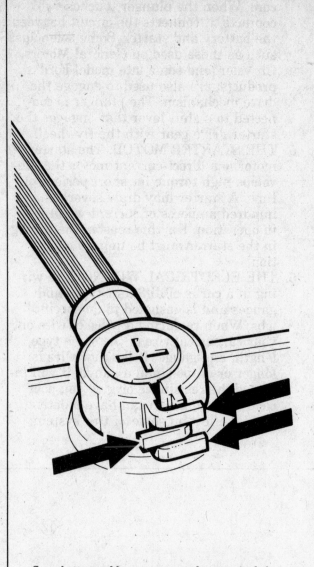

Some battery cables are connected to terminals by spring-type cable clamps. This type of clamp is removed by squeezing the prongs with pliers.

KEEPING YOUR battery clean is one of the most essential services you can do for your car, and it is one of the easiest. Obviously, we are not talking about the aesthetic factor of a clean battery; we are concerned about cleanliness to prevent power loss.

On every battery, there is a positive and negative terminal (or connector). If a wire were to be placed across these two terminals, you would have a short circuit and plenty of sparks. A wire is a superb conductor of electricity.

Dust and dirt are conductors of electricity, too, especially when they are damp. Without your realizing it, they can form a nearly invisible conductor of electricity on a dirty battery that slowly bleeds away its power. It may not be strong enough to create sparks, but nevertheless, the "leakage" is there.

Another, and more common, power loss is caused by poor connections at the battery terminals. We are all familiar with the buildup of whitish-green corrosion that accumulates on the battery terminals on the tops of some batteries. This material is the result of the chemical action due to gases coming from inside the battery. This corrosion is an excellent insulator and often forms between a battery cable and its terminal. The connection may look good, but there may be just enough corrosion to prevent electricity from flowing.

Cleaning the Battery

A survey by the Car Care Council of garage mechanics pointed to battery cables and battery terminals as some of the most neglected parts of customers' cars. Here is how to clean your car's battery.

1. Wear old clothes. The substance you are going to be cleaning off the battery contains strong acid. Do not let it touch your skin, and if it does, be sure to wash it off immediately. ***Caution:** Do not smoke or tackle this job in the vicinity of an open flame. Batteries can be highly explosive.*

2. If there are vent caps on top of the battery, cover the holes in the caps with masking tape to prevent your cleaning solution from getting into the battery. You do not want to neutralize the acid that makes the battery work. This is not necessary for sealed, maintenance-free batteries; they have no vent caps.

3. Remove the battery cable clamps. This is done on most batteries by loosening a nut and bolt with a wrench. But if your cables are equipped with spring-type cable clamps, you will have to squeeze the prongs with pliers to free them. Use a terminal puller to lift the clamp off the ground cable *first.* ***Caution:** On most cars, this is the negative terminal. If the positive cable is disconnected first, you could accidentally ground the wrench or pliers against the body or some other parts of the car and create a spark. On cars with positive-ground systems, remove the positive cable first. There is the possibility of the battery exploding, ruining the wrench, or burning your hand with the heavy current flow. So always remember, follow the instructions to be safe.*

Because of the highly corrosive nature of battery acid, you may find that the cable clamp nuts have been so eaten away that they are virtually impossible to remove. In this case, you may have to apply some penetrating oil for a while until whatever remains of the nut can be turned. This is a good case for owning a battery terminal puller; it is

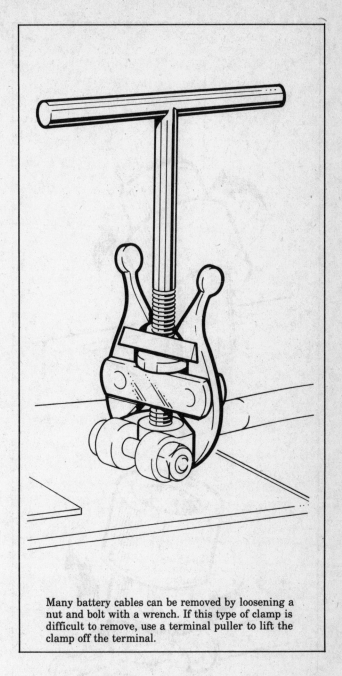

Many battery cables can be removed by loosening a nut and bolt with a wrench. If this type of clamp is difficult to remove, use a terminal puller to lift the clamp off the terminal.

especially useful when the cable clamp is too corroded for normal measures. If so, it is advisable to replace the cable when the job is finished or at least to replace the clamp if the wire in the cable is still good. Avoid putting a new clamp on a wire where the insulation is bad or where too many strands of wire have deteriorated. (See the instructions for replacing a cable and for replacing a cable clamp at the end of this section.)

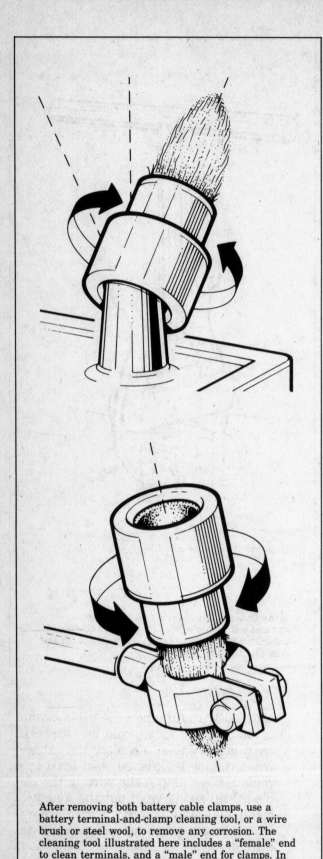

After removing both battery cable clamps, use a battery terminal-and-clamp cleaning tool, or a wire brush or steel wool, to remove any corrosion. The cleaning tool illustrated here includes a "female" end to clean terminals, and a "male" end for clamps. In both cases, use a twisting motion.

Note: Many late model cars have side-terminal batteries. These terminals are less likely to corrode but still should be checked periodically and cleaned if necessary.

4. When both cable clamps are removed, use a battery terminal-and-clamp cleaning tool, wire brush, or steel wool to clean any corrosion on the battery terminals and clamps. The metal parts must be shiny to provide good electrical contact. The inside of the clamps can be cleaned with sandpaper, or lightly scraped with a penknife. A good investment is a battery terminal-and-clamp cleaning tool. This tool can be bought in kit combinations that include the terminal puller and battery pliers. The terminal cleaner has a round "female" brush that is slipped over the battery terminal and twisted to remove traces of corrosion. On the other side of the brush is a "male" end that slips inside the battery cable clamp.

5. Mix ½ cup of baking soda in a pint of water, pour the solution over the top of the battery, and wait until it stops fizzing and foaming. Scrub the top of the battery with a wire brush to remove dirt, grease, and corrosion; rinse the battery thoroughly with water and dry it with a rag.

6. Replace the cable clamps on the proper terminals, securing the *ungrounded* cable first—the opposite of the way you disconnected the cables—and then the grounded cable, the one connected to the car's frame or engine. Be sure they fit well down onto the terminals. Do not hammer a clamp down or overtighten a nut, as this could damage the battery case or the clamp. If the old nuts are in bad condition, they should be replaced with a special type that can be obtained at an auto parts store.

Battery Cables

Part of the battery cleaning and checking process should include a close examination of the cables. Sometimes a cable may look fine at the terminal end, but closer to the engine you may find the insulation cracked, brittle, or even split open. Be sure to replace any cable that has defective insulation or frayed or broken strands of wire. And always replace the cable with one of the same conductor quality, at least the same gauge and the same length. Otherwise you are likely to have starting problems. An inadequate gauge or incorrect length of battery cable creates a resistance that prevents sufficient current from getting to the starter motor. The result will be a slow-turning starter and eventual damage to the starter motor. Play it safe by taking the old battery cable to an auto parts store to replace it with one of equivalent quality and capacity. Here is the correct procedure for replacing a battery cable.

1. Whether you are replacing a negative cable, a positive cable, or both, remove the ground cable first. Loosen the nut on the clamp with a wrench. Use a battery terminal puller to remove the clamp from the terminal. If your battery has the spring-type clamp, use battery pliers to squeeze the clamp for removal. *Caution: On late model cars with computerized engine controls, make sure the ignition switch is off before removing either battery cable. Failure to have the key off may cause a voltage spike in the electrical system which could damage the computer.* **Note:** Disconnecting either battery cable on vehicles with electronic clocks or radios will erase the unit's memory. Don't forget to reset the clock or radio after replacing the cables.

2. Remove the other end of the cable or cables that you intend to replace. The negative cable can be loosened by removing a bolt with a wrench. It is connected to the engine block or some other good ground. The positive cable is connected to the starter motor solenoid, which is mounted either on the starter motor or on the inside of the fender well, depending on the make and model of car. The positive cable can be disconnected by removing a nut with a wrench at the starter motor solenoid. (Remember, if your vehicle has a positive-ground system, the negative cable will be connected to the starter motor solenoid and the positive cable will go to ground. Remove the positive cable from the battery terminal first on this system.)

On side-terminal batteries, either cable can be removed by loosening a retaining bolt from the clamp. The cable and clamp will then come loose. The other ends of the negative and positive cables are connected and removed in the same way as conventional cables.

3. Clean the cable clamps, battery terminals, and the top of the battery following the instructions given earlier in this section.

4. After having obtained the correct type and length of replacement cable, reverse Steps 1 and 2 for proper replacement.

5. Coat the cable clamps and battery terminals with petroleum jelly or grease to help protect them from corrosion.

Cable Clamps

If the battery cable is still good, but the cable clamp needs to be replaced, here is a quick procedure for replacing it.

1. Whether you intend to replace the negative clamp, positive clamp, or both, first remove the ground cable from the battery terminal as previously outlined.

2. Use a cable cutter or hacksaw to cut off the old clamp where it joins the thick cable and strip the insulation on the cable back 1 inch.

3. Make sure the cable will still be long enough to reach the battery terminal, otherwise you will have to replace the entire assembly—cable and clamp. Also be sure that the battery terminal is clean to insure a good connection.

4. Install a good quality replacement clamp, available at auto supply stores. This is done by loosening the two bolts on the clamp, placing the stripped end of the cable into the clamp, and tightening the two bolts. The insulation of the cable must be flush against the bottom of the clamp so that no uninsulated cable is exposed.

5. Regardless of which cable clamp or clamps you replaced, the positive clamp

is connected to the battery first, then the negative clamp, as previously outlined. (This procedure is reversed on positive-ground systems.)

Battery Testing

Tools and Materials

- Hydrometer
- Voltmeter
- Clip-On Jumper Wire
- Water—Plain or Distilled
- Toothpick

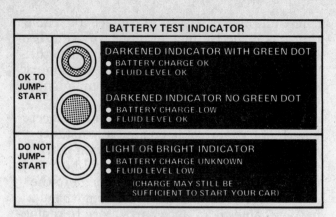

On maintenance-free batteries, the state of the battery's charge is checked by looking at its test indicator.

BECAUSE THE starting system of a car is engineered to operate with a battery that is fully charged, a battery hydrometer is an indispensable tool for checking the performance of a conventional battery—one that has vent caps on top. The hydrometer compares the density (specific gravity or weight) of the battery fluid (electrolyte) to that of water. The acid in your battery is heavier than plain water. Therefore, the more fully charged your battery, the heavier the fluid. This, of course, is the tip-off to the degree of charge in your battery. The "heavier" the fluid, the higher the degree of charge.

Hydrometer Test

A hydrometer test of your battery should be made seasonally to avoid strain on the car's electrical system as well as to detect battery trouble before outright failure befalls it. **Note:** If your car is equipped with a sealed, maintenance-free battery, check the state of the battery's charge by looking at its test indicator. If there is a green dot, the battery is charged. If the indicator is light or bright, the battery should be replaced; do not attempt to charge

it. If, however, the indicator is dark, the battery should be charged until a green dot appears in the indicator. On sealed batteries without a test indicator, a voltmeter must be used to check the state of charge. Such a battery must test at 12.6 volts with no load (all auto accessories turned off) to be fully charged.

Before performing a hydrometer test on a conventional battery, or visually checking a maintenance-free battery, make sure the battery is in good condition. Inspect the case for cracks and other damage. Loose hold-down frames, freezing, or flying stones are the most likely cause of battery cracking. A bulging battery case can cause starting failure, too. The bulging can be caused by overcharging or freezing. A bulged battery will probably have buckled plates and cracked partitions. Once you have judged your battery to be in good shape, you can perform the hydrometer test on a conventional battery as follows.

1. With the engine off, remove the vent caps and check the fluid level of the battery. If the level is too low, add plain or distilled water. If this is the case, run your engine for approximately 20 minutes to let the fresh water mix thoroughly with the fluid already in the battery. Then let the car cool for 15 minutes before performing the hydrometer test.

2. Test each cell of the battery with the hydrometer, one at a time. Squeeze the

hydrometer's bulb and release it to suck enough battery fluid into the hydrometer to float the indicator inside the tube and take a reading. On a bulb float-type tester, you will get a false reading if the indicator touches the sides or the top of the instrument.

A reading from 1.260 to 1.300 in each cell means the battery is healthy. A consistent reading of approximately 1.225 probably means the battery is satisfactory but low on charge. Any cell that varies more than 0.050 from the others indicates a defective cell, and the battery should be replaced.

Note: The specific gravity of a fully charged battery should be between 1.260 and 1.280, with the electrolyte temperature at 80°F. The accompanying illustrations depict the relationship between specific gravity and state of charge. If the electrolyte temperature is above or below 80°F, the specific gravity reading must be corrected by *adding* 0.004 for each 10° above 80°F or *subtracting* 0.004 for each 10° below 80°F.

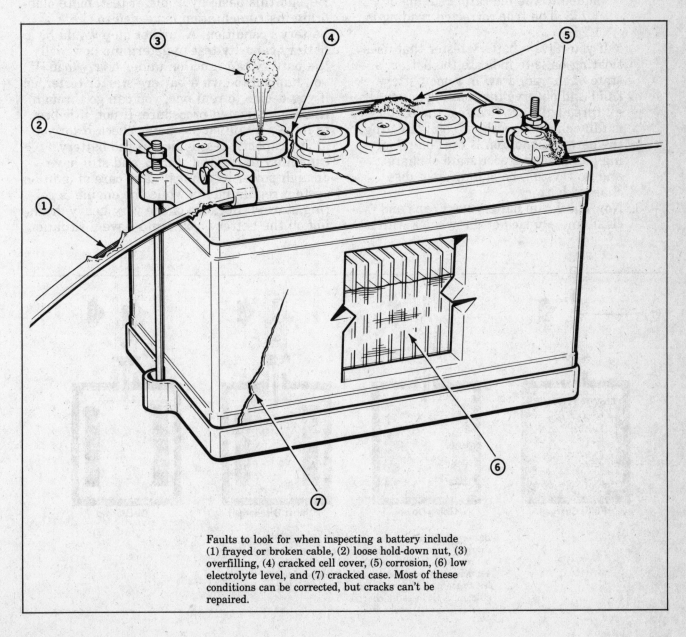

Faults to look for when inspecting a battery include (1) frayed or broken cable, (2) loose hold-down nut, (3) overfilling, (4) cracked cell cover, (5) corrosion, (6) low electrolyte level, and (7) cracked case. Most of these conditions can be corrected, but cracks can't be repaired.

Here are two examples.

A. The indicator reading is 1.230, and the temperature reading is 10°F. The temperature must be corrected for a variation of 70°, or 28 points (0.004 × 7 = 0.028) must be subtracted from the indicator reading of 1.230. The true corrected reading is 1.202.

B. The indicator reading is 1.235, and the temperature reading is 120°F. Since the temperature reading is 40° above the standard of 80°F, 16 points (0.004 × 4 = 0.016) must be added to the indicator reading of 1.235. The true corrected reading is 1.251.

If you have a battery tester that uses floating balls to indicate the battery's state of charge, draw in some battery fluid and observe the floating action. If all three balls are floating, the battery is fully charged; with two balls floating, the battery condition is fair; one floating ball means a poor state of charge; and no floating balls indicate a discharged battery.

3. Now check the battery vent caps and clean any plugged or dirty holes with a toothpick. This will help prevent acid fumes from building up dangerously in the battery. **Note:** Under normal driving conditions and weather conditions, a battery will lose up to 2 ounces of its fluid every 1000 miles. If the fluid loss is greater than this amount, check other parts of the car's charging system. Maintenance-free batteries are designed in such a way that they do not use much water.

Capacity Test

Beyond this basic hydrometer test, more elaborate instrumentation is needed to check a battery's condition. A further step would be a battery capacity test to determine how well the battery can function under heavy load. If you happen to own a battery-starter tester, or if you decide to rent one, you can go through this sophisticated procedure. If not, it is best to have a qualified mechanic check it for you.

The capacity test indicates the battery's capability to run the starter and still have enough power left in it to take care of ignition system requirements while the engine is getting started. Because of the very heavy draining on the battery, you could have a situation

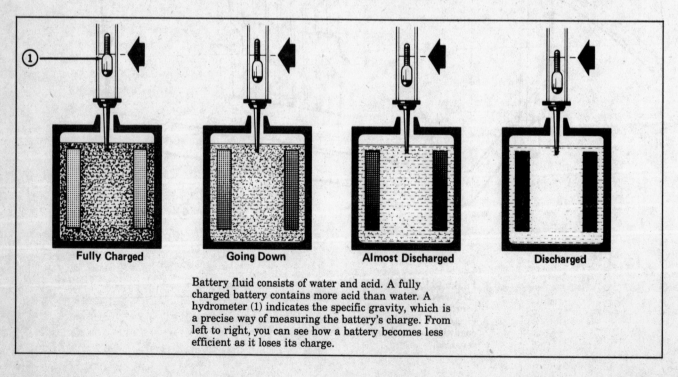

Fully Charged   **Going Down**   **Almost Discharged**   **Discharged**

Battery fluid consists of water and acid. A fully charged battery contains more acid than water. A hydrometer (1) indicates the specific gravity, which is a precise way of measuring the battery's charge. From left to right, you can see how a battery becomes less efficient as it loses its charge.

where the battery is capable of turning the starter but because of a borderline situation in the ignition system, there just is not enough electricity to cause a spark at the spark plugs.

In lieu of investing in a battery-starter tester, you might try the following procedure. In effect, you will be using the starter motor itself as a loading test device. However, you will need a voltmeter.

1. Lift the secondary high-tension lead from the center tower of the distributor cap and ground it to some part of the car body or frame with a clip-on jumper wire. On General Motors HEI distributors, disconnect the ignition lead from the distributor. Do not ground the lead.
2. Connect the terminals of your voltmeter to the battery. Be sure you are connecting positive terminal to positive terminal and negative to negative.
3. Turn the ignition key to crank—do not start—the engine for 15 seconds while observing the reading of the voltmeter. If you cannot position the voltmeter where you can see it while you crank the engine, have someone crank it for you. At the end of the continuous 15-second test, the voltmeter still should read 9.6 volts or more on a 12-volt system. If the voltage drops below 9.6 volts, you have a battery in poor condition. **Note:** Never operate the starter for more than 30 seconds without stopping for a while to cool it off.

Battery Charging

THERE IS probably nothing more aggravating than hurrying out to your car on a cold morning and, upon attempting to start it, hearing a clicking sound or nothing at all. This no-start condition does not necessarily

Tools and Materials

- Wrenches or Battery Pliers
- Battery Terminal Puller
- Battery Terminal-and-Clamp Cleaning Tool
- Battery Charger
- Hydrometer
- Water—Plain or Distilled

mean that your battery is completely dead; it may just be a little tired.

Batteries can become run down for a number of reasons: a defective alternator, faulty voltage regulator, too much corrosion on the terminals, damaged cables, and so on. In addition, studies have shown that batteries are often blamed for trouble that can be traced to other areas of the car. For example, you may call a motor club for a battery boost, explaining that your battery has failed, when actually your problem is a faulty choke on the carburetor, or your car is in desperate need of a tune-up.

Another way to run down a battery is through carelessness. If you accidentally leave your headlights on for several hours, you will most assuredly end up with a dead battery. In this case, you will need to recharge your battery. Battery chargers are designed to bring life back to the chemicals in your battery. These chemicals in turn provide the electrical current necessary to start your engine time and time again.

Whatever the reason your battery is dead, the question is, what is the best way to bring it back to life?

Getting a boost with a good set of jumper cables will get the car started and, if you intend to do a lot of driving right away, the battery will probably recharge itself as you are driving. (See the section in this chapter on "Using Jumper Cables.") Your charging system, consisting of an alternator and regulator, must be in good shape, however. (Cars made before the early 1960s were equipped with a generator, which has since been replaced by the alternator. The alternator is further explained in "The Charging System" chapter.)

If you are not planning to go anywhere after you jump-start your car's battery, you cannot take the chance that your car will start the next time you need it. If your battery has been drained of its electrical current for any length of time, then it will probably need to be charged up.

A battery in good condition can be recharged by passing a specific amount of direct current through the battery. Fast charging and slow charging are the two most frequently used methods to do this. Slow charging induces a small amount of current, usually 5 to 15 amperes, through the battery over a period of 12 to 14 hours or more. Fast charging will induce between 50 and 60 amperes through the battery in just an hour or two.

If it is at all possible, take the time to give your battery a slow charge. While this takes much longer than a quick charge, it is best for your battery in terms of preventing damage to the inside of the battery, and the battery will also hold its charge longer.

Fast charging will give your battery a quick boost, but it can be harmful to its health. The principle of quick charging is that the battery can be brought up to an *acceptable* rate of charge (not full charge) before the electrolyte reaches damaging high temperatures. The real question is whether you have the experience to cut back the charge rate soon enough to prevent damage. The more sophisticated equipment used by professional mechanics has protection devices to prevent overheating. Even after a fast charge, however, the battery should be brought up to its full state of charge by slow charging.

If you think a battery charger would be a good investment for you, then buy one that features an automatic cutoff or taper charging which prevents your battery from overheating, so that your battery can be allowed to charge overnight. Some of the more sophisticated units have rate-of-charge adjustments so that you can get a quicker charge if you so desire. Here is how to hook up and use a battery charger.

1. Remove the battery vent caps from the

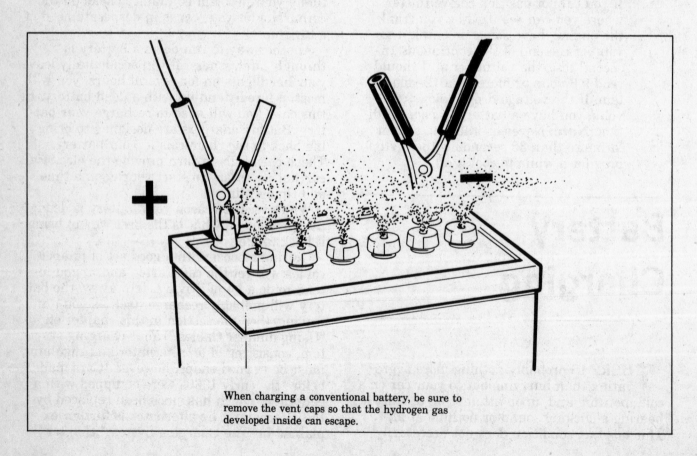

When charging a conventional battery, be sure to remove the vent caps so that the hydrogen gas developed inside can escape.

top of a conventional battery. Vent caps are either pulled off or unscrewed by hand. *Caution: This is important because the buildup of hydrogen gas in your battery during the charging process can be dangerous. Always remove rings and watches when working around batteries to prevent the possibility of electrical burns. Be careful that metal tools do not contact the positive battery terminal (or any metal in contact with that terminal) and any other metal on the car at the same time. A short circuit could occur.* **Note:** If your car is equipped with a sealed, maintenance-free battery, there is no need to do this; there are no removable vent caps.

2. Make sure the battery fluid in each cell is up to the proper fill mark; this step is not necessary for sealed, maintenance-free batteries. Instead, check the charge indicator "eye" on top. If it is dark, the battery may be charged. Do not charge it if the indicator is light or yellow. A green dot indicates that it is charged. In a conventional battery, the proper level will be indicated by a slot, notch, lip, or ring. If you can see the tops of the plates in the battery, or if the fluid level is below the fill mark, add plain or distilled water. If the water in your area has a high mineral content, use distilled water. *Caution: Do not overfill!*

3. If you intend to leave the battery in the car while you charge it, disconnect both battery cables (negative cable first) to prevent damage to the car's electrical system (make sure the ignition key is off first) and the accessories. (On cars that have a positive-ground system, with the positive cable connected to ground, disconnect the positive cable first.) To remove the battery cables, use a wrench to loosen the nuts on the battery cable clamps. If the cable clamps do not pull off easily, use a battery terminal puller to get them off. Do not use a screwdriver or any other similar tool to pry the clamps off as this can result in a cracked battery case. With spring-type cable clamps, battery pliers should

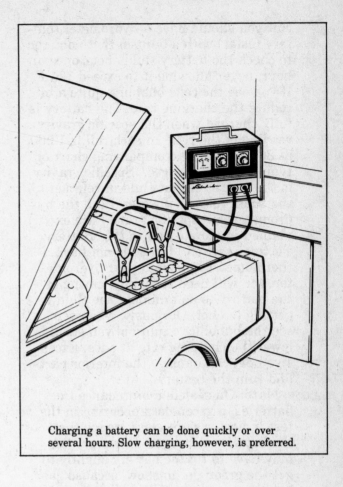

Charging a battery can be done quickly or over several hours. Slow charging, however, is preferred.

be used to release them.

4. Clean the battery terminals with a battery terminal-and-clamp cleaning tool, as described in the "Battery Maintenance" section, so that the cables from the battery charger can make good contact.

5. Connect the positive (+) cable of the battery charger to the positive battery terminal, then connect the negative (−) cable of the charger to the negative battery terminal. Plug the charger cord into an electrical wall outlet or other 110-volt power source.

6. Turn the charger to the on position. If you have an adjustable unit, set it at a rate of between 5 and 15 amperes, or at the slow-charging rate indicated by the manufacturer. Also set the charger for the battery voltage; for virtually all cars this will be 12 volts.

7. If your battery charger does not have an automatic cutoff or taper charge cir-

cuit you should have a hydrometer (battery tester) with a built-in thermometer to check the battery fluid about once an hour, never allowing it to exceed 125°F. If you see the cells bubbling quite a bit, reduce the charging rate. The battery is fully charged when the specific gravity reading of the fluid in each cell is 1.260 at 80°F; see the accompanying chart of typical specific ranges. (Specific gravity is the weight of that fluid in relation to the same volume of water. Both the hydrometer and specific gravity are explained in more detail in the "Battery Testing" section.) If you do not have a thermometer built into your hydrometer, you will need to feel the casing of the battery to determine if the fluid is getting too hot. Obviously, when you see the bubbling condition, you should lower the charging rate at once. Excessive heat can damage the interior parts and ruin the battery.

    Note: On sealed, maintenance-free batteries, a green dot appearing in the test indicator sight glass means that the battery is charged. However, you may have to tip the battery slightly to get the green dot to show, because gas bubbles may have collected around the indicator.

8. Once the charging process has been completed, turn off the battery charger and disconnect the charger's cables from the battery. Remove the charger cord from the 110-volt power source. Store the charger in a safe, dry place. Reconnect the battery cables—positive cable first. Replace the battery vent caps after cleaning the vent holes.

If your battery is in sound condition, the battery charge should hold. If it does not,

TYPICAL RANGES OF SPECIFIC GRAVITY AT 80°F

1.260 to 1.280 Specific Gravity	100% Charged
1.230 to 1.250 Specific Gravity	75% Charged
1.200 to 1.220 Specific Gravity	50% Charged
1.170 to 1.190 Specific Gravity	25% Charged
1.140 to 1.160 Specific Gravity	Very Little Useful Capacity
1.110 to 1.130 Specific Gravity	Discharged

then you must track down the source of trouble. Some causes are improper regulator settings, a faulty alternator, excessive cranking from a defective starting motor, and bad wiring. You will learn more about these in later chapters.

Using Jumper Cables

Tools and Materials

- Water—Plain or Distilled
- Rag
- Jumper Cables
- Hydrometer

DURING COLD weather, there is one question that creates a bond within a neighborhood: ". . . can you give me a boost?" To cement your friendship with neighbors, you must know what you are doing with your jumper cables.

    Using jumper cables to start a dead battery from a healthy one is the most common method used to revive a dead battery. Electrical current, sufficient to start the ailing car, is supplied through the jumper cables from the good battery. With jumper cables and power from the battery of any car having the same voltage, you can probably start your car with no trouble.

    The procedure is easy when done right, but you can damage a car's electrical system by not connecting the cables correctly. If you have the talent to lift the hood of the car, you should be able to hook up the jumper cables properly in the correct sequence without any trouble. *Caution: Always remove rings and watches when working around batteries and*

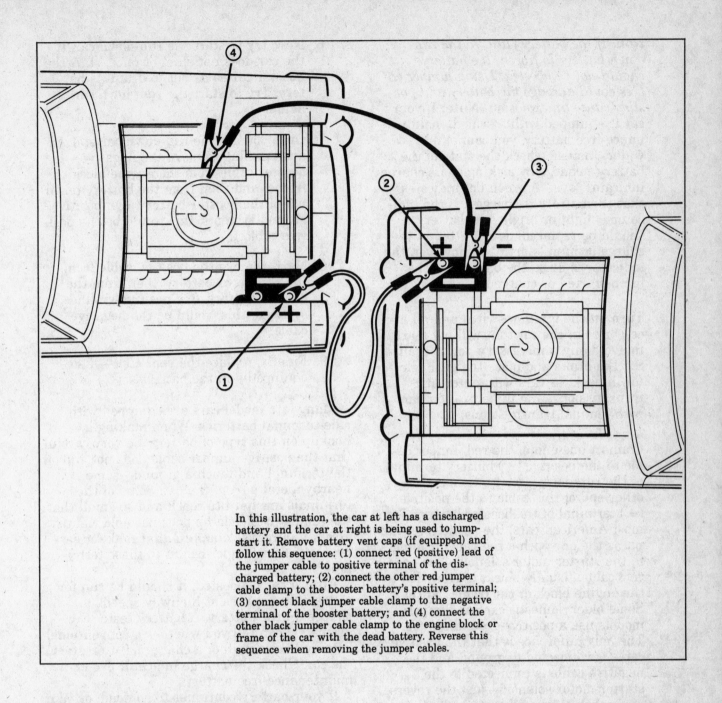

In this illustration, the car at left has a discharged battery and the car at right is being used to jump-start it. Remove battery vent caps (if equipped) and follow this sequence: (1) connect red (positive) lead of the jumper cable to positive terminal of the discharged battery; (2) connect the other red jumper cable clamp to the booster battery's positive terminal; (3) connect black jumper cable clamp to the negative terminal of the booster battery; and (4) connect the other black jumper cable clamp to the engine block or frame of the car with the dead battery. Reverse this sequence when removing the jumper cables.

jumper cables to prevent the possibility of electrical burns. Be careful that jumper cables do not contact the positive battery terminal (or any metal in contact with that terminal) and any other metal on the car at the same time. A short circuit could occur. Never expose the battery to an open flame or electrical spark.

Here is how it should be done.

1. To jump-start your car's dead battery, line up the two cars so they are facing each other. Do not allow them to touch; this could lead to electrical shorts and dangerous sparks.

2. Remove the battery vent caps from both the run-down battery and the good battery. Look inside and check the electrolyte level in both batteries. If the level is low, add water. Use distilled water if the water in your area has a high mineral content. Leave all vent caps off during the jump-starting procedure and keep the holes covered with a rag. *Cau-*

tion: If the battery fluid in the run-down battery is frozen, the battery should not be boosted. Using jumper cables could damage the battery and possibly cause an explosion. **Note:** If your car is equipped with a sealed, maintenance-free battery, you cannot add water. Instead, check the state of the battery's charge by looking at its charge indicator "eye." A green dot indicates that the battery is charged. If the indicator is light or bright, the battery should be replaced; do not attempt to charge or jump-start it. If, however, the indicator is dark, the battery can be jump-started or charged.

3. Turn off the ignition switch and all accessories in the car that will not start to avoid any unnecessary power drains. Set the brake and place the gear selector in park for cars with automatic transmissions, and in neutral for cars with manual transmissions.

4. Connect one end of the red jumper cable to the positive (+) battery terminal of the run-down battery. Connect the other end of this cable to the positive (+) terminal of the booster battery. In most American cars, the positive terminal is the one with a red cable leading to the starter motor solenoid. The negative cable, usually black, is grounded to the engine block or car frame. **Note:** Some older domestic cars and import models use a positive-ground system. The only difference is that the positive cable is connected to ground and the negative cable is connected to the starter motor solenoid—just the reverse of a negative-ground system. On this system, the negative jumper cable is connected first and removed last.

5. Connect one end of the black jumper cable to the negative (−) battery terminal of the booster battery, and the other end of this cable to the run-down car's engine block or frame. Always connect positive to positive and negative to negative.

6. Now, try to start the run-down car. If the car does not start at once, start the booster car so as not to drain its battery. Try to start the run-down car again.

7. Once you get the run-down car started and running, remove the negative booster cable from the engine block or frame, and then from the battery terminal of the booster battery. (On positive-ground systems, this would be the positive cable.)

8. Next, remove the positive cable from the run-down battery, then from the booster battery. (On positive-ground systems, this would be the negative cable.)

9. Finally, replace the vent caps—if so equipped—on the batteries.

Many late model cars are equipped with side-terminal batteries. When making a hookup on this type of battery, be very careful that the positive jumper cable does not slip off the terminal and touch a ground—some nearby metal part of the car. Some of these terminals are hard to reach and so small that the jumper cable clamp does not hold tightly. You can purchase adapters that make it easier to connect jumper cables to these terminals.

After a car is boosted, it should be run for at least 20 minutes at highway speeds to charge up the battery. A battery tester (hydrometer) can tell you whether a conventional battery has enough of a charge left to restart the car. Check the charge indicator eye on a maintenance-free battery.

If your battery continues to go dead, or your alternator light or gauge indicates trouble, you will have to do some further checking of the battery and of the charging system, which is covered in "The Charging System" chapter.

When purchasing a set of jumper cables, buy some with a good electrical conductor, such as copper. Copper carries electrical current much better than aluminum and most other metals. Also, make sure the cables are flexible. Good cables should not feel brittle or kink when you bend them.

Battery Selection and Replacement

Tools and Materials

- Wrenches or Battery Pliers
- Battery Terminal Puller
- Battery Carrier Strap
- Paintbrush
- Hydrometer
- Replacement Battery
- Penetrating Oil
- Water—Plain or Distilled
- Baking Soda
- Rust-Inhibiting Paint
- Silicone Spray or Corrosion Inhibitor
- Grease or Petroleum Jelly

WHEN BUYING a new battery, invest in one with at least as much capacity as the original equipment battery or the one you are replacing, unless you intend to be disposing of the car in the relatively near future. And even then, a heavy-duty battery can be a good sales point if you are selling the car yourself.

Batteries are rated according to cold-cranking performance, which indicates how much current a battery can supply to the starter in extremely cold weather. The cold-cranking performance test shows the number of amps that can be drawn from a 12-volt battery at 0°F for 30 seconds before the voltage drops to 7.2 volts. Ratings are expressed in amperes—for example, a 280-ampere battery.

As a rule of thumb, you should select a battery with a cold-cranking amp capacity that's at least equal to your engine's displacement in cubic inches. For example, a 250 cubic inch V6 would require a battery with at least 250 amp capacity. For engines that have additional accessories such as air conditioning, power windows and seats, and high-output stereos, a higher capacity battery should be installed. If cold weather starting is a concern, then buy the highest capacity battery that will physically fit in your engine compartment. Remember, at zero degrees your battery will have only about 40 percent of its fully charged capacity. That means the same 250 cubic inch V6 engine may need a battery rated at 625 amps to get going on a subzero winter morning.

As opposed to some parts of the car, such as belts and hoses, batteries are a highly competitive commodity at the retail level and often can be bought at substantial savings by watching for sales. For this reason, be aware of your battery's age and condition; be able to anticipate when it will be ready for replacement and you will be able to buy your new one at the best price rather than possibly be forced into buying one under emergency conditions when you cannot shop for the best price.

In addition to the sizes and capacities of batteries, there are several types to choose from. The pre-charged or wet-charged type, with the battery fluid (electrolyte) already in it, ready for installation, is most common.

The dry-charged battery has to have electrolyte added to it. This fluid comes with the battery in a plastic pour container. While the battery will be absolutely "fresh," never having had any electrolyte in the case, it does present the problem of filling. (See caution below.) Each cell should be filled to the top of the plates.

Caution: Battery fluid is a corrosive acid. Do not allow it to contact your eyes, skin, or clothes, or painted surfaces. Flush any contacted area with water immediately and thoroughly. Never expose a battery to an open flame or electric spark. Batteries generate a gas that is flammable and explosive. Always remove rings and watches when working around batteries and jumper cables to prevent the possibility of electrical burns. Be careful that metal tools or jumper cables do not contact the positive battery terminal (or any metal in contact with that terminal) and any other

The fluid in a battery contains acid. If you get any in your eye, flush it immediately with water.

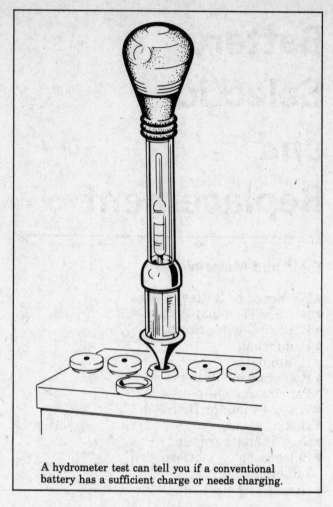

A hydrometer test can tell you if a conventional battery has a sufficient charge or needs charging.

metal on the car at the same time. A short circuit could occur.

The Maintenance-Free Battery

If you have a car that is a number of years old and you have been replacing the original parts such as tires, shock absorbers, and mufflers with the best you can buy, you probably are driving a car that is, in many respects, better than it was when it was new. That is one of the benefits the "automotive aftermarket" has to offer the motoring public.

A good example of this is the maintenance-free battery, well worth considering when replacing your battery. Its main feature is that it should never need the addition of water. But, keep in mind there are various types of maintenance-free batteries, and unless you happen to be a chemical engineer, you might

have trouble determining which kind you want.

There are some maintenance-free batteries that still have the vent/filler caps on the top. This is generally the "low-antimony" type that probably will cost less than a calcium-lead battery and, according to some manufacturers, will last just as long as the more expensive type. Antimony is a chemical that is used with metals to harden them and increase their resistance to chemical action.

The sealed, maintenance-free battery, now being used on newer cars and sold by some of the big retail companies, has no vent/filler caps on top. Instead of the traditional lead-acid compound called electrolyte (which uses antimony in the mixture), this new type uses a calcium-lead approach that permits the manufacturers to seal the top of the battery. The calcium reduces the amount of gas that is produced by the charging action and the lack of antimony is supposed to eliminate the need to add water.

Whether you opt for the completely sealed, maintenance-free battery or the less expensive type with filler caps, you are probably still going to get a better replacement battery than what came in your older model car.

One of the benefits of all maintenance-free batteries is that there is little or no acid buildup. Therefore, there is a considerable reduction in the amount of corrosion on the terminal posts, cable clamps, and on the case itself. Nevertheless, it is still a good idea to clean the battery occasionally because there can be an accumulation from other under-the-hood contaminants.

Because sealed, maintenance-free batteries do not have caps and holes for checking their condition with a hydrometer, a typical unit will usually have a test indicator to show its condition. When the indicator shows a green dot, the charge is good. When it shows a dark color, it needs charging, and when the indicator is clear or a light color, the electrolyte

level is too low to charge. Do not attempt to charge a maintenance-free battery under this last condition; it must be replaced.

After charging a maintenance-free battery that uses such an indicator, you may have to tip the battery slightly from side to side in order to get the green color to show, because gas bubbles may have collected around the test indicator.

If after following instructions in the "Battery Testing" section, you find that your battery needs to be replaced, here is how it should be done.

1. Use a wrench to remove the hold-down frame bolts that secure the battery in the car. Planning ahead always makes for easiest serviceability. If you think that you may have to change the battery, go out at least a couple of hours before you are going to change it and cover the hold-down nuts with penetrating oil so they will be easier to remove.

2. Remove the battery cable clamps as outlined in the section on "Battery Charging." Make sure the ignition is off.

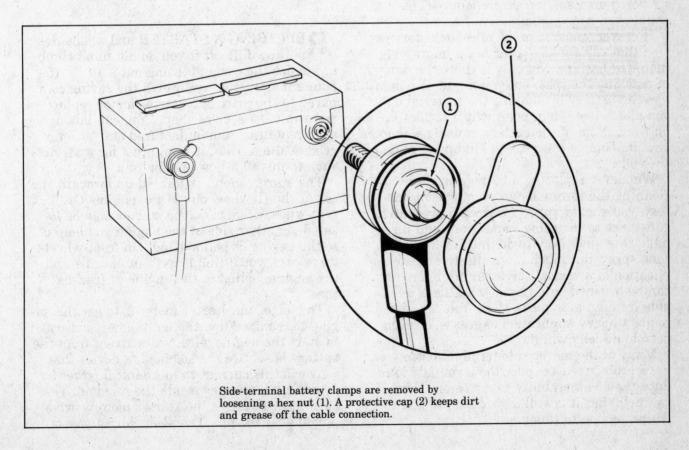

Side-terminal battery clamps are removed by loosening a hex nut (1). A protective cap (2) keeps dirt and grease off the cable connection.

3. Remove the old battery from the car. A battery carrier strap will make the removal much easier. Clean the hold-down frame with a baking soda and water solution. It is a good idea to paint this frame after cleaning and drying it to retard further corrosion (any type of rust-inhibiting paint can be used).

4. Install the new battery, making sure that the same cables go to the same terminals as on the old battery. The negative terminal is almost always the cable that is grounded against the engine block or frame. Only some older cars and import models have positive-ground systems where the positive cable is connected to a good ground.

5. Always be sure that the new battery is fully charged after installation. If it is a conventional battery, check it with a hydrometer. If the battery needs charging, refer to the section on "Battery Charging" for instructions.

There are several dangers to an insecurely mounted battery. One of the most obvious ones is the possibility of the battery falling off its perch on a sudden severe jounce. This could even cause an electrical fire.

However, another problem is the deterioration that can rapidly occur in an improperly mounted battery. Not only is there the danger of cracking the case, but you might also damage the battery by shaking the material on the plates loose, to a point where it piles up on the bottom of the battery, causing a short circuit. This, of course, will kill one or more of the cells.

Whenever replacing a battery or after cleaning the terminals on your present battery, you should apply a corrosion preventive substance to the cable connections and terminals. One quick way to do this is with a silicone spray, but much more effective is the application of a special corrosion inhibitor that can be brushed onto the metal. This is available from an auto parts store. You can also apply a heavy application of grease, or even petroleum jelly will do.

Many of the newer side-terminal batteries have protective caps over the terminals to reduce their vulnerability to corrosion. These can help, but it is still a good idea to add extra protection to this metal.

Replacing a Starter and Solenoid

Tools and Materials

- Wheel Chocks
- Jack and Safety Jack Stands
- Creeper
- Wrenches
- Battery Pliers
- Battery Terminal Puller
- Starter Motor
- Solenoid
- Lock Washers or Internal Tooth Washers

REPLACING A STARTER and solenoid is not too difficult if you do not mind climbing under the car and lifting out a 10- to 15-pound motor. It is well worth the saving compared to the price of a starter motor replacement in most service shops. You can buy a good rebuilt or remanufactured starter for a good deal less than it would cost for a service shop to install a new one for you.

The starter motor is located underneath the car at the flywheel end of the engine. On rear-wheel-drive cars, the starter may be located on either side of the engine and bolted to the engine or bellhousing. On front-wheel-drive cars, you'll find it in front of or behind the engine, bolted to the engine or transaxle case.

The job of the starter motor is to get the engine to crank. When the ignition key is turned to start the engine, electrical current from the battery is sent to the solenoid, a device that converts this current to mechanical power by activating a plunger inside the solenoid. The current also causes the starter motor's drive pinion gear to spin. The solenoid plunger is

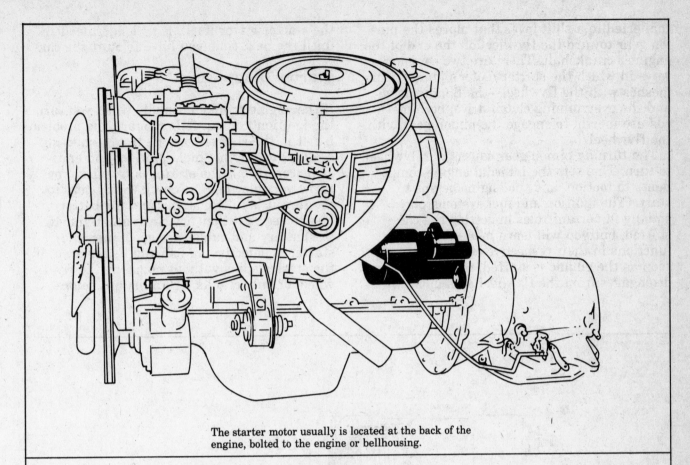

The starter motor usually is located at the back of the engine, bolted to the engine or bellhousing.

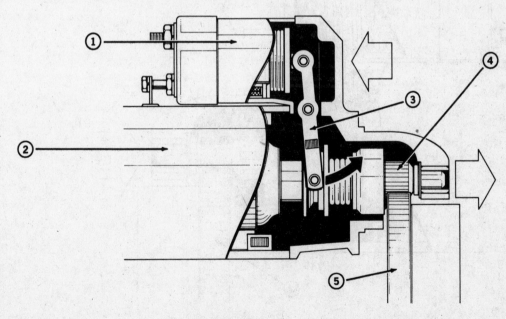

The solenoid (1) is located on top of the starter motor (2). When the ignition key is turned to start the car, electrical current is sent to the solenoid, causing a shift lever (3) to engage the drive pinion gear (4) with the flywheel (5).

connected to a shift lever that moves the pinion gear toward the flywheel on the end of the engine's crankshaft. There are two common ways in which the starter motor's pinion gear meshes with the flywheel—the Bendix drive and the overrunning clutch drive; both methods use inertia to engage the pinion gear with the flywheel.

The turning pinion gear causes the flywheel to turn. This sets the internal engine components in motion, and the engine begins to start. (The ignition and fuel systems play equally important roles in getting the car started, but you will learn more about their functions in their respective chapters.) As soon as the engine is started, the pinion gear disengages from the flywheel and, along with

the starter motor itself, is no longer needed until the next time you have to start the car.

Starter Diagnosis

If the engine cranks normally when you turn the ignition key but fails to start, the problem is not in the starter (see the troubleshooting sections on engine, fuel, ignition, and emissions control). If the starter only "clicks" or turns very slowly, first check the battery to see that it is fully charged and the battery cables to see that they are clean and tight. If the battery and cables are good, then the starter is defective and should be replaced. If the starter spins without engaging the flywheel or only cranks for an instant before

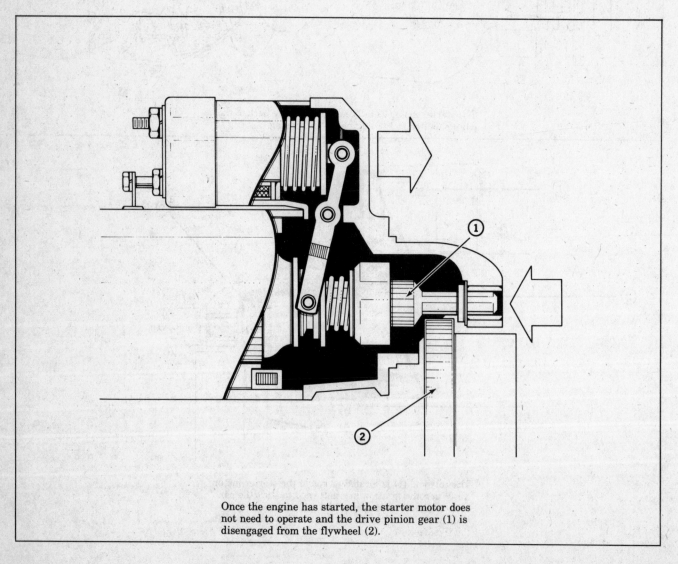

Once the engine has started, the starter motor does not need to operate and the drive pinion gear (1) is disengaged from the flywheel (2).

slipping, then the solenoid and/or starter drive is defective and should be replaced.

Starter Removal

Removing a starter motor varies from car to car and from model to model. For example, on some cars you will have to maneuver the starter motor around exhaust pipes and suspension linkage, which can be tricky without an air lift.

Solenoids are mounted either on the inner fender well or on the starter motor itself. There is no problem in taking one off a fender well, but when the solenoid is mounted on the starter motor, the starter motor usually has to be removed to get at the solenoid.

In either case, the following procedures for removing a starter motor and solenoid are general procedures that can be used as guidelines. By following the instructions and carefully examining how the components are installed, you should not have any problems.

Some special equipment that will make your replacement job easier includes a jack, a pair of safety jack stands, and a creeper. The jack will get your car high enough off the ground so that you will have more room to remove the starter motor. The jack stands will support the front end of your car safely while you are underneath it. And with a creeper, you can lie on your back and easily roll under the car. Here is how to remove and install a starter motor.

1. Park the car on a level surface and engage the parking gear.
2. Place a wheel chock at the front and rear of each rear tire.
3. Using the car jack, raise the front of the car until the front wheels are off the ground, unless you can reach the starter from above.
4. Place jack stands under the front of the car to support it safely, and lower the car onto the jack stands with the jack.
5. Before you roll under the car to remove the starter motor, disconnect the ground cable from the battery terminal (use a wrench, pliers, or battery terminal puller). Then locate the starter motor. It is usually near the bottom and rear of the engine on the driver's side of the car.

6. Brush off any dirt on the starter motor (protect your eyes). Use a wrench to remove all wires connected to the starter motor and solenoid. It is a good idea to tag these wires in some way so that you can be sure they go back to the same connections. Incorrectly connected wires can cause serious problems in the electrical system.
7. Loosen the starter motor mounting bolts, but do not take them all the way out. Find some way to support the starter motor so that you can brace yourself to accept its weight, approximately 10 to 15 pounds.
8. After bracing the starter, remove the bolts and pull the starter motor forward and out. **Note:** On some cars, especially General Motors models, there may be a bracket on the top of the starter motor that braces it to the engine or is attached to one of the three starter motor bolts. This bracket must be removed before the starter motor can come out.
9. To install the starter motor, reverse Steps 6, 7, and 8. Use lock washers or internal tooth washers on all wire connections. **Note:** Be sure the starter motor has a clean connection around the mounting bolt holes, without corrosion or paint.
10. Reconnect the battery ground cable.
11. Lower the car by reversing Steps 1, 2, 3, and 4, and test the starter motor for normal operation by starting the engine.

General Motors cars and some Ford Motor Company and Chrysler Corporation products have the solenoid mounted on the starter motor, so the starter motor must be removed in order to replace the solenoid. This is done by following the procedure we have just described. Once you have the starter motor and solenoid assembly out of the car, place it on a workbench and follow these steps.

1. Remove the two bolts that secure the solenoid to the starter motor.
2. At one end of the solenoid is a connection that attaches the starter motor field lead or leads to the solenoid. After removing this connection, rotate and re-

move the solenoid. **Note:** Be sure to replace the old plunger spring with the one supplied with the new solenoid.

3. Install the new solenoid, reversing Steps 1 and 2. Make sure that the spring seats properly on the plunger.
4. Secure all connections using lock washers or internal tooth washers.
5. Reinstall the starter motor and solenoid assembly as previously outlined.

Ford Motor Company, American Motors Corporation, and import cars that have the solenoid mounted on the inner fender require the following procedure for removal.

1. Disconnect the battery ground cable.

2. Disconnect all wire connections on the solenoid. Be sure to tag them so you will not get confused when reconnecting them.
3. Remove the mounting bolts.
4. Mount the new solenoid in the same place as the old one.
5. Reconnect the wires using internal tooth or lock washers on all connections.
6. Reconnect the battery cable to the terminal.

Some Chrysler Corporation and import cars use a solenoid built directly into the starter motor that should only be changed by someone familiar with this type of starter motor and solenoid assembly.

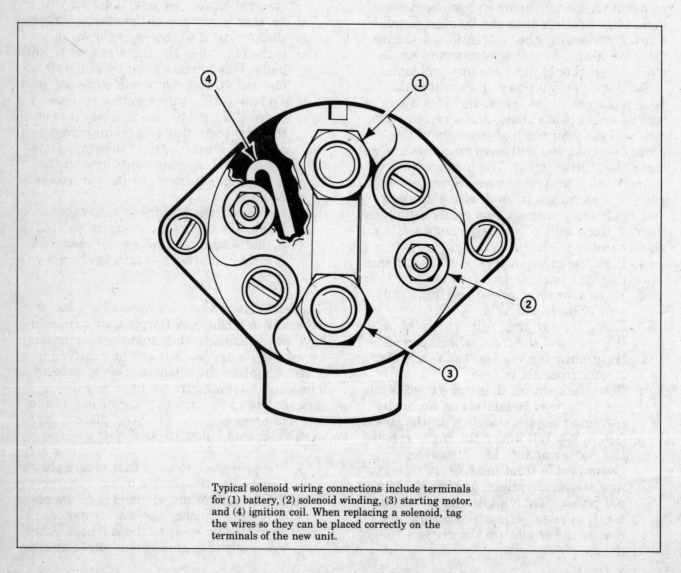

Typical solenoid wiring connections include terminals for (1) battery, (2) solenoid winding, (3) starting motor, and (4) ignition coil. When replacing a solenoid, tag the wires so they can be placed correctly on the terminals of the new unit.

THE CHARGING SYSTEM

AS WE LEARNED in the previous chapter, the battery supplies the initial electrical current needed to start the engine. Once the engine is started, however, the electrical current is generated by an alternator. Because about one half of all automotive problems are electrically related, it is important to understand as much as possible about the function and basic repairs of the charging system.

The charging system basically consists of the battery, alternator, voltage regulator, and the necessary switches and wiring. For a complete discussion of the battery, see the chapter on "The Starting System."

To keep up with the increased electrical demands of modern automobiles, the direct-current generator has been replaced by the alternator, which also has the capability of producing a greater level of electrical current at low engine speeds.

The alternator is located at the front of the engine and is mechanically driven by a drive belt connected to the crankshaft pulley that turns the fan.

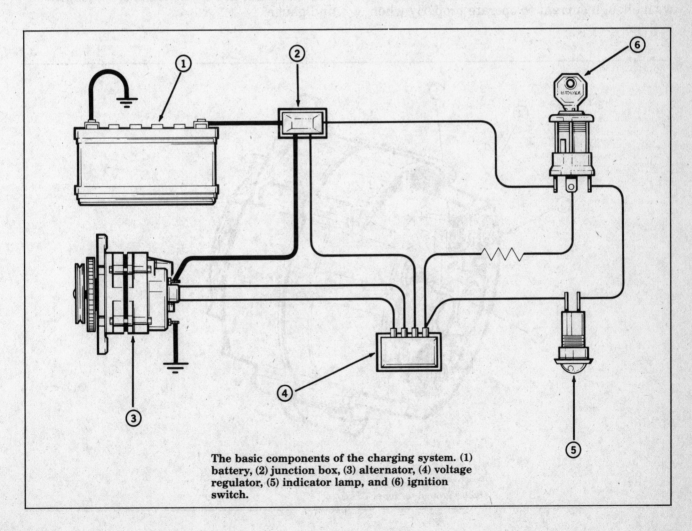

The basic components of the charging system. (1) battery, (2) junction box, (3) alternator, (4) voltage regulator, (5) indicator lamp, and (6) ignition switch.

The voltage regulator is the "brains" of the charging system because it controls the amount of electricity produced by the alternator. It prevents the alternator from delivering too much current to the battery, a condition that can burn out all of the car's electrical components. The voltage regulator is usually silver or black in color, square or rectangular in shape, with "Regulator" usually stamped on its top, and flat metal tabs or terminals at its bottom edge. Generally, it is mounted on or near the alternator—sometimes on the fender well, sometimes on the firewall between the engine and the passenger compartment. In some charging systems, the voltage regulator is mounted inside the alternator.

The purpose of the charging system is to keep the battery charged and to furnish the electrical accessories—lights, horn, air conditioning, AM/FM radio, tape deck, windshield wipers, power windows, and other devices—with enough current to operate properly when the engine is running. In addition to meeting all the electrical needs of the engine and other electrically powered devices, the alternator also returns electricity to the battery where it will be stored until it is needed again. It must be remembered that the battery can only store electrical energy; it cannot produce it.

Other parts of the charging system include the ignition switch, indicator "charge" lamp, and electrical wiring. The ignition switch controls the flow of electrical current by turning it on and off. It generally has five positions: accessories, lock, off, on, and start. The indicator lamp acts as a warning signal by lighting up on the instrument panel when trouble develops in the charging system. The electrical wiring connects all the components in the charging system. The wiring in a car is of different types and gauges designed for specific jobs. Therefore, always replace old wires with new ones that are of the same type, length, and gauge.

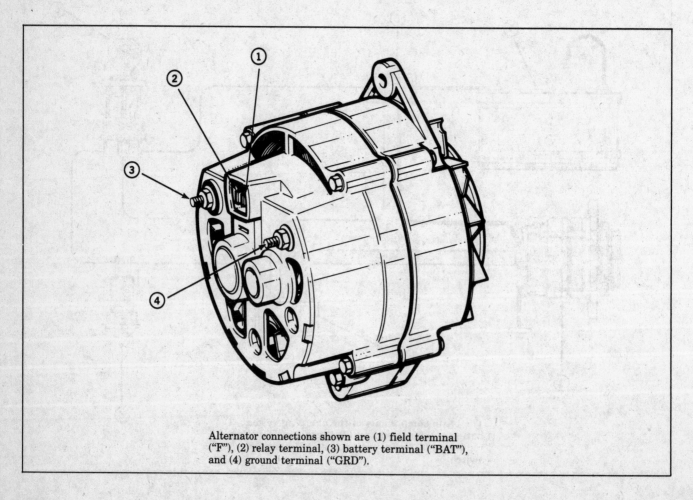

Alternator connections shown are (1) field terminal ("F"), (2) relay terminal, (3) battery terminal ("BAT"), and (4) ground terminal ("GRD").

Replacing an Alternator Drive Belt

Tools and Materials

- Belt Tension Gauge
- Wrenches
- Pry Bar
- Drive Belt

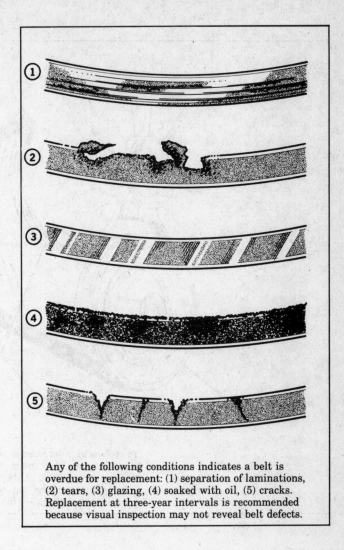

Any of the following conditions indicates a belt is overdue for replacement: (1) separation of laminations, (2) tears, (3) glazing, (4) soaked with oil, (5) cracks. Replacement at three-year intervals is recommended because visual inspection may not reveal belt defects.

A PROBLEM in your car's charging system can start out small and gradually get worse. These are indications, however, that will let you know when the system is malfunctioning.

An overcharged battery is a common sign that the charging system needs attention. An overcharged battery is indicated by its constant need for additional water. If this condition is not remedied immediately, your battery could be seriously damaged.

An undercharged battery can be just as serious. Signs are slow cranking of the engine and dim headlights.

Whether your car has an indicator lamp or an ammeter gauge on its instrument panel, either of these devices will signal early trouble. An indicator light should only come on when the ignition switch is in the on position with the engine not running. If it comes on while the engine is running or the ignition switch is off, then a problem exists in the charging system. The reading on the ammeter indicates if the battery is overcharging, undercharging, or not charging at all.

If the battery is charged and in good condition, the drive belt is the next logical part to inspect, then the voltage regulator. If both the charge and temperature warning lights are on, it means the drive belt is slipping or broken.

One of the biggest causes of charging system failure is a loose, overly tight, or defective drive belt. (If this is not the cause of your problem, read the section on "Testing the Alternator and Voltage Regulator" in this chapter.) A loose drive belt means slippage, and the alternator will not produce enough power to charge the battery. So the red "charge" light on the instrument panel may brighten and stay lit, the headlights will dim at idle speeds, and the battery will run down repeatedly. A drive belt that is too tight can burn out the alternator bearings and strain the water-pump bearings.

Drive belts, like most parts made of rubber, usually last about 3 years. Many careful car owners replace the drive belt at 3-year intervals to avoid both mechanical problems and electrical system damages. The only sound a

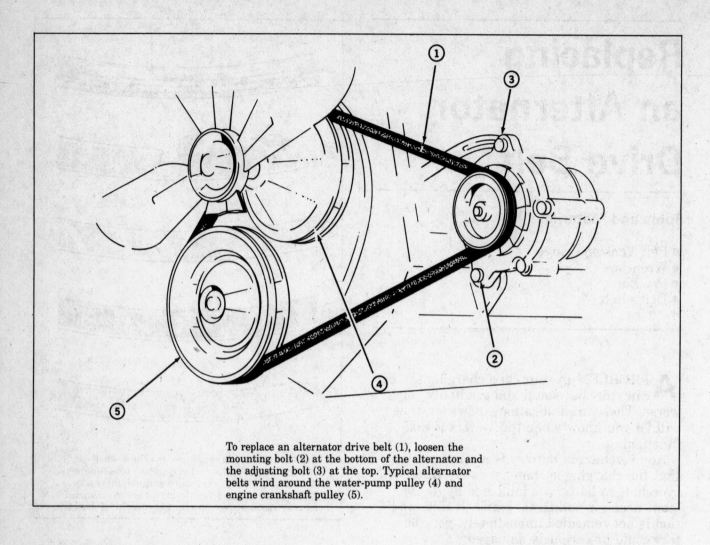

To replace an alternator drive belt (1), loosen the mounting bolt (2) at the bottom of the alternator and the adjusting bolt (3) at the top. Typical alternator belts wind around the water-pump pulley (4) and engine crankshaft pulley (5).

loose drive belt makes is an occasional squeak or wail during acceleration.

You can check drive belt tension with a belt tension gauge, which can be obtained at auto supply stores. If you do not have a tension gauge, with the engine off, place your finger on the drive belt midway between the pulleys. Press on the drive belt with your finger. If the belt depresses more than ¾ inch, then the drive belt is too loose and could be the cause of your charging system troubles. Inspect the drive belt for cracks, brittleness, or oil on its surface. An oil-soaked drive belt may appear tight, but it will still slip and prevent the battery from recharging. Here is the correct procedure for adjusting or replacing an alternator drive belt.

1. Use a wrench to loosen the alternator mounting bolt at the bottom of the al-ternator and the adjustment bolt at the top. **Note:** For engines equipped with "serpentine" drive belts (one flat belt drives all the engine accessories), such belts are removed by using a large screwdriver or pry bar to relieve tension on the belt tensioner pulley. The belt can then be slipped off and re-placed. Route the belt according to the illustration shown on the underhood de-cal (if the decal is missing, refer to the shop manual). No belt tension gauge or other adjustments should be necessary.

2. Slide the alternator in the direction of the fan just enough to loosen the ten-sion on the drive belt. If your car has other accessory units such as power steering, air conditioning, or an emis-sion-control air pump, these belts may have to be loosened or removed to gain

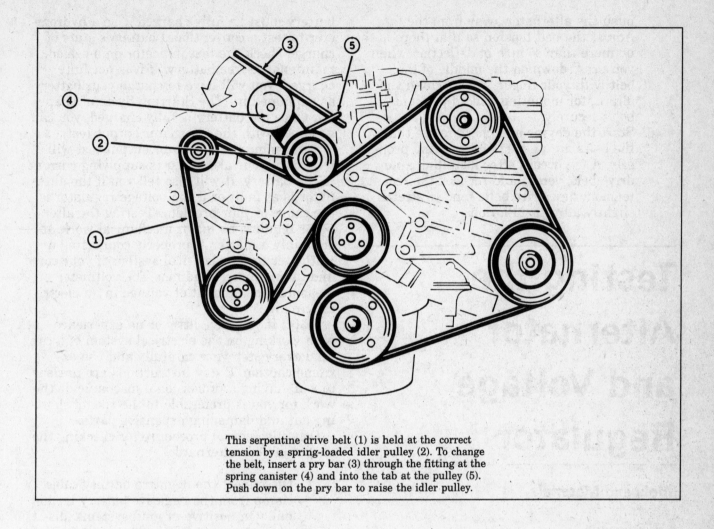

This serpentine drive belt (1) is held at the correct tension by a spring-loaded idler pulley (2). To change the belt, insert a pry bar (3) through the fitting at the spring canister (4) and into the tab at the pulley (5). Push down on the pry bar to raise the idler pulley.

access to the alternator drive belt. Be sure to note which belt rides in which groove so you can reinstall them in the correct way.

3. Remove the old drive belt from the pulleys. Do not cut the drive belt to remove it unless you already have the correct replacement belt in hand. When buying a replacement drive belt from an auto supply store, be sure to get the correct size of belt for your car.

4. Install the new alternator drive belt over the pulleys that it rides in. **Note:** If other belts are to be replaced, be sure you put the belts back on starting with the belt closest to the engine block. Do not try to stretch a new belt over the pulley with a screwdriver; this will weaken it.

5. Tighten the belt using a pry bar to

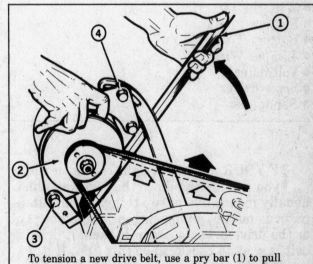

To tension a new drive belt, use a pry bar (1) to pull the alternator (2) away from the fan. Then tighten the alternator mounting bolt (3) and adjustment bolt (4). When properly tensioned, the belt should not depress more than ¾ inch.

push the alternator away from the fan. Adjust the belt tension so that there is no more than ¾ inch of deflection when you press down on the middle of the belt with your finger. Then tighten the alternator mounting and adjustment bolts securely.

6. Start the engine and check to see that the belts are aligned and working properly. A few weeks after installing a new drive belt, you should recheck the belt tension; new drive belts tend to stretch slightly after installation.

Testing the Alternator and Voltage Regulator

Tools and Materials

- Hydrometer
- Wrenches
- Battery Pliers
- Battery Terminal Puller
- Jumper Wire
- Voltmeter
- Screwdriver
- Sandpaper

IF YOUR alternator light comes on while you are driving down the highway, this usually means one of two things—your alternator is not supplying current to the battery, or the drive belt is loose or broken. A drive belt is easy to check, so do this first. If it needs to be replaced or tightened, follow the directions in the section on "Replacing an Alternator Drive Belt" in this chapter.

Before performing any alternator tests, the battery must be fully charged. Use a hydrometer to test a conventional battery's state of charge; check the test indicator on a sealed, maintenance-free battery. If it is not fully charged, you will have to charge your battery as explained in "The Starting System" chapter. Once the battery is fully charged, you can go ahead with the alternator output test.

Performing an alternator output test will tell you if your alternator is supplying current to the battery. It will also tell you if the alternator is at fault or if the voltage regulator is the cause of your problem. Testing the alternator requires no major mechanical work. It is mainly a matter of properly connecting a voltmeter to the electrical system of your car and taking meter readings. The voltmeter measures the amount of voltage in an electrical circuit.

Note: If you have little or no experience with working on the electrical system of a car, read every step very carefully and use extreme caution. If any instructions are unclear to you, having a professional mechanic do the work for you is preferable to the risk of shorting out and damaging expensive parts.

Use this general procedure for checking the output of your alternator.

1. Disconnect the negative battery cable clamp from the negative battery terminal. (On positive-ground systems, disconnect the positive cable clamp.) Side-terminal battery cable clamps will come off by removing a hex-head bolt from the clamp with a wrench. Spring-type clamps require pliers to squeeze the tabs on the end of the clamp and to lift the clamp off the terminal. Conventional clamps can be removed by using a wrench to loosen a bolt on the clamp. A battery terminal puller will help lift the clamp from the terminal.
2. Disconnect the field lead from the alternator. The field lead can be disconnected by pulling off a plug-on connector, or by removing a nut with a small wrench. This lead will generally be marked with an "F" on the alternator housing. If there is no mark, then you will have to find out which terminal is the field terminal by using your car's service manual.

Note: If you have a 1973 or newer General Motors car, an alternator output test can be performed without disconnecting any wires. On the back of the alternator, there is a D-shaped opening used for checking full alternator output. Start the engine and carefully insert a small screwdriver blade about ½ inch into the hole, grounding the screwdriver against the metal tab and the alternator housing. This bypasses the regulator, which is inside, and the voltage should start to climb. *Caution: Do not insert the screwdriver* *more than ¾ inch into the opening. If you do not get a reading on the voltmeter after inserting it this far, something is wrong with the alternator or you are not grounding it properly. Further insertion may damage vital alternator components.*

If the regulator is faulty, an auto parts store or repair shop may sell you the alternator with the regulator inside for little more than the internal regulator plus labor charge to install it. If your car is under warranty, talk to your dealer's service department to deter-

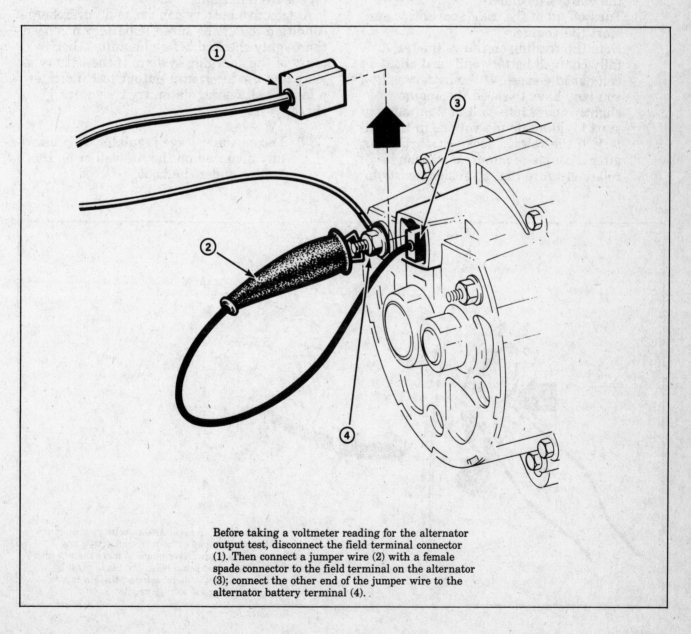

Before taking a voltmeter reading for the alternator output test, disconnect the field terminal connector (1). Then connect a jumper wire (2) with a female spade connector to the field terminal on the alternator (3); connect the other end of the jumper wire to the alternator battery terminal (4).

mine whether the entire unit is covered, rather than only the regulator.

3. Connect one end of a jumper wire to the field terminal. You are now eliminating the regulator from the charging system to make the alternator charge at full output. Connect the other end of the jumper wire to the battery terminal on the alternator, marked "BAT."

4. Hook up the leads of the voltmeter—the red wire to the "BAT" terminal on the alternator, and the black one to a good ground on the alternator frame.

5. Reconnect the negative battery cable to the battery terminal.

6. Turn off all of the car's accessories and start the engine.

7. Note the reading on the voltmeter. A fully charged battery will read about 14 volts at idle speed. If the battery is low, you may have to speed the engine slightly above idle for 1 or 2 minutes to start building up the voltage in the battery. If the voltage does not start rising after a couple of minutes, you can be relatively sure that a problem exists in

the alternator. If the voltage does start to climb, the regulator is causing the problem and should be replaced. *Caution: Never let the voltage climb over 15 volts when performing this test; it can damage the alternator or some other part of the electrical system.*

One of the most common problems that results from a faulty voltage regulator is overcharging of the battery. If you must continually add water to the battery or if a voltmeter reads 15 volts or higher when the car is running at idle, it is a sign that the battery is overcharging.

A defective battery can cause an overcharge condition too. So be sure the battery has been thoroughly checked before blaming other parts of the charging system. If the battery is okay and the alternator output test indicates a faulty voltage regulator, try this quick check.

8. Locate the voltage regulator. It is usually mounted on the firewall or on the fender under the hood.

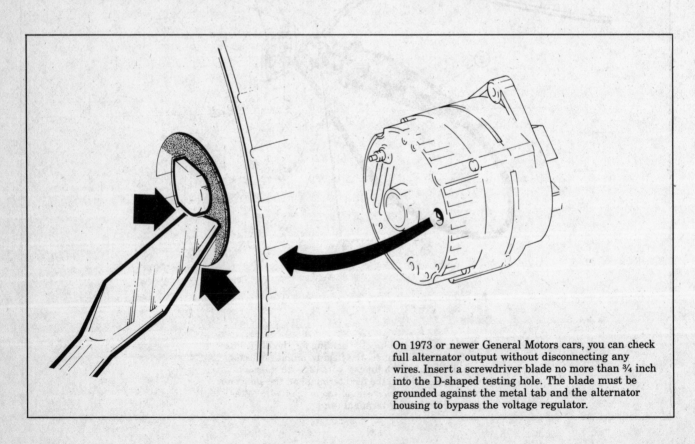

On 1973 or newer General Motors cars, you can check full alternator output without disconnecting any wires. Insert a screwdriver blade no more than ¾ inch into the D-shaped testing hole. The blade must be grounded against the metal tab and the alternator housing to bypass the voltage regulator.

9. Remove the screws holding the voltage regulator with a screwdriver.

10. Use a piece of sandpaper to clean the area around the screws on the regulator and where it mounts on the body of the car.

11. Remount the regulator and start the car to see if the voltage reduces to a normal rate of charge. If overcharging still exists, install a new voltage regulator as covered in the next section.

12. Reverse Steps 1 through 5 to disconnect the voltmeter and reconnect the alternator, voltage regulator, and battery ground cable.

Replacing the Alternator and Voltage Regulator

Tools and Materials

- Wrenches
- Battery Pliers
- Battery Terminal Puller
- Pry Bar
- Screwdriver
- Alternator
- Voltage Regulator

THE SYMPTOMS of troublesome voltage regulators and alternators are the general signs of electrical problems: the red charge light on the instrument panel remains lit after the engine is started (or the ammeter shows a low reading), the lights dim significantly at idle, and the battery repeatedly runs down. If you have checked the battery connections, performed hydrometer tests or otherwise checked the battery's state of charge, examined drive belts and checked pulleys for restrictions and sideplay, you have narrowed the problem to either the voltage regulator or the alternator.

If you have never worked with the electrical wiring of a car and have no experienced friend to assist you, you should consider leaving the repair of these parts to a trained mechanic. Once learned, however, the processes are easy.

Replacing the Alternator

An alternator is generally not too difficult to replace, so if you question its condition, remove it from the car and bring it to a parts store or to a rebuilder who can give it a thorough check.

Here is how to remove and replace an alternator.

1. Make sure the ignition is off, then disconnect the negative battery cable clamp from the battery terminal (disconnect positive clamp if your car has a positive-ground system). Use a wrench to loosen the bolt on the clamp. Remove

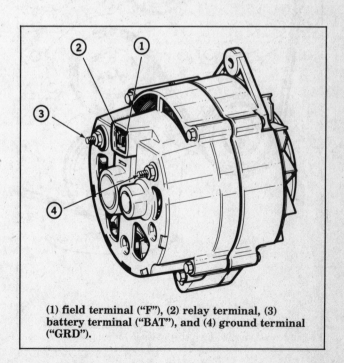

(1) field terminal ("F"), (2) relay terminal, (3) battery terminal ("BAT"), and (4) ground terminal ("GRD").

the clamp from the terminal with a battery terminal puller if the clamp cannot be lifted off by hand. Do not hammer or pry the terminal or clamp. You could break or crack the battery case. If you have a spring-type cable clamp, use pliers to squeeze the tabs on the clamp and lift it off. Side-terminal battery cables are removed by loosening a small hex bolt and unscrewing it from the battery.

2. Loosen the mounting bolts for the alternator with a wrench. There is usually one mounting bolt that secures the alternator to the engine block and one adjustment bolt at the top.

This serpentine belt drives all accessories, and is held in correct tension by a spring-loaded idler pulley.

3. Move the alternator to create slack in the belt and slip the drive belt off the pulley.
4. Disconnect the wires that are attached to the alternator. Note and mark their locations so that you will not get confused when you have to reconnect them.
5. Remove the mounting bolts and the alternator from the car.
6. After your alternator has been thoroughly checked, reinstall the alternator or its replacement by reversing Steps 1 through 5.
7. The drive belt must be properly tensioned when it is put back on. Place the belt on the pulleys. Then, using a pry bar, pull the alternator away from the fan until the belt is taut. Finally, tighten the mounting bolts. Depress the middle of the belt with your finger; it should not depress more than ¾ inch.

Replacing the Voltage Regulator

Installing a new voltage regulator whenever an alternator is replaced is a good policy. The step may be unnecessary, but it does insure against the likelihood that the old regulator will be responsible for the ruin of the replaced alternator. **Note:** Many late model cars have their voltage regulator mounted inside the alternator. Replacing this type of regulator is a job that should be left up to a professional mechanic. However, here is the procedure for replacing an external voltage regulator.

Caution: The battery ground cable must be disconnected as previously outlined.

1. Locate the voltage regulator. It is usually mounted on the firewall or on or near the fender under the hood.
2. Remove the wires, noting and marking their locations, from the voltage regulator. **Note:** Some model cars have a plug-type connector that, when removed, disconnects all regulator wires.
3. Remove the unit from its mounting. Use a screwdriver to remove the screws that hold it in place.
4. Attach the new voltage regulator in the same location as the old one and install the attaching screws.
5. Reconnect the wires properly.

THE COOLING SYSTEM

THE INTERNAL combustion engine, which powers almost all automobiles, works on the principle of "burning inside." Burning the air/fuel mixture in the engine creates a tremendous amount of heat—enough heat to melt a 200-pound engine block in 20 minutes. In normal driving, temperatures inside the cylinders may be as high as 4500°F. Pistons may run 600° at the crown (very top).

The function of the cooling system is to keep the engine at a temperature where it performs best. Two methods have been employed to regulate this performance—air-cooling and water-cooling. However, water-cooling systems are by far the most common.

For efficient operation, each automobile engine has an optimum temperature range. Without an efficient cooling system, the en-

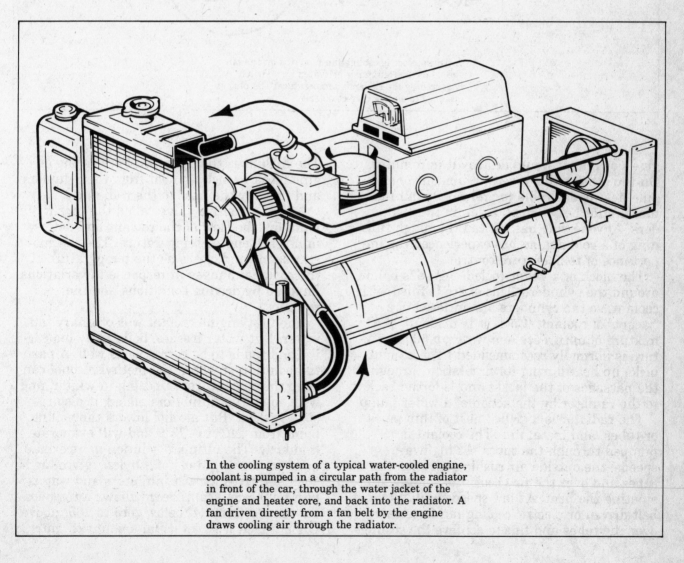

In the cooling system of a typical water-cooled engine, coolant is pumped in a circular path from the radiator in front of the car, through the water jacket of the engine and heater core, and back into the radiator. A fan driven directly from a fan belt by the engine draws cooling air through the radiator.

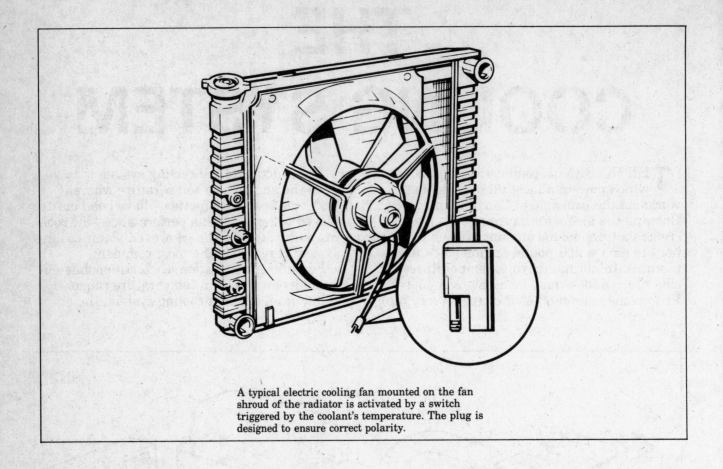

A typical electric cooling fan mounted on the fan shroud of the radiator is activated by a switch triggered by the coolant's temperature. The plug is designed to ensure correct polarity.

gine's own heat would destroy it in minutes. On the other hand, a certain amount of engine heat is desirable to preheat the air/fuel mixture for better combustion in the cylinders. Anyone who has noticed the rough running of a cold engine has experienced the importance of temperature control.

The block of a water-cooled engine is hollow around the cylinders. This space is filled with coolant, so the cylinders are enclosed in a "jacket" of coolant. (Coolant is made up of a mixture of antifreeze and water; a 50/50 mixture is normally recommended.) The coolant picks up heat during its circulation through the passages of the jacket and is forced back to the radiator by the action of a water pump.

The radiator is a grilled nest of thin pipes, or tubes, and metal fins. The coolant is pumped through the tubes. At highway speeds, the outside air rushing between the tubes and over the fins cools the solution, dissipating the heat. At low speeds and at idle, a belt-driven or electric cooling fan forces air over the tubes and fins to achieve the cooling.

The coolant is then pumped back to the engine block to pick up heat from the cylinders and to carry the heat to the radiator.

A heat-sensitive valve called the thermostat monitors the flow of the coolant and determines the engine temperature. The thermostat opens and closes as the temperature of the coolant changes in response to variations imposed by driving conditions and the weather.

The first engine coolant was ordinary tap water. But water freezes, boils away too easily, and tends to be corrosive as well. A partial solution of water and methyl alcohol can keep the coolant from freezing in winter, and with some rust inhibitors added, it also resists rusting. But alcohol lowers the boiling point from 212° to 173°F and will evaporate regularly. The ultimate solution is a permanent antifreeze. Made of ethylene glycol and such additives as rust inhibitors and water-pump lubricant, antifreeze allows a temperature range from 34° below zero to 265° above when mixed with an equal amount of water.

If anything, the modern cooling system with permanent antifreeze works too well. Not being the wheel that squeaks, it usually receives little attention. However, no antifreeze is really permanent—the additives do wear out. Neglecting the cooling system can result in leaks from connections to the engine block, from worn hoses, from radiator tubes, and from pumps—all causing overheating and doing irreversible damage to the engine.

With proper care, the cooling system can last for many years with only minor service such as replacement of hoses, belts, and possibly a radiator pressure cap or thermostat. It is strictly a matter of keeping the coolant in the system clean with all components working properly. Here are the components of your car's cooling system.

1. RADIATOR. The radiator is a honeycomb of small tubes and fins. The hot coolant flows through the tubes and is cooled by the air passing around the tubes and the fins.

2. FAN. At idle and in slow operation, the fan draws air from the outside through the radiator core to cool the coolant as it passes through the radiator.

3. FAN CLUTCH. On some vehicles, the fan is mounted on a fan clutch that allows the fan to turn at a slower speed or to coast when maximum cooling is not required, as when the engine is cold or when the car is traveling fast enough to force sufficient air through the radiator. The fan clutch reduces the parasitic horsepower drag on the engine and helps to improve fuel economy.

4. ELECTRIC COOLING FAN. On front-wheel-drive cars with transverse-mounted engines, an electric cooling fan is used to draw air through the radiator. The fan is switched on and off by a thermostat in the radiator or engine block. The fan normally remains off until coolant temperatures rise above 190° to 200°F, at which point the fan turns on and remains on until coolant temperatures drop back below the thermostat threshold.

5. WATER PUMP. The water pump carries coolant through the radiator (or through the radiator bypass) and circulates it through the cylinder block and head. It circulates as much as 7500 gallons per hour.

6. FAN BELT. The fan belt drives both the fan and the water pump. If it is slipping or if it breaks, your engine will be overheating very shortly.

7. THERMOSTAT. The amount of coolant that flows through the radiator is controlled by the thermostat. Its purpose is to keep the engine operating at a specified temperature, and frequently, in cold weather or easy driving, it is nearly closed. The pump then recirculates coolant through the engine through a radiator bypass.

8. RADIATOR PRESSURE CAP. The radiator pressure cap controls the pressure in the cooling system. Coolant, just as water, boils at a higher temperature under pressure than it does without pressure (as does a pressure cooker). Therefore, the cooling system is designed to function at high temperatures with the system working under pressure.

9. COOLANT. The coolant in the cooling system consists of a mixture of antifreeze and water. The automobile manufacturers recommend a 50/50 mixture for year-round protection. Be sure to buy a quality antifreeze, one that contains ethylene glycol, plus rust and corrosion inhibitors.

10. HOSES AND CLAMPS. The radiator and heater each have two hoses. One hose lets the coolant in and the other hose lets it out. Many cars also have a radiator bypass hose. The bypass hose allows the coolant to flow through the cooling system when the thermostat is closed. **Note:** A few cars have an internal bypass passage built into the water pump. All hose connections use hose clamps to ensure a tight seal. The two popular types of hose clamps are the screw-type and spring-type. The screw-type has a screw on the clamp that is turned to either tighten or loosen the clamp. Spring-type clamps have tabs. By squeezing these tabs with pliers, the tension is relieved and the clamp can be removed or installed.

11. COOLANT RECOVERY SYSTEMS.

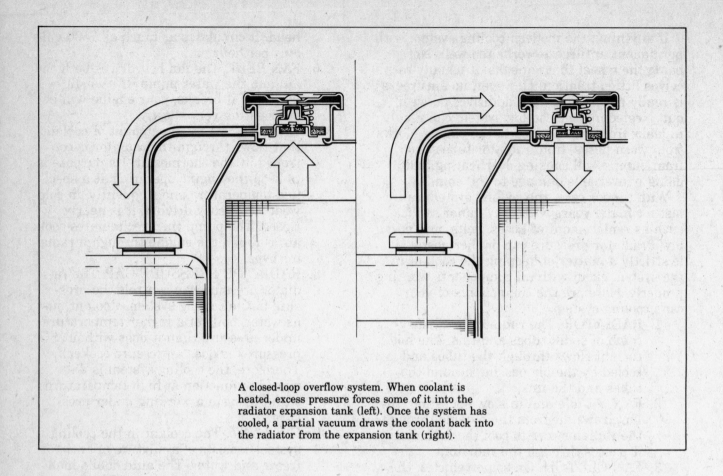

A closed-loop overflow system. When coolant is heated, excess pressure forces some of it into the radiator expansion tank (left). Once the system has cooled, a partial vacuum draws the coolant back into the radiator from the expansion tank (right).

Coolant recovery systems are part of most cooling systems on late model cars. A coolant recovery system uses a reservoir to hold the overflow of coolant as it is heated and expands. After the engine has been stopped and cools down, a partial vacuum exists that draws the coolant back into the radiator. Coolant recovery system kits are available at auto supply stores.

12. OTHER COMPONENTS. Gaskets, freeze plugs, and a heater control valve are the other components of the cooling system. Gaskets are used to provide a leakproof seal between two mating surfaces. Freeze plugs are located on the sides of the engine block. If the coolant should ever freeze, the expanding coolant will force the freeze plugs out of the engine block. In many cases, this will prevent serious engine damage. The heater control valve is usually located in the inlet heater hose. It controls the flow of coolant to and from the heater.

Cooling System Inspection

Tools and Materials

- Flashlight or Trouble Light
- Small Mirror
- Stop-Leak Additive

A UNITED STATES Department of Transportation survey showed cooling system failure is the third most common cause of highway breakdowns, led only by running out of gas and tire failure. One reason may be that cooling systems are often overlooked by car owners and servicemen. This section deals with the preventive measures of checking for leaks and impending failures in your car's cooling system.

Ideally, you should make a quick visual check of your cooling system every time you raise the hood and the engine is turned off. A thorough check should be made every 3 or 4 months. Follow this systematic process in checking your cooling system for leaks.

1. HOSES. The cooling system uses several hoses to carry hot coolant, under pressure, from one place to another. They include upper and lower radiator hoses, inlet and outlet heater hoses, and on some cars, a radiator bypass hose. Hoses have to perform in an atmosphere that may be a deep freeze one day and a baking oven the next. The emphasis is on heat because in recent years engine temperatures have jumped dramatically due to the maze of emission-control devices. This increased underhood heat has put a greater strain on these rubber parts. Average hose life today is about 25,000 miles.

Check hoses when the engine is cold, so cooling system pressures do not mislead you. With a good flashlight, or trouble light, check for seepage of coolant, especially around the ends of hoses. Look for spots where hoses may be rubbing against parts of the engine or body, causing abrasion. Feel the hoses for condition of the rubber. Often, outside appearances are misleading and what appears to be a good hose is really ready to leak or burst.

By feeling the hoses, we mean really squeezing and flexing them. To get experience in this area, check hoses on a new car with fewer than 10,000 miles on it. Radiator and heater hoses when squeezed and flexed should have a firm feel and should spring back into shape immediately. If they are mushy and squeeze together like a limp rag, replace them. If they are so brittle and hard they will not flex, replace them. Hoses must be pliable enough to absorb any engine movement and vibration

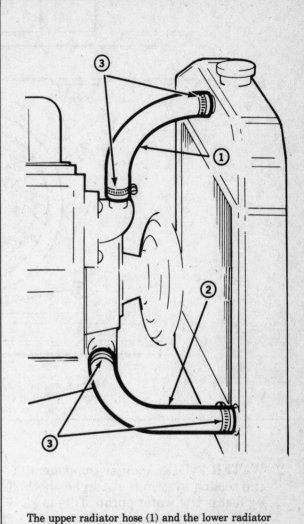

The upper radiator hose (1) and the lower radiator hose (2) are held onto their respective fittings by hose clamps (3). The average life span of a radiator hose is about 25,000 miles, so they should be replaced every two years or so.

without breaking, but not so yielding that they will fail on the next trip you take.

If there is any doubt about the quality of the hoses you are looking at and the car has over 25,000 miles on it, especially if it is a late model with air conditioning (which adds to underhood heat), change all the hoses. (See the section on "Hose Removal and Installation.") If your car has a short bypass hose near the thermostat housing, do not forget to change that one, too. It is important and frequently breaks.

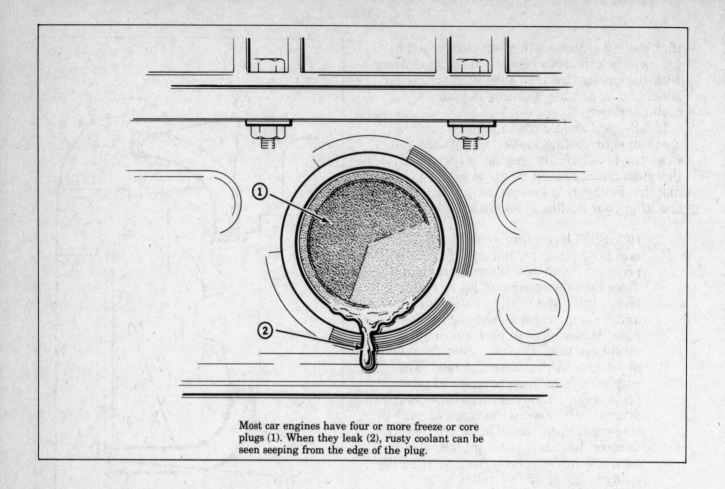

Most car engines have four or more freeze or core plugs (1). When they leak (2), rusty coolant can be seen seeping from the edge of the plug.

2. WATER PUMP. Another component of the cooling system that can be checked by feel is the water pump. This is located directly behind the fan pulley and is checked in this manner. Grip the fan blades horizontally across from one another and wiggle them. There should be no lateral movement in the fan and pulley. On front-wheel-drive cars with transverse-mounted engines, there's no fan attached to the water-pump pulley, so you'll have to wiggle the pulley itself. If there is any slackness, this indicates water-pump bearing looseness, because the pump bearing supports the fan and its pulley. If the pump bearing is loose, this will eventually cause coolant loss from the pump.

To check for leaks at the water pump, look carefully for moisture behind the pulley. There is a small vent hole at the bottom of the pump behind the pulley. This is where leakage is visible. On some cars it is difficult to see, so you may have to use a small mirror, or inspect the pump from underneath the car. If the pump shows any traces of seepage from this vent hole, the only remedy is replacement, as these are sealed units and cannot be repaired.

3. FREEZE PLUGS. Engine freeze plugs (also called core plugs) are another source of leaks, especially on cars three or more years old. Most engines have four or more freeze plugs. They are located in the engine block. If one is leaking, you will see telltale signs of rusty coolant seeping from the edge of the plug.

Some cooling system additives, often called stop-leak, may forestall repairs by sealing tiny leaks. A more permanent repair is replacement of the plug. (See section on "Replacing Freeze Plugs.")

4. HEAD GASKETS. Head gaskets are another source of coolant loss. Head gaskets are located between each cylin-

der head and the engine block. Again, visual inspection for traces of coolant residue is the tip-off. Since replacement of a leaky head gasket requires removing the cylinder head, you'd better leave the job to a professional mechanic unless you're a very skilled do-it-yourselfer.

5. HEATER CONTROL VALVES. Here is a common source of coolant leaks. These can be either manually or vacuum operated water valves, usually located in series with one or two of the heater hoses. You will find a control cable or vacuum hose coming from the valve. Check the valve carefully for leaks, especially near the hose connections. You may see traces of coolant at small vent holes on the underside of the unit. If so, replacement is necessary.

They are easy to replace. Drain the radiator, remove the hoses connected to the heater control valve and unscrew the valve from its mounting. Reverse this procedure to install the new valve, which is available from an auto parts store.

6. RADIATOR. A thorough visual inspection of the radiator is essential. Use a good light to look for loose side straps and supports. Solder joints may have loosened and caused these pieces to separate from the radiator. Look for signs of seepage on the front and rear finned area of the radiator. A real tip-off is greenish-white corrosion, either on or near the top of the radiator tank. Stop-leak may help this kind of seepage for a while, but sooner or later the radiator will have to be removed and re-

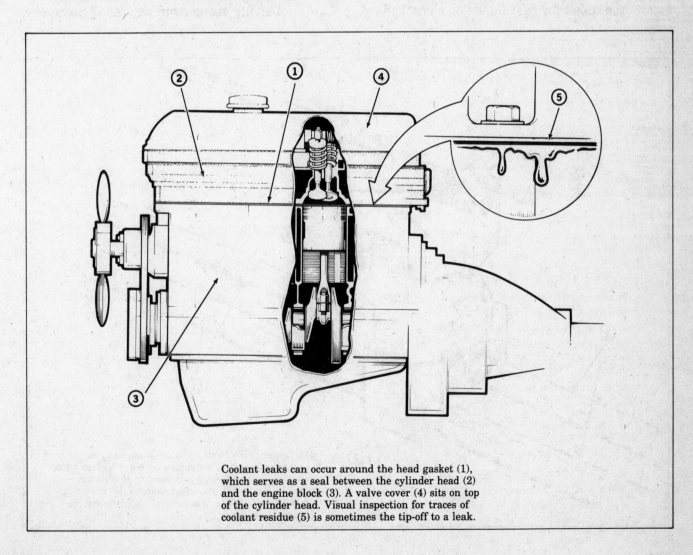

Coolant leaks can occur around the head gasket (1), which serves as a seal between the cylinder head (2) and the engine block (3). A valve cover (4) sits on top of the cylinder head. Visual inspection for traces of coolant residue (5) is sometimes the tip-off to a leak.

paired. You can remove the radiator yourself and take it to a radiator shop to have it repaired. (See section on "Replacing the Radiator.")

Loose fins—the tiny thin pieces of brass folded between the tubes of the radiator—must be securely fastened between the tubes. If they are not, the radiator may overheat because it cannot conduct its heat into the air with poorly bonded fins. While you are looking, make sure the surface of the radiator is not clogged with dirt, bugs, and debris, also affecting its efficiency. If you suspect dirt is clogging your radiator's surface, blow it out with compressed air. Use the air supply at your service station if necessary.

7. RADIATOR PRESSURE CAP. Take the radiator pressure cap off and check it too. Look for rust inside or a cracked

rubber seal inside the cap. These keep the cap from functioning as it should, resulting in coolant loss and eventual overheating. If you need a replacement cap, be sure to ask for the correct cap for your car. You can buy one at any service station or auto supply store. ***Caution:*** *Do not remove the radiator pressure cap when the system is hot. The system is under pressure and when the cap is removed, hot coolant could rush out of the filler neck and burn you. Some caps have a lever lift to relieve this pressure. But it is best to let the system cool down before removing the cap for inspection.*

8. PETCOCK. The little drain at the bottom of most radiators can develop leaks too. Feel around it for moisture. Is it tightly closed? Has it been damaged by a flying stone from the road? Some en-

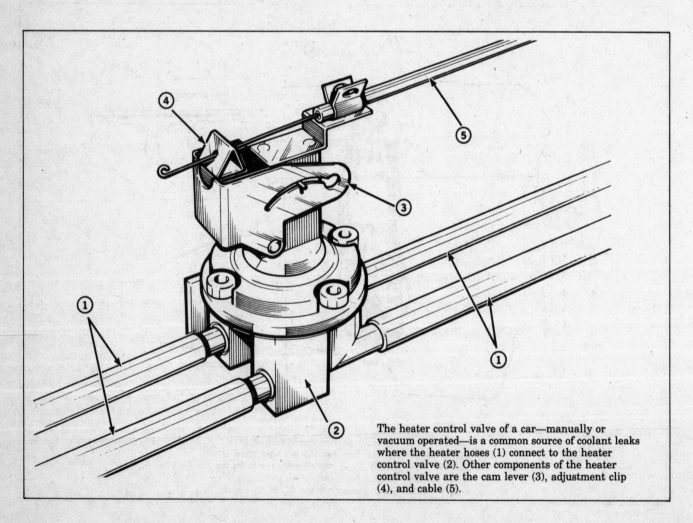

The heater control valve of a car—manually or vacuum operated—is a common source of coolant leaks where the heater hoses (1) connect to the heater control valve (2). Other components of the heater control valve are the cam lever (3), adjustment clip (4), and cable (5).

gine blocks also have a drain petcock. Check this for leakage too. Leakage can develop at the threads even though the petcock is in good condition. Replacement petcocks can be purchased at an auto supply store.

9. FAN CLUTCH. A slipping or inoperative fan clutch can result in overheating because the fan won't be able to turn fast enough to keep up with the cooling demands of the engine. There are several ways to check the fan clutch. With the engine off, grasp the fan blades and try to wiggle the fan back and forth. Any visible free play (assuming the water-pump shaft bearings are okay) means the fan clutch should be replaced. Another telltale symptom of a bad clutch is oily streaks radiating outward from the clutch hub. The clutch is filled with a silicone-based fluid; once the fluid is lost the clutch will slip all the time. Another way to check for a defective clutch is to start the engine and run it at fast idle until it reaches normal operating temperature. A piece of cardboard in front of the radiator will speed things up. Then rev up the engine while listening to the fan (or you can use a timing light aimed at the fan to observe its apparent motion). If the fan fails to speed up with the engine hot, it indicates the clutch is bad and should be replaced.

10. ELECTRIC COOLING FAN. An inoperative fan motor or a defective thermostat switch that prevents the fan from coming on can result in overheating. To check the electric cooling fan circuit, insert a piece of cardboard in front of the radiator, start the engine and run it at fast idle until it reaches normal operating temperature. If the fan doesn't come on within a few minutes, it indicates a problem in the electrical circuit or fan motor. Your next step is to shut the engine off and check the fan motor. By disconnecting the motor leads and using jumper wires, you can connect the fan directly to the car's battery. If the motor is good, the fan should spin. If not, replace the motor. If the fan checks out okay, remove the thermostat switch

and check it by dipping the end in boiling water. An ohmmeter or self-powered test light will tell you if the switch is closing or not. Should the thermostat check out okay, there may be a problem in the circuit wiring, fan relay, or circuit fuse. If the thermostat has a single wire lead, grounding the wire should turn on the fan if the circuit is working correctly. For two-wire thermostats, use a jumper wire to connect them together. If nothing happens after bypassing the thermostat, check the circuit fuse and circuit continuity with an ohmmeter. Refer to your shop manual for the location of the fan relay.

Pressure-Testing the Cooling System

Tools and Materials

- Cooling System Pressure Tester
- Adapter for Cooling System Pressure Tester
- Safety Goggles
- Water
- Rags

IF YOUR COOLING system passes visual inspection, the next step is to test it under pressure for leaks. Your safest and most efficient means of pressure-testing the cooling system is to use a testing device such as the kind used by professional mechanics. A cooling system pressure tester is a small hand-operated pump that attaches to the radiator in place of the radiator pressure cap. You pump up the filled cooling system to the pressure indicated on the radiator pressure cap, then examine the system for leaks.

Here is how to pressure-test the cooling sys-

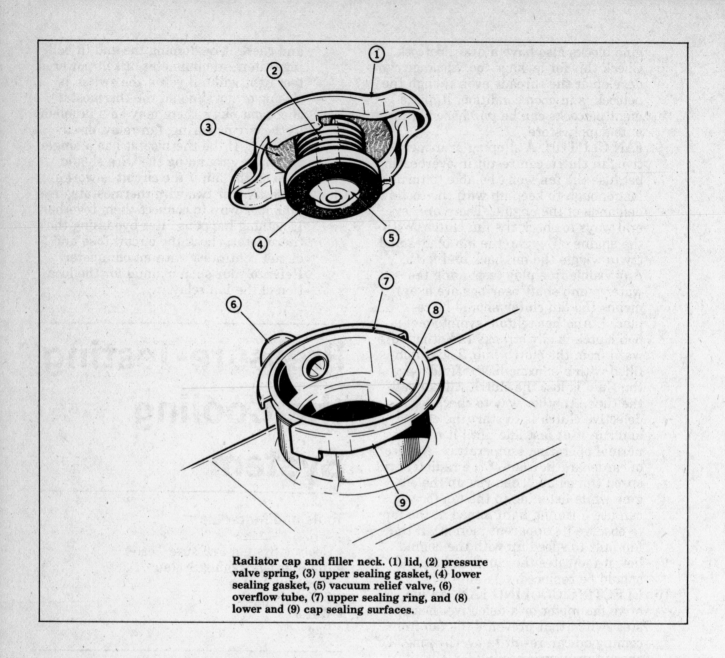

Radiator cap and filler neck. (1) lid, (2) pressure valve spring, (3) upper sealing gasket, (4) lower sealing gasket, (5) vacuum relief valve, (6) overflow tube, (7) upper sealing ring, and (8) lower and (9) cap sealing surfaces.

tem. **Note:** Perform the test when the engine is cold.

1. Open the hood. Remove the radiator pressure cap. This test should be performed with the engine cold and turned off, so there should be no pressure buildup in the cooling system. Nevertheless, always use caution when removing a radiator pressure cap.

2. Visually check the coolant level. It should be up to the proper level—1 inch below the top of the radiator filler neck. If it is not, fill the radiator to the proper level with water.

3. Attach the cooling system pressure tester to the radiator filler neck. It goes on just like the radiator pressure cap. Pump the tester up to the amount of pressure indicated on the radiator pressure cap.

4. Watch for a drop in pressure on the pressure tester gauge. Pumped up to normal pressure, it should hold without dropping for at least two minutes. A very slight loss in pressure (1 or 2 pounds) over several more minutes is negligible. But if the pressure drops rapidly within several minutes, there is

a leak somewhere in the system.

5. Look for any bulged out spots on the radiator or heater hoses. This would indicate an internal fabric weakness and future rupture. Squeeze and flex the hoses. Be sure to wiggle each hose at the end of its connection to be sure it will not give way now that the system is under pressure. *Caution: Wear safety goggles and be careful not to be in the line of spray if a hose should break off in your hand.*

6. Visually inspect the areas around the water pump, freeze plugs, head gaskets, radiator, and heater control valve. If you find any signs of leakage, the problem should be corrected immediately.

7. Remove the pressure tester from the radiator filler neck. Most testers have a relief valve to allow the pressure buildup to escape.

8. You can also use this tester to pressure-test the radiator pressure cap. The radiator pressure cap is designed to release at a given pressure. There is an adapter available for your tester to test the cap. Instructions are provided. If the cap releases either too soon or too late, replace it.

9. Remove the radiator pressure cap from the tester and reattach the tester to the radiator filler neck. Start the engine and run it for 15 to 20 minutes until it reaches its normal operating temperature. Do not turn off the engine.

10. Pump up the pressure tester again to the specified amount (if it isn't already at that level).

11. Look for leaks around the water pump (watch out for moving parts) and the heater control valve, as these components may show leaks only when warmed up. Also, work the heater controls from inside the car to discover any hidden leak at the valve.

12. If you find a leak, take immediate action to correct it. If there are no leaks, turn the engine off—your test is completed.

13. Remove the pressure tester from the radiator filler neck.

14. Reinstall the radiator pressure cap.

Checking the Coolant

Tools and Materials

- Antifreeze Tester
- Pliers
- Rags
- Container
- Antifreeze
- Water

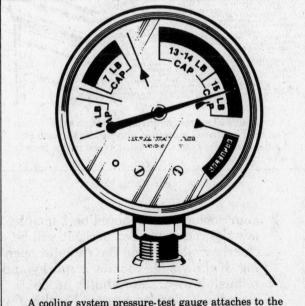

A cooling system pressure-test gauge attaches to the radiator filler neck. The gauge indicates where the cooling system is leaking.

THE COOLANT in your car's cooling system consists of antifreeze and water. The ideal mixture is a 50/50 solution. If the solution is too weak (more water, less antifreeze), it can lead to overheating, especially at low speeds. At the other extreme, weak coolant can freeze at low temperatures, possibly cracking the engine block as the freezing coolant expands.

When purchasing antifreeze, buy only an ethylene-glycol-based product with rust and corrosion inhibitors for year-round protection. Read the label carefully. The product is not up to standard if the label indicates that the content's half-and-half solution of ethylene glycol and water will not provide protection against freezing to −34°F.

Newer cars usually have a coolant recovery system. It takes the expanded volume of coolant from a heated radiator and sends the excess to a reservoir, where it stays until the radiator cools again. You can check the coolant at the reservoir—a plastic container near the radiator at one side of the engine—where a mark indicates the proper level.

If your car has an aluminum engine block, any antifreeze you add should state on the container that it is safe for this type of engine. Your owner's manual will tell you if you have an aluminum engine block.

To check the coolant in your car's radiator, you will need an antifreeze tester. The antifreeze tester, also called a hydrometer, is much like the hydrometer used to test the battery. Follow this procedure to check the degree of freeze protection in your car's radiator.

1. Coolant testing should be done after the engine has been run for a least a few minutes. This assures the coolant will be well mixed and will give you an accurate reading on the antifreeze tester. *Caution: Never remove the radiator pressure cap when the engine is hot because the boiling coolant can geyser under pressure. If your car is excessively warm, wait at least 15 minutes with the hood raised and the engine turned off before removing the cap. Then do so with several thicknesses of rags for protection.*

   Remove the radiator pressure cap slowly. Be prepared to move out of the way quickly if hot coolant sprays out. **Note:** There are two ways to relieve the pressure in the cooling system. Some radiator pressure caps have a lever or a button. Flipping the lever up or holding the button in will release the pressure buildup. Other caps are designed to be turned to a notch. Once the pressure escapes, push down on the cap and continue turning it for removal.

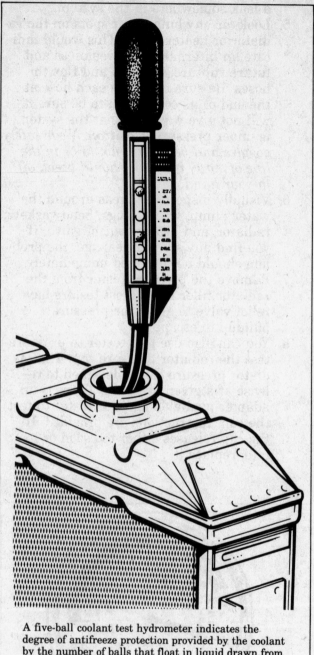

A five-ball coolant test hydrometer indicates the degree of antifreeze protection provided by the coolant by the number of balls that float in liquid drawn from a radiator.

2. Your coolant level should be 1 inch below the radiator filler neck. It will be clearly visible inside the radiator opening. If the visible coolant is murky and reddish brown, the radiator needs cleaning. ("Cooling System Flushing" is covered elsewhere in this chapter.)

3. If the fluid appears clean and clear, re-

start the engine and draw a sample into the antifreeze tester and take a reading. This is done by squeezing the bulb on top of the tester, inserting it into the coolant, and then releasing the bulb. Draw enough coolant into the tester to allow the float inside the glass body to move upwards slightly. Read the scale on the float where the fluid level is highest. Compare this reading with the chart on the tester; most antifreeze testers have a chart on the tester itself that will tell you the degree of protection. Another type of tester uses floating balls to indicate the degree of protection. Instructions for the use of this antifreeze tester are right on the instrument itself.

4. If the antifreeze tester reading is −20°F, the protection should be adequate for most climates. However, if you live in an extremely cold climate, you may want to get your cooling system down to −34°F. With the engine turned off, open the radiator drain petcock with pliers and drain approximately 2 quarts of radiator coolant into a container. *Caution: The coolant will be hot.* Close the petcock immediately after 2 quarts have drained out. Then add 2 quarts of pure antifreeze. If you have a coolant recovery system, you can add the antifreeze to this tank. **Note:** If you have a car that does not have a radiator drain petcock, you can remove the lower radiator hose to drain the coolant. But be careful, this can get pretty messy.

   If your antifreeze tester reading is between +10°F and −19°F, you will have to drain as much as 4 quarts of solution from the radiator and replace it with antifreeze. If the reading is +11°F or higher, the best method is to drain the entire cooling system and refill it with a 50/50 mixture of antifreeze and water. Your owner's manual will tell you how many quarts of coolant your radiator will hold.

5. Reinstall the radiator pressure cap.
6. Start the engine to mix the coolant, and check to be sure that the level is correct.

Cooling System Flushing

Tools and Materials

- Pliers
- Screwdriver
- Utility Knife
- Garden Hose
- Drain Pan
- Rags
- Radiator Hose
- Chemical System Flush
- Antifreeze
- Water
- Flushing Kit

YOUR CAR'S COOLING system can be trouble-free for years if you keep it clean and replace antifreeze at least every two years. Antifreeze loses its rust-inhibiting ability in time and must be replaced if the cooling system is to function properly during the life of the car.

There are several methods of cleaning the cooling system, some of which require professional equipment. Unless you have a badly clogged system that requires professional reverse flushing, one of the two methods explained in this section can be used to flush the cooling system. If you do the job annually, a good chemical system flush may be all you will need. Buy a good quality product and follow the directions. You should have no problem maintaining your cooling system. Essentially, it is a matter of draining your old coolant and filling the cooling system with water. Then pour in the cleaner and drive the car for a short time or run the engine at normal operating temperature. Next, drain the system and flush it with clear water. Finally, add the new antifreeze/water solution. **Note:** Be sure you have a leak-free system before adding antifreeze. See the "Cooling System Inspection" section in this chapter for advice on checking for leaks. This is one way to flush your cooling system.

1. You must drain your car's cooling system completely. To make this job simple, place a drain pan under the radiator. The pan should be able to hold at least 5 gallons of liquid. Then remove the radiator pressure cap to allow the coolant to drain easier. *Caution: Never remove the radiator pressure cap from a hot radiator; when the coolant is suddenly reduced to atmospheric pressure, it will turn to steam.* Instead, allow the engine to cool. Then, with several cloth rags over the radiator pressure cap, turn it slowly to the first notch to release the pressure. Then push down on the cap and carefully remove the radiator pressure cap after all pressure has escaped. Some cars have radiator pressure caps with a button or lever that will release the pressure buildup before you remove the cap. Simply push the button in and hold it or flip the lever up to release the pressure.

2. Using pliers, open the radiator drain petcock near the bottom of the radiator. *Caution: The coolant may be hot if your car has been driven for a while.* On a few older model cars, there is no radiator drain petcock. To drain this type of radiator, you will have to remove the lower radiator hose.

Radiator hose connections are secured by one of two types of hose clamps. Screw-type clamps can be loosened by turning a screw on the clamp with a screwdriver. Once it is loose enough, the clamp can be slid back along the hose and out of the way.

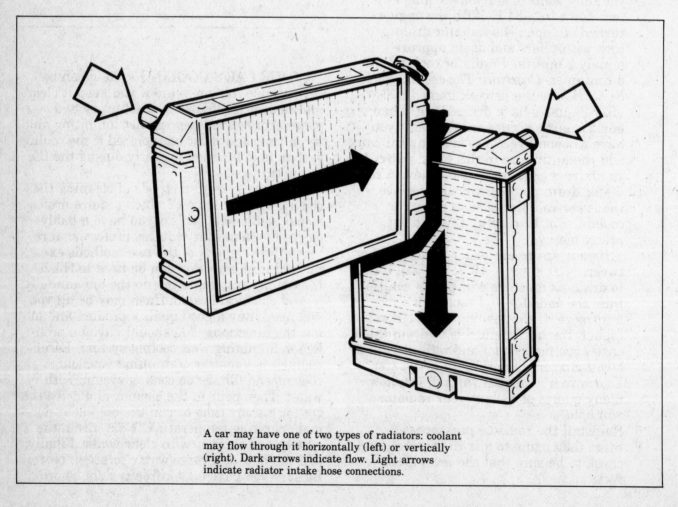

A car may have one of two types of radiators: coolant may flow through it horizontally (left) or vertically (right). Dark arrows indicate flow. Light arrows indicate radiator intake hose connections.

Spring-type clamps require pliers for removal. Simply squeeze the tabs on the clamp to release the pressure and slide it back along the hose.

Once the clamp is out of the way, you can remove the hose from its mounting. Often, hoses are firmly attached and require a hard twisting action to get them off. If that does not work, a sharp knife can be used to cut them off. However, that means you will have to buy a new hose.

3. Observe the condition of the coolant being drained. If it is rusty, a strong chemical system flush is needed, preferably one with oxalic acid. If the coolant is not brown-red in color, any fast-flush product will do. *Caution: After cleaning a system with a coolant reservoir or recovery system, flush the reservoir with water. A contaminated reservoir could be harmful to your cooling system.*

4. When draining is complete, tighten the petcock or reconnect the lower radiator hose. Pour a canful of the flushing chemical (available at an auto supply store) into the radiator. Use a garden hose to fill the radiator to the full level with water. The full level is approximately 1 inch below the filler neck in the radiator.

5. Replace the radiator pressure cap.

6. Start the engine and let it run for the length of time specified in the instructions accompanying the flushing chemical, usually about 15 minutes. Turn the heater controls on all the way; this assures the flushing solution will flow through the entire system, cleaning the heater core as well.

7. Stop the engine and drain the cooling system as before.

8. Remove the radiator pressure cap and then flush the system with water a second time to remove all traces of the flushing chemical that could later have a corrosive action. If the water is not clear after the second flushing, repeat until the water does run clear.

9. Tighten the drain petcock or reconnect the lower radiator hose once more, and fill your radiator with fresh water and antifreeze. Most manufacturers recom-

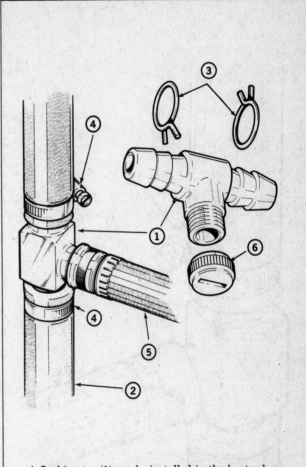

A flushing tee (1) can be installed in the heater hose (2) that runs to the engine block, using either spring hose clamps (3) or screw-type hose clamps (4). Water for flushing the cooling system can then be supplied by a garden hose (5). At other times, the tee is plugged by a cap (6).

mend a 50/50 mixture. To determine how many quarts your cooling system holds, check your owner's manual. **Note:** This is a good time to wash away, with the hose, all of the bugs and dirt that have collected on the cooling fins of the radiator.

10. Replace the radiator pressure cap.

Using a Flushing Tee

This method involves the use of a flushing kit that is becoming popular among both do-it-yourself and professional mechanics. The flushing kit contains a flushing tee, a cap for the flushing tee, two hose clamps, and a

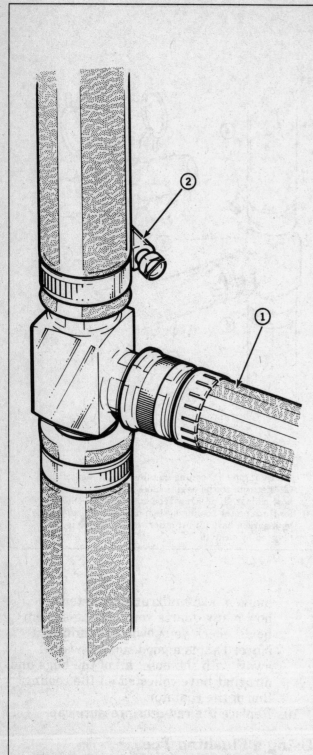

When flushing a radiator through a flushing tee, water from the garden hose (1) should run until the fluid coming out of the deflector placed in the radiator filler neck is clear. Turn off the water and remove the hose. The clamps (2) holding the tee in the heater hose should be tight; otherwise leaks can occur once the cooling system is operating.

water deflector. Here is how to install the kit and use it to flush your cooling system.

1. Locate the inlet heater hose. This is one of two hoses coming from the firewall on the left side of the engine compartment. It is connected to the engine block or manifold—not the heater hose leading to the water pump.
2. Cut through this hose in the middle with a sharp utility knife. Slip a hose clamp on the end of each cut piece. Install the flushing tee between the two cut pieces. Make sure the tee fits snugly into both cut pieces of hose. Move the hose clamps into position and tighten the hose clamps with a screwdriver; use pliers for spring-type clamps.
3. Remove the cap on the flushing tee. Then screw the end of a garden hose onto the tee.
4. Remove the radiator pressure cap. Do this slowly and carefully. It is best to allow the engine to cool.
5. Place the water deflector pipe into the radiator filler neck. This will deflect the water when the system is being flushed.
6. Turn the dashboard heater control on all the way to make sure the heater is flushed clean too. Then, turn on the garden hose and flush the cooling system until the water coming out of the deflector is clear.
7. Turn off the water and remove the garden hose from the flushing tee—do not replace the cap on the flushing tee yet. Also remove the water deflector from the radiator filler neck.
8. Pour enough antifreeze into the radiator for a 50 percent concentration—for example, 2 quarts of antifreeze into a 1-gallon system. As the antifreeze is poured in, clear water will pour out of the flushing tee so that when the proper amount is added, there will be a 50/50 mixture. To determine how many quarts your cooling system holds, check your owner's manual.
9. Replace the flushing tee cap.
10. Start and run the engine until it reaches its normal operating temperature. Then turn off the engine and

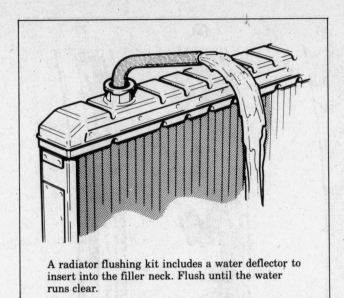

A radiator flushing kit includes a water deflector to insert into the filler neck. Flush until the water runs clear.

check the coolant level. If more coolant is needed, add pure antifreeze.

11. Finally, be sure that all connections are tight and replace the radiator cap.

Replacing a Fan Belt

Tools and Materials

- Wrenches or Ratchet Wrench and Sockets
- Pry Bar
- Belt Tension Gauge
- Fan Belt
- Other Drive Belts

THE COOLING system uses one of the several drive belts that power such components as an alternator, an air conditioning compressor, a power steering pump, and an emission-control air pump. The cooling system drive belt, also called the fan belt, powers the fan and water-pump assembly.

There are two things to check when examining the cooling system fan belt. The condition of the fan belt should be checked first. This can be done while the belt is still on the car (with the engine off). If it is in poor condition, replace it. If it is in good shape, the second thing to check is proper belt tension. A fan belt that is too loose cannot provide adequate cooling at low speeds; a fan belt that is too tight can strain the bearings in the water pump.

Note: Nearly all transverse-mounted engines and some longitudinal-mounted engines have electric fans that are not driven by a belt. However, the water pump on these engines will still be driven by a belt, often the same one that drives the alternator.

Replacing a fan belt is not a difficult task. You may have to remove a power steering belt or an air conditioning compressor belt to reach the fan belt. However, each component that uses a drive belt can be loosened and moved so you can get the drive belt off. Just loosen the mounting and adjustment bolts and move the component toward the fan. This will loosen the belt so it can be removed. Be sure to make a note of which pulley groove each belt rides in so that they can be put back in the same place. Belts are usually of different sizes and are not interchangeable.

Fan belts, like most parts made of rubber, usually last about three years. Here is how to inspect and, if necessary, replace your fan belt.

1. Most fan belt wear shows up on the underside of the belt—the side that contacts the pulley groove. Twist the belt and check it for damage. Look for cracks, brittleness, oil spots, frayed edges, tears, cuts, or polished sides. If any of these conditions are present, replace the fan belt.

2. The cooling system fan belt also drives the alternator on many cars. If drive belts on other components are in the way, loosen their mounting and adjustment bolts. You will need either a wrench or a ratchet wrench and socket to loosen them. Beginning with the belt closest to the radiator, slide the component(s) toward the fan and remove the

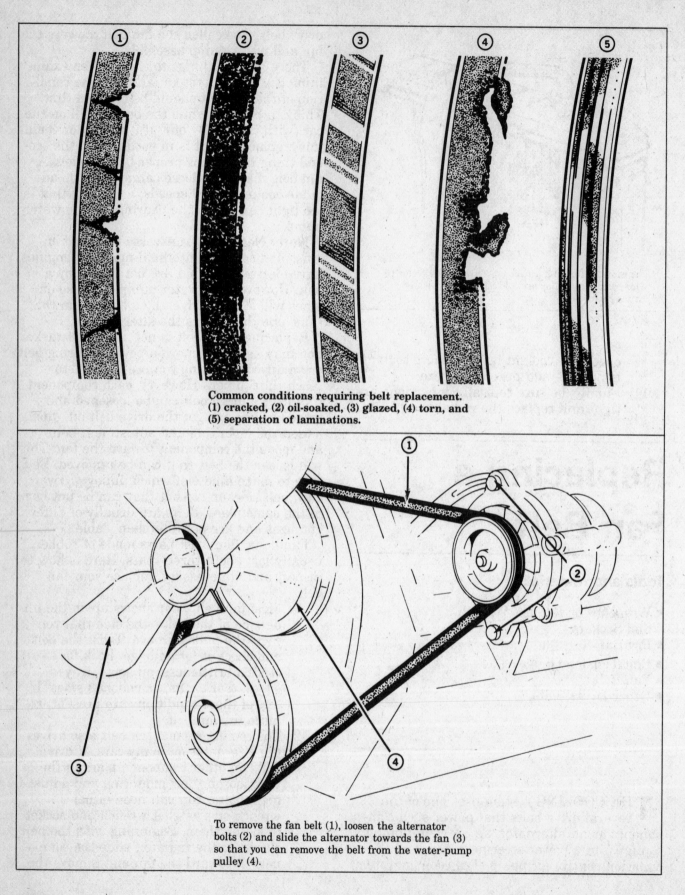

Common conditions requiring belt replacement.
(1) cracked, (2) oil-soaked, (3) glazed, (4) torn, and
(5) separation of laminations.

To remove the fan belt (1), loosen the alternator
bolts (2) and slide the alternator towards the fan (3)
so that you can remove the belt from the water-pump
pulley (4).

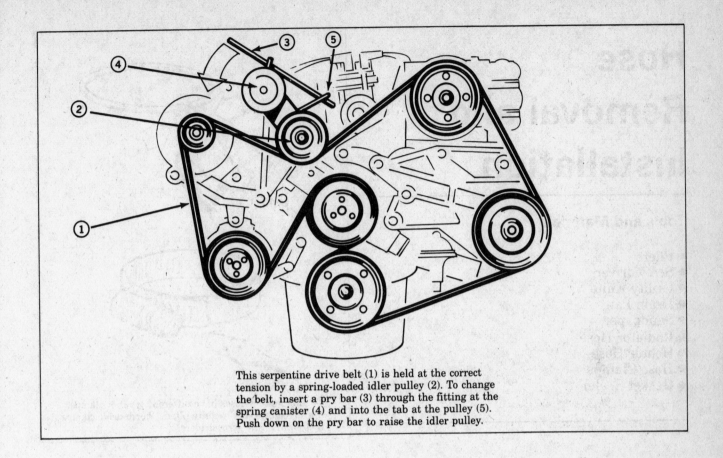

This serpentine drive belt (1) is held at the correct tension by a spring-loaded idler pulley (2). To change the belt, insert a pry bar (3) through the fitting at the spring canister (4) and into the tab at the pulley (5). Push down on the pry bar to raise the idler pulley.

belt(s). Inspect these belts for the same conditions as in Step 1. Replace any as required.

3. Loosen the alternator mounting bolt (bottom of alternator) and adjustment bolt (top of alternator). Push the alternator toward the fan and remove the fan belt. **Note:** Do not cut any belt to remove it unless you already have the replacement belt in hand. Be sure to purchase new belts of the correct size. **Note:** On engines equipped with a single serpentine belt to drive all accessories, the belt can be removed by prying against the belt tensioner pulley to relieve tension. Using a large screwdriver or pry bar to push the tensioner back, the belt can be slipped off and a new one installed. No further adjustments should be necessary, as the tensioner will automatically set the correct belt tension.

4. To reinstall the fan and drive belts, start with the belt closest to the engine and work toward the radiator. **Note:** Do not try to stretch a new belt over the pulleys with a screwdriver; this will weaken it.

5. Once all the belts are in place, use a pry bar to tighten them. Be careful that you do not damage any part that you pry against. While holding a belt taut, tighten the mounting bolt and the adjustment bolt. Adjust belt tension so that there is not more than ¾ inch of deflection when you press down with your finger. You can buy a belt tension gauge for a more accurate reading.

6. Check to be sure that all belts are installed on their proper pulleys. Start the engine and check them again. A third belt tension check should be made in about three or four weeks because new fan belts tend to stretch after installation. Periodic checking of the fan belt is a good idea. This can help prevent a breakdown, which usually occurs at the most inconvenient times. Carrying a set of spare belts, a pry bar, and suitable wrenches is also a good idea.

Hose Removal and Installation

Tools and Materials

- Pliers
- Screwdriver
- Utility Knife
- Drain Pan
- Sandpaper
- Radiator Hose
- Heater Hose
- Hose Clamps
- Gasket Sealer

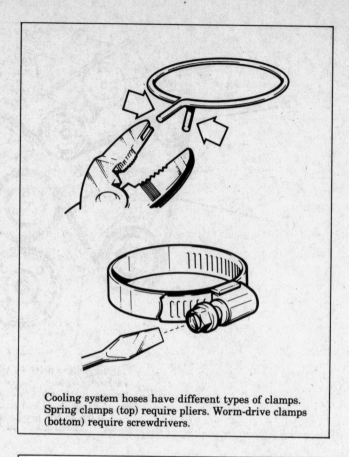

Cooling system hoses have different types of clamps. Spring clamps (top) require pliers. Worm-drive clamps (bottom) require screwdrivers.

RADIATOR AND HEATER hoses generally have a life expectancy of about three years. Most experienced mechanics recommend that you replace all hoses when one of them needs replacement. It saves a lot of labor later on and reduces the possibility of hose failure.

There are up to five hoses in a cooling system. There is an upper and a lower radiator hose, an inlet and an outlet heater hose, and a bypass hose for the water pump. The job of replacing hoses is not as bad as it appears when you first raise the hood. *Caution: This is a job that should be done when the engine is cool.* To replace the hoses, follow these steps.

1. Drain the cooling system. If you have recently added antifreeze, you will want to save the coolant by draining it into a clean pan. To drain the cooling system, remove the radiator pressure cap. Using pliers, loosen the radiator drain petcock located near the bottom of the radiator. **Note:** On some older models, there is no radiator drain petcock. To drain a car without a radiator drain

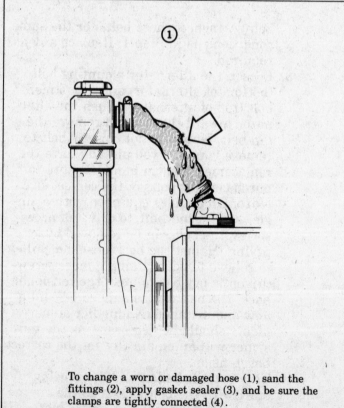

To change a worn or damaged hose (1), sand the fittings (2), apply gasket sealer (3), and be sure the clamps are tightly connected (4).

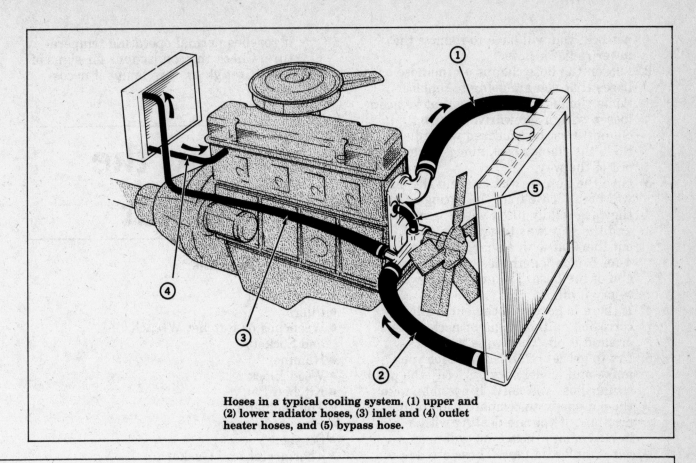

Hoses in a typical cooling system. (1) upper and
(2) lower radiator hoses, (3) inlet and (4) outlet
heater hoses, and (5) bypass hose.

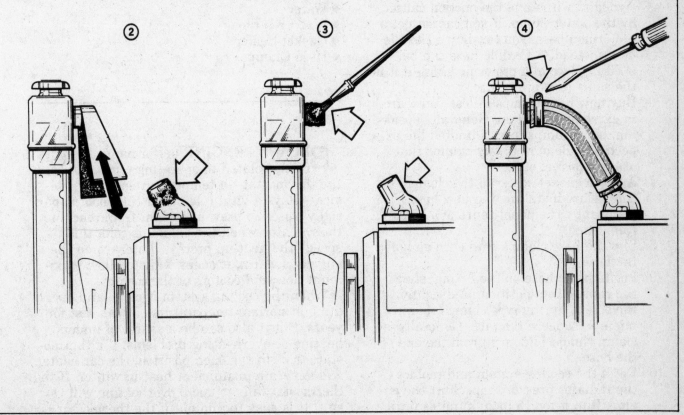

petcock, you will have to remove the lower radiator hose.

2. Loosen the hose clamps on the hose or hoses that you are going to replace. Some clamps have a screw that you can loosen with a screwdriver. Spring clamps must be squeezed with pliers. Slide the clamps back along the hose out of the way.

3. Give the hose a twist to see if the ends will break loose from the fittings. Often, they are solidly fused with the metal and the only way to get them off is to cut them off with a sharp knife; cut a 4- or 5-inch lengthwise slit from the end of the hose. Then use a screwdriver to pry it off.

4. If there is hardened cement, sealer, or corrosion on the fitting or neck, scrape or sand it off. Then wipe it clean.

5. Try to get a preformed hose for your make and model of car. Specify the particular hose you need. If possible, take the old one in to compare it with the new one. If you are dealing with a lower radiator hose, you will need a wire-reinforced type. These are designed to withstand the suction caused by the water pump. If you cannot get a preformed hose, you can buy a flexible hose instead. A flexible hose can be used in place of a preformed hose if it is the same length and size.

6. Buy new hose clamps unless yours are in excellent condition. Generally speaking, hose clamps have a limited life expectancy. Be sure to buy clamps that are the correct size.

7. Apply a gasket sealer to the cleaned fitting before installing the new hose if you want to be doubly sure of a good connection.

8. Slip the hose clamps onto each end of the hose.

9. Position the hose on the fitting, slide the clamps into position, and tighten the screw. Spring-type clamps require pliers to squeeze the tabs. Generally, a clamp should be 1 inch from the end of the hose.

10. Refill the cooling system and replace the radiator pressure cap. Start the engine. Run it for 15 to 20 minutes until it reaches normal operating temperature. Check the connections for signs of leaks. Retighten the clamps if necessary.

Servicing the Thermostat

Tools and Materials

- Screwdriver
- Pliers
- Wrenches or Ratchet Wrench and Sockets
- Hammer
- Wood Block
- Kitchen Pan
- Thermometer
- Piece of Wire
- Scraper
- Thermostat and Gasket
- Water
- Lint-Free Rags
- Gasket Sealer
- Hose Clamps

BECAUSE ENGINE performance is so directly related to operating temperature, the thermostat—a temperature-sensitive device—plays a vital role under the hood. It partially closes to prevent coolant from reaching the radiator when the engine is cold; this speeds the heat-up process. Later, when the engine is warm, it opens wide to allow maximum flow and cooling of the coolant.

When the cooling system is clean and operating at normal temperatures, it can last for years. But it also can be a source of underheating or overheating problems. If a thermostat sticks in the open position, the car heater will generate insufficient heat in winter. If the thermostat fails to open, overheating will result. It is easy to find out if the thermostat is

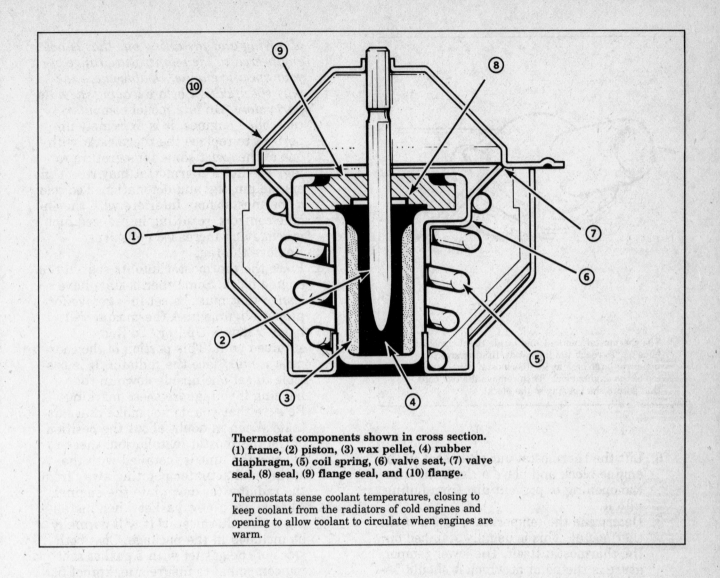

Thermostat components shown in cross section. (1) frame, (2) piston, (3) wax pellet, (4) rubber diaphragm, (5) coil spring, (6) valve seat, (7) valve seal, (8) seal, (9) flange seal, and (10) flange.

Thermostats sense coolant temperatures, closing to keep coolant from the radiators of cold engines and opening to allow coolant to circulate when engines are warm.

creating your cooling system troubles. Here is how to go about it.

1. Drain the cooling system radiator. See the section in this chapter on "Cooling System Flushing" for instructions.
2. Find the thermostat housing, which contains the thermostat. It is generally located on the engine block at the top front of the engine. It is connected to the upper radiator hose. On front-wheel-drive cars with transverse-mounted engines, the thermostat housing may be located on the front side or end of the engine. On some vehicles, you'll find it in a special housing attached to the upper radiator hose. Refer to a shop manual if you're not sure of the thermostat's location.
3. Remove the upper radiator hose clamp at the thermostat housing. Use a screwdriver to loosen the screw on the clamp. If you have a spring-type clamp, use pliers to remove it. Slide the clamp along the hose out of the way. Remove the end of the hose from the fitting.
4. Remove the two bolts that secure the thermostat housing to the engine block. If you cannot fit a wrench over these bolts, use a ratchet wrench and the proper-size socket.
5. Lift off the thermostat housing. This may require some gentle tapping if the gasket has hardened. If so, put a block of wood against the housing and tap gently with a hammer until it comes loose.

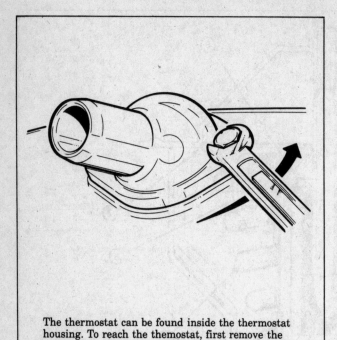

The thermostat can be found inside the thermostat housing. To reach the themostat, first remove the upper radiator hose at the thermostat housing on the top of the engine block. Then remove the two bolts that secure the housing to the block.

6. Lift the thermostat out of its seat in the engine block and place a clean rag into the opening to prevent dirt from falling into it.

7. Determine the temperature range of the thermostat. This is usually stamped on the thermostat itself. The lower temperature is the point at which it should begin to open. The higher temperature marks the full-open position.

8. Place a pan of water on a stove or hot plate and insert a kitchen thermometer. Heat the water to 10° or 15°F *below* the thermostat's low temperature setting.

9. Suspend the thermostat in the water with a piece of wire and continue heating. If the thermostat opens early, it should be replaced.

10. Continue heating the water to about 20°F *above* the low temperature setting for the thermostat. It should open fully. If it does not, it should be replaced.

11. Before installing a new thermostat, scrape the old gasket material and sealer off the mounting surface on the engine block. *Caution: Most thermostats look alike, so there is a possibility*

of buying and installing one that is not engineered to the temperature range of your specific engine. Double-check the part specification before leaving the auto parts store. On late model computer-controlled engines, it is extremely important to replace the thermostat with one of the exact same temperature rating. Too hot a thermostat may result in engine pinging and detonation. Too cold a thermostat may interfere with the engine controls, resulting in reduced fuel mileage and increased emissions.

12. Remove the rag.

13. Place the thermostat into its seat in the engine block. Some thermostats have a flange that must be set in a groove for proper alignment. A thermostat will have "Front," "Up," or "To Rad" stamped on it. This portion of the thermostat *must* face the radiator. It is possible to get one upside down in the housing if you ignore these markings. Be sure that you do not make that mistake. When in doubt about the position of the thermostat installation, check to be sure the unit is installed with the spring and actuator pointing away from the radiator (or down into the engine).

14. Always use a new gasket when installing a new thermostat. It will normally be included in the package. Coat both sides of the gasket with a gasket sealing compound to insure a leakproof fit. Then carefully place the gasket over the thermostat and the mounting surface of the engine block.

15. Place the thermostat housing over the thermostat and gasket. Install the two housing bolts and tighten. *Caution: Do not overtighten. The thermostat housing can be easily cracked or broken by overtightening.*

16. Unless your hose clamps are in excellent condition, use new ones. Slide the hose clamp onto the hose and place the upper radiator hose over the thermostat housing. Slide the clamp along the hose until it is about 1 inch from the end of the hose. If you have a spring-type clamp, you will need pliers to do this; on screw-type clamps, tighten the screw securely.

17. Once you are satisfied that all hose connections are secure, it is time to refill the cooling system. Be sure the petcock drain on the bottom of the radiator is shut tight, or the lower radiator hose is secure. Fill the system with a 50/50 mixture of water and antifreeze. (Refer to the section in this chapter on "Cooling System Flushing" for instructions.)

18. Reinstall the radiator pressure cap. Start the engine and run it for 15 or 20 minutes to allow the engine to reach normal operating temperature. With the engine still running, carefully check for leaks where the upper radiator hose and thermostat housing are joined. Also check around the thermostat housing and engine block connection. If there are no leaks, your job is done. If a leak is present, try tightening the hose clamp some more. If the leak is at the housing-to-block connection, use a wrench of the proper size and carefully turn each bolt in quarter-of-a-turn increments. If after a couple of turns on each bolt the leak does not stop, you will have to remove the housing and start over.

19. If there are no leaks, shut off the engine and let it cool. Remove the radiator pressure cap. *Caution: Some pressure will remain in the cooling system. Be careful. Slowly turn the radiator pressure cap to the first notch to relieve this pressure. Place rags around the radiator pressure cap to prevent coolant from splashing out and possibly burning you.*

20. Recheck the cooling system level. Any air pockets that were in the cooling system before it was put under pressure will now have been filled. The system should be filled to within 1 inch below the radiator filler neck. Add coolant as necessary.

21. Replace the radiator pressure cap.

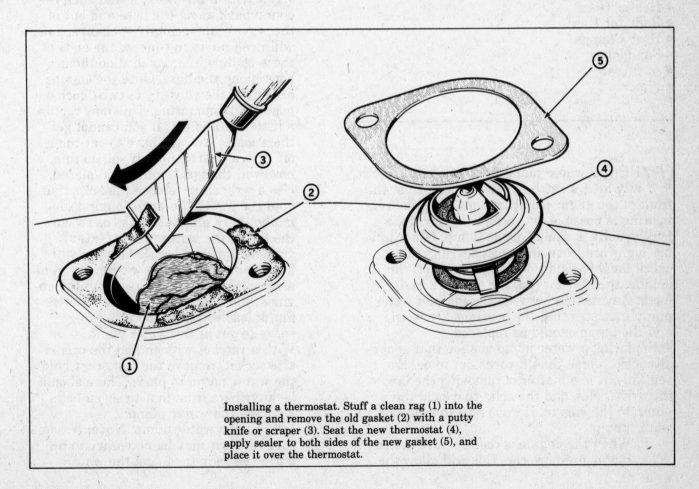

Installing a thermostat. Stuff a clean rag (1) into the opening and remove the old gasket (2) with a putty knife or scraper (3). Seat the new thermostat (4), apply sealer to both sides of the new gasket (5), and place it over the thermostat.

Water-Pump Replacement

Tools and Materials

- Pliers
- Wrenches
- Screwdriver
- Utility Knife
- Ratchet Wrench and Sockets
- Scraper
- Pry Bar
- Cooling System Pressure Tester
- Antifreeze Tester
- Drain Pan
- Lint-Free Rag
- Gasket Sealer
- Water Pump and Gasket
- Heater Hose
- Radiator Hose
- Hose Clamps
- Sandpaper
- Antifreeze
- Water

WHEN A water pump fails, you will usually hear a rattling noise coming from the front of the engine compartment. Engine overheating is possible, but before this occurs, a leak usually is visible at the pump. Other failure signs are loose and worn bearings. To check for this condition, simply turn off the engine, then try moving the fan back and forth. Any motion between the fan and water pump indicates that the bearings are worn and the pump should be replaced.

Replacing a water pump is a job that generally looks worse than it turns out to be. Essentially, it is a matter of removing the fan, the drive belts, and the bolts that hold the pump to the engine. Here is how to replace a water pump.

1. When the engine is cool, remove the radiator pressure cap; this will allow the coolant to drain easier. Use pliers to loosen the petcock—located near the bottom of the radiator. If you want to reuse this coolant, drain it into a clean pan. Once the coolant has completely drained out of the radiator, tighten the petcock. **Note:** Some older models do not have a radiator drain petcock. To drain this type of radiator, you will have to remove the lower radiator hose as described in Step 3.
2. Next, you will have to remove all drive belts; you will need a wrench for this job. A complete discussion on this subject is covered in the "Replacing a Fan Belt" section elsewhere in this chapter.
3. Remove all hoses connected to the water pump. There may be up to three hoses: lower radiator hose, heater hose, and bypass hose. It is a good idea to mark each hose, so you will know where to put them back on. On hoses with screw-type clamps, loosen the screw with a screwdriver and slide the clamp back along the hose and out of the way. With spring-type clamps, you will need pliers to squeeze the ends of these clamps in order to slide them back along the hose. Once the clamps are out of the way, try to twist each hose off its mounting. This may require a little extra effort. If you cannot get them loose, you will have to cut them off with a sharp knife. If you do this, however, the hoses must be replaced.
4. Use a wrench to remove the bolts that hold the fan to the water pump. Normally, there are four bolts that secure the fan to the water pump. **Note:** If your car has an electric fan, you will have to disconnect the wiring. On front-drive cars with transverse-mounted engines, you will not have to remove the fan unless you need more working space to get at the water pump.
5. With a ratchet wrench and the proper-size socket, remove the bolts that hold the water pump in place. There should be anywhere from four to seven bolts securing the water pump.
6. Lift out the water pump. **Note:** In some rare cases, it may be necessary to remove the radiator to get the water

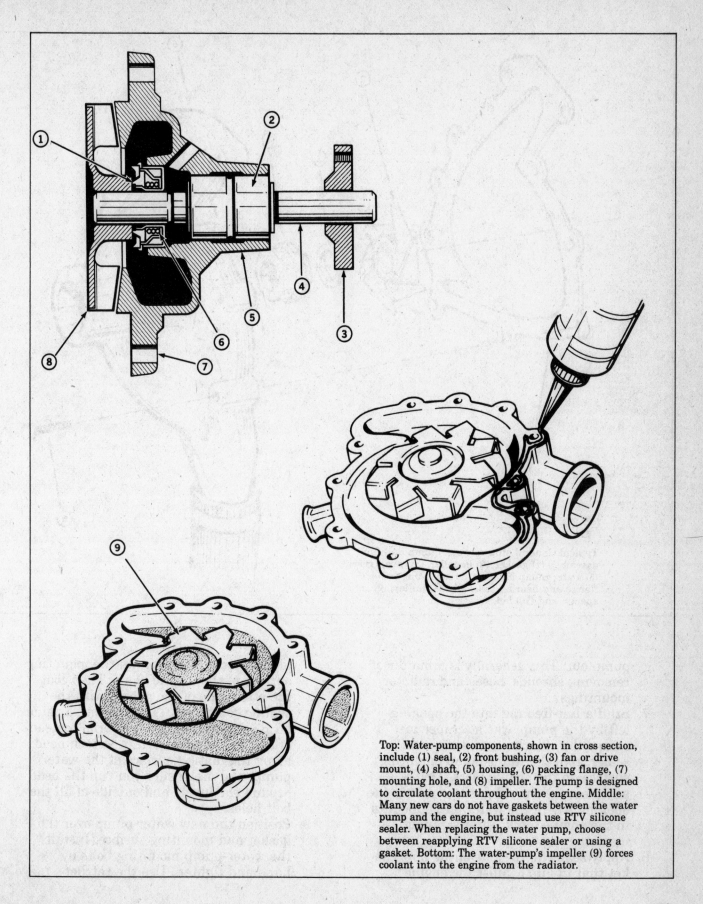

Top: Water-pump components, shown in cross section, include (1) seal, (2) front bushing, (3) fan or drive mount, (4) shaft, (5) housing, (6) packing flange, (7) mounting hole, and (8) impeller. The pump is designed to circulate coolant throughout the engine. Middle: Many new cars do not have gaskets between the water pump and the engine, but instead use RTV silicone sealer. When replacing the water pump, choose between reapplying RTV silicone sealer or using a gasket. Bottom: The water-pump's impeller (9) forces coolant into the engine from the radiator.

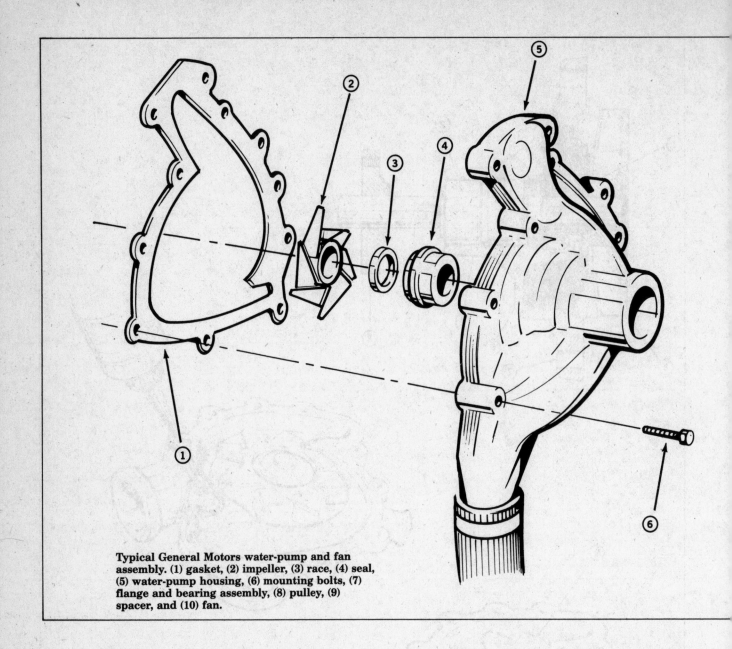

Typical General Motors water-pump and fan assembly. (1) gasket, (2) impeller, (3) race, (4) seal, (5) water-pump housing, (6) mounting bolts, (7) flange and bearing assembly, (8) pulley, (9) spacer, and (10) fan.

pump out. This generally is a matter of removing shrouds, hoses, and radiator mountings.

7. Stuff a lint-free rag into the opening left by the pump. Use a scraper to scrape the old gasket material and sealer from the water-pump mounting surface on the engine block. Do not let any pieces of the old gasket fall into the opening where the water pump mounts to the engine block. After scraping, remove the rag.

8. Apply sealer to the side of the new gasket that fits up against the engine

block. Place the gasket on the mounting surface of the engine block. Then coat the other side of the gasket with the sealing compound. **Note:** If you're using an RTV silicone sealer material instead of a gasket, apply about a 1/8-inch bead along the mating surface of the water pump, and make sure you run the bead around the inside and outside of all the bolt holes.

9. Position the new water pump over the gasket and mounting surface. Install the water-pump mounting bolts by hand and tighten. Use the ratchet

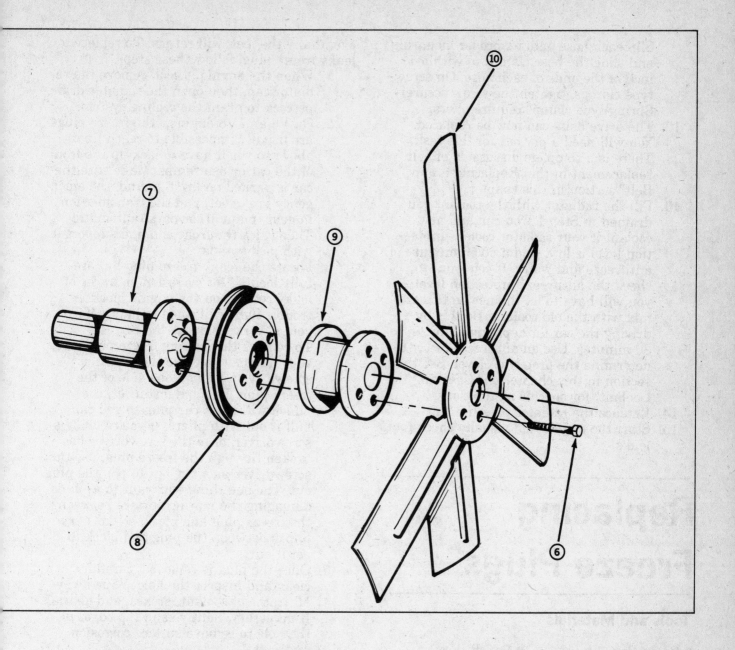

wrench and the proper-size socket to
tighten the bolts securely. *Caution:
Water pumps are very similar in appearance, so be sure you get the right replacement pump for your car. Take the
old one with you to the auto supply store
if you can.* **Note:** You can save yourself
about half the price of a new pump by
installing a rebuilt unit. Generally,
these will work as well as a new one.
Check with an auto supply store for information on rebuilt or remanufactured
parts.

10. Place the fan or pully over the end of
the new water pump and install the
mounting bolts. Tighten them securely
with a wrench.

11. Replace all hoses. If you had to cut any
to remove them, you will have to install
new ones. See the section on "Hose Removal and Installation" in this chapter.
Always use new hose clamps unless the
old ones are still in excellent condition.
Scrape or sand any sealing compound
off the hose mounting surfaces. Place a
new clamp over each hose. If the old
ones are being reused, be sure they are
on the hoses before you reinstall them.

Slip each hose onto its proper mounting and slide the hose clamps to within 1 inch of the ends of each hose. On screw-type clamps, tighten the screw securely. Spring-type clamps require pliers.

12. The drive belts can now be replaced. You will need a pry bar for this task. There is a complete discussion of belt replacement in the "Replacing a Fan Belt" section in this chapter.

13. Fill the radiator with the coolant you drained in Step 1. You can add new coolant if your radiator coolant protection level is low. Add a 50/50 mixture of antifreeze and water. If you want to check the antifreeze protection level, you will have to let the new antifreeze mix with the old coolant. Do this by driving the car for approximately 20 to 30 minutes. Use an antifreeze tester to determine the protection level. See the section in this chapter on "Checking the Coolant" for specific instructions.

14. Replace the radiator pressure cap.

15. Start the engine and visually check for leaks.

Replacing Freeze Plugs

Tools and Materials

- Drain Pan
- Pliers
- Hammer
- Trouble Light
- Sandpaper
- Punch
- Screwdriver
- Gasket Sealer
- Antifreeze
- Water

WHEN YOU'RE FACED with a leaky freeze plug, the only permanent cure is to replace the plug with a new one. Stop-leak additives may provide temporary relief, but eventually the leak will return. To replace a leaky freeze plug, follow these steps.

1. When the engine is cool, remove the radiator cap, then open the radiator drain petcock to drain the cooling system.

2. On V6 and V8 engines, the freeze plugs are usually impossible to reach from above so you'll have to jack up the front of the car or use ramps. Make sure the car is parked on level ground, the emergency brake set, and the transmission in gear (manual) or park (automatic). Then raise the front end and support it with jack stands.

3. Locate the leaky freeze plug by carefully looking for corrosion or traces of leaky coolant on the engine block. A trouble light will come in handy if you're working under the car.

4. To remove the leaking freeze plug, use your hammer to drive the punch or screwdriver through one side of the freeze plug. In some instances, the punch will twist the plug so you can pull it out with pliers. If you're using a screwdriver, once the screwdriver has broken through the freeze plug, use the screwdriver as a pry bar to pop the plug out. The one thing you want to avoid is damaging the mating surface between the freeze plug and block, so don't try to pry between the plug and block to get it out.

5. Once the plug is removed, carefully clean and inspect the hole. Wipe away all traces of coolant, grease, and debris. If necessary, lightly sand the edges of the hole to remove surface corrosion and rust.

6. There are several types of replacement freeze plugs. If you're installing an original equipment type metal plug, apply sealer to the edges of the plug and carefully drive it into place, trying to keep it from twisting or becoming cocked in the plug hole. For replacement plugs that use an expanded rubber grommet, use no sealer. Just position the plug in the hole and tighten the plug bolt until the plug is held firmly in place.

7. Refill the cooling system with a 50/50 mixture of antifreeze and water. Start the engine and allow it to run until the

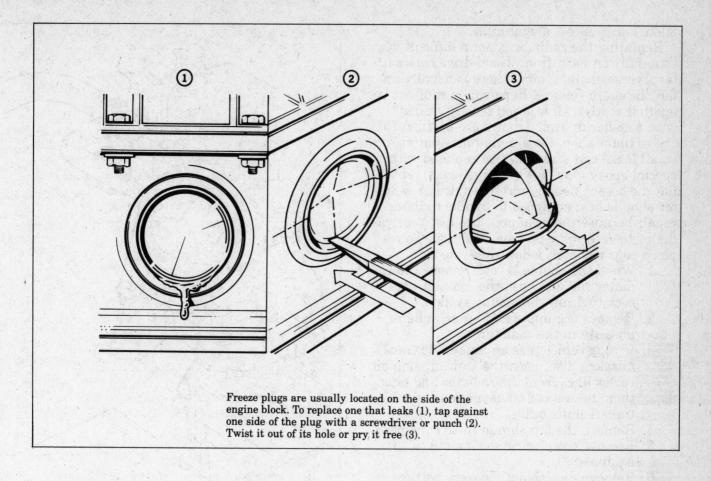

Freeze plugs are usually located on the side of the engine block. To replace one that leaks (1), tap against one side of the plug with a screwdriver or punch (2). Twist it out of its hole or pry it free (3).

engine warms up. Add coolant as needed to top off the system.

8. Replace the radiator cap and let the engine run for several minutes to build up pressure inside the cooling system. Then shut the engine off and check for leaks.

Replacing the Radiator

WHEN YOUR COOLING system inspection reveals a leaky, damaged, or deteriorated radiator, it's time to remove the radiator for repair or replacement. Minor damage and leaks can usually be repaired at minimal cost, but a badly damaged or deteriorated radiator

Tools and Materials
- Drain Pan
- Pliers
- Wrenches
- Screwdriver
- Antifreeze
- Water

will require "recoring" or replacement. Recoring is where the radiator shop removes the end tanks from your old radiator and installs them on a brand new core. This is usually less costly than buying a new radiator because you're only paying for a new center section and the labor to put the radiator together. In some instances, though, the end tanks can't be salvaged, so your only option is to replace the radiator. New radiators are available through radiator shops, car dealers, and most auto parts stores. Used radiators are also available at reasonable prices at salvage yards, but buying a used radiator can be risky since you don't know what its condition is inside. If you do opt for a used radiator, make sure you get a guarantee.

Replacing the radiator is not a difficult job, especially on most front-wheel-drive cars with transverse engines, since there is usually no fan shroud to remove. Repairing a radiator is another matter. Unless you're very skilled with a soldering iron, repairs are best left to the radiator shop. On aluminum radiators, small leaks can sometimes be repaired with special epoxy glue, but for large leaks, replacing the core is usually recommended. A radiator shop is best equipped to handle radiator repair because they can pressure-test your radiator to determine its true condition. To replace your radiator, follow these steps.

1. When the engine is cool, remove the radiator cap and open the radiator petcock to drain the cooling system.
2. Remove the upper and lower radiator hoses from the radiator.
3. If your vehicle has an automatic transmission, disconnect the transmission oil cooler lines from the radiator and plug them to prevent transmission fluid from leaking out.
4. Remove the fan shroud (if so equipped).
5. Remove the electric cooling fan (if so equipped).
6. Remove the coolant recovery bottle from the radiator, or disconnect the hose that runs from the radiator cap to the recovery bottle.
7. Remove the bolts that hold the upper radiator brackets and remove the brackets. Most radiators can now be lifted up and out of the engine compartment. On others, bolts along the side of the radiator must be removed or lower brackets unbolted. *Caution: Be careful not to damage the radiator if you think it can be repaired.*
8. To reinstall the repaired radiator (or new radiator), repeat the above steps in reverse order. Refill the cooling system with a fresh mixture of antifreeze and water, then run the engine and check for leaks. If the radiator is equipped with a fan shroud, don't forget to put it back on. Leaving the shroud off will reduce the efficiency of the cooling fan and may result in overheating. **Note:** If the radiator is being replaced because of age deterioration, now would be an

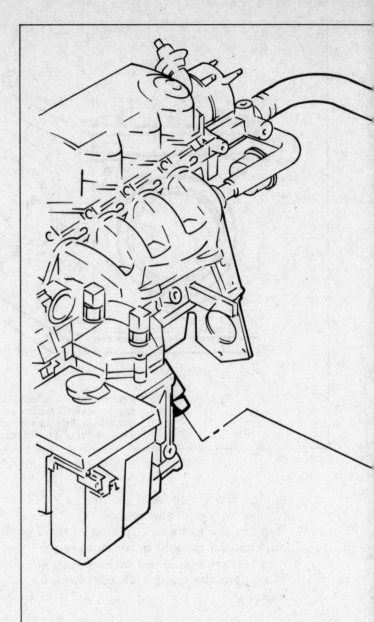

To remove a radiator from a front-wheel-drive car that has a transversely mounted engine, disconnect the radiator hoses from the radiator. Then remove the fan and fan shroud. Remove the coolant recovery bottle connections and other various clips, caps, and bolts that hold the radiator to the support frame. It should be ready to lift out of the car.

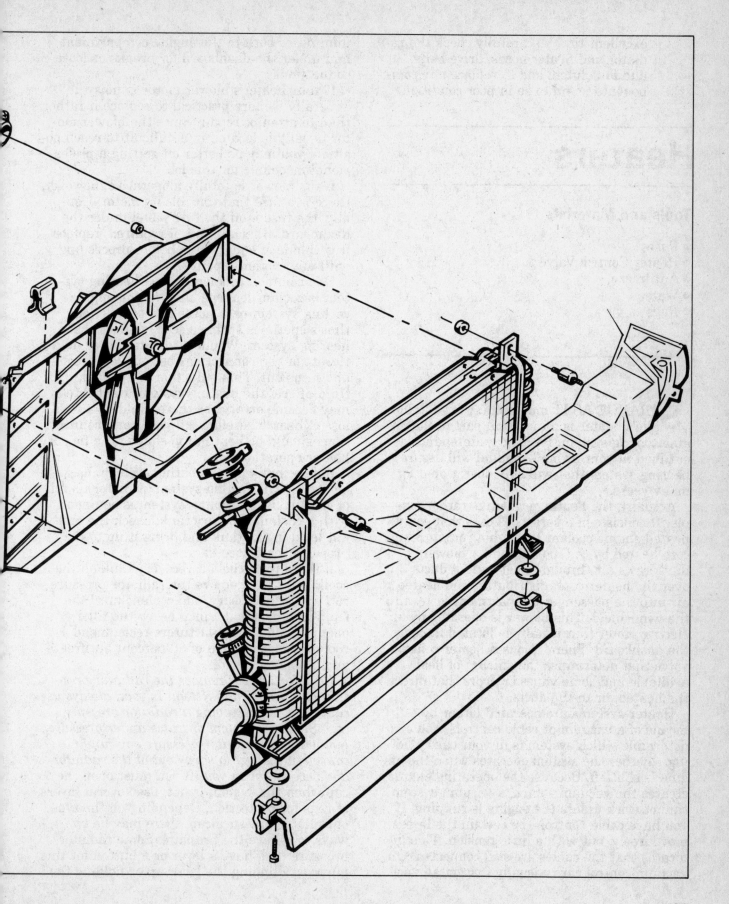

excellent time to carefully check the radiator and heater hoses, drive belts, and fan clutch, and to replace any components found to be in poor condition.

Heaters

Tools and Materials

- Fuses
- Heater Control Valve
- Antifreeze
- Water
- Rags

STRANGE AS IT may seem, your automobile's heater is an integral part of the engine cooling system. Periodic maintenance as outlined in your owner's manual will assure a heating system that will stay operational for many years.

Actually, the heating system is rather simple. It consists of a series of hoses that carry heated engine coolant through a radiatorlike core heated by the coolant, and a blower that draws air through a network of ducts over the heater core, distributing the heated air into the passenger compartment or toward the windshield. This blower is operated by an electric motor that usually is located under the dashboard. There also is a heater control valve that determines the amount of heat available and some vanes or doors that direct the heated air in the ducts.

Heater systems are operated either by means of a vacuum or cable controls. You can determine which system is in your car by noting whether the system operates when the engine is shut off. Because the operating engine creates the vacuum source, a vacuum system cannot work unless the engine is running. If you have cable controls, be certain the levers move freely, but with a little tension. This indicates that the cables are still connected. On vacuum-control cars, visually inspect all vacuum hoses both in the engine compartment and under the dashboard for breaks or loose connections.

If your heater's blower motor is noisy, it generally is more practical to replace it rather than to attempt repair. Since the blower motor usually is located in a difficult-to-reach position, you may be better off getting a professional mechanic for this job.

If the blower is totally inoperative, however, there is a fuse that controls its motor. Usually, the fuse is in the fuse panel under the dashboard. Check it and, if required, replace it with one of equal value before proceeding with any system repairs.

One common problem with a heating system is coolant leakage. Just as the engine cooling system uses hoses and connections that sometimes spring a leak, so does the heating system. Whenever heater hoses deteriorate or the connections become loose, coolant seeps out. This reduction of available fluid affects the heating system. Heat levels may become erratic, or there could be a total loss of heat. Therefore, all hoses and connections should be kept in top shape for efficient heater operation.

Before making any heating system checks, be certain the cooling system (radiator) is full of coolant. If the cooling system is equipped with a coolant recovery tank, check the coolant level in the tank and bring it up to the proper level if necessary.

If there is no coolant recovery tank on the cooling system, remove the radiator pressure cap and, if necessary, add coolant until the fluid level is about 1 inch below the filler opening. Most manufacturers recommend a coolant concentration of 50 percent antifreeze and 50 percent water.

Caution: Never remove the radiator pressure cap from a hot system. In fact, always use caution when removing a radiator pressure cap. Since the system operates under pressure, removing the radiator pressure cap might cause hot coolant to spray out of the radiator and severely burn you. If you must open the cap when the system is hot, use several layers of rags for protection. Depending on the type of radiator pressure cap, there may be two ways to relieve the pressure. Some radiator pressure caps have a lever or a button for this purpose. Flipping the lever up or holding the

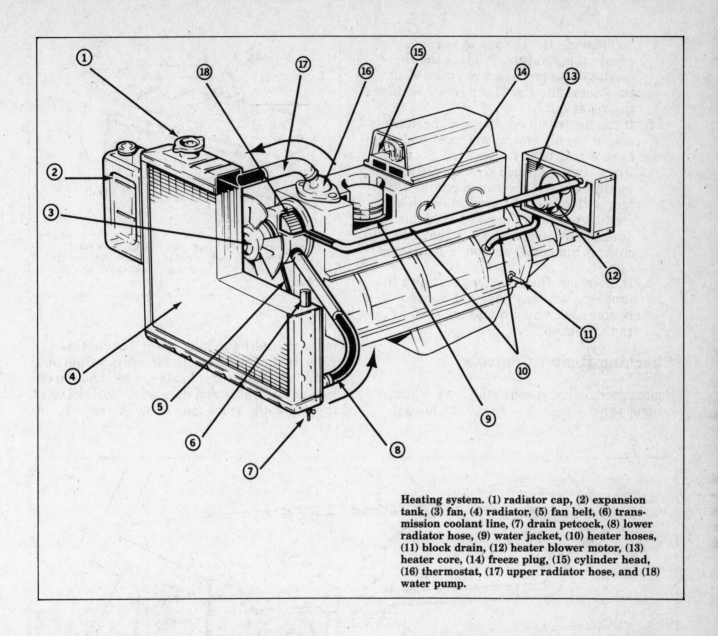

Heating system. (1) radiator cap, (2) expansion tank, (3) fan, (4) radiator, (5) fan belt, (6) transmission coolant line, (7) drain petcock, (8) lower radiator hose, (9) water jacket, (10) heater hoses, (11) block drain, (12) heater blower motor, (13) heater core, (14) freeze plug, (15) cylinder head, (16) thermostat, (17) upper radiator hose, and (18) water pump.

button in will release the pressure buildup. Other radiator pressure caps, meanwhile, are designed to be turned counterclockwise to a notch. Once the pressure has been relieved, you push the cap down and turn it counterclockwise for removal.

Checking for Low Heat or No Heat

You should be certain the engine is at normal operating temperature before heating system checks are made. Allow the engine to run for about 20 minutes. Then, to check for low heat or no heat at all, follow these steps.

1. Determine whether coolant is flowing through the heater core. First, turn the heater to on and the temperature to hot. Feel the two heater hoses. These are long hoses coming from the engine that connect to the heater core on the engine side of the firewall. Generally, heater hoses are about 1 inch in diameter. With the heater system operating, both heater hoses should be hot to the touch.

2. If the heater hoses are only warm (and there is coolant in the radiator and the engine is at operating temperature), you may have a malfunctioning thermostat in your cooling system. It may not

be allowing the coolant to reach the proper temperature. Replace the thermostat. This procedure is outlined in the "Servicing the Thermostat" section in this chapter.

3. If one heater hose is hot and the other is not, or is only warm, you most probably have a restricted heater core. Sometimes, this condition may be corrected by flushing out the entire cooling system with one of the products designed for this purpose. They are available at auto supply stores. Refer to the "Cooling System Flushing" section in this chapter.

4. If, however, flushing does not solve the problem, you may have to have the heater core removed and repaired by a radiator shop.

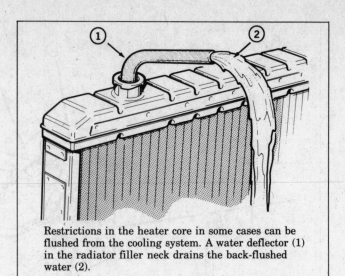

Restrictions in the heater core in some cases can be flushed from the cooling system. A water deflector (1) in the radiator filler neck drains the back-flushed water (2).

Checking Heater Controls

Some automobiles, meanwhile, have a heater control valve attached to one of the heater hoses (usually the inlet hose). Locate this valve by following each of the hoses from one end to the other. If a heater hose is hot on one side of this valve and only warm (or cool) on the other, the valve may be defective or be in-

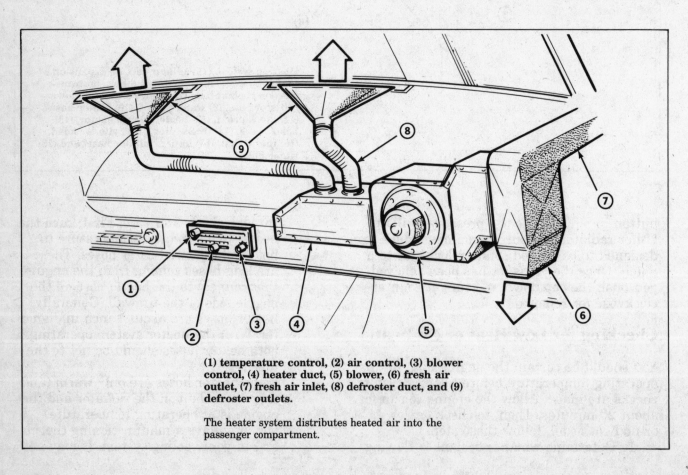

(1) temperature control, (2) air control, (3) blower control, (4) heater duct, (5) blower, (6) fresh air outlet, (7) fresh air inlet, (8) defroster duct, and (9) defroster outlets.

The heater system distributes heated air into the passenger compartment.

operative due to faulty cable or vacuum operation. Here are some steps to determine the nature of the problem.

1. If your heater is cable-operated, have someone in the car move the temperature control from low to high as you closely watch the control valve. If the cable connected to it does not move, it is either broken or it has come loose at the lever end.
2. Inspect the cable connection at both ends. If they are secure, the cable is broken and must be replaced by a mechanic. Otherwise, resecure the cable.
3. If the car's system is vacuum-operated, have someone move the temperature control from low to high with the engine running. Observe the control valve.
4. If it does not operate, check for vacuum leaks and repair them. Otherwise, replace the heater control valve. To replace it, drain the radiator, remove the hoses connected to the heater control valve, and unscrew the valve from its mounting. Reverse this procedure to install the new valve, which is available from an auto parts store.

Checking Blend Doors

If both heater hoses are hot, then you know the coolant is flowing through the system. However, if there still is no heat, one of the "blend doors" may not be working properly. A blend door is like a "flapper" valve, or vane, that directs the air passing through the heat duct. If this does not open or close properly, heat may not be directed into the passenger area (or you may not be able to shut off the heat). Check this in the following way.

1. Follow the heater duct, usually under the dashboard, and locate the blend door or doors.
2. Make certain they swing freely on their hinges.
3. If the system is cable-operated, make sure the cable is securely connected to the door.
4. If the blend doors are vacuum-operated, check for leaks and repair them, replacing any defective vacuum hoses.

Sometimes, a heating system will produce heat all the time, regardless of where the control levers are positioned. In such a case, check the heater control valve for operation as outlined previously. If the valve is stuck in the open position and the controls to the valve are operating, have the valve replaced. Also check the blend doors. If they are not closing fully, heat will be delivered into the passenger compartment at all times. Once again, check the controls, especially the blend doors, for warpage or sticking hinges. If you cannot get the doors to close properly, you should have a professional mechanic check them.

Air Conditioning

Tools and Materials

- Safety Goggles
- Work Gloves
- Belt Tension Gauge
- Box-End Wrench
- Pry Bar
- Air Conditioner Drive Belt
- Fuses
- Rag

PERFORMING any service or repair on an automotive air conditioning system requires a high level of knowledge and experience, and special tools. It can also be a dangerous undertaking if you don't know what you're doing. Because of this, most do-it-yourself mechanics leave air conditioning work to the professionals. There are, however, some items you can check yourself including the drive belt, compressor clutch, and system charge. You can also add refrigerant to the system to recharge your air conditioner.

Shown here is the layout of a typical air conditioning system to show you how complex

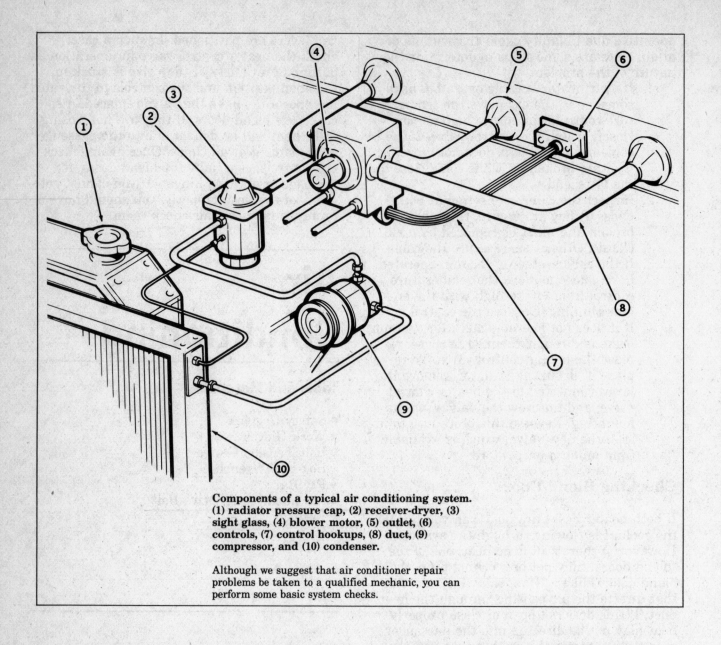

**Components of a typical air conditioning system.
(1) radiator pressure cap, (2) receiver-dryer, (3)
sight glass, (4) blower motor, (5) outlet, (6)
controls, (7) control hookups, (8) duct, (9)
compressor, and (10) condenser.**

Although we suggest that air conditioner repair
problems be taken to a qualified mechanic, you can
perform some basic system checks.

they can be. Whether or not you want to delve
into anything more than basic checks depends
on the level of your expertise and, to some extent, courage. We offer this caution because
air conditioning systems use a refrigerant
called R-12, commonly called Freon (a regis-
tered trademark of E.I. du Pont de Nemours
& Co.). If Freon touches your skin, it could
cause severe frostbite. If it touches your eye,
it could cause blindness. And, unfortunately,
you are dealing with this refrigerant when
you are recharging your system.

If you should decide to buy a recharge kit,
available from most auto supply stores, and

if you carefully follow the manufacturer's
instructions (most accidents are caused by
failure to follow instructions), you can save
yourself some money. However, our recommendation is that you take your air conditioning troubles to a qualified mechanic. The specialty tools, gauges, and vacuum pump needed
for full-fledged air conditioning work are too
expensive for a home mechanic to use only
rarely.

But if you suspect your air conditioning system is not working as well as it should, there
are some basic checks you can perform before
bringing the car into a repair shop. Common

sense and a few minutes spent looking the car over could save you a lot of money in unnecessary repairs. *Caution: Remember, be cautious and always wear safety goggles and protective work gloves whenever working on or around air conditioning systems.*

Checking the Drive Belt

To check the air conditioner's drive belt, follow this procedure.

1. Put on your safety goggles and work gloves. Open the hood of your car and locate the air conditioner drive belt. Some people refer to this drive as the "fan belt." It looks like the fan belt but, if you look carefully, there will be a belt that is driven from the pulley at the lower front of the engine that may or may not go around the fan pulley and on to the air conditioning system compressor. Usually, the compressor is located on the side of the engine opposite the alternator. The compressor, which looks like a motor, will have a large and a small tube attached to it, and a pulley on the forward end. This is the heart of the air conditioning system, and it must be running at proper speed for the system to operate.

2. Check the air conditioner drive belt for proper belt tension. Depress the belt with your finger about halfway between the compressor pulley and the drive pulley. There should be no more than 1 inch of deflection. You also can check belt tension with a drive belt tension gauge, available from most auto supply stores.

3. If there is more than about 1 inch of deflection, use a box-end wrench and loosen the bolts that hold the compressor to its brackets.

4. With the bolts loose, move the compressor outward with a pry bar to tighten the belt.

5. Retighten the compressor bracket bolts.

6. While you are at it, check the condition of the fan belt and any other belts by looking for cracks or any signs of fraying or deterioration.

7. Change any belts that are suspect. For removal and installation, see "Replac-

ing an Alternator Drive Belt" in "The Charging System" chapter and "Replacing a Fan Belt" in this chapter.

Once the drive belts are tight and in good condition, start the engine and turn on the air conditioning system. You should hear the compressor clutch engage when the system is turned on. As mentioned, the compressor has a drive pulley at the front end. This pulley rotates while your car's engine is running. When you turn on the air conditioning system, a magnetic drive clutch is activated (a click should be heard) that causes the compressor to become operational.

Checking the Compressor Clutch

To check if the compressor clutch is operating, follow these steps.

1. Have someone sit in the car with the engine running and turn the air conditioning system on and off while you listen for the engaging and disengaging of the compressor's drive clutch.

2. If this clutch is not working, check for a blown fuse. It may be in the fuse panel under the dashboard or in one of the thin wires leading to the compressor. Your owner's manual will give you the correct fuse location. If the fuse under the dashboard is not burned out, locate the in-line fuse on a wire leading to the compressor. Usually, it is in a small black fuse-holder that is opened by rotating one end.

3. Replace any defective fuse with one of equal value. The size of the fuse is marked on the end of the fuse. If you have doubts about which fuse to use, check the owner's manual again or ask an auto parts dealer.

4. If the compressor still will not operate after the fuses have been checked or replaced, you need the services of a professional air conditioning repairman.

Checking the Sight Glass

The next air conditioning check is performed while sitting in your car. With the air conditioning system turned on, note the amount of air coming through the air vents around the dashboard or wherever they may be located.

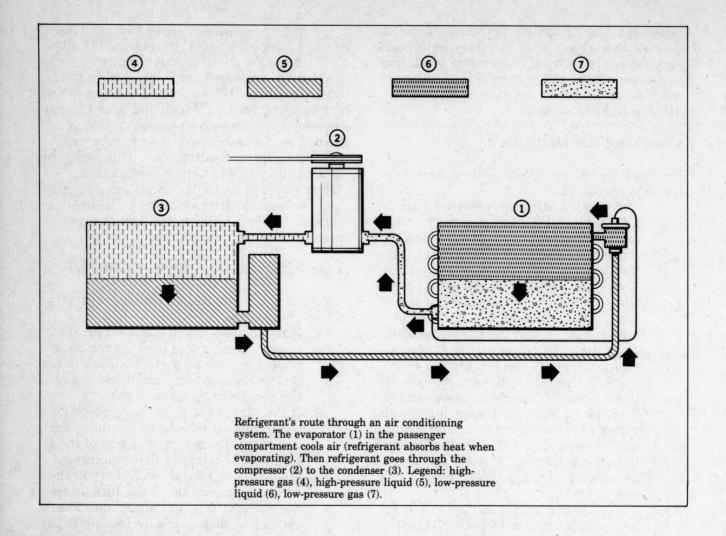

Refrigerant's route through an air conditioning system. The evaporator (1) in the passenger compartment cools air (refrigerant absorbs heat when evaporating). Then refrigerant goes through the compressor (2) to the condenser (3). Legend: high-pressure gas (4), high-pressure liquid (5), low-pressure liquid (6), low-pressure gas (7).

Move the fan switch to all speeds and feel the airflow. If the air does not flow out of the vents at different speeds, check the blower fuse. Usually this is located in the fuse panel under the dashboard. If a blown fuse is not the problem, have the blower motor checked by a qualified mechanic.

If everything you have checked so far is working and the air conditioning system is blowing out warm air, or air that is only slightly cool, the next thing to check is the sight glass. This will indicate whether the system needs to be recharged. Here is how to go about it.

1. The sight glass is located on a component called the receiver-dryer, or in one of the lines leading to this unit. The receiver-dryer is a long cylinderlike device that resembles a thermos jug. Usually, it is connected to the special air conditioning radiator, called the condenser. Generally, this is located in front of the cooling system radiator. **Note:** Many air conditioning systems do not have a sight glass, so the only way to accurately determine if the system is properly charged is with an air conditioning gauge set. Again, this is a job best left to a professional.

2. The sight glass normally is dirty and must be cleaned before you can see anything.

3. With the engine running and the air conditioning system turned on, observe the sight glass. For the first few minutes the system is operating, you should see tiny bubbles passing under the sight glass. This is normal. However, if the bubbles continue to be seen after approximately 5 minutes or so of

operation, it indicates that the system has leaked and is low on refrigerant. A system low on refrigerant will not cool properly. If this is the case, you should have a qualified mechanic check the system for leaks, repair them, and recharge your system with refrigerant.

One final note: Most air conditioning system problems are the result of a leak in the system. Much of the time, this is caused by seals in the system drying out from lack of use. Throughout the year, even in winter, it is a good practice to operate your air conditioning system for a few minutes every other week. But even if you do this, it is best to have the system checked out at least once a year by a qualified air conditioning mechanic.

Recharging the Air Conditioner

Tools and Materials

- Recharging Hose Kit and Valve
- 1 to 3 Cans of Freon
- Safety Goggles
- Work Gloves
- Wrench or Pliers

FREON SHOULD ONLY be added to an air conditioning system after it has been determined that the system is low, by using the sight glass inspection method or a gauge set. Do not overcharge an air conditioner. Adding too much refrigerant can damage the compressor and reduce system performance.

It's also important to remember that if your air conditioner is low, it probably means there is a leak somewhere. Recharging the system

may temporarily restore cooling, but the Freon will eventually leak out unless the leak is repaired. A professional mechanic can find the leak for you by using an electronic leak detector (plain old soapy water also works—just watch for the bubbles) but don't try to fix the leak yourself. The system is under pressure and must first be safely discharged before any hose connections are opened. The system must also be evacuated with a vacuum pump after repairs are made, to remove all traces of air and moisture that can cause corrosion and interfere with cooling performance.

When recharging an air conditioning system, Freon is added to the Schrader valve on the *low-pressure* side of the system. This valve can be found on the suction port of the compressor or the suction line leading from the evaporator to the compressor. If the system is still working, you can determine the low-pressure suction line by feeling the compressor hoses. The cooler one is the suction line. The hot one is the discharge line and contains high-pressure Freon. *Caution: DO NOT connect your recharging hose to this line. As a safety precaution, most suction and discharge hose Schrader valve fittings are of different size, to prevent an accidental hookup.*

To recharge the system, follow the directions provided with the recharge kit or the following steps (**Note:** Always give preference to the manufacturer's directions over ours, since some steps may vary slightly).

1. Start the engine and turn the A/C controls to high.
2. Make sure you have your work gloves and safety goggles on, then connect the recharge adapter valve to the can of Freon. Momentarily open the valve to blow any air or moisture out of the recharge hose.
3. Locate the *low-pressure* Schrader valve and attach the recharge hose to it.
4. Open the valve on the can of Freon. Hold the can upright so only vapor enters the recharge hose. If the valve attaches to the side of the can, position the can sideways so the valve is on top. Holding the can upside down can allow liquid Freon to enter the recharge hose, which could damage the compressor.
5. Suction in the low-pressure side of the system will draw Freon vapor through

the recharge hose until the can is empty. This can take a number of minutes, so be patient. When the can feels empty, turn the valve off and disconnect the recharge hose from the Schrader valve.

6. Recheck the sight glass or note the coldness of the air blowing out of the air conditioner. If the system is still low, add another can of Freon repeating steps 2 through 5. If the system is com- pletely empty, you can add three cans of Freon, but for partially charged systems, add only one or two cans. Stop adding Freon once the bubbles have disappeared from the sight glass.

7. After recharging, check system performance by noting the temperature of the air blowing out of the air conditioner. If it still doesn't feel cold enough, take your car to a professional for futher diagnosis.

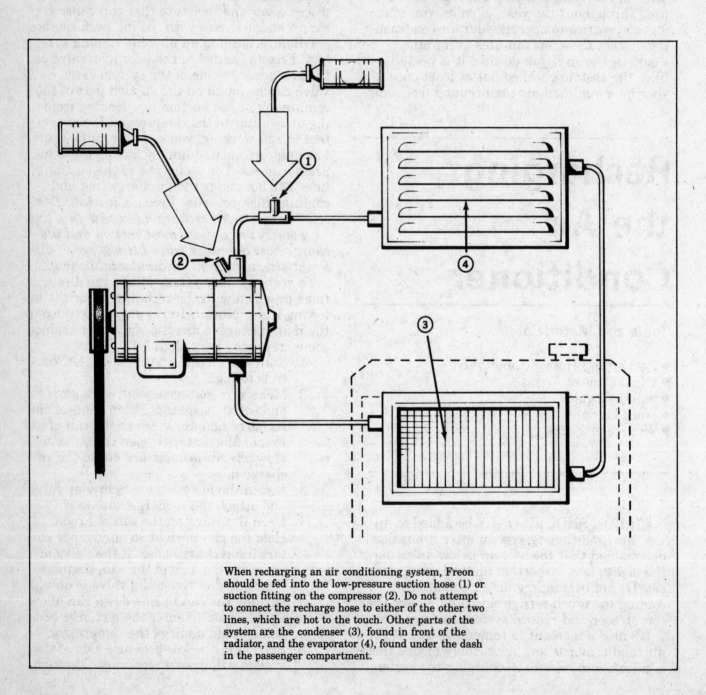

When recharging an air conditioning system, Freon should be fed into the low-pressure suction hose (1) or suction fitting on the compressor (2). Do not attempt to connect the recharge hose to either of the other two lines, which are hot to the touch. Other parts of the system are the condenser (3), found in front of the radiator, and the evaporator (4), found under the dash in the passenger compartment.

THE FUEL SYSTEM

GETTING MORE miles per gallon of fuel from your car should be of concern to all of us, given the ever-present threat that prices can increase suddenly and dramatically. Some automobiles may never get really good gas mileage due to the engine size or weight of the car itself. Larger engines usually require more fuel to operate than smaller engines do. And, as the weight of the car increases, so does the power needed to move it. The more power required, the higher the fuel consumption will be.

The way you drive also affects fuel consumption. If you are in the habit of making "jackrabbit" starts, you are going to get less gas mileage because rapid acceleration causes more fuel to be pumped into the engine. Also, fuel economy suffers at high speed. However unpopular highway speed limits may be, it still is a fact that most automobile engines operate much more efficiently at a speed of 55 mph than they do at 70 mph.

Let us assume here that we are dealing with auto engines using gasoline for fuel, al-

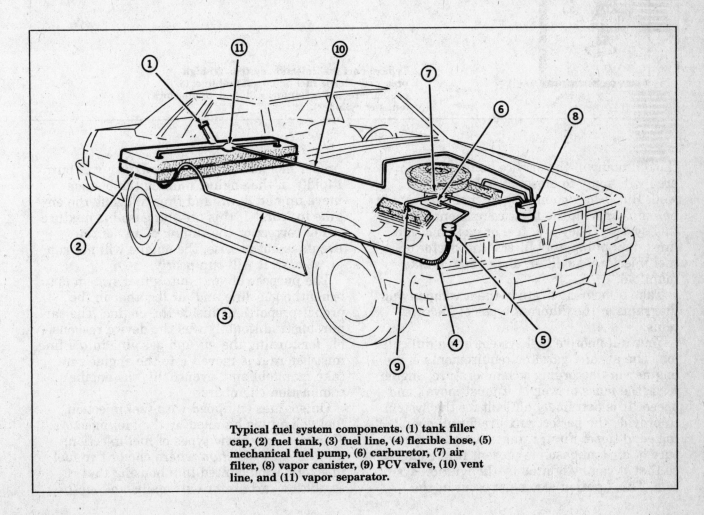

Typical fuel system components. (1) tank filler cap, (2) fuel tank, (3) fuel line, (4) flexible hose, (5) mechanical fuel pump, (6) carburetor, (7) air filter, (8) vapor canister, (9) PCV valve, (10) vent line, and (11) vapor separator.

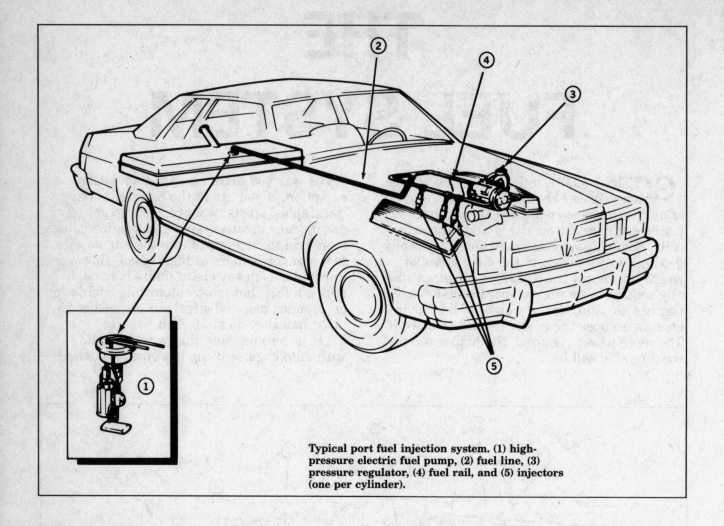

Typical port fuel injection system. (1) high-pressure electric fuel pump, (2) fuel line, (3) pressure regulator, (4) fuel rail, and (5) injectors (one per cylinder).

though many of the service points to be covered will apply to diesel-fueled engines as well. But before going any further, you should be familiar with the basic components of any fuel system. They are: fuel or gas tank, fuel lines, fuel pump, fuel filters, carburetor or fuel injectors, air filter, and engine intake manifold.

Take a moment to study the accompanying diagrams of the different types of fuel systems.

Your automotive fuel system has a difficult job. The air and gasoline requirements of an engine vary according to temperature, engine load (the mass or weight it must move), and speed. It is extremely difficult for the system to provide the perfect mixture for all operating conditions. First, it takes a certain mixture of air and gasoline present in the engine so that it can be ignited by the ignition system. This ignition also must occur at the

proper moment so that the mixture will burn rapidly in the engine, making the pistons move up and down and thus allowing the engine to "run." If this air and gasoline mixture is not correct or the timing of any of the events is not precise, the engine will not run or, at best, it will run poorly.

The purpose of your auto's fuel system is to bring the gasoline and air together in the proper proportions inside the engine. The carburetor traditionally was the device responsible for turning the air and gasoline into a fine mist before it is moved into the engine's intake manifold and, eventually, the engine's combustion chambers.

On engines equipped with fuel injection, fuel delivery is handled by the fuel injectors. There are two basic types of fuel injection: *throttle-body injection* where one or two fuel injectors are mounted in a housing that resembles a carburetor externally, and *multi-*

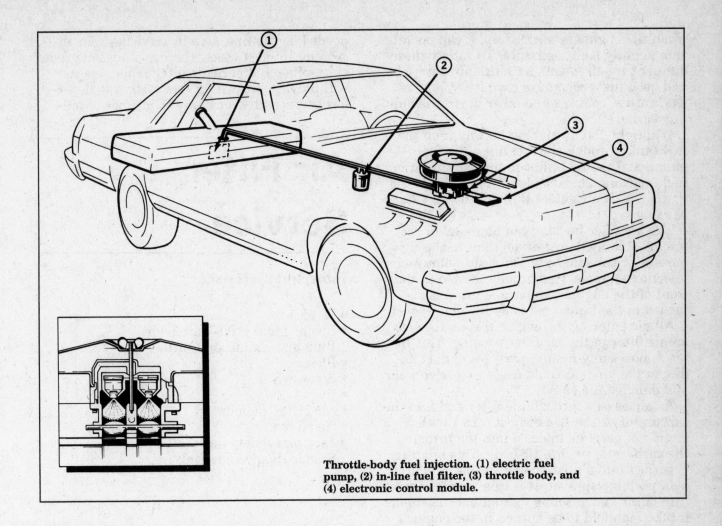

Throttle-body fuel injection. (1) electric fuel
pump, (2) in-line fuel filter, (3) throttle body, and
(4) electronic control module.

point injection where there is one injector per cylinder, and the injectors are mounted directly on the intake manifold. With either type of system, the fuel injector sprays a mist of fuel into the intake manifold where it mixes with incoming air to form the proper air/fuel ratio.

Let us pause for a moment to explain the term "mixture." You may have heard that a good fuel mixture should be about 15 to 1; that is, 15 parts of air to 1 part of gasoline. Here is how that ratio is determined.

It requires 9000 gallons of air to support the combustion of 1 gallon of gasoline. If these figures were to be used, we would be working with a formula such as 9000 to 1. This becomes rather cumbersome. So, for simplicity, figures are converted into weight.

Converting our original ideal mixture of 9000 gallons of air to weight, we find that 9000 gallons of air weigh 90 pounds (100 gallons of air weigh 1 pound). One gallon of gasoline, meanwhile, weighs 6 pounds. When you divide 90 by 6, you obtain 15. Therefore, we arrive at an air/gasoline ratio of 15 to 1 by weight.

Furthermore, if a mixture is "lean," it means there is proportionately more air than gasoline. This affects engine operation in several ways. A lean-running engine will accelerate poorly, run slightly hotter than normal, idle roughly and not operate well at high speeds.

If the mixture is "rich," it means there is proportionately less air. A rich-running engine usually has high fuel consumption, tends to stall at low speeds and often will emit dark smoke from the tailpipe.

Keeping this explanation in mind, let us also remember that when the engine is cold (not up to operating temperature), it requires a richer mixture to operate satisfactorily. But when the engine is warmed up, it can operate on a slightly leaner mixture. To satisfy these different requirements for efficient operation and good fuel economy, a complex system of jets, valves, controls, and other devices is built into carburetors.

While the fuel is making its way from the fuel tank, through the fuel lines, the fuel pump, and the fuel filter to the carburetor or fuel injectors, air is being introduced into the system. This air enters through the air filter housing.

The air filter housing can be round or rectangular, located over or adjacent to the carburetor or throttle-body. On multi-point fuel injection systems, it is usually located in the front of the engine compartment and is attached to the intake manifold by a large duct.

All air entering the engine travels through an air filter in the air filter housing. This filter removes any minute particles of dust and dirt in the air that could cause excessive wear and damage the engine.

As air passes through the filter and into the carburetor or throttle-body, it mixes with a stream of gasoline injected into the throat of the carburetor or throttle-body. This mixture is turned into a mist similar to that produced by a perfume sprayer. It is this atomized mixture of air and gasoline that enters the engine intake manifold to be burned in the engine's combustion chambers.

On engines with multi-port fuel injection, air passes through the filter and then through a device that measures how much air is entering the engine. This is called an air flow sensor. Fuel isn't mixed with the air until it reaches the intake ports of the cylinders. At that point, the fuel injector sprays fuel into the port, and the air and fuel are carried into the cylinder.

One thing you should keep in mind: dirt is the biggest enemy of your fuel system. Dirt may enter the system through the carburetor due to a dirty air filter. Dirt also may get into the fuel system from the fuel tank. If this happens, the gasoline flowing through the system will carry the dirt with it, contaminating the system. This is the reason for fuel filters.

Simple routine maintenance can prevent most fuel system problems. Changing the air and fuel filters when recommended, or when needed, is the first step in servicing your fuel system. In most cases, the use of a good grade of gasoline and periodic filter replacements will provide you with a fuel system that performs efficiently for many thousands of miles.

Air Filter Service

Tools and Materials

- Wrenches
- Bright Light (100-Watt Light Bulb and Extension Cord)
- Pliers
- Screwdriver
- Rags
- Air Filter Element
- Golf Tees
- Jack and Safety Jack Stands (Some Cars Only)

YOUR AUTOMOBILE'S air filter element is usually changed whenever your engine is tuned—at least it should be. Most automakers recommend changing this filter element more often if you operate your car under dirty or dusty conditions. A dirty air filter restricts the flow of air to the engine and increases fuel consumption. Either way, it is a good idea to check your filter at least every 3000 to 4000 miles of driving, and to replace the element when necessary.

The filter element is inside the air filter housing, which is mounted on top of the carburetor or throttle-body, or just ahead of the fuel injection air flow sensor. Here is how to check and, if necessary, to replace the element.

1. Open the car's hood and locate the air filter housing.
2. Generally, there will be a wing nut in

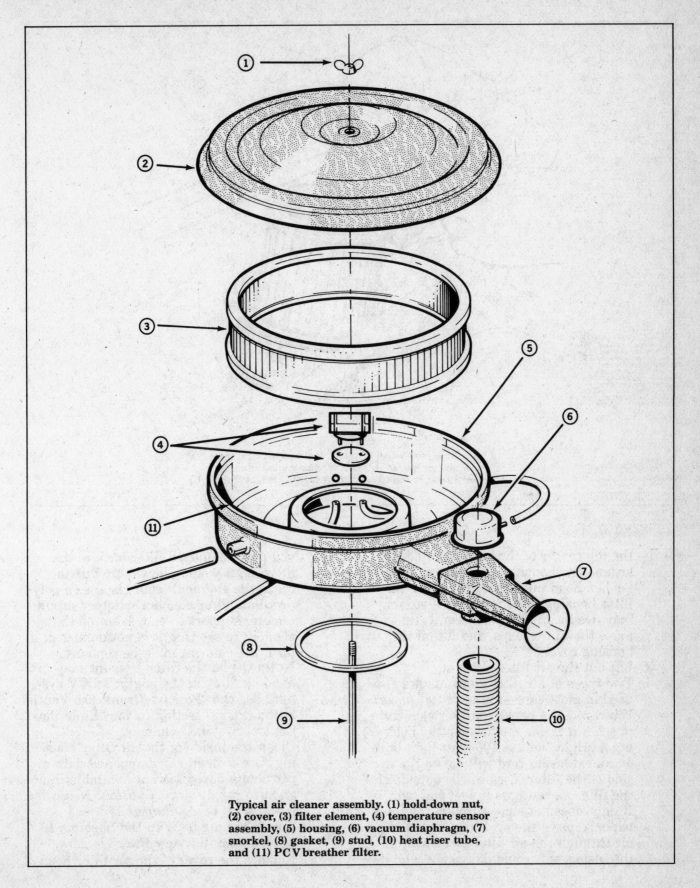

Typical air cleaner assembly. (1) hold-down nut, (2) cover, (3) filter element, (4) temperature sensor assembly, (5) housing, (6) vacuum diaphragm, (7) snorkel, (8) gasket, (9) stud, (10) heat riser tube, and (11) PCV breather filter.

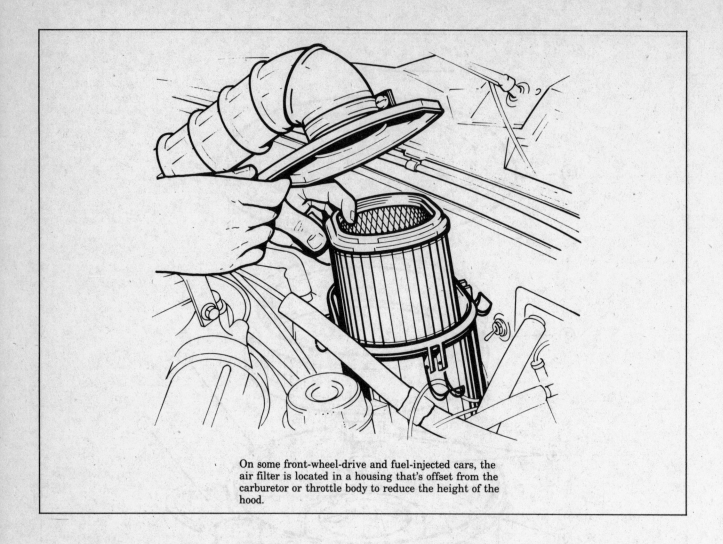

On some front-wheel-drive and fuel-injected cars, the air filter is located in a housing that's offset from the carburetor or throttle body to reduce the height of the hood.

the top center of the housing or clips around the housing. Sometimes, a regular hex-head nut is used to secure the filter housing cover in place. If so, you may need a wrench to loosen it. Remove the nut or clips, and lift off the housing cover.

3. Lift out the air filter element.
4. Two types of air filter elements are used in most cars—round or flat paper. You can test a paper air filter element to see if it needs replacement by holding a bright light (a 100-watt light bulb on an extension cord will do) on the inside of the filter. Look at the outside of the filter as you pass it over the light. If light does not show through the filter paper, replace the air filter. Do not blow air through the air filter element from the inside; this could damage it, and if

you put a damaged filter back in the housing, it would allow more dirt to reach the engine. If your car uses a polyurethane filter element wrapped around a metal support screen, examine the element to see that it is not damaged; if torn, the element must be replaced. **Note:** Oil on the filter element may indicate a fault in the engine's PCV system. See the "Positive Crankcase Ventilation (PCV)" section in the "Emissions Control Systems" chapter.

5. Clean the inside of the air filter housing. Use a clean rag dampened with a petroleum-based solvent available from an auto supply store. *Caution: Never use gasoline; it is too dangerous.*
6. Install the air filter in the housing. If needed, install a new filter element.
7. Replace the cover of the air filter hous-

ing. Finger-tighten the wing nut, tighten the hex-head nut, or resnap the clips. Be sure the cover is on properly and no wires or hoses from the engine compartment are caught between the cover and the housing. To operate efficiently, the air filter housing should have no air gaps around the cover.

Removing the Entire Housing

On occasion, such as during a tune-up, you may have to remove the entire air filter housing from the engine. Here is how to do this.

1. Remove the air filter housing cover and air filter element as outlined above.
2. Check the "snorkel" arm (air intake) of the housing for any clamps or hose connections. Loosen any clamps with pliers or a screwdriver and pull off any hoses, noting their position. You may want to mark them to make reinstallation easier.
3. If you do remove any vacuum hoses, plug the ends with golf tees. This will

prevent dirt from entering and, if you have to run the engine, you will not have a vacuum leak.

4. Some model cars route the PCV ("Positive Crankcase Ventilation") filter hose to the air filter housing. This hose must also be removed. If so, you will see a pipe or hose coming from an engine valve cover. Usually, there is a small piece of hose at the end of the pipe connecting it to the housing. Actually, the hose is connected to the PCV filter, which is inside the air filter housing. Simply pull the hose away from the air filter housing. (Refer to the section on "Positive Crankcase Ventilation (PCV)" in the "Emissions Control Systems" chapter.
5. When all clamps and hoses are removed and their positions noted, lift the air filter housing off the carburetor or throttle-body.
6. When replacing the air filter housing, reverse Steps 1 through 5. Be certain all connections are secure.

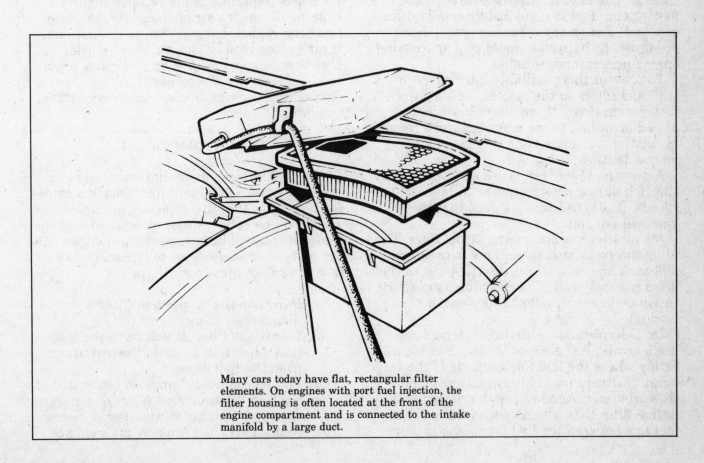

Many cars today have flat, rectangular filter elements. On engines with port fuel injection, the filter housing is often located at the front of the engine compartment and is connected to the intake manifold by a large duct.

Fuel Filter Replacement

Tools and Materials

- Pliers or Screwdriver
- Open-End Wrenches
- Flare-Nut or Tubing Wrenches, 9/16 or 5/8 Inch
- Fuel Filter
- Fuel Line Hose
- Rags

TO RUN PROPERLY, an engine must have an adequate supply of fuel at all times. And, this available fuel must be as clean as possible. As it passes through the fuel system, fuel is regulated by small orifices or jets. If dirt or any other foreign particles are present, the system could clog up, causing engine performance to suffer.

To prevent this possibility, carmakers install fuel filters in the system. To keep the fuel system clean, these filters must be replaced according to the manufacturer's recommendations, or more often if engine performance declines.

A dirty fuel filter can cause an engine to act sluggish during acceleration or at high speeds. It also can be so clogged that the engine will not run.

All vehicles use some form of fuel filter. The filter will be located somewhere between the fuel tank and carburetor, throttle-body, or fuel injector supply rail. To determine its exact location on your car, refer to your owner's manual.

On older vehicles with carburetors, some use a small filter element mounted inside a fitting where the fuel line connects to the carburetor. Others use a filter that screws into the carburetor. Another popular design is the in-line filter that is located somewhere in the fuel line between the fuel pump and carbure-tor. This type of filter is easy to identify because it looks like a small metal or plastic canister connected to the fuel line with two short lengths of rubber hose and clamps. On some imported cars, a third hose may be connected to the filter to route vapors back to the fuel tank.

On many newer vehicles with fuel injection, the fuel filter is located under the car, near the fuel tank. The filter may be either an in-line or screw-on design. *Caution: Fuel injection systems typically operate at high pressure. The vehicle should be allowed to sit for some time before loosening the filter, or the pressure within the fuel lines should be relieved following the manufacturer's particular procedure or the one described on the following pages.*

Diesel-equipped cars normally have a filter housing located somewhere in the engine compartment. The housing can be screwed open and the filter replaced. Many of these filters also serve as water traps, and the filter housing contains a small drain that allows you to periodically drain water from the housing. The presence of water does not mean the filter needs replacing. Some systems require priming to remove air bubbles after the filter has been replaced. Again, follow the manufacturer's recommendations for your vehicle. *Caution: A potential fire hazard exists whenever fuel lines are disconnected. Avoid open flames and working in confined areas without ventilation.*

In-Line Filter Replacement

Chrysler, AMC, and many imported cars generally use an in-line fuel filter. This is a canister-type filter that is completely discarded. There will be rubber hoses on both ends of the filter, so you will have hose clamps, either spring-type or screw-type, to loosen. Here's how to replace these fuel filters.

1. Purchase the proper fuel filter at an auto supply store.
2. Locate the filter. It will be in the fuel line (pipe) that leads to the carburetor from the fuel pump.
3. Loosen the hose clamps on either end of the fuel filter, using a pliers or screwdriver, depending on the type of clamp.
4. Remove the fuel filter by pulling back

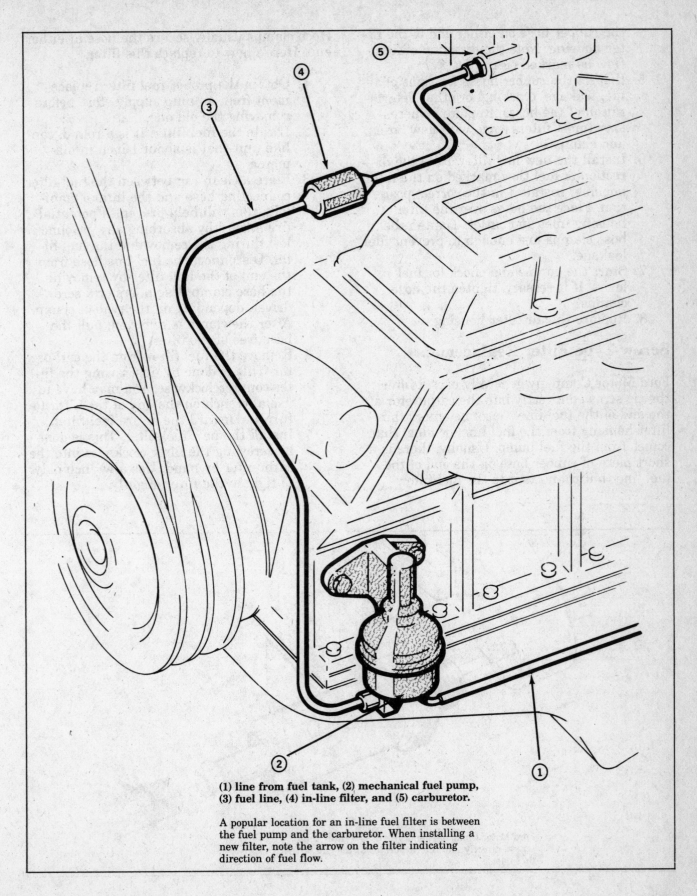

(1) line from fuel tank, (2) mechanical fuel pump,
(3) fuel line, (4) in-line filter, and (5) carburetor.

A popular location for an in-line fuel filter is between
the fuel pump and the carburetor. When installing a
new filter, note the arrow on the filter indicating
direction of fuel flow.

the rubber hose on either end of the filter housing. Note the direction of fuel flow as marked on the filter.

5. Inspect the rubber hoses for signs of fuel leakage, cracking, or other deterioration of the hoses. Replace as necessary (most filters come with new hoses and clamps).

6. Install the new fuel filter. Note the direction of fuel flow marked on the filter housing. Install it in the correct position. Place the hoses over the filter housing inlet and outlet. Tighten the hose clamps just enough to prevent fuel leakage.

7. Start the engine and check for fuel leaks. If necessary, tighten the hose clamps.

8. Replace the air filter housing.

Screw-Type Filter Replacement

Ford Motor Company generally uses a filter that is screwed directly into the carburetor at the end of the fuel line. Gasoline enters the filter housing from the fuel line (or pipe) that comes from the fuel pump. Usually, there is a short piece of rubber hose on the end of the fuel line that connects it to the fuel filter.

Hose clamps usually secure the hose at either end. Here's how to replace this filter.

1. Obtain the proper fuel filter replacement from an auto supply store before removing the old one.

2. Locate the fuel filter. It is a round, can-like unit that is about 1 inch in diameter.

3. Place a clean rag between the fuel filter connecting hose and the intake manifold; this will help prevent a potential fire hazard by absorbing any gasoline lost during the removal of the fuel filter. Disconnect the fuel line hose from the end of the fuel filter by removing the hose clamp. Use pliers or a screwdriver, depending on the type of clamp. After the clamp is removed, pull the hose free of the filter.

4. Remove the fuel filter from the carburetor. This is done by unscrewing the filter counterclockwise. You may have to use a wrench on the end of the filter to turn it. Discard the entire fuel filter.

5. Install the new fuel filter. This is done by screwing the filter clockwise into the carburetor by hand. Use a wrench only to tighten the filter slightly.

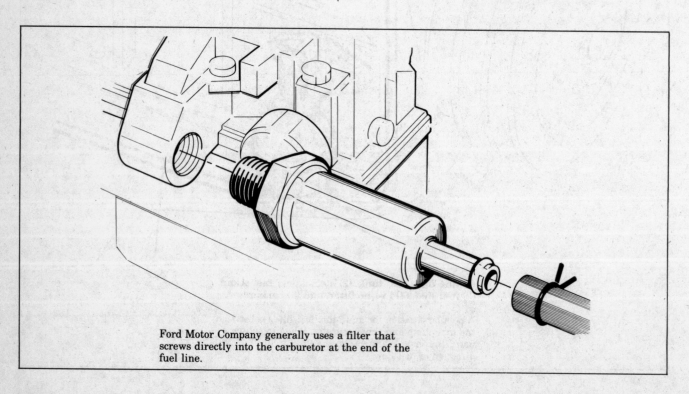

Ford Motor Company generally uses a filter that screws directly into the carburetor at the end of the fuel line.

6. Reinstall the fuel line hose located on the end of the fuel line by pushing it onto the end of the fuel filter. Tighten the clamp. Remove any gasoline that may have spilled onto the intake manifold with the rag and then discard the rag in a safe place.

7. Start the engine and check for fuel leaks. Stop any leaks by tightening the filter or hose clamp as necessary.

8. Replace the air filter housing.

Internal Filter Replacement

Most General Motors cars with carburetors have the fuel filter housed right in the carburetor where the fuel line from the fuel pump is connected. Generally, the fuel filter element is made of bronze or paper. In this case, only the element itself is replaced. Be sure to obtain the correct replacement element before removing the old element. Here's how to replace this fuel filter.

1. Locate the fuel line (pipe) that comes from the fuel pump to the carburetor.

2. Place a clean rag between the fuel inlet nut at the carburetor and the intake manifold; this will help absorb any gasoline lost during removal of the filter. Disconnect the fuel line at the carburetor. You will need two wrenches for this, about a 1-inch open-end wrench and a flare-nut or tubing wrench, usually 9/16 or 5/8 inch in size. **Note:** A flare-nut wrench looks like a box-end wrench with a section of the box cut out so that the wrench may be placed around a fluid line and then moved into position to loosen or tighten a fitting. Use the open end wrench to keep the larger nut on the carburetor from turning, which can damage the fuel line, as you loosen the smaller nut on the end of the fuel line with the flare-nut wrench.

3. With the fuel line disconnected, loosen the larger nut (the filter housing nut on the carburetor) with the larger wrench. This one holds the fuel filter. There is a light spring inside the filter element housing that could pop out if you are not careful, so remove this nut slowly. Also, notice the positions of the spring and filter as you remove them.

4. Install the new fuel filter in the carburetor—do not forget the spring—and tighten the nut that holds it in the housing with the wrench.

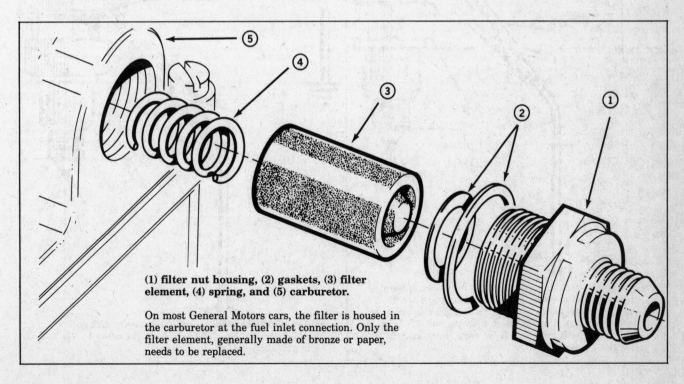

(1) filter nut housing, (2) gaskets, (3) filter element, (4) spring, and (5) carburetor.

On most General Motors cars, the filter is housed in the carburetor at the fuel inlet connection. Only the filter element, generally made of bronze or paper, needs to be replaced.

5. Reconnect the fuel line to the carburetor and tighten the nut with the flare-nut wrench. Remove any gasoline that may have spilled on the intake manifold during the removal and installation of the filter.
6. Start the engine and check for fuel leaks. Repair them if necessary by tightening the nuts on the fuel line and carburetor.
7. Replace the air filter housing.

Fuel Injection Filter Replacement

On vehicles with either throttle-body fuel injection or multi-point injection, an in-line or screw-on filter can usually be found under the car near the fuel tank. Refer to your owner's manual for its exact location.

Caution: Most fuel injection systems are under high pressure. No attempt should be made to loosen or remove the filter until pressure within the fuel lines and filter have been relieved. To relieve pressure, follow the manufacturer's recommended procedure or the one that follows. An alternate method is simply to let the car sit overnight. System pressure will diminish over time, so waiting several hours after the car has been shut off will usually allow internal pressure to drop so the filter can be safely changed.

To replace the filter, follow this procedure.

1. If the filter is located under the rear of the car, block the front wheels, raise the car, and support it with jackstands. It's extremely important to block the front wheels, because the emergency

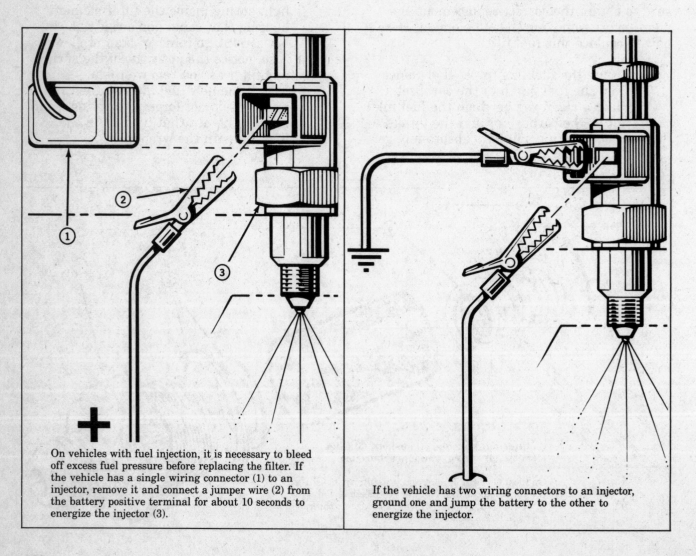

On vehicles with fuel injection, it is necessary to bleed off excess fuel pressure before replacing the filter. If the vehicle has a single wiring connector (1) to an injector, remove it and connect a jumper wire (2) from the battery positive terminal for about 10 seconds to energize the injector (3).

If the vehicle has two wiring connectors to an injector, ground one and jump the battery to the other to energize the injector.

brake only locks the rear wheels on most vehicles, and if they're raised off the ground, they can't hold the car. With front-wheel-drive vehicles, put the transaxle in gear or park.

2. Loosen the gas cap to relieve any pressure in the fuel tank.
3. With the ignition off, pull the wiring connector off one of the injectors.
4. If the injector has one electrical lead, use a jumper wire from the battery positive terminal to energize the injector for about 10 seconds. If the injector has two leads, ground one and jump the other from the battery to energize it. This will cause the injector to spray fuel into the engine and relieve pressure in the fuel lines.
5. Reconnect the electrical connector to the injector and proceed with your fuel filter replacement.
6. Unscrew the filter from its housing, or loosen and remove the clamps from the in-line filter to replace it. Install the new filter, retighten the gas cap, and start the engine to check for leaks.

Diesel Fuel Filter Replacement

Many diesel fuel filters separate water as well as dirt, and thus have a water drain valve and tube at the bottom. On those with a clear plastic housing, the water level inside can be observed to determine when the water needs draining. On those with metal housings, a water level sensor may be included as part of the filter. When the water level inside reaches a certain depth, a warning light on the dash is illuminated, signaling that it's time to drain the filter.

To drain water from a filter, the engine must be off. Open the drain valve at the bottom of the filter and leave it open until diesel fuel dribbles out. The hand prime pump can be used to force the water out more quickly. Catch the water and diesel fuel in a small pan. *Caution: Do not allow diesel fuel to splash on a hot exhaust manifold or pipe.*

To replace the filter, use the following procedure.

1. With the engine and ignition off, open the drain valve and drain the filter.

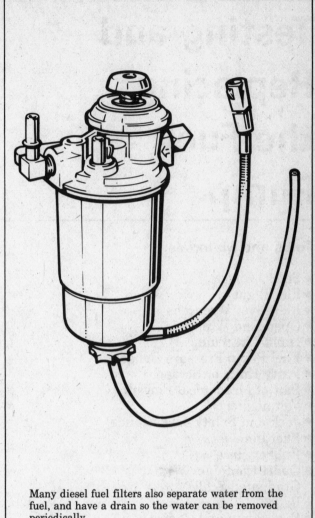

Many diesel fuel filters also separate water from the fuel, and have a drain so the water can be removed periodically.

2. Disconnect the drain tube and water sensor wiring connector (if so equipped) from the bottom of the filter.
3. Unscrew the filter housing, turning it counterclockwise as viewed from below.
4. Replace the filter element inside, or install a new screw-on filter assembly. Prefill the filter housing with clean diesel fuel, and after screwing it back on, hand tighten about ½ turn after the housing seat makes contact with the O-ring seal.
5. Prime the system by pumping on the hand pump until resistance is felt, or until fuel is observed flowing from the filter housing to the injection pump.
6. Start the engine and check for leaks.

Testing and Replacing the Fuel Pump

Tools and Materials

- Safety Goggles
- Flashlight
- Flare-Nut Wrenches
- Open-End Wrenches
- Hand/Tire Pump
- Fuel Pump Pressure Gauge
- Putty Knife or Scraper
- Pair of Mechanical Fingers
- Voltmeter
- Jack and Safety Jack Stands
- Fuel Line
- Rubber Hose
- Quart Container With Graduated Scale
- Rags
- Fuel Pump and Gasket
- Gasket Sealer
- Fuse
- Gas-Cleaning Chemicals

THE FUEL PUMP is the device that draws the fuel in the fuel tank through the fuel lines or pipes to the engine's carburetor or fuel injectors. Basically, there are two types of fuel pumps—mechanical and electrical.

Mechanical Fuel Pumps

The mechanical fuel pump is the type found on most carbureted engines. Usually, it is located on the engine block near the front of the engine. If you have difficulty locating the fuel pump, simply follow the fuel line (pipe) leading from your carburetor. The fuel line will be connected to the fuel pump.

Mechanical fuel pumps are also referred to as the diaphragm type because there is a diaphragm inside the pump that is actuated by the engine's camshaft. As the camshaft rotates during engine operation, a shaft or actuating arm in the pump is moved up and down or back and forth, depending on the fuel pump's position on the engine. This causes the diaphragm to move back and forth, drawing fuel from the fuel tank, through the fuel lines and to the carburetor.

Once, fuel pumps were designed to be disassembled and rebuilt. This is not the case today. Therefore, if the fuel pump does not operate, replacement is necessary.

Fuel pumps are designed to deliver a certain amount of fuel to the carburetor with a certain amount of pressure. Any pump that fails to do this must be replaced.

Other factors, however, can sometimes affect fuel pump operation. Leaks—air or fuel—will cause the pump to function improperly. A visual inspection of the entire fuel system is in order before any volume or pressure tests can be made. Also, if you suspect you are not getting the proper amount of fuel to the carburetor, make certain your problem is not caused by a clogged fuel filter. Refer to the section on "Fuel Filter Replacement" in this chapter and make appropriate repairs or replacements before proceeding with fuel pump tests. *Caution: A potential fire hazard exists whenever fuel lines are disconnected. Avoid open flames and working in confined areas without ventilation.*

Visual Inspection

Visual inspection involves getting under your car to check the fuel system, so you should be prepared with appropriate clothing and safety goggles.

1. Starting at the fuel tank, locate the fuel line (pipe) at the front of the tank. This is the line that runs to the fuel pump.
2. Look for any signs of fuel leakage where the line connects to the fuel tank. With a flare-nut wrench of the

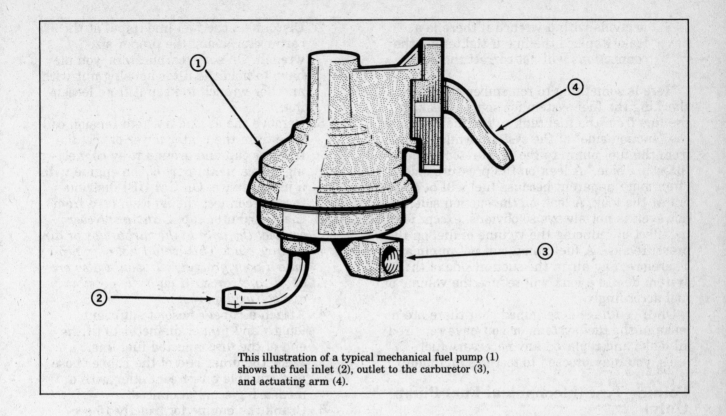

This illustration of a typical mechanical fuel pump (1)
shows the fuel inlet (2), outlet to the carburetor (3),
and actuating arm (4).

proper size, tighten the nut on the fuel line to stop any leak.

3. Using a flashlight, follow the fuel line toward the front of the car, checking for fuel leaks. If you suspect leaks at any connections, tighten the connecting nuts with a flare-nut wrench of the proper size.

4. If the fuel line is leaking as a result of rust or from chafing on some part of the car, the line must be replaced. Replacement fuel line is available from an auto supply store. To replace the line, disconnect it at both ends, using open-end and flare-nut wrenches of the proper size. Remove the line from under the car and replace it with the new one, securing the nuts at both ends.

5. Continue inspecting the fuel line as you move toward the fuel pump. Because the pump is mounted on the engine, vibration could cause this connection to work loose. Tighten if necessary with a flare-nut wrench of the proper size.

6. Now inspect the fuel pump itself. In this case, you are looking for the presence of oil or gasoline. Most fuel pumps have a small diaphragm breather hole under them. This hole will show evidence of fuel leakage if the pump's diaphragm is damaged. In some cases, when the diaphragm is severely damaged, engine oil will be present on the outside of the fuel pump. In either case, the fuel pump must be replaced if oil or gasoline is present.

If you find gasoline leaking at the fuel pump, check the motor oil dipstick. It is possible that gasoline has entered the engine crankcase through the fuel pump mounting hole. If this is the case, drain the crankcase, replace the oil filter, and put fresh oil into the engine. Refer to the "Changing the Oil and Filter" section in the "Maintaining Your Car" chapter for this procedure. *Caution: Gasoline in the engine crankcase is dangerous because it could cause the engine to explode. Also, diluted motor oil will not lubricate properly, causing premature engine wear.*

7. Finally, check the fuel line that runs between the fuel pump and the carburetor. Once again, tighten any loose con-

nections with a wrench if there is a leak. Replace the line if tightening the connections will not correct the leak.

Here is something to remember when checking the fuel system for signs of leakage: the line from the fuel tank to the fuel pump is the "suction side" of the system, while the line from the fuel pump to the carburetor is the "pressure side." A leak on the pressure side is often more apparent because fuel will be present at the leak. A leak on the suction side, however, is not always so obvious, except for its effect of reducing the volume of fuel on the pressure side. A fuel pump will not pump air. Therefore, any air in the suction side of the system due to a leak will reduce the volume of fuel accordingly.

Once you have determined that there are no leaks in the fuel system, or you have repaired all leaks and replaced any necessary fuel lines, you may proceed to test the fuel pump.

Volume Test (Mechanical Fuel Pump Only)

This test is to determine whether the fuel pump is capable of delivering the proper amount of fuel to the carburetor at all times. To test for volume, follow this procedure.

1. Remove the air filter housing. Refer to the section on "Air Filter Service" in this chapter for procedure.

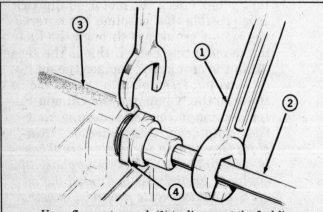

Use a flare-nut wrench (1) to disconnect the fuel line (2) at the carburetor (3). It may be necessary to hold the filter housing nut (4) with another wrench to keep it from loosening.

2. Disconnect the fuel line (pipe) at the carburetor, using the proper-size wrench. On some carburetors, you may have to hold the filter housing nut with another wrench to keep it from loosening.
3. Remove the secondary high-tension coil wire from the center tower of the distributor cap and ground it by connecting it to a metal part of the engine with a jumper wire. On GM HEI distributors, disconnect the ignition lead from the distributor cap. *Caution: Never connect the wire to the carburetor or air cleaner stud. This would not only provide a poor ground, but would also create a safety hazard with the possibility of electrical sparks.*
4. Attach a rubber hose of sufficient length and proper diameter to fit the end of the disconnected fuel line.
5. Place the other end of the rubber hose in a suitable quart container with a measuring scale in ounces.
6. Crank the engine for exactly 15 seconds, allowing fuel to run into the container.
7. Measure the amount of fuel in the container and multiply by 4. The sum will yield the amount of fuel the pump will deliver in 1 minute.
8. Check your car's repair manual for the fuel pump volume specification and compare your results with the specification. If the amount is within the specified limits, reconnect the secondary high-tension coil wire and proceed to the fuel pump pressure test. If the volume does not meet specifications, proceed as follows.
A. Reconnect the fuel line at the carburetor, using the proper-size wrench.
B. At the fuel pump, disconnect the fuel line that runs to the fuel tank.
C. Connect one end of the rubber hose to the disconnected fuel pump fitting.
D. Place the other end of this rubber hose in a quart container of gasoline.
E. Repeat the volume test as outlined in Steps 6 through 8. If the amount

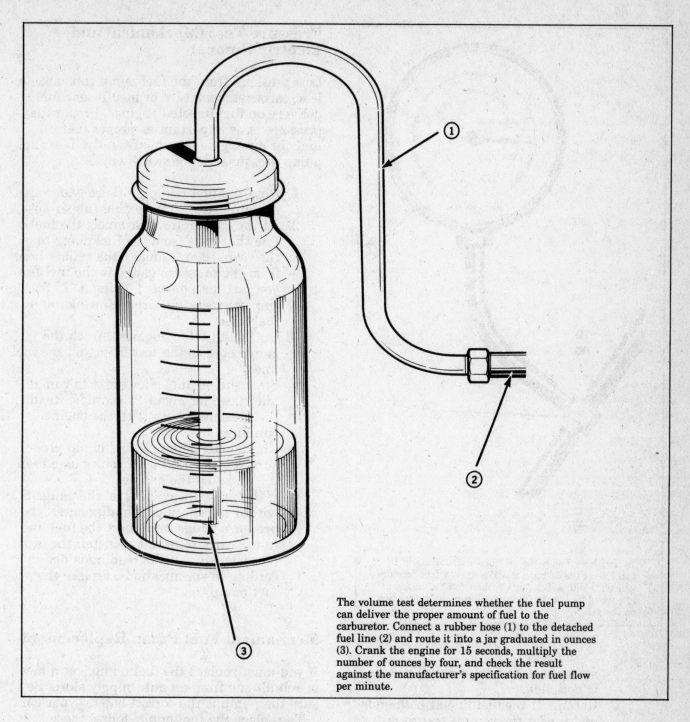

The volume test determines whether the fuel pump can deliver the proper amount of fuel to the carburetor. Connect a rubber hose (1) to the detached fuel line (2) and route it into a jar graduated in ounces (3). Crank the engine for 15 seconds, multiply the number of ounces by four, and check the result against the manufacturer's specification for fuel flow per minute.

of fuel *withdrawn* from the container is according to specifications in the repair manual, it may indicate the line between the fuel tank and the fuel pump is blocked.

9. If you suspect the fuel line is clogged, perform the following test.
   A. Disconnect the fuel line at the fuel tank, using the proper-size wrench.

The fuel line is now open at both ends.

B. Blow out the fuel line with air. Always force the air into the line in the direction that is opposite the normal fuel line flow. You can use a hand tire pump to do this. *Caution: Blowing into the line with your*

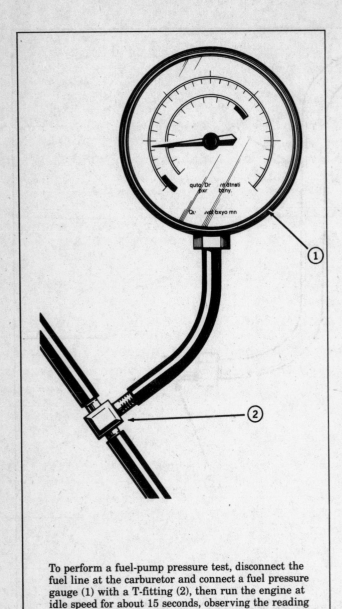

To perform a fuel-pump pressure test, disconnect the fuel line at the carburetor and connect a fuel pressure gauge (1) with a T-fitting (2), then run the engine at idle speed for about 15 seconds, observing the reading on the gauge.

Pressure-Test (Mechanical and Electric Pumps)

Low pressure from the fuel pump can cause a lean carburetor mixture or insufficient fuel delivery on fuel injected engines. Proper fuel pressure is as important as proper fuel volume for an engine to run efficiently. Test fuel pump pressure the following way.

1. Obtain a fuel pump pressure gauge that is equipped with a flexible rubber hose.
2. At the carburetor, disconnect the fuel line that runs from the fuel pump to the carburetor. Connect the rubber hose from the pressure gauge to the fuel line you just disconnected, using a "T" fitting between the carburetor inlet and fuel lines.
3. On fuel injected engines, attach the gauge hose to the test fitting on the fuel line.
4. Start the engine, allowing it to run at idle speed for about 15 seconds. Read the pressure gauge with the engine running.
5. Check your manual's fuel pump pressure specification with your gauge reading and stop the engine.
6. If the pressure reading on the gauge is within the specification, disconnect the pressure gauge, reconnect the fuel line to the carburetor and reinstall the air filter housing. If the reading is not according to specifications, replace the fuel pump.

Mechanical Fuel Pump Replacement

If you must replace the fuel pump, get a new or rebuilt one from an auto supply store. Be sure the pump is the correct one for your car.

To replace the fuel pump, follow these steps.

1. Disconnect the fuel lines at the fuel pump. Remember to use two wrenches for this job—one to hold the fitting on the fuel pump (to keep it from turning) while you are loosening the nuts on the fuel lines. This will eliminate possible damage to the fuel lines.

mouth is not recommended; gasoline is poisonous.

C. Reconnect the fuel line at both ends and repeat the volume test as outlined in Steps 2 through 8. If the volume is still not according to manual specification, the fuel pump should be replaced. The procedure is covered later in this section. If, however, the volume is according to specification, reconnect the distributor-to-coil primary wire and proceed to the pressure-test.

2. Using a wrench of proper size, remove the bolts holding the fuel pump to the engine block.

3. Remove the fuel pump. **Note:** On some engines, the fuel pump is actuated by a pushrod in the engine that runs off the camshaft. Use care in removing the fuel pump so that the rod does not fall out of the engine. If it does, wipe it with a clean rag and place it back in the engine.

4. Stuff a clean rag into the hole in the engine exposed by removal of the pump and scrape off any gasket material around the fuel pump mounting flange. Use a putty knife or scraper. The rag will prevent gasket scrapings from getting into the engine. Do not forget to remove the rag when you are through cleaning the mounting surface.

5. Compare the old and new fuel pumps. You may have to transfer the fuel line fittings from the old fuel pump to the new one. If so, unscrew the old fittings with a wrench and install them on the new pump. Make certain the fittings are pointing in the same direction as they were on the old fuel pump. This will make reconnecting the fuel lines much easier.

6. Apply gasket sealer to both sides of the new gasket that is supplied with the new fuel pump and place the gasket in position on the fuel pump mounting surface.

7. Place the new fuel pump in position on the engine. **Note:** If the fuel pump is actuated by a pushrod in the engine, be certain that the pushrod is in position and sits properly in the fuel pump. You may need a pair of mechanical fingers to hold the pushrod in place while you are working the fuel pump into position.

8. Reinstall the fuel pump mounting bolts and tighten them snugly with a wrench.

9. Reconnect the fuel lines to the fuel pump. Tighten the fuel line nuts using two wrenches as explained in Step 1.

10. Start the engine and check for fuel leaks. Repair any leaks by tightening connections.

11. Reinstall the air filter housing.

Electric Fuel Pumps

Many foreign cars with carbureted engines and most American and foreign cars with fuel injection use an electric fuel pump. Unlike the mechanical fuel pump that requires an operating engine to be actuated, the electric fuel pump begins to operate as soon as the car's ignition switch is turned on. Therefore, if a little piece of dirt or other contaminant gets under the needle valve in your carburetor, this electric pump could flood the engine or even pump the fuel tank dry if the ignition switch were left on for a length of time.

Some electric fuel pump equipped cars have eliminated this problem by having a switch that keeps the fuel pump shut off until the engine builds up oil pressure. Unfortunately, if one of these cars equipped with such a switch has been idle for a while, it may be difficult to start because the oil pressure may take some time to increase and there will be no fuel flow.

If you have a car with an electric fuel pump and you suspect fuel problems, do this.

1. Check to see if the fuse protecting the fuel pump's electrical circuit has been blown. Most electric fuel pump systems have such a fuse. Generally, it is located in the fuse box under the dashboard. Your owner's manual will give you its location. A visual inspection will tell you if this fuse is blown or not. If it is blown, replace it with one of equal value.

2. Locate the electric fuel pump. Usually these pumps are in or near the fuel tank. Simply follow the fuel line (pipe) from the carburetor, moving back toward the fuel tank. There will be inlet and outlet connections on the fuel pump. There also will be an electrical connection.

3. First, determine if you have electric current flowing to the fuel pump by using a voltmeter. With the ignition switch turned on, connect the voltmeter ground lead (black wire) to a good ground on the car frame. Touch the positive lead (red wire) of the voltmeter to the electrical connection on the elec-

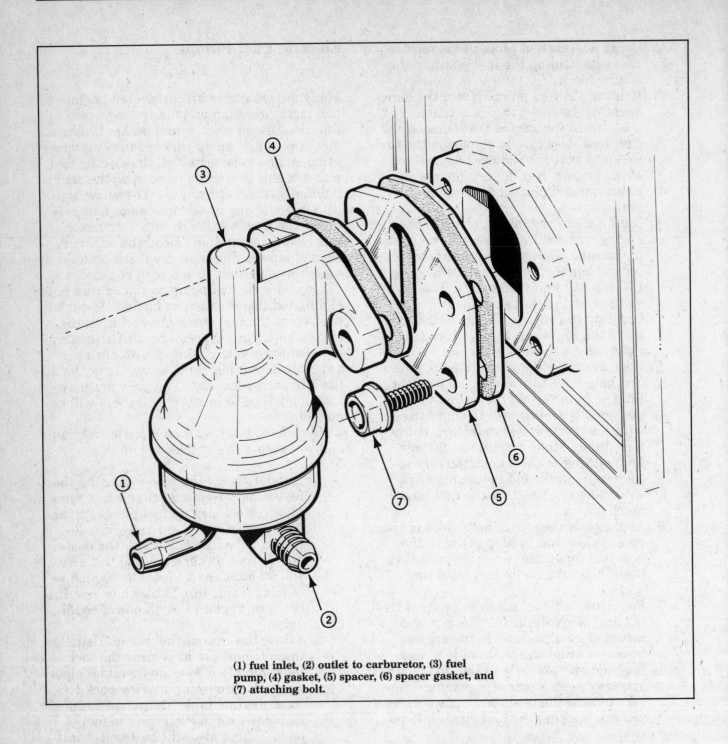

(1) fuel inlet, (2) outlet to carburetor, (3) fuel pump, (4) gasket, (5) spacer, (6) spacer gasket, and (7) attaching bolt.

tric fuel pump. You should obtain a reading of 12 volts at this connection.

4. If you do obtain this reading and the pump will not operate, replace the pump. If you do not obtain the correct voltage, the problem is somewhere between the fuel pump electrical connection and the ignition switch. You might be better off to consult a professional mechanic in this case.

5. Turn off the ignition switch.

If you determine that the electric fuel pump needs to be replaced, be sure you obtain one that meets the minimum requirements of pressure and volume for your particular car. Consult an auto supply store counterman if you have any questions.

Replacing an Electric Fuel Pump

Here's how to replace an electric fuel pump.

1. For pumps mounted underneath the car, block the front wheels, then raise the back of the car and support it on safety stands. On front-wheel-drive cars, put the transaxle in gear or park.
2. Disconnect the ground terminal at the battery.
3. Disconnect the electrical connector(s) on the electric fuel pump with a wrench of the proper size. Label the wire(s) to aid in connecting it to the new pump.
4. Disconnect the fuel lines as described in the procedure on mechanical fuel pumps. You may wish to label these fuel lines to assist you in reconnecting them to the new pump.
5. Using a wrench of proper size, remove the fuel pump mounting bolts. There may be two or four mounting bolts, depending on the unit.

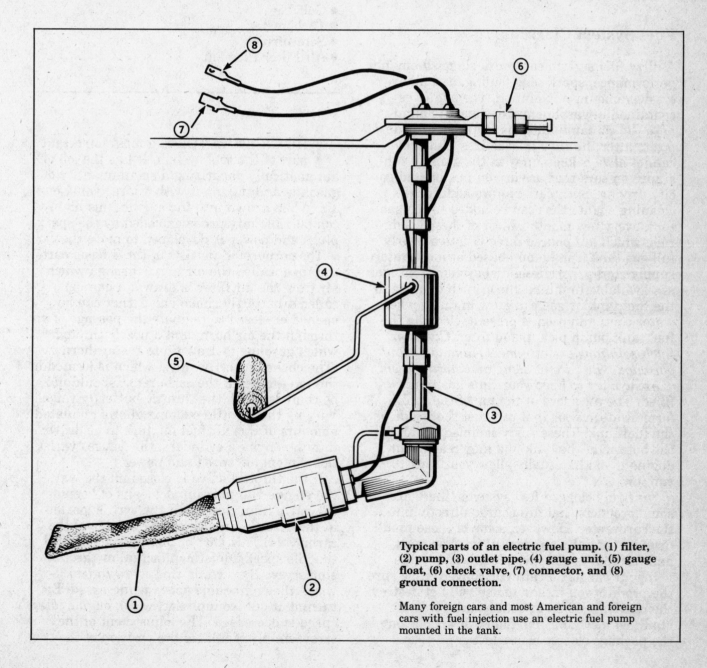

Typical parts of an electric fuel pump. (1) filter, (2) pump, (3) outlet pipe, (4) gauge unit, (5) gauge float, (6) check valve, (7) connector, and (8) ground connection.

Many foreign cars and most American and foreign cars with fuel injection use an electric fuel pump mounted in the tank.

6. Compare the new electric fuel pump with the old one. If necessary, transfer any fuel line fittings from the old pump to the new one.
7. Mount the new pump by securing the mounting bolts with the wrench.
8. Reconnect the fuel lines.
9. Reconnect the electrical connector(s).
10. Reconnect the ground terminal at the battery.
11. Start the engine and check for fuel leaks. Repair any leaks.

Fuel System Cleaning

A dirty fuel system can cause sluggish engine performance, spark plug fouling, and an excessive amount of pollution. The additives contained in gasoline are designed to eliminate the contaminants that form gummy deposits after the gasoline oxidizes. But they cannot always keep up with the gummy substance on cars that are driven in stop-and-go city driving. Such cars require additional cleaning agents that can be added to the gas tank every few months. Most of these chemicals, which are poured directly into a nearly full gas tank, can be purchased at most auto supply stores. For diesel fuel systems, biocides are available to inhibit the growth of algae in the fuel tank. Algae can grow in tanks where water contamination is present, clogging the fuel tank pump pickup and filter. *Caution: Such solutions are extremely flammable and poisonous. Be careful using and storing them.*

Always try to keep your car's gas tank filled. The air space at the top of the tank forms water vapor that can rust the inside of the fuel tank. These rusty sediments sink to the bottom of the tank and may reach your engine if you habitually allow your tank to run low.

For badly clogged fuel systems, there are some products that are poured directly into the carburetor. However, some of these products can actually do more harm than good and can foul your spark plugs.

If your car has a catalytic converter, be sure the product you intend to use will not destroy the catalyst. When in doubt, check with a qualified mechanic and follow directions on the package closely before using.

Carburetor Adjustments

Tools and Materials

- Wheel Chocks
- Wrenches
- Golf Tees
- Tachometer
- Screwdriver
- Air Filter Element

THE CARBURETOR is a most important part of the fuel system. It has the job of automatically vaporizing a small quantity of gasoline and mixing it with a large volume of air. When drawn into the engine, this highly combustible mixture is exploded by the spark plugs and power is developed to move the car.

The carburetor consists of three basic parts: the tube, called the air horn, through which air from the air filter is drawn; a damper, called a butterfly choke valve, that can be opened or closed to regulate the passage of air through the air horn; and a nozzle through which gasoline is drawn into the air horn. (The choke butterfly valve, which is located in the top section of the carburetor, should not be confused with the throttle butterfly valve. Varying the throttle opening allows regulated amounts of this air/fuel mixture to be drawn into the engine's cylinders; this causes variations in engine speed and power.)

If the throttle valve is closed all the way, the engine will not run. A means of keeping the valve from closing all the way is located in the throttle linkage on the outside of the carburetor. This part of the linkage is called the idle speed adjustment screw, or throttle stop screw. By turning this screw in (clockwise), the engine idle speed is increased. By turning it out (counterclockwise), engine idle speed is decreased. The adjustment of the screw simply regulates the position of the

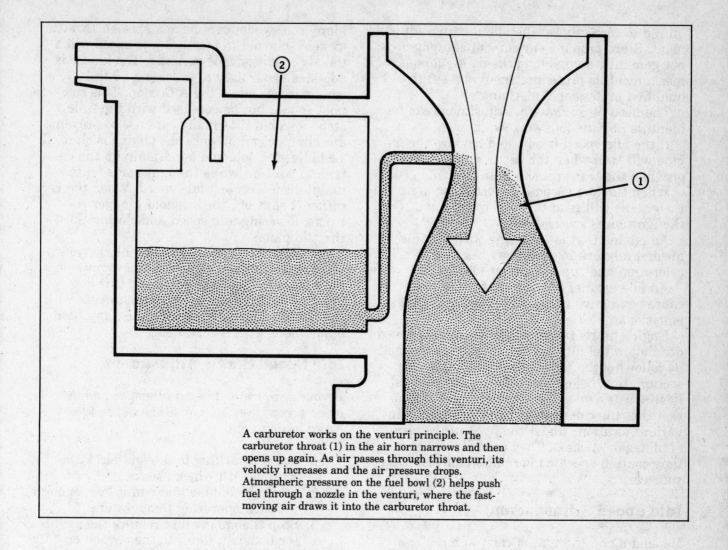

A carburetor works on the venturi principle. The carburetor throat (1) in the air horn narrows and then opens up again. As air passes through this venturi, its velocity increases and the air pressure drops. Atmospheric pressure on the fuel bowl (2) helps push fuel through a nozzle in the venturi, where the fast-moving air draws it into the carburetor throat.

throttle valve inside the carburetor and should not be confused with the idle *mixture* adusting screw. **Note:** Some carburetors are equipped with an anti-dieseling solenoid. This unit operates as part of the throttle linkage and must be considered when adjusting engine idle speed. Many late model vehicles with computerized engine controls have computer-controlled idle speed. Since the computer maintains idle speed within pre-programmed limits, no idle speed adjustment is possible.

Depending on the size of the carburetor, there will be one or two idle mixture screws located in its base casting. The idle mixture screw is a simple valve that regulates the amount of gasoline being mixed with the air flowing through the carburetor at low engine speeds. If the idle mixture screw is turned in (clockwise), the gasoline mixture is reduced and the air/fuel mixture becomes "lean." When the idle mixture screw is turned out (counterclockwise), the flow of gasoline is increased and the air/fuel mixture becomes "rich."

Basically, these adjustments are intended to correct two minor faults that detract from driving pleasure. However, they also are important final steps to every complete engine tune-up. **Note:** Most late model cars have sealed idle mixture adjustment screws or screws that can only be adjusted within a very narrow range due to "limiter caps." The idle mixture is factory set and should not require readjustment unless the carburetor is being overhauled or installed on a different engine. On many of these carburetors a special "propane enrichment" procedure is required to correctly set the idle mixture adjustment. Since propane enrichment equipment is not generally available to the do-it-yourself mechanic, this procedure should be left to a qualified professional mechanic.

The need for carburetor adjustment can be identified by the following symptoms.

If the idle speed is adjusted too low, the engine will stall when the car is slowed to a stop or when the transmission is shifted into gear.

When the idle speed is adjusted too high, the engine will tend to diesel or run on after the ignition is switched off.

An engine that is operating with the idle air/fuel mixture too lean may hesitate on acceleration and run roughly at idle speed.

An idle air/fuel mixture that is too rich causes excessive use of fuel and high exhaust emissions.

Engine faults traced to the wrong idle speed or idle air/fuel mixture can be easily corrected by following the procedures outlined in this section. But, before you begin making adjustments, it is a good idea to check the information that the car manufacturer has posted in various locations under the hood in the form of plates or stickers. They are helpful because they contain specific information for servicing your car.

Idle Speed Adjustments

Depending on the type of car you have, the idle speed is adjusted either by means of an idle speed adjustment screw or by an idle solenoid and idle screw. Consult your service manual or the tune-up decal in the engine compartment if you are in doubt as to which adjustment you have. Also, check to determine at what speed your engine should idle and if adjustments should be made with the transmission in drive, park, or neutral, or if any electrical accessories should be switched on or off. Power from the engine is used to drive these components and their use places a load on the engine that affects the idle speed.

For example, shifting an automatic transmission into drive range takes power from the engine and lowers the idle speed. Also, turning on accessories such as air conditioning adds to the engine load. These power-using loads must be taken into consideration when the engine idle speed needs to be adjusted.

Many late model cars have a special "throttle kicker" solenoid to increase idle speed when the air conditioner is running. The kicker is adjusted separately to provide a 50 to 100 rpm increase when the A/C is on. This solenoid should not be confused with the "idle stop" solenoid that many cars use to prevent dieseling or run-on once the engine is shut off. The idle stop solenoid is normally in the extended position while the ignition is on to maintain the correct idle speed. When the ignition is shut off, the solenoid plunger retracts, lowering idle speed and closing the throttle plates.

Because the air filter housing blocks your view of the linkage and adjusting screws on most cars, it should be removed. It is good practice to make the initial adjustments with the air filter housing removed and any final adjustment with it installed.

Idle Speed Screw Adjustment

If your carburetor has an idle speed adjustment screw, here is how to make the idle speed adjustment.

1. Set the parking brake and block the wheels with wheel chocks.
2. Start the engine and run it long enough to reach operating temperature.
3. Stop the engine and remove the air filter housing. Refer to the section on "Air Filter Service" in this chapter for the removal procedure. **Note:** Any vacuum hoses that have been removed from the air filter housing must be plugged. A golf tee is a good plugging tool. Vacuum lines that are left open will affect the engine idle speed.
4. Connect a tachometer, which measures revolutions per minute (rpm), to the engine. The instrument has two lead wires—one red, one black. Connect the black lead to any metal part of the engine, such as a bolt head or bracket, to ground the tachometer. Connect the red lead to the ignition coil at the primary terminal that leads to the distributor.
5. Start the engine.
6. Set the transmission and any accessories according to the tune-up plate or sticker, or directions in the service

manual for your car.

7. Observe the tachometer reading. Compare the indicated speed with the recommended speed. If adjustment is necessary, proceed to Step 8. If no adjustment is required, go to Step 9.

8. Using a screwdriver, turn the idle speed adjustment screw clockwise to increase rpm, counterclockwise to decrease rpm. You will find that a ¼ turn of the screw in either direction will usually bring the idle speed into specification.

9. Stop the engine.

10. Replace the air filter housing, but leave the tachometer hooked up.

11. Start the engine and check the tachometer reading. If the reading is within specification (±20 rpm), proceed to Step 12. If it is not, make a final adjustment at this time. **Note:** If you experience a decline in the engine idle speed after you replace the air filter assembly, the filter element could be restricting the air flow (it may be dirty). If so, it should be cleaned or replaced. Refer to the section on "Air Filter Service" in this chapter.

12. Stop the engine.

13. Remove the tachometer, reversing Step 4.

14. Remove the wheel chocks from the wheels.

15. Test drive the car.

Idle Solenoid and Idle Speed Screw Adjustments

If your carburetor is equipped with an idle solenoid and idle speed screw, here is how to make the idle speed adjustments.

1. Set the parking brake and block the wheels with wheel chocks.

2. Start the engine and run it long enough to allow it to reach operating temperature.

3. Stop the engine and remove the air filter housing. Refer to the section on "Air Filter Service" in this chapter for removal procedure. **Note:** Any vacuum hoses that have been removed from the air filter housing must be plugged. A golf tee is a good plugging tool. Vacuum

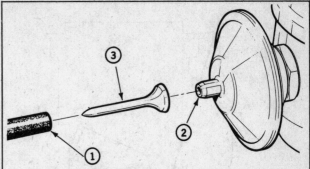

When adjusting idle speed, any vacuum line removed from the air filter housing or carburetor must be plugged. In this illustration, the vacuum hose (1) to the distributor vacuum advance diaphragm (2) is being plugged with a golf tee (3).

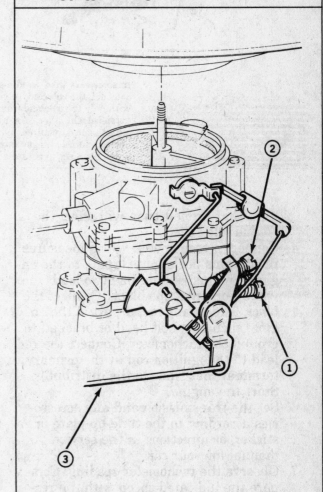

Idle mixture adjustment screws (1) can be turned clockwise or counterclockwise to make the air/fuel ratio leaner or richer. The idle speed adjustment screw (2) operates on the throttle linkage (3) to increase or decrease engine speed. On most late model carburetors, however, the mixture screws are sealed or covered with caps that prevent or limit adjustment.

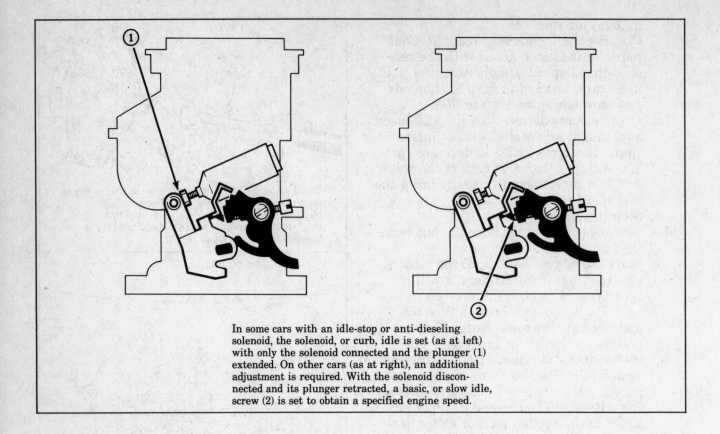

In some cars with an idle-stop or anti-dieseling solenoid, the solenoid, or curb, idle is set (as at left) with only the solenoid connected and the plunger (1) extended. On other cars (as at right), an additional adjustment is required. With the solenoid disconnected and its plunger retracted, a basic, or slow idle, screw (2) is set to obtain a specified engine speed.

lines that are left open will affect the engine idle speed.

4. Connect a tachometer, which measures revolutions per minute (rpm), to the engine. The instrument has two lead wires—one red, one black. Connect the black lead to any metal part of the engine, such as a bolt head or bracket, to ground the tachometer. Connect the red lead to the ignition coil at the primary terminal that leads to the distributor.

5. Start the engine.

6. Set the transmission and any accessories according to the tune-up plate or sticker, or directions in the service manual for your car.

7. Observe the tachometer reading. Compare the indicated speed with the recommended speed. If adjustment is necessary, proceed to Step 8. If no adjustment is required, go to Step 9.

8. This is the solenoid rpm adjustment. Using a wrench, turn the solenoid adjusting nut clockwise to increase rpm, counterclockwise to decrease rpm. Adjust until the specified rpm is reached.

9. This is the basic, or slow idle rpm adjustment. Disconnect the solenoid wire at the spade or bullet connector. This will cause the solenoid plunger to retract.

10. Observe the tachometer. If the indicated speed is at the specified basic idle rpm, no adjustment is required. If it is not, use a screwdriver to turn the idle speed screw until the tachometer indicates the specified rpm.

11. Reconnect the solenoid wire.

12. Depress the accelerator or move the carburetor throttle linkage by hand to increase the engine rpm. This will allow the solenoid plunger to extend to the position of the first adjustment. Release the pressure on the linkage so the engine rpm will come back to idle speed.

13. Observe the tachometer reading. It should be at the specification you set in Step 8. If it is not, make the adjustment at this time.

14. Stop the engine.

15. Replace the air filter housing, but leave the tachometer hooked up.

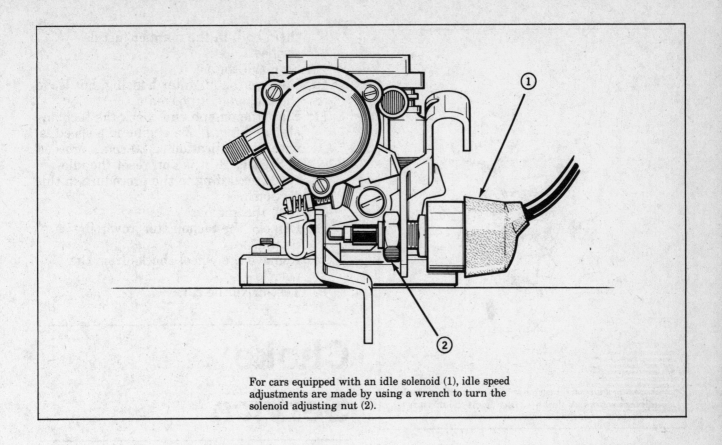

For cars equipped with an idle solenoid (1), idle speed adjustments are made by using a wrench to turn the solenoid adjusting nut (2).

16. Start the engine and check the tachometer reading. If the reading is within specification (± 20 rpm), proceed to the next step. If it is not, make the final adjustment at this time.
17. Stop the engine.
18. Remove the tachometer, reversing Step 4.
19. Remove the wheel chocks from the wheels.
20. Test-drive the car.

Idle Air/Fuel Mixture Adjustments

To make the idle air/fuel mixture adjustments, follow these steps.

1. Set the parking brake and block the wheels with wheel chocks.
2. Start the engine and run it long enough to allow it to reach operating temperature.
3. Stop the engine and remove the air filter housing. Refer to the section on "Air Filter Service" in this chapter for the removal procedure. **Note:** Any vacuum hoses that have been removed from the air filter housing must be plugged. A golf tee is a good plugging tool. Vacuum lines that are left open will affect the engine idle speed.
4. Connect a tachometer, which measures revolutions per minute (rpm), to the engine. The instrument has two lead wires—one red, one black. Connect the black lead to any metal part of the engine such as a bolt head or bracket to ground the tachometer. Connect the red lead to the ignition coil at the primary terminal that leads to the distributor.
5. Start the engine.
6. Set the transmission and any accessories according to the tune-up plate or sticker, or directions in the service manual for your car.
7. Locate the idle air/fuel mixture screws. **Note:** Single-barrel carburetors have one adjusting screw; two- and four-barrel carburetors have two adjusting screws. **Note:** On carburetors with sealed mixture adjustment screws, adjustment is not possible without first

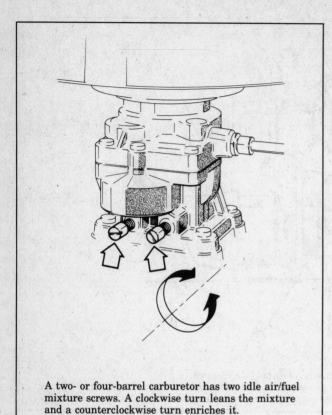

A two- or four-barrel carburetor has two idle air/fuel mixture screws. A clockwise turn leans the mixture and a counterclockwise turn enriches it.

them both in the manner just described.

9. Stop the engine.
10. Replace the air filter housing, but leave the tachometer hooked up.
11. Start the engine and check the tachometer reading. If the engine idle speed is within specification (± 20 rpm), proceed to Step 12. If it is not, reset the idle speed according to the procedure in this section.
12. Stop the engine.
13. Remove the tachometer, reversing Step 4.
14. Remove the wheel chocks from the wheels.
15. Test-drive the car.

Choke Service

Tools and Materials

- Wrench
- Screwdriver
- Rag
- Carburetor and Choke Cleaner Spray
- Thermostatic Spring

drilling or punching out the anti-tamper screw covers. Plastic idle limiter caps can generally be pried or pulled off. Most late model carburetors also have orifice restrictions in the idle mixture metering passages to limit the amount of mixture adjustment that's possible. If correct idle cannot be achieved after repeated attempts to make adjustments, it indicates a problem elsewhere in the carburetor or a vacuum leak.

8. Note the rpm indicated on the tachometer. Using a small screwdriver, carefully turn the adjusting screw in (clockwise) until the engine falters and there is a drop in rpm. When the engine falters, this condition is called the leanroll rpm. Now turn the adjusting screw out (counterclockwise) until the engine speed reaches its highest rpm. This point is said to be the optimum or balanced rpm, and the engine should run very smoothly. If your carburetor has two mixture adjusting screws, adjust

ALL AUTOMOBILES with carburetors use a choke or air valve system to regulate the amount of air that passes into the throat of the carburetor. A cold engine requires a richer mixture of fuel than an engine that is at operating temperature. A richer mixture means that more fuel is allowed into the carburetor. The choke system uses a butterfly-type valve on the top of the carburetor to regulate the flow of air.

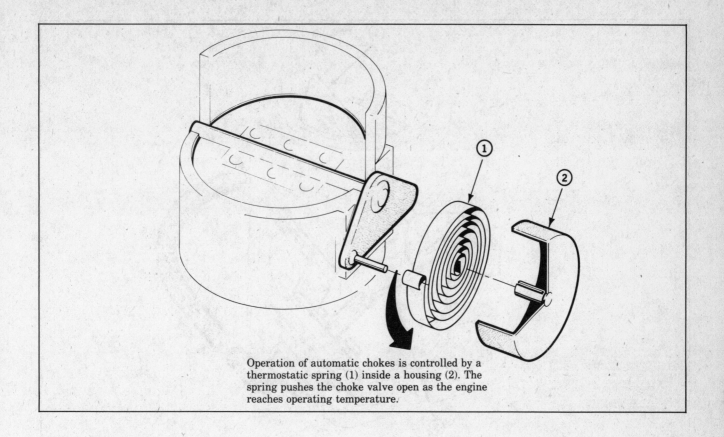

Operation of automatic chokes is controlled by a thermostatic spring (1) inside a housing (2). The spring pushes the choke valve open as the engine reaches operating temperature.

The Automatic Choke

On an automatic choke, the main control is a temperature-sensitive (thermostatic) coil spring. It can be located in the engine intake manifold, where it reacts to engine temperature, or on the carburetor. When the manifold and choke are cold, the spring will tighten, moving the choke linkage to close the butterfly valve, letting in less air and providing a richer air/fuel mixture. But as the engine warms up, the spring will uncoil, opening the choke and thus letting in more air and providing a leaner air/fuel mixture.

A vacuum diaphragm also is located on the carburetor to pull the choke butterfly valve open slightly as soon as the engine starts, to prevent excessive choking and an extra-rich mixture.

There are two main automatic choke problems. The choke butterfly valve may be sticky or the automatic choke thermostatic spring needs adjustment or replacement. As explained, the choke valve—the butterfly-type flap in the top of the carburetor—is designed to close when the car is cold and open when it is warmed up. If the choke does not close when your engine is cold, you will have starting trouble. The mixture will not be rich enough. If it does not open partially when the engine is started, you may get black exhaust smoke, indicating too rich a mixture, and your car will be a "gas gobbler."

Here is how to service an automatic choke.

1. Allow your car to sit long enough to thoroughly cool the engine. Overnight is best.
2. Open the hood and have someone depress the accelerator pedal. You should hear the choke butterfly valve snap shut. If it does not snap shut, slowly loosen the nut on the cover of the air filter housing, listening for the valve to snap shut. If it closes as you are turning the nut, probably something from the air filter housing assembly is restricting the operation of the choke valve. Find the restriction and you will probably solve your choke problem.
3. If the choke butterly valve does not

197

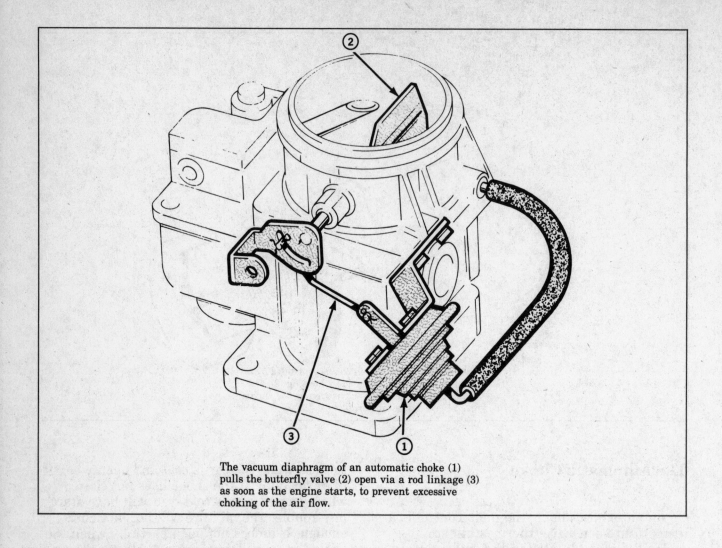

The vacuum diaphragm of an automatic choke (1) pulls the butterfly valve (2) open via a rod linkage (3) as soon as the engine starts, to prevent excessive choking of the air flow.

shut, completely remove the air filter housing as described in the section in this chapter on "Air Filter Service" and have someone depress the accelerator slightly.

4. Now move the choke valve linkage by hand to see if it binds in any position. The choke valve linkage tends to get gummy and sticky and often needs cleaning.

5. Use a carburetor and choke spray cleaner on the linkage and valve. Work the linkage by hand to make certain the parts move freely. Dry all of the parts as much as possible with a clean rag. Wet cleaner on the linkage tends to attract dirt and cause gumming quicker.

6. If all the linkage moves freely and the choke butterfly valve still does not shut, the valve may need adjusting, the thermostatic coil spring may have lost its tension or the spring may be broken. Keep in mind that the butterfly valve is not designed to snap shut if the car is even slightly warmed up. Even if the car is warm, however, you still can check to see if the linkages move freely.

As explained earlier, some cars have the choke thermostat in a metal housing at the base of the carburetor. The spring inside this housing also may lose tension. Generally, the housing and spring are replaceable at a reasonable price. You can also disconnect this linkage at its connection to the carburetor and move it slightly up and down. You should feel spring tension. If you do not, the spring probably is broken, and the unit needs replacement.

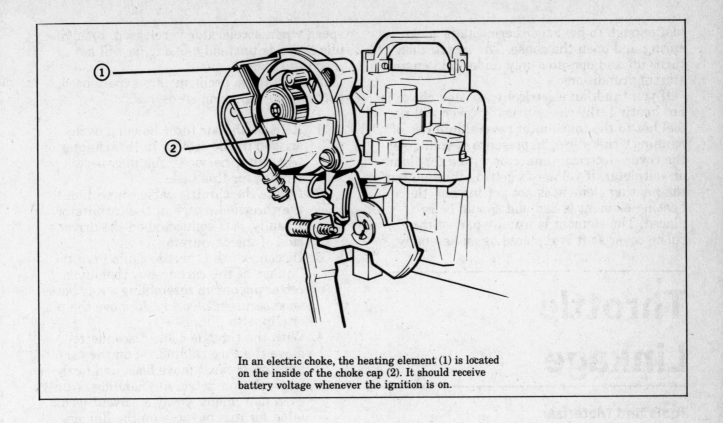

In an electric choke, the heating element (1) is located on the inside of the choke cap (2). It should receive battery voltage whenever the ignition is on.

Servicing an Automatic Adjustable Choke Thermostat

Some cars with an automatic choke still have an adjustable choke thermostat. This component is housed in a round box attached to the outside of the carburetor. Here's how to adjust this.

1. Check the service manual for the correct choke setting.
2. With a screwdriver, loosen—do not remove—the screws holding the unit in place.
3. Slightly turn the cover counterclockwise to feel the spring tension. If there is none, the spring is probably broken and needs replacement. If you feel tension, adjust the choke to specification by lining up the marks on the cover plate.
4. Retighten the screws and check for proper operation.

Electric Assist Chokes

Many cars use an electrically assisted choke. The electric assist is designed to open the choke faster at temperatures of about 60°F or more. This should help reduce exhaust pollution and promote gas economy.

There is a small thermostatic switch near the carburetor that works automatically. When it is on, the switch heats a small coil

The choke thermostat is adjusted by loosening the screws (1) of the choke cover (2) and rotating the cover to line up with indexing marks (3) on the choke housing (4).

just enough to heat the thermostatic choke spring and open the choke. The switch then turns off and operates only under cold engine starting conditions.

If you think an electrically assisted choke is not heating (the choke housing cover will not feel hot to the touch after several minutes of running), check for the presence of voltage at the cover electrical connector with a test lamp or voltmeter. If voltage is getting through but the heating element is not getting hot, the heating element is bad and should be replaced. The element is usually part of the choke cover so it is replaced as an assembly.

Throttle Linkage

Tools and Materials

- Carburetor and Choke Cleaner Spray
- Idle-Return Spring
- Wrench
- Pliers
- Lubricant

THE THROTTLE linkage plays an important role in the overall operation of the automobile engine because it links the driver and the engine. The linkage is attached to the carburetor and a throttle cable or rod connects this linkage to the accelerator pedal. A driver depressing the accelerator pedal moves the throttle linkage, which opens the throttle valve in the carburetor. This action allows more air and fuel to enter the carburetor intake, increasing the speed or revolutions per minute (rpm) of the engine.

For efficient and safe engine operation, the throttle linkage must operate smoothly without sticking or binding. Signs of linkage problems include: a) engine will not return to idle

speed when accelerator is released; b) engine idle speed is unsteady; c) engine will not reach full rpm.

If any of these problems are experienced, perform the following steps.

1. Remove the air filter housing as described in the section in this chapter on "Air Filter Service." You may need a wrench for this task.
2. Locate the throttle cable connection to the throttle linkage at the carburetor. Usually, it is connected on the driver's side of the carburetor.
3. Disconnect the throttle cable from the linkage at the carburetor. Usually, a cotter pin or clip resembling a tiny horseshoe secures the cable. Remove the pin or clip with pliers.
4. With the throttle cable disconnected, move the throttle linkage on the carburetor. It must move back and forth freely. If you detect any binding or uneven movement, spray a solvent formulated for this purpose on the linkage and inside the carburetor at the shaft holding the throttle valve in place. Often, any binding or uneven movement here can be corrected by cleaning with a solvent. If this does not correct the problem, the carburetor should be repaired.
5. With the throttle cable still disconnected from the linkage (and any binding corrected), move the accelerator pedal up and down. If any binding or uneven movement is discovered here, start at the carburetor and follow the throttle cable housing toward the engine compartment firewall. Inspect the cable and its housing for sharp bends or kinks. Minor relocation of the cable and its housing will usually correct binding if sharp bends are found. Never attempt to straighten a cable or its housing if there are kinks in it. If kinks exist, replacement is necessary.
6. In the passenger compartment, check the accelerator pedal and its mounting. Sometimes a small drop of lubricant on the pedal's hinge will correct any binding here.
7. Reconnect the throttle cable to the

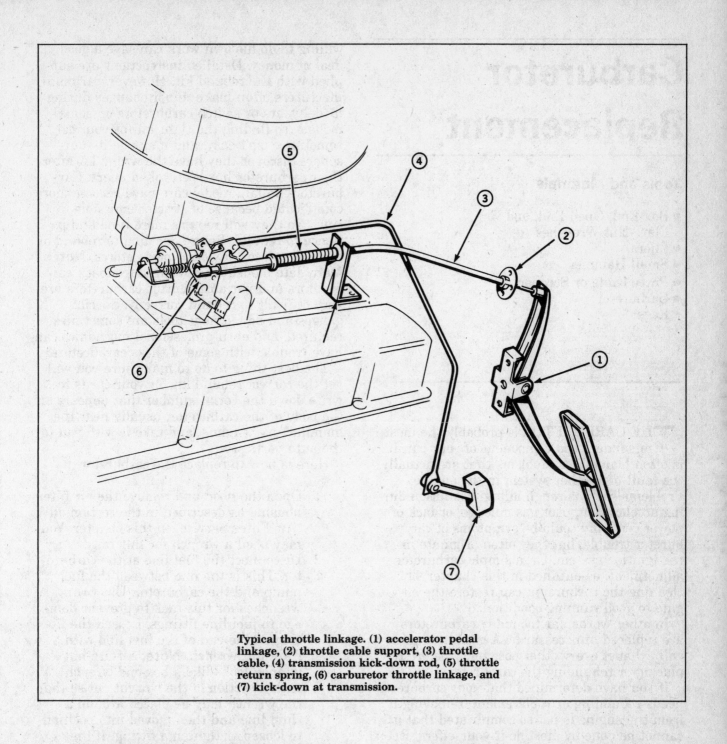

Typical throttle linkage. (1) accelerator pedal linkage, (2) throttle cable support, (3) throttle cable, (4) transmission kick-down rod, (5) throttle return spring, (6) carburetor throttle linkage, and (7) kick-down at transmission.

throttle linkage on the carburetor.

8. Have someone depress the accelerator all the way to the floor while you check at the carburetor to see if the throttle valve goes to the full open position when the accelerator is depressed. Use a wrench to adjust the throttle cable (turn the adjusting nut clockwise or counterclockwise as necessary) to obtain a full open throttle valve position.

9. Release the accelerator pedal, allowing it to return to the idle position. If it does not return to the idle position smoothly, replace the idle return spring on the carburetor. The idle return spring is between the carburetor and the throttle linkage.

10. Replace the air filter housing.

Carburetor Replacement

Tools and Materials

- Box-End, Open-End, and Flare-Nut Wrenches
- Pliers
- Small Hammer
- Putty Knife or Scraper
- Carburetor
- Rags

THE CARBURETOR is probably the most misunderstood component of your car. It is often blamed for problems that are actually the fault of another system in the engine. Problems such as rough idling, hesitation during acceleration, poor gas mileage, or lack of power certainly could be symptoms of carburetor trouble, but they often originate in the ignition system. Or, a simple carburetor adjustment, as outlined in this chapter, or cleaning the carburetor, can restore the engine to good running condition.

In other words, far too many carburetors are replaced unnecessarily. A good mechanic will exhaust every other possibility before replacing or rebuilding the carburetor.

If you have determined that your carburetor needs rebuilding or replacement, removing it from the engine is not so complicated that it cannot be done by most do-it-yourselfers. Remember, however, every car manufacturer has its own carburetor design, so removal and replacement procedures will vary to some degree. As a general rule, though, the guidelines presented here will apply to most installations.

Most rebuild kits for carburetors cost less than $25, while a remanufactured carburetor will cost far more, so the car owner who is willing to do his own work can save a good deal of money. Detailed instructions are supplied with the rebuild kit. However, car manufacturers often make minor changes during model years or switch carburetors on some models, so finding the right kit for your car sometimes isn't easy, and many do-it-yourselfers discover they have the wrong kit after their carburetor has been taken apart. Carburetors on late model cars have become more complicated because of stricter emissions rules, so they will require more time and patience to rebuild. Before deciding to rebuild or replace, ask for advice at parts stores. **Note:** Many late model computerized feedback carburetors and variable venturi carburetors are very difficult to rebuild correctly. Special gauges and adjustment tools are sometimes required, and even professional mechanics can have trouble with some of these carburetors.

The best thing to do to make sure you will get the correct rebuild kit for your car is to write down the serial number that appears on the body of the carburetor, usually near the manufacturer's name, and take it with you to the auto parts store.

Here is how to replace the carburetor.

1. Open the hood and remove the air filter housing as described in the section on "Air Filter Service" in this chapter. You may need a wrench for this task.
2. Disconnect the fuel line at the carburetor. This is the line between the fuel pump and the carburetor. Use two wrenches for this task to prevent damage to fuel line fittings. Loosen the fitting on the end of the fuel line with a flare-nut wrench. **Note:** A flare-nut wrench looks like a box-end wrench with a section of the box cut out so that the wrench may be placed around a fluid line and then moved into position to loosen or tighten a fitting. If the larger fitting on the carburetor also turns, use an open-end wrench to keep it from turning. This is necessary so that you will not damage the fuel line when disconnecting it.
3. Disconnect all other hose connections. Tag these hoses so that it will be easier to reconnect them. **Note:** There may be wires to such things as a transmission

kick-down switch, throttle position sensor, idle switch, air conditioning idle speed-up switch, or an anti-dieseling solenoid. Be sure to mark each of these wires as they are removed so that you can replace them.

4. Disconnect the throttle cable from the throttle linkage at the carburetor. Usually, this is held in place by a cotter pin or a clip that resembles a tiny horseshoe. Use pliers to remove it.

5. Disconnect the choke cable from the choke linkage at the carburetor. Here, too, there will either be a clip or pin. Use pliers to remove it. Also, note the location of the choke rod. Sometimes, it can fit into more than one hole.

6. Using a wrench of proper size, remove the carburetor's mounting nuts, turning them counterclockwise. These nuts are at the base of the carburetor and secure the component to studs on the engine intake manifold. Depending on the type of carburetor, there will be two or four mounting nuts.

7. With the mounting nuts removed, lift the carburetor upward and remove it from the engine compartment. **Note:** There is a gasket between the carburetor and the intake manifold. Sometimes this gasket will prevent the carburetor from being removed easily. If this is the case, use a small hammer to tap lightly around the base of the carburetor to loosen it.

8. As you remove the carburetor, see if there is one or more gaskets or metal plates between the carburetor and intake manifold. Make a note of this for reinstallation.

9. Place a clean rag into the intake manifold inlet and scrape the carburetor mounting surface clean of any old gasket material. Use a putty knife or scraper. Do not allow any of this material to fall into the intake manifold.

10. When the mounting surface is clean, remove the rag from the intake manifold and position a new carburetor gasket. It will be supplied with the carburetor. At this time, also reinstall any gaskets or plates removed in Step 8. **Note:** A new carburetor base gasket should always

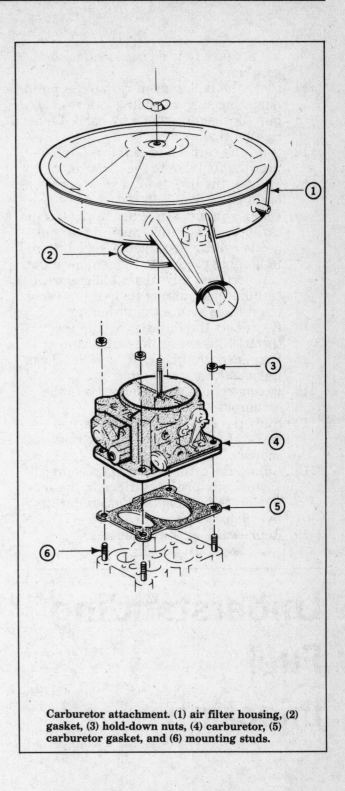

Carburetor attachment. (1) air filter housing, (2) gasket, (3) hold-down nuts, (4) carburetor, (5) carburetor gasket, and (6) mounting studs.

be used to prevent leaks. The application of a thin coating of gasket sealer to both sides of the gasket is also recommended to form an airtight seal. Do not use RTV silicone type sealants on carburetor gaskets or to form a base gasket because they do not stand up to gasoline.

11. Place the replacement carburetor on the mounting surface and replace the carburetor mounting nuts by hand. Do not tighten them.

12. With the carburetor still loose, reconnect the fuel line to the carburetor. Tighten the line, using two wrenches as outlined in Step 2.

13. Using a proper-size wrench, tighten the carburetor mounting nuts. Be careful not to overtighten them. Use a diagonal tightening pattern to tighten down the carburetor evenly. You could crack the carburetor mounting flange. Just snug the nuts to secure the carburetor.

14. Reconnect the throttle cable to the throttle linkage at the carburetor.

15. Reconnect the choke cable to the choke linkage at the carburetor.

16. Reconnect all hoses and wires to the carburetor.

17. Start the engine and check for fuel leaks. If any are found, locate the source of the leak and repair it.

18. Adjust the carburetor idle speed and air/fuel mixture as outlined in the section on "Adjusting the Carburetor" in this chapter.

19. Replace the air filter housing.

Understanding Fuel Injection

ALTHOUGH FUEL INJECTION has been around for many years, the advent of electronic fuel injection has numbered the days of the carburetor. Fuel injection's advantages are numerous: easier cold starting, better performance, more precise control over air/ fuel mixtures for improved fuel economy and reduced emissions. It also eliminates the need for a choke, accelerator pump, and idle stop solenoid. With so much in its favor, it's not surprising that most new cars today are being equipped with one form or another of electronic fuel injection.

The main difference between a carburetor and fuel injection is that fuel is drawn into the engine by vacuum in a carburetor, whereas with fuel injection it is sprayed or injected into the engine under pressure. When air passes down through the narrow part of a carburetor's throat (called the venturi), it creates a difference in pressure between the air in the venturi and that in the carburetor fuel bowl. This difference in pressure draws the fuel through the carburetor's main jets and metering passages and into the venturi where it mixes with the air and passes into the intake manifold.

With fuel injection, fuel metering is not dependent on differences in air pressure. Fuel is sprayed into the incoming air stream, creating a much finer fuel mist that promotes better fuel atomization and mixing. The amount of fuel that's injected depends only on the volume of air entering the engine and engine load. This is where the electronic part comes in, because it takes a computer and various engine sensors to calculate how much fuel is needed to maintain the correct air/fuel ratio.

There are essentially two types of electronic fuel injection: throttle-body injection and multi-point injection. In throttle-body systems, one or two injectors are mounted in a throttle-body housing that resembles a carburetor externally. But instead of all the fuel metering circuits and components you'd expect to find in a carburetor, the throttle-body is essentially a hollow shell that serves only to position the fuel injectors over the throttle plates. The throttle-body is mounted in the same position as a carburetor would be. The throttle-body system consists of a high-pressure electric fuel pump (usually mounted in or near the fuel tank), a fuel filter, a pressure regulator (to maintain even fuel pressure to the injectors), the throttle-body with one or two injectors, and the engine-control computer and its sensors.

The injectors are nothing mysterious. They're simply spray nozzles that are opened

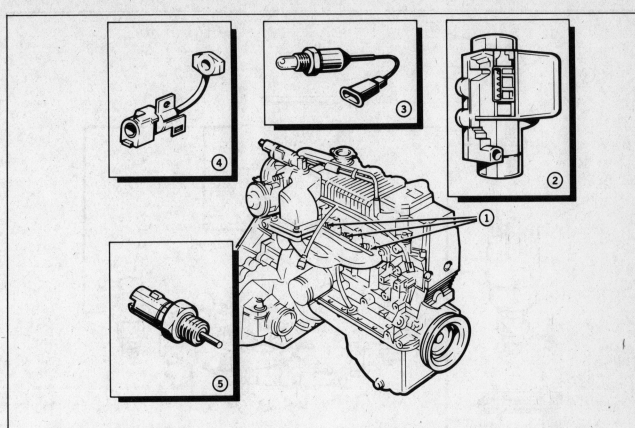

A port (or multi-point) fuel injection system has an injector (1) for each cylinder mounted in the intake manifold. The injectors spray fuel directly into the intake ports. This type of system requires an air flow sensor, in this case a vane-type (2) to measure the volume of air entering the engine so the computer can determine proper fuel metering. Other common sensors include those for oxygen (3), throttle position (4), and coolant temperature (5).

by applying voltage to a built-in solenoid. In other words, when the injector is energized, the solenoid pulls open a pintle valve allowing fuel to spray out of the injector. The injectors do not spray continuously but rather in short bursts. The duration of these bursts is controlled by engine speed and the engine-control computer. This is how the computer regulates the air/fuel ratio.

In multi-point electronic fuel injection systems, the basics are still the same except that each cylinder has its own fuel injector. A V6, for example, would have six fuel injectors while a four cylinder would have four injectors. Instead of mounting the injectors in a centrally located throttle-body, the injectors are mounted on the intake manifold so that they spray fuel directly into the intake ports of each cylinder (which is why it's sometimes called "port" injection). This promotes better cylinder-to-cylinder fuel distribution and eliminates any air/fuel separation that might otherwise occur in the intake manifold. That's why multi-point injection is considered to be the "performance" fuel injection system.

Air entering a multi-point fuel injection system first passes through a device known as an *air flow sensor*. This tells the computer how much air is entering the engine so the computer can add the right amount of fuel. A *throttle position sensor* on the throttle plates tells the computer how wide open the throttle is, and additional inputs from a *barometric pressure sensor, inlet air temperature sensor,* and *manifold pressure sensor* tell the computer if it should compensate for changes in air density and engine load. An *oxygen sensor* in the exhaust manifold keeps the computer informed about the relative richness or leanness of the fuel mixture, and an *engine tem-*

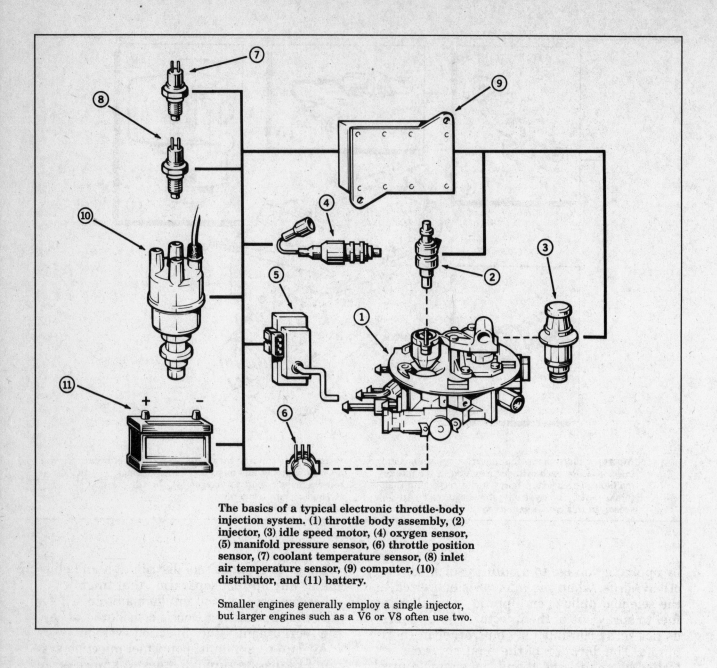

The basics of a typical electronic throttle-body injection system. (1) throttle body assembly, (2) injector, (3) idle speed motor, (4) oxygen sensor, (5) manifold pressure sensor, (6) throttle position sensor, (7) coolant temperature sensor, (8) inlet air temperature sensor, (9) computer, (10) distributor, and (11) battery.

Smaller engines generally employ a single injector, but larger engines such as a V6 or V8 often use two.

perature sensor monitors engine coolant temperature. The computer receives inputs from all these sensors and then calculates according to its built-in program how rich or how lean to make the fuel mixture depending on the operating circumstances of the engine. It does this by increasing the duration the injectors are open to richen the mixture, or decreasing the duration to lean the mixture. It's a complex system, but one that allows very precise control over fuel delivery, exhaust emissions, and performance.

It should be obvious that to function properly, all the engine sensors must be working and feeding correct information to the computer. If one or more of the sensors are faulty, the computer will not be able to determine the correct fuel mixture. Most electronic fuel injection systems have a certain amount of built-in self-diagnostics to detect sensor problems. If a sensor is not producing a signal, the computer will note it and store a "trouble code" in its internal memory. Depending on the nature of the failure, it may cause a warning light such as the check engine light on your dash to come on. At that point, you should take your car to someone who knows how to troubleshoot electronic fuel injection for repair. Correct diagnosis depends on following the step-by-step instructions in the manufacturer's repair manual; trying to figure out what's wrong without the right manual is next to impossible.

When the mechanic gets your car, he will put the computer into a self-diagnostic mode so it will give him any trouble codes stored in memory. On some vehicles, the codes are read by counting the flashes of the check engine light while on others special diagnostic test equipment is needed to read the codes. From there, he'll proceed through a step-by-step test sequence until the fault is isolated.

It's important to note that the engine computer and its sensors are considered part of your vehicle's emission-control system. They are therefore covered under the manufacturer's 5-year/50,000 mile emissions warranty. This warranty applies to all vehicles sold in the United States since 1981, and covers all emission-control devices, as well as related systems which can affect emissions, such as fuel delivery, ignition, and computerized engine controls. The warranty entitles you to free repairs for the duration of the warranty period at an authorized dealer on defective emission-control components, but does not cover scheduled replacement parts.

As a do-it-yourself mechanic, there aren't a lot of things you can service on most electronic fuel injection systems unless you're fairly knowledgeable and have the right repair manuals and test equipment. And unless you know what you're doing, there's the possibility of damaging the computer and/or sensors. Never pull any wiring connectors apart on the engine control system while the ignition is on and never attempt to jump, ground, or test sensors unless you're specifically told to do so in a repair manual. The computer and sensors are very vulnerable to voltage overloads; crossing up the wrong wires or grounding out a live circuit could easily damage a component in the system.

Even without a lot of detailed knowledge, though, you can still get an idea of what's wrong should a problem develop. Electronic fuel injection requires several things to function properly: adequate fuel pressure (which requires a good pump and clean filter), accurate measurement of the incoming air and engine functions (which requires that all the sensors be working correctly) and proper operation of the fuel injectors (which requires a good electrical contact with the control wire, correct fuel pressure and opening and closing of the pintle valve). We've already covered how to check and replace an electric fuel pump, as well as filter service, earlier in this chapter. Troubleshooting sensor problems, as we said earlier, is best left to someone who knows what they're doing. As for the fuel injectors, an inoperative injector (no voltage reaching the injector, a faulty pintle valve, or a clogged orifice) won't spray fuel, resulting in a dead engine on systems with only one injector, a severe loss of power on throttle-body systems with two injectors, or a noticeable miss and rough idle on multi-point systems. If an injector fails to close completely, it will dribble fuel, resulting in excessive fuel consumption, a rich mixture, and possibly a rough idle. On multi-point injection systems, you can use a power balance test to isolate a problem injector (see the chapter on "The Engine"). For throttle-body systems, direct observation can tell you a lot. If the injector(s) is working correctly, you should see a cone-shaped spray pattern when the engine is revved.

If you encounter idle problems on a fuel injection system (too fast or too slow) you'll quickly discover there's no place to adjust the idle speed as with a carburetor. On fuel injection systems, the idle is controlled by a small air bleed passageway and idle speed control motor. The computer monitors engine speed and adjusts the size of the air bleed passageway by running a small plunger on the end of the idle speed motor in or out. If the motor fails or the passageway becomes blocked, it should be obvious that the engine will experience idle problems, but an often overlooked problem is a vacuum leak that permits "unmetered" air to enter the engine. Since the computer thinks this air is coming through the idle circuit, it will attempt to shut it off. This only serves to further compound the problem of metering the air, so idle quality suffers. It's important, therefore, to make sure the air filter is clean and to check for vacuum leaks whenever a performance problem is noticed.

Understanding Diesel Injection

THE POPULARITY of diesel engines for automotive applications seems to wax and wane with the price and availability of gasoline, but diesel engines do have inherent advantages (and disadvantages) when compared to gasoline powerplants. On the plus side, diesel engines have a much higher thermal efficiency rating which means they generally deliver much better fuel mileage. A diesel can run on much leaner fuel mixtures and exhaust emissions (with the exception of soot and nitrous oxides) are fairly low. Since there's no ignition system, periodic spark plug replacement and all of the maintenance associated with an ignition system are eliminated.

On the other hand, diesels have some drawbacks that make them less attractive than gasoline engines for certain applications. Because of increased cylinder blow-by, more frequent oil changes are usually recommended for diesel engines. They tend to be noisy and can be hard to start during cold weather. The diesel injection system is also vulnerable to water contamination as well as dirt, making clean fuel an absolute must for trouble-free operation.

The basic difference between a diesel engine

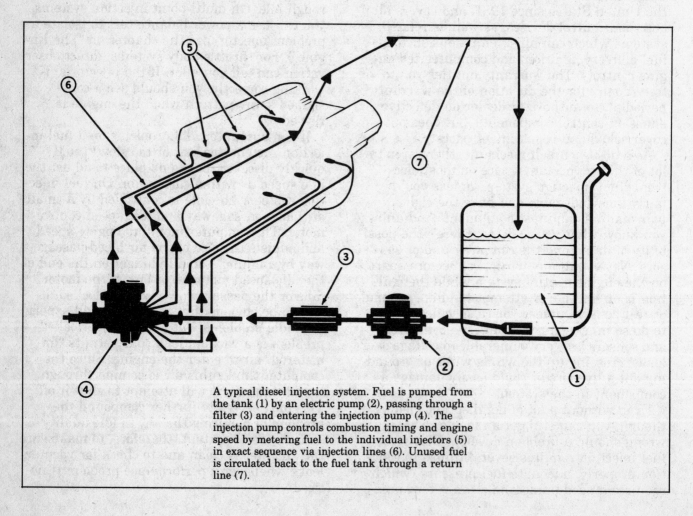

A typical diesel injection system. Fuel is pumped from the tank (1) by an electric pump (2), passing through a filter (3) and entering the injection pump (4). The injection pump controls combustion timing and engine speed by metering fuel to the individual injectors (5) in exact sequence via injection lines (6). Unused fuel is circulated back to the fuel tank through a return line (7).

and a gasoline engine is that a diesel engine uses the heat of compression to ignite the fuel, whereas gasoline engines use a spark provided by a spark plug and ignition system. To accomplish this, diesel engines run much higher compression ratios, say 16:1 up to 22:1. Compressing the air to such an extent heats it up to close to 1000°F, which is hot enough to ignite fuel spontaneously when fuel is injected directly into the combustion chamber.

Unlike a gasoline fuel injection system, where fuel is shot into the intake manifold or into the cylinder intake ports, a diesel injector is mounted in the cylinder head where it sprays fuel directly into the combustion chamber. To overcome the pressure in the cylinder, therefore, the injector must operate at a very high pressure: 1100 to 4000 psi depending on the system and type of injector it uses.

A diesel engine also has no throttle. Air enters the engine through the air filter and proceeds directly into the intake manifold. There is no carburetor or throttle-body to restrict the air flow, so there is no vacuum in the intake manifold on a diesel engine. And, unlike a gasoline engine where engine speed is controlled by opening and closing the throttle, engine speed in a diesel is controlled entirely by fuel metering through the diesel injection pump.

The diesel injection pump is the brains of the system. It's a complex and precisely machined piece of equipment. It takes diesel fuel from the incoming fuel line, boosts it to extremely high pressure and directs metered amounts of fuel to each of the engine's individual injectors in timed pulses. The amount of fuel delivered determines how much power is produced and how fast the engine runs.

Since there is no ignition system, the instant at which fuel is injected into the cylinder must be timed exactly to control combustion. At fast idle, say around 1200 rpm, injection timing for most engines will be around 4 to 8 degrees before top dead center. As engine rpms increase, the injection pump will compensate and advance injection timing so the fuel will have adequate time to burn.

When starting a diesel engine, especially on a cold morning, the heat of compression may not be sufficient to ignite the fuel, so an auxiliary heating sytem is required. This is the *glow plug* system. Each cylinder has a small screw-in heating element (the glow plug) that glows red hot when voltage is applied. The glow plugs are energized when the ignition is first turned on and remain energized until a timer turns them off within a minute or so after the engine starts. Cold starting problems, therefore, can often be traced to a faulty glow plug system or burned out glow plugs. Glow plugs can be replaced like spark plugs if they become defective. Glow plugs are checked by measuring their electrical resistance with an ohmmeter.

A diesel engine will continue to run once started as long as the injection pump continues to receive fuel. The only way to shut it off is to shut off the flow of fuel. When you turn the ignition off, a fuel shut-off solenoid on the injection pump closes, blocking the flow of fuel. An engine that fails to start can sometimes be caused by a loose wire on this solenoid, or a problem in the circuit that supplies voltage to it.

In terms of maintenance, clean fuel is extremely important. Water can corrode the closely fitted components in the injection pump, causing them to stick and rendering the pump useless. Dirt can do the same thing, so regular fuel filter inspection and replacement is very important. Fuel filter service is covered earlier in this chapter.

The injection pump itself is a precision assembly, which means that under no circumstances should you attempt to take it apart. Rebuilding an injection pump is akin to a surgical procedure requiring special skills and very expensive test equipment. If your pump calls it quits, turn it over to a professional for service. You can change the pump yourself, but on some vehicles timing is rather tricky and requires special gauges for accurate adjustment. Timing is basically a matter of rotating the pump in its mount (with the engine off) until the pump is positioned to deliver fuel at the right number of degrees before top dead center. On some vehicles a reference mark is provided to align the pump. On others there are none. Refer to a shop manual *before* you attempt to change a pump yourself.

As for troubleshooting diesel injection problems, the injectors are subject to clogging and leaking. A clogged injector won't deliver fuel to its cylinder, so a miss and loss of power will be obvious. You can sometimes spot an in-

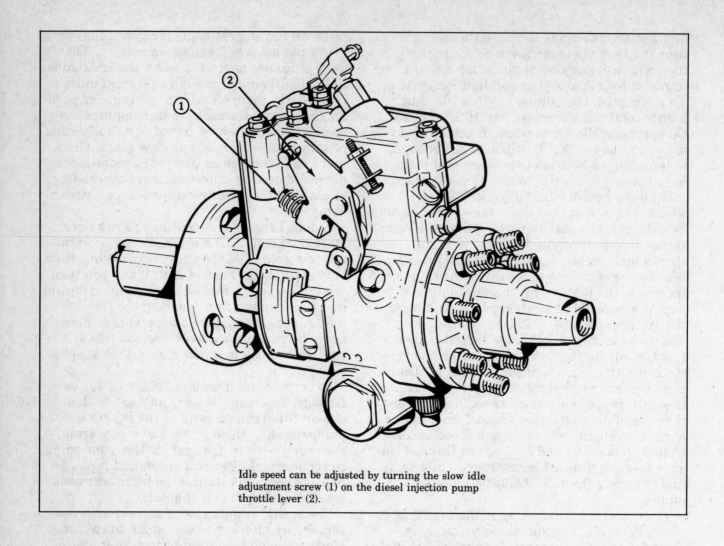

Idle speed can be adjusted by turning the slow idle adjustment screw (1) on the diesel injection pump throttle lever (2).

operative injector by carefully feeling the exhaust manifold after starting a cold engine. *Caution: The exhaust manifolds will become extremely hot very quickly, so use care not to burn yourself. But a cylinder that is misfiring will not produce heat, so the exhaust outlet for that cylinder will not heat up as quickly.*

A leaking injector will dribble fuel into the cylinder and a weak injector will open too soon. In either case, combustion will be affected, resulting in increased exhaust soot, loss of power, and increased fuel consumption. If the injection pump is not timed correctly (over or under advanced), the engine will be excessively noisy and increased exhaust soot will be noticed.

Idle Speed Adjustment

You can adjust the idle speed on most diesel injection pumps by simply turning an idle screw on the throttle linkage. To adjust idle, proceed as follows.

1. Locate the position of the idle speed adjustment screw. Refer to a shop manual for the exact location on your vehicle's pump.
2. Connect a diesel tachometer that can read rpm based on rotation of the crankshaft pulley to the engine. Some of these use a magnetic pickup, an optical pickup, or a rotating wheel to measure engine speed.
3. Start the engine, allow it to reach normal operating temperature, then turn the idle speed adjusting screw until the desired idle speed is achieved. Idle specs should be included on the under-hood emissions decal or in your shop manual.

Turbocharging

TURBOCHARGING has become a popular technique for boosting the power output of small-displacement engines without adversely affecting fuel mileage. A turbocharger is nothing more than an exhaust-driven compressor that forces more air into the engine on demand. By forcing more air into the engine, it makes a little engine behave as though it had a much larger displacement. Thus, turbochargers are used to boost power and enhance performance.

The amount of boost pressure developed by the turbocharger depends on engine speed and throttle opening. In other words, the greater the volume of air passing through the engine, the greater the boost pressure developed. The turbocharger is driven by hot exhaust gases exiting through the exhaust manifold. Exhaust gases are routed into the turbine housing to spin the turbine wheel. A shaft connects the turbine wheel to a compressor wheel at the other end of the turbocharger. The faster the turbo spins, the more air it draws through the compressor housing and rams into the engine. At full throttle, the turbo can be spinning in excess of 150,000 rpm. Maximum boost pressure depends on the size of the unit, but most factory installed turbochargers develop boost pressures in the 6- to 14-pound range.

Boost pressure is what makes horsepower, and the greater the boost pressure, the

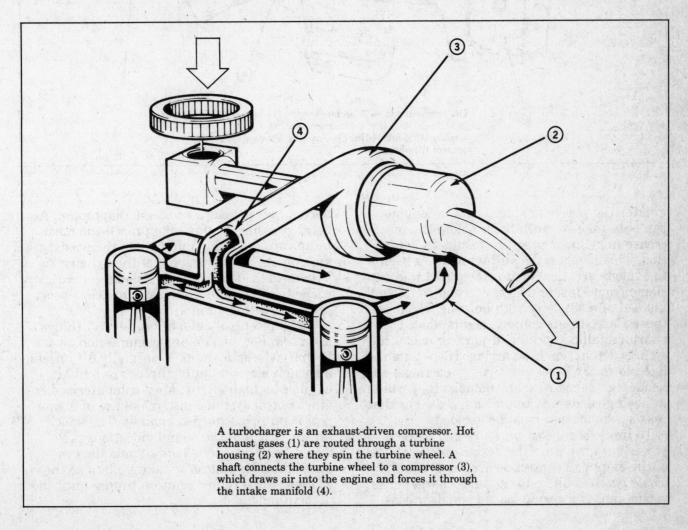

A turbocharger is an exhaust-driven compressor. Hot exhaust gases (1) are routed through a turbine housing (2) where they spin the turbine wheel. A shaft connects the turbine wheel to a compressor (3), which draws air into the engine and forces it through the intake manifold (4).

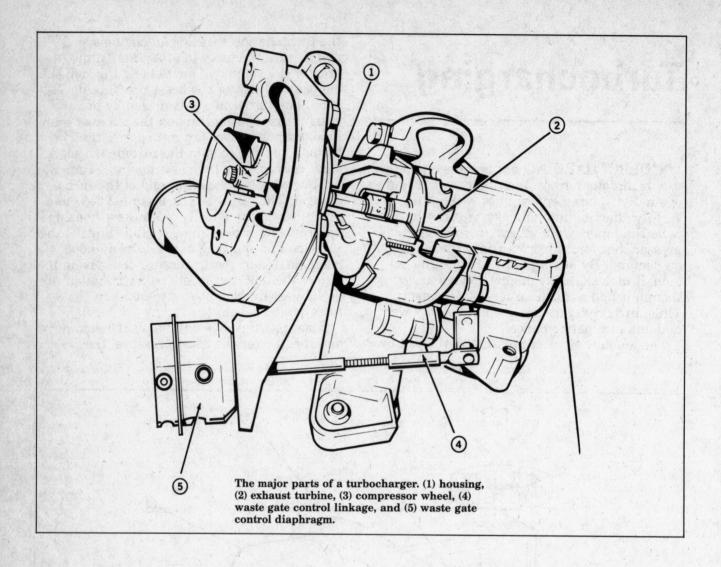

The major parts of a turbocharger. (1) housing, (2) exhaust turbine, (3) compressor wheel, (4) waste gate control linkage, and (5) waste gate control diaphragm.

greater the power produced. But an engine can only take so much boost before the increase in cylinder pressure results in detonation. This is when the air/fuel mixture begins to explode erratically, producing multiple flame fronts inside the combustion chamber instead of a single smooth-burning flame. As these flame fronts collide, they produce the sharp metallic knocking or pinging noise that signals detonation is occurring. These hammer-like blows can crack pistons, piston rings, and heads, not to mention the damage they can do to head gaskets and connecting rods. For that reason, detonation must be avoided.

To limit total boost pressure and to keep power output within the design specifications of the engine, a control device known as the *waste gate* is built into the turbocharger. The waste gate is a spring-loaded trapdoor con-

nected to a pressure-sensitive diaphragm. As boost pressure begins to approach the maximum rating for the application, the waste gate opens, allowing some of the exhaust to bypass the turbine wheel. This keeps the turbo from spinning too fast and keeps boost pressure within limits.

To help control detonation, several things are used. For one, engine compression on turbocharged applications is normally 8:1 or less, although a few manufacturers are building engines as high as 9:1. Most computerized engine control systems also make use of a *knock sensor* on turbocharged engines. The knock sensor reacts to the sound vibrations produced by detonation. This signals the computer that detonation is taking place so the computer can retard ignition timing until the detonation stops.

Turbocharger Precautions

Because of the high rotational speeds at which the turbocharger operates, lubrication of the turbo shaft bearings is extremely important. The oil used in a turbocharged engine should be a top-quality lubricant meeting or exceeding the manufacturer's recommendations. Oil change intervals of 3000 miles are also recommended because the temperatures inside the turbocharger housing can sometimes exceed 300°F. At such elevated temperatures, motor oil begins to oxidize and form charred deposits that can interfere with shaft lubrication.

When changing the oil and filter, the system should always be primed prior to starting by cranking the engine for 10 to 15 seconds with the coil wire grounded or the ignition lead removed. This will prevent a dry start which could otherwise damage the turbocharger shaft bearings.

In terms of general driving techniques, you should never start a turbocharged engine and drive it hard until the oil has had a chance to warm up. When shutting the engine off, allow it to idle for at least 15 seconds or so to give the turbocharger time to slow down. As soon as the engine stops running, oil pressure is lost. If the turbo is still spinning at high speed, the bearings will quickly run out of oil and may be damaged. Because of this, never rev the engine as you're about to shut it off. Some manufacturers have added water-cooling circuits to turbochargers to extend bearing life.

Turbocharger Diagnosis

There are three common problems you may encounter on turbocharged engines: turbocharger noise, overboost, and underboost. Scraping or rubbing noises mean the bearings are worn or damaged and the turbo wheels are scraping against their housings. This will reduce turbo speed and limit boost pressure. The cure is to replace the turbocharger.

Overboost causes detonation. Assuming the problem is not due to over-advanced ignition timing and/or a faulty knock sensor, the most likely cause is a defective waste gate. A ruptured waste gate diaphragm, loose or ob-structed waste gate hose, or a buildup of rust or carbon in the waste gate housing can prevent it from opening when it should. The easiest way to tell whether or not the waste gate is working is simply to watch the linkage while an assistant revs the engine. If it doesn't move, remove the waste gate and try to manually operate the linkage to check for binding. The waste gate diaphragm can be checked with a handheld vacuum pump for leaks. If the waste gate diaphragm is defective, it should be replaced with an identical unit. Installing a waste gate that opens at a higher boost pressure may increase horsepower, but it may also exceed your engine's ability to handle it.

Underboost can be caused by a waste gate control door that's stuck open, or by a sluggish turbo. By sluggish, we mean a turbocharger whose bearings are worn or damaged to the point where they prevent the turbo from achieving full speed or allow the turbocharger wheels to drag against their respective housings. Anything that interferes with the free rotation of the turbo will limit boost and engine performance. To check for this condition, remove either the compressor inlet or outlet duct. Use a flashlight to look inside the housing for signs of rubbing or compressor wheel damage. Dirt or debris can sometimes get into the system and damage the wheel. If everything looks okay, try spinning the turbocharger by hand. It should turn freely and smoothly. There should be no free-play if you try to push the wheel in or pull it out (actual tolerances range from .001 to .003 inches).

Turbocharger Replacement

If your turbocharger is found to be damaged, worn, or otherwise defective, you can replace it yourself. It's basically a matter of unbolting and removing the old unit and installing a new one in its place. Be sure to use new gaskets where gaskets are required and tighten all fasteners to the manufacturer's recommended specifications. Be careful not to allow any dirt, debris or old gasket material to fall into the turbo ducting as this could damage the new unit. Don't forget to prime the turbocharger oil supply line by cranking the engine prior to starting the engine.

Computerized Engine Controls

COMPUTERIZED ENGINE CONTROL systems are widely used on most 1981 and newer automobiles, though some earlier model vehicles also have them. Auto manufacturers went to computerized engine controls as a means of achieving lower exhaust emissions and better fuel economy. Such systems are considered far superior to the older mechanical and vacuum engine control systems, because the computer can react almost instantly to changing operating conditions. It also does so with far greater precision and accuracy than mechanical control devices. What's more, since there are no mechanical components to wear out, maintenance is reduced and reliability improved.

Computerized engine controls are used to control three main engine functions: fuel, ignition, and emissions. By constantly changing the air/fuel ratio either through a variable *mixture control solenoid* in a carburetor or by varying the pulse duration of the fuel injectors, it can maintain the best fuel mixture under all operating conditions for performance, economy, and low emissions. The computer also monitors spark timing and advances or retards ignition timing as needed. Finally, it regulates when certain emission-control devices are activated, so they don't interfere with engine warm-up or driving performance.

The heart of a computerized engine control system is obviously the computer, a small microprocessor similar in function and design to a personal computer. The computer is often referred to as the *electronic control module* (ECM). The computer monitors up to a dozen or more engine functions through its sensors. The functions monitored include engine coolant temperature, throttle position, intake manifold pressure, barometric pressure, inlet air temperature, exhaust oxygen content, battery voltage, vehicle speed, air conditioning compressor engagement, transmission gear selection, boost pressure (turbocharged engines only), engine speed and, on some, even brake pedal engagement. On many turbocharged engines, a knock sensor is also included to detect detonation.

Based on what the sensors tell it, the computer calculates the optimum air/fuel ratio for the particular set of operating conditions, as well as spark timing and which emission control functions should be activated. On many systems, the computer also controls idle speed. For carbureted engines, a small stepper motor is used to open or close the throttle, while on fuel injected engines, a small motor opens and closes an air bypass valve.

The emission-control functions usually regulated by the computer include the *exhaust gas recirculation* (EGR) valve, the *charcoal canister,* and the *air pump diverter valve.* For example, the computer won't allow the EGR valve to open until the engine has warmed up and is running above idle. Opening the EGR valve while the engine is cold or during idle would cause rough running. The computer also waits to purge the charcoal canister of fuel vapors until the engine is warm and is running at cruising speed. The computer must also determine how to divert the air pump's output so air goes either to the exhaust manifold or to the catalytic converter.

On cars with automatic transmissions and lockup torque converters, the computer will monitor vehicle speed and engage the torque converter lockup solenoid when the vehicle reaches a predetermined speed.

How the computer makes its decisions and calculations is determined by its calibration unit, sometimes called the *PROM* (Program Read Only Memory). The PROM tells the computer how to control the various engine functions based on a complex set of circumstances. In effect, this creates a map for the computer to follow so it will know what to do at any given instant in time. The computer's PROM is programmed by the vehicle manufacturer for a specific application. Things such as engine size, fuel system, axle ratio, transmission, vehicle make and model, high or low altitude application, and accessories all have

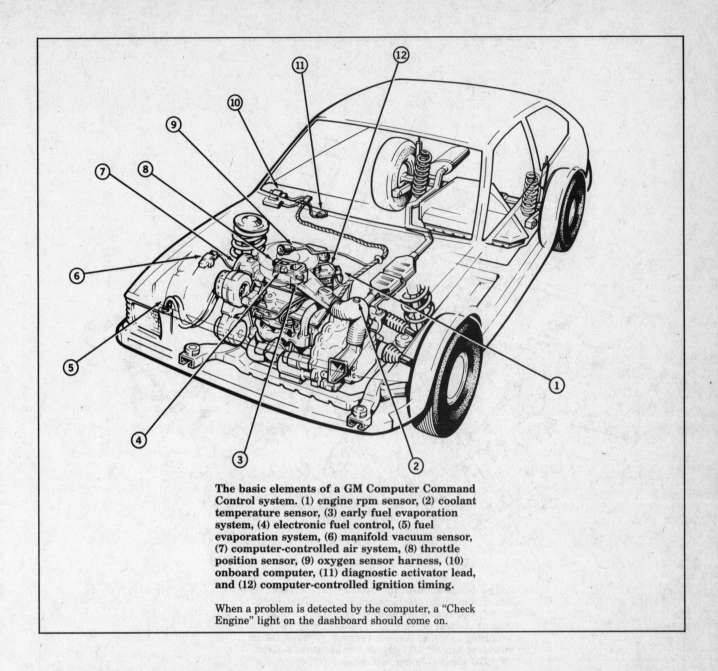

The basic elements of a GM Computer Command Control system. (1) engine rpm sensor, (2) coolant temperature sensor, (3) early fuel evaporation system, (4) electronic fuel control, (5) fuel evaporation system, (6) manifold vacuum sensor, (7) computer-controlled air system, (8) throttle position sensor, (9) oxygen sensor harness, (10) onboard computer, (11) diagnostic activator lead, and (12) computer-controlled ignition timing.

When a problem is detected by the computer, a "Check Engine" light on the dashboard should come on.

a bearing on how the PROM is programmed. There are hundreds of different PROMs, and each has its own part number. If your vehicle's computer ever has to be replaced, make sure it is fitted with the right PROM, because installing the wrong one can result in poor vehicle performance.

Loops and Computer Feedback

Computerized engine control systems have two basic modes of operation: open loop and closed loop. When the engine is first started and is warming up, the system runs in the open loop mode. Open loop means the computer is not varying the air/fuel mixture because (1) the engine is still cold and requires a fixed rich fuel setting to idle smoothly, and (2) the oxygen sensor is not yet warm enough to provide a feedback signal.

As soon as the oxygen sensor reaches about 600°F, it begins to produce a voltage signal that corresponds to the relative amount of oxygen in the exhaust. The higher the voltage signal, the richer the fuel mixture. The computer can then use this information to make

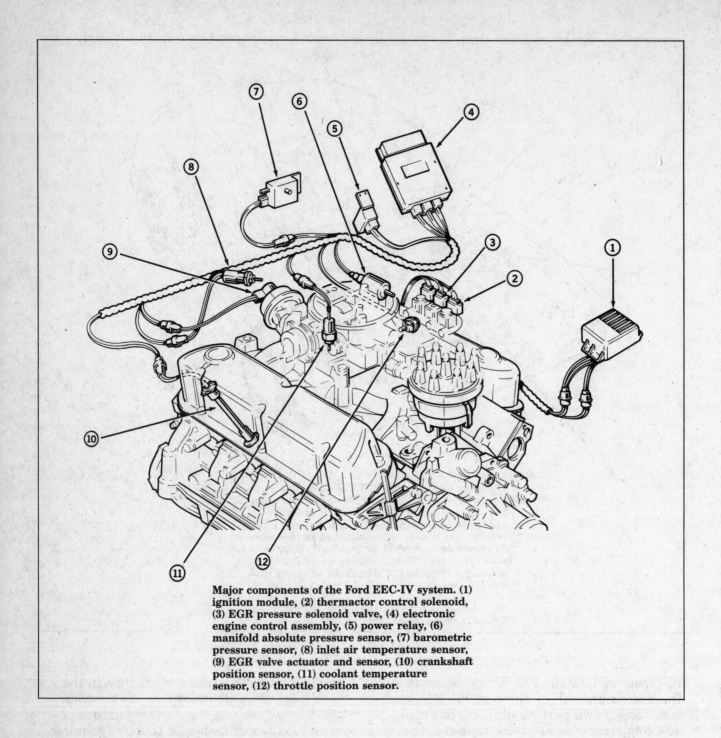

Major components of the Ford EEC-IV system. (1) ignition module, (2) thermactor control solenoid, (3) EGR pressure solenoid valve, (4) electronic engine control assembly, (5) power relay, (6) manifold absolute pressure sensor, (7) barometric pressure sensor, (8) inlet air temperature sensor, (9) EGR valve actuator and sensor, (10) crankshaft position sensor, (11) coolant temperature sensor, (12) throttle position sensor.

any necessary corrections in the air/fuel ratio. In operation, what happens is this: if the oxygen sensor reads rich, the computer compensates by making the fuel mixture leaner; if the oxygen sensor reads lean, the computer compensates by making the mixture richer. The ideal fuel ratio is 14.7:1, so by flip-flopping rapidly back and forth from rich to lean, the average air/fuel ratio is held fairly close to

the ideal setting. This process of reading the exhaust oxygen sensor signal and varying the air/fuel ratio is called the closed loop operation. In other words, the computer is using the oxygen sensor feedback signal to control the fuel mixture.

On engines equipped with feedback carburetors, the computer changes the air/fuel ratio by rapidly opening and closing a fuel metering jet, called the *mixture control solenoid*. The mixture control solenoid may be turned on and off 10 times a second, and the percentage of on time versus off time determines how rich or lean the mixture will be. The longer it is on, the leaner the mixture. The cycling of the mixture control solenoid can be read with an ordinary dwell meter, thus fuel mixture readings are often cited in so many degrees of dwell. A rich mixture would have a short dwell, and a lean mixture a long dwell.

Because of all the variation from one manufacturer's engine control system to another, and the changes made from year to year, it's essential to have up-to-date service information when attempting to troubleshoot or service one of these systems.

Diagnosis

Most computerized engine control systems have a certain amount of self-diagnostic capability that allows the computer to detect gross malfunctions in engine sensors, control circuits, and even the computer itself. When a problem is detected, the check engine light or similar light on the dash will be your warning. Many systems (but not all) then record a trouble code that corresponds to a specific fault in the computer's memory to be later recalled by the service technician.

On a computerized engine control system such as those found in most General Motors vehicles, you can read out the trouble codes by grounding the diagnostic connector under the dash and counting the flashes of the

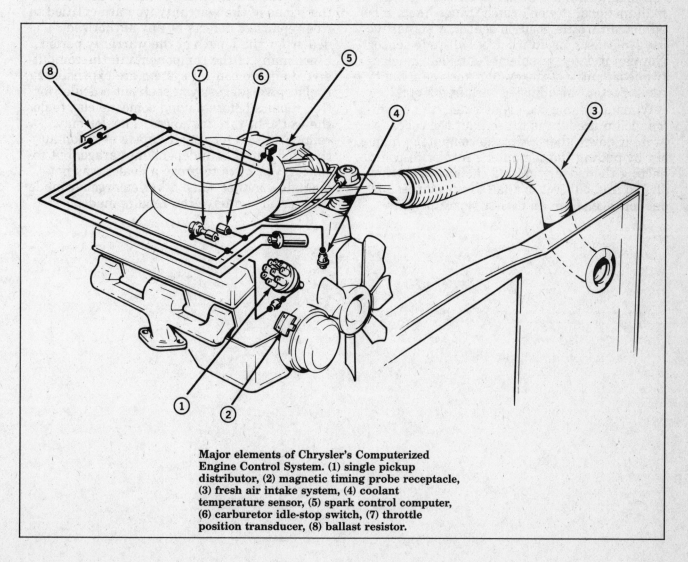

Major elements of Chrysler's Computerized Engine Control System. (1) single pickup distributor, (2) magnetic timing probe receptacle, (3) fresh air intake system, (4) coolant temperature sensor, (5) spark control computer, (6) carburetor idle-stop switch, (7) throttle position transducer, (8) ballast resistor.

"Check Engine" light. There are also special testers that plug into the diagnostic connector to allow you to read the trouble codes as a two-digit display. These testers also allow you to monitor most engine sensors and switches while the car is running or being driven.

The presence or absence of trouble codes doesn't always mean there's a problem or the engine is alright. Sometimes "false" trouble codes can be triggered by certain types of service work, noise in the electrical system, or even using the wrong starting procedure. The presence of a trouble code, therefore, doesn't necessarily mean there is a real problem in the system. On the other hand, just because there are no trouble codes stored in memory doesn't mean everything is working perfectly either. As mentioned earlier, the computer's self-diagnostics are designed to catch gross malfunctions. It won't catch things like a misadjusted throttle position sensor, a borderline oxygen sensor, or an incorrect altitude sensor. Nor can it detect problems "outside" the electronic circuitry of the system such as a faulty fuel injector, misadjusted carburetor, etc.

When a trouble code is detected, the recommended procedure is to read out the code, write it down, then clear the computer's memory by pulling the computer's fuse or disconnecting the battery ground cable with the key off. To find out if it is a false code or possibly one left over from an earlier repair or prob-

lem, drive the car for awhile to see if the same code reappears. If it does, then it warrants further investigation. The meaning of each trouble code number can be found in your shop manual. One thing to watch out for here is that the same number may have different meanings from one year to the next, or from one model car to another, so make sure you have the right application. Then follow the step-by-step diagnostic sequence for pinpointing the source of the problem. Skipping steps or not following directions to the letter almost guarantees an inaccurate diagnosis.

Note: Your vehicle's engine control system is considered part of the emission-control package, and is therefore included under the manufacturer's 5-year/50,000-mile emissions warranty. This warranty applies to all cars sold in the United States since 1981. Under the terms of the warranty, you are entitled to free repairs of defects at any authorized dealer for the length of the warranty period. Since many of the components in the computerized engine control system are expensive to replace, we suggest you seek out a dealer for free repairs before paying someone else to do the work. In rare instances, a dealer may reimburse you for repairs made at a non-authorized outlet or independent garage, but to collect, you have to prove a dealer was not available or that some other emergency made it necessary to have the repairs made.

EMISSIONS CONTROL SYSTEMS

TO BETTER UNDERSTAND the reasons behind automotive emissions control and why things are the way they are today, we need to take a quick look back to the beginnings of emissions control. Up until the late 1960s, little had been done to limit the amount of pollutants automobiles released into the atmosphere. In the early days of automotive history, nobody gave much thought to the question of air pollution. But as our vehicle population grew to over 100 million and our cities became congested with traffic, air quality in many metropolitan areas became a serious concern. Los Angeles, due to its location in a mountain basin where air tends to be trapped over the city, is where the word "smog" originated, so it's not surprising California was the first state to pass legislation requiring automakers to control vehicle emissions.

A growing body of scientific evidence pointing to the automobile as one of the major sources of air pollution and the growth of the environmental movement on college campuses focused public attention on the issue. This led to the enactment in 1970 of the Clean Air Act, which created the Environmental Protection Agency (EPA) and gave it responsibility for establishing air quality and vehicle emission standards for the country. Following what was already underway in California, the Federal program set standards that were approximately a year behind California's standards. This would give the automakers more time to comply with the new rules, as well as a year's experience in California before going nationwide with new emission controls.

The automakers complained bitterly that the new standards could not be met and that such standards would drive up the cost of new cars. But in 1973, the industry experienced its worst crisis since World War II. The Arab oil embargo disrupted gasoline supplies and sent fuel prices skyrocketing. Motorists were in a panic and Congress reacted by imposing Corporate Average Fuel Economy (CAFE) goals on the automakers to force them to build more fuel efficient cars. Again the automakers cried foul and said it would be impossible to meet the conflicting air quality and fuel economy standards—yet they managed to do it anyway. But it wasn't easy, and the changes it brought with it created a revolution in automotive technology.

The Basics of Emissions Control

Within a few short years, automakers had moved from simple add-on emission-control devices to complex fuel, ignition, and emissions management systems. Some of the early emission-control systems were cumbersome as well as troublesome, and professional as well as do-it-yourself mechanics reacted by simply removing all the "pollution-control junk" from the engine. Although this tactic may have solved a few drivability problems and improved fuel economy on some of the 1973-74 vintage cars, changes in vehicle technology were starting to weave fuel, ignition, and emissions into one package, making it more difficult to tamper with one system without affecting the others. To help discourage the practice of tampering, the EPA established heavy fines for professional mechanics caught altering emission controls. Some states and municipalities also passed laws making it illegal for anyone, including the vehicle's owner, to remove any pollution-control devices. Rules were also set up for the vehicle manufacturers, requiring them to make certain carburetor adjustments and other items "tamper-resistant" to discourage mechanics from

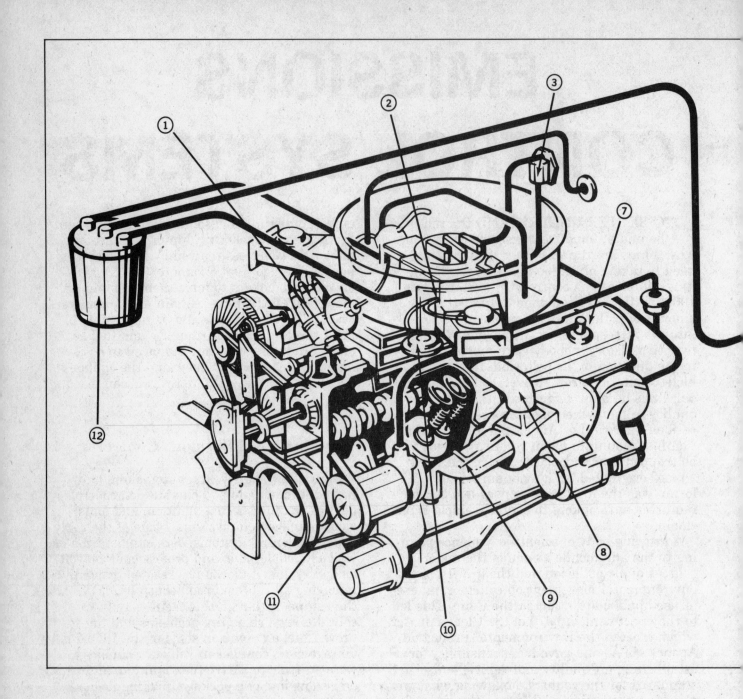

defeating the pollution-control devices.

The ultimate solution for this problem, however, was the creation of periodic vehicle inspection and testing programs in areas with the worst air quality. Set up by state government and run by either licensed independent testing stations or government contracted inspection centers, emissions testing identified vehicles that failed to meet the emissions standards and required their owners to have the necessary repairs made to bring them into compliance. Most large metropolitan areas now have such programs.

The reason for giving you this short historical perspective is twofold: one is to illustrate just how far we've come in a relatively short period of time. Although today's cars are not 100 percent pollution-free, they are as clean-running as is economically and technically practical. Two of the major automotive exhaust pollutants, hydrocarbons (HC) and carbon monoxide (CO), have been reduced 96 per-

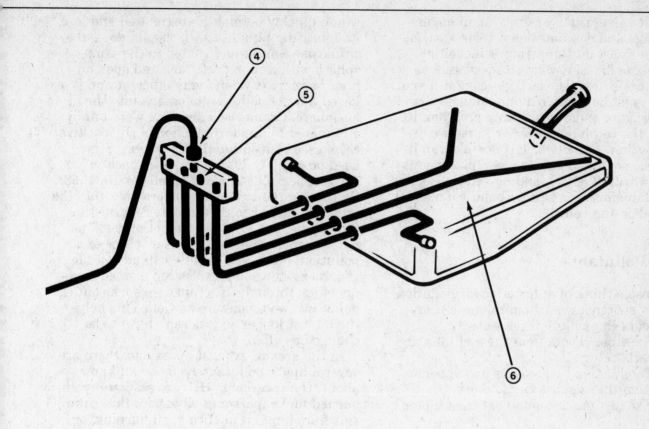

Some of the emission-control devices that are
used to limit air pollution. (1) electronic ignition,
(2) electronically controlled carburetor or fuel
injection, (3) transmission-controlled spark, (4)
overfill limiting valve, (5) vapor-liquid separator,
(6) fuel tank, (7) positive crankcase ventilation, (8)
heated intake air, (9) exhaust-port air injection,
(10) exhaust gas recirculation, (11) air pump, and
(12) charcoal canister.

cent compared to pre-control era engines. At
the same time, today's sophisticated engine-
control systems combine fuel, ignition, and
emissions control into one engine management system that can deliver far superior fuel
economy. This, combined with vehicle down-
sizing, has doubled Corporate Average Fuel
Economy figures. The average CAFE in the
early 1970s for the domestic carmakers was
only about 13 to 14 mpg. Today it's 26 to 27
mpg!

The second reason for this short overview is
to discourage any ideas you might have about
tampering with your vehicle's emission controls to "improve" fuel economy, performance,
or drivability. Except for a few of those early
1970s vintage cars, tampering will likely hurt
fuel economy and performance rather than
help it. On today's engine-control systems, it's
impossible to tamper with or disconnect some
emission-control devices without affecting
something else. For example, disconnecting

the EGR valve usually results in an engine that pings and detonates on acceleration. Besides the fact that tampering is illegal in many areas for do-it-yourself mechanics as well as professionals, you'll get caught if your vehicle must be inspected annually as part of a city or state emissions testing program. Removing the catalytic converter to reduce exhaust backpressure (which it doesn't) can be an expensive mistake, because replacements cost upwards of $100—and no vehicle is going to pass an emissions test without it if one is required on the vehicle.

Basic Pollutants

Most people think of automotive air pollution as being strictly exhaust emissions, but actually, cars can pollute three ways:

1. Gasoline vapors from the fuel tank and carburetor
2. Combustion by-products and vapors from the engine's crankcase
3. Exhaust gases coming out the tailpipe

Gasoline fuel vapors, or evaporated emissions as they are called, include a variety of hydrocarbons (HC). If allowed to escape into the atmosphere, they react with air and sunlight to form smog. Evaporative emissions can be a major source of pollution because they continue even when the car isn't running. But evaporative emissions have been greatly reduced as a source of air pollution by sealing off the fuel system from the atmosphere. The gas tank and carburetor are no longer vented to the atmosphere. Vapors are now routed through hoses to a special canister usually located in the engine compartment. This is the charcoal canister and its job is to trap and store the vapors until the engine can burn them later.

Crankcase emissions can be another major source of vehicle pollution. When fuel burns in the engine's cylinders, the tremendous pressure created by combustion pushes some of the exhaust gas and unburned fuel past the piston rings. This is called blow-by, and is the major source of oil contamination inside the engine. Since the blow-by gases also contain a lot of water vapor, some means of getting rid of these gases must be provided, or the oil

would quickly become contaminated and lose its lubricating qualities. In the old days, the crankcase was simply vented to the atmosphere with a road draft tube and open oil breather cap. It wasn't very efficient and it allowed a lot of pollution to escape into the atmosphere. Crankcase emissions were totally eliminated by the introduction of the positive crankcase ventilation (PCV) system. First used on some California vehicles back in 1961, it became standard on all cars in 1963. By routing the crankcase vapors back into the intake manifold so they can be reburned in the engine, the PCV system not only eliminates crankcase emissions as a source of air pollution, but it also greatly extends oil life. Using engine vacuum to sweep a steady supply of air through the crankcase sucks out the pollutants and moisture as well. This helps the oil last longer so it doesn't have to be changed as often.

In the area of exhaust emissions, there are several major pollutants you should know about. Hydrocarbons (HC) are essentially unburned fuel vapors and oil vapors that can result from ignition misfiring, oil burning, or other mechanical problems in the engine or fuel system. Hydrocarbons by themselves are not directly toxic, although some research has linked them to certain types of cancer. The EPA's main concern with hydrocarbons is that they are a major source of smog. Hydrocarbons react with air and sunlight to form a variety of secondary chemical compounds, and this is what contributes to smog.

A more dangerous exhaust pollutant is carbon monoxide (CO). Carbon monoxide is a byproduct of incomplete combustion. Increased carbon monoxide levels are produced when there's too much fuel and not enough oxygen in the combustion chamber. A rich air/fuel ratio, a clogged air filter, or a sticking choke can all contribute to excessive CO emissions. Carbon monoxide is a killer because it is absorbed by red blood cells 200 times faster than oxygen. That's why a leaky exhaust system can quickly lead to unconsciousness and death if the exhaust finds its way into the car. Carbon monoxide is colorless and odorless, and that's what makes it so dangerous.

Both hydrocarbon and carbon monoxide emissions are controlled by calibrating the air/fuel ratio to maintain as close to an ideal ratio as possible for clean combustion. The catalytic converter is also an important control device for reducing these two pollutants. The converter is essentially an afterburner that combines oxygen with these two pollutants to turn them into carbon dioxide, a harmless gas, and water vapor, which we exhale ourselves with every breath.

Another group of exhaust pollutants are oxides of nitrogen (NOx). This includes several different oxygen/nitrogen compounds that are formed when combustion temperatures inside an engine exceed 2500°F. Approximately 78 percent of the earth's atmosphere is nitrogen (only about 20 percent is oxygen). Normally, nitrogen doesn't do much of anything except fill space. But inside a hot combustion chamber, it reacts with oxygen to form a variety of chemical compounds. One such compound is nitrous oxide, more commonly known as laughing gas. Maybe that's one pollutant we need more of, but most NOx compounds are poisonous. NOx forms the reddish-brown haze that hangs over heavily polluted areas and also contributes to the formation of ozone, another toxic pollutant. NOx is responsible for many of the direct symptoms of air pollution such as headaches, watery eyes, and difficult breathing. There is also strong evidence that suggests NOx is one of the major ingredients in acid rain, along with sulfur. NOx emissions have not been eliminated, but they have been significantly reduced by exhaust gas recirculation (EGR). Your engine's EGR valve recirculates a small amount of burned exhaust gas back into the intake manifold to dilute the incoming air/fuel mixture. This helps to reduce combustion temperatures and keep them under the 2500°F threshold where NOx becomes a problem. Beginning in 1981, the catalytic converter also became part of the NOx control team. The newer catalytic converters contain a second chamber with a different type of catalyst that reduces NOx to less toxic compounds. This type of converter is sometimes called a three-way converter or an oxidation-reduction converter.

Another automotive exhaust pollutant that is rapidly becoming history is lead. Gasoline refiners long ago discovered that adding small amounts of tetraethyllead to gasoline improved its octane rating (its ability to resist detonation under high compression). Not only

did this advance allow the automakers to build higher compression engines for more power and fuel economy, but it also enabled refiners to make better gasoline out of lower grade crude oil stocks. Unfortunately, we've come to learn that lead, as well as other heavy metals, can accumulate in our bodies and cause a variety of ailments. Engineers also discovered that leaded gasoline wouldn't work with catalytic converters and that only a couple of tankfuls of leaded gas can render the converter useless. Because the catalytic converter was considered the only viable solution to cleaning up HC and CO exhaust emissions, unleaded gasoline was introduced back in the early 1970s for the new generation of pollution controls. Virtually every domestic car built since 1975 is designed to burn unleaded gasoline, and burning leaded gasoline in one of these cars not only ruins the converter, but also the oxygen sensor on computerized engine control systems. Unleaded gasoline costs more because it requires more refining to achieve a high octane rating, but on the plus side, there's no lead in it to foul our environment or your engine's spark plugs. In fact, the spark plugs in an engine burning unleaded gasoline will last 3 to 5 times longer than those in an engine using leaded fuel. Unleaded fuel can be used in older vehicles, but the exhaust valves will probably not last as long, since most older engines relied on lead in the fuel to lubricate and cool the exhaust valve seats.

Emission-Control Systems

The subject of emissions control is a fairly complex one. To adequately cover it, we'd need a manual twice the size of this one, so we'll limit our coverage to basic systems you can check yourself. For in-depth troubleshooting, we strongly recommend using a shop manual that details the emission-control system for your particular vehicle. As with computerized engine controls, there is a great deal of difference between one manufacturer's vehicles and another's, as well as differences within a car line and from one year to the next. If you don't have access to the right manuals or don't feel competent trying to do the work yourself, better leave it to a qualified professional.

Positive Crankcase Ventilation (PCV)

Tools and Materials

- Pliers
- Screwdriver
- Utility Knife
- Wrench
- PCV System Hose
- Motor Oil
- PCV Valve
- PCV Breather Filter

AS YOUR AUTOMOBILE operates and combustion is taking place, a highly corrosive gas is produced. In addition, for every gallon of gasoline burned, more than a gallon of water is formed. During the last part of the engine's combustion stroke, some unburned fuel and products of combustion—water vapor, for instance—leak past the engine's piston rings into the crankcase. This leakage is the result of four things.

1. High pressures in the engine combustion chamber. This condition is created by the normal compression stroke in the engine under operation.
2. The necessary working clearance of piston rings in their grooves. Without this normal ring clearance, the engine's piston rings would not have room to ex-

pand from heat created by normal engine operation and would not seal properly against the cylinder walls.
3. The normal shifting of piston rings in their grooves that sometimes lines up the clearance gaps of two or more rings. This, too, is a normal condition. As the piston rings continue to turn in their grooves, the situation will correct itself.
4. The reduction in piston ring sealing contact area as the piston moves up and down in the cylinder.

This leakage into the engine crankcase often is referred to as "blow-by," which must be removed from the engine before it condenses in the crankcase and reacts with oil to form sludge. If sludge does form and is allowed to circulate with the engine oil, it will corrode and accelerate the wear of pistons, piston rings, valves, bearings, and other internal working parts of the engine.

Complete burning of the air/fuel mixture in the engine never occurs, so blow-by carries a certain amount of unburned fuel from the engine's combustion chamber into the crankcase. If this unburned fuel is not removed, the oil in the crankcase will be diluted. Oil diluted with gasoline will not lubricate the engine properly, causing excessive wear.

The combustion gases that do enter the engine crankcase are removed from the crankcase by means of a system using engine vacuum to draw fresh air through the crankcase. This system is called Positive Crankcase Ventilation (PCV).

This fresh air, which dissipates the harmful gases, enters through the air filter on top of the carburetor or through a separate PCV breather filter located on the inside of the air filter housing.

Because the vacuum supply for the PCV system is from the engine's intake manifold, the air flow through this system must be controlled in such a way that it varies in proportion to the regular air/fuel ratio being drawn into the intake manifold through the carburetor. Otherwise, the additional air being drawn into the system would cause the air/fuel mixture to become too lean for efficient engine operation.

The air flow through the PCV system into the intake manifold is regulated by the PCV

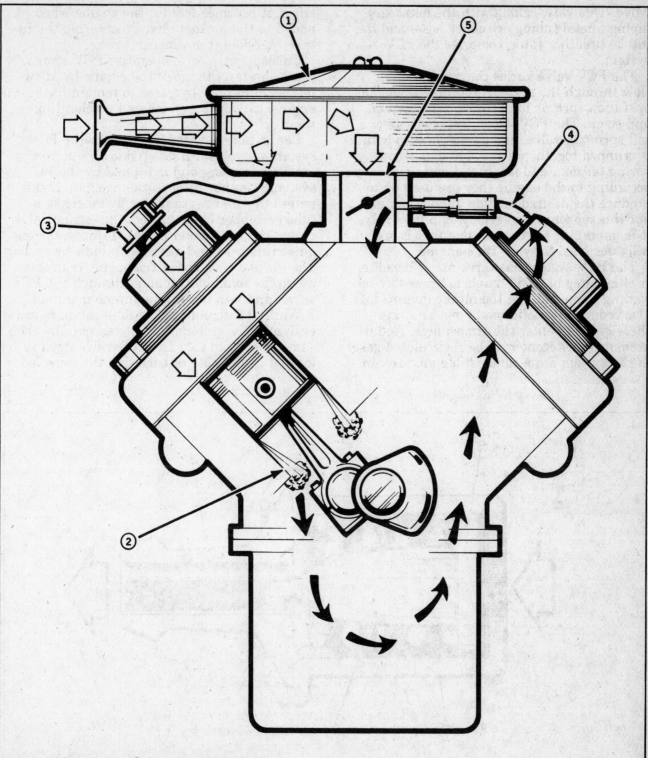

A typical PCV system. Air enters the engine through the air filter (1). During combustion, blow-by gases (2) enter the crankcase. A PCV breather filter (3) allows fresh air to enter the crankcase, to dissipate the gases, which then pass through the PCV valve (4) below the carburetor throttle (5) and reenter the engine for combustion.

valve. This valve, along with the necessary piping (metal tubing or rubber hose) and the intake breather filter, comprise the PCV system.

The PCV valve varies the amount of air flow through the system according to engine operation such as idle, cruise, acceleration, and so on. The PCV valve itself consists of a coil spring, a valve, and a two-piece body that is crimped together. The valve dimensions, spring tension, and internal dimensions vary according to the engine they are used on to produce the desired air flow requirements. For this reason, when replacing a PCV valve, it is important to get the valve that is specifically designed for your car's engine.

The PCV system has three major benefits. It eliminates harmful crankcase gases by re-routing them through the intake manifold. It also reduces air pollution by not allowing these gases to enter the atmosphere. And it promotes fuel economy. The recirculated gases in the system are a combustible mixture. In effect, it becomes fuel for the engine when added to the air/fuel mixture entering the intake manifold from the carburetor.

Consequently, an inoperative PCV system could shorten the life of the engine by allowing harmful blow-by gases to remain in the engine, causing corrosion and accelerating wear.

Let us take a closer look at how the PCV system operates. First, outside air enters the air filter housing and is filtered by the PCV system breather filter in the housing. It then enters the engine crankcase by means of a tube or rubber hose through the engine valve cover. The air then circulates through the engine crankcase and mixes with blow-by gases. The air is drawn out of the engine crankcase by intake manifold vacuum, through the PCV valve, and into the engine intake manifold.

While the accompanying illustration is general, all PCV systems operate essentially the same way. Note that the PCV valve itself is located in the hose or tube that is connected

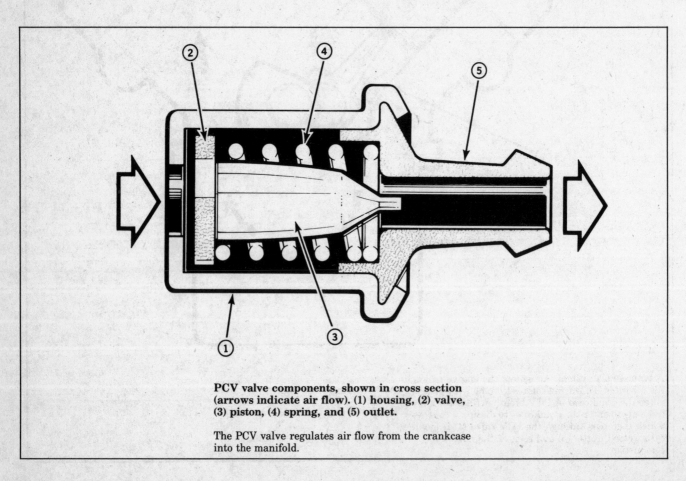

PCV valve components, shown in cross section (arrows indicate air flow). (1) housing, (2) valve, (3) piston, (4) spring, and (5) outlet.

The PCV valve regulates air flow from the crankcase into the manifold.

between the engine valve cover and a vacuum source fitting at the intake manifold below the carburetor. Depending on the particular engine, the actual location of the PCV valve will vary. It may be inserted into a rubber grommet in the engine valve cover, or it may be closer to the intake manifold with rubber hoses connected to each end of the valve. If you have any doubt as to the location of the PCV valve on your vehicle, ask a professional mechanic or a knowledgeable individual at an auto supply store.

Note, too, how fresh air enters the PCV system from the air filter housing. There is a rubber hose or tubing with one end connected to the air filter housing and the other end connected to the engine, usually at the valve cover. In-line four- and six-cylinder engines will have one valve cover; V6 and V8 engines will have two, one on each side.

Carmakers may vary on their recommendations for PCV system servicing and PCV valve replacement. But as a general rule, you should check the PCV system for satisfactory operation every 12 months or 12,000 miles of driving, whichever comes first. Also, the PCV valve should be replaced at least every 24 months or 24,000 miles of driving, whichever comes first.

If you operate your car under dusty conditions, subject your engine to long periods of idling, or make mostly short trips in cold weather, you should check your PCV system more often.

You may be having trouble with your PCV system if you have a rough-running engine at idle speed, discover oil in the air filter housing, find oil leaks at any of the PCV system hose or tube connections, or see oil leaks around the engine. Also, when you check the oil level of your engine and find that it is sludged up or appears to be diluted with gasoline (you can smell it), you probably have problems with the PCV system.

Checking the PCV System

If you experience any of the symptoms described, a check of the PCV system is in order. Here is how to do it. **Note:** Before you replace a PCV valve or hoses, take a few minutes to look over the entire system. Locate the hoses in the system and locate the PCV valve. You

will see that one hose is connected to the air filter housing and to the engine at the valve cover. This hose carries filtered air from the air filter to the engine crankcase. It seldom needs service, other than making sure the connections are secure. The line formed by this hose is unrestricted and never contains the PCV valve.

Next, you will see a hose connected between the engine valve cover and a fitting at the intake manifold just below the carburetor hose. The PCV valve will be installed as part of this line. Usually, the PCV valve will be installed in the end of the hose at the engine valve cover. However, the PCV valve will always be located somewhere in this line. Because the crankcase vapors and other contaminants are being drawn through the PCV valve and hose into the intake manifold, system problems are usually confined to this area.

Some rubber hoses have hose clamps requiring pliers or a screwdriver to loosen or tighten them. Most hose connections, however, simply slip over the PCV valve or connection at the intake manifold.

Start the engine and listen for vacuum leaks in the PCV system hose. If there is a leak, you will hear a slight hissing sound. Stop the engine. Inspect the hoses for cracks or any sign of deterioration. Since the PCV blockage system must be airtight to operate efficiently, a leaking hose must be replaced. It is a good idea to replace the hose when replacing the PCV valve. Here's how to replace a hose.

1. Disconnect the hose at both ends using either a screwdriver or pliers if the hose is secured with a hose clamp. If no clamp is used, simply pull the hose from its connection. Remove the hose.

2. Purchase a length of PCV system hose from an auto supply store. Specify the make and model of your car. In this way you will get the correct diameter hose. Or, take the old hose with you and buy only the length that you need.

3. Using a sharp utility knife, cut the new hose to the same length as the one you removed.

4. Install the new PCV system hose, reversing Step 1.

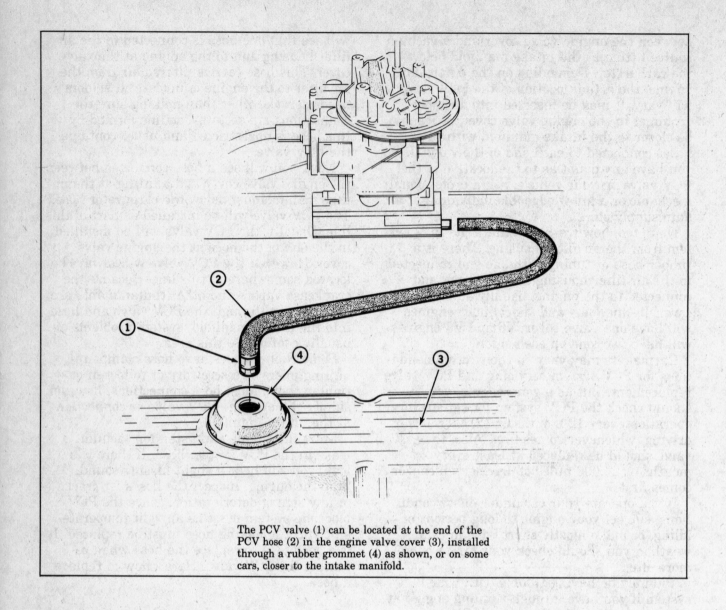

The PCV valve (1) can be located at the end of the PCV hose (2) in the engine valve cover (3), installed through a rubber grommet (4) as shown, or on some cars, closer to the intake manifold.

Testing the PCV Valve

Having visually checked out the PCV system and having replaced any defective hose, the next step is to test the PCV valve. Here is how to do it.

1. Open the hood and remove the air filter housing as outlined in the section on "Air Filter Service" in this chapter. You may need a wrench or pliers to remove the air filter housing cover nut.

2. Look at the area near the carburetor base. There will be a hose about ¾ inch in diameter. The PCV valve will be located near the carburetor end of this hose or at the other end entering the engine valve cover through a rubber grommet.

3. Start the engine and let it run at idle speed.

4. Using your hand, pinch the hose connected to the PCV valve. If the valve is operating, you will be able to hear the engine idle speed decline. If the engine idle speed does drop, the PCV system and valve are operating satisfactorily. Stop the engine and replace the air filter housing.

5. If no drop in engine speed is noted, replace the PCV valve.

Replacing the PCV Valve

If the PCV valve must be replaced, here is how to do it.

1. Locate the PCV valve as explained earlier.
2. Disconnect the PCV system hose from the PCV valve. This may be done by simply pulling the hose from the valve or by removing a hose clamp with pliers or a screwdriver and then pulling the hose free of the valve.
3. If the valve is in-line, use pliers to remove it or just pull off the hoses, depending on the hose connection. If the valve is located in a rubber grommet in the engine valve cover, remove it with pliers. Wiggle it back and forth while pulling it from the grommet. **Note:** If the grommet comes out with the PCV valve, it can be difficult to replace. Soaking the grommet with motor oil will make it easier to reinstall.
4. Purchase the correct PCV valve for your car's engine.

5. Replace the new PCV valve by reversing Steps 2 and 3.
6. Replace the air filter housing as outlined in the section on "Air Filter Service" in this chapter.

Replacing the Breather Filter Element

On most model cars, there also is an intake breather filter element for the PCV system. It is located inside the air filter housing. If your car has one, this element also should be replaced periodically. Consult your owner's manual for replacement recommendations. Here's how to replace this element.

1. Remove the air filter housing cover using pliers or a wrench, if necessary, to remove the hold-down nut.
2. Remove the air filter element.
3. Remove the PCV breather filter retaining clip with pliers.
4. Remove the PCV breather filter.
5. Purchase a new PCV breather filter and replace it by reversing Steps 1 through 4.

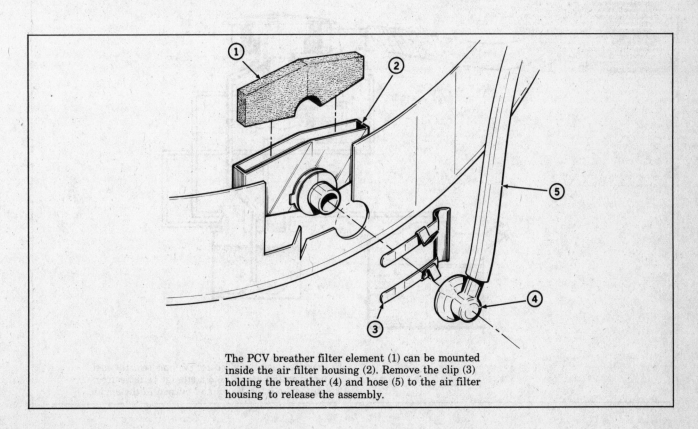

The PCV breather filter element (1) can be mounted inside the air filter housing (2). Remove the clip (3) holding the breather (4) and hose (5) to the air filter housing to release the assembly.

Evaporative Emissions Control

YOUR VEHICLE'S evaporative emission-control system is designed to prevent the escape of fuel vapors into the atmosphere. The gas tank and carburetor are vented to a vapor storage canister, the charcoal canister as it is commonly called, where the vapors are trapped and held by charcoal crystals. The crystals act like a sponge to soak up the vapors. When the engine is started, fresh air is circulated through the canister to sweep out the trapped vapors. The vapors are then drawn into the intake manifold and burned inside the engine. This is called purging.

Many evaporative emission-control systems are designed to delay purging until the engine has had a chance to warm up. A purge control solenoid or ported vacuum switch may be included in the canister plumbing for this purpose. On computer-controlled engines, the computer often regulates this function by monitoring engine coolant temperature.

The evaporative emission-control system requires virtually no maintenance or service on most cars. On some vehicles, a replaceable filter element must be changed periodically on the bottom of the charcoal canister, but most systems today use a sealed canister. Refer to your owner's manual for specific service recommendations.

About the only things that can go wrong with the system are cracked, loose, or misrouted vent and vacuum hoses (refer to your underhood emissions decal for hose routing), a

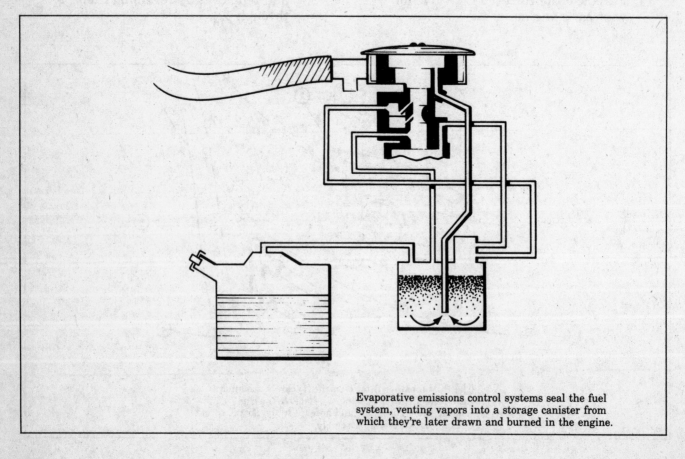

Evaporative emissions control systems seal the fuel system, venting vapors into a storage canister from which they're later drawn and burned in the engine.

plugged up vent line between the fuel tank and canister, or a defective purge valve or control solenoid. In most instances, you won't know anything is wrong with your car because a system failure normally doesn't affect drivability. A vacuum leak can cause lean misfiring or hesitation during acceleration, or a purge valve that's stuck open can allow fuel vapors to be continually drawn into the engine, contributing to rough idling, but usually there are no symptoms. If the vent line to the fuel tank becomes plugged, you may notice a "whoosh" when you remove the gas cap to fill the tank. Many systems use gas tank filler caps with spring-loaded pressure relief valves to vent the tank just in case the filler line should become plugged.

Heated Air System Service

Tools and Materials

- Hand Vacuum Pump

ALL ENGINES today have a thermostatically controlled heated air intake system to supply warm air to the air cleaner when the engine is first started or during cold weather driving. The heated air system actually serves a dual purpose. It improves engine warm-up and cold drivability by supplying much needed heat to help vaporize fuel, and this helps to reduce hydrocarbon emissions by reducing misfiring during warm-up. It also allows for leaner fuel calibration, which helps cut carbon monoxide and improve fuel economy.

The heated air system consists of a shroud or "stove" around the exhaust manifold to pre-

heat air, a duct assembly to carry the warm air up to the air cleaner, a vacuum-controlled door to determine how much warm air is allowed into the air cleaner, and a temperature sensor inside the air cleaner to regulate the operation of the whole system. The temperature sensor is preset to pass vacuum to the control door whenever the temperature inside the air cleaner is below a certain temperature, usually around 70° to 90°F.

When the engine is first started, the control door is closed to outside air. All air coming into the air cleaner is routed through the heat stove on the exhaust manifold (where it is heated), up the duct and into the air cleaner. As the engine warms up, and less supplemental heat is required, the temperature sensor begins to reduce vacuum to the control door. This allows more outside cool air to enter the air cleaner and less pre-heated air. Finally, when the engine is warmed up and no supplemental heat is needed, the temperature sensor shuts off all heated air and fully opens the door to outside air.

Several things can go wrong with this system, and the impact on drivability will be immediately noticeable. If anything happens to render the system inoperative (missing heat riser duct between the exhaust stove and air cleaner, a jammed open control door, or a defective temperature sensor), heated air cannot reach the air cleaner. During warm weather this might not create much of a problem, but during cold weather the engine would likely idle rough and stumble during acceleration, especially during the warm-up period. Cold air is much denser than warm air, and on older vehicles without self-adjusting carburetors or fuel injection, the change in air density can throw the air/fuel mixture off, resulting in lean misfire.

If a malfunction occurs that causes the air control door to remain closed (defective vacuum motor, vacuum leak, or defective temperature sensor) so that the air cleaner receives warm air all the time, the result can be detonation and a rich fuel condition during hot weather. Again, older vehicles without computerized engine controls are more adversely affected by problems of this nature.

Maintenance and service on the heated air intake system is relatively basic. The condition of the air duct between the exhaust stove

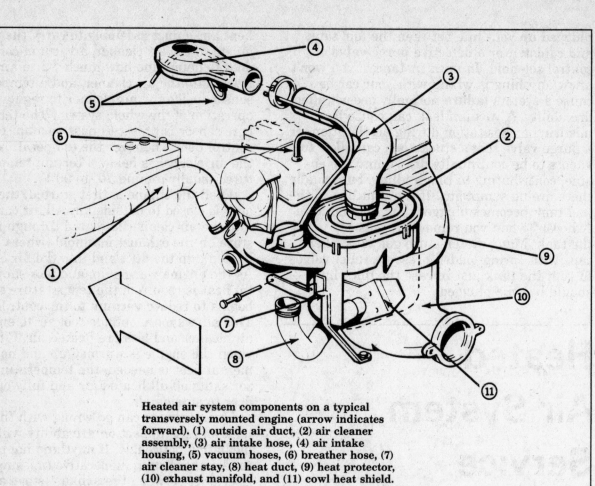

Heated air system components on a typical transversely mounted engine (arrow indicates forward). (1) outside air duct, (2) air cleaner assembly, (3) air intake hose, (4) air intake housing, (5) vacuum hoses, (6) breather hose, (7) air cleaner stay, (8) heat duct, (9) heat protector, (10) exhaust manifold, and (11) cowl heat shield.

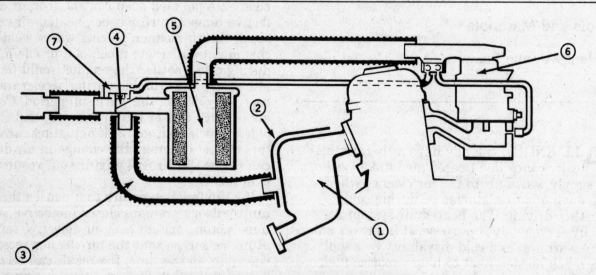

Air heated by passing over the exhaust manifold (1) under the heat cowl or stove (2) follows the air duct (3) through a temperature-controlled door (4), then enters the air cleaner (5) on its way to the carburetor (6). The control door's operation depends on the temperature inside the air cleaner. A sensor passes vacuum to the control door motor (7) only after the engine warms up.

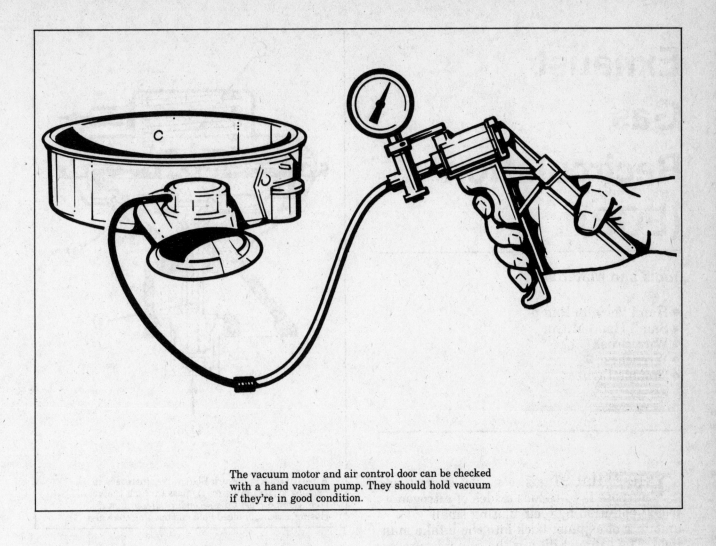

The vacuum motor and air control door can be checked
with a hand vacuum pump. They should hold vacuum
if they're in good condition.

and air cleaner should be checked periodically to see that it is tight and free from cracks. If the duct is missing on your car, be sure to replace it.

Operation of the air control door can be checked by disconnecting the outside air duct from the air cleaner inlet. Look inside the inlet. The control door should be in the closed position when the engine is off, the engine is cold and the outside temperature is below about 80°F or so. Start the engine and watch to see what happens. Again, if the engine is cold and it's not hot outside, the flap should remain closed for a few minutes then begin to gradually open as the engine warms up. By the time the engine reaches normal operating temperature, the control flap should be wide open.

If the system isn't operating properly, the vacuum motor on the control door can be checked by applying vacuum to it with a hand-held pump. If it holds vacuum, it's okay. If not, replace the motor.

The temperature sensor can be checked in a similar manner. Many sensors are designed to bleed air when cold, but to pass vacuum when hot. You'll have to check the exact specs for your temperature sensor in a shop manual, but if it continues to bleed air regardless of how warm it gets, it's probably defective and should be replaced.

Leaky vacuum hoses or loose hose connections are other common faults in this system. Inspect the length of each vacuum hose, looking carefully for cracks or cuts. Check the hose fittings to see if they're loose or if the hose has become brittle with age. Replace any hoses found to be damaged, leaking, or deteriorated.

Exhaust Gas Recirculation (EGR)

Tools and Materials

- Hand Vacuum Pump
- Small Hand Mirror
- Wire Brush
- Wrenches
- Trouble Light

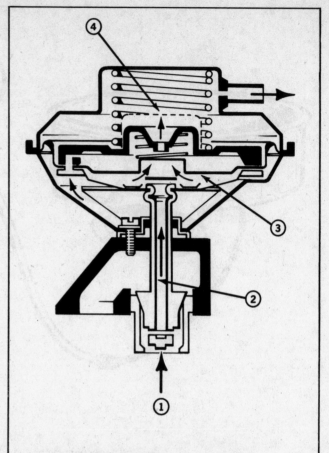

A positive backpressure EGR valve. Increases in exhaust system pressure (1) pass through the valve stem (2) and push up a secondary diaphragm (3), closing a vacuum bleed hole and opening the valve (4).

THE EXHAUST gas recirculation system's purpose is to reduce oxides of nitrogen (NOx) pollution by recirculating small amounts of exhaust back into the intake manifold. The exhaust dilutes the fuel mixture and helps to reduce combustion temperatures to a point where NOx formation is sharply limited.

The system consists of an EGR valve, some type of EGR valve control circuit, and plumbing to connect the exhaust and intake manifolds. The EGR valve itself is a fairly simple open-and-close poppet valve. The EGR valve tip extends into a fixture usually located on the exhaust manifold and rests against a small port. The valve is normally closed, held shut by spring tension until the vacuum working against the valve's diaphragm lifts the valve off its seat and opens the exhaust port. Engine vacuum then pulls exhaust into the intake manifold, diluting the fuel mixture somewhere between 6 to 10 percent.

EGR is not a full-time emission control because it has the same effect on performance as a small vacuum leak. Because of this, the EGR system is designed not to open during idle or during engine warm-up. The valve's control circuitry is designed so the EGR's vacuum supply is taken above the carburetor throttle plates. This is called ported vacuum, and it prevents the valve from opening until the engine is running at part throttle. A ported vacuum switch or solenoid is also included in the vacuum supply line to prevent vacuum from reaching the valve until the engine has had a chance to warm up. On late model computerized engine control systems, a computer controlled solenoid may be used to turn vacuum on and off to the valve depending on operating conditions.

Although the basic principle behind EGR is essentially the same for all vehicles, there is a great amount of difference between systems. Some are relatively simple while others are

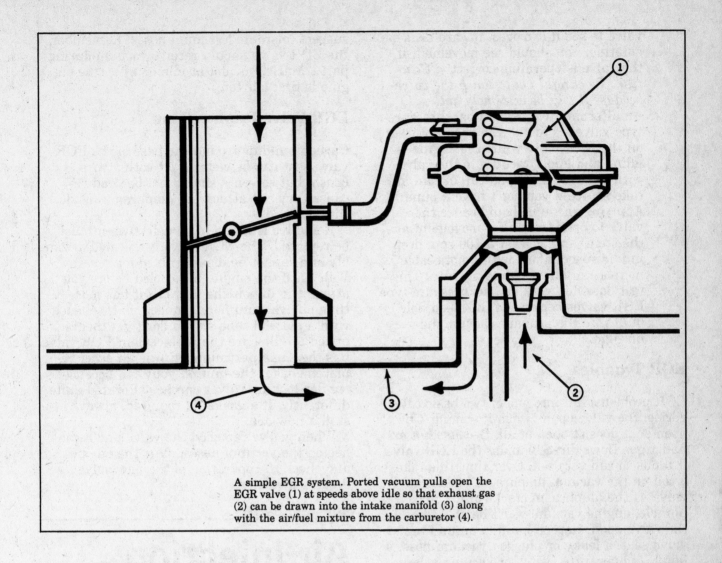

A simple EGR system. Ported vacuum pulls open the EGR valve (1) at speeds above idle so that exhaust gas (2) can be drawn into the intake manifold (3) along with the air/fuel mixture from the carburetor (4).

fairly complex. The differences can be found in the design and location of the EGR valve, as well as the control circuitry used to determine when and how much EGR is used. For the specifics on your engine's EGR system, refer to your shop manual.

One of the differences in EGR systems is the use of exhaust backpressure to "fine tune" how much exhaust is allowed to flow back into the intake manifold. Since NOx formation increases during acceleration and when the engine is under load, some means of increasing EGR flow during these times can help reduce NOx. Exhaust backpressure also increases during these times, so making the valve respond to changes in exhaust pressure solves the problem. The EGR valve can be designed so that it responds to either increased backpressure or decreased backpressure. A

small hole up through the valve's stem allows pressure to pass into a small chamber. A pressure sensitive diaphragm across one side of this chamber inside the EGR valve then opens or closes a bleed hole, which causes the valve to open wider, increasing EGR flow. This type of valve typically oscillates with changing backpressure, averaging out the amount of flow to suit conditions.

Testing the EGR System

To check EGR valve operation, do the following.

1. With the engine warmed up and at normal operating temperature, rev it up to about 2000 rpm. Using your trouble light and/or a mirror, try to watch the EGR valve stem at the base of the EGR

valve to see if it moves upward or is oscillating. You should see movement if the valve is operating correctly. *Caution: Be careful not to touch the valve because it will be extremely hot.*

2. An alternate test for non-backpressure-type valves is to pull the vacuum hose off the EGR valve while the engine is idling and apply vacuum to the valve with a hand pump (you can use an intake source if you don't have a pump). Applying vacuum should cause the valve to open (watch for movement at the stem) and at least a 100 rpm drop in idle speed, along with a noticeable increase in idle roughness. **Note:** This test does not work on backpressure-type EGR valves because of the bleed hole built into the primary vacuum diaphragm.

EGR Troubles

EGR problems fall into one of two basic categories: the valve opens when it shouldn't be open or it doesn't open at all. Because hot exhaust gas flows directly under the EGR valve, it tends to run very hot. Over time this takes a toll on the vacuum diaphragm inside the valve. If the diaphragm cracks or develops a pinhole, engine vacuum won't be able to pull the valve open. Carbon buildup around the valve seat, a leaky or plugged vacuum hose, a faulty temperature switch or vacuum solenoid, or misrouting of the vacuum hoses can all keep the valve from working. If the EGR valve fails to open, the most noticeable complaint will be pinging during acceleration.

What happens if the valve remains open all the time or opens at the wrong time? A valve that's stuck open because of carbon buildup around the valve seat, a broken spring inside the valve, stem corrosion, or misalignment acts just like a vacuum leak in the intake system. The result will be rough idle, hard starting, and hesitation or stumbling during acceleration. Misrouted vacuum hoses or a temperature switch or warm-up solenoid that's stuck open, allowing vacuum to reach the valve all the time or at the wrong time, will produce the same results. Check the vacuum hose routing diaphragm on your underhood emissions decal or in your manual if you

suspect misrouted vacuum hoses. Remember, the EGR valve should receive vacuum during part throttle, but not at idle or when the engine is first started.

EGR Valve Replacement

Carbon buildup around the base of the EGR valve seat can be cleaned off with a wire brush, but solvents should not be used because they can attack the diaphragm inside the valve.

If a valve is found to be defective, it must be replaced. The EGR valve is a sealed assembly and cannot be disassembled for repair. Wait until the engine has cooled before you attempt to unbolt the valve. If it has more than one vacuum hose connection, label each with a piece of tape so you don't get them mixed up. Be sure the replacement EGR valve has the same part number or is an exact replacement for the unit on your car, because similar-looking valves can be calibrated quite differently. If a gasket is required, always install a new one.

When you've replaced the valve and reconnected the vacuum hoses, start the engine and check the operation of the new valve as described earlier.

Air Injection and the Catalytic Converter

THE AIR INJECTION system and catalytic converter work together to clean up hydrocarbon (HC) and carbon monoxide (CO) emissions in the engine's exhaust. The system does this by reburning the pollutants inside

Tools and Materials

- Hand Vacuum Pump
- Wrenches
- Pliers
- Screwdriver
- Vacuum Gauge

the converter. On 1981 and newer cars, the system also reduces oxides of nitrogen (NOx) emissions.

Before we explain exactly how this happens, let's take a look at the various components that make up the air injection systems. On 1980 and older systems that just handle HC and CO, there is a belt-driven air pump, a diverter valve, a check valve, and some plumbing to carry the air to the exhaust manifold. The air pump is usually driven off the crank-

shaft pulley, although on some engines, it may be driven off another accessory drive. The air pump is a simple vane pump that draws air in one side and pushes it out the other. At the pump's discharge side is the diverter valve, which either diverts the air to the exhaust manifold or dumps it back to the atmosphere if air isn't needed. A vacuum line connected to the diverter valve usually cuts off air flow to the exhaust manifold during deceleration to prevent backfiring. A check valve in the plumbing between the diverter valve and exhaust manifold prevents the hot exhaust gases from flowing back through the air plumbing, where it would damage the diverter valve and air pump.

A variation on this basic system is the "pulse air" approach where no air pump is used. With this type of system, fresh air is drawn into the exhaust manifold through a one-way pulse air valve that allows air to enter between cylinder firings. This is possible because as the "pulses" of exhaust move out of

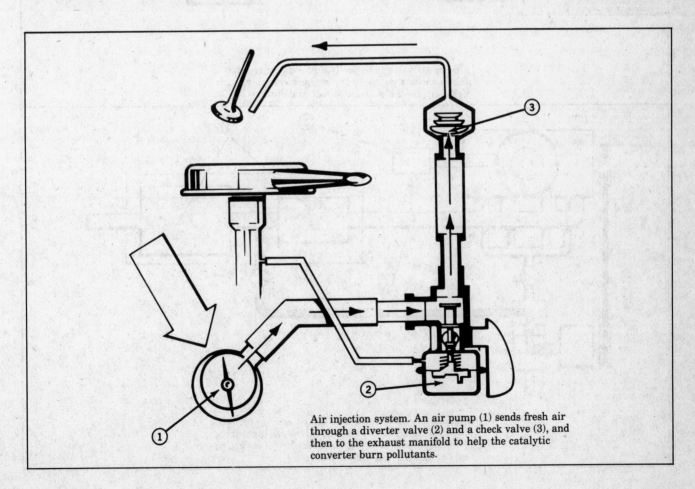

Air injection system. An air pump (1) sends fresh air through a diverter valve (2) and a check valve (3), and then to the exhaust manifold to help the catalytic converter burn pollutants.

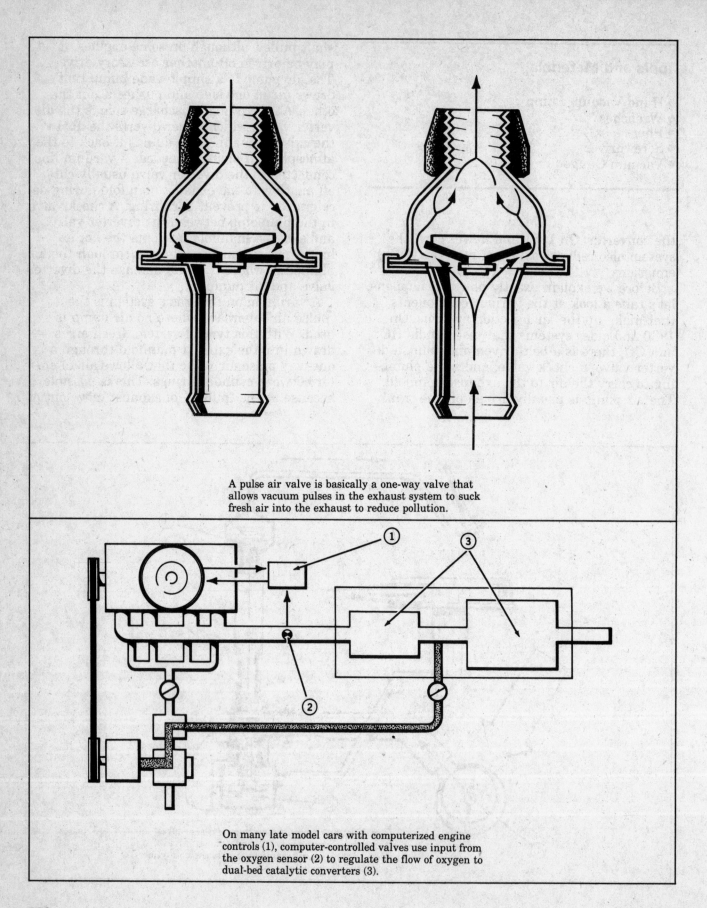

A pulse air valve is basically a one-way valve that allows vacuum pulses in the exhaust system to suck fresh air into the exhaust to reduce pollution.

On many late model cars with computerized engine controls (1), computer-controlled valves use input from the oxygen sensor (2) to regulate the flow of oxygen to dual-bed catalytic converters (3).

each cylinder, they create a momentary vacuum between pulses. The one-way valve allows air to be sucked into the exhaust between every pulse, thus eliminating the need for an air pump.

On the 1981 and newer systems that also handle NOx, the air pump has two diverter valves. The first one serves exactly the same purpose as the diverter valve on the older systems, diverting air to either the air plumbing or back to the atmosphere. A second air switching valve is added to the system to route the air either to the exhaust manifold or to the converter. The system is set up to route air to the exhaust manifold when the engine is cold to help oxidize the high levels of HC and CO that are produced during warm-up. Once the engine reaches normal operating temperature, the air is rerouted directly to the converter. The reason for doing this is because the later model converters have two catalyst chambers. The forward chamber reduces NOx back into nitrogen and oxygen, and to work efficiently it doesn't require extra oxygen. The second chamber is where the HC and CO are burned, so extra oxygen is needed to complete the process. A pipe is connected to the middle of the converter so air can be injected right at the point where the exhaust has just been scrubbed of NOx and is now ready to be reburned to get rid of the HC and CO.

The catalyst part of the converter contains either a ceramic honeycomb or ceramic pellets. This substrate material offers a huge surface area to the exhaust gases flowing over it—the equivalent of a football field. The substrate has a thin coating of platinum and palladium metal that serves as the catalyst to trigger the chemical reaction that converts HC and CO into water vapor and carbon dioxide. The reaction generates a tremendous amount of heat, so the converter runs much hotter than the rest of the system. In the later "three-way" converters that also reduce NOx, the forward chamber contains substrate coated with rhodium. This metal causes NOx to break down into nitrogen and oxygen.

Problems

Several problems can render this very efficient system virtually useless. One is to use

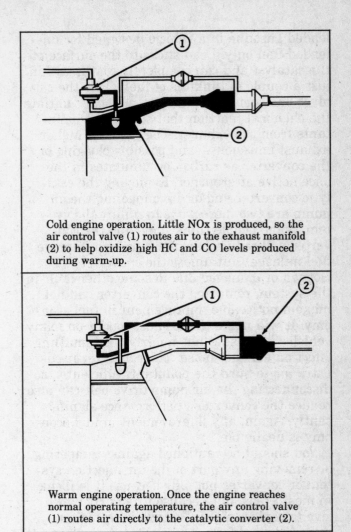

Cold engine operation. Little NOx is produced, so the air control valve (1) routes air to the exhaust manifold (2) to help oxidize high HC and CO levels produced during warm-up.

Warm engine operation. Once the engine reaches normal operating temperature, the air control valve (1) routes air directly to the catalytic converter (2).

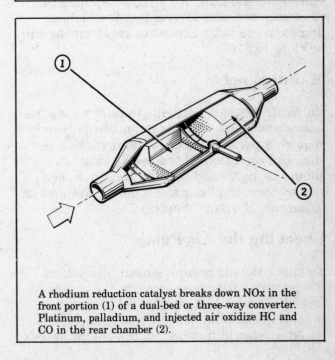

A rhodium reduction catalyst breaks down NOx in the front portion (1) of a dual-bed or three-way converter. Platinum, palladium, and injected air oxidize HC and CO in the rear chamber (2).

leaded gasoline in a vehicle designed for unleaded fuel only. Lead sticks to the surface of the catalyst and can completely coat it within just a couple of tankfuls of fuel. Once the catalyst has been ruined, it can no longer initiate the chemical reaction that scrubs the pollutants from the exhaust. The result is higher exhaust emissions—and possibly clogging of the converter as carbon accumulates in the once active afterburner. Removing the catalytic converter and/or disconnecting the air pump are two more ways to nullify the system. Some people think removing the converter will reduce backpressure and improve fuel mileage. But unless the converter is clogged or damaged due to some other fault in the system, removing the converter will not make a noticeable improvement in fuel economy. It will make the exhaust louder on many vehicles because it has a fairly good muffling effect on exhaust noise. The converter needs extra air to burn the pollutants efficiently, so disconnecting the air pump drive belt can also reduce the converter's performance significantly. Again, any improvement in fuel economy is negligible.

You should be cautioned against tampering or removing any part of the air injection system or converter not only because it is illegal in most areas, but because it is fairly expensive to replace if your vehicle is tested for emissions and fails. An original equipment converter can cost several hundred dollars and even the least expensive replacement will be close to $100.

Maintenance

Pulse air systems normally require no maintenance and those with air pumps usually only require a periodic check of the drive belt tension and condition. If the belt is loose, it should be tightened (see the section on belt replacement in either the "Cooling System" or "Charging System" chapters).

Checking the Air Pump

To check the air pump's output, disconnect the pump's outlet hose and run the engine at fast idle (about 1500 rpm). Feel the air coming out of the pump as you increase engine speed. It should increase as the engine speeds up. If there is no increase, or little air output, the pump is defective and should be replaced.

A noisy pump also indicates trouble, usually in the form of worn or damaged shaft bearings or pump vanes. Air pumps are not rebuildable by do-it-yourselfers, so you'll have to replace it with either a new or remanufactured unit. Oiling a noisy pump isn't recommended because oil can gum up the pump and attack the pump's seals and diverter valve diaphragm.

Checking the Diverter Valve

With the engine warm and idling, feel for air exhausting from the diverter valve vent or muffler. You should feel nothing as all air should be going to the exhaust manifold. Accelerate the engine momentarily, and as it returns to idle, air should now be vented out of the diverter valve or its muffler. Air should exhaust for several seconds. If nothing happens, check to see that vacuum is reaching the valve during engine deceleration by removing the vacuum hose from the valve and feeling for vacuum with your finger, while again accelerating the engine speed and letting it drop back to idle. If there is vacuum, but the diverter valve fails to respond, the valve is defective and should be replaced (backfiring would be common with this type of situation). If you don't feel any vacuum, the problem is in the vacuum line and not the valve. Check for a loose or plugged hose, or possibly a misrouted hose.

On the 1981 and newer systems, this same test applies to the first valve (or air control valve as it is sometimes called). The second air switching valve can be checked by noting which way it pumps air depending on engine temperature. When the engine is cold, air should be routed to the exhaust manifold. When the engine is hot, air should be sent to the converter. You can check air flow by removing one of the output hoses and feeling for air while the engine runs at fast idle.

Checking the Check Valve

To test a check valve, remove the valve from the engine while the engine is off. (Wait for the engine to cool if it is hot.) Then try to blow through the valve in both directions. It

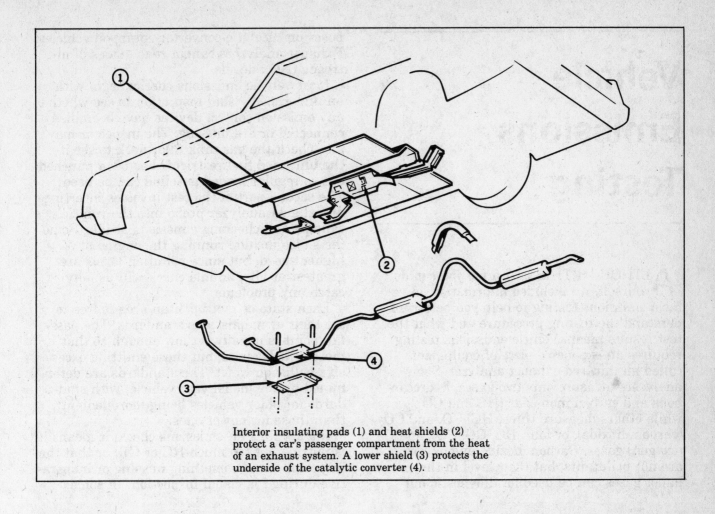

Interior insulating pads (1) and heat shields (2) protect a car's passenger compartment from the heat of an exhaust system. A lower shield (3) protects the underside of the catalytic converter (4).

should pass air towards the engine but not the other way. If you can blow through it both ways, or can't blow through it either way, the check valve is defective and should be replaced.

Checking the Pulse Air Valve

Disconnect the pulse air hose from the valve assembly, and use a hand vacuum pump to apply vacuum to the rubber hose end of the pulse air valve. Vacuum should drop no less than 5 inches in 2 seconds. Replace the valve if vacuum drops in less than two seconds.

Checking the Catalytic Converter

Although there's no way you can check the operating efficiency of the converter itself without an emissions analyzer, you can check for excessive backpressure in the exhaust system that might be due to a clogged or collapsed converter. Excessive temperatures inside the converter caused by flooding it with raw fuel while the engine is running (a misfiring cylinder, fuel leak in the engine, etc.) can sometimes cause the catalyst inside the converter shell to melt, partially or completely blocking the flow of exhaust. Symptoms of a plugged converter would be loss of power or stalling after the engine starts and runs a few minutes (if completely plugged).

To check for excessive backpressure, connect a vacuum gauge to the intake manifold and observe the readings while the engine idles. If the readings gradually drop and the engine idles slower and slower until it stalls, a plugged converter is at fault and should be replaced. A partially plugged converter won't cause the engine to stall, but it will limit power above idle and slow speeds. Again, a low vacuum gauge reading at 2500 to 3000 rpm (below 10 inches of mercury) indicates an exhaust restriction.

Vehicle Emissions Testing

ALTHOUGH THIS isn't a job you can do yourself, we included information on vehicle emissions testing to help you better understand the testing procedure and what the test results mean. Vehicle emissions testing requires an expensive piece of equipment called an infrared exhaust analyzer. Some analyzers measure only two gases, hydrocarbons and carbon monoxide (HC and CO), while others measure three, HC, CO, and CO_2 (carbon dioxide), or four, HC, CO, CO_2, and O_2 (oxygen) gases. Carbon dioxide and oxygen are not pollutants, but their level in the exhaust gases can be used for diagnostic pur-

poses on catalytic-converter-equipped vehicles. Exhaust analyzers cannot read oxides of nitrogen (NOx) levels.

Most vehicle emissions checks begin with an underhood visual inspection to see whether any emission-control devices have been disconnected or are missing. The inspector may also check the gas tank filler neck to see if the unleaded fuel restricter has been punched out so regular leaded gasoline can be used. The second part of the test involves inserting an exhaust analyzer probe into the vehicle's tailpipe and checking emissions at idle. Some tests also include running the engine at a higher speed, but since pollution levels are greatest at idle, an idle check will usually catch any problems.

Each state or metropolitan area is free to set their own emissions standards. The pass-fail point is usually set low enough so that most vehicles pass, but those emitting excessive pollution won't. The standards are determined by the model year vehicle, with standards for older vehicles being more lenient than those for newer ones.

If a car fails an emissions check, it means it is putting out too much HC or CO, or that the inspector found something missing or inoperative during his visual inspection. In some

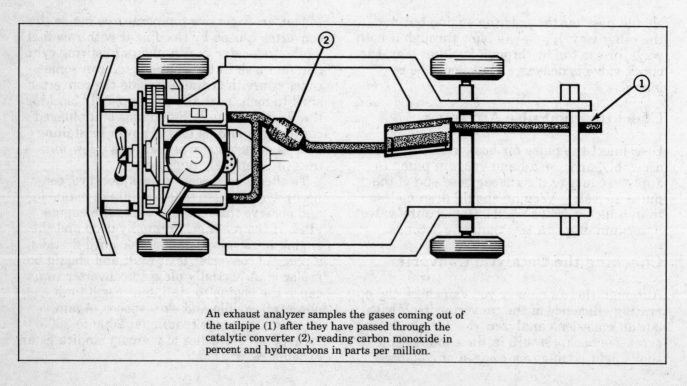

An exhaust analyzer samples the gases coming out of the tailpipe (1) after they have passed through the catalytic converter (2), reading carbon monoxide in percent and hydrocarbons in parts per million.

states, there is a cost waiver that says if repairs to bring a vehicle into compliance with the law will exceed a certain dollar amount, then the vehicle will be passed anyway. This is to avoid an undue financial hardship on those who can't afford to keep their vehicles in good repair. Other states have no such waiver. And even in those states that do have a waiver, there is no waiver allowed for cars that have been deliberately tampered with. In other words, if the inspector finds that you've replaced the catalytic converter with a piece of exhaust pipe or disconnected any emission control device, the vehicle must be restored to its original condition before it will be passed. Any missing or intentionally disconnected emission-control systems must be replaced regardless of cost.

Since the specifics of vehicle emissions testing vary considerably from one area to another, we suggest you contact your state department of transportation or environmental control for details.

Even if you live in an area where no periodic emissions checks are required, having your car's emissions checked at a local garage or dealership as part of a tune-up or diagnostic checkup can tell you a lot about your en-

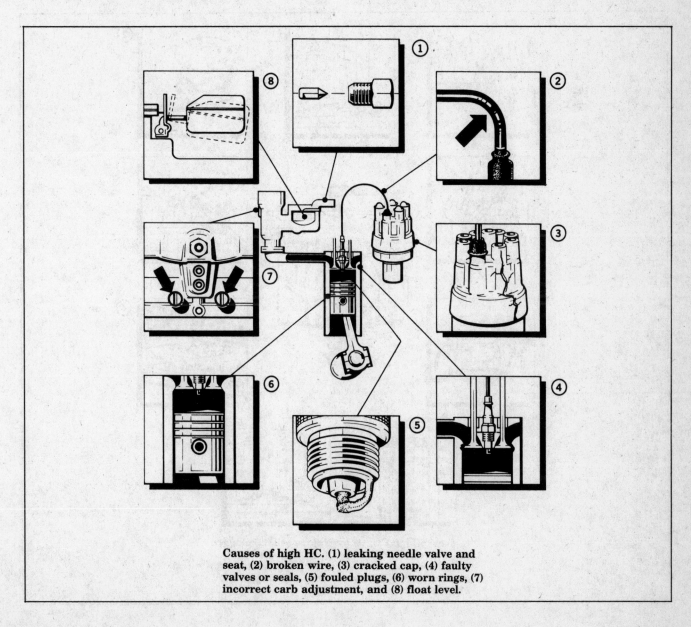

Causes of high HC. (1) leaking needle valve and seat, (2) broken wire, (3) cracked cap, (4) faulty valves or seals, (5) fouled plugs, (6) worn rings, (7) incorrect carb adjustment, and (8) float level.

gine's health. Or, if your car fails a state required emissions check, knowing the causes of high HC and CO emissions can help you determine the repairs needed.

High HC emissions often indicate an ignition problem such as a misfiring or fouled spark plug, a cracked distributor cap, or bad plug wire. Anything that interferes with good ignition will permit unburned fuel to pass through the engine and into the exhaust. Badly worn piston rings and/or valve guides that allow your engine to burn oil will also cause high HC readings. Carburetor flooding or an excessively rich fuel mixture likewise can contribute to high HC levels. Loss of compression due to a leaky valve or blown head gasket can pass unburned fuel into the exhaust, too.

Carbon monoxide indicates incomplete combustion resulting from too much fuel and/or not enough air. Things to check for here include a clogged air filter, sticking choke, misadjusted carburetor, plugged or inoperative PCV system, or a problem in the air pump or air injection system. Overadvanced ignition timing can also send CO levels soaring.

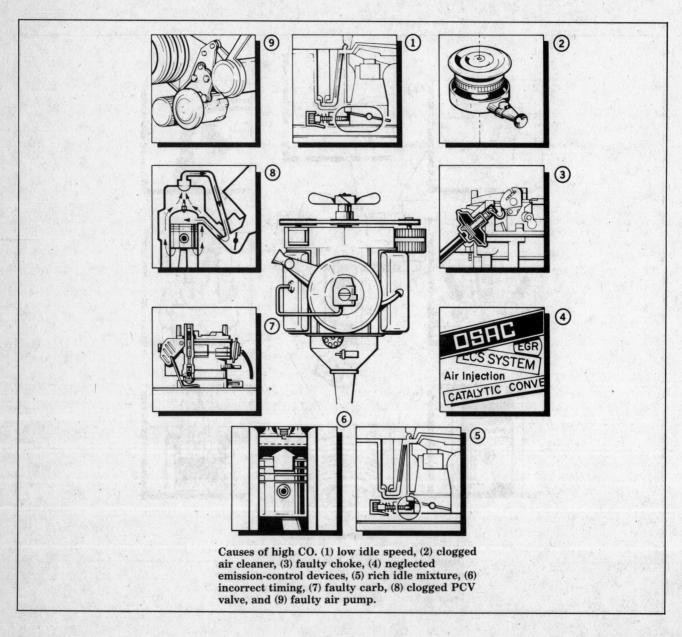

Causes of high CO. (1) low idle speed, (2) clogged air cleaner, (3) faulty choke, (4) neglected emission-control devices, (5) rich idle mixture, (6) incorrect timing, (7) faulty carb, (8) clogged PCV valve, and (9) faulty air pump.

THE IGNITION SYSTEM

THE IGNITION SYSTEM, one of several electrical systems in your car, is designed to ignite the air/fuel mixture inside your engine's cylinders. The ignition system is separated into two circuits. These circuits are the primary or low-voltage circuit and the secondary or high-voltage circuit. However, they function together and are interdependent.

The primary circuit consists of the battery, the ignition switch, the primary part of the ignition coil (the coil has a dual circuit), the primary side of the distributor (the distributor also has a dual circuit)—which includes the ignition breaker points and condenser on older cars, or the electronic ignition module, pickup coil, and armature on newer vehicles with electronic ignition—and, finally, the wires connecting each of these components to complete the electrical circuitry.

Components of the secondary circuit include the secondary part of the ignition coil, the secondary side of the distributor (distributor cap, rotor, and secondary wires), and, finally, the spark plugs.

The primary circuit depends on the battery for voltage to function when the car is being started. After the engine is running, the ignition system depends on the charging system for its voltage source.

When the ignition switch is turned on, the primary circuit (the low-voltage or battery circuit) of the ignition system is activated. Voltage is applied to the primary side of the coil and to the ignition breaker points in the distributor. On vehicles with electronic ignition, voltage is applied to the pickup coil module. The ignition coil has three wires connected to it. Two wires are small and connect to two small primary terminals on opposite sides of the coil. The third wire—the secondary high-tension wire—is heavier than the other two

(about the diameter of an ordinary pencil). It has a friction clip on one end, and is fastened by simply pushing it into a receptacle, called the coil tower, in the center of one end of the coil.

Ignition coil location varies from one type of engine to another. On V6 and V8 engines, however, the coil is usually mounted on top of the engine, very close to the distributor (or in the distributor on many General Motors cars with electronic ignition). Four- and six-cylinder in-line engines usually have the coil mounted on the side of the engine, near the distributor, opposite the carburetor and intake manifold.

This is a good place in our description of the ignition system to explain the concept of any electrical circuit in an automobile. It is simply a path for the flow of electric current (amperage) from a source (in this case, the battery or charging system) to one or more electrically operated units or devices and back to the source.

If the current's path is interrupted by a switch or a break in the path continuity (a broken wire or a loose or poor connection), the circuit is said to be *open* and no current (amperage) will flow. In your car, one side of the battery (the source of power) is connected directly to the car frame, floor pan, body, or the engine. For most electrical devices, the path of the circuit back to the battery is the car's frame, engine, or other metal part—because all of them are connected (grounded) to one side of the battery. A wire from the other side of an electrical device is connected to the other side of the battery, completing the circuit.

For example, a test light is composed of two wires hooked to a filament or bulb. If you touch one wire to one terminal of the battery and the other wire to the other terminal, current will flow through the wires to light the bulb. The test light also will light when one wire is touched to the battery terminal that is not connected to the engine or other metal parts of the car, and the other wire is touched to any metal part that is connected to the battery.

The Primary Ignition Circuit

Now that you have an idea of what a circuit is, let us get back to the primary ignition circuit. The two small wires connected to the ignition coil are the primary leads or wires. One of these wires is connected to the ignition switch, which, in turn, is connected by a wire to one terminal of the battery—the side not

connected to the metal parts of the engine block. When the ignition switch is turned on, this completes a path from the battery, through the ignition switch, and on to the ignition coil terminal on the ignition switch side of the coil.

Inside the ignition coil, there is a continuous series of wire loops or coils fastened between the primary coil terminals. The small wire connected to the other ignition coil terminal enters the distributor housing and is connected to one side of the ignition breaker points. The other side of the points is connected to the distributor housing. The points are a simple switch that is opened and closed as a shaft in the distributor is turned. On electronic ignition systems, the negative coil terminal is connected to the triggering circuit

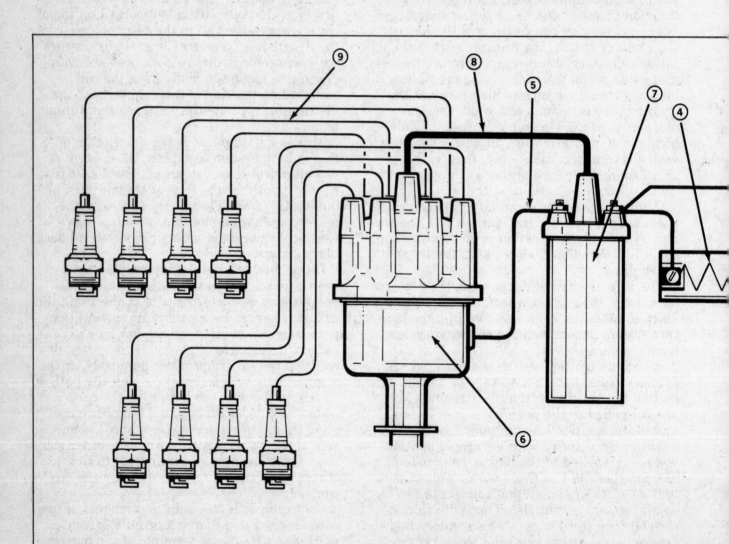

in the pickup control module. The module fires the coil by switching a ground circuit on and off.

The distributor housing is grounded to the engine block, which is connected to one side of the battery. When the ignition breaker points are closed by rotation of the distributor shaft, a circuit is completed and current flows through the primary circuit. When the rotation of the distributor shaft causes the ignition points to open, the flow of current is interrupted. With electronic ignitions, the same basic principle holds true except that instead of mechanically opening and closing of a set of contact points to complete the coil circuit, a solid state switching device grounds the coil.

When the distributor is properly adjusted for ignition timing, the distributor shaft rotates, opening and closing the ignition breaker points or triggering the pickup module which times the pulses of electrical energy that cause an arc at the electrodes of the spark plugs. The points, or module, however, do not cause the arc at the spark plugs; they merely trigger the secondary circuit. It is the secondary circuit that causes the arc.

The one remaining component in a contact point type primary circuit is the *condenser,* which is mounted in the distributor. It has two connections. One is connected to the ignition coil side of the ignition breaker points; the other is connected to the distributor's frame. The condenser has only one function—to act as an electrical "shock absorber" when the points open and close. It is designed to absorb a surge of high voltage and gradually

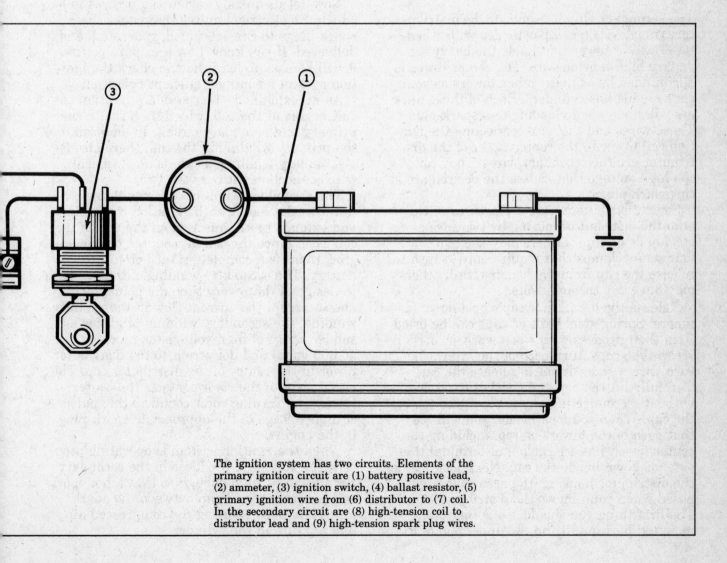

The ignition system has two circuits. Elements of the primary ignition circuit are (1) battery positive lead, (2) ammeter, (3) ignition switch, (4) ballast resistor, (5) primary ignition wire from (6) distributor to (7) coil. In the secondary circuit are (8) high-tension coil to distributor lead and (9) high-tension spark plug wires.

feed it back into the ignition circuit.

The ignition system will malfunction if the condenser is bad. If the points are open and the condenser is unable to absorb some of the high voltage, the points will flash and burn.

As we explained, a circuit is established between the ungrounded battery terminal and the windings of the primary coil when the ignition switch is turned on. When the ignition breaker points close, the circuit is completed through the coil, the engine block, and back to the battery. When the points are opened, the circuit is interrupted and the flow of current ceases. The condenser absorbs the voltage surge when the circuit is broken and gradually feeds it back into the circuit to prevent arcing or flash.

The Secondary Ignition Circuit

The secondary circuit begins at the distributor. This device has a plastic cap with a center crown or tower that holds the heavy secondary high-tension wire. The center tower is surrounded by as many other towers as your car's engine has cylinders. Each of these towers will have a wire leading to a spark plug. These wires and the wire connecting the ignition coil tower to the center tower of the distributor are the secondary wires. They carry the high voltage that causes the desired arc at the spark plugs.

Some distributors have a plastic cap held onto the distributor housing by two spring-steel bails or clips. Others may use two or four screw clamps that require only ½ turn to release the cap from the housing. Still others may have two through-bolts.

Release the distributor cap's hold-down fasteners. Spring-steel bails or clips can be pried from their grooves with a screwdriver. For screw-type caps, turn each of the screws ½ turn with a screwdriver to release the cap. Carefully lift the cap and gently turn it over without disconnecting any wires in the top of the cap. When you look inside, you will see that each of the towers on top, including the center tower, has a large metal terminal that extends down inside the cap. Next, look inside the distributor housing (the area that is exposed when you remove the distributor cap). The first thing you should see is the rotor, mounted horizontally on the upper end of the distributor shaft. This plastic piece has a metal strip that extends from the center toward the round distributor housing. The rotor turns with the distributor shaft. Below the rotor, you should be able to see the ignition breaker points and condenser or pickup coil and armature.

Place the distributor cap back into position and secure it with the hold-down fasteners. The cap can only seat one way on the housing because of a "guide key." Once the cap is on, look at the metal unit fastened to the side of the distributor housing. It has a small hose connected to it. This device, called the vacuum advance unit, automatically adjusts spark timing as the load on the engine varies. On many engines with computerized engine controls, spark timing is controlled electronically, so no vacuum advance unit is used.

Now, let us quickly review the process in which the electrical pulses that cause the spark plugs to fire are timed, generated, and delivered. If you know how the spark occurs, it will be easy to learn how to check the ignition system for proper, efficient operation.

As we explained, the secondary ignition circuit begins at the coil, which serves both the primary and secondary circuit. In addition to the primary winding in the coil, there also is a secondary winding. There is no electrical wire connection between the two.

The secondary winding connects to the tower in the center of the ignition coil casing and extends to a connection on the end of the coil case. Since the coil is mounted on the engine, there is a complete return circuit to the battery. The secondary winding of the coil is so designed that every time the points open and interrupt the current flow in the primary winding, the secondary winding produces a sudden surge of high voltage (as much as 40,000 volts) and delivers it to the distributor tower in the center of the distributor cap. The metal strip in the rotor contacts the center tower. The turning rotor conducts this pulse of high voltage to the appropriate spark plug in the engine.

When the ignition system is operating properly, the voltage it produces in the secondary circuit will be high enough so that a hot spark will jump the small gap between the spark plug electrodes, igniting the compressed air/fuel mixture in the cylinder.

Point Ignition Systems

Tools and Materials

- Screwdriver
- Ignition Wrenches
- Steel Feeler Gauge
- Clean Cloth
- Solvent
- High-Temperature Grease (Cam Lubricant)
- Breaker Points and Condenser
- Felt Wick Lubricator
- Motor Oil

IF YOUR car's engine is equipped with an electronic ignition system, you may skip this section because electronic ignition systems have no distributor breaker points or condenser.

The ignition system, as we said in the introduction to this chapter, works by the opening and closing of a switch in the ignition's primary circuit. This stops the primary current and develops secondary current in the ignition coil by induction. This induced secondary current is ultimately used to fire the spark plugs.

While all components of the ignition system are important and must be functioning properly for an efficiently running engine, the distributor breaker, or contact, points are perhaps the most vulnerable component in the system.

The breaker points are located inside the distributor and are attached to the breaker plate by screws. Two wires are connected to the points. One is the condenser wire; the other is the ignition primary wire from the ignition coil's primary terminal.

The breaker points are constructed of a low-resistance metal, usually tungsten. Electrical current flows from the wire connection, through the movable arm of the points assembly, across the closed points to the stationary part of the assembly, and on to the ground to complete the circuit.

The assembly is adjustable. Depending on the make and model of your engine, the adjustment screws will be either slotted or hex-head screws, and you will need that type of screwdriver. Whichever adjustment your car has, it accomplishes the same thing—it allows you to vary the amount of space, or gap, between the points.

This gap is critical. If it is too large, the points will not stay closed long enough. If the gap is too small, the points will stay closed too long. The length of time the points stay closed, referred to as "dwell time," has a direct effect on the operation of the ignition system.

If the dwell time is too brief, the primary circuit of the ignition will not have enough time to build up a sufficient magnetic field in the coil. Therefore, when the points do open and the primary circuit is interrupted, the induced secondary voltage will not be strong enough to properly fire the spark plug. In such a case, a rough-running engine will result. At times, even a no-start condition will result or, perhaps, you will have an engine with no power.

If the dwell time is too long, there will not be enough time for the induced secondary voltage to do its job before primary current will again flow through the circuit. This, too, creates a low power situation or roughly running engine, because the basic ignition timing is affected.

High electrical resistance across the points is a common condition. This resistance impedes the primary ignition system from completing its circuit on time, so loss of engine power will be experienced. In addition, the points will wear rapidly.

Replacing breaker points sometimes takes a bit of patience, because you have to work inside the distributor with small tools. But once you get the knack of it, it is a fairly simple job. The first time you do it, you may want to

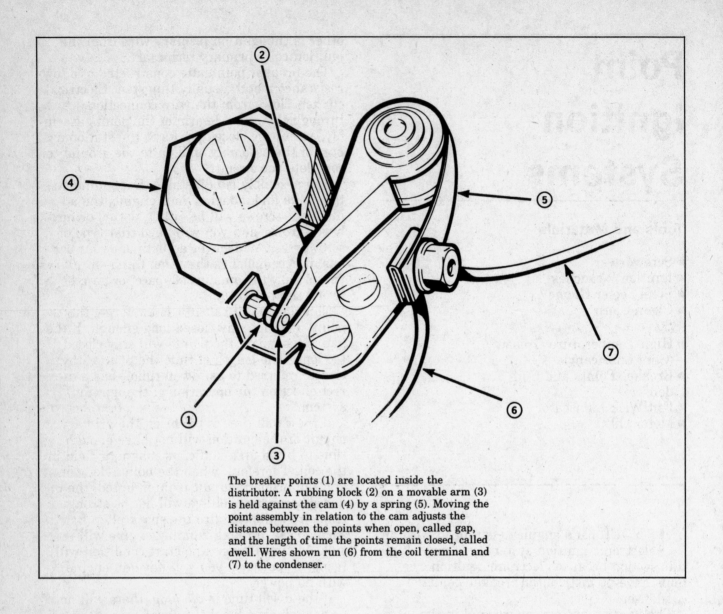

The breaker points (1) are located inside the distributor. A rubbing block (2) on a movable arm (3) is held against the cam (4) by a spring (5). Moving the point assembly in relation to the cam adjusts the distance between the points when open, called gap, and the length of time the points remain closed, called dwell. Wires shown run (6) from the coil terminal and (7) to the condenser.

have the help of someone who has done the job before, just in case you experience some difficulty.

There are certain safety rules to be observed when you are working on any part of the electrical or ignition system. The rule that applies here is that the ignition switch must be turned off all the time you are touching or handling the components inside the distributor. If the ignition switch is turned on, the primary ignition circuit is energized and current will flow as the circuit is completed. Your body will complete the circuit to ground if you are touching a metal part of the car and at the same time touch any energized part or wire in the distributor. **Caution:** *You may re-*

ceive a disagreeable shock. If you are shocked, there is little danger of harm because the current flow at this point is low. The real danger lies in striking a sharp object with your hand or arm when you pull away as a result of surprise at being shocked.

The information contained in this section is factual, but it does not apply to some General Motors and American Motors Corporation cars in respect to adjusting the breaker points. If your distributor cap is held in place by clamp screws, you will need a dwell-tachometer. Turn to the section on "Adjusting Dwell" and follow the adjustment procedure for "Dwell Adjustment for Window-Cap Distributors." Here is how to replace and adjust the points if your distributor has bails or spring clips that hold the distributor cap in position.

1. Verify that the ignition is in the off position. Remove the distributor cap. To release the cap from the distributor housing, simply pry the bails or spring clips loose from grooves in the distributor cap. Raise the cap and carefully move it away from the distributor housing.

2. Remove the rotor. The majority of cars have a rotor that is placed on top of the distributor shaft. To remove it, lift it up and off the shaft. Other rotors are secured to the shaft by two screws. Use a screwdriver to loosen these screws to remove the rotor.

3. Some distributors on older model cars have a radio frequency interference (RFI) shield covering the points. If your distributor is so equipped, remove it. This involves removing two screws holding down the shield. Note their placement to ease reassembly. A spring-loaded, screw-holding screwdriver works well here.

4. Disconnect the wire leads attached to the movable arms of the breaker points. There are two of them—the primary wire and the condenser wire. Use either a wrench or screwdriver, whichever is applicable, to loosen the fasteners and disconnect the wires. **Note:** Some General Motors cars have a points-condenser combination called a Uniset assembly. In such a case, the condenser is removed with the points and only the primary wire needs to be removed.

5. Remove the breaker points. With a screwdriver, loosen the one or two screws holding the points. The points can sometimes be removed without removing the screws entirely.

6. Remove the condenser mounting screw that holds the condenser in place, but

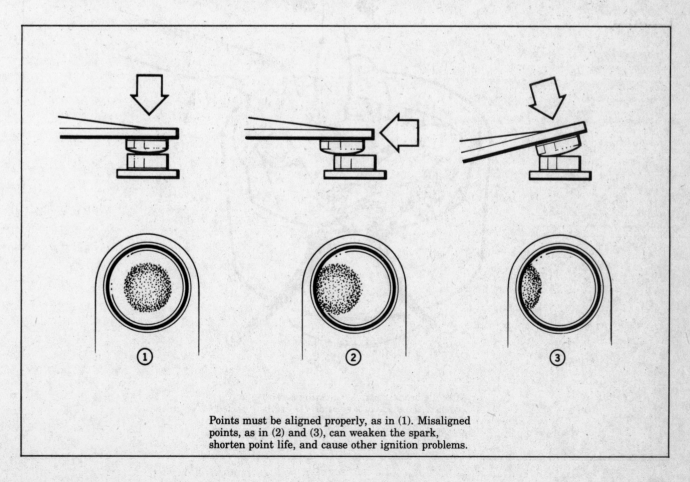

Points must be aligned properly, as in (1). Misaligned points, as in (2) and (3), can weaken the spark, shorten point life, and cause other ignition problems.

remember in which direction the wire lead faces for easier reinstallation.

7. Remove the condenser. If the distributor has a cam lubricator or wick under the rotor, remove it too.

8. Look into the distributor for any signs of rust, corrosion, oil, or grease. Use a clean cloth dampened with solvent to clean inside the distributor housing and shaft, removing all varnish and gum deposits. Clean any grease and dust from the breaker plate at the base of the distributor and the cam with a clean cloth. Dry the entire assembly thoroughly.

9. Lubricate the distributor cam with a light coating of high-temperature grease called cam lubricant. **Note:** Some replacement points are packed with a small amount of grease to be used for lubricating the cam. Be sure to keep the lubricant off the points, cap, rotor, and all electrical connections. *Caution: Be sure you have obtained the correct replacement points and condenser before installation.*

10. Install the new points and condenser. Reverse Steps 2 through 7. Do not tighten the points, hold-down screws until the points' spacing, or gap, has been set. Screws on GM and AMC V8

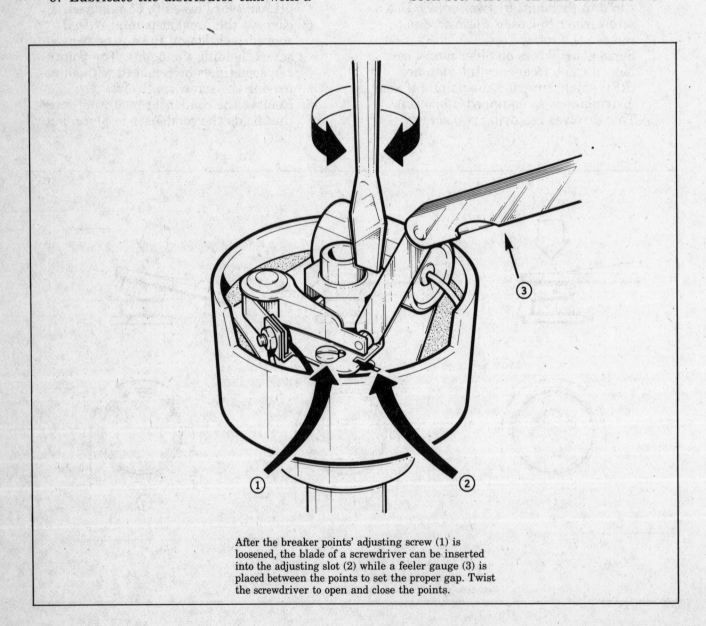

After the breaker points' adjusting screw (1) is loosened, the blade of a screwdriver can be inserted into the adjusting slot (2) while a feeler gauge (3) is placed between the points to set the proper gap. Twist the screwdriver to open and close the points.

engines with window distributor caps, however, may now be tightened because the adjustment is made with a hex-head screw that is part of the points assembly. (See the section on "Adjusting Dwell" in this chapter.)

If it is not part of a set, install the new condenser, positioning it so the condenser lead end is flush with its mounting bracket to take the slack out of the lead. Then, tighten the bracket hold-down.

11. Align the points by having someone crank the engine with the ignition switch until the rubbing block on the points assembly is resting on the peak of one of the distributor cam lobes. The ignition switch should be flicked on just to bump the engine to get the proper point-cam position. Remember to turn the ignition switch *off* once the proper position is obtained.

12. Check the specifications for the precise opening for the points. It will be listed in your service manual. This information is given in thousandths of an inch. For example, 0.017 inch. **Note:** Some tune-up charts give no specification for ignition point gap. However, there will always be a specification for dwell. If the point gap specification is not known, divide the dwell value by two and the result will be the approximate point opening. For example, if the dwell specification is 30, then the point opening should be set at 15 thousandths of an inch, or 0.015.

Note: Some General Motors and American Motors Corporation cars are equipped with ignition breaker points that cannot be set by using a flat feeler gauge. Points of this type have a bi-metal saddle installed between the movable, spring-loaded arm and stationary (ground) arm of the points assembly. Do not attempt to remove this saddle in order to insert a feeler gauge between the contact points. If your car is so equipped, a dwell meter must be used to establish the point setting. Refer to the "Adjusting Dwell" section in this chapter.

13. Insert a clean steel feeler gauge of the specified thickness between the points.

14. Carefully move the stationary base of the points to adjust the opening. Use a screwdriver to turn the adjusting screw or open and close the adjusting slot to obtain the correct opening. When the feeler gauge can be slid in and out of the points opening with only a slight drag, the points opening is correctly set and the points assembly hold-down screws may be tightened.

Note: If you have removed a felt wick lubricator, install a new one after the points have been installed and gapped. Apply only a few drops of ordinary motor oil to the wick. Also apply a drop of oil or a light film of lubricant to the breaker point pivot whenever you replace the points.

15. If an RFI shield was removed, replace it reversing Step 3.

16. Reinstall the rotor, reversing Step 2.

17. Reinstall the distributor cap, reversing Step 1.

Using a Dwell-Tachometer

The dwell-tachometer is a basic but very valuable instrument that can perform several important tests. The most common model is a hand-held instrument with several scales on one dial face and a multi-position switch or switches. Usually, there are only two connections required to make the unit function. However, the selector, or mode switch, must be set for the test that is being performed.

With a good but inexpensive dwell-tachometer, you can test for engine revolutions per minute (rpm), dwell angle, and points condition.

Dwell, as we explained elsewhere, is the period during which the distributor points remain closed for an ignition cycle. The dwell meter electrically measures this period and registers the average for all cylinders in terms of degrees of the distributor cam rotation. You can find the specifications for dwell in your car's service manual or tune-up guide. When checking for points condition, you are actually measuring the continuity at the points. This simply means measuring the ability or inability of the points to conduct primary voltage.

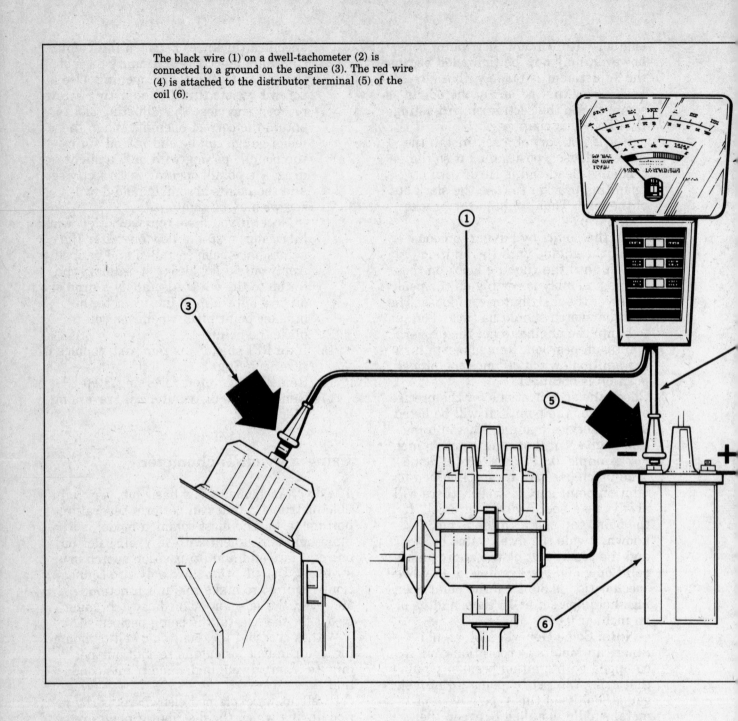

The black wire (1) on a dwell-tachometer (2) is connected to a ground on the engine (3). The red wire (4) is attached to the distributor terminal (5) of the coil (6).

Meter Operation

On the face of the average dwell-tachometer, there will be at least three scales. One represents engine rpm on a tachometer scale from 0 to about 15. Each division represents engine rpm multiplied by 100. Therefore, if you read 7 on the tachometer scale, the engine will be turning at 700 rpm. Since most dwell-tachometers are set up to be used on six- or eight-cylinder engines, you must divide the reading shown on the eight-cylinder scale in half if the engine you are working on has only four cylinders.

The second scale is engine dwell. As explained, this is the period of time, measured in degrees, that the points are closed during each ignition cycle. A single cycle is the open-close action required for each spark plug to fire. An important point is that there is a di-

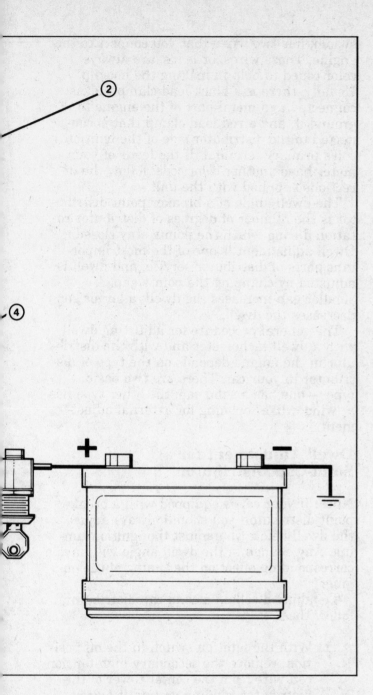

When you look at your dwell-tachometer, you will see that there is a switch position for six-cylinder or four- and eight-cylinder readings. It is important that this switch be in the correct position when testing because the meter automatically computes dwell and tachometer readings based on the number of times the points open and close during a complete revolution of the distributor shaft, depending on the number of cylinders the engine has. Because a six-cylinder engine has six lobes on the distributor cam and an eight-cylinder has eight, the reading obtained would be incorrectly computed by the meter if it were not set correctly.

Another function of most all dwell-tachometers is points condition. Usually, this is indicated on the scale at the bottom of the meter. This scale will have at least two divisions—"Good" and "Bad." With the ignition switch at the on position and the meter switched to the "Points" position, the scale will indicate whether or not the points are in satisfactory condition. If the scale reads "Bad" and you believe the points are still good, "bump" the ignition switch to crank the engine slightly. This will allow the breaker points to close so the meter will give a correct reading. If a "Good" reading cannot be obtained after several attempts at this procedure, you will have to replace the ignition breaker points. Of course, dwell and tach readings are taken while the engine is running, but points are checked while the engine is stopped.

Dwell-Tachometer Hookup

Since dwell-tachometers vary, it is necessary to follow the correct procedure for the instrument you are using. The following, however, is a basic procedure for connecting a dwell-tachometer.

1. On most units, you will find two wire leads, one red and one black. The black lead should be connected to a good ground, such as the negative (−) battery terminal or a part on the engine block. **Caution:** *Never connect the lead to the carburetor or air cleaner stud. This would not only provide a poor*

rect relationship between dwell and setting the points air gap, another tune-up procedure. The number of degrees for a single ignition cycle is 360° (one full revolution of the distributor cam) divided by the number of cylinders in the engine. For example, a six-cylinder engine would be 60° for each cylinder, only 36° of which will represent dwell. A wider point setting will result in less dwell; a smaller point setting will increase the dwell.

ground, but would create a safety haz-ard—the possibility of electrical sparks near gasoline.

2. The red wire lead should be connected to the primary side of the ignition coil. This will be the side to which the distributor breaker points are connected. On some cars, especially Fords, you will need an adapter to allow you to connect this lead and still have electrical contact between the coil terminal and the primary lead. These adapters usually are provided with the test instrument.

Adjusting Dwell

Tools and Materials

- Jumper Wire
- Screwdriver
- Golf Tees
- Remote Starter Switch
- Dwell-Tachometer
- Hexagonal Allen Wrench

NEW POINTS may be set with reasonable accuracy using a clean feeler gauge. However, used points that may be slightly pitted or burned *must* always be gapped with a dwell meter, as well as new or used points in a window-cap distributor that allows adjustment with the distributor fully assembled.

The use of a remote starter switch will make dwell adjustment a one-person operation. The switch allows you to control the cranking of the engine while you are working under the hood. This remote switch has two wires, or leads, that you connect to the starter solenoid. Follow the directions included with the switch. They will explain exactly how the wires are to be connected.

The dwell meter, like the remote starter switch, has two wires that you connect to the engine. These wires, or leads, are always color-coded to help in making the hookup. Usually, there is a black lead-clamp that is connected to a metal part of the engine to ground it, and a red lead clamp that is connected to the distributor side of the ignition coil's primary terminal. If the leads of your meter have another color code, follow the directions supplied with the unit.

The dwell angle of a breaker point distributor is the number of degrees of distributor rotation during which the points stay closed. Dwell adjustment is one of the most important parts of distributor service, and dwell is adjusted by changing the points gap. A smaller gap increases the dwell; a larger gap decreases the dwell.

The general procedure for adjusting dwell with a dwell-tachometer and with the distributor in the engine depends on the type of distributor in your car. There are two basic types—one has a solid cap; the other type has a "windowlike" opening for external adjustment.

Dwell Adjustment for a Solid-Cap Distributor

Note: If your car is equipped with a breaker point distributor, you should always adjust the dwell before you adjust the ignition timing. Any change in the dwell angle will have a corresponding effect on the timing of the engine.

To adjust dwell on a solid-cap distributor, follow these steps.

1. With the ignition switch in the off position, remove the secondary high-tension coil wire from the center tower of the distributor cap and ground it by connecting it to a metal part of the engine with a jumper wire. *Caution: Never connect the wire to the carburetor or air cleaner stud. This would not only provide a poor ground, but would create a safety hazard—the possibility of electrical sparks near gasoline.*
2. Remove the distributor cap. Release the spring clips or turn each clamp hold-down ½ turn clockwise or counterclockwise while pushing down on a screw-

driver to release the cap.
3. Remove the rotor. Most can simply be lifted off the distributor's center shaft with your hand; others may be secured by two screws and can be removed with a screwdriver.

   Note: Some distributors on older model cars have a radio frequency interference (RFI) shield covering the points. If your distributor is so equipped, remove it. This involves removing two screws holding down the shield. Note their placement to ease reassembly. A spring-loaded, screw-holding screwdriver works well here.
4. Disconnect and plug vacuum lines with golf tees if required.
5. Connect a remote starter switch to the starter solenoid, following the directions supplied with the switch. If you do not have this convenient device, someone will have to assist you by cranking the engine with the ignition switch at certain steps.
6. Connect the dwell-tachometer to the engine according to the manufacturer's instructions. The following, however, is a basic procedure for connecting this instrument.
   A. On most units, you will find two wire leads—one red and one black. Connect the black lead to a good ground, such as the negative (−) battery terminal or a part on the engine block. If the leads of your meter have another color code, follow the directions supplied with the unit. *Caution: Never connect the lead to the carburetor or air cleaner stud. This would not only provide a poor ground, but would create a safety hazard—the possibility of electrical sparks near gasoline.*
   B. Connect the red wire lead to the primary side of the ignition coil. This will be the side to which the distributor breaker points are connected. On some cars, especially Fords, you will need an adapter to allow you to connect this lead and still have electrical contact between the coil terminal and the primary lead. These adapters usually are provided with

the test instrument.
7. Turn the ignition to the "on" position. *Caution: This is an important step! Failure to do so can result in damage to the ignition switch ground circuit.*
8. Loosen the point adjusting screw or shift point bracket in the distributor with a screwdriver.
9. While observing the dwell-tachometer, crank the engine using the remote starter switch. Turn the point adjusting screw or shift point bracket to obtain specified degrees of dwell. Some points are adjusted by turning an eccentric adjustment screw; others are adjusted by moving the mounting bracket with a screwdriver placed in a slotted hole.
10. After adjusting the dwell, retighten the point adjustment screws and turn the ignition to the "off" position.
11. Wipe the distributor cam with a clean cloth and apply a film of cam lubricant. If a cam lubricator or wick is used in the distributor, turn it to expose fresh lubricant to the cam, or replace the lubricator.
12. If you have removed an RFI shield, reinstall it at this time but make sure that the primary or condenser leads are not caught under the edge of the shield before tightening the two shield retaining screws. Failure to install the shield will result in radio interference.
13. Reinstall the rotor. If your rotor was secured by two screws, place the rotor on the distributor shaft. There will be a round and a square peg on the rotor that will fit into a round and square hole in the rotor mount. Do not try to force the rotor. You will break it. Using a screwdriver, tighten the screws. If your rotor slips over the distributor's center shaft, you should note a flat side on the shaft. This will correspond to the flat area inside the rotor. It, too, will only go on the shaft one way.
14. Replace the distributor cap, reversing the procedure used for removal.
15. Remove the jumper wire and reconnect the secondary high-tension coil wire.
16. Remove the remote starter switch.
17. Disconnect the dwell-tachometer, reversing Step 6.

Dwell Adjusting for a Window-Cap Distributor

Note: General Motors V6 and V8 breaker-point distributors have a "window" in their distributor caps so that the dwell angle can be adjusted with the cap in place and with the engine running at idle speed. If the spark plugs have been removed from the engine

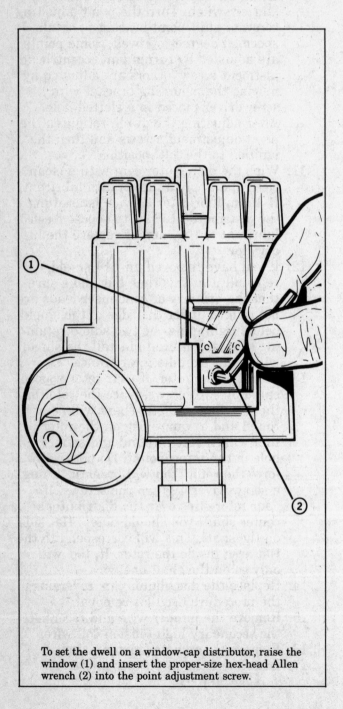

To set the dwell on a window-cap distributor, raise the window (1) and insert the proper-size hex-head Allen wrench (2) into the point adjustment screw.

during the course of a tune-up, install them before proceeding. Refer to the section on "Evaluating and Installing Spark Plugs" in this chapter.

If your car has a window-cap distributor, follow these steps.

1. With the ignition switch in the off position, connect the dwell-tachometer to the engine according to the manufacturer's instructions. The following, however, is a basic procedure for connecting this instrument.
   A. On most units, you will find two wire leads—one red and one black. Connect the black lead to a good ground, such as the negative (−) battery terminal or a part on the engine block. If the leads of your meter have another color code, follow the directions supplied with the unit. *Caution: Never connect the lead to the carburetor or air cleaner stud. This would not only provide a poor ground, but would create a safety hazard—the possibility of electrical sparks near gasoline.*
   B. Connect the red wire lead to the primary side of the ignition coil. This will be the side to which the distributor breaker points are connected. On some cars, especially Fords, you will need an adapter to allow you to connect this lead and still have electrical contact between the coil terminal and the primary lead. These adapters usually are provided with the test instrument.
2. Start the engine and let it idle.
3. Raise the window in the distributor cap and insert the proper-size hexagonal Allen wrench into the point adjustment screw.
4. While observing the dwell-tachometer, turn the adjustment screw clockwise to increase the dwell; counterclockwise to decrease it. The adjustment is self-locking.
5. After the dwell has been adjusted, remove the wrench and close the cap window.
6. Disconnect the dwell-tachometer, reversing Step 1.

Electronic Ignition

Tools and Materials

- Insulated Pliers
- Voltmeter and Ohmmeter or Volt/Ohmmeter (VOM)
- Jumper Wires
- Remote Starter Switch
- Screwdriver
- Coil Spring Adapter
- Timing Light
- Dwell-Tachometer
- Golf Tee

ONE OF THE most troublesome components in a car's ignition system always has been the distributor's breaker points. Today, however, the points and condenser of conventional systems have been replaced by electronic ignition systems, which cause far fewer problems.

Some advantages of electronic ignition systems are: more available secondary circuit voltage to reduce engine misfiring; less spark plug fouling, hence longer plug life; less high-speed missing to improve fuel economy and reduce emissions; and more reliable starting.

Although the differences between an electronic ignition system and the conventional point system it replaces are great, there are few differences in servicing. Fortunately, most of these differences make the task easier.

In electronic ignition systems, for example, the distributor cam is replaced by a round part with teeth that resembles a pointed wheel. Chrysler calls this device a "reluctor;" Ford calls it an "armature;" and General Motors calls it a "timing core." Ford's name probably comes closest to describing the part's

function, so "armature" is the term we will use here.

Along with the armature is a magnetic pickup coil, which replaces the breaker points of a conventional system, and a transistorized control box or electronic control unit. As the distributor shaft turns, the teeth of the armature pass the pickup coil and establish a magnetic impulse that then is directed to the electronic control unit. The control unit is designed to break the coil's primary circuit each time an impulse is received from the pickup coil. Breaking the coil's primary circuit will allow the coil's secondary circuit to produce the high voltage necessary to fire the spark plug.

Electronic ignitions can raise voltage to the spark plugs up to 40,000 volts as compared with 15,000 to 20,000 volts in conventional systems. With this greater voltage, spark plugs can be gapped wider for better performance. This high voltage, however, imposes greater demands on spark plug wiring. So, you must be sure that the wires' insulation is in good shape and that all connections are clean and tight. (See the section on "Spark Plug Wires" in this chapter.) Also, you must check the distributor cap and rotor for cracks, dirt, and corrosion.

As stated earlier, there are significant differences between electronic and conventional ignition systems. There are also significant differences between the electronic ignition systems as used by the various car manufacturers, so it is important to take a look into some of the systems used and how they can be serviced.

Servicing Electronic Ignition Systems

Servicing electronic ignitions generally requires detailed service information with technical specifications and test procedures. This kind of information can be found in a shop manual for your vehicle, but unless you're a fairly competent do-it-yourselfer, you'd probably be better off leaving electronic ignition troubleshooting and repair to a knowledgeable professional. If, however, your car does not start and you suspect the electronic ignition system, you can perform a spark intensity test without special test instruments to prove

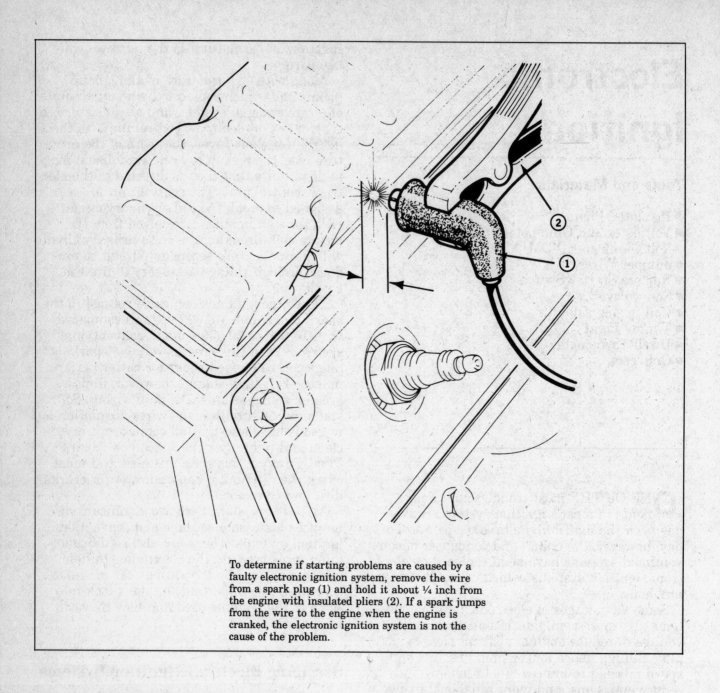

To determine if starting problems are caused by a faulty electronic ignition system, remove the wire from a spark plug (1) and hold it about ¼ inch from the engine with insulated pliers (2). If a spark jumps from the wire to the engine when the engine is cranked, the electronic ignition system is not the cause of the problem.

there is a problem in the system. *Caution: When making a spark intensity test, do not remove the following spark plug wires.*

- V8 Engines—No. 1 or No. 8 spark plug wire
- Inline Six-Cylinder Engines—No. 3 or No. 5 spark plug wire
- V6 Engines—No. 1 or No. 4 spark plug wire
- Inline Four-Cylinder Engines—No. 1 or No. 3 spark plug wire

If one of these wires is used, it can cause the distributor rotor to arc and crossfire to the pickup coil. This will damage the coil or rotor, or both. To perform the spark intensity test, follow these steps.

1. Disconnect a spark plug wire (see caution above) at the spark plug. Grasp the rubber boot and twist, carefully pulling the wire from the spark plug by hand. Do not pull on the wire itself. You can easily damage it.

2. Hold the end of the spark plug wire with a pair of insulated spark plug pliers near a metallic part of the engine—about ¼ to ⅜ inch is sufficient.
3. Have someone crank the engine.
4. While the engine is cranking, look for a spark to jump from the spark plug wire you are holding to the engine. You also may hear a crackling sound. This is the high-voltage spark jumping the gap.

If there is a spark jump, your no-start condition is not caused by the electronic ignition system. If there is no spark jump, you may find the problem in the electronic ignition by using a voltmeter and an ohmmeter, or a single instrument that combines these two devices—a volt/ohmmeter or VOM. No matter which instrument you use, it will have two wires—a red lead and a black lead.

Testing Electronic Ignition Systems

To troubleshoot the electronic ignition system in your car, proceed to the appropriate series of tests, arranged by manufacturer. The following tests must be performed in sequence to locate the defective component in the system. In addition to a volt/ohmmeter, jumper wires are required for some tests. A remote starter switch is also helpful in performing many tests, otherwise you will have to have someone assist you.

Note: In the following procedures, all tests conducted with a voltmeter, or the voltmeter section of a volt/ohmmeter (VOM), are made with the ignition switch turned to the "on" or "start" position. With the ignition switch in either of these positions, the voltage from the car battery should be present in the circuit wiring and all parts of the ignition system. Voltmeter tests must be made when the system circuits are "alive," or completed, and battery voltage is available at the test connections to be valid. All tests conducted with an ohmmeter, or the ohmmeter section of a volt/ohmmeter (VOM), are made with the ignition switch turned to the "off" position and no voltage is present in any part of the ignition system beyond the ignition switch. Ohmmeter tests *must* be made while the system circuits are "dead" and *no* battery voltage is available at the test connections. ***Caution:*** *Never attempt to test a live circuit with an ohmmeter; doing so will damage the test instrument.*

General Test Procedures

Whether you drive a domestic or import automobile, the basic procedures for troubleshooting an electronic ignition are generally similar:

1. You first check the battery voltage to see that there is sufficient charge in the battery to power the ignition. Most electronic ignitions need a minimum of 9 volts.
2. Next you turn the key on and check to see if voltage is reaching the positive (+) side of the ignition coil. Your voltmeter should read battery voltage.
3. If the ignition system passed the spark test described earlier, then you can assume the coil, distributor pickup, and control module are working. The only exception here would be a system that misfires or dies intermittently. This problem indicates an intermittent short or open somewhere in the module or pickup, or in the wiring between them.

   If the ignition system failed to produce a spark, you have to figure out whether it is the coil, the pickup, the module, or the wiring somewhere in between.
4. To rule out the coil, you turn the ignition off and check both the primary and secondary resistance of the coil. Always refer to the exact specifications listed by the manufacturer, but generally speaking, the primary resistance between the coil positive and negative terminals will be between 0.5 and 3 ohms. A very high reading indicates an open in the coil primary windings, so replace it if that's what you find. Secondary resistance between the coil negative terminal and high-voltage lead is usually somewhere between 8000 to 12,000 ohms. A very low reading would indicate a ground whereas a very high reading would indicate an open. (See

the section on "The Ignition Coil" at the end of this chapter.)

If the coil's primary and secondary resistance readings are within the manufacturer's specs, you can rule it out as the source of trouble.

5. The next item to check is the pickup coil in the distributor. To test it, unplug the pickup connector and measure its resistance with your ohmmeter. Again, refer to the manufacturer's specs. The general range of values here is 150 to 1200 ohms. A very high reading would indicate an open in the coil or its leads, while a very low reading would indicate a short. You should also check to see that the pickup coil is not grounded by checking resistance between both pickup coil leads and the distributor housing. Your meter should read infinity if the pickup is not grounded.

If the pickup passes these tests, you can rule it out as a possible cause of ignition problems.

Note: On some Chrysler systems, the distance between the pickup coil and the arms on the distributor shaft armature can have a bearing on ignition performance. This is referred to as the *air gap* setting, and it must be within specs for the application.

On electronic ignition systems that use a "Hall Effect" pickup, you should check to see that the shutter on the underside of the rotor is grounded. If it isn't, the Hall pickup won't generate a signal to the control module.

6. Now you're down to two things that could be responsible for your no-start or intermittent spark condition: the ignition control module or the wiring. To check the wiring, you'll need to refer to your shop manual again to determine which connector leads do what. Basically, you rule out wiring problems by checking the wires between the module and pickup for continuity, then checking the module power connector for battery voltage when the key is on. Many modules are also grounded through this connector. If your test shows no opens or shorts in the wiring between the module and pickup, and the module is

receiving power and ground, it should work. If it isn't, or if the car works sometimes and sometimes not, the module is probably defective and should be replaced. Make sure it is not a wiring problem by wiggling all the connectors while you're doing your wiring checks.

Checking out an electronic ignition system really isn't that difficult if you understand the basics of what it is you're doing and you have the right service information.

Because of the great amount of diversity and complexity that has become common in recent ignition systems, we won't attempt to duplicate all the specific service information that's available in numerous shop manuals. We will, however, give you some basics on a few of the more common systems so you can appreciate what's involved in checking out the electronic ignition system.

American Motors

Note: In 1978, some American Motors Corporation cars were equipped with the Dura-Spark II electronic ignition system. Refer to the tests for Ford for this procedure.

BATTERY CONDITION TEST

1. Set the volt/ohmmeter (VOM) selector to 16 volts.
2. Connect the VOM red lead to the positive (+) battery terminal.
3. Connect the VOM black lead to the negative (−) battery terminal.
4. Disconnect the secondary high-tension wire from the center tower of the distributor and ground it to a metal part of the engine with a jumper wire.
5. Crank the engine long enough to obtain a meter reading. The meter should read at least 9.0 volts. If it does, turn the ignition switch off, disconnect the jumper wire, disconnect the VOM red lead, reconnect the secondary high-tension wire

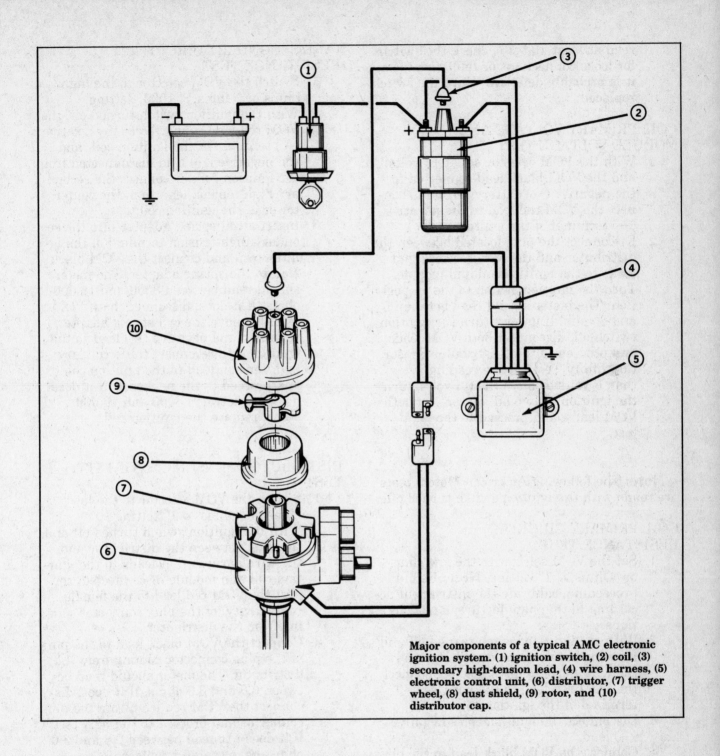

Major components of a typical AMC electronic ignition system. (1) ignition switch, (2) coil, (3) secondary high-tension lead, (4) wire harness, (5) electronic control unit, (6) distributor, (7) trigger wheel, (8) dust shield, (9) rotor, and (10) distributor cap.

to the distributor, and proceed to the next test. If it does not read at least 9.0 volts, recharge the battery and repeat the test.

IGNITION SWITCH TEST
1. With the VOM selector set at 16 volts and the VOM black lead connected to

the negative (−) battery terminal, connect the VOM red lead to the positive (+) terminal of the ignition coil.
2. Turn the ignition switch to the on position. The meter should read at least 10 volts. If it does, turn the ignition switch off, disconnect the VOM red lead, and proceed to the next test. If it does not

read at least 10 volts, check the switch for loose connections or faulty contacts; it is probably defective. Have the switch replaced.

COIL PRIMARY VOLTAGE AND MODULE VOLTAGE TEST

1. With the VOM selector set at 16 volts and the VOM black lead connected to the negative (−) battery terminal, connect the VOM red lead to the negative (−) terminal of the ignition coil.
2. Disconnect the plug located between the distributor and the wire harness that leads to the ignition coil and module.
3. Turn the ignition switch to the on position. The meter should read between 5 and 8 volts. If it does, turn the ignition switch off, disconnect both VOM leads, and proceed to the "Distributor Sensor Continuity Test." If the reading is less than 5 volts or more than 8 volts, turn the ignition switch off, disconnect both VOM leads, and proceed to the next test.

Note: The following American Motors tests are made with the ignition switch turned off.

COIL PRIMARY CIRCUIT RESISTANCE TEST

1. Set the VOM selector to the low ohms or "Ohms × 1" setting. **Note:** Before proceeding, calibrate the instrument according to the manufacturer's instructions.
2. With the ignition switch turned off and the plug between the distributor and the wire harness disconnected, connect the VOM red lead to the positive (+) terminal of the ignition coil.
3. Disconnect the ignition coil's negative (−) lead.
4. Connect the VOM black lead to the negative (−) terminal of the ignition coil. The meter should read between 0.7 and 2.5 ohms. If it does, disconnect the VOM black lead, reconnect the plug between the distributor and the wire harness, and proceed to the next test. If it does not read between 0.7 and 2.5 ohms, replace the ignition coil.

COIL SECONDARY CIRCUIT RESISTANCE TEST

1. Switch the VOM selector to the high ohms or "Ohms × 1000" setting.
2. With the ignition switch turned off, the VOM red lead connected to the positive (+) terminal of the ignition coil, and the negative (−) lead disconnected from the ignition coil, disconnect the secondary high-tension lead from the center tower of the ignition coil.
3. Insert a coil spring adapter into the secondary high-tension terminal of the ignition coil and connect the VOM black lead to the spring adapter. The meter should read between 8000 and 16,000 ohms. If it does, disconnect both VOM leads, remove the coil spring adapter, reconnect the negative (−) lead to the ignition coil, reconnect the secondary high-tension lead to the ignition coil, and proceed to the next test. If it does not read between 8000 and 16,000 ohms, replace the ignition coil.

DISTRIBUTOR SENSOR CONTINUITY TEST

1. Switch the VOM selector to the low ohms or "Ohms × 1" setting.
2. With the ignition switch turned off and the plug between the distributor and the wire harness that leads to the ignition coil and module disconnected, connect the VOM red lead to the female part (cavity) of the plug connector coming from the distributor.
3. Connect the VOM black lead to the pin of the plug connector coming from the distributor. The meter should read between 0.8 and 3.0 ohms. If it does, disconnect the VOM red lead from the plug connector and proceed to the next test. If it does not read between 0.8 and 3.0 ohms, have the unit replaced.

DISTRIBUTOR SENSOR GROUND TEST

1. Switch the VOM selector to the high ohms or "Ohms × 1000" setting.
2. With the ignition switch turned off and the VOM black lead connected to the pin of the plug connector coming from the distributor, connect the VOM red

lead to the negative (−) battery terminal. The meter indicator should not move at all. If this is the case and you have not found a defective component in the preceding tests, have the electronic module replaced. If the meter indicator does move, have the distributor sensor unit replaced.

Chrysler
(Domestic Only)

BATTERY CONDITION TEST
1. Set the volt/ohmmeter (VOM) selector to 16 volts.
2. Connect the VOM red lead to the positive (+) battery terminal.
3. Connect the VOM black lead to the negative (−) battery terminal.
4. Disconnect the secondary high-tension wire from the center tower of the distributor and ground it to a metal part of the engine with a jumper wire.
5. Crank the engine long enough to obtain a meter reading. The meter should read at least 9.0 volts. If it does, turn the ignition switch off, disconnect the VOM red lead, and proceed to the next test. If it does not read at least 9.0 volts, recharge the battery and repeat the test.

PRIMARY RESISTOR TEST
(COMPENSATING SIDE)
1. With the VOM selector set at 16 volts, the secondary high-tension wire still grounded, and the VOM black lead connected to the negative (−) battery terminal, connect the VOM red lead to the positive (+) terminal of the ignition coil.
2. Turn the ignition switch to the on position. The meter should read between 3.5 and 7.5 volts. If the reading is less than 3.5 volts or zero, turn the ignition switch off, disconnect the VOM black lead, disconnect the jumper wire, reconnect the secondary high-tension wire to the distributor, and proceed to the "Coil

Secondary Continuity Test." If the reading is above 7.5 volts, crank the engine; the meter should read at least 9.0 volts. If it does, turn the ignition switch off, disconnect the VOM black lead, disconnect the jumper wire, reconnect the secondary high-tension wire to the distributor, and proceed to the next test. If it does not read at least 9.0 volts, check the ignition switch for loose connections or faulty contacts; it is probably defective. Have the switch replaced.

COIL PRIMARY CIRCUIT
RESISTANCE TEST
1. Set the VOM selector to the low ohms or "Ohms × 1" setting. **Note:** Before proceeding, calibrate the instrument according to the manufacturer's instructions.
2. With the ignition switch turned off and the VOM red lead connected to the positive (+) terminal of the ignition coil, connect the VOM black lead to the negative (−) terminal of the ignition coil. The meter should read between 1.0 and 3.0 ohms. If it does, disconnect the VOM black lead and proceed to the next test. If it does not read between 1.0 and 3.0 ohms, replace the ignition coil.

COIL SECONDARY CONTINUITY TEST
1. Switch the VOM selector to the high ohms or "Ohms × 1000" setting.
2. Disconnect the secondary high-tension wire from the center tower of the ignition coil.
3. With the ignition switch turned off and the VOM red lead connected to the positive (+) terminal of the ignition coil, insert a coil spring adapter into the secondary high-tension terminal of the ignition coil and connect the VOM black lead to the spring adapter. The meter should read between 5000 to 25,000 ohms. If it does, disconnect both VOM leads, remove the coil spring adapter, reconnect the secondary high-tension wire to the ignition coil, and proceed to the next test. If it does not read between 5000 and 25,000 ohms, replace the ignition coil.

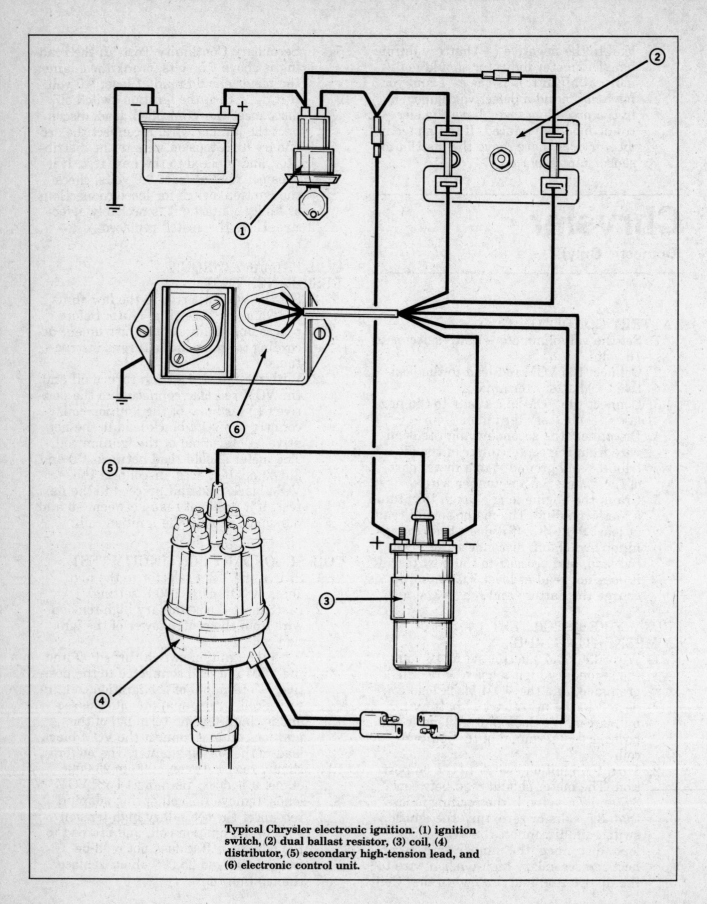

Typical Chrysler electronic ignition. (1) ignition switch, (2) dual ballast resistor, (3) coil, (4) distributor, (5) secondary high-tension lead, and (6) electronic control unit.

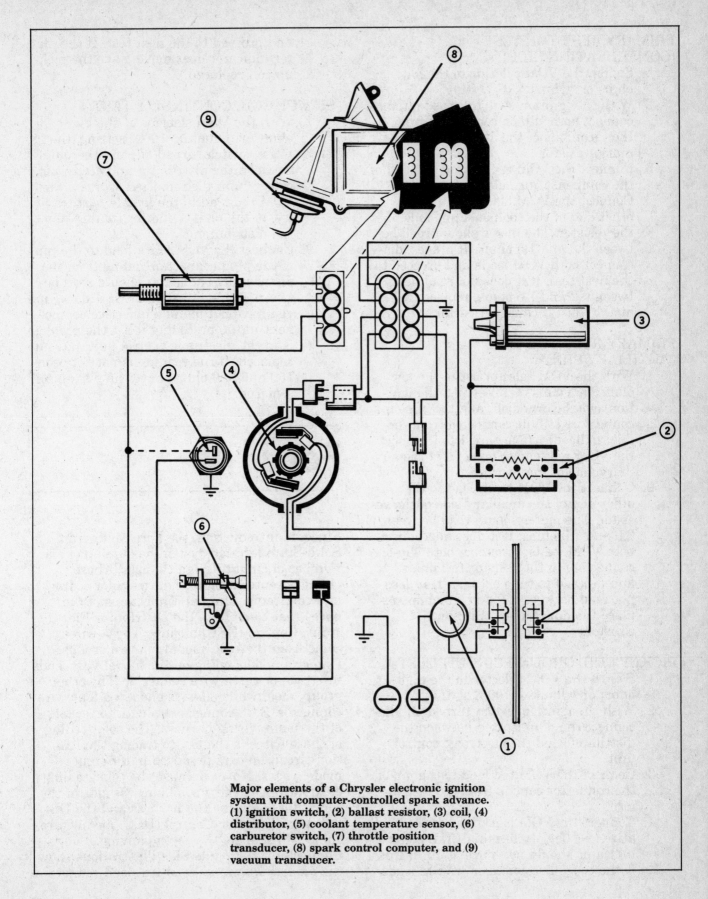

Major elements of a Chrysler electronic ignition system with computer-controlled spark advance. (1) ignition switch, (2) ballast resistor, (3) coil, (4) distributor, (5) coolant temperature sensor, (6) carburetor switch, (7) throttle position transducer, (8) spark control computer, and (9) vacuum transducer.

PRIMARY RESISTOR TEST (COMPENSATING SIDE)

1. Switch the VOM selector to the low ohms or "Ohms × 1" setting.
2. With the ignition switch turned off, disconnect both slip-on connectors from the terminals of the dual ballast (primary) resistor.
3. Connect the VOM red lead to one end of the compensating side of the resistor.
4. Connect the VOM black lead to the other end of the compensating side of the resistor. The meter should read between 0.2 and 1.5 ohms. If it does, disconnect both VOM leads and proceed to the next test. If it does not read between 0.2 and 1.5 ohms, replace the dual ballast (primary) resistor.

PRIMARY RESISTOR TEST (AUXILIARY SIDE)

1. With the VOM selector set to the low ohms or "Ohms × 1" setting, the ignition switch turned off, and the slip-on connectors still disconnected from the dual ballast (primary) resistor, connect the VOM red lead to one end of the auxiliary side of the resistor.
2. Connect the VOM black lead to the other end of the auxiliary side of the resistor. The meter should read between 3.0 and 7.0 ohms. If it does, disconnect both VOM leads, reconnect both slip-on connectors to the resistor terminals, and proceed to the next test. If it does not read between 3.0 and 7.0 ohms, replace the dual ballast (primary) resistor.

PICKUP COIL GROUND CIRCUIT TEST

1. Switch the VOM selector to the high ohms or "Ohms × 1000" setting.
2. With the ignition switch turned off, disconnect the plug located between the distributor and the electronic control unit.
3. Connect the VOM red lead to the pin of the connector coming from the distributor.
4. Connect the VOM black lead to the negative (−) battery terminal. The meter indicator should not move at all. If this is the case, disconnect both VOM leads and proceed to the next test. If the meter indicator does move, have the pickup coil replaced.

PICKUP COIL CONTINUITY TEST

1. With the VOM selector at the high ohms or "Ohms × 1000" setting, the ignition switch turned off, and the plug between the distributor and electronic control unit disconnected, connect the VOM red lead to the female part (cavity) of the plug connector coming from the distributor.
2. Connect the VOM black lead to the pin of the plug connector coming from the distributor. The meter should read between 150 and 900 ohms. If it does, and you have not found a defective component in the preceding tests, the problem is in the electronic control unit; have it replaced. If the reading is not between 150 and 900 ohms, have the pickup coil replaced.

Ford

Since its introduction, the Ford Motorcraft Solid-State Ignition system has undergone a number of circuit design changes. These changes center around the wire color-coding and connector terminal connections of the wires that come from the Distributor Electronic Control (DEC) module. These wires come from the DEC module in two groups. One group, depending on the model year, ends in a two- or three-wire connector. The other group, meanwhile, always ends in a four-wire connector. Both connectors plug into sockets of the main wiring harness. The color-coding of these wires is the key to tracing the ignition circuit on cars produced in different model years. **Note:** Because the color-coding of the wires on the wiring harness side of the connectors between the harness and the Distributor Electronic Control (DEC) module are subject to change, the accompanying Blade Connectors on Module Side illustrations show the *blade connectors*. VOM test lead connec-

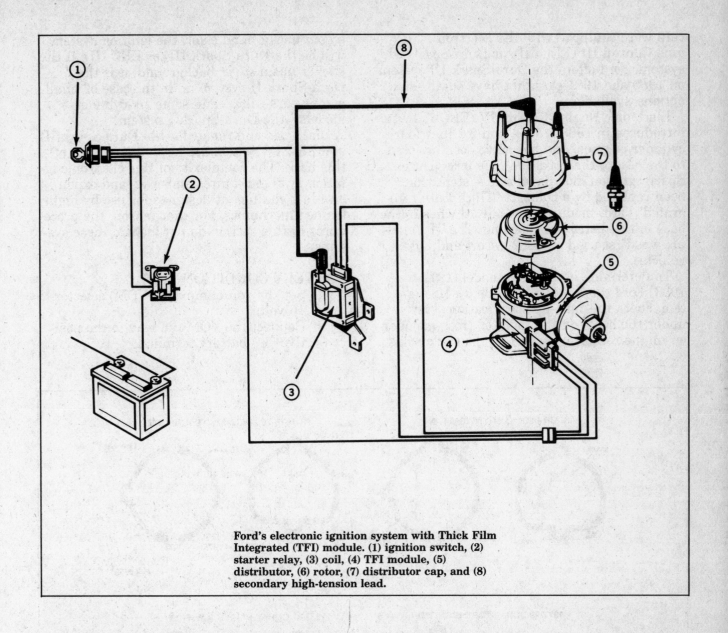

Ford's electronic ignition system with Thick Film Integrated (TFI) module. (1) ignition switch, (2) starter relay, (3) coil, (4) TFI module, (5) distributor, (6) rotor, (7) distributor cap, and (8) secondary high-tension lead.

tions, however, are to be made at the *socket connectors*. Therefore, connect the test instrument leads to the appropriate socket terminal that mates with the blade terminal specified.

Power (voltage) from the ignition switch reaches the control module through the WHITE wire when the engine is cranking (ignition switch is in the start position). Power (voltage) reaches the control module through the RED wire when the ignition switch is in the on position. Distributor signals (voltage pulses) are received at the module by means of the ORANGE and PURPLE wires.

Voltage from the ignition coil (the primary circuit) is received at the module by the

GREEN wire. The BLACK wire, meanwhile, is a ground connection between the electronic control module and the distributor; it carries no readable current (voltage or amperage).

All 1973, 1974, and 1975 Ford Motorcraft systems have a BLUE wire that is designed to protect the system against high-voltage surges. It was, however, eliminated in ignition systems beginning in 1976.

Beginning in 1977, Dura-Spark I and II ignition systems were introduced. The color-coding for both of these systems is the same, but the terminal connections are slightly different.

In 1979, Lincoln Continental and Mark VI

cars were equipped with the Electronic Engine Control III (EEC III), or Dura-Spark III, system. Ford offers the Dura-Spark III system on 1980 and 1981 cars that have engine-size options available.

Electronic Engine Control IV (EEC-IV) was introduced in 1983 on 1.6- and 2.3-liter four-cylinder engines, and has since been adapted to the rest of the Ford line. The large Dura-Spark ignition module on this system has been replaced by a compact "Thick Film Integrated" (TFI) module chip that attaches to the base of the distributor housing. The TFI module was first used on 1982 Escort and Lynx vehicles.

To determine if your late model (1979 to 1983) Ford car has the Dura-Spark III system, check the tune-up specifications sticker under the hood, on the radiator cross-member or engine rocker arm cover. If the sticker has

a *gold* background color, the ignition system will be the Dura-Spark III (or EEC III). If the sticker has a *silver* background, it is the Dura-Spark II system or, in the case of small-engine cars—four- and some six-cylinder models—the Dura-Spark I system.

Diagnosis and repair for the Dura-Spark III and EEC-IV system are beyond the scope of this book. The complexity of this electronic ignition system requires elaborate and expensive test equipment designed for use by highly trained mechanics. For that reason, the procedures in this section do not include these systems.

BATTERY CONDITION TEST
1. Set the volt/ohmmeter (VOM) selector to 16 volts.
2. Connect the VOM red lead to the positive (+) battery terminal.

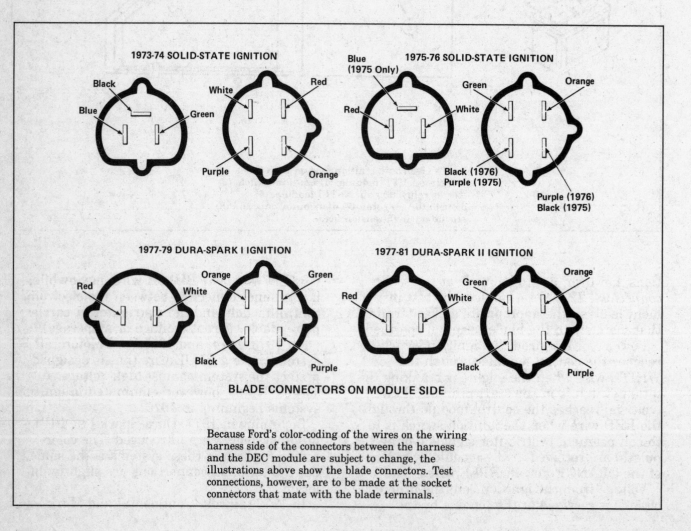

BLADE CONNECTORS ON MODULE SIDE

Because Ford's color-coding of the wires on the wiring harness side of the connectors between the harness and the DEC module are subject to change, the illustrations above show the blade connectors. Test connections, however, are to be made at the socket connectors that mate with the blade terminals.

3. Connect the VOM black lead to the negative (−) battery terminal.
4. Disconnect the secondary high-tension wire from the center tower of the distributor and ground it to a metal part of the engine with a jumper wire.
5. Crank the engine long enough to obtain a meter reading. The meter should read at least 9.0 volts. If it does, turn the ignition switch off, disconnect the jumper wire and both VOM leads, reconnect the secondary high-tension wire to the distributor, and proceed to the next test. If it does not read at least 9.0 volts, recharge the battery and repeat the test.

RESISTANCE WIRE TEST

1. Switch the VOM selector to the low ohms or "Ohms × 1" setting. **Note:** Before proceeding, calibrate the instrument according to the manufacturer's instructions.
2. Study the accompanying Blade Connectors on Module Side illustrations to determine which ignition system is on your car. Then, make sure that the ignition switch is turned off, and select the proper test connection procedure.

   A. For 1973-74 systems: (1) Disconnect both connectors coming from the Distributor Electronic Control (DEC) module; (2) Connect the VOM red lead to the socket terminal that mates with the blade terminal for the RED wire; (3) Connect the VOM black lead to the socket terminal that mates with the blade terminal for the BLUE wire.

   B. For 1975 systems: (1) Disconnect the three-wire connector coming from the DEC module; (2) Connect the VOM red lead to the socket terminal that mates with the blade terminal for the RED wire; (3) Connect the VOM black lead to the socket terminal that mates with the blade terminal for the BLUE wire.

   C. For 1976 and 1977-81 Dura-Spark I and II systems: (1) Disconnect the two-wire connector coming from the DEC module; (2) Connect the VOM red lead to the socket terminal that

mates with the blade terminal for the RED wire; (3) Connect the VOM black lead to the battery (BAT) terminal on the ignition coil.

The meter should read between 1.0 and 2.0 ohms. If it does, disconnect both VOM leads, reconnect the DEC module connector(s), and proceed to the next test. If the meter reading is zero or more than 2.0 ohms, have the primary resistance wire replaced.

COIL PRIMARY CIRCUIT RESISTANCE TEST

1. With the VOM selector set at the low ohms or "Ohms × 1" setting and the ignition switch turned off, connect the VOM red lead to the battery (BAT) terminal on the ignition coil.
2. Connect the VOM black lead to the DEC terminal on the ignition coil. The meter should read between 1.0 and 3.0 ohms. If it does, disconnect the VOM black lead and proceed to the next test. If the meter does not read between 1.0 and 3.0 ohms, replace the ignition coil. On later model Ford ignitions with the TFI module, primary coil resistance should be 0.3 to 1.0 ohms, and secondary resistance 8000 to 11,500 ohms.

COIL SECONDARY CONTINUITY TEST

1. Switch the VOM selector to the high ohms or "Ohms × 1000" setting.
2. With the ignition switch turned off, disconnect the secondary high-tension wire from the center tower of the ignition coil.
3. With the VOM red lead connected to the BAT terminal on the ignition coil, insert a coil spring adapter into the secondary high-tension terminal of the ignition coil and connect the VOM black lead to the spring adapter. The meter should read between 5000 and 25,000 ohms. If it does, disconnect both VOM leads, remove the coil spring adapter, reconnect the secondary high-tension wire to the ignition coil, and proceed to the next test. If it does not read between 5000 and 25,000 ohms, replace the ignition coil.

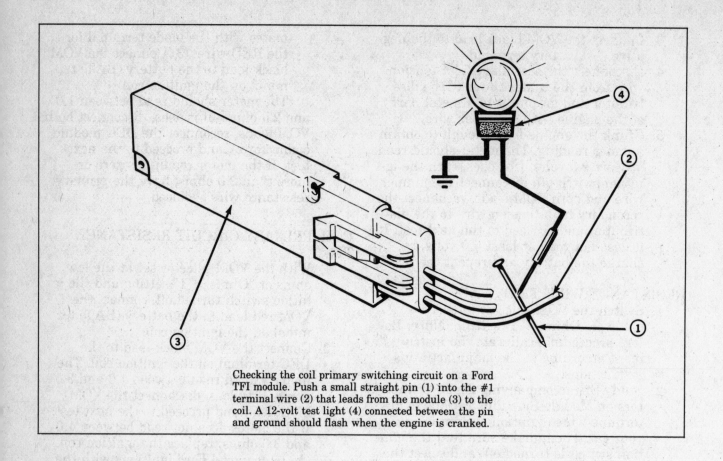

Checking the coil primary switching circuit on a Ford TFI module. Push a small straight pin (1) into the #1 terminal wire (2) that leads from the module (3) to the coil. A 12-volt test light (4) connected between the pin and ground should flash when the engine is cranked.

RESISTANCE WIRE VOLTAGE DROP TEST

1. Switch the VOM selector to 16 volts.
2. Connect the VOM red lead to the positive (+) battery terminal.
3. Connect the VOM black lead to the battery (BAT) terminal on the ignition coil.
4. Turn the ignition switch to the on position. The meter should read between 5.0 and 7.0 volts. If the meter reading is higher than 7.0 volts, repeat the Resistance Wire Test. If the meter reading is lower than 5.0 volts, turn the ignition off, disconnect both VOM leads, and proceed to the next test.

VOLTAGE TO MODULE TEST

1. With the VOM selector set at 16 volts, disconnect the connector coming from the DEC module that has a GREEN wire.
2. Connect the VOM red lead to the socket terminal that mates with the blade terminal for the GREEN wire.
3. Connect the VOM black lead to the negative (−) battery terminal.
4. Turn the ignition switch to the on position. The meter should read between 10 and 13 volts. If the reading is lower than 10 volts or zero, repeat the Resistance Wire Voltage Drop Test. And, if this test still shows a meter reading between 5.0 and 7.0 volts, have the ignition switch replaced. If the reading is between 10 and 13 volts, turn the ignition switch off, disconnect the VOM red lead, reconnect the connector, and proceed to the next test.
5. To check the coil primary switching circuit on Ford systems with the TFI module, push a small straight pin into the #1 terminal wire that leads from the module at the base of the distributor to the coil negative terminal. Do not allow the pin to touch anything else. With a 12-volt test light connected between the pin and ground, crank the engine. If the light flashes, the TFI module is triggering properly. If the light does not flash (either stays on or does not light) check

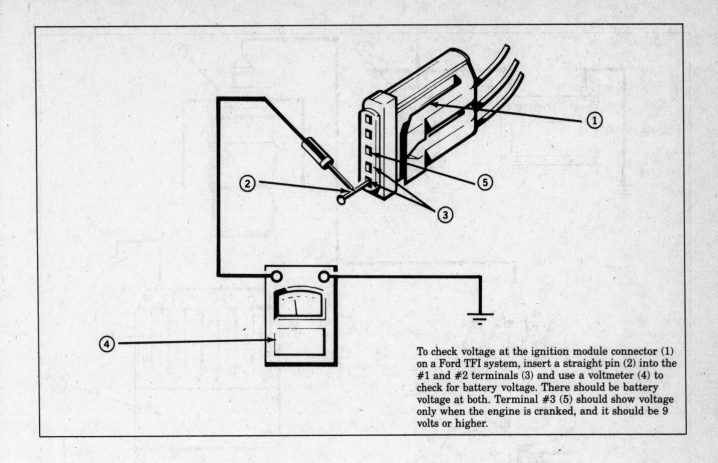

To check voltage at the ignition module connector (1) on a Ford TFI system, insert a straight pin (2) into the #1 and #2 terminals (3) and use a voltmeter (4) to check for battery voltage. There should be battery voltage at both. Terminal #3 (5) should show voltage only when the engine is cranked, and it should be 9 volts or higher.

the module connector terminals #1 and #2 with the key on for battery voltage. Use the straight pin to probe each terminal. There should be voltage at both. Terminal #3 should show voltage when the engine is cranked only, and it should be 9 volts or higher.

PICKUP COIL GROUND CIRCUIT TEST

1. Switch the VOM selector to the high ohms or "Ohms × 1000" setting. **Note:** Before proceeding, recalibrate the instrument.
2. With the ignition switch turned off, disconnect the connector in the wires coming from the distributor that lead to the wire harness going to the DEC module.
3. With the VOM black lead connected to the negative (−) battery terminal, connect the VOM red lead to the ORANGE wire (blade—not socket) terminal in the connector coming from the distributor. The meter indicator should not move at all. If this is the case, disconnect the VOM black lead and proceed to the next

test. If the meter indicator moves or if there is a full-scale reading, have the pickup coil assembly replaced.

PICKUP COIL CONTINUITY TEST

1. With the VOM selector at the high ohms or "Ohms × 1000" setting and the VOM red lead connected to the OR-ANGE wire terminal in the connector coming from the distributor, connect the VOM black lead to the PURPLE wire (blade—not socket) terminal in the connector coming from the distributor. The meter should read between 400 and 800 ohms. If the reading is not between 400 and 800 ohms, and you have not found a defective component in the preceding tests, the problem is in the DEC module; have it replaced. If the reading is lower or higher than this range, have the pickup coil assembly replaced. On Ford TFI module systems, the pickup resistance should be between 800 and 975 ohms.

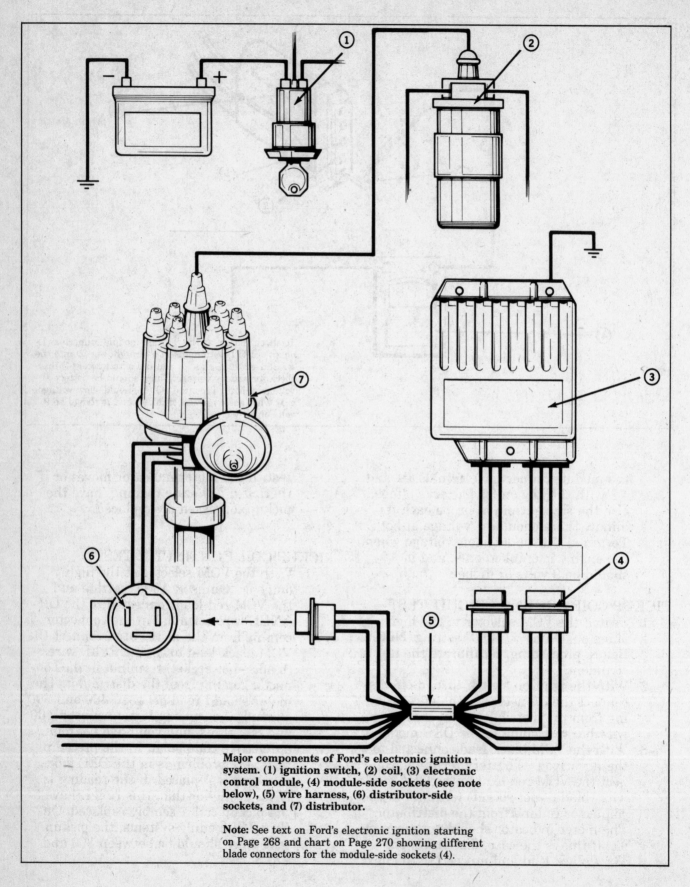

Major components of Ford's electronic ignition system. (1) ignition switch, (2) coil, (3) electronic control module, (4) module-side sockets (see note below), (5) wire harness, (6) distributor-side sockets, and (7) distributor.

Note: See text on Ford's electronic ignition starting on Page 268 and chart on Page 270 showing different blade connectors for the module-side sockets (4).

General Motors

(Delco HEI System
With Separate Coil)

BATTERY CONDITION TEST
1. Set the volt/ohmmeter (VOM) selector to 16 volts.
2. Connect the VOM red lead to the positive (+) battery terminal.
3. Connect the VOM black lead to the negative (−) battery terminal.
4. Disconnect the ignition switch feed wire from the ignition coil connector.
5. Crank the engine long enough to obtain a meter reading. The meter should read at least 9.6 volts. If it does, turn the ignition switch off, disconnect the VOM red lead, and proceed to the next test. If it does not read at least 9.6 volts, recharge the battery and repeat the test.

IGNITION SWITCH TEST
1. With the VOM selector set at 16 volts and the VOM black lead connected to the negative (−) battery terminal, connect the VOM red lead to the disconnected ignition switch feed wire.
2. Turn the ignition switch to the on position. The meter should read at least 10 volts. If it does, turn the ignition switch off, disconnect both VOM leads, and proceed to the next test. If the meter reads less than 10 volts or zero, have the ignition switch replaced.

COIL PRIMARY CIRCUIT
RESISTANCE TEST
1. Switch the VOM selector to the low ohms or "Ohms × 1" setting. **Note:** Before proceeding, calibrate the instrument according to the manufacturer's instructions.
2. With the ignition switch turned off, disconnect the ignition coil connector.
3. Connect the VOM red lead to ignition coil terminal "X." (See illustration.)
4. Connect the VOM black lead to ignition coil terminal "Y." (See illustration.) The

meter should read between 0.2 and 0.7 ohms. If it does, disconnect both VOM leads and proceed to the next test. If the meter reading is less than 0.2 ohms, have the coil replaced. If the reading is more than 0.7 ohms, clean the connections and repeat the test.

COIL SECONDARY CIRCUIT
RESISTANCE TEST
1. Switch the VOM selector to the high ohms or "Ohms × 1000" setting.
2. With the ignition switch turned off, disconnect the ignition coil secondary high-tension wire.
3. Connect the VOM red lead to the coil secondary high-tension terminal.
4. Connect the VOM black lead to ignition coil terminal "X." The meter should read between 6000 and 12,000 ohms. If it does, reconnect the secondary high-tension wire on the ignition coil, disconnect both VOM leads, and proceed to the next test. If the meter does not read between 6000 and 12,000 ohms, replace the ignition coil.

HOUSING HARNESS CONTINUITY TEST
1. Switch the VOM selector to 16 volts.
2. Remove the distributor cap and rotor.
3. Reconnect the coil connector and ignition switch feed wire to the coil.
4. Connect the VOM red lead to the "B" terminal on the distributor module.
5. Connect the VOM black lead to the negative (−) battery terminal.
6. Turn the ignition switch to the on position. The meter should read at least 10 volts. If it does, turn the ignition switch off, disconnect the VOM red lead, and proceed to the next test. If the meter reads less than 10 volts, have the housing harness repaired or replaced.

HOUSING HARNESS CONTINUITY TEST
1. With the VOM selector at 16 volts and the VOM black lead connected to the negative (−) battery terminal, connect the VOM red lead to the "C" terminal on the module in the distributor.
2. Turn the ignition switch to the on position. The meter should read at least 10 volts. If it does, turn the ignition switch

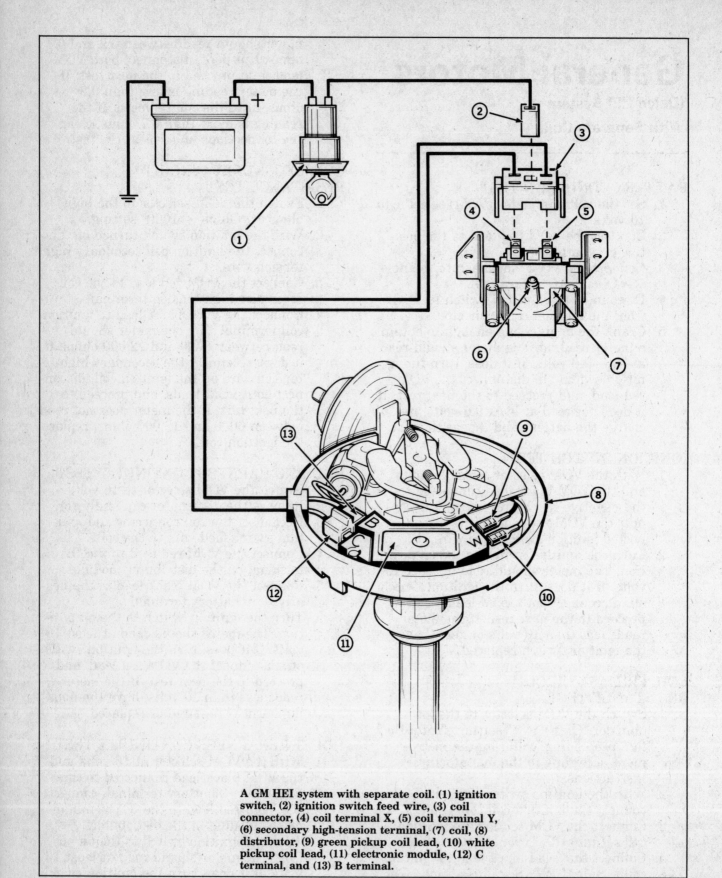

A GM HEI system with separate coil. (1) ignition switch, (2) ignition switch feed wire, (3) coil connector, (4) coil terminal X, (5) coil terminal Y, (6) secondary high-tension terminal, (7) coil, (8) distributor, (9) green pickup coil lead, (10) white pickup coil lead, (11) electronic module, (12) C terminal, and (13) B terminal.

off, disconnect both VOM leads, and proceed to the next test. If the meter reads less than 10 volts, have the housing harness repaired or replaced.

PICKUP COIL RESISTANCE TEST

1. Switch the VOM selector to the high ohms or "Ohms × 1000" setting. **Note:** Before proceeding, recalibrate the instrument.
2. With the ignition switch turned off, disconnect the white (W) and green (G) pickup leads in the distributor.
3. Connect the VOM red lead to the white (W) pickup lead.
4. Connect the VOM black lead to the green (G) pickup lead. The meter should read between 500 and 1500 ohms. If it does, disconnect the VOM black lead, and proceed to the next test. If the meter does not read between 500 and 1500 ohms, have the pickup coil assembly replaced.

PICKUP COIL GROUND CIRCUIT TEST

1. With the VOM selector at the high ohms or "Ohms × 1000" setting, the ignition switch turned off, and the VOM red lead connected to the white (W) pickup lead, connect the VOM black lead to the negative (−) battery terminal. **Note:** Check to make sure that the green (G) pickup lead is not touching any metal surface. The meter indicator should not move at all. If this is the case and you have not found a defective component in the preceding tests, have the electronic module replaced. If the meter does move, have the pickup coil assembly replaced.

General Motors

(Delco HEI System

With Coil in Distributor)

BATTERY CONDITION TEST

1. Set the volt/ohmmeter (VOM) selector to 16 volts.

2. Connect the VOM red lead to the positive (+) battery terminal.
3. Connect the VOM black lead to the negative (−) battery terminal.
4. Disconnect the PINK lead from the "BAT" terminal on the connector on the distributor cap.
5. Crank the engine long enough to obtain a reading on the meter. The meter should read at least 9.6 volts. If it does, turn the ignition switch off, disconnect the VOM red lead, and proceed to the next test. If the meter does not read at least 9.6 volts, recharge the battery and repeat the test.

IGNITION SWITCH TEST

1. With the VOM selector at 16 volts and the VOM black lead connected to the negative (−) battery terminal, connect the VOM red lead to the end of the PINK lead disconnected from the distributor cap.
2. Turn the ignition switch to the on position. The meter should read at least 10 volts. If it does, turn the ignition switch off, disconnect both VOM leads, leave the PINK lead disconnected, and proceed to the next test. If the meter reading is less than 10 volts, have the ignition switch replaced.

COIL PRIMARY CIRCUIT RESISTANCE TEST

1. Switch the VOM selector to the low ohms or "Ohms × 1" setting. **Note:** Before proceeding, calibrate the instrument according to the manufacturer's instructions.
2. With the ignition switch turned off, remove the distributor cap and rotor.
3. Disconnect the three-wire housing harness coming from the distributor.
4. Connect the VOM red lead to the "C−" terminal on the connector on the distributor cap.
5. Connect the VOM black lead to the "BAT" terminal on the connector on the distributor cap. The meter should read between 0.2 and 0.7 ohms. If it does, disconnect both VOM leads and proceed to the next test. If the meter does not read between 0.2 and 0.7 ohms, have

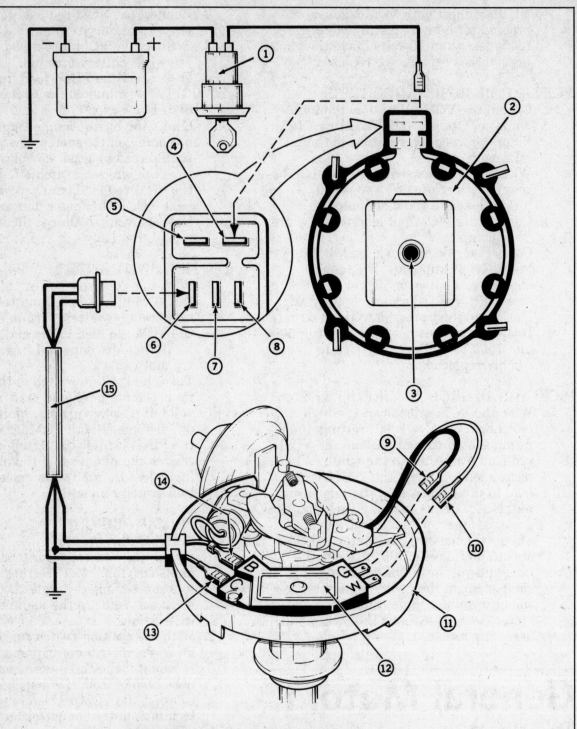

A GM HEI system with coil in distributor. (1) ignition switch, (2) distributor cap (underside), (3) secondary high-tension terminal button, (4) BAT terminal, (5) TACH terminal, (6) C− terminal, (7) GND terminal, (8) B+ terminal, (9) green pickup coil lead, (10) white pickup coil lead, (11) distributor, (12) electronic module, (13) C− terminal (brown wire), (14) B+ terminal (orange wire), and (15) three-wire housing harness.

the ignition coil in the distributor cap replaced.

COIL SECONDARY CIRCUIT RESISTANCE TEST

1. Switch the VOM selector to the high ohms or "Ohms × 1000" setting.
2. With the ignition switch turned off, connect the VOM red lead to the secondary high-tension terminal button inside the distributor cap.
3. Connect the VOM black lead to the ground ("GND") terminal on the connector on the distributor cap. The meter should read between 10,000 and 30,000 ohms. If it does, disconnect both VOM leads and proceed to the next test. If the meter does not read between 10,000 ohms and 30,000 ohms, have the ignition coil assembly replaced.

COIL PRIMARY CIRCUIT CONTINUITY TEST

1. Switch the VOM selector to 16 volts.
2. Reconnect the PINK lead to the "BAT" terminal on the connector on the distributor cap.
3. Connect the VOM red lead to the "C–" terminal on the connector on the distributor cap.
4. Connect the VOM black lead to the negative (–) battery terminal.
5. Turn the ignition switch to the on position. The meter should read at least 10 volts. If it does, turn the ignition switch off, disconnect the VOM red lead, and proceed to the next test. If the reading is less than 10 volts, have the ignition coil assembly replaced.

VOLTAGE TO MODULE TEST

1. With the VOM selector at 16 volts and the VOM black lead connected to the negative (–) battery terminal, connect the VOM red lead to the "B+" terminal on the connector on the distributor cap.
2. Turn the ignition switch to the on position. The meter should read at least 10 volts. If it does, turn the ignition switch off, disconnect the VOM red lead, and proceed to the next test. If the reading is less than 10 volts or zero, repeat the Ignition Switch Test. If the reading is

still low, check the terminals and connections inside the distributor cap cover.

HOUSING HARNESS CONTINUITY TEST

1. With the VOM selector at 16 volts and the VOM black lead connected to the negative (–) battery terminal, connect the VOM red lead to the "B+" terminal (orange wire) on the electronic module in the distributor.
2. Reconnect the three-wire housing harness coming from the distributor.
3. Turn the ignition switch to the on position. The meter should read at least 10 volts. If it does, turn the ignition switch off, disconnect the VOM red lead, and proceed to the next test. If the reading is less than 10 volts or zero, have the three-wire housing harness repaired or replaced.

HOUSING HARNESS CONTINUITY TEST

1. With the VOM selector at 16 volts and the VOM black lead connected to the negative (–) battery terminal, connect the VOM red lead to the "C–" terminal (brown wire) on the electronic module in the distributor.
2. Turn the ignition switch to the on position. The meter should read at least 10 volts. If it does, turn the ignition switch off, disconnect the VOM leads, and proceed to the next test. If the reading is less than 10 volts or zero, have the three-wire housing harness repaired or replaced.

PICKUP COIL CONTINUITY TEST

1. Switch the VOM selector to the high ohms or "Ohms × 1000" setting. **Note:** Before proceeding, recalibrate the instrument.
2. With the ignition switch turned off, disconnect the white (W) and green (G) pickup leads in the distributor.
3. Connect the VOM red lead to the white (W) pickup lead.
4. Connect the VOM black lead to the green (G) pickup lead. The meter should read between 550 and 1500 ohms. If it does, disconnect the VOM black lead and proceed to the next test.

If the meter does not read between 550 and 1500 ohms, have the pickup coil assembly replaced.

PICKUP COIL GROUND CIRCUIT TEST

1. With the VOM selector at the high ohms or "Ohms × 1000" setting, the ignition switch turned off, and the VOM red lead connected to the white (W) pickup lead, connect the VOM black lead to the negative (−) battery terminal. **Note:** Check to make sure that the disconnected green (G) pickup lead is not touching any metal surface. The meter indicator should not move at all. If this is the case and you have not found a defective component in the preceding tests, have the electronic module replaced. If the meter does move, have the pickup coil assembly replaced.

Timing the Engine

Tools and Materials

- Timing Light
- Ratchet Wrench, Extension, and Socket
- Rags
- Chalk
- Golf Tees

THE PURPOSE of engine timing is to ensure that each spark plug will fire at exactly the right moment for maximum engine efficiency. The spark occurs in microseconds and is measured in terms of degrees "Before Top Dead Center" (BTDC) in relation to each piston as it goes through its cycle.

Most engines have the basic timing index, in the form of a line, a dent, or the like, marked on the rim of the vibration damper.

The vibration damper is the heavy steel wheel that is connected to the crankshaft at the front of the engine. Some engines will have several marks on the vibration damper and a single pointer on the timing cover. Others will have only one mark on the damper and a plate extending from the timing cover with several divisions indicating varying degrees of engine timing. Timing is set by aligning two of these points while the engine is running.

The timing is generally set by using a strobe lamp (a light that is triggered by high-voltage surges from the No. 1 spark plug wire at the No. 1 cylinder). After the contact point gap (or dwell) is accurately set, the strobe lamp is connected to a power source and to the No. 1 spark plug wire. The engine is started and idled slowly. Usually, the vacuum line to the vacuum advance unit at the distributor is removed and plugged.

The strobe light is aimed so it shines on the pointer over the vibration damper. Each time the No. 1 spark plug fires, the strobe lamp will light. Since the spark plug fires with the damper in the same position in relation to the pointer, the timing marks will appear to be standing still.

Alternate Timing Light Hookups

Because of options such as air conditioning and pollution control devices that are mounted on engines, it may be difficult to connect a timing light to the No. 1 spark plug. There is, however, a way around this problem—alternate timing. Simply stated, correct timing can be obtained by the "companion cylinder method." This also applies to electronic ignition timing.

This companion cylinder method allows you to hook the timing light to a spark plug other than the No. 1 cylinder and still set the proper basic timing. **Note:** This tip only applies to engines with an *even* number of cylinders and will not work on exotic three- and five-cylinder engines.

The companion cylinder to an engine's No. 1 cylinder can be quickly determined by the engine's firing order as follows.

In a four-cylinder engine, the companion cylinder is the third cylinder in the firing order.

In a six-cylinder engine, the companion cyl-

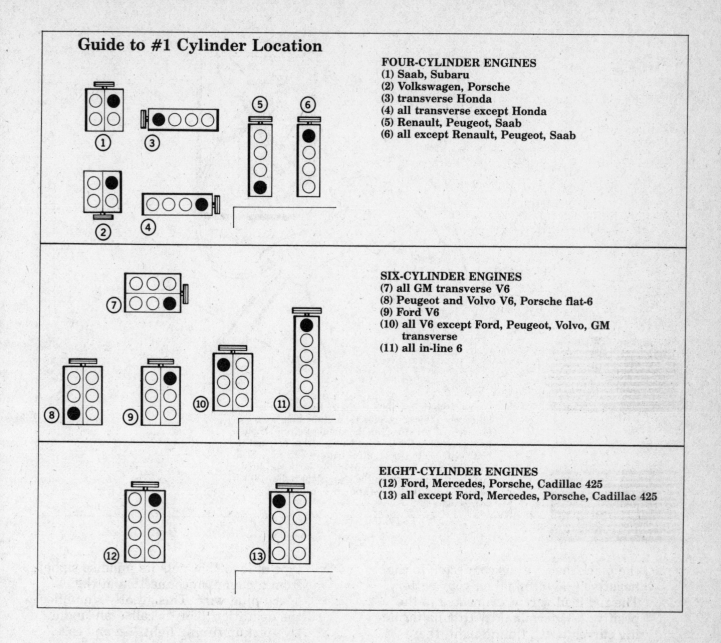

Guide to #1 Cylinder Location

FOUR-CYLINDER ENGINES
(1) Saab, Subaru
(2) Volkswagen, Porsche
(3) transverse Honda
(4) all transverse except Honda
(5) Renault, Peugeot, Saab
(6) all except Renault, Peugeot, Saab

SIX-CYLINDER ENGINES
(7) all GM transverse V6
(8) Peugeot and Volvo V6, Porsche flat-6
(9) Ford V6
(10) all V6 except Ford, Peugeot, Volvo, GM
    transverse
(11) all in-line 6

EIGHT-CYLINDER ENGINES
(12) Ford, Mercedes, Porsche, Cadillac 425
(13) all except Ford, Mercedes, Porsche, Cadillac 425

inder is the fourth cylinder in the firing order.

In an eight-cylinder engine, the companion cylinder is the fifth cylinder in the firing order.

Firing order can be found either by looking at the engine's intake manifold where it will be stamped into the metal, or by consulting tune-up specifications in the service manual for your car.

Timing Procedure

To set basic engine timing on cars without computer spark timing follow these steps.

1. With the engine not running, clean the timing marks on your engine with a rag.
2. On the clean surface, put a chalk mark on the two points that you want to align in the timing process so that they will be visible. Check the service manual timing specifications for your engine. On late model engines, the timing setting is provided on an engine tune-up data plate or sticker in the engine compartment.
3. Connect a timing light to your engine. With a direct current (DC) timing light,

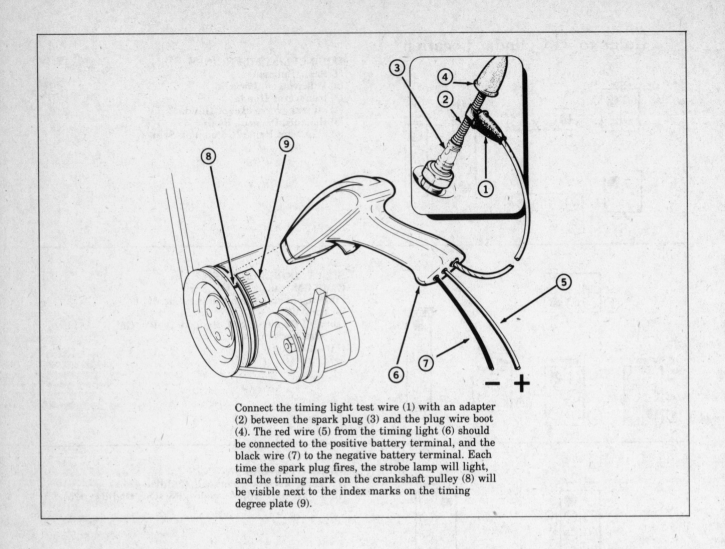

Connect the timing light test wire (1) with an adapter (2) between the spark plug (3) and the plug wire boot (4). The red wire (5) from the timing light (6) should be connected to the positive battery terminal, and the black wire (7) to the negative battery terminal. Each time the spark plug fires, the strobe lamp will light, and the timing mark on the crankshaft pulley (8) will be visible next to the index marks on the timing degree plate (9).

the black lead wire is connected to the negative (−) terminal on your battery. The red lead wire is connected to the positive (+) terminal. With an alternating current (AC) timing light, these connections are not necessary because the light draws its power from a 110-volt source (drop light, extension cord, etc.). In either case, there is an additional wire or lead from the timing light. This is connected to the No. 1 spark plug or to the spark plug wire of the No. 1 cylinder of your engine. Adapters to make this connection come with the timing light. Refer to the tune-up guide in your service manual for the location of the No. 1 cylinder on your engine.

Note: If you are planning to buy a timing light, try to get one with the type of lead that gets its impulse signal from a clamp-on connection at the spark plug wire. This greatly simplifies the operation. This is called an "inductive-pickup timing light." In any case, *never* puncture a spark plug cable or boot with a sharp probe to connect a timing light!

4. On some engines, the vacuum hose is left connected during timing, but for most it is disconnected and plugged. If this is the case, locate the distributor's vacuum advance unit. Disconnect the rubber vacuum hose by pulling it off the unit and plugging the end of the hose with a golf tee. A vacuum leak here will cause the engine to run rough, and a true timing check will not be possible. On dual-diaphragm distributors, both vacuum lines must be discon-

nected and plugged. Note the position of the lines before disconnecting them so that they can be reinstalled correctly.

5. Make sure all wires are clear of the fan and other moving engine components.

6. On point ignition systems only, adjust the dwell and run the engine for about 15 minutes to reach normal operating temperature before adjusting timing. Refer to the "Adjusting Dwell" section in this chapter.

7. Point the light at the timing marks, being careful to keep the light and your hands away from the engine fan. If the chalk marks are lined up, your engine is properly timed and you may proceed to Step 11. If they are not lined up, proceed to the next step.

8. With the engine still running, loosen the distributor hold-down bolt found at the outside base of the distributor where it attaches to the engine. This bolt actually holds a bracket that keeps the distributor in place. You will need a wrench for this.

9. Now with the engine running and the activated timing light pointing at the timing marks, carefully rotate the distributor a fraction of an inch at a time—clockwise or counterclockwise—until the timing marks line up. Rotate it *against* rotor rotation to advance the timing; *with* rotor rotation to retard the timing. The engine is now basically timed.

10. Retighten the distributor hold-down bolt. Recheck the timing after you have tightened the bolt to be sure that the distributor has not moved.

11. Shut off the engine.

12. Disconnect the timing light from the battery or power source. Also, disconnect the hookup at the No. 1 cylinder.

13. Remove any golf tees and reconnect distributor vacuum advance rubber hoses.

Computerized Ignition Special Instructions

On cars with computerized spark control, special preliminary steps must be taken prior to checking basic timing.

AMC FOUR-CYLINDER (GM 2.5-liter Iron

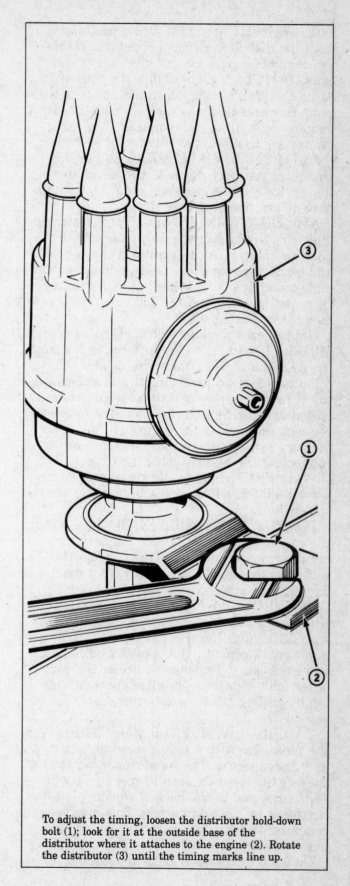

To adjust the timing, loosen the distributor hold-down bolt (1); look for it at the outside base of the distributor where it attaches to the engine (2). Rotate the distributor (3) until the timing marks line up.

Duke engine). Unplug the four-wire connector from the distributor. This procedure disables the computer spark control circuit and will cause the "Check Engine" light to come on. After checking timing, reconnect the four-wire connector and clear the computer fault code memory by pulling the computer fuse or disconnecting the battery cable for 10 seconds.

AMC/RENAULT ALLIANCE. Locate the electronic control module at the left center of the firewall. Disconnect and plug the vacuum hose before checking base timing.

AMC SIX-CYLINDER (uses Ford electronic ignition). Disconnect the distributor vacuum hose and plug it. Also disconnect the yellow and black wire connector and jump across the male terminals before checking basic timing. Increase engine speed to 1600 rpm. Then make your timing check.

GM (all except those with fuel injection or MISAR). Unplug the four-wire connector from the distributor. This procedure disables the computer spark control circuit and will cause the "Check Engine" light to come on. After checking basic timing, reconnect the four-wire connector and clear the computer fault code memory by pulling the computer fuse or disconnecting the battery cable for 10 seconds. On cars with computer idle speed control, do not attempt to adjust or disconnect the idle speed control.

PONTIAC WITH FUEL INJECTION. Find the computer terminal under the dash and jump terminals A and B. This triggers the self-test mode so the computer will provide a fixed timing advance.

CHEVROLET WITH FUEL INJECTION. Unplug the tan wire connector from the four-wire distributor harness to eliminate computer spark control. The "Check Engine" light will come on, so remember to clear the computer fault code memory after checking timing by pulling the fuse or battery cable for 10 seconds.

CADILLAC WITH FUEL INJECTION. Find the pink wire with a light green connector and disconnect it. The connector is located on the left side next to the idle speed motor on 1981 cars, and in the back of the engine compartment in 1982-83 models. This disables computer spark advance so you can check basic timing.

On 1980 Seville and Eldorado models, a pink wire with light green connector on the right rear of the engine near the distributor should be grounded before checking ignition timing. The connector doesn't connect to anything and is provided for this purpose only. Do not ground the connector on any Cadillac after 1980 or you may ruin the computer.

1977 OLDSMOBILE WITH MISAR (Toronado). Locate the computer under the dash at the glove box and find the unconnected purple wire taped to the computer harness. Ground the purple wire and start the engine. The "Check Engine" light will come on. To adjust the timing on this engine, a pickup at the front of the engine near the crankshaft pulley must be loosened and repositioned. Do not do this while the engine is running. Make your initial timing check, shut the engine off and reposition the pickup. Sliding it in the same direction that the pulley rotates will retard timing. Sliding it in the opposite direction will advance timing. Then restart the engine and recheck timing.

CHRYSLER (with spark advance computer). Ground the carburetor throttle switch with a jumper wire before checking basic timing. This will eliminate all computer spark advance.

FORD WITH EEC-I & EEC-II. Find the computer and remove the program unit from it (key off). Then check base timing.

FORD WITH EEC-III. Find the computer and remove the program unit from it (key off). Then check base timing. Or put the computer into the self-diagnostic mode by installing a vacuum gauge between the diverter valve and diverter valve solenoid on the right side fender apron. Run the engine at idle, and with a hand-held vacuum pump, apply 20 inches or more of vacuum to the vent neck (plainly labeled) of the barometric-manifold pressure sensor. Wait 15 seconds and then release the vacuum. The vacuum gauge needle should pulse 2 or 4 times, indicating the computer is going into the self-diagnostic mode. Idle speed will increase (throttle kicker is activated by the computer). Timing at the increased speed should be 27 to 33 degrees.

FORD WITH EEC-IV. Connect a voltmeter to terminal 4 of the 6-terminal diagnostic connector and the positive battery terminal. Then jump terminals 2 and 5. This will send the computer into self-diagnostic mode with the

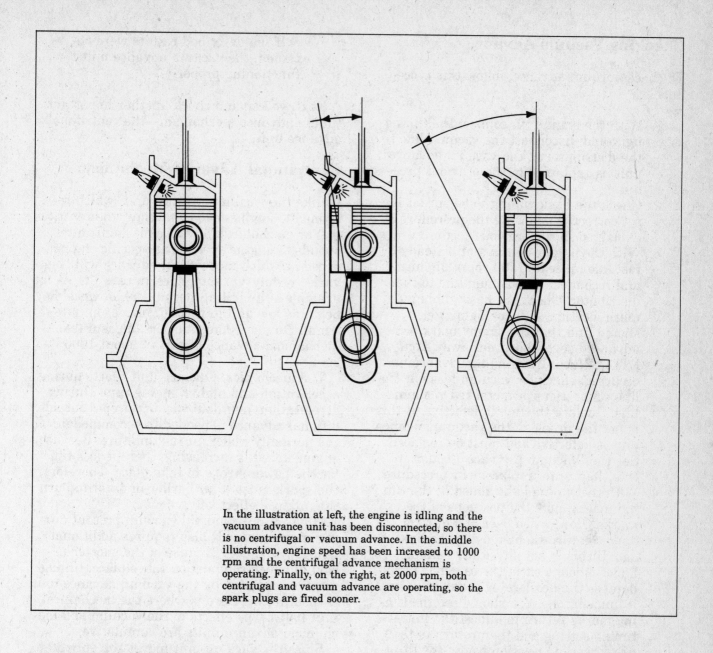

In the illustration at left, the engine is idling and the vacuum advance unit has been disconnected, so there is no centrifugal or vacuum advance. In the middle illustration, engine speed has been increased to 1000 rpm and the centrifugal advance mechanism is operating. Finally, on the right, at 2000 rpm, both centrifugal and vacuum advance are operating, so the spark plugs are fired sooner.

engine idling. The voltmeter will pulse twice and the engine speed will increase to 2000 rpm. Ignition timing at this point should be about 27 to 33 degrees.

FORD WITH MCU. The ignition module has a built-in retard feature. Bypass the retard by disconnecting the yellow and black wire connector and jumping the two male terminals together. You can now check basic timing.

Setting the engine's basic ignition timing only assures you that the timing is correct at one speed. If an automobile engine is to operate efficiently at all speeds and under all load

conditions, it is essential for each spark plug to fire at exactly the right time. As engine speed and load change, so does the ignition timing requirement. To achieve maximum efficiency, there are two devices in the distributor to control ignition timing under various speed and load conditions—the vacuum advance unit and the centrifugal advance mechanism.

It is necessary for these mechanisms to be operating properly in order to realize maximum fuel economy. Therefore, a check of those units should be included in each tune-up operation.

Checking Vacuum Advance

To check vacuum advance, follow this procedure.

1. With the engine off, connect the timing light and disconnect the vacuum line to the distributor at the vacuum advance unit as explained in the previous procedure.
2. Check the basic timing to be sure it is set correctly, following the procedure explained in the previous section.
3. With the engine running at a steady fast idle (at least 1500 rpm), unplug and reconnect the vacuum line to the distributor. Check the basic timing mark location with the light. You should find that the timing mark has advanced several degrees away from BTDC. **Note:** If no timing advance has occurred, check for vacuum leaks at the line connections or a cracked vacuum line. Replace the line if defective. If this is not the problem, the vacuum advance unit is defective and must be replaced. See the "Vacuum Advance" section in this chapter for replacement procedure.
4. With the timing light aimed at the timing marks, note the positions of the marks. Now, reach over and quickly open the throttle by moving the linkage. If this is not physically possible, have someone sit in the car and sharply depress the accelerator pedal, releasing it immediately. You should see the timing marks return to almost the initial timing setting and then return to the first observed position before the throttle was opened. This is due to the sudden decrease in manifold vacuum when the throttle is opened. The decreased vacuum allows the return spring in the vacuum advance unit to move the distributor breaker plate in a "retard" direction.

   If the timing marks did not appear to move, the breaker plate may be binding inside the distributor housing, or the return spring in the vacuum advance unit is too weak. Repair of the distributor or replacement of the vacuum advance unit will be necessary.

If the described results were obtained, the vacuum advance unit is functioning properly.

Next, you should check another important timing advance mechanism—the centrifugal advance unit.

Centrifugal Advance Mechanism

Unlike the vacuum advance unit, which responds to engine load conditions, the centrifugal, or mechanical, advance mechanism responds to engine speed. The specific engine speed at which mechanical advance will begin varies widely. On some foreign cars—Opel, for example—the initial mechanical advance may begin as low as 150 revolutions per minute (rpm). On most domestic cars, measurable mechanical advance begins at about 1000 rpm.

The mechanical advance unit reacts during acceleration and higher engine rpm. During acceleration, manifold vacuum drops, but additional advance is needed to accommodate the normally richer air/fuel mixture. Because engine speed is increasing, there is less time for the power stroke to take place. Therefore, the spark must occur earlier in order to burn the mixture effectively.

High intake manifold vacuum present during cruising speeds also requires additional ignition advance. Because of the shorter period in which combustion takes place, timing advance supplied by the vacuum advance unit is insufficient. Here is where the mechanical unit helps. The effects of the vacuum and mechanical advance units are cumulative.

Since the vacuum unit moves the entire breaker plate mechanism, mechanical advance can still occur. In essence, vacuum and mechanical advance are compounded to advance timing to a degree much higher than either the vacuum or mechanical units could create separately.

Here is how to check your mechanical advance unit.

1. With the engine not running, connect the timing light as explained earlier in this section.
2. Disconnect the vacuum line to the distributor and plug it with a golf tee to

eliminate any vacuum advance that might affect the test.

3. Start the engine and increase engine speed while observing the timing marks. You may need someone to help you here too. If the mechanical advance mechanism is functioning properly, the timing will advance (move against engine rotation) as the engine speed is increased above 1000 rpm. The observed timing marks should appear to move as engine speed is changed. If they do not, then the unit is defective and professional help is required to correct it.

4. Shut off the engine.

5. Disconnect the timing light from the battery or power source. Also, disconnect the hookup at the No. 1 cylinder.

6. Remove the golf tee and reconnect the vacuum advance hose to the distributor.

Troubleshooting

Problems that can result from over-advanced timing include the following.

- Detonation (spark knock or pinging on acceleration or when the engine is under load)
- Overheating
- Engine run-on (dieseling)
- Burned valves (too much total advance at high rpms)
- Hard starting (too much initial advance)

The causes of over-advanced timing include: incorrect basic timing adjustment; broken or weak springs in the centrifugal advance mechanism; centrifugal advance weights stuck in the "out" position; wrong vacuum advance connection to the distributor (most engines should not provide vacuum to the distributor at idle); defective vacuum delay valve, coolant vacuum switch, or solenoid in the vacuum advance plumbing.

Problems that can result from retarded timing include the following.

- Poor fuel economy
- Lack of power
- Hard starting

The causes of retarded timing include: incorrect basic timing adjustment; centrifugal advance weights sticking; leaking vacuum diaphragm or hose; binding breaker plate in the distributor; wrong vacuum hose connec-

tion; defective or plugged vacuum delay valve, coolant vacuum switch, or solenoid that prevents vacuum from reaching the distributor during cruise conditions.

Vacuum Advance

Tools and Materials

- Screwdriver
- Pliers
- Vacuum Advance Unit

IF AN AUTOMOBILE engine is to operate efficiently at all speeds and under all load conditions, it is essential for each spark plug to fire at exactly the right time. Setting the ignition timing only assures you that the timing is correct at one speed. As engine speed and load change, so must the ignition timing. To achieve this, there are two devices in the distributor to control ignition timing under various speed and load conditions—the vacuum advance unit and the centrifugal advance mechanism.

Under part throttle (low engine rpm), a high vacuum develops in the engine's intake manifold and a smaller amount of air and fuel enters the cylinders. Under these conditions, the additional spark advance needed to operate the engine efficiently is provided by the distributor's vacuum advance unit (the centrifugal advance unit is covered elsewhere in this chapter). To achieve maximum power and fuel economy, ignition must take place earlier in the compression cycle when the throttle is partly open.

In operation, the vacuum advance unit causes the distributor's breaker plate assembly to rotate several degrees, advancing the ignition timing to meet the load demands of the engine. The vacuum-operated unit contains a spring to allow the breaker plate to return to its original position when not under the influence of engine vacuum. This would occur during heavy acceleration or when the engine is not operating.

Checking the Vacuum Advance Unit

The vacuum advance unit can be checked without a timing light. Here is how.

1. With the engine not running, remove the distributor cap as explained in the section on "The Distributor."

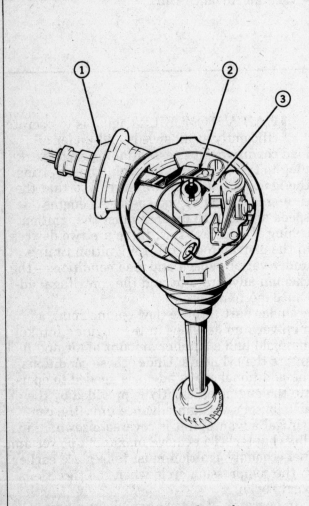

The vacuum advance unit (1) attaches to the distributor, and the diaphragm operates the vacuum advance arm (2), which rotates the breaker plate (3) to change timing.

2. Remove the rotor. It will be secured to the center shaft by two screws, which should be removed with a screwdriver, or be simply slipped onto the shaft, in which case it can be lifted off.
3. Move the distributor breaker plate mechanism in the distributor forward against its spring and hold it.
4. Pinch the vacuum advance hose (or hoses) with your fingers. This is the hose leading from the engine manifold to the vacuum advance unit.
5. While pinching the hose, release the distributor breaker plate mechanism. It should move back slightly and then hold its position. If it does not hold, the vacuum advance unit is leaking and should be replaced. **Note:** If you have determined that the vacuum advance unit must be replaced, proceed to "Replacing the Vacuum Advance Unit" in this section.
6. Release the vacuum advance hose. The breaker plate should then slip back to its original position. If it does not, the return spring on the plate is binding, requiring replacement of the vacuum advance unit. Proceed to "Replacing the Vacuum Advance Unit" in this section.
7. Reinstall the rotor.
8. Reinstall the distributor cap.

Note: On most computerized engine control systems, a vacuum advance mechanism is not used on the distributor. However, the computer still adds the equivalent of vacuum advance electronically by monitoring engine load through a vacuum sensor connected to the intake manifold.

On Chrysler electronic spark control engines, the vacuum diaphragm is located on the computer. It serves the same function as a mechanical vacuum advance diaphragm on a distributor, except that the computer adjusts timing electronically to compensate for changes in engine vacuum.

Replacing the Vacuum Advance Unit

If you have determined that you must replace the vacuum advance unit, here is how to do it.

1. Obtain the correct replacement unit from an auto supply store.

2. Remove the distributor cap and rotor as described in "The Distributor" section in this chapter. **Note:** If you have just completed the checking operation, these parts have already been removed.

3. Disconnect the vacuum hose (or hoses) connected to the outside of the vacuum advance unit. It will simply pull off.

4. Disconnect the vacuum advance control arm. This is the arm coming from the vacuum advance unit and attaching to the distributor breaker plate assembly. In some cases, it is connected to the breaker plate with a slotted screw or a spring clip, in which case you will need a screwdriver or pliers to disconnect it. In other cases, it is merely linked to the breaker plate in a slot. If this is the case, the entire unit must be loosened in order to disconnect the arm (see Step 5).

5. Remove the screws holding the vacuum advance unit to the distributor. Usually, there are two slotted screws securing the unit. Use a screwdriver to remove them.

6. Install the new vacuum advance unit by reversing Steps 2 through 5.

Centrifugal Advance

Tools and Materials

- Screwdriver

IN THE introduction to this chapter, we explained how the ignition's primary and secondary systems work together to produce a high-voltage charge that is sufficient to ignite the compressed air/fuel mixture in the engine. Because the engine is designed to operate over a wide range of speed and power require-

ments, ignition timing must vary to accommodate these varying conditions.

The vacuum advance and the centrifugal, or mechanical, advance mechanisms work together to provide flexibility in ignition timing. Both of these mechanisms are installed in or on the distributor and are working parts of the spark or timing system.

The vacuum advance unit, which is highly sensitive to the changes in intake manifold

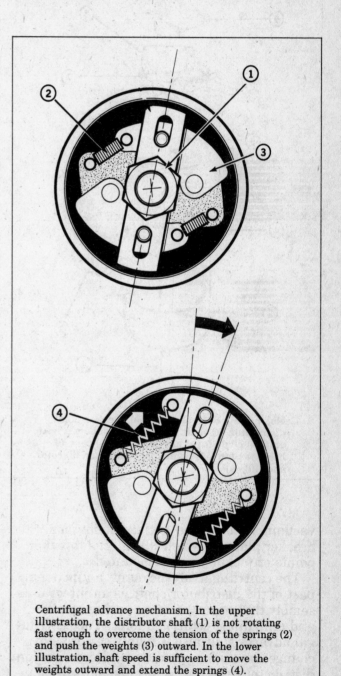

Centrifugal advance mechanism. In the upper illustration, the distributor shaft (1) is not rotating fast enough to overcome the tension of the springs (2) and push the weights (3) outward. In the lower illustration, shaft speed is sufficient to move the weights outward and extend the springs (4).

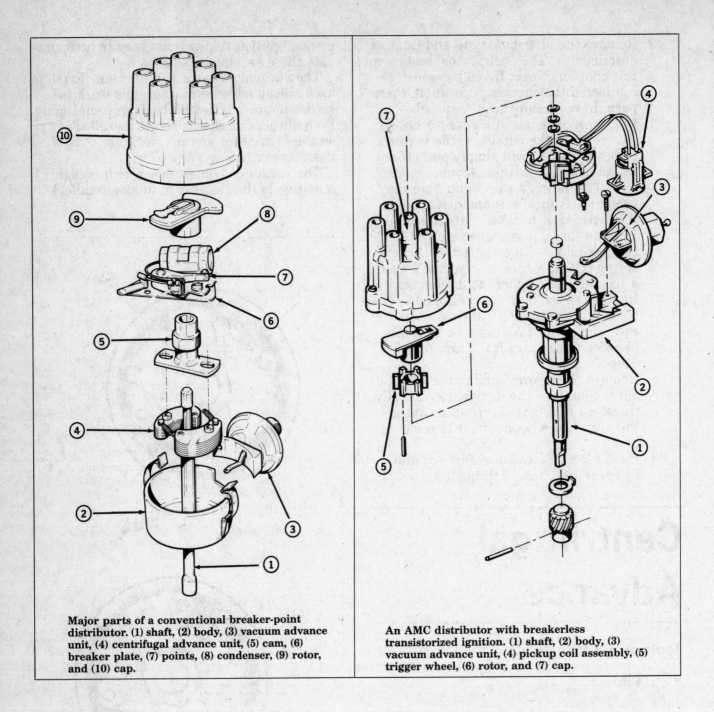

Major parts of a conventional breaker-point distributor. (1) shaft, (2) body, (3) vacuum advance unit, (4) centrifugal advance unit, (5) cam, (6) breaker plate, (7) points, (8) condenser, (9) rotor, and (10) cap.

An AMC distributor with breakerless transistorized ignition. (1) shaft, (2) body, (3) vacuum advance unit, (4) pickup coil assembly, (5) trigger wheel, (6) rotor, and (7) cap.

vacuum, is connected to the distributor's breaker plate on which the ignition breaker points or pickup coil are mounted.

The centrifugal advance unit, a functional part of the distributor shaft, is an integral assembly that operates under spring tension and centrifugal rotational force. The centrifugal advance unit also is highly sensitive to changes in engine speed (rpm). Depending on distributor design, this mechanism will be in-stalled above or below the breaker plate assembly. If your distributor's rotor is retained by two screws, the centrifugal advance unit will be located above the breaker plate. If the rotor is the press-on type, the mechanism will be located under the breaker plate. Location, however, does not change the function of the mechanism. The operation is the same in either case.

The centrifugal advance unit is connected

between the upper end of the distributor shaft and the cam that causes the ignition breaker points to make and break the primary ignition circuit. This mechanism consists of two weights and two springs. When the distributor shaft rotates, it turns the centrifugal unit, which then turns the cam. At engine speeds below 1000 rpm, the weights are held closed by the springs. There is, however, a small initial movement of the weights designed into the component's assembly. This looseness is taken into consideration in the initial timing of the engine and is not reflected in basic timing adjustments.

At engine speeds above 1000 rpm, the centrifugal weights overcome the spring tension and begin to move outward. Centrifugal force, as a result of the distributor shaft speed, forces them out. As these weights move outward, they cause the breaker cam or armature to move ahead in relation to the distributor shaft. This advances coil triggering and thus advances ignition timing. The action of the weights, when they are moving outward, causes the ignition timing to advance. And, as engine speed increases, the weights continue to move out until they finally reach the limit of their travel.

When engine speed decreases, the centrifugal force on the weights is reduced and the springs start to pull the weights together, retarding the timing cycle. Complete centrifugal retard, however, does not occur at the same rpm as centrifugal advance begins (1000 rpm). Complete retard takes place at approximately 800 rpm.

The mechanical action of the centrifugal mechanism can easily be checked.

1. Remove the distributor cap. Refer to the section on "The Distributor" in this chapter.
2. Grasp the rotor and gently turn it in a clockwise direction.
3. Release the rotor. It should spring back to its original position. If it does not, or it returns slowly, then you may have to replace the centrifugal advance mechanism. This should be done by a qualified mechanic.

Other test procedures for the vacuum and centrifugal advance mechanisms are covered in the "Timing the Engine" section.

The Distributor

Tools and Materials

- Screwdriver
- Open-End Ignition Wrenches
- Small Wire Brush
- Rags
- Solvent
- Internal Distributor Wires
- Rotor
- Distributor Cap

THE DISTRIBUTOR, as its name implies, distributes high-voltage electricity to each spark plug at the proper time. Depending on your car's engine, the distributor can be located in one of several places. On some four- and six-cylinder in-line engines, you will find the distributor on the side of the engine, opposite the carburetor; on V6 and V8 engines, the distributor will be in the front or at the rear of the engine. In every engine, the distributor and ignition coil will be installed close to each other. Look at the accompanying illustrations to see what the distributor looks like and you will not have any trouble locating it on your engine.

The distributor, when it is operating efficiently, combines the functions of the primary (low-voltage) and the secondary (high-voltage) ignition system circuits. It opens and closes the primary ignition circuit between the source of electrical energy (battery or charging system voltage) and the ignition coil so that the primary winding in the coil is supplied with intermittent electrical current. This is accomplished by the opening and closing of the distributor breaker points.

When the distributor points are closed, the primary system circuit is complete and current flows through the primary winding of the

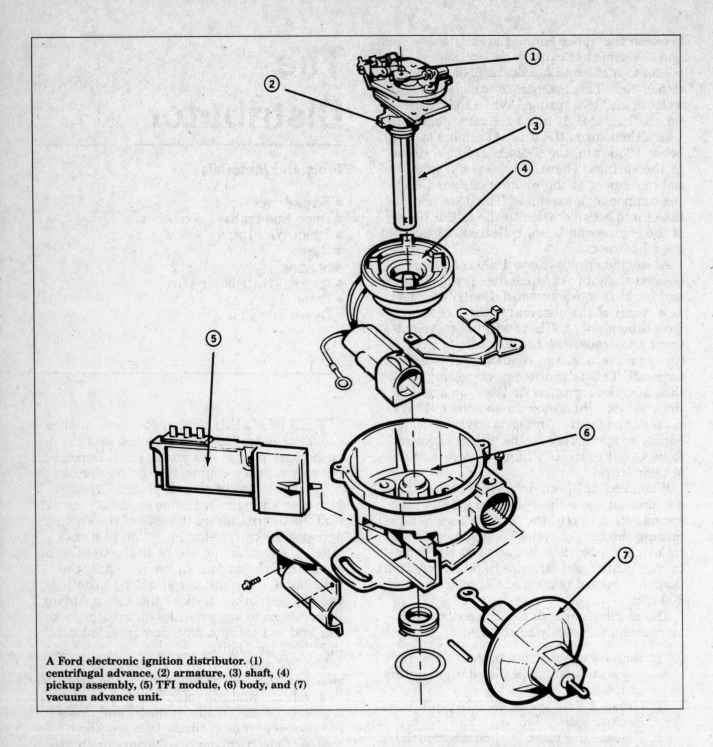

A Ford electronic ignition distributor. (1) centrifugal advance, (2) armature, (3) shaft, (4) pickup assembly, (5) TFI module, (6) body, and (7) vacuum advance unit.

the magnetic field collapses. The voltage in the primary windings is transformed and multiplied as it travels through the path created by the magnetic field to the secondary winding in the coil. This high voltage surges through the coil secondary wire into the distributor cap and then on to the rotor. At this point, the rotor conveys the high voltage to

coil. As current flows through the primary winding, a magnetic field is built up that surrounds both the primary and the secondary windings in the coil. This magnetic field, when interrupted, acts as a conductor and multiplies the voltage in the coil many times. When the distributor breaker points are opened, the primary circuit is interrupted and

the distributor cap terminals. From here, the voltage flows through the secondary wires to the spark plugs, where the secondary circuit is completed by a spark at the plug's electrodes.

In addition to combining the primary and secondary electrical systems, the distributor must be capable of timing the sparks that occur at the spark plug electrodes. This timing is very important—it allows the engine to produce the desired speed and power. This is partially accomplished by means of centrifugal and vacuum advance mechanisms that are contained in and on the distributor housing. The centrifugal advance unit controls the timing of the high-voltage surges according to engine speed requirements; the vacuum advance unit controls timing of the high-voltage surges according to engine load requirements. The engine timing will be thoroughly covered in another section of this chapter.

The basic components of the distributor are the cap, rotor, distributor cam or armature, shaft, and housing. Other components depend on whether it has ignition points or electronic ignition. The distributor cap, rotor, and secondary wires carry high voltage to the spark plugs at the proper time and in correct sequence.

The distributor cap sits on the top of the distributor. It is the component that has one wire from the ignition coil connected to its center tower and four, six, or eight other wires (depending on the number of cylinders in your engine) coming out of towers surrounding this center tower.

The distributor cap is secured to the distributor housing by means of screw clamps or bails. If you look at your distributor cap from the top, you will see how it is secured. There will either be two slotted screws (four on some electronic ignitions) opposite each other on the outside edge of the cap at its base, or two springlike bails that are secured to the distributor housing below the cap; these hold the distributor cap in place by snapping into slots or grooves in the lower part of the cap.

If the cap is held by screw clamps, use a screwdriver and turn each screw ½ turn, either clockwise or counterclockwise, while pushing down on the screwdriver. This will release the cap from the distributor housing. Reverse this procedure to install a cap.

If the distributor cap is held secure by the bails, use a screwdriver and pry the bails from the grooves in the distributor cap. This will release the cap from the distributor housing. To install this type of cap, put the cap in place on top of the distributor housing and, with your hand, snap the bails in place. Only a small amount of effort is needed to accomplish this.

Checking the Distributor

If you are having engine performance problems such as hard starting, rough running, poor acceleration, and so on, trouble in the ignition system could be the cause. The place to start looking for the trouble is at the distributor. Here is how to check it.

1. Remove the air filter housing. Refer to the section on "Air Filter Service" in "The Fuel System" chapter. **Note:** This may not be necessary on some cars if the distributor is easily accessible.
2. Locate the distributor as explained earlier in this section.
3. Remove the distributor cap according to

Some distributor caps are secured by spring bails that can be pried loose with a screwdriver.

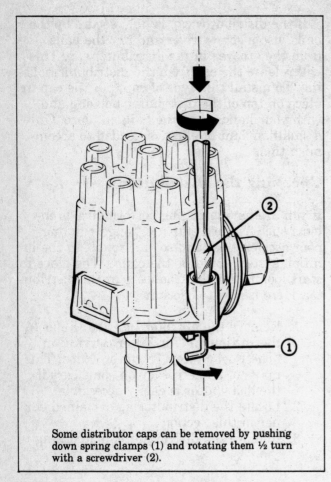

Some distributor caps can be removed by pushing down spring clamps (1) and rotating them ½ turn with a screwdriver (2).

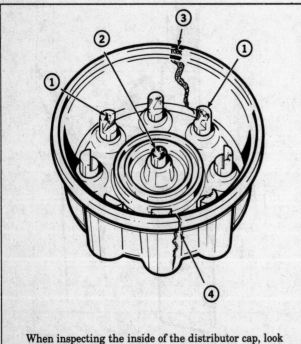

When inspecting the inside of the distributor cap, look for burned metal spikes (1), a deteriorated carbon button (2), carbon tracks (3), and cracks (4).

instructions explained earlier. **Note:** It is not necessary to remove the high-tension coil wire or spark plug wires from the cap tower connections at this time. There should be enough slack in these wires to allow you to turn the cap over and look inside.

4. Turn the cap over in your hands and examine the inside. You will find metal spikes under each high-tension wire connection (the spikes are inside the cap, the connections on the outside). There also will be a black "button" made of carbon under the center tower inside the cap. This is where the rotor connects with the cap.

5. Inspect the inside of the distributor cap. Look for signs of burned metal spikes, a deteriorated carbon button, or any other signs of cracks or damage.

6. Inspect the outside of the cap. Look for cracks or signs of other damage to the cap. Also, carefully inspect for cracks around the wire tower connections.

7. Inspect both the inside and outside of the distributor cap for signs of carbon tracks. These will appear as black lines running from a wire connection tower or metal spike.

8. If you find any of the conditions described, you will have to install a new distributor cap. **Note:** Do not remove any wires from the cap at this point; this will be done in a later procedure in this section.

9. Inspect the rotor. You will find the rotor on top of the distributor center shaft after you remove the distributor cap. It will be secured to the center shaft by two screws (remove them with a screwdriver) or it will be simply slipped onto the shaft (lift it off the shaft with your hand). Look for carbon tracks, cracks, or signs of other damage, including any signs of burning on the metal "finger" on top of the rotor.

10. If you find any of the conditions described, you will have to install a new rotor.

11. If the cap and rotor pass inspection, clean each with a clean rag dampened with a solvent such as alcohol.

12. Look into the distributor. Check for any

signs of rust, corrosion, oil, or grease. Use a clean rag soaked with solvent to clean inside the distributor.

13. Wiggle the center shaft of the distributor with your fingers. It should be secure in the distributor. If it is loose, the distributor must be replaced. See the section on "Removing and Installing the Distributor."

14. Inspect the distributor breaker points or pickup coil. These should be clean and secure.

15. Check any wires and/or wire connections inside the distributor. Look for signs of deteriorated wire insulation and loose connections. The wires to the pickup coil on many distributors are very vulnerable to damage caused by flexing when the vacuum advance mechanism rotates the pickup coil into a more advanced position. Carefully inspect these wires for looseness, and wiggle each to see that the connections are not broken or frayed. If the wires to the pickup are damaged, loose, or broken, the entire pickup assembly must be replaced.

If the distributor passes inspection or if you have replaced any defective parts, complete the following steps.

16. Reinstall the rotor. If your rotor was secured by two screws, place the rotor on the distributor shaft. There will be a round and a square peg on the rotor that will fit into a round and square hole in the rotor mount. Do not try to force the rotor. You will break it. Using a screwdriver, tighten the screws.

If your rotor simply slips over the distributor's center shaft, you should note a flat side on the shaft. This will correspond to the flat area inside the rotor. It, too, will only go on the shaft one way.

17. Reinstall the distributor cap, reversing the procedure described earlier in this section, unless it must be replaced. One of the following procedures in this section describes replacement.

Note: The spark plug wires (secondary ignition) that are connected to the distributor cap tower connections should be pushed all the

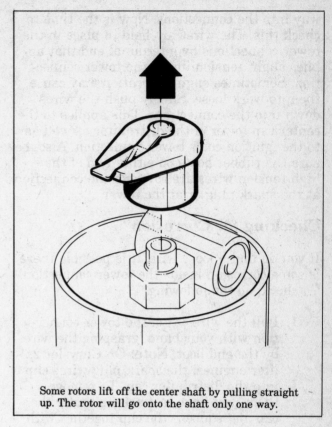

Some rotors lift off the center shaft by pulling straight up. The rotor will go onto the shaft only one way.

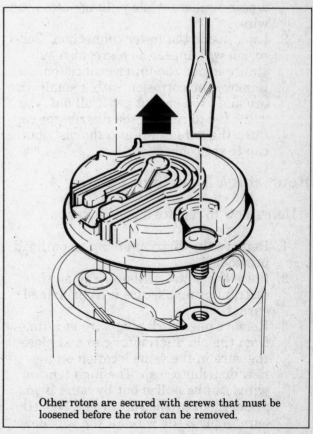

Other rotors are secured with screws that must be loosened before the rotor can be removed.

way into the connections. Now is the time to check this. The wires are held in place in the tower connections by a terminal end that applies slight tension inside the tower connection. Sometimes engine vibration may cause them to work loose. Simply push the wires down into the connections. This applies to the center cap tower of the distributor as well as to the ignition coil's tower connection. Also, be sure the rubber boots on either end of the high-tension wires are covering the connection at the spark plug or at the tower.

Checking for Corrosion

If you do find a loose wire, it is possible there is some corrosion inside the tower connection. To check, do the following.

1. Pull the wire out of the tower connection with your hand, grasping the wire by the end boot. **Note:** On Chrysler 2.2-liter engines, the spark plug wires clip into the distributor cap. To remove them, you have to reach up under the cap and squeeze the clip together with a pair of pliers while pulling out on the wire.
2. Look inside the tower connection. Corrosion will appear as a greenish substance inside the tower connection.
3. Remove the corrosion with a small wire brush. If you cannot get it all out, you will have to replace the distributor cap.
4. Push the wire down into the distributor cap tower connection.

Replacing a Distributor Cap

Here's how to replace a distributor cap.

1. Remove the distributor cap as outlined previously.
2. Place the new distributor cap on the distributor and secure it as explained earlier.
3. Remove one spark plug wire at a time from the old distributor cap and place the wire in the same location on the new distributor cap. The high-tension wires can be pulled out by hand if you grasp them by the rubber end boot. Be sure to push the wire all the way down

in the new cap tower.

Note: Most professional mechanics replace the distributor cap and rotor at the same time. This is good practice. Be sure to purchase the distributor cap and rotor designed for your car's engine. Also, be sure the distributor cap and rotor are from the same manufacturer. This will assure you that the parts are compatible.

Removing and Installing the Distributor

Tools and Materials

- Screwdriver
- Ratchet Wrench, Extension, and Socket
- Small Wrench
- Chalk
- Golf Tee(s)

THE DISTRIBUTOR is a complex mechanism. And, because of the several important roles it plays in the operation of your automobile's engine, it must be functioning correctly at all times.

Most of the checking and servicing of distributor and its parts may be performed while it is still mounted on the engine. In fact, we recommend that replacement of the ignition breaker points, condenser, distributor cap, rotor, and the vacuum advance unit be done without removing the distributor.

There may be a time, however, when distributor removal is necessary. For example, if you have a problem with the centrifugal advance unit (except for those General Motors

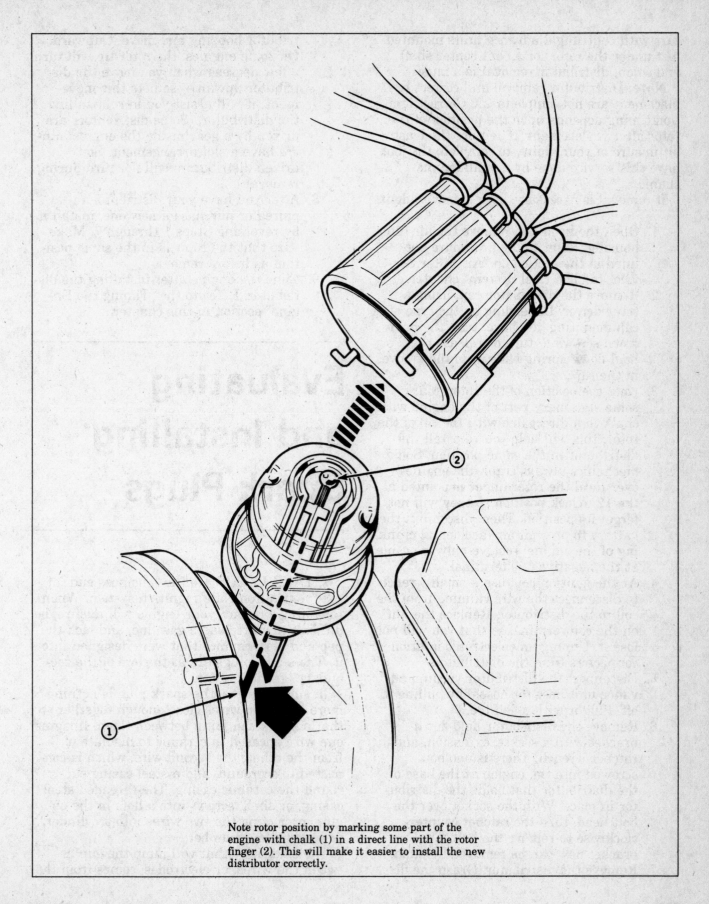

Note rotor position by marking some part of the engine with chalk (1) in a direct line with the rotor finger (2). This will make it easier to install the new distributor correctly.

cars with centrifugal advance units mounted just under the rotor) or a bent center shaft, and so on, distributor removal is a must.

Note: Distributor removal and correct replacement are not simple tasks. Correct ignition timing depends upon the position of the rotor after replacement. If you are the least bit unsure of your ability to complete the job, have this service done by a qualified mechanic.

If removal is necessary, here is how to do it.

1. Open the hood and remove the air filter housing. Refer to the procedure outlined in the section on "Air Filter Service" in "The Fuel System" chapter.
2. Remove the distributor cap, using a screwdriver. Depending on the type of cap mounting you have, turn the hold-down screws ½ turn or release the hold-down spring bails from the grooves in the cap.
3. Note the position of the rotor. Mark some stationary part of the engine with chalk in a direct line with the tip of the rotor; this will help you reinstall the distributor in the same position. Some mechanics always crank the engine over until the rotor finger is pointed at the 12 o'clock position so they will not forget its position. Then, disconnect the battery to prevent any accidental cranking of the engine; remove only the cable at the negative (−) terminal.
4. At the ignition coil, use a small wrench to disconnect the wire running from the coil to the distributor. Replace the nut on the coil terminal so that you will not lose it. Unplug any electronic ignition connectors from the distributor.
5. Disconnect the distributor vacuum advance unit hose (or hoses) by pulling it off. Plug it with a golf tee.
6. Remove the distributor hold-down bracket with a socket, extension, and ratchet wrench. There is one bolt screwed into the engine at the base of the distributor that holds the distributor in place. With the socket over the bolt head, turn the ratchet counterclockwise to remove the bolt. The bracket now can be removed by hand.
7. Remove the distributor. Grasp the dis-

tributor housing and move it upward. On some engines, the rotor tip will turn a few degrees when you move the distributor upward—so note this movement; it will assist you in reinstalling the distributor. (Some distributors are driven by a gear inside the engine; others have a slot arrangement. Slot-driven distributors will not turn during removal.)
8. After you have your distributor repaired or purchase a new one, install it by reversing Steps 1 through 7. Make sure that the rotor is in the same position as before removal.
9. Time the engine after installing the distributor. Refer to the "Timing the Engine" section in this chapter.

Evaluating and Installing Spark Plugs

SPARK PLUGS are the "business end" of your automobile's ignition system. When they are worn out, your engine will misfire, be difficult to start, waste gasoline, and lack the pep and performance that were designed into it. The spark plugs are at the end of the secondary ignition system.

In simple terms, the spark plug is nothing more than two wires close enough together so that a spark can jump between them. Imagine one wire encased in ceramic to insulate it from the other; the second wire, which is connected to a ground, and a steel casing surround the ceramic casing. The threaded steel casing, or shell, screws into a hole in the engine, projecting the two wires into a cylinder, or combustion chamber.

The electricity that will jump the gap between the wires, or electrodes, comes from the

Tools and Materials

- Spark Plug Ratchet Wrench, Extension, and Spark Plug Socket
- Safety Goggles
- Wire Brush
- Ignition Point File
- Round Wire Spark Plug Gap Gauge
- Torque Wrench
- Spark Plugs
- Masking Tape
- Rags
- Solvent
- Penetrating Oil
- Short Length of Heater Hose

distributor. It flows through the ceramic-encased wire and jumps to the other wire, which is connected to a ground to complete the circuit.

Because the highly compressed mixture of gasoline and air present in the cylinder is a difficult environment in which to create a spark, it requires a great deal of voltage to jump that gap. As spark plugs age, the gap erodes or widens from use, making it increasingly difficult for the spark to leap from the center wire or electrode to the ground. When spark plugs are sufficiently worn, electricity cannot make the jump, so it follows the path of least resistance and short-circuits its way to a ground. This is called "misfiring."

Sometimes, a lack of spark is not the fault of the spark plug, but of some other part of the ignition system such as the wiring, breaker points, or ignition coil. In this case, the voltage requirements of the spark plug may not have been excessively high but the voltage available from the ignition system was too low.

There are times when spark plugs appear to be performing adequately but, in truth, they are in a borderline condition. This is difficult for most drivers to determine. If one or more spark plugs occasionally misfire, you are wasting gas. Tests have shown that most drivers cannot sense a misfire on an eight-cylinder engine operating at normal light load and road conditions.

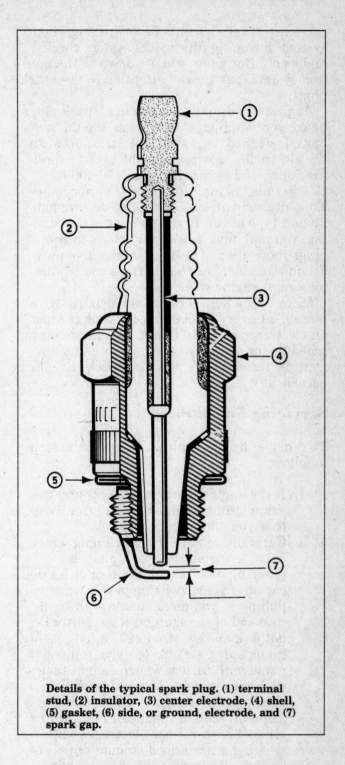

Details of the typical spark plug. (1) terminal stud, (2) insulator, (3) center electrode, (4) shell, (5) gasket, (6) side, or ground, electrode, and (7) spark gap.

The spark plug is a vital part of engine maintenance and, indeed, on late model cars with electronic ignition (no points or condenser), the spark plugs are the main things you will have to be concerned about as far as ignition service goes. In a tune-up, of course, there are other elements beyond the ignition system, including filters, fuel system check, and so on. But when you get down to the ignition system, pay careful attention to the spark plugs.

As part of normal maintenance, spark plugs on conventional ignition systems should be removed, cleaned, regapped (the space between the electrodes or wires brought back to specifications), and reinstalled every 10,000 to 12,000 miles to maintain proper performance. This interval varies according to driving habits and type of car. If you do a lot of city driving, you may find it necessary to clean the plugs more often. This is also true if you are driving an older car that burns some oil due to normal engine wear.

Many carmakers recommend spark plug replacement every 30,000 miles if your car has an electronic ignition. Check the maintenance schedule for your car to see what the manufacturer recommends, but also check the plugs periodically.

Servicing Spark Plugs

To remove the spark plugs, here are the steps to follow.

1. If the engine is warm, allow it and the exhaust manifold to cool sufficiently so that you do not burn yourself.
2. Carefully remove the spark plug wires, or cables, from the spark plugs by grasping each one by the boot or hooded cap shield and twisting gently while pulling so you do not damage the delicate end of the ignition wire. **Note:** Do not jerk on the wire itself. It is probably composed of strands of nylon impregnated with carbon, which cannot take such punishment. As mentioned elsewhere in this chapter, ignition wiring is a special kind of conductor designed to conduct high-voltage electricity while creating a prescribed amount of resistance to eliminate radio interference. These wires must be treated with care. The best way to loosen the connection is to twist the boot slightly while gently pulling outward.
3. Make a careful note of where each spark plug wire goes. If necessary, label them with pieces of masking tape before removal. On some cars, the lengths are similar and it is possible to reinstall them incorrectly. Wipe the wires clean.
4. Loosen each spark plug *only* one or two turns, turning counterclockwise with a ratchet wrench and spark plug socket of the proper size. Use a special spark plug socket with a rubber or plastic insert and ratchet wrench. These sockets help prevent cracking the insulator on the plug and also hold the spark plugs in the socket for easier removal and replacement. You may need a flexible spark plug ratchet and possibly an extension for certain locations because the plugs are not easy to reach on some engines.
5. Using a cloth dampened with solvent, wipe any dirt from around the base of each spark plug. It is best to put on a pair of safety goggles and blow the dirt away with compressed air to keep it from falling into the cylinders when the plugs are completely removed. But since this is not always feasible, an alternate method is to turn on the car's ignition switch to crank the engine for a few seconds, so that any loose dirt around the spark plug will be blown away.
6. Remove the spark plugs one at a time and arrange each one in a tray or on your workbench by cylinder number or in order of removal for inspection. **Note:** On gasketed plugs, be sure the metal gasket is removed with the plug. Chrysler six-cylinder engines, hemispherical V8 engines, and some import engines use gasket-type plugs installed in tubes without gaskets.

Inspecting Spark Plugs

An experienced mechanic can tell you plenty about your car's engine by removing and examining its spark plugs. You can do the same.

First, keep in mind that the atmosphere within which the spark plug operates is indicated by the condition of the firing end of the spark plug. Since it was installed, the plug will have changed in color and may be coated and encrusted with a variety of materials that

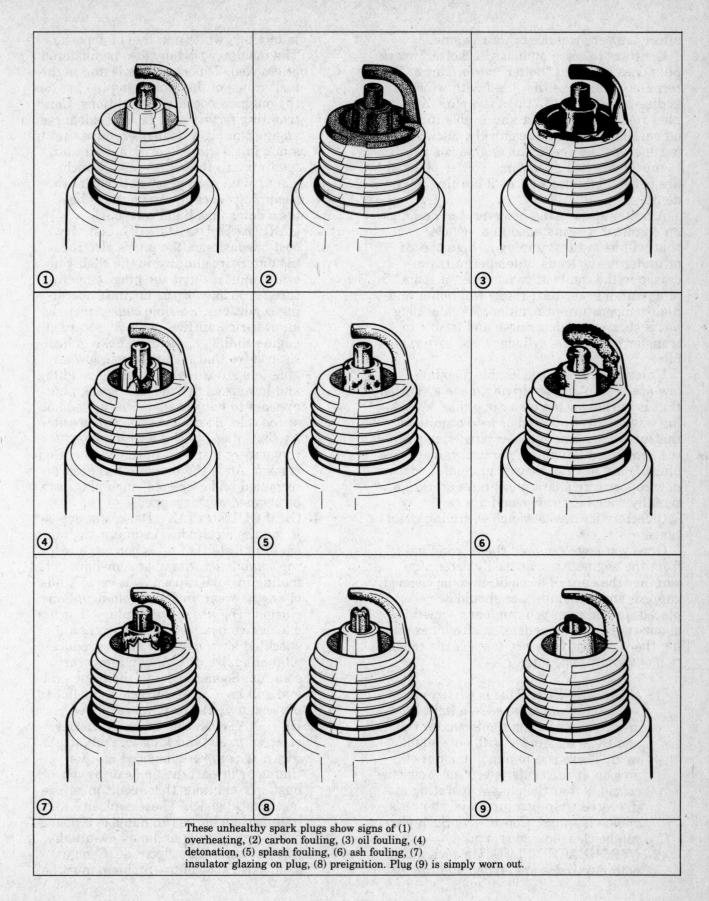

These unhealthy spark plugs show signs of (1)
overheating, (2) carbon fouling, (3) oil fouling, (4)
detonation, (5) splash fouling, (6) ash fouling, (7)
insulator glazing on plug, (8) preignition. Plug (9) is simply worn out.

affect the performance of your engine.

Contrary to some opinions, a "hotter" spark plug does not yield "hotter" performance. The term only indicates the speed with which heat is dissipated from the tip of the plug. A hotter plug retains heat longer and is able to burn off carbon deposits more quickly. Such a plug is generally used when an engine is subjected to much stop-and-go driving. Hotter plugs also are used in engines where oil burning is evident.

A hotter spark plug, however, can destroy an engine if it is installed in a vehicle that will be mostly running at high speeds or under heavy loads. If temperatures increase in the combustion chamber, a spark plug with a lower heat range will help avoid high-temperature preignition. A colder plug has a shorter insulator nose and is able to transfer heat to the cylinder head very rapidly.

Unless you do a considerable amount of low-speed stop-and-go driving, have a vehicle that is burning some oil, or one that is working under extreme speed or load conditions that would demand a colder plug, stay with the recommendation for "normal" range spark plugs found in your owner's manual. Today's new copper core spark plugs have an exceptionally wide heat range and are generally satisfactory for a wide range of driving conditions.

Once you have removed the spark plugs from the engine, you can easily determine whether they are in a condition to be cleaned, gapped, and reinstalled, or should be replaced. In addition, you can learn something about your engine's general health by examining them closely. Here are some of the conditions you may encounter.

1. NORMAL PLUG. This is what you would always like to see—a light brown or gray-tan color on the insulator tip and clean electrodes with only slight wear. There is a minimal amount of erosion at the center electrode. You can conclude that the plug is operating at the correct temperatures and the car's engine is sound. Conclusion: Such plugs can be cleaned and regapped.
2. OVERHEATED PLUG. On such plugs, both electrodes are eroded and the insulator tip is white and free of deposits. The insulator tip may also be blistered or cracked. This condition is due to the heat range of the plug being too hot for the engine's operating conditions. Contributing factors may be over-advanced engine timing, a heat-riser valve that is stuck in the closed position, or an air/ fuel mixture that is too lean. Conclusion: It is a good practice to replace such plugs once the basic cause has been determined and corrected.
3. CARBON-FOULED PLUG. Soft, dry, sooty deposits on the plug's electrodes, insulator tip, and inside the shell generally indicate that the plug temperature is too low for the engine's operating conditions. Possible causes include an over-rich air/fuel mixture, retarded engine timing, a sticking choke, a heat-riser valve that is stuck open, low engine temperatures, and excessive idling and low-speed driving. If a spark plug appears to have been operating too hot or too cold, do not overlook the possibility that plugs with the wrong heat range were installed in the engine. Conclusion: After the problem has been determined and corrected, such plugs can be cleaned and regapped.
4. OIL-FOULED PLUG. Dark, wet deposits on the electrodes, insulator tip, and shell indicate that oil is getting into the combustion chamber somehow. Oil-fouling may be caused by several kinds of engine wear, including old age. Conclusion: The use of spark plugs that are one or two heat ranges hotter than specified for the engine should reduce oil-fouling, but it is only a temporary solution. Sooner or later, the basic problem will have to be corrected. Oil-fouled plugs can be cleaned and regapped.
5. DETONATION. Detonation, generally referred to as "knocking" or "pinging," occurs when over-advanced ignition timing or low-octane fuel causes combustion conditions that result in severe mechanical shock. These explosive, hammerlike blows can damage a piston or the spark plug, and may eventually fracture the plug's electrode. Conclusion: The cause of the problem must be

corrected, and the damaged plug should be replaced.

6. SPLASH-FOULED PLUG. This condition is caused by deposits in the combustion chamber suddenly breaking loose from pistons and valves and "splashing" against a hot plug insulator. It can occur after a long-delayed tune-up. Conclusion: Too much splash-fouling can short out the plug. Before this occurs, the plugs should be cleaned and regapped.

7. CORE- OR GAP-BRIDGED PLUG. Core- or gap-bridging is usually due to the same conditions as splash-fouling. The difference is mainly in degree. Excessive deposits can form a bridge between the plug's insulator and the shell, producing a short. This is most common in engines where oil control is poor or in engines that are used in slow-speed, stop-and-go driving. This splashing can also bridge the gap across the electrodes to short out the plug. Conclusion: Sometimes the plug can be cleaned and regapped.

8. INSULATOR-CHIPPED PLUG. A cracked or broken insulator usually results from bending the center electrode to set the correct spark gap. To avoid such damage, bend only the side electrode when gapping a spark plug. Under certain conditions, a chipped insulator can result from severe detonations. Conclusion: Such plugs must be replaced.

9. ASH-FOULED PLUG. If there are excessive deposits of light brown or white ash on the ground and center electrodes, the cause may be the type of fuel or oil being used. Conclusion: In this case, you may clean or replace the plug and first try changing the brand of gasoline to see if that solves the problem. If it does not, you know you are faced with at least an oil and filter change with a different brand of oil and, most likely, some engine work.

10. INSULATOR GLAZING ON PLUG. On such plugs, normal combustion deposits on the firing tip do not have an opportunity to burn off. Instead, they melt to form a conductive coating. Conclusion:

Generally, glazing cannot be removed by normal cleaning procedures and it is better to replace the plugs. If the condition persists, you may have to use a plug that is one step colder to solve the problem.

11. PREIGNITION. This is just what it implies—ignition of the fuel charge prior to the timed spark. It can be caused by combustion chamber deposits that become incandescent; hot spots in the combustion chamber due to poor control of engine heat; piston scuffing, caused by inadequate lubrication or improper clearance of engine parts; detonation; cross-firing; or a spark plug heat range that is too high for the engine. Often, preignition can damage the piston head and the electrodes of a spark plug. Conclusion: The cause must be determined and corrected. Damaged plugs must be replaced.

12. WORN-OUT PLUG. Worn center and ground electrodes indicate that a plug has given its full service life and should be replaced. A brownish-gray color on the insulator tip shows that the plug's heat range is correct. Conclusion: Since the ground electrode cannot be squared with the center electrode, such plugs should be replaced.

Cleaning Spark Plugs

Considering the amount of time and effort involved in removing and reinstalling spark plugs, once you have them out you are generally better off to install new ones if the old plugs are approaching the end of their life expectancy. But if you have followed a frequent cleaning interval, they are probably in good condition and can be serviced as follows.

1. Using a clean cloth, wipe oil and grease from the outside of the plugs. If necessary, use a small amount of solvent. Dry the plugs thoroughly with a clean cloth.
2. Put on a pair of safety goggles and use a hand-held wire brush to clean the threads and electrode ends of the plugs.
3. File the center electrode of each plug with a ignition point file until it is

clean and flat. File the inside surface of the ground electrode of each plug until the surface appears shiny.

Gapping Spark Plugs

Before installation, both new and used spark plugs must be gapped to the engine manufacturer's specifications. This information can be found in the owner's manual for your car. Although new plugs may be pregapped by the manufacturer, do not assume that they are gapped correctly. In addition, spark plugs used with many electronic ignition systems require wide gaps—in the 0.060- to 0.080-inch range. Plug manufacturers supply special plugs for wide-gap applications. Wide-gap and narrow-gap plugs are made in identical heat ranges, the only difference is in the preset gap. *Caution: Do not attempt to set a narrow-gap plug to wide-gap specifications, or vice versa. Electrode damage will result.*

To check a spark plug's gap, you need a round-wire gap gauge; a flat gap gauge is likely to give you an inaccurate reading. To change the gap, use the bending part of the plug-gapping tool. Carefully bend the side electrode—and only this electrode—to the required gap. Recheck the gap.

To check spark plug gap, use a round-wire gauge; a flat feeler gauge will not give an accurate reading.

SPARK PLUG TORQUE SPECIFICATIONS

Plug Thread Size	Iron Head	Aluminum Head
14mm, gasketed	25-30 lb./ft.	18-22 lb./ft.
14mm, tapered	7-15 lb./ft.	7-15 lb./ft.
18mm, tapered	15-20 lb./ft.	15-20 lb./ft.

Reinstalling the Spark Plugs

After cleaning and gapping, or buying and gapping, your spark plugs, here is the procedure for installing them.

1. Wipe any remaining dirt and grease from the plug seats in the engine with a dry clean rag.
2. Be sure that the metal gaskets on gasketed plugs are in good condition and are properly seated on the plugs.
3. Install the plugs into the engine finger-tight. If you have trouble getting the plugs started in their holes by hand, the threads in the cylinder head may require cleaning. Usually, these threads can be cleaned by applying penetrating oil to them. Soak a corner of a clean cloth with oil. Twist the oil-soaked cloth into the spark plug hole, turning it clockwise. Remove the cloth by turning it counterclockwise. Repeat as often as is required to remove the dirt. If the threads are clean and you still have trouble, try slipping the end of a short length of scrap heater hose over the end of the plug to form a flexible handle. You can also use a thread chaser, available at parts stores, to clean threads. **Note:** Some car manufacturers recommend using an anti-seize lubricant when installing spark plugs; check your owner's manual.
4. Tighten the plugs with a torque wrench to the foot-pound values shown in the accompanying table. If a torque wrench is not available, use a spark plug ratchet and socket and give each finger-tight plug another ¼ to ½ turn, making it snug, but not too tight! If your car uses tapered plugs, which do not have gaskets, there will be a metal-to-metal

contact so only about ¼ turn is required for a proper seal.

5. Reconnect each spark plug cable to the proper plug. Push the wire's rubber boot firmly over the tip of the plug with your hand. Remove the masking tape labels from the cables.

Spark Plug Wires

WHETHER you are performing a complete engine tune-up, just replacing spark plugs, or looking for the reason why your car's engine is not running properly, be sure to check the spark plug, or ignition, wires. If

Tools and Materials

- Wrench
- Spark Plug Wire Set
- Non-Ammoniated Soap or Silicone Spray

damage to one or more of these cables is not apparent, they are assumed—often incorrectly—to be in good shape. The spark plug wires often are only checked when everything else fails to produce a smoothly running engine.

If your car's engine is misfiring, or if some of your spark plugs are carbon-fouled (see the section in this chapter on "Evaluating and Installing Spark Plugs"), the spark plug wires could be the cause.

Although a spark plug wire may appear to be in good condition, it still could be defective. A professional mechanic using a special tester or a volt/ohmmeter can tell you if wires are

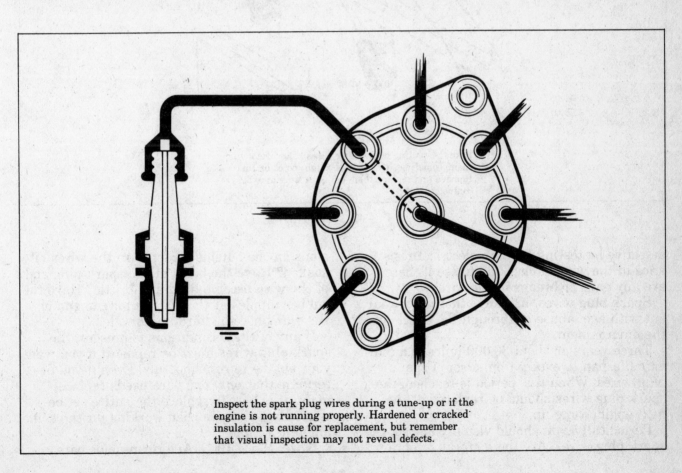

Inspect the spark plug wires during a tune-up or if the engine is not running properly. Hardened or cracked insulation is cause for replacement, but remember that visual inspection may not reveal defects.

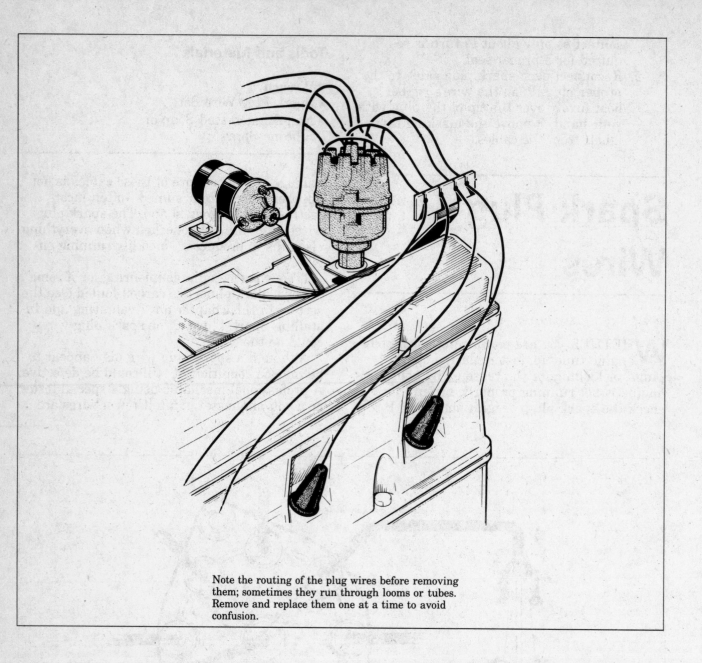

Note the routing of the plug wires before removing them; sometimes they run through looms or tubes. Remove and replace them one at a time to avoid confusion.

defective by testing for high electrical resistance in the wire or checking to see if there are any gaps or breaks in the wire.

Spark plug wires, like any other part, wear out with age, abuse or through the effects of the environment.

Three years or about 30,000 miles is a realistic lifespan to expect from a set of spark plug wires. When this period is reached, the spark plug wires should be replaced at the next engine tune-up.

Periodically, you should visually inspect the spark plug wires. Are there cracks or abrasions on the outside jacket? Are the wires oil-soaked? Have the boots at the spark plug end of the wire become hard and brittle? Have the rubber nipples at the distributor cap end of the wires become hard and brittle?

If any of these conditions is present, the spark plug wires must be replaced if you want your engine to run smoothly. Even if you determine that only one wire needs replacement, it is best to replace the entire set because they all have been working for the same amount of time.

Note: Since 1963, American-made cars

have used a carbon resistance wire for spark plug wires. This often is referred to as TVRS wire, which is an acronym for television and radio suppression. This wire is constructed with a 12-strand nylon center core impregnated with carbon. Because there is no metal core in this kind of wire, it is more easily damaged and likely to burn out. Resistance wire is heavily insulated with a silicone rubber material for high resistance to heat—one major enemy to this type of wire.

Spark plug wire replacement can be performed by any home mechanic on most any car engine. Some engines, however, have the spark plug wires run under parts of the engine, through tubes, looms, or separators, and through some unusual locations. Always visually inspect the job before attempting replacement to be certain you can handle it.

Replacing Conventional Spark Plug Wires

When changing spark plug wires, make sure you have the correct wire set for your particular engine. You can purchase a spark plug wire set that has the wires already tailored to the correct length for your car's engine with the nipples, connectors, and boots in place. **Note:** If your car has a High Energy Ignition (HEI) system, use the procedure at the end of this section.

To replace spark plug wires, follow these steps.

1. If the engine is warm, allow it and the exhaust manifold to cool sufficiently so that you do not burn yourself.
2. Remove the air filter housing. Refer to the section on "Air Filter Service" in "The Fuel System" chapter. This may be necessary for access to all spark plug wires.
3. Starting at the spark plug farthest from the distributor (on V8 or V6 engines, you may start on either side of the engine), carefully remove the spark plug wire by grasping the rubber boot or hooded cap shield and twisting gently while pulling.
4. Follow the wire you have disconnected at the spark plug up to the distributor.
5. Pull the other end of the wire out of the

distributor cap with your hand. Once again, a slight twisting motion will make it easier to remove the wire.
6. Remove the spark plug wire from the engine. If the spark plug wire is threaded through any tubes or looms or held in place by separators, make a note of this to assist you when installing the new wire.
7. Select a spark plug wire from the new set you have purchased that is the same length as the wire you have just removed. Compare both wires to be sure.
8. Install this new spark plug wire by reversing Steps 3 through 6. Be careful to route the new wire in the same manner as the one you removed.
9. At both the spark plug end of the wire as well as the distributor cap end, be sure to push the rubber boot and the nipple in as far as they will go to obtain a good connection.
10. Continue this same procedure, one spark plug wire at a time, until you have replaced the entire set.
11. Remove the secondary high-tension wire from the ignition coil tower; this is the wire that is connected to the distributor at the other end. Pull it out of the tower with a slight twisting motion.
12. Remove the other end of this high-tension wire from the center tower connection of the distributor cap. Once again, twist slightly as you pull the wire out.
13. Using the wire supplied in the wire set you purchased for your car's engine, replace the secondary high-tension wire by reversing Steps 11 and 12. Once again, be sure to push the rubber nipples—there is one on each end of this wire—all the way down to assure a good connection.

High Energy Ignition Systems

If you are working on a car equipped with a High Energy Ignition (HEI) system, the distributor cap and the way the wires attach to the distributor cap will differ. You will also discover that the diameter of the spark plug

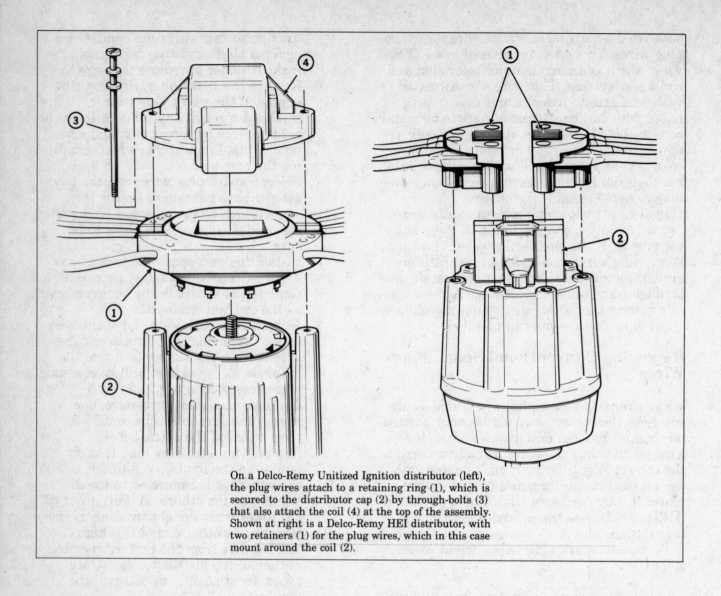

On a Delco-Remy Unitized Ignition distributor (left), the plug wires attach to a retaining ring (1), which is secured to the distributor cap (2) by through-bolts (3) that also attach the coil (4) at the top of the assembly. Shown at right is a Delco-Remy HEI distributor, with two retainers (1) for the plug wires, which in this case mount around the coil (2).

wires is larger. And, because the ignition coil is an integral part of the distributor cap assembly in an HEI system, there also will be no secondary high-tension wire at the coil.

Here's how to remove a spark plug wire on an HEI system.

1. Lift off the retaining ring from the distributor cap. This is done by removing the retaining clips (marked "Latch") outward and lifting the ring up. All the spark plug wire connections will remain in the retaining ring.

   Note: Some HEI systems have spark plug wires going to two retainers. Simply remove the wires and retainers from the distributor cap. On Delco-Remy Unitized systems, two through-bolts and the coil must be removed before the spark plug wires and harness assembly may be removed. Use a screwdriver to remove the through-bolts. Then, remove the coil, and finally, the spark plug wires and harness assembly.

2. Remove the nipple end of the spark plug wire from the distributor cap's retaining ring by pressing down on the nipple with your thumb.

   Note: On Delco-Remy Unitized systems, the end of each spark plug wire is held in the harness assembly by a setscrew. Loosen the setscrews to remove the wires; tighten them to secure the wires.

3. Remove the opposite end of the wire from the spark plug. Carefully remove the wire by grasping the rubber boot or hooded cap shield and twisting gently while pulling. Do not jerk on the cable or you may damage it.

4. Select a matching length of spark plug wire from the replacement set.

5. To install the new wire in the retaining ring, lubricate the nipple with a non-ammoniated soap or silicone spray and press the nipple into the retaining ring. On Delco-Remy Unitized systems, insert the wire into its opening and tighten the setscrew.

6. Repeat Steps 2 through 5 for each spark plug wire until you have replaced the entire set. Remember, do one wire at a time to avoid confusion and time-consuming mistakes.

7. When all spark plug wires have been replaced, reverse Step 1 to complete the procedure.

Remember, all procedures for replacing spark plug wires on HEI systems are the same as for conventional systems except for those differences at the distributor cap as outlined above. If you have any doubts as to whether you can perform this task, consult a professional mechanic.

Ignition Coil

Tools and Materials

- Spark Plug Adapter
- Ignition Coil
- Volt/Ohmmeter
- Open-End Wrenches

IN MOST cars, the ignition coil is a black, cylindrical or rectangular unit about the size of a 12-ounce can of orange juice. Normally, it is located near the distributor. If you have a problem finding it, begin by tracing the heavy secondary high-tension ignition wire from the distributor cap. The ignition coil will be at the other end of this wire.

A visual inspection is your first step in checking the ignition coil. Make certain that the coil is mounted tightly to assure a good ground and that all wire connections are clean and secure. Loose or dirty wire connections cause high resistance to flow in the wires. High resistance at these points could cause poor ignition system performance. Look for cracks at the top of the coil, a dented housing, or oil leaking from inside the coil. If you find any of these conditions, the ignition coil must be replaced.

The ignition coil is actually a small trans-

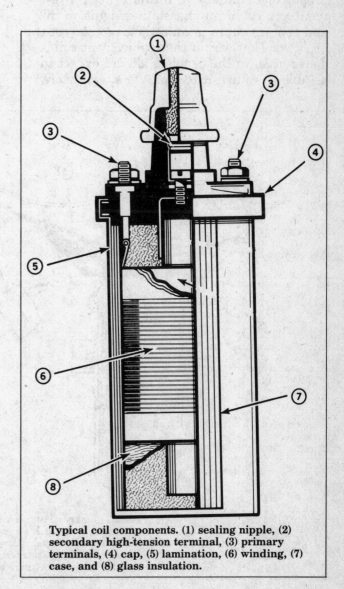

Typical coil components. (1) sealing nipple, (2) secondary high-tension terminal, (3) primary terminals, (4) cap, (5) lamination, (6) winding, (7) case, and (8) glass insulation.

former that boosts the 12-volt primary part of the ignition system up to 30,000-plus volts in the secondary system. High voltage is required to jump the spark plug gap to ignite the air/fuel mixture inside the engine.

Even though the ignition coil may appear from the outside to be in good condition, it could be defective electrically. Some signs of a defective ignition coil, or in some cases at least a weak one, include a loss of power at higher engine speeds, a hesitation of the engine during acceleration, or in extreme cases, a no-start condition.

If you experience any of these symptoms, it would be best to have your ignition coil checked by a service repairman who has the proper test equipment. If this is not convenient you could purchase a new ignition coil and replace yours in an attempt to correct the problem. However, if the replacement coil does not solve the problem, do not expect to be able to return it to the auto supply store

once you put it in your car. Most auto stores will not accept used electrical components for refunds once they have been installed. If, however, you own or have access to a volt/ohmmeter (VOM) or other automotive "analyzer" capable of testing the ignition coil, you can perform these test procedures yourself.

Primary Resistance Test

To perform a primary resistance test on the ignition coil, follow these steps.

1. Set the volt/ohmmeter's selector knob to the "Ohms × 1" position. If necessary, connect the proper test lead plug into the instrument.
2. Calibrate the test instrument according to the manufacturer's instructions.
3. With the ignition switch turned off, disconnect the two wires connected to the primary terminal near the top of the

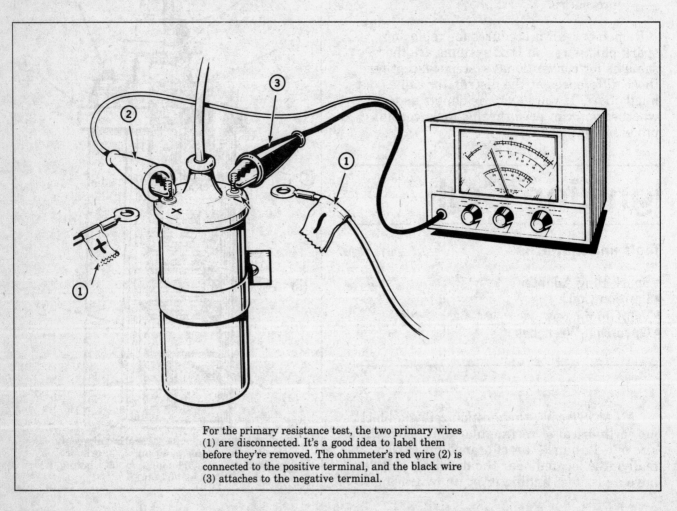

For the primary resistance test, the two primary wires (1) are disconnected. It's a good idea to label them before they're removed. The ohmmeter's red wire (2) is connected to the positive terminal, and the black wire (3) attaches to the negative terminal.

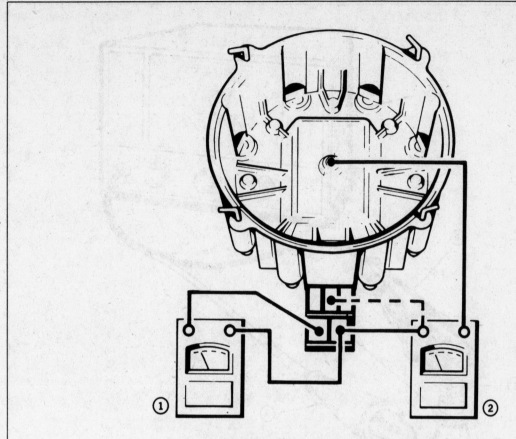

For GM HEI systems with the coil in the distributor cap, ohmmeter connections are as shown for (1) primary and (2) secondary resistance.

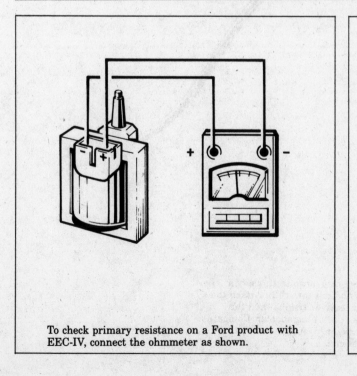

To check primary resistance on a Ford product with EEC-IV, connect the ohmmeter as shown.

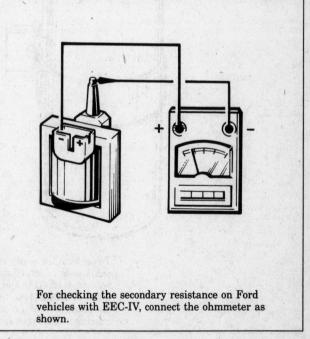

For checking the secondary resistance on Ford vehicles with EEC-IV, connect the ohmmeter as shown.

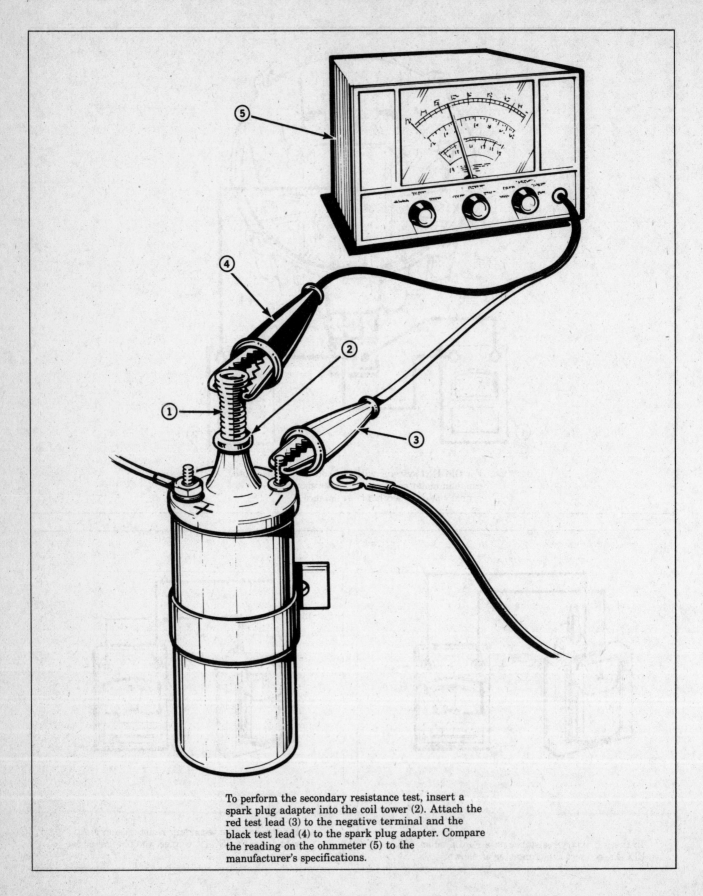

To perform the secondary resistance test, insert a
spark plug adapter into the coil tower (2). Attach the
red test lead (3) to the negative terminal and the
black test lead (4) to the spark plug adapter. Compare
the reading on the ohmmeter (5) to the
manufacturer's specifications.

coil. Some wires have press-on fittings that can be pulled free; others have nuts on the binding posts that can be removed with a small open-end wrench. The terminals are marked in various ways. Most often, the marks will be "POS" or (+), meaning positive, and "NEG" or (−), meaning negative. Tag the wires as you remove them for correct reconnection later.

4. Connect the red and black leads of the test instrument to the primary terminals.
5. Observe the meter reading on the instrument's low ohms scale. The reading should meet the carmaker's specification; this can be found in the service manual for your vehicle. Generally, however, the coil's primary winding resistance should be between 0.5 and 3 ohms. If the reading is considerably above or below the specification, the ignition coil is defective and should be replaced.
6. If the coil is defective, remove the test leads from the primary terminals and replace the coil following the procedure outlined at the end of this section. If the coil is within specification, proceed to the secondary resistance test.

Secondary Resistance Test

To perform the secondary resistance test on the ignition coil, follow these steps.

1. Set the volt/ohmmeter's selector knob to the "Ohms × 1000" position.
2. Calibrate the test instrument according to the manufacturer's instructions.
3. Remove the high-tension lead from the center tower of the ignition coil. *Caution: Before removing the lead, make certain that the ignition switch is in the off position.* The lead can be removed by grasping the end, and twisting it as you pull.
4. Connect one of the instrument's test leads to either primary terminal.
5. Connect the instrument's other lead to a spark plug, or coil spring, adapter and insert it into the coil tower.
6. Observe the instrument's meter reading on the "Ohms × 1000" scale. The read-

ing should meet the carmaker's specification. The specifications for various manufacturers are listed below. If your car is not listed, check the service manual for your car.

Manufacturer	Secondary Resistance
American Motors	6500 to 9500
Chrysler	9500 to 11,500
Ford	7500 to 9000
Ford TFI	8000 to 11,500
General Motors (Delco-Remy)	5500 to 9500

If the meter reading is higher or lower than the manufacturer's specification, the ignition coil is defective and should be replaced.

7. If the coil is defective, remove the test lead from the coil and replace the coil following the procedure below. If the coil is within specification, remove the test lead and reconnect the primary wires and the high-tension lead.

Replacing the Ignition Coil

If you determine that your ignition coil is defective and must be replaced, here is how to do it.

1. Obtain the correct replacement ignition coil for your car. Many coils look similar but they may not be able to provide sufficient secondary voltage to operate your car's ignition system.
2. If you have not done so, turn the ignition switch off and disconnect the two wires connected to the primary terminals near the top of the ignition coil. Some wires have press-on fittings that can be pulled free; others have nuts on the binding posts that can be removed with a small open-end wrench. The terminals are marked in various ways. Most often, the marks will be "POS" or (+), meaning positive, and "NEG" or (−), meaning negative. Tag the wires as you remove them for correct reconnection later.
3. Disconnect the secondary high-tension wire from the center tower of the ignition coil.

4. With a wrench, loosen the ignition coil mounting bracket bolt. Generally, this bolt screws into the engine block.
5. Remove the old coil.
6. To install the new ignition coil, reverse Steps 1 through 4.

Ignition Primary Resistor

Tools and Materials

- Jumper Wire
- Wrench
- Primary Resistor

IN MANY cars, the ignition system is designed to operate on less than full battery voltage when the engine is running. To accomplish this, a primary (ballast) resistor is installed between the ignition switch and the ignition coil. This resistor lowers battery voltage (called charging voltage when the engine is running) by 3 volts. However, since full battery voltage is required for starting the engine, this primary resistor is bypassed when the engine is being started.

If your car's engine starts, but stops as soon as the ignition switch moves from the start to the on or run position, the primary resistor most likely is causing the problem.

Testing the Resistor

The following procedure will verify that the resistor is inoperative.

1. Make sure the ignition switch is turned off. Connect a jumper wire from the positive (+) terminal of the battery to the positive (+) terminal on the ignition coil, which is the small coil terminal opposite the one with the distributor primary wire connected to it.
2. Start the engine. If the engine stays running with the jumper wire connected, the problem is in the primary resistor. It must be replaced.

Caution: It must be kept in mind that this temporary connection is intended to be used as a means of testing only—not as a permanent repair. If you run your engine for even a few hundred miles with the jumper wire connected, the increased heat created by this hookup

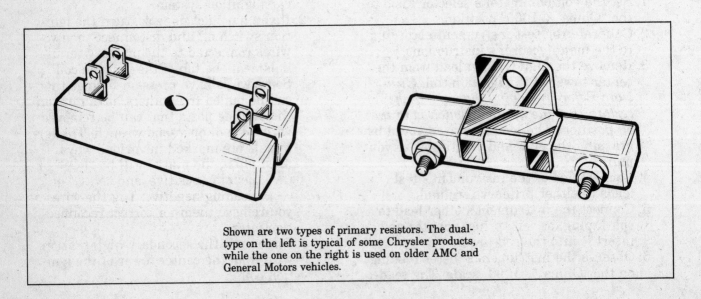

Shown are two types of primary resistors. The dual-type on the left is typical of some Chrysler products, while the one on the right is used on older AMC and General Motors vehicles.

the firewall of the engine compartment. To replace it, do the following.

1. Disconnect the wires at the resistor assembly. Label them to make reinstallation easier.
2. With a wrench, remove the primary resistor mounting cap screw.
3. Remove the primary resistor from the firewall.
4. Reverse Steps 1 through 3 to install a new primary resistor. **Note:** Be sure to obtain the correct resistor for your car.
5. Start the engine. If it starts and continues to run, you have repaired the problem.

Ignition Switch

A FEW YEARS AGO, an automobile's ignition switch had only one job—turning the primary circuit on and off. Now, it also actuates the starter motor, connects the alternator and accessories, locks the steering wheel, and sounds a buzzer if you leave the key in it.

As the functions of the ignition switch became more complex, so too did its construction. On most ignition switches found in today's cars, you will find that there are five positions, each with a separate function: "accessories," "lock," "off," "on" or "run," and "start." The first position, "accessories," allows you to operate various electrically operated components on the car without supplying voltage to the car's ignition circuit, which would not only drain the battery needlessly, but also could "burn up" the ignition system. On most cars, options such as electrically powered windows and seats can only be operated when the switch is in the "on" position for reasons of safety.

When the switch is turned to the "lock" position, all power that is supplied through the ignition switch is cut off. Power that does not go through the ignition switch, such as that for the headlights and the cigarette lighter, is constantly supplied by the battery. In the "lock" position, the ignition key can be removed. On older cars—pre-1966 models—the

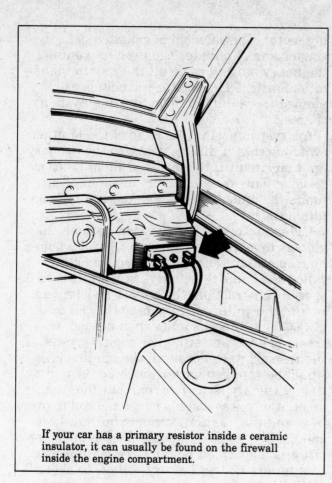

If your car has a primary resistor inside a ceramic insulator, it can usually be found on the firewall inside the engine compartment.

would probably burn out your ignition coil, breaker points, and other components of your ignition system.

3. Turn off the engine. Disconnect the jumper wire.

Note: On late model GM cars, the primary resistor is actually a resistor wire between the ignition switch and the ignition coil. If, after performing the test procedure outlined above on your GM car, you determine there is trouble in the primary resistor, leave the jumper wire connected as described in Step 1, note the caution in Step 2, and drive your car to the nearest professional mechanic. This repair is *not* a job for the beginning technician.

Replacing the Resistor

On many cars, especially older models, the primary resistor is simply a small coil of wire inside a ceramic insulator. It is mounted on

key could be removed in all but the "start" position. On later models, there is a theft prevention device that locks the steering wheel and the gearshift lever against movement. On almost all cars with the locking steering wheel system, there is an "off" position just to the right of "lock" that allows the steering wheel and gear selector lever to be operated without draining the battery. This position is used when steering or suspension service is being performed or when adjusting the selector linkage.

When the key is turned to the "on" or "run" position, power is supplied to the circuits that would be used during normal operation of the automobile. These include the radio, blower motor, power accessories such as windows and seats, the windshield wipers, backup lights, cruise control, and so on.

In the "start" position, battery voltage is supplied to the starting motor through the starter solenoid. The solenoid has several functions, one of which is to act as a relay switch. When voltage is applied to the solenoid by the ignition switch, a circuit is completed, allowing power to be sent to the start-

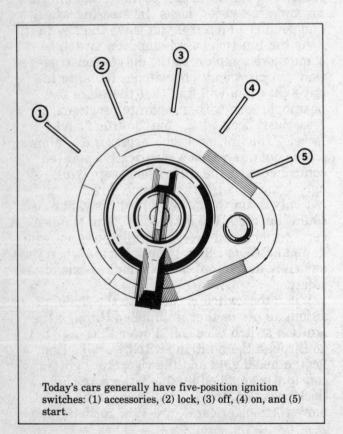

Today's cars generally have five-position ignition switches: (1) accessories, (2) lock, (3) off, (4) on, and (5) start.

ing motor. The solenoid is mounted near the starter and eliminates the need for running the heavy battery cable all the way to the ignition switch. The starter solenoid is explained more fully in "The Starting System" chapter.

Another important function of the ignition switch is that it directs power to the primary ignition circuit through the primary ignition resistor. This resistor, as its name implies, limits the amount of voltage reaching the ignition coil.

Older cars use a resistor that reduces the voltage to a specified amount regardless of engine operation. The modern component is called the ballast (primary) resistor. Due to its special construction, the ballast resistor can reduce the voltage available to the coil at lower engine speeds and, when needed, increase the voltage at higher engine speeds. If the resistor were not used, the ignition coil would be supplied with enough power to function efficiently at higher rpm, but the same amount of voltage would cause the coil to overheat and the ignition points to burn at lower speeds. The most commonly used primary resistor is a specified length of resistance wire that lowers 12-volt battery voltage to about 9 to 10.5 volts during normal engine operation.

An engine needs all the voltage it can get in order to start efficiently, especially on cold winter mornings when cranking speed is already hindered by thickened motor oil and higher electrical resistance due to lower temperatures. Because of this, the ignition switch incorporates a special bypass circuit that allows full voltage to be supplied to the ignition coil during cranking.

If your automobile engine suddenly quits running, then restarts easily only to die again at an odd moment, the ignition switch may be the problem. You should, however, have a trained mechanic check this condition thoroughly. If your key fits loosely in the switch and you get erratic operation of the ignition or accessories when you wiggle the key, then the switch probably needs replacement.

Cars with steering wheel locks require a special tool to remove the ignition switch. Home mechanics should not attempt to replace these switches due to the difficulty and potential damage involved without the use of proper equipment.

THE ENGINE

TECHNICALLY speaking, your car's engine is not a motor—although everyone uses the two words interchangeably. A "motor" converts *electrical* energy into mechanical work such as the starter motor that cranks your engine. An "engine," on the other hand, is a machine that converts *heat* energy into mechanical work. Your engine does this by burning gasoline inside its combustion chambers.

When gasoline and air are mixed together in the right proportions (14.7 parts of air to one part gasoline is considered ideal) and ignited by a spark, the mixture explodes, creating tremendous heat and pressure. Although combustion occurs in a split-second, it does so in a controlled manner. When the spark ignites the mixture, a "flame front" sweeps out from the point of ignition like a rapidly expanding balloon until all the fuel mixture is consumed. This causes a sharp rise in cylinder pressure, which pushes the piston down and turns the crankshaft. Thus, heat energy is transformed into useful mechanical work to power your car down the road.

Pressing down on the accelerator pedal opens up the throttle, which allows more air and fuel to be drawn into the engine. This increases the density of the fuel mixture in each of the engine's cylinders, which in turn increases the intensity of cylinder pressures when the mixture is ignited. As a result, the engine develops more power, allowing it to either run faster or work harder, depending on the load. Let off on the accelerator pedal and the amount of air and fuel are decreased. Cylinder pressures drop and the engine slows down.

In a way, you can think of an internal combustion engine as an air pump. Opening up the throttle allows it to pump more air through itself, and the greater the volume of air (and fuel), the greater the power output.

That's why bigger engines generally produce more horsepower than smaller ones. They have a greater pumping capacity.

Unfortunately, internal combustion engines are not very efficient when it comes to making good use of the heat energy produced by combustion. Only about a third of the heat energy is actually used to drive the vehicle. Nearly a third is lost when the hot exhaust gases exit out the tailpipe. By the time the piston reaches the lower limit of its travel, cylinder pressure has dropped considerably from its peak which occurred shortly after ignition. The engine has gotten all it can from the expanding combustion gases, yet heat energy remains which must now be dumped out the exhaust so the cylinder can repeat the process over again with a fresh charge of air and fuel.

Another 20 to 25 percent of the heat produced during combustion is lost to the cooling system. As the engine burns fuel, it begins to heat up. Were it not for the cooling system, the engine would continue to build up heat until it eventually melted. So heat loss through this path is unavoidable.

Another form of loss is overcoming internal friction: piston rings rubbing against the cylinders; cam lobes rubbing against their lifters; valves sliding up and down in their valve guides; the crankshaft turning in its bearings; etc. Yet frictional losses aren't as great as you might imagine. It's only about 5 to 8 percent for most engines. Even so, it's another loss that comes out of the useful work produced by combustion.

A percentage of the engine's remaining power is also required to drive "parasitic" accessories such as the water pump, alternator, power steering pump, and air conditioning compressor. There are also frictional losses in the engine's drive belts, transmission, drivetrain, and tires (rolling resistance). The remaining power available to drive the vehicle

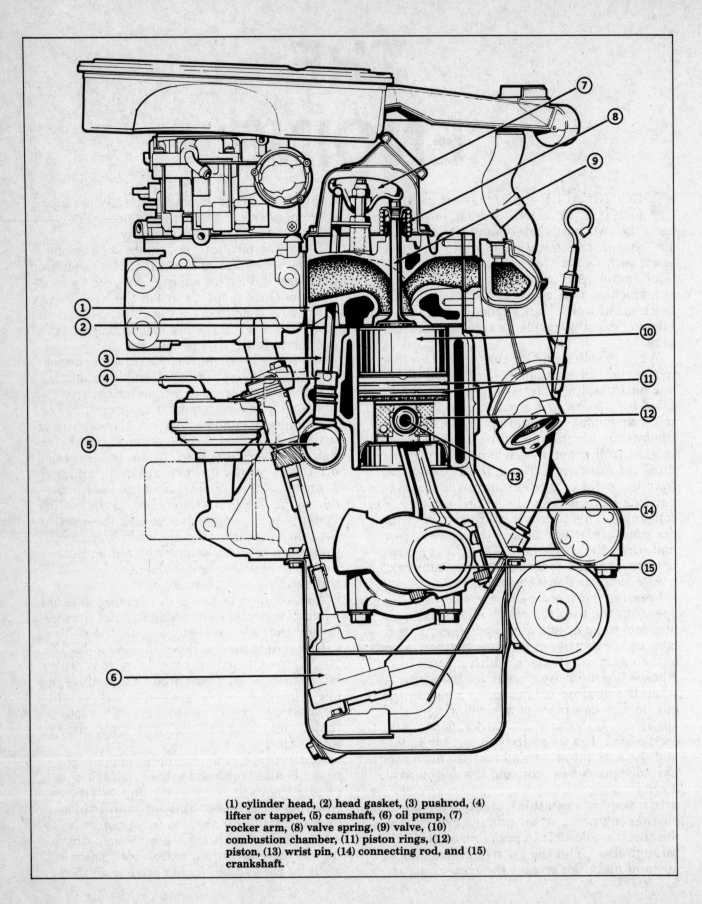

(1) cylinder head, (2) head gasket, (3) pushrod, (4) lifter or tappet, (5) camshaft, (6) oil pump, (7) rocker arm, (8) valve spring, (9) valve, (10) combustion chamber, (11) piston rings, (12) piston, (13) wrist pin, (14) connecting rod, and (15) crankshaft.

is only a small percentage of the total power produced when the fuel mixture was ignited.

Engineers are searching for ways to make the internal combustion engine more efficient. Designing an engine out of heat-resistant materials so it could run at higher temperatures or possibly without a cooling system would reduce heat losses. Much work is being done to develop ceramic materials, either as complete engine components, or as coatings on pistons, valves, cylinders, and combustion chambers. Recapturing some of the waste heat from the exhaust is possible by using it to spin a turbocharger. Yet turbochargers are expensive, generally limiting their use to luxury and sports models only. Low-friction oils and mechanical improvements which cut frictional losses also help, but again, the gains are small compared to the costs. Until engineers come up with a better way to recapture much of this lost heat energy economically, the internal combustion engine will continue to be a less than efficient workhorse for powering our vehicles. However, it is still the most efficient, cost-effective workhorse available today.

Speaking of workhorses, an engine's power output is often measured in horsepower. One horsepower is the equivalent of lifting 33,000 pounds one foot in one minute. The figure was arrived at by observing the amount of work a typical horse could do when lugging coal out of a coal mine. Another measure of engine output is torque, or the amount of twisting force the engine can exert. This is expressed in foot-pounds (lbs./ft.), and is determined by the rotation of the crankshaft and maximum cylinder pressure.

Engine Fundamentals

As a do-it-yourself mechanic interested primarily in maintenance and light repairs, you really don't have to understand a lot about the internal workings of your engine. But you should realize the importance of lubrication to the engine's longevity. An adequate supply of clean oil is essential to prevent metal-to-metal contact and engine wear. Oil change and lubrication information is covered in the "Maintaining Your Car" chapter at the front of this book.

If you maintain your engine properly, it should last the life of your car; 100,000 to 150,000 miles is possible with adequate care. The only items that may not go the distance are the exhaust valves and possibly some of the engine's gaskets or seals.

All valves eventually wear themselves out. The rapid opening and closing that hammers the valves against their seats, combined with the high temperatures in the combustion chamber, eventually wear away the mating surface of both valve and seat. The intake valves are fortunate in that they are constantly cooled by the incoming fuel mixture, but the exhaust valves don't have this advantage. Instead, they see only the searing heat of the exhaust gases. The only cooling they receive, therefore, is the small amount of heat conducted up the valve stem to the valve guide, and during the brief time the valve is closed and resting on its seat. Heat is conducted across the valve seat to the head. But once the valve seat starts to deteriorate with high mileage, the contact surface is reduced and thus the valve is unable to shed as much heat as before. Consequently, the exhaust valve runs hotter, which accelerates metal fatigue and deterioration of the valve even further. Eventually the valve starts to leak. Once this happens, the hot combustion gases shoot through the gap, which causes a blowtorch effect on the valve. The gap gets wider as more and more metal is literally burned away until the valve is destroyed. This condition is called a "burned valve" and it can be accelerated by lean fuel mixtures, incorrect ignition timing, incorrect valve lash adjustment, or poor filtration of incoming air.

Sometimes a valve will crack, chip, or even pull apart when it fails. This can result in severe engine damage, requiring a complete overhaul to repair the engine. But for ordinary valve wear, a "valve job" is usually all that's required to restore the valves to good operating condition. A valve job involves removing the cylinder head, disassembling the valves and replacing any worn components such as valve guides, valve guide seals, or springs. Worn intake valves are usually reground to restore their mating surface. Exhaust valves are usually replaced with new ones. The seats in the cylinder head must likewise be reground to restore their surfaces. Worn valve guides can often be "knurled" to restore original clearances, or reamed so over-

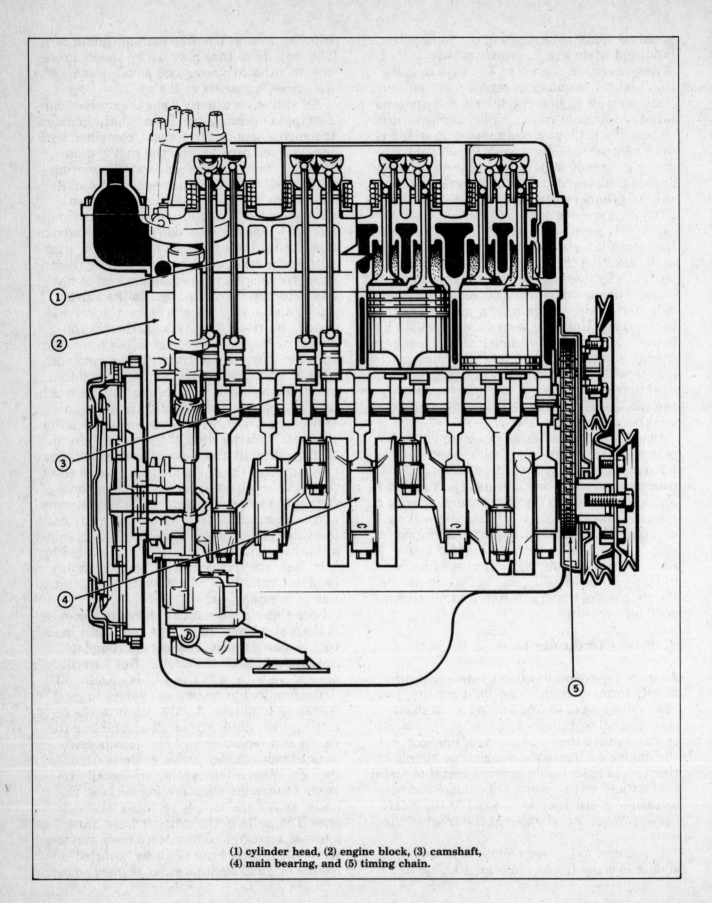

(1) cylinder head, (2) engine block, (3) camshaft,
(4) main bearing, and (5) timing chain.

sized valve stems can be installed. This is a job for an experienced machinist and is beyond the abilities of most do-it-yourselfers. It requires not only a knowledge of what must be done, but also the right kinds of tools and machine equipment to do the work. Even so, you can save some of the labor cost of doing a valve job by removing the cylinder head(s) yourself and taking them to an automotive machine shop for the necessary work. Pulling a cylinder head is an involved job, so we didn't include it in this book. But if you think your abilities are up to the task, you can look up the necessary disassembly and installation instructions in any shop manual.

One job you can do yourself is to maintain correct valve lash clearances. This is essential on engines that use "solid" valve lifters or mechanical followers rather than "hydraulic" lifters. This includes many import engines. A certain amount of space (called lash) between the top of the valve stems and their rocker arms or followers must be maintained to compensate for thermal expansion in the engine and valve stretching that occurs over time on some exhaust valves. Depending on the type of alloys used in the engine block and head, and how the engine is constructed, the valve lash may increase or decrease as the engine heats up. Because of this, the vehicle manufacturer will specify that the valve lash be set either hot or cold. This procedure is covered later on in this chapter.

Another item you may find yourself replacing at some point in time is the timing belt or timing chain. A rubber/fiberglass timing belt is often used to drive the camshaft on overhead cam engines while a chain or gear set is used for the same purpose on most overhead valve, or pushrod, engines. Over time a belt will deteriorate and develop cracks and weak spots. If it snaps, the engine will quit running because the valves will cease to open and close. On some engines, this can result in major engine damage if a piston strikes an open valve. On other engines, the engine is "freewheeling" which means it can continue to spin without the pistons striking the valves. On engines with timing chains, the chain tends to stretch with age. This introduces slop into the valve timing mechanism, which leads to a gradual deterioration in engine performance. On many engines, the camshaft drive gear on

which the chain runs has nylon/plastic teeth. The relatively soft teeth reduce engine noise but they also tend to wear rapidly. If they wear to the point where the chain can slip and jump a tooth, valve timing will be lost and in most cases the engine will stop running. The cure here is to replace both chain and drive gear. This too is covered in this chapter.

Replacing a leaky gasket is another job you can do yourself in most instances, although some gaskets are far easier to repair than others. A head gasket may be more than you want to tackle, but valve cover, intake manifold, and oil pan gaskets should be within your abilities. There are a couple of reasons why gaskets develop leaks with age. Cork/rubber type gaskets tend to become brittle as a result of heat and mileage. Mechanical vibration combined with a loose bolt or screw can cause a crack or leak to develop. Sometimes simply tightening a few bolts or screws is all that's needed to stop a leak. But if the gasket has cracked or slipped out of place, it should be replaced. Many engines today come from the factory without precut cork/rubber gaskets. To reduce manufacturing costs, most vehicle manufacturers now use RTV (Room Temperature Vulcanizing) silicone sealer to seal many mating surfaces. RTV sealer makes an excellent gasket, but unless it is applied properly and allowed to cure it can develop leaks—especially on valve covers, which tend to work themselves loose over time anyway. When attempting to repair a leak of this nature, you have the option of reapplying fresh RTV sealer or installing a precut cork/rubber gasket in its place. This is covered in this chapter too.

Engine Troubleshooting

THIS CHAPTER also contains information for three kinds of diagnostic tests you can perform to detect internal engine problems. A compression test is useful for pinpointing bad valves, worn piston rings/cylinders, and/or leaky head gaskets. A vacuum test can help you spot vacuum leaks in the intake manifold or carburetor, low engine compression, a leaky head gasket, late ignition timing, a restricted exhaust system, sticking valves, burned or damaged valves, or even worn valve guides. The third test, a power balance test, can help you spot a problem cylinder when trouble-shooting a miss or loss of power.

Some of the common types of problems engines are prone to are described as follows.

● **Oil burning**—Blue smoke in the exhaust indicates oil is being burned due to worn piston rings, broken piston rings, a cracked piston, or worn valve guides. Anything that allows oil to get into the combustion chamber will result in oil burning. If the condition is not accompanied by any unusual engine noises or a loss of power, the most likely cause is worn valve guides. This can cause an engine to use a quart of oil every 250 to 350 miles. The cure is to do a complete valve job and to restore or replace the guides and seals. The offending cylinder can usually be identified by removing the spark plugs and looking for heavy black oily deposits on the plugs. Oil burning due to worn piston rings or cylinders usually means a complete engine overhaul is in order. A cracked piston or cracked piston rings are usually the result of severe detonation.

● **Oil leakage**—Symptoms include oil puddles on the driveway or street, oil on the outside of the engine or under the car, or oil consumption with no visible blue smoke in the exhaust. The most common points for oil leakage include the rear main crankshaft oil seal (at the back of the engine on rear-wheel-drive vehicles, or at the transaxle end on transverse engines in front-wheel-drive cars), the valve cover(s), the front crankshaft pulley seal, or on V6 and V8 engines, sometimes the intake manifold gaskets. The oil pan is another gasket that can sometimes leak. The cure is to identify and replace the offending gasket or seal.

● **Leaky head gasket**—This causes a loss of compression if it occurs between cylinders or a cylinder and the outside world. Two adjacent cylinders that show little or no compression when checked usually indicate a blown head gasket. A leaky gasket can also allow coolant to seep into a cylinder (which quickly destroys the cylinder because of excessive heat) or into the crankcase (where again it causes problems, because coolant is a lousy lubricant). An oily residue in the radiator combined with a mysterious coolant loss and overheating could indicate a leaky head gasket. A compression check of the engine and a pressure-test on the cooling system should be performed to diagnose the problem.

● **Bad valves**—A burned or worn exhaust valve will allow a loss of compression in the affected cylinder. A compression check will show little or no compression if this is the problem. A bad intake valve will likewise allow a loss of compression, as well as a popping or backfiring into the intake manifold. Bad valves must be replaced, requiring a valve job to be performed on the engine.

● **Engine noises**—A sharp pinging, knocking, or clattering sound that is heard only while accelerating under load indicates detonation is occurring in the engine. This can be the result of over-advanced ignition timing, too lean an air/fuel mixture, an overheated engine, or too much compression due to carbon buildup in the combustion chambers. An inoperative or disconnected EGR valve can also cause detonation. The cure is to find out what's causing the detonation and to eliminate it before serious engine damage can result. Sometimes switching to higher octane gasoline helps if everything else seems to be okay. Mild detonation is generally considered harmless but severe detonation over time can crack pistons, piston rings, and heads, or damage connecting rod bearings.

A sharp metallic knock that matches engine speed and increases in intensity with speed indicates a worn rod bearing or main bearing. A worn piston wrist pin can also produce such noises. Major engine work is indicated by these kinds of noises.

A clattering or tapping noise that's only heard when the engine is first started is usually due to the hydraulic lifters. When the lifters become worn, they bleed down, increasing valve lash and causing noise when the engine is first started. As oil pressure builds up, the lash is reduced and the lifters quiet down. This is a normal condition if an engine sits for a long time without running, but if it happens every time the engine is started, it could indicate lifter replacement is needed.

A steady clattering or tapping noise usually indicates excessive valve lash on one or more valves. This could be due to misadjustment, an adjustment that's come loose, a worn rocker arm, bent pushrod or worn lifter, or a combination of the above. A collapsed hydraulic lifter will cause the same kind of noise.

A rumbling noise or growl that increases with engine speed can usually be traced to noisy water-pump bearings. Check the pump shaft for looseness. If loose, or if the pump is seeping coolant, it should be replaced.

Compression Testing

Tools and Materials

- Wrench or Pliers
- Spark Plug Wire Pliers
- Spark Plug Socket and Ratchet Wrench
- Jumper Wire
- Compression Tester
- Pump-Type Oil Can
- Motor Oil

A COMPRESSION test reveals the condition of an engine. No engine is able to operate as it is designed to unless every cylinder is operating at peak efficiency—that is, at specified compression. Specifications for compression are expressed in pounds per square inch (psi). For example, a particular engine may have a cranking compression pressure of 200 psi.

It may be helpful to understand how these compression specifications are determined. When the piston reaches the bottom limit of its travel on the intake stroke (BDC—bottom dead center), the intake valve closes and the piston begins upward travel, thus compress-

ing the air/fuel mixture. When the piston reaches the top of its travel (TDC—top dead center), the air/fuel mixture is compressed to its fullest. It is the amount of pressure at this point, measured in psi, that is referred to as compression.

An engine in good condition will have equal compression readings in all cylinders, and the readings will be up to at least the minimum compression specified by the manufacturer. Unequal cylinder compression causes the engine to run rough at all speeds. Low compression on all cylinders will cause the engine to lack power.

To determine the condition of your engine, a compression test should be taken. This test should be performed at every tune-up or whenever your engine is running poorly.

To perform a compression test, you first must gain access to each cylinder. Since the only possible access to the cylinders from outside the engine is through the spark plug holes, you must remove the spark plug from each cylinder. Depending on the type of engine you have, there will be either 4, 6, or 8 spark plugs—one for each cylinder. These are located in the engine cylinder head or engine block.

On four- and six-cylinder in-line engines, the spark plugs will be readily visible because they will be lined up on one side of the engine. You will find a high-voltage wire connected to each spark plug. The wires are connected to the ignition's distributor cap at the other end. On V8 and V6 engines, there will be either 4 or 3 spark plugs on each side of the engine.

Here is how to perform the compression test.

1. Remove the air filter housing. You may need a wrench for this task. See the section on "Air Filter Service" in "The Fuel System" chapter.
2. Disconnect the spark plug wires from each spark plug. This is done by grasping the boot on the end of each wire with your hand or a spark plug wire pliers and, with a twisting motion, pull the wire away from the spark plug. It is best to label each spark plug wire as you remove it to be sure you reconnect it to the proper spark plug.

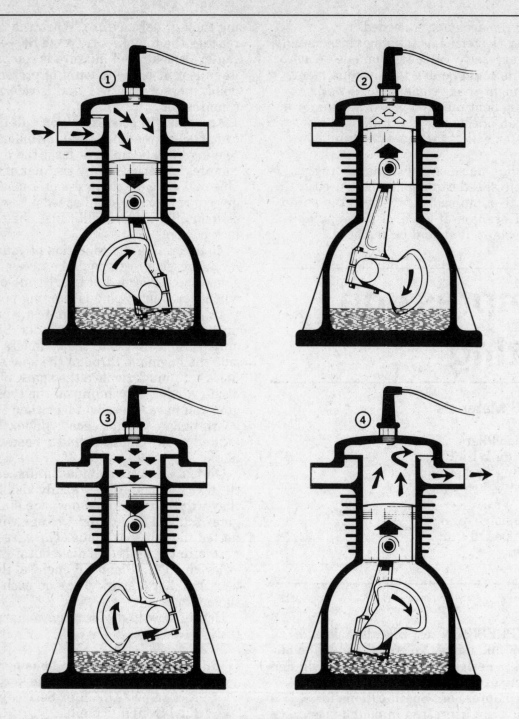

(1) intake stroke, (2) compression stroke, (3) power stroke, and (4) exhaust stroke.

During the intake stroke, the intake valve opens and the downward motion of the piston draws the air/fuel mixture into the combustion chamber. During the compression stroke, both valves are closed and the mixture is squeezed. The spark plug fires the mixture during the power stroke, forcing the piston down. The exhaust valve opens during the exhaust stroke and the spent gases are expelled as the piston moves up.

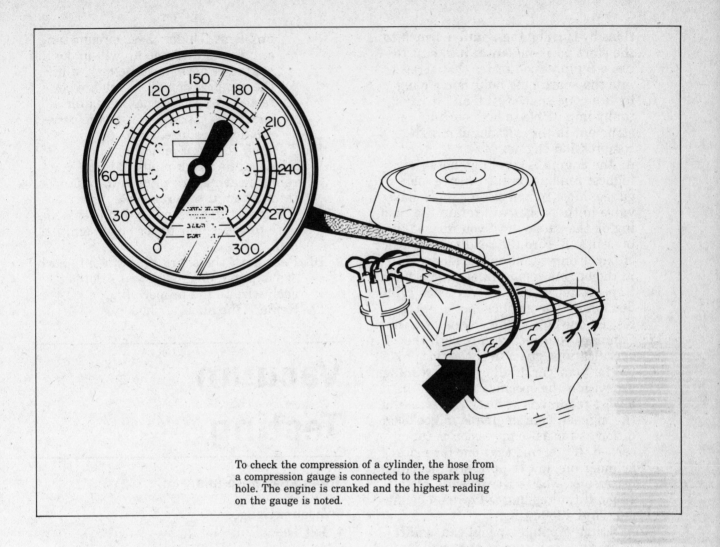

To check the compression of a cylinder, the hose from a compression gauge is connected to the spark plug hole. The engine is cranked and the highest reading on the gauge is noted.

3. Using a spark plug socket and ratchet wrench, loosen each spark plug about ½ turn. Do not remove the spark plug yet.
4. Disconnect the secondary high-tension wire from the center tower of the distributor cap, which leads to the ignition coil, and connect it to a good ground on the engine with a jumper wire.
5. With the spark plugs slightly loose and the secondary (high-tension) ignition coil wire grounded, crank the engine for about 5 seconds by turning the ignition switch to the start position. The reason for this cranking is to reduce the possibility of dirt or foreign material entering the compression chambers when the spark plugs are removed. Engine compression will blow any debris away from the spark plugs while the engine is cranking.
6. Remove the spark plugs with the spark plug socket and ratchet wrench.
7. Place the spark plugs on a bench or table in such a way so you will know from which cylinder they were removed. As pointed out in the section on "Evaluating and Installing Spark Plugs" in "The Ignition System" chapter, the condition of a spark plug can aid you in diagnosing engine problems.
8. Move the throttle linkage and block it in the open position or have someone sit in the car and hold the accelerator pedal to the floor. This allows the greatest amount of air to enter the engine during the compression test.
9. Starting with the cylinder closest to the car's radiator, insert the compression tester into the spark plug hole and have someone crank the engine 4 or 5 revolu-

tions by turning the ignition switch to the start position. **Note:** It is best to use a compression tester that screws into the spark plug hole. Some gauges have a cone-shaped end, and it is virtually impossible to hold such an instrument in the cylinder of a high-compression engine.

10. As the engine is cranking, note the highest reading on the compression gauge. Most compression gauges have a valve in them that will retain the reading on the gauge until you release the pressure. Record the reading on a piece of paper or write it on the fender well in the engine compartment with chalk.

11. Repeat Steps 9 and 10 with each cylinder. On V-type engines, perform the test on one side of the engine at a time.

12. Compare your test results with the specifications given in the service manual for your car. If all cylinder readings are within the specifications and the lowest reading is at least 75 percent of the highest, your engine is in good condition as far as compression is concerned. If you find that one (or more) cylinder has low compression, it may be because of a bad valve or worn piston rings. If the reading is low on a cylinder, do the following.

A. Using a pump-type oil can, squirt about a teaspoon of motor oil into the spark plug hole.

B. Repeat the compression test. If the compression test reading increases to almost normal, this indicates worn piston rings. (The oil you inserted into the cylinder has sealed the rings, causing compression pressure to increase.)

If the reading is still low, this most likely indicates a bad valve.

If two adjacent cylinders have low compression readings, chances are the engine cylinder head gasket is defective.

Compression readings that are higher than specifications indicate an engine with an excessive buildup of carbon in the cylinders.

Low, high, or uneven compression readings indicate serious engine problems. Under these circumstances, no engine tune-up will make the engine perform satisfactorily until the compression problems are corrected. A professional mechanic should be consulted as to the correct repair procedure.

13. Turn off the ignition switch.

14. Replace the spark plugs. Be sure you replace each spark plug in the cylinder from which it was removed.

15. Reconnect the secondary high-tension wire to the center tower of the ignition coil.

16. Reconnect the spark plug wires to each spark plug. Make sure you reconnect each wire to the proper plug.

17. Replace the air filter housing.

Vacuum Testing

Tools and Materials

- Vacuum Gauge
- Golf Tee

IN THESE DAYS of increasing concern about obtaining better fuel efficiency and economy, a vacuum gauge is one of the most valuable instruments you can have permanently installed on your engine. Properly used, it can tell you when you are obtaining the maximum efficiency from your car's engine and indicate poor driving habits such as jackrabbit starts. You can easily determine the most efficient driving speed simply by checking the gauge's indicator. The engine operates most efficiently when the gauge reaches its highest position. The lower the reading, the more fuel you are using. This, coupled with a continuous check of your engine's operation, gives you a general idea of

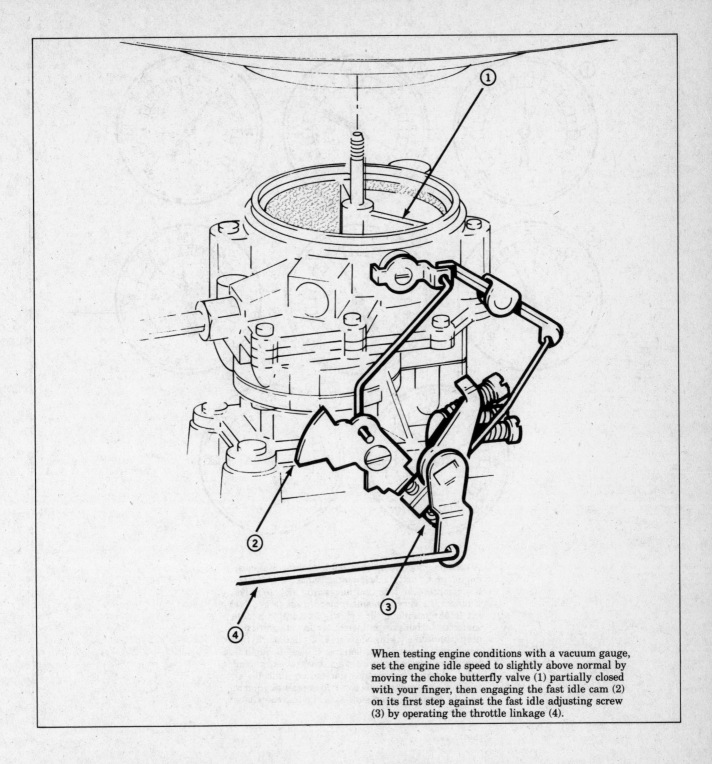

When testing engine conditions with a vacuum gauge, set the engine idle speed to slightly above normal by moving the choke butterfly valve (1) partially closed with your finger, then engaging the fast idle cam (2) on its first step against the fast idle adjusting screw (3) by operating the throttle linkage (4).

what is going on inside the engine and helps you avoid future problems.

A vacuum gauge reads the level of vacuum in the intake manifold while the engine is running. Vacuum is measured in inches of mercury (Hg), so gauges are marked in inches. To explain the principle of vacuum measurement would be too complex for the scope of this book, but what is important is that a vacuum gauge is an extremely practical instrument.

If your car does not have a permanently installed vacuum gauge, there is a great deal to be learned about the internal workings of the

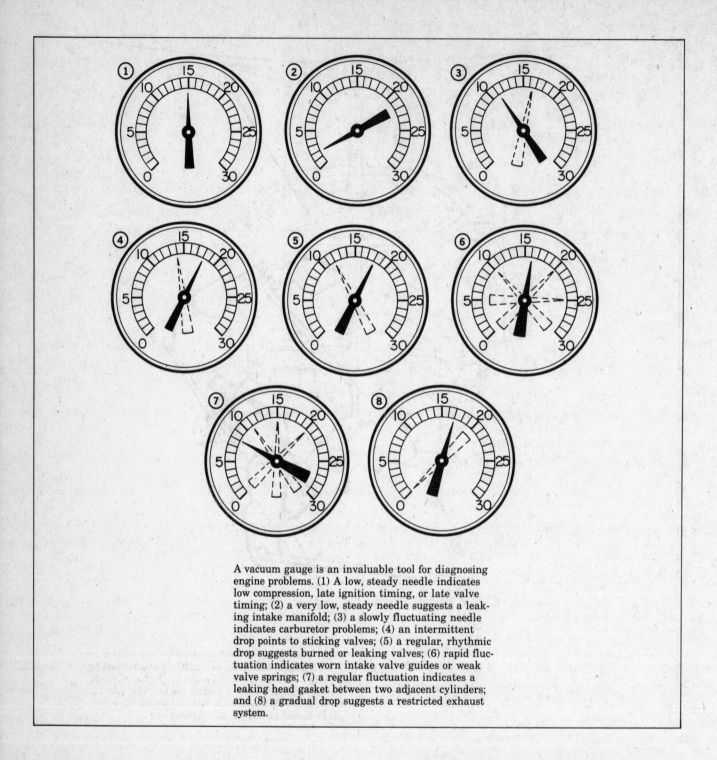

A vacuum gauge is an invaluable tool for diagnosing engine problems. (1) A low, steady needle indicates low compression, late ignition timing, or late valve timing; (2) a very low, steady needle suggests a leaking intake manifold; (3) a slowly fluctuating needle indicates carburetor problems; (4) an intermittent drop points to sticking valves; (5) a regular, rhythmic drop suggests burned or leaking valves; (6) rapid fluctuation indicates worn intake valve guides or weak valve springs; (7) a regular fluctuation indicates a leaking head gasket between two adjacent cylinders; and (8) a gradual drop suggests a restricted exhaust system.

engine by taking a vacuum test with a vacuum tester. And, you can learn as much by watching the action of the needle on the instrument as you can by reading the dial numbers. With a vacuum gauge, you can tell the condition of the engine's intake and exhaust valves, piston rings, cylinder head gasket, and carburetor air/fuel mixture.

Vacuum gauges are available at auto supply stores for permanent installation in your car. They are one of the most popular test instruments bought by knowledgeable car enthusiasts. No professional mechanic would be without one.

Vacuum Gauge Hookup

To make tests of engine condition with a vacuum gauge, follow these steps.

1. Warm up your car's engine to normal operating temperature. To do this, run the engine for about 15 to 20 minutes.
2. Open the hood and remove the air filter housing. Refer to the procedure outlined in the section on "Air Filter Service" in "The Fuel System" chapter.
3. Set the engine idle speed to slightly above normal by setting the throttle linkage on the first step of the fast idle cam. This can be done by moving the choke butterfly valve partially closed with your finger. Engine speed will be increased slightly by a very small movement of the valve, and this position should set the linkage on the first step of the fast idle cam.
4. Connect the vacuum gauge to the engine intake manifold. (You can leave the engine running when you do this.) This connection location will vary from car to car. Most vacuum gauges have a rubber hose that is attached to the gauge itself. This hose is of a size that will slip over most vacuum connections on the engine. In general, a rubber vacuum hose connected directly to the engine intake manifold is best when making tests with a vacuum gauge. If you have any doubts as to the proper place, consult the instructions provided with the gauge. Remember though, when you disconnect a vacuum line to connect the test gauge, plug the disconnected vacuum line with a golf tee so that it will not leak and provide inaccurate test readings.
5. With the engine running at slightly higher than idle speed, observe the vacuum gauge dial and watch the needle. If your engine is running normally, the vacuum gauge needle will be steady between about 15 and 20 inches of vacuum.
6. Have someone sit in the car and quickly depress the accelerator pedal to the floor and release it. The vacuum gauge needle should drop to about 5 inches and then climb up to about 25 inches, and then slowly return to the original idle reading.
7. If the vacuum gauge reacts as explained in Step 6, your car's engine is operating normally.
8. If the engine is not operating normally, you may be able to pinpoint the problem by means of the vacuum gauge.

The following are some of the conditions you can diagnose.

LEAKING HEAD GASKET: When the gauge needle fluctuates regularly, the cylinder head gasket probably has blown between two adjacent cylinders.

WORN PISTON RINGS (LOW COMPRESSION): This is indicated by a fairly steady needle but with a slightly lower than normal reading, about 3 to 4 inches of vacuum below normal.

LEAKING INTAKE MANIFOLD: When you have a very low reading, 10 to 12 inches of vacuum below normal for example, but the needle remains steady, you probably have a leaking intake manifold or a vacuum leak at the carburetor.

LATE IGNITION TIMING: A steady but low reading, when the compression is known to be good, indicates late ignition timing. This can also be an indication of worn timing gears and/or chain in the engine.

CARBURETOR PROBLEMS: Slow fluctuation of the needle indicates carburetor problems, probably in the adjustment of the idle or air/fuel mixture.

RESTRICTED EXHAUST SYSTEM: A needle that gradually drops when the engine is idling indicates a restriction in the exhaust system.

VALVE PROBLEMS: A rapidly fluctuating needle is a tip-off that your engine intake valve guides are probably worn. If the needle fluctuates rapidly as the engine is accelerated, you may have weak engine valve springs. An intermittent drop of 3 to 4 inches of vacuum indicates sticking engine valves. When the variation is rhythmical and regular, you probably have a burned or leaking engine valve.

9. Turn off the engine.
10. Disconnect the vacuum gauge, reversing Step 4, and reconnect the vacuum hose.

Power Balance Test

Tools and Materials

- Tachometer
- Insulated Spark Plug Wire Pliers

THIS IS a fairly simple test that can be used to identify quickly a weak or misfiring cylinder. Once the "problem" cylinder has been identified, the nature of the problem can be further diagnosed by removing the spark plug and performing a compression test. If the cylinder has good compression, the problem is in the ignition system (fouled spark plug, bad spark plug wire or distributor cap), or on multi-point fuel injected engines it could indicate a bad fuel injector. If the compression is weak, then a bad valve or blown head gasket is the likely cause.

The basic idea behind a power balance test is that each of the engine's cylinders should contribute roughly the same amount of power to the engine's total output. Momentarily disconnecting each spark plug wire, one at a time, should therefore result in an equal drop in idle speed if all the cylinders are performing equally. Professional mechanics can perform this test with an ignition scope or diagnostic analyzer that automatically shorts out each cylinder one-by-one while displaying the resulting rpm drop. But to do this test yourself, you have to momentarily disconnect each spark plug wire either from the spark plug or the distributor cap using your insulated plug wire pliers.

Caution: Do not lean against the car while doing this test. The high voltage in the spark plug wire will try to seek a path to ground. If you happen to be leaning against the metal fender, you're the path of least resistance and you'll likely receive a nasty shock. The insulated plug wire pliers will protect against this, but lacking such pliers, keeping yourself clear of the vehicle body will prevent you from being shocked.

Note: On vehicles equipped with catalytic converters, a spark plug should not be disconnected for more than 15 to 20 seconds. When the plug is disconnected, it allows unburned air and fuel to pass through to the converter. This can cause the converter to overheat and possibly damage the catalyst.

On vehicles equipped with computerized idle speed control, the computer will attempt to compensate for any drop in idle speed from disconnecting a plug wire by increasing the throttle opening. Since this makes accurate diagnosis impossible, you must first disconnect the idle speed control motor before starting the test. This must be done with the ignition key off to prevent possible damage to the system electronics. Unplugging the electrical connector from the idle speed control motor may set a trouble code in the computer, so this should be cleared following completion of the power balance test by turning off the ignition and disconnecting the computer's fuse or the battery for 10 seconds.

To perform a power balance test, proceed as follows.

1. Connect a tachometer to the engine and disconnect the wiring harness from the idle speed control motor on the throttle linkage if so equipped.
2. Start the engine and allow it to idle. The engine should be at normal operating temperature.
3. Using your insulated spark plug wire pliers, momentarily disconnect each spark plug wire one at a time, and note the resulting drop in idle speed. The cylinder or cylinders that fail to produce a drop in idle speed or not as great a drop as the other cylinders are

the problem cylinders. A compression check on these cylinders should be performed to identify the problem.

4. After completing the test, turn the ignition off, remove your tachometer, and reconnect the idle speed control motor if necessary.

Gasket/ Sealer Replacement

Tools and Materials

- Hand Wrenches
- Screwdriver
- Gasket Scraper or Chemical Remover
- Trouble Light
- Clean Rags
- Replacement Cork/Rubber Gasket or RTV Silicone Sealer

TO REPAIR a leaking gasket, you first have to identify the gasket that's leaking. In most instances, it will be obvious, but sometimes you can be fooled if the oil or coolant follows a seam before making itself visible. A trouble light, a clean rag, and a careful visual examination can help pinpoint the exact source of the leak.

Once you've found the leak, you might try tightening the bolts around it to see if that will stop the leak. This often works on valve covers, oil pans, transmission oil pans, and timing covers. Be careful not to over-tighten the bolts because the stamped metal flanges on these components can easily be deformed. Once this happens, the gasket immediately under the bolt is pinched tightly, but the gas-

ket between bolt holes has little or no tension against it. As a result, it leaks. Over-tightening the bolts can also crush the gasket and literally squeeze it out of place.

If tightening the bolts doesn't help, or if the gasket is obviously defective, it will have to be replaced.

The basic procedure for replacing a conventional cork/rubber gasket goes as follows.

1. Disassemble the components and remove the old gasket.
2. Thoroughly clean both mating surfaces, removing all traces of the old gasket and sealer material with a gasket scraper or chemical cleaner. Wipe both mating surfaces clean with a dry rag to remove any traces of oil or other chemicals.
3. Inspect both mating surfaces for damage. If either surface is heavily scratched or gouged, a good seal may not be possible without resurfacing, repairing, or replacing the damaged surface. On stamped steel covers (valve covers, oil pans, transmission pans, etc.), check the sealing surface for flatness by laying a straightedge or ruler on it. If there are big gaps between the

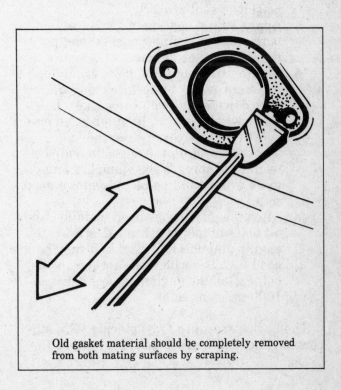

Old gasket material should be completely removed from both mating surfaces by scraping.

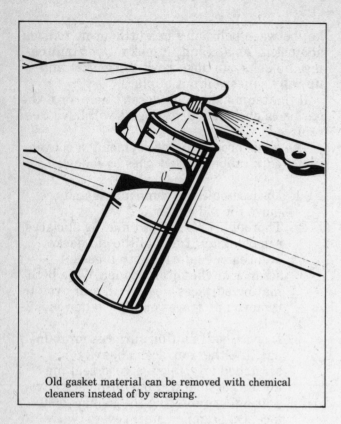

Old gasket material can be removed with chemical cleaners instead of by scraping.

1. Disassemble the components.
2. Thoroughly remove all traces of the old sealer from both mating surfaces with a scraper, being careful not to damage either surface.
3. Inspect both mating surfaces for damage. Both surfaces must be relatively flat and in good condition to provide a lasting seal.
4. Before applying new RTV sealer, wipe both mating surfaces clean. It is extremely important that the surfaces not be wet or oil contaminated as this will interfere with the bonding of the sealer to the surface.
5. Carefully apply a ⅛-inch bead of RTV silicone along the middle of one mating surface. When bolt holes are encountered, run the bead around both sides of the hole to completely encircle it.
6. While the sealer is still wet, assemble the components and tighten the bolts evenly, using a cross-pattern approach to bring both surfaces together smoothly.
7. Allow the RTV sealer to cure for 30 to 45 minutes before adding fluids or restarting the engine.

bolt holes, try to flatten out the deformed areas by gently pounding on them with a hammer. The surface must be flat to seal properly.
4. Apply a light coating of gasket sealer to both sides of the new gasket, and position the gasket in place.
5. Tighten the mounting bolts evenly using a cross-star pattern to bring the part down equally on the gasket. In other words, first tighten a bolt on one side of a valve cover, then the one across from it on the opposite end. This technique spreads the clamping force more evenly and helps to assure a good seal.
6. After the gasket has been installed and all bolts properly tightened, start the engine and check for leaks. It may be a good idea to recheck the torque on the bolts after the engine has been driven 1000 miles or so.

The basic procedure for replacing RTV silicone or "formed-in-place" gaskets goes as follows.

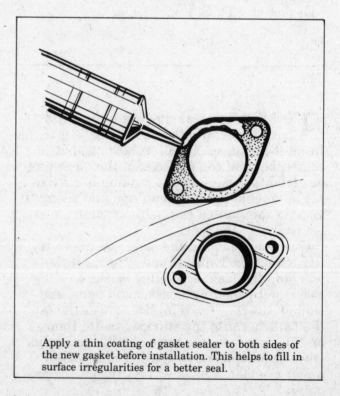

Apply a thin coating of gasket sealer to both sides of the new gasket before installation. This helps to fill in surface irregularities for a better seal.

Note: If any of the sealer is accidentally wiped off during assembly, it may leak. The same holds true if the sealer is put to the test before it has had a chance to cure.

Caution: Always follow the instructions provided with the product when using any type of chemical sealer. Some types of chemical sealers are "anaerobic," which means they cure in the absence of air. These often involve a two-part preparation: the sealer is applied to one mating surface and the "hardener" or "fixer" is applied to the other. The sealer does not cure until the two parts are mated and bolted together. It should also be noted that RTV silicone sealers do not work well when exposed to gasoline. The material softens and falls apart, so don't use RTV for carburetor base gaskets or fuel line connections.

Note: You also have the option of not replacing RTV sealer with the same. If you prefer to install a conventional precut cork/rubber gasket, such replacement gaskets are generally available for most applications. In some instances, longer mounting bolts must be used to compensate for the added thickness of the gasket.

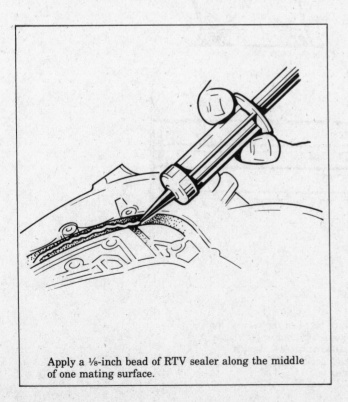

Apply a ⅛-inch bead of RTV sealer along the middle of one mating surface.

Adjusting the Valves: Pushrod Engines

Tools and Materials

- Hand Wrenches
- Feeler Gauge Set
- Deep Sockets and Ratchet
- Remote Starter Switch or a Screwdriver

PERIODIC ADJUSTMENT of the valve lash on pushrod engines with solid valve lifters or mechanical followers is necessary to maintain the correct amount of clearance between the tip of the valve stem and the rocker arm or follower. A certain amount of clearance is necessary to compensate for thermal expansion in the engine. Over time, this gap can close up as the valve stretches or recedes on its seat, or it can open up as wear in the valve train increases tolerances. Since valve lash determines to some extent valve timing and the duration of the valve's opening time, it can have a pronounced effect on both engine performance and valve cooling. If the gap becomes too large, the valves will be noisy and they will not open as long or as far as they would with the proper lash. This interferes with breathing and reduces engine power. If the gap closes up, the valve will open sooner, close later, and open further (all of which can help performance), but it also means the valve can be held off its seat, allowing loss of compression and poor valve cooling. The result can be valve failure and a severe loss in

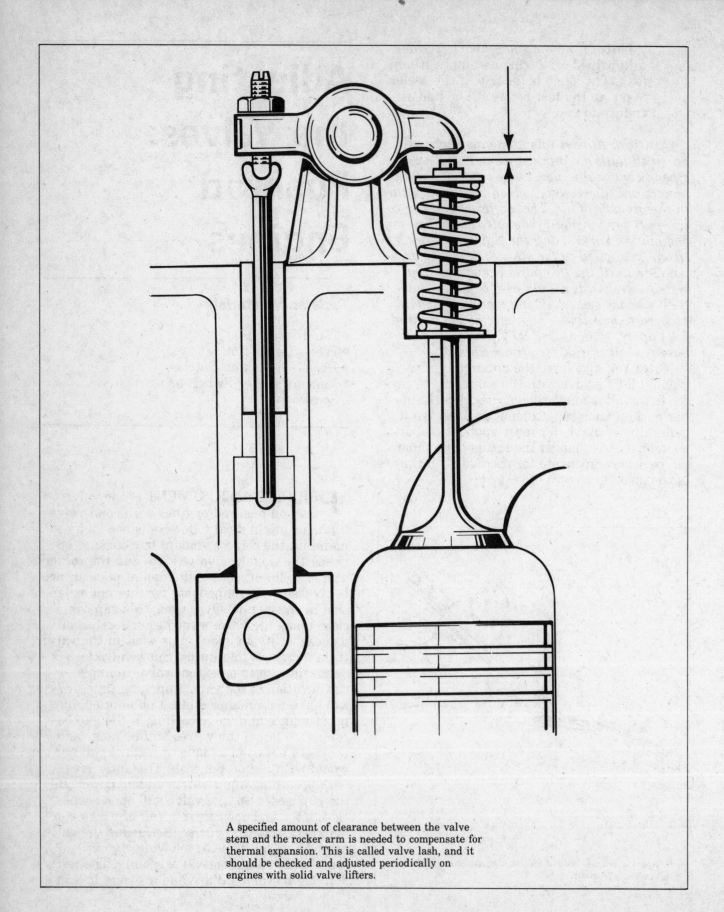

A specified amount of clearance between the valve stem and the rocker arm is needed to compensate for thermal expansion. This is called valve lash, and it should be checked and adjusted periodically on engines with solid valve lifters.

power due to loss of compression.

The valves should be adjusted to the manufacturer's specifications and at the specified mileage intervals. Generally speaking, this ranges from 15,000 to 30,000 miles. The recommended valve lash adjustment usually coincides with the recommended tune-up intervals for the vehicle.

The manufacturer's recommended lash will be specified in inches or millimeters, as well as "hot" or "cold." If the spec says to adjust the valves hot, it means to set them after the engine is at normal operating temperature. If the spec says "cold," then set the valves with the engine at room temperature. The reason for doing this is to compensate for thermal expansion in the engine. Since there are no hard and fast rules about the valve gap opening or closing as the engine heats up (because every engine is different), always follow the manufacturer's recommendations.

The basic procedure for setting the valves goes as follows.

1. Look up the valve lash specs in your manual or on the underhood emissions and tune-up decal. If the specs say cold, then the engine should be allowed to sit for several hours (preferably overnight) until it cools to room temperature. If the specs say hot, then the engine should be started and run at fast idle until it reaches normal operating temperature.

   Note: The valve lash for intake and exhaust valves will usually differ. Exhaust valves generally require greater clearance because they run hotter. Make sure you know which is which.

2. With the engine off, remove the valve cover.

3. Identify the intake and exhaust valves. The intakes will be those that line up with the intake ports on the intake manifold. The exhausts will align with the exhaust ports in the exhaust manifold.

4. To set the lash, the engine must be turned so the lifter or follower is on the lowest part of the cam lobe. This occurs when the piston is at the top dead center of its compression stroke. Turning the engine over until the timing marks line up at zero degrees TDC will allow you to adjust the valves on the number one cylinder.

5. Loosen the adjustment lock nut (if so equipped) and slide the appropriate feeler gauge between the top of the valve stem and the rocker arm or follower. If the gap is too narrow and the feeler gauge won't fit, back off on the adjustment nut until the feeler gauge just slips through with slight resistance. If the gap is too wide, tighten the adjustment nut until the gauge fits with slight resistance. Then tighten the lock nut (if so equipped).

6. Next, rotate the crankshaft using your remote starter switch, or by jumping the starter solenoid with a screwdriver blade or momentarily activating the ignition switch so the next cylinder in the firing sequence is brought to its top dead center position. On a four-cylinder engine, you simply rotate the crank 180 degrees. On a straight 6 or V6, 120 degrees will bring the next cylinder up to top dead center. On a V8, 90 degrees of crank rotation will do the trick. If you're unsure of which cylinder is next in the firing sequence, just follow the spark plug wires from the distributor cap to each of the cylinders. The one that comes after number one will be second in the firing sequence, and so on.

   Another technique for determining when the piston is at the top of its compression stroke is to remove the spark plugs, then hold a finger over the spark plug hole. When you feel air being pushed out as you crank the engine, the piston is coming up on the compression stroke. To tell if it's top dead center of the compression stroke, just watch the valves as you crank the engine. If both valves are closed while the piston is coming up, it's the compression stroke. If the exhaust valve is closing, it's the exhaust stroke. Once more around will bring it up to the compression stroke.

Adjusting the Valves: Overhead Cam Engines

Tools and Materials

- Hand Wrenches
- Feeler Gauge
- Remote Starter Switch or Screwdriver
- Special Valve Spring Compressor Tool (required on some cars)
- Valve Follower Shims

FOR OVERHEAD CAM engines that use rocker arms to actuate the valves, the same procedure for adjusting the valves as described for pushrod engines should be used. For overhead cam engines that do not use rocker arms but instead use followers mounted on top of the valve springs, a special procedure is required.

There are two basic designs used in this approach. In one, a tapered adjustment screw is positioned between the follower that rides against the cam and the top of the valve stem. By turning the screw, the amount of clearance between the follower and cam can be adjusted. This system can be found on some Chevrolet Monza and Vega engines.

The other setup, which is used on Volkswagen Rabbits and others, is to use a small shim between the follower and cam to adjust clearances. To change the adjustment, the shim is removed and a thicker or thinner one installed in its place. To accomplish this, the valve spring must be pushed down so the shim can be slipped out and replaced. This requires a special tool in most instances.

The basic procedure goes as follows.

1. Look up the valve specs for the engine on which you're working, and make sure you set them hot or cold as specified.
2. With the engine off, remove the valve cover.
3. Identify the intake and exhaust valves.
4. Turn the engine over so the number one piston is at top dead center of its compression stroke. You can check for this by aligning the timing marks on the crankshaft pulley or flywheel, and then opening the distributor cap to see if the rotor is aligned with the spark plug wire leading to the number one cylinder.
5. Check the valve lash clearance by sliding your feeler gauge between the follower and cam. If the correct gauge won't fit, try narrower gauges until you find the one that just slips through with slight resistance. Subtract this gauge reading from the one specified by the manufacturer. This is how much you'll have to increase the gap by installing a narrower shim.

   If the specified feeler gauge slips right through, it indicates too much clearance. Keep trying thicker gauges until you find the one that fits. Then subtract the specified gauge thickness from the one you found that fits. This is how much thicker the shim must be to provide the desired clearance. You'll have to buy the appropriate shims at a parts store.
6. Push the valve spring down using the compressor tool, and remove the shim from the follower. Then install a thicker or thinner shim as required to achieve the desired clearance. Release the valve spring and recheck the clearance with your feeler gauge.
7. Repeat this procedure for each of the remaining valves, rotating the crankshaft as needed to bring each of the consecutive cylinders to top dead center in their firing order.

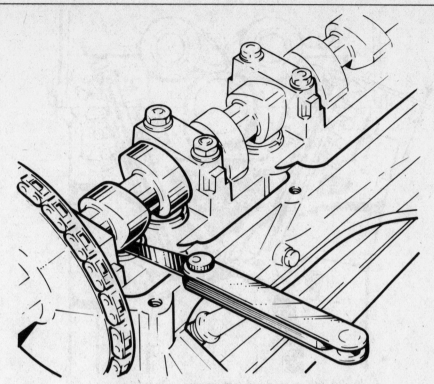

To check valve clearances on overhead cam engines, insert the feeler gauge between the cam and the follower.

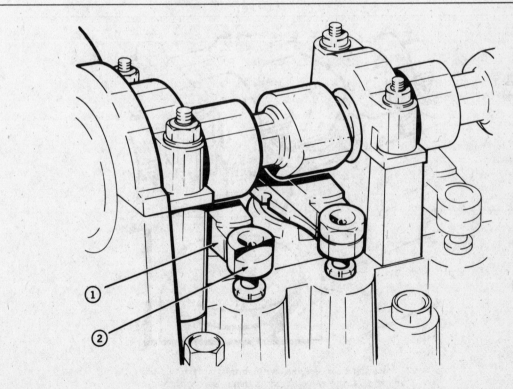

On some overhead cam engines, rocker arms (1) are used with lash-adjusting screws (2).

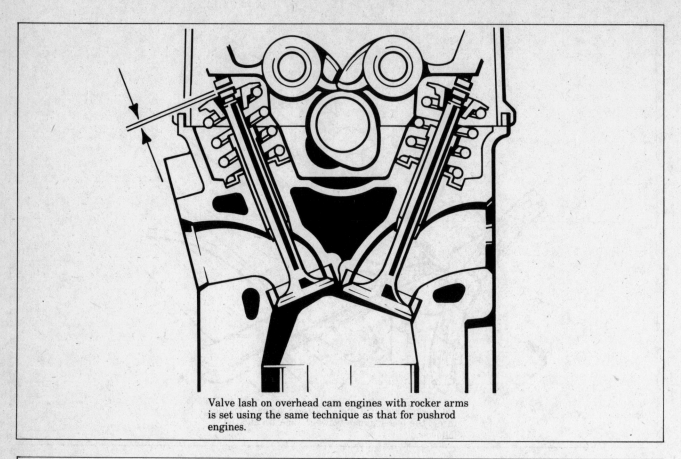

Valve lash on overhead cam engines with rocker arms is set using the same technique as that for pushrod engines.

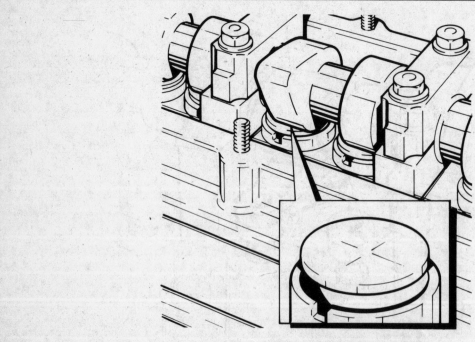

On overhead cam engines with shim-type lash adjustment, the valve spring is compressed with a special tool to allow insertion of a shim of the appropriate thickness.

Timing Belts

Tools and Materials

- Hand Wrenches
- Large Screwdriver or Pry Bar
- Trouble Light
- Replacement Belt
- Torque Wrench

IN MANY OVERHEAD cam engines, a cogged rubber/fiberglass reinforced timing belt is used to drive the camshaft. This type of belt is popular because it tends to run more quietly than a steel timing chain, it doesn't require any lubrication, it won't stretch with age (or when new for that matter), and it's less costly for the vehicle manufacturer.

On the other hand, rubber belts do deteriorate over time, developing age cracks and weak points in the internal reinforcing material. Oil contamination can also shorten their life. Rather than a gradual deterioration in engine performance as you might expect from a timing chain which stretches with age, a rubber timing belt will run fine—until it snaps. Then the engine quits cold. The failure can also sometimes cause major engine damage if the engine is not designed to free-wheel and the pistons collide with the valves.

Because of these characteristics, some vehicle manufacturers now recommend inspecting the timing belt periodically (at major tune-up intervals is a good time to do this) and replacing the belt at 50,000 to 60,000 mile intervals. Even though a belt may appear sound, a belt with a lot of miles on it will likely have weakened reinforcing material. Since the rate of failure increases sharply after 50,000 to 60,000 miles of driving, replacing it without waiting for it to fail is a preventative measure you should consider doing.

Belt Inspection and Adjustment

To check the timing belt, it is necessary to remove the protective shrouding that normally keeps hands, tools, dirt, and grease away from the belt. With the engine off, remove the shrouding and carefully examine the entire circumference of the belt inside and out for fraying or severe cracks. If the belt is damaged or obviously worn, it should be replaced.

Also check belt tension. If the belt is not tight and there is more than about ½ inch of deflection between the two furthest pulleys when you push against the belt with your hand, it is probably too loose and should be tightened.

Caution: Over-tightening the belt can shorten its life, too. Most vehicle manufacturers specify belt tension using a belt tension gauge. Since you won't have one of these in your toolbox, using the ¼ to ½ inch of deflection rule between the two furthest pulleys when pressing with moderate finger pressure should allow you to set belt tension correctly.

To adjust belt tension, simply loosen the bolt that holds the tensioner pulley. Then pry against the pulley with a large screwdriver or pry bar until you get the right tension on the belt. Hold the tension and tighten the pulley bolt.

Belt Replacement

To replace a timing belt, proceed as follows.

1. Turn the engine until the timing marks line up on the crankshaft pulley or flywheel.
2. With the engine off, remove the protective shrouding from around the timing belt.
3. Carefully note the relative position of any timing marks that are located on the cam gear, balance shafts, or other pulleys.
4. Loosen the adjustment bolt on the ten-

sioner pulley, and relieve tension on the belt.

5. You should now be able to slip the old belt off. Be careful not to turn either the crankshaft or camshaft.

6. Double-check the timing marks to see that nothing has moved, then slide the new timing belt onto the pulleys, routing it exactly the same as the old one.

7. Tighten the belt by prying against the tensioner pulley until you get the ¼ to ½ inch of deflection between the two

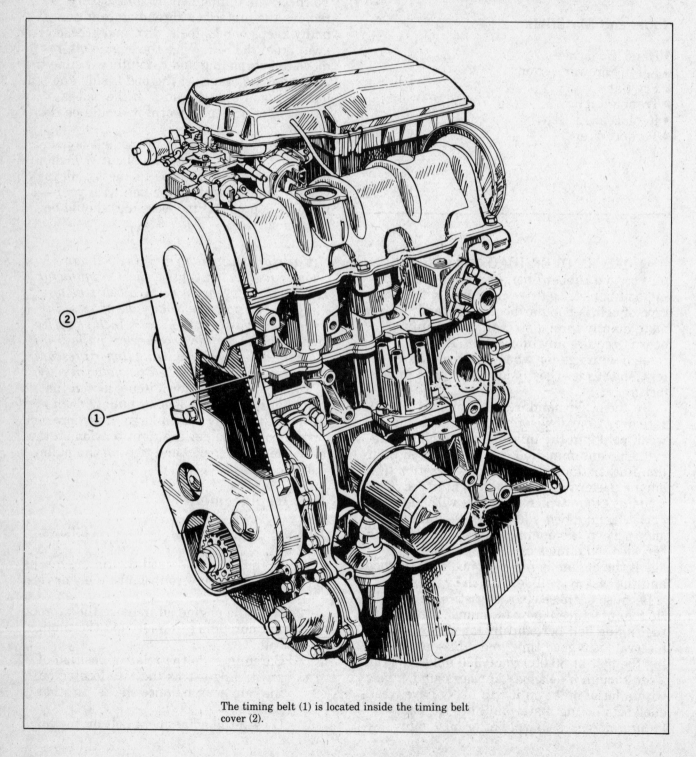

The timing belt (1) is located inside the timing belt cover (2).

furthest pulleys. Then tighten the bolts on the tensioner pulley while maintaining pressure against the belt.

8. Start the engine to see that it runs. If all is okay, shut the engine off and replace the protective shrouding to finish the job. If you've mislocated the belt, the engine probably won't start if you're off by more than a notch or two. Accurate timing is extremely important, so always double-check the timing marks when replacing the belt.

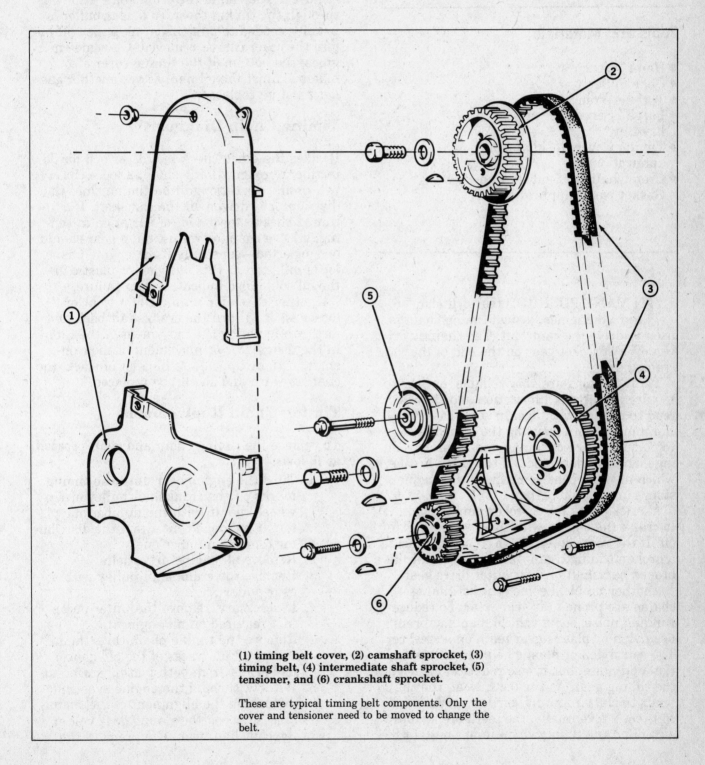

(1) **timing belt cover, (2) camshaft sprocket, (3) timing belt, (4) intermediate shaft sprocket, (5) tensioner, and (6) crankshaft sprocket.**

These are typical timing belt components. Only the cover and tensioner need to be moved to change the belt.

Timing Chains

Tools and Materials

- Hand Wrenches
- Gear Puller
- Torque Wrench
- Large Screwdriver or Pry Bar
- Timing Cover Gasket (some applications)
- Crankshaft Oil Seal/Oil Pan Gasket (some applications)

IN MANY PUSHROD four-cylinder, V6, and V8 engines, a steel timing chain is used to drive the camshaft. The chain is driven off a sprocket gear on the end of the crankshaft.

Timing chains are very reliable, but they require a source of lubrication and they do tend to stretch with age. In some cases they can jump a tooth, causing the camshaft to come out of correct timing and severely reducing engine performance. If the chain breaks, which also happens sometimes, the engine stops running altogether.

A quick check for a broken timing chain is to crank the engine with the distributor cap off. If the rotor doesn't turn, it could indicate a broken timing chain (it could also indicate a broken camshaft or distributor drive gear).

Another problem some types of timing chains are prone to is gear wear. To reduce running noise, some vehicle manufacturers use nylon or plastic gear teeth on a steel core. The soft nylon or plastic helps to reduce friction and noise, but it also reduces longevity of the timing gear. As the teeth wear, the chain tends to clatter around, further eroding the soft teeth. Eventually, the teeth are stripped away and the timing chain jumps out of time.

When this happens, the engine quits running and the chain and gear must be replaced.

Because a timing chain requires oil lubrication, it is usually housed inside a metal timing cover. This makes replacement more of a job because the cover and its gasket must be removed. The end of the crankshaft also runs through the timing cover, so a gear puller is usually needed to pull the crank pulley off before the cover can be removed. On some engines, the bottom of the timing cover also mates against the oil pan, so yet another gasket must be replaced.

Timing Chain Diagnosis

Besides the quick check just described for detecting a broken timing chain, a loose chain will produce erratic ignition timing since the distributor is driven off the camshaft. If a timing check shows a lot of variation in timing, a loose chain or worn timing gear should be suspected—especially if the engine has a lot of miles on it. Bits of nylon or plastic in the oil could also indicate a gear failure.

Another check for timing chain wear or looseness is to turn the crankshaft back and forth while noting the movement of the rotor in the distributor or movement of the camshaft. If there appears to be a lot of slack, the chain is worn and should be replaced.

Timing Chain Replacement

To replace the timing chain and gear, proceed as follows.

1. Turn the engine over until the timing marks on the crankshaft pulley or flywheel line up with the number one piston at top dead center and the distributor rotor on number one.
2. Remove all engine drive belts.
3. Remove the crankshaft pulley with a gear puller.
4. If necessary, remove the water pump (not required on all engines).
5. Remove the timing chain cover, and scrape off all traces of the old gasket and sealer from both mating surfaces.
6. Without turning the engine over and disturbing the alignment of the timing marks, loosen the timing gear bolt on the camshaft gear. Then remove the

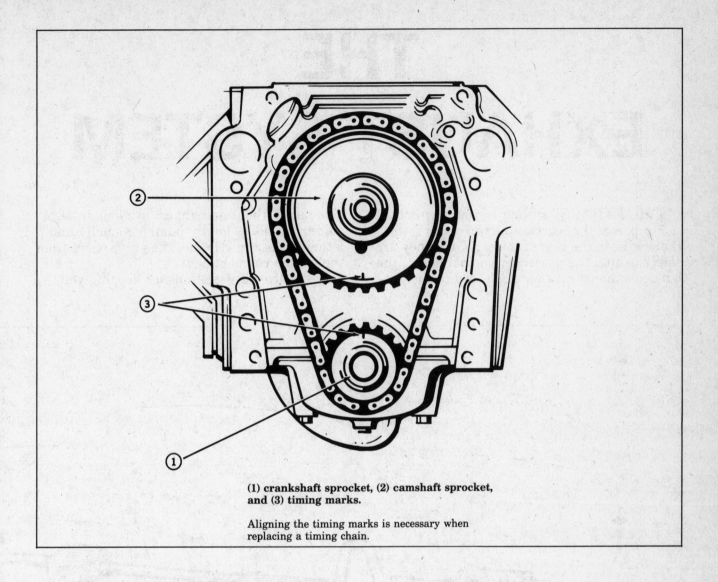

(1) crankshaft sprocket, (2) camshaft sprocket, and (3) timing marks.

Aligning the timing marks is necessary when replacing a timing chain.

bolt and pull the gear off the end of the cam using a large screwdriver, pry bar, or gear puller.

7. Drape the new timing chain over its new gear, then slip the bottom of the chain around the gear on the crankshaft, being careful to align the gear so it will fit right onto the camshaft without disturbing the timing marks. **Note:** If you turn either the crankshaft or the camshaft before the timing gear is installed, you'll destroy the timing relationship between them. But all is not lost because timing marks are provided on the crank and cam gears for reference. Simply realign the timing marks and install the timing chain and gear.

8. After the timing gear is in place, double-check the timing marks, then torque the cam bolt to the manufacturer's specs (usually 60 to 90 foot-pounds).

9. If the crankshaft runs through the timing cover, replacing the crankshaft oil seal at this time is recommended.

10. Coat both sides of the timing cover gasket with sealer, then hold it in place and reinstall the timing cover.

11. Put the crankshaft pulley back on, and replace all the drive belts. **Note:** If the engine was equipped with a plastic timing gear that failed, the oil should also be changed at this time to flush all debris out of the crankcase. Be sure to include a new filter.

THE EXHAUST SYSTEM

THE EXHAUST system in your car is the pipeline that carries burned gases from the engine to the rear of the car. Once they are safely behind the passenger compartment, the burned exhaust gases are released to the outside air. Without an exhaust system, an auto engine would be loudly pumping smelly and lethal fumes directly into the atmosphere from the engine compartment.

There are many reasons for keeping your

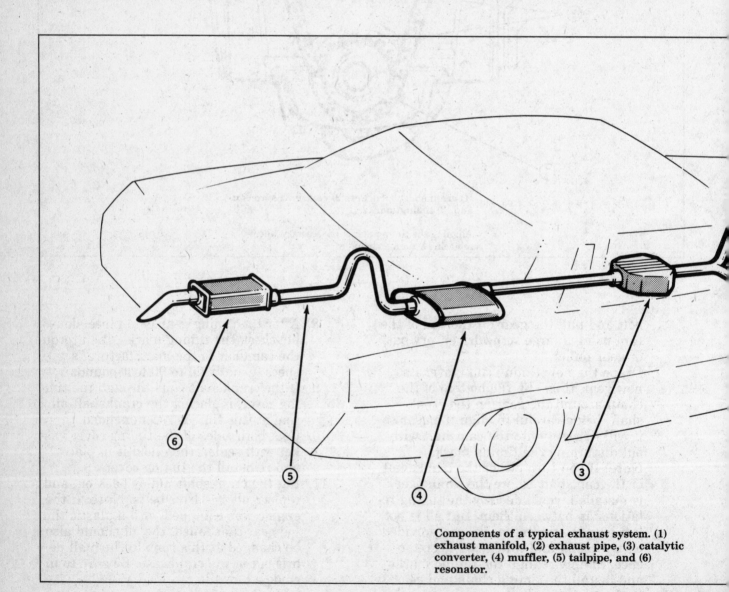

Components of a typical exhaust system. (1) exhaust manifold, (2) exhaust pipe, (3) catalytic converter, (4) muffler, (5) tailpipe, and (6) resonator.

exhaust system in good condition. First, a good system prevents dangerous carbon monoxide gas from getting into the passenger compartment. Second, it keeps the exhaust system quiet. Third, an engine will perform better when the exhaust system is in good condition.

The exhaust system consists of several components. Together, these components safely and quietly get rid of engine exhaust. Here are the components that make up the exhaust system.

1. EXHAUST MANIFOLD. As burned exhaust gases leave each cylinder in the engine, they enter separate passages in an exhaust manifold. The exhaust mani-

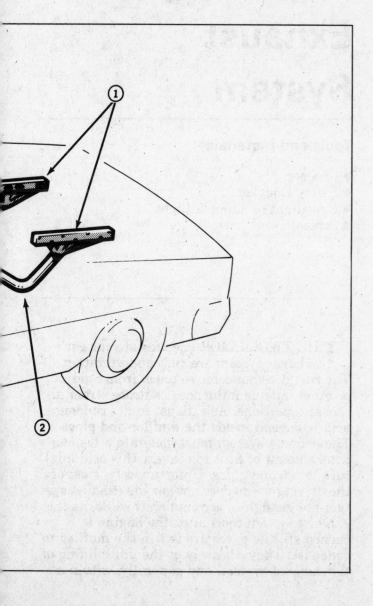

fold, generally made of cast iron, is connected to the cylinder head on the engine by several bolts. Straight line engines, those with all the cylinders in a row, will have one exhaust manifold. Engines of the V-type will have an exhaust manifold on each side of the engine. An exhaust manifold will have either three, four, or six passages (depending on the type of engine) at one end. These passages blend into a single passage at the other end, which connects to an exhaust pipe. From here, the flow of exhaust gases continues to the back of the car.

2. EXHAUST PIPE. The exhaust pipe is a heavy-gauge steel pipe that runs under the car between the exhaust manifold and the muffler. **Note:** On 1975 and newer cars equipped with catalytic converters, the exhaust pipe is connected to a catalytic converter first. Then a short pipe connects the catalytic converter to the muffler.

On most V-type engines, an exhaust pipe resembling the shape of a Y is used. The two ends at the top of the Y are connected to the two exhaust manifolds used on V-type engines. The bottom of the Y connects to either the catalytic converter or the muffler. On large V8 engines, you may find a dual exhaust system. This system has separate exhaust system components for each side. A separate exhaust pipe extends from each exhaust manifold and runs along each side of the car to its own muffler system.

3. CATALYTIC CONVERTER. If you have a 1975 or newer car, you probably have a catalytic converter in the exhaust system. It is normally located between the exhaust pipe and the muffler. The catalytic converter is not a muffler, although it looks somewhat like one. It is a device to convert unburned exhaust gases into environmentally acceptable water vapor and carbon dioxide. Because the catalyst does such a good job of reducing the level of hydrocarbons and carbon monoxide in the exhaust, your engine can be tuned for more economical operation instead of solely for

emissions reduction. All this is part of the Clean Air Act of 1970, which requires that automobile exhaust emissions be reduced to help clean up the air.

There are two types of catalytic converters in general use. The "monolithic" converter, such as used in Ford and Chrysler products, involves a sort of honeycomb through which the exhaust must pass. Because the honeycomb is coated with platinum and palladium catalyst, the exhaust is rendered harmless by the time it leaves the converter.

General Motors and American Motors use a "pelletized" converter arrangement, in which a stainless steel case containing thousands of small porous ceramic beads coated with catalyst is connected into the system. The exhaust gases pass through these beads, which clean them up.

Because lead, used in leaded fuel, can destroy the catalyst, all cars equipped with catalytic converters must run on unleaded fuel. **Note:** Certain other additives that can be poured into the gas tank or through the carburetor can also damage the catalytic converter. Check the label on any product you use or check with your car dealer's service department to be safe.

4. MUFFLER. This is a cylindrical or oval-shaped component, generally about 2 feet long. It is mounted in the exhaust system about midway or toward the rear of the car. Consisting of a series of baffles and tubes to break up the sound pattern, it silences the exhaust.

5. RESONATOR. On some cars, there is an additional muffler, known as a resonator, to further reduce the sound level of the exhaust. This is located toward the back end of the system and generally looks like a smaller, rounder version of a muffler.

6. TAILPIPE. This is the end of the pipeline carrying exhaust fumes to the atmosphere beyond the back end of the car. On cars equipped with a resonator, the resonator may be located in the middle of the tailpipe.

7. CLAMPS, HANGERS, AND BRACK-

ETS. These components are used to properly join and support various exhaust system components. When replacing a muffler, tailpipe, or some other component, always use a new clamp, hanger, or bracket of the proper size.

8. HEAT-RISER VALVE. Part of the exhaust system on most cars is a valve that deflects heat to the carburetor when the engine is cold. It is called a manifold heat control valve or, more commonly, a heat-riser valve.

Inspecting the Exhaust System

Tools and Materials

- Creeper
- Safety Goggles
- Flashlight or Trouble Light
- Screwdriver

THE TWO MAJOR enemies of your car's exhaust system are rust and vibration. The rust does not come so much from road salt or other outside influences as it does from internal conditions. As exhaust fumes condense, acid is formed inside the muffler and pipes. The exhaust system must generate a tremendous amount of heat to convert this acid mixture to harmless gas. Unfortunately, most of the driving we do does not get the exhaust system hot enough to accomplish this. So, as the exhaust system cools after the engine is turned off, the gases are left in the muffler to condense. They eat away at the inner lining of the exhaust system, and generally, within a

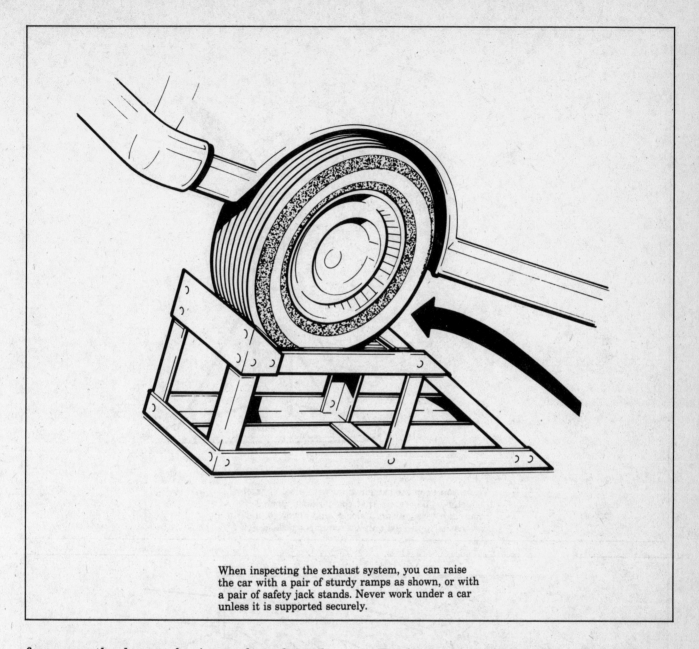

When inspecting the exhaust system, you can raise the car with a pair of sturdy ramps as shown, or with a pair of safety jack stands. Never work under a car unless it is supported securely.

few years, the damage begins to show through.

But even a sound exhaust system can be damaged by the unavoidable shaking, jouncing, and vibration from normal driving conditions that cause the hangers—the supports that hold the exhaust system—to break.

A periodic check of your car's exhaust system is one of the most important safety measures you can take. Exhaust gas is poisonous. A leaking muffler or exhaust pipe connection allows lethal carbon monoxide to work its way into the car, causing headaches, drowsiness, nausea, and even death. Do not gamble with a leaking exhaust system.

The best way to check out your exhaust system is on a lift where the car is above eye level. Unfortunately, this is not always convenient. Instead, you should occasionally plan to slide under the car on a creeper and probe these important connections. Since rust and dirt accumulate on exhaust system parts, you would be well advised to wear safety goggles anytime you crawl under the car.

1. Before making a visual inspection, listen closely for the hissing or rumbling sound that indicates the beginning of exhaust system failure. With the engine

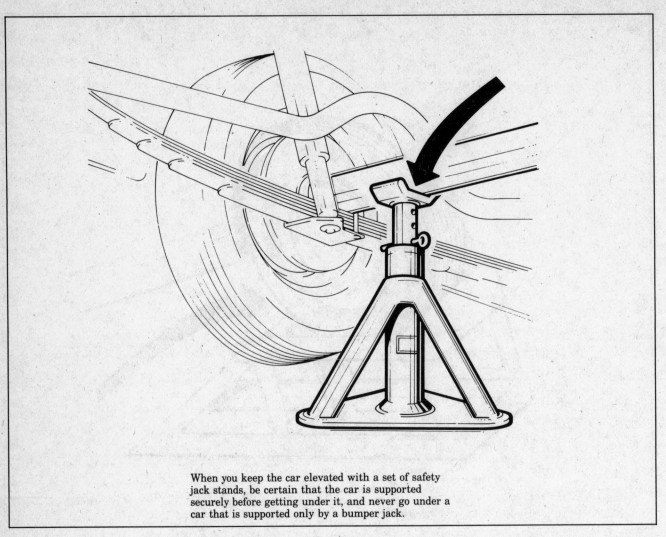

When you keep the car elevated with a set of safety jack stands, be certain that the car is supported securely before getting under it, and never go under a car that is supported only by a bumper jack.

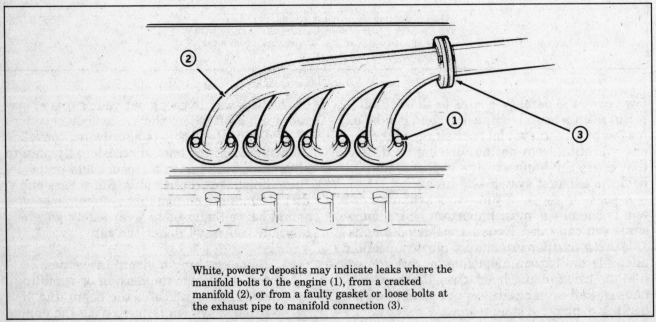

White, powdery deposits may indicate leaks where the manifold bolts to the engine (1), from a cracked manifold (2), or from a faulty gasket or loose bolts at the exhaust pipe to manifold connection (3).

idling, slowly move along the entire system and listen for leaks. It is generally quite easy to locate the source of your leak. *Caution: Be careful. Remember that the exhaust system gets hot. Do not get your face too close when listening for leaks.*

2. With a flashlight or trouble light and a screwdriver, examine and poke every part of the exhaust system that shows signs of excessive rusting. Look for holes, cracks, and any other possible damage. Check all pipes for kinks and dents that may restrict the flow of exhaust gases. A bent, kinked, or dented pipe should be replaced immediately because this restriction causes excessive backpressure and poor engine performance.

3. Take a close look at each connection. Check the exhaust manifold to exhaust pipe connection. If you see any white powdery deposits here, the bolts could be loose, or the gasket may be leaking. Check for loose connections at the muffler by pushing up on the muffler slightly.

4. Tap the pipes, muffler, and resonator, if your car has one, to hear whether there is a "thudding" sound, which is due to deterioration, or a solid metallic clink, which means that it is still in good condition. If you hear any rattles, this indicates loose parts inside the muffler. When you begin to see or hear such deterioration, it is an indication that you should soon begin shopping for good replacement parts at the best price you can find.

5. Shake the exhaust system to determine whether or not all the hangers that hold the system to the car are secure. Most exhaust system hangers are made of combined rubber and fabric, not unlike the sidewall cross section of a tire. If the hanger breaks, you may soon lose a valuable exhaust system along the highway. Check each hanger for cracks, damage, fraying, or rusty conditions.

Exhaust System Service

Tools and Materials

- Jack and Safety Jack Stands
- Wheel Chocks
- Wrenches
- Hacksaw or Exhaust Pipe Cut-Off Tool
- Locking-Jaw Pliers
- Hammer
- Chisel
- Chain Wrench
- Small File
- Ratchet Wrench, Extension, Universal, and Sockets
- Exhaust Pipe Shaper
- Penetrating Oil
- Fine Sandpaper
- Hangers, Brackets, and Clamps
- Tailpipe
- Exhaust System Sealer
- Muffler
- Exhaust Pipe
- Gasket
- Graphite-Based Lubricant
- Manifold Heat Control Valve Solvent

IF YOUR EXHAUST system has gotten to the point where it is too noisy to put up with any longer, it is time to replace it. A thorough inspection will point out any need for replacing an exhaust system component, or the whole system for that matter. Follow the steps in the section on "Inspecting the Exhaust System" elsewhere in this chapter.

Before tackling the job of replacing the exhaust system, make sure that you will be able to get the replacement parts you need. There

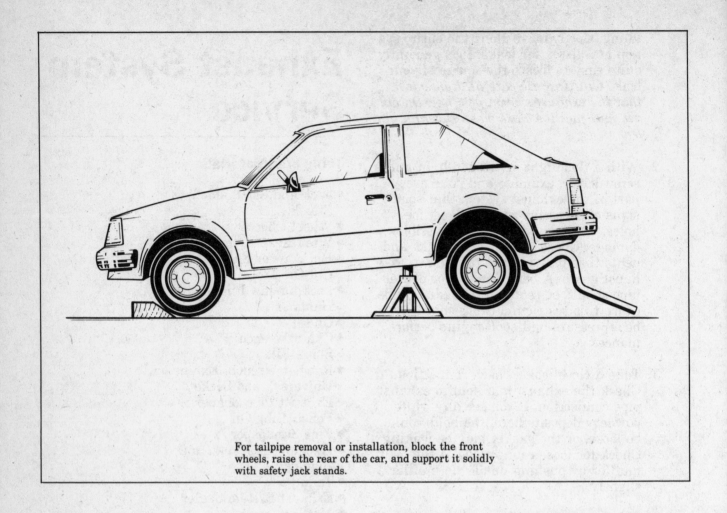

For tailpipe removal or installation, block the front wheels, raise the rear of the car, and support it solidly with safety jack stands.

are literally hundreds of combinations of exhaust pipes, mufflers, and tailpipes to fit the numerous American and foreign makes and models. So there is no use removing the parts until you know that you can replace them. If you have any doubts as to what you need, ask an auto parts dealer for assistance.

If your car still has the original exhaust system, you may find that some of the components are welded together. However, when you purchase replacement parts, the new components may be separate. This usually requires extra clamps and brackets or hangers, depending on the make and model of car you have. So be sure you get all the necessary parts from an auto supply store before you begin.

If you have an air lift available to you, use it. It can make the job a lot easier. Otherwise, use a good jack and the best set of safety jack stands you can find to get the car as high as possible for easy maneuverability.

The following procedure for replacing the

exhaust system has been divided into three sections: "Tailpipe Removal and Installation," "Muffler Removal and Installation," and "Exhaust Pipe Removal and Installation." If you need to replace the muffler only, you can go right to that section, skipping the other two. If you need to replace the whole system, follow the entire sequence in the order of appearance. If your car is equipped with a dual exhaust system, work on one side at a time. **Note:** Whenever you replace a complete exhaust system, manufacturers recommend that you start at the rear of the car and work toward the front to disassemble the system. Reverse this procedure for reassembly.

Here is something else to consider: chances are if one component of the exhaust system is rusted or otherwise needs replacement, the other components might be in almost as bad a shape. Although it will cost you a little more, much time and labor will be saved by replacing the entire system at once.

Tailpipe Removal and Installation

1. Raise the rear of the car off the ground by using a good jack. Block the front wheels with wheel chocks. Support the rear of the car with a good set of jack stands as shown in the accompanying illustration. **Note:** On some cars, it may be helpful to remove the rear wheels. This will give you more maneuverability for removing and installing the tailpipe.
2. With the car securely elevated, soak the nuts and bolts on the tailpipe hangers, clamps, and brackets with penetrating oil. Also squirt penetrating oil into the tailpipe to muffler connection. Let the oil penetrate for a few minutes.
3. Using the proper-size wrench, remove the nuts and bolts that hold the rear tailpipe hanger to the tailpipe. There should also be a bolt that holds the bracket to the car frame. Remove it with the proper-size wrench.
4. Remove the rear muffler hanger or clamp and bracket bolts with a wrench at the muffler to tailpipe connection. If you are lucky, the tailpipe will twist free from the muffler. In most cases, however, it is necessary to do some chiseling to separate the two parts. The best way to do this is to cut the tailpipe with a hacksaw a few inches from the muffler. Then work the stub of the pipe out of the muffler connection using a pair of locking-jaw pliers. **Note:** Depending on the make and model of car you have, some tailpipes fit *over* the muffler connection. Other tailpipes fit *into* the muffler connection.
5. Clean the connection on the muffler with fine sandpaper.
6. Always use new clamps and brackets or hangers. Slide the new hanger or clamp and bracket over the end of the new tailpipe that connects to the muffler.
7. Apply a coating of exhaust system sealer to the mating surfaces of both the muffler and tailpipe. Slide the tailpipe into or onto the muffler. There should be approximately 2 inches of overlap for a proper connection. Position the rear muffler clamp and bracket or hanger over the muffler to tailpipe connection. Install the two bolts; do not tighten them yet.

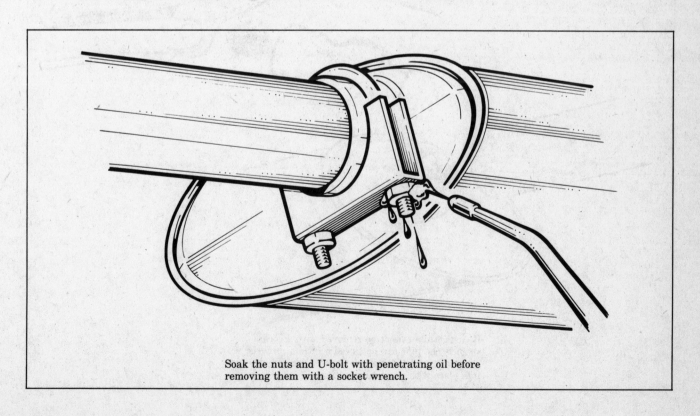

Soak the nuts and U-bolt with penetrating oil before removing them with a socket wrench.

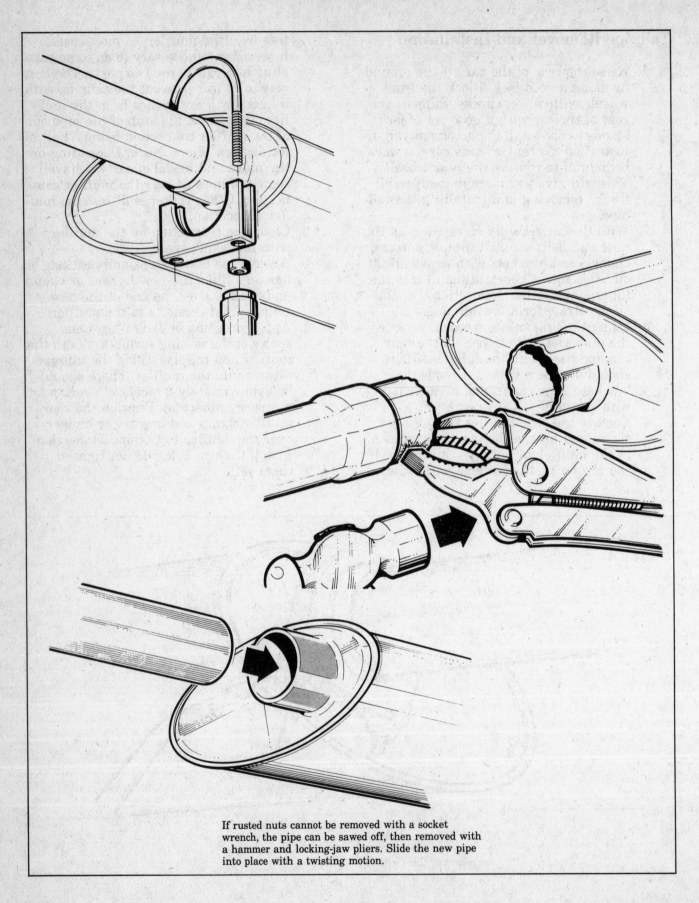

If rusted nuts cannot be removed with a socket
wrench, the pipe can be sawed off, then removed with
a hammer and locking-jaw pliers. Slide the new pipe
into place with a twisting motion.

8. Install a new rear tailpipe hanger loosely over the end of the tailpipe; do not tighten it yet. Install the bolt that holds the hanger to the car frame and tighten it securely.

9. Make sure that the new tailpipe is in its proper position. It should not be touching any part of the car such as the frame, body, or rear suspension parts.

10. Now tighten the hanger or clamp and bracket bolts at the muffler connection, then the hanger to tailpipe bolts. Recheck to make sure that the tailpipe does not touch any part of the car by shaking it. If the clearance is not just right, you will get an annoying rattle when you drive your car.

11. Remove the jack stands and lower the car.

Muffler Removal and Installation

1. Using the car jack, raise the rear of the car until the wheels are off the ground. Place a good set of jack stands under the frame of the car to support it solidly. Block the front wheels with wheel chocks before raising the car.

2. Soak both front and rear muffler clamp and bracket nuts with penetrating oil. Some cars may use a hanger to support the muffler. Also soak the rear tailpipe hanger nuts and bolts. It also may be helpful to soak the front and rear muffler to pipe connections with penetrating oil.

3. Use a wrench to remove the rear tailpipe hanger from the tailpipe; you do not need to remove the rear tailpipe hanger from the frame.

4. Remove the rear muffler bracket and clamp from the muffler to tailpipe connection.

5. Assuming you intend to keep the old tailpipe, carefully work it up and down until it separates from the muffler. If it does not come loose easily, you may have to do the following.
   A. If the tailpipe fits inside the muffler, cut slits in the muffler outlet connection with a hammer and chisel.
   B. If the tailpipe fits over the muffler outlet connection, use a chain

wrench to get a firm grip on the pipe. Then twist it off.

6. Loosen the front muffler clamp and bracket bolts with a wrench.

7. If the muffler cannot be easily pulled off the exhaust pipe (or the pipe to the catalytic converter if so equipped), follow the procedure in Step 5 with the exhaust pipe and muffler connection. **Note:** Sometimes the original factory installation has a welded connection between the exhaust pipe and the inlet on the muffler. In this case, you can use an exhaust pipe cut-off tool or hacksaw to separate the two parts.

8. Remove any burrs from the exhaust pipe with a small file for a smooth reinstallation. Then check all connections to make sure they are perfectly round to accommodate your new muffler. The professionals have special tools for reshaping exhaust connections. You may have to use a bit of ingenuity or obtain such tools from a tool rental shop if the parts do not fit properly.

9. Slip new clamps and brackets (do not use the old ones) into position over both pipe ends—exhaust pipe and tailpipe.

10. Lift the new muffler into position, making sure that you have the inlet end toward the front of the car. Replacement mufflers are always so marked. **Note:** It is wise to apply some exhaust system sealer to the mating surfaces before installation. This is available at an auto parts store.

11. Slide the exhaust pipe into the muffler approximately 2 inches, but no more than that. Be sure that the slits in the muffler tube are covered for a gas-tight fit. Position the muffler so that it cannot touch the body, frame, or underside of the car.

12. Slide the front clamp and bracket over the muffler to exhaust pipe connection and tighten the bolts by hand; do not use the wrench to tighten yet.

13. Slide the tailpipe into—or onto, depending on the setup on your car—the rear muffler connection. Position the pipe so that it does not touch the car body, frame, or rear suspension parts.

14. Slide the rear clamp and bracket over

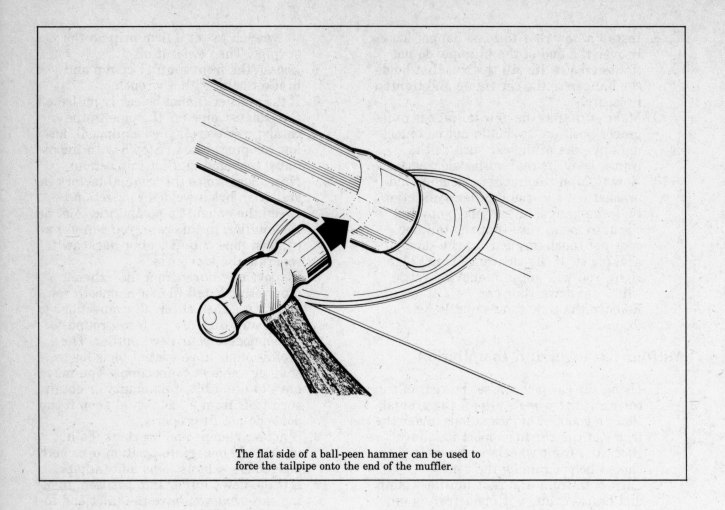

The flat side of a ball-peen hammer can be used to
force the tailpipe onto the end of the muffler.

the muffler to tailpipe connection and
hand-tighten the bolts.

15. Reconnect the rear tailpipe hanger to
the tailpipe. Before doing so, however,
check its condition to see if it, too,
should be replaced. Hand-tighten these
bolts as well.

16. Make sure all exhaust system parts are
properly positioned. There should be no
contact with the car body, frame, or any
other parts. Starting at the exhaust
pipe to muffler connection, and working
towards the rear of the car, tighten all
connections securely with a wrench.
After you have done this, shake the exhaust system with your hands. Again,
no exhaust system part should touch
any part of the car.

17. Remove the jack stands and lower the
car. Start the engine and listen to the
exhaust system. If all is quiet, you have
done your job successfully.

Exhaust Pipe Removal and Installation

1. To remove the exhaust pipe, it will be
easier to raise the front of the car as
well as the rear. Use a good jack to do
this, and support the car with good jack
stands. You can also drive the car onto a
sturdy pair of ramps. Then you can use
the jacking procedure to support the
rear end on jack stands.

2. To help in removing the nuts and bolts
on clamps and hangers, soak all connections—from front to back—with penetrating oil. Because you will be removing the forward end of the pipe from the
exhaust manifold, be sure to soak those
nuts thoroughly.

3. Loosen and remove the clamp and
bracket nuts at the muffler to exhaust
pipe connection with a wrench. **Note:**
Late model cars have a catalytic con-

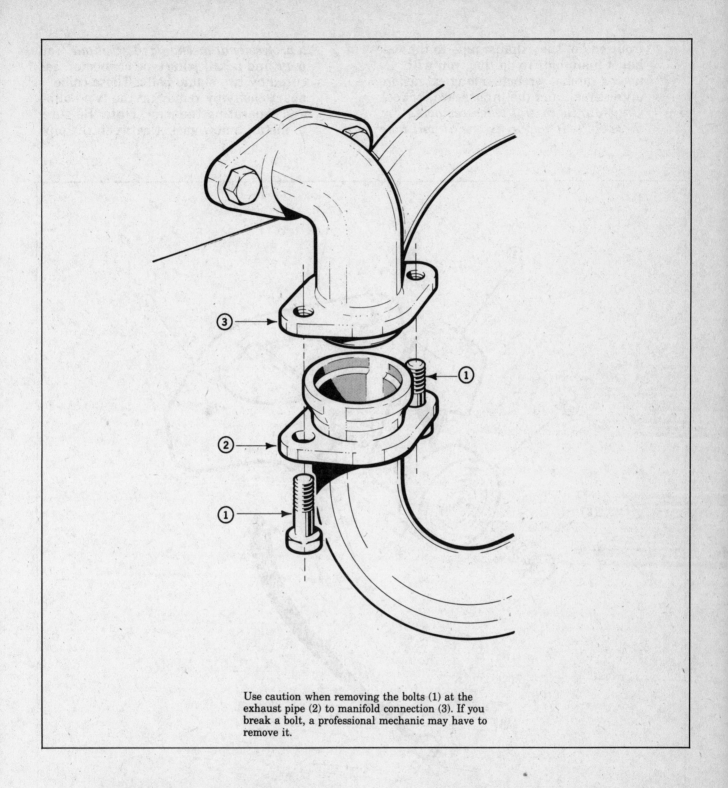

Use caution when removing the bolts (1) at the exhaust pipe (2) to manifold connection (3). If you break a bolt, a professional mechanic may have to remove it.

verter installed between the muffler and the exhaust manifold. If this is the case, it will have to be removed in order to replace sections of exhaust pipe in front of and behind the converter. However, the catalytic converter must not be tampered with, bypassed, or removed permanently.

4. Loosen—but do not remove—the brackets and hangers that support the muffler and tailpipe assembly.

5. Remove the nuts or bolts that secure the

front end of the exhaust pipe to the exhaust manifold. To do this, you will need a ratchet wrench, a long extension, a universal, and the proper-size socket. *Caution: Be careful when removing these bolts. If you break one, it will take* *a professional mechanic to get it out.* You may find a ball joint type connector, secured by two clamp bolts. These come apart easily by removing the two bolts and separating the joint. **Note:** Be sure to install a new gasket between the pipe

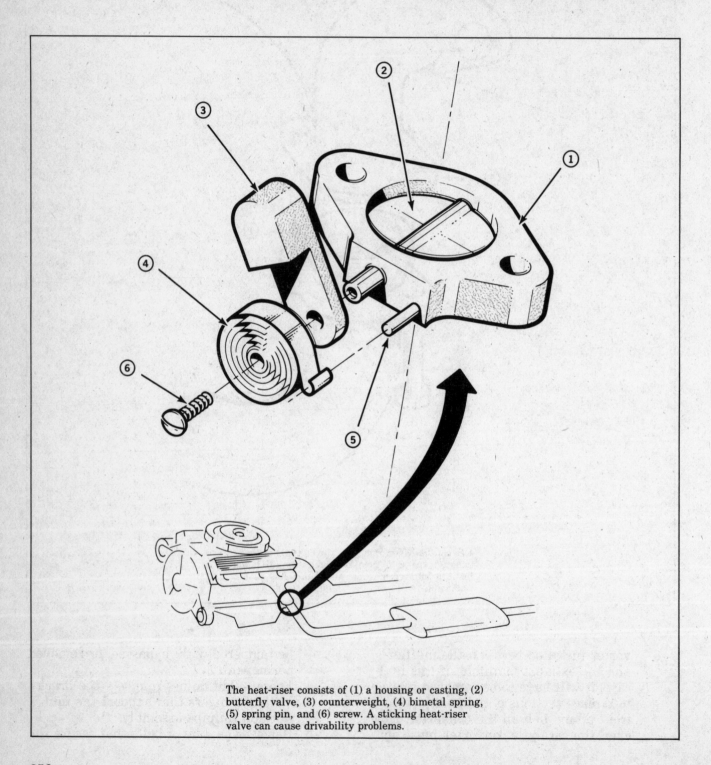

The heat-riser consists of (1) a housing or casting, (2) butterfly valve, (3) counterweight, (4) bimetal spring, (5) spring pin, and (6) screw. A sticking heat-riser valve can cause drivability problems.

and the manifold if your car is equipped with this type of connection. Most cars require a gasket at the connection point of the exhaust manifold and exhaust pipe.

6. If your muffler is welded to the exhaust pipe, it will be necessary to cut it free. You can use a cut-off tool or a hacksaw to do this. If you have clamps, loosen them as well as the tailpipe clamps just enough so that the muffler and the tailpipe can be shifted backward until they separate from the exhaust pipe.

7. Remove the exhaust pipe from the car. **Note:** At this time, you should check out the heat-riser valve if your car is so equipped.

   The heat-riser valve may slide off along with the exhaust pipe as part of the connection. Examine the heat-riser valve and lubricate it with a graphite-based lubricant. In fact, this should be a normal part of your lubrication service.

   To check for proper heat-riser valve operation when the exhaust system is intact, see if the counterweight moves freely; the valve should open and close freely when the engine is accelerated. If it sticks, saturate it thoroughly with manifold heat control valve solvent or penetrating oil until it works freely. *Caution: On some cars such as late model, eight-cylinder Chrysler products, the exhaust pipe passes close to the terminals of the starter motor. Whatever make of car you are working on, be sure to watch for this so that you do not accidentally short the pipe on the terminals. It is best to disconnect the ground battery cable.*

8. Install the new exhaust pipe. Position the front end onto the exhaust manifold and install the bolts using the ratchet wrench, extension, universal, and socket. Do not tighten yet.

9. Position a new clamp and bracket over the exhaust pipe. Slide the muffler onto or into the exhaust pipe and tighten the nuts by hand.

10. Make sure all exhaust system parts are properly positioned with no parts touching the car frame, body, or suspension. Tighten all connections securely, start-

ing at the exhaust pipe to exhaust manifold connection and working towards the rear of the car.

11. Remove the jack stands and lower the car. **Note:** If auto ramps were used to support the front end, back the car down off the ramps.

12. Start the engine and listen for the same quietness that your car had when it was new.

Catalytic Converter Service

Tools and Materials

- Jack and Safety Jack Stands
- Wheel Chocks
- Wrenches
- Penetrating Oil
- Vacuum Gauge
- Replacement Catalytic Converter
- Propane Torch
- Hammer and Chisel

MOST PASSENGER CARS and light trucks since 1975 are equipped with a catalytic converter. On 1975 through 1980 vehicles, the converter's purpose is to reduce carbon monoxide and hydrocarbons in the exhaust. On 1981 and newer vehicles, the converter also reduces oxides of nitrogen. The converter's operation is explained in the chapter on "Emissions Control Systems".

The converter may require replacement for one of three reasons: in some instances, it can

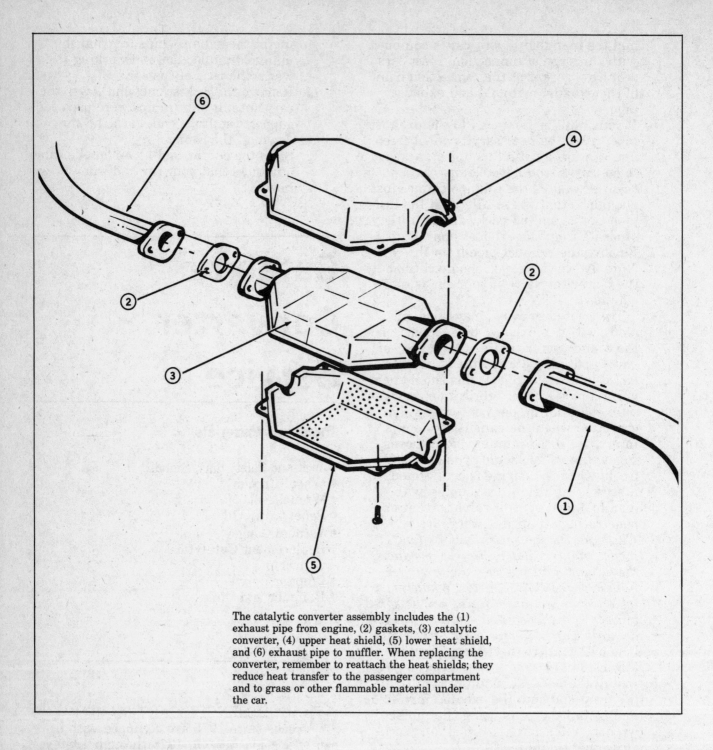

The catalytic converter assembly includes the (1) exhaust pipe from engine, (2) gaskets, (3) catalytic converter, (4) upper heat shield, (5) lower heat shield, and (6) exhaust pipe to muffler. When replacing the converter, remember to reattach the heat shields; they reduce heat transfer to the passenger compartment and to grass or other flammable material under the car.

suffer internal damage causing a partial blockage in the exhaust system or a restriction; it eventually wears out with age; or it can be rendered useless by using leaded gasoline. A plugged up converter will have a noticeable loss of power, but an inoperative or worn out converter will cause no noticeable effect on drivability or performance except with respect to emission control. The only accurate way to determine whether or not it is working is to perform an exhaust emissions check—something that is now required in many states and large cities as part of a vehicle emissions testing program. If the inspection finds the converter to be defective or inoperative, the law usually requires that the converter be replaced. Although some states have a cost waiver as part of the law, limiting the total amount of money a motorist must spend to have his or her car repaired to bring it into compliance with the law, the limit is, in most cases, set high enough so the cost of a replacement converter is not excluded. An original equipment type converter can cost up to $300 but less costly aftermarket replacement converters are available for less than $100. The aftermarket replacement converters sell for less, because they do not contain as much catalyst as an original equipment converter, nor do they have as long a service life. Two years or 24,000 miles is the guarantee offered on this type of unit. However, they are good enough to get a car through inspection and they do perform adequately to satisfy the requirements of the law.

Note: The catalytic converter is part of your vehicle's emission-control system, and as such it is covered by the 5-year/50,000 mile emissions warranty required on all new cars built since 1981. If your vehicle is still within this warranty period, you should be able to take it back to the dealer for free repairs if anything goes wrong with the converter.

How to Check for Excessive Backpressure

It the converter becomes partially blocked internally, it will obstruct the flow of exhaust gases and create excessive backpressure in the exhaust system. The result will be a noticeable loss of power, especially at high speed. If the blockage is severe, the engine may only idle but barely run or even die when the throttle is opened.

What causes the blockage? On some General Motors converters with a dual-bed pellet construction, the support structure between the two layers of pellets collapses and causes a blockage. If a converter is severely overheated (which can result from running excessive amounts of raw fuel through it, as when a spark plug is disconnected or fouled, a carburetor leaks fuel, etc.), the heat can partially melt the catalyst. In some instances, it can completely block the flow of exhaust. A third cause of clogging is carbon buildup in a worn out or lead-fouled converter. Once the converter becomes inoperative, it isn't able to continually burn off the pollutants, so carbon can build up and restrict the flow of exhaust.

To check for excessive backpressure, all you need is a vacuum gauge. Vacuum testing is covered in the previous chapter, but basically all you do is hook up your vacuum gauge to a vacuum source on the intake manifold, start the engine, and watch for a gradual drop in the needle reading at idle. If the vacuum slowly decreases, it means pressure is backing up in the exhaust system. The cure is to remove the blockage.

Keep in mind that a blockage can also occur inside the muffler if it has collapsed internally, in a tailpipe if it has been bent or damaged by a road hazard, or by a double-walled exhaust pipe that has collapsed internally. So before you condemn the converter, make a careful visual inspection of the entire exhaust system.

Converter Replacement

To replace a defective converter, you follow the same basic procedure as when replacing a muffler, except that the converter usually has bolt-together flanges rather than slip-pipe and U-bolt connections.

The basic replacement procedure goes as follows.

1. Wait until the exhaust system has cooled before starting work, then raise the car and support it on safety jack stands.
2. The converter is usually enclosed in a protective heat shield. In some cases, it will be necessary to remove the lower portion of the heat shield to replace the converter.
3. Disconnect the converter from the head pipe and exhaust pipe. Penetrating oil and/or a propane torch can help loosen rusted bolts. If all else fails, use a hammer and chisel to remove the nuts on the bolts. The converter can now be removed from the car.
4. Check both pipe connections for corrosion or damage, then lift the replacement converter into place and put new flange gaskets in place if required.
5. Install new bolts and nuts, tighten all pipe connections, and replace the lower heat shield if it was removed.

THE DRIVELINE

IN THIS chapter, we are introducing the technical term "driveline," which covers a lot of things. On a conventional rear-wheel-drive car, it includes all of the components it takes to transfer power from the end of the engine's rotating crankshaft to the drive wheels—the clutch (if the car is so equipped), transmission, universal joints, drive or propeller shaft, rear axle, and finally, rear axle shafts.

The transmission—manual or automatic—provides the driver with a selection of gears to permit the car to operate under a variety of conditions and engine loads. The majority of

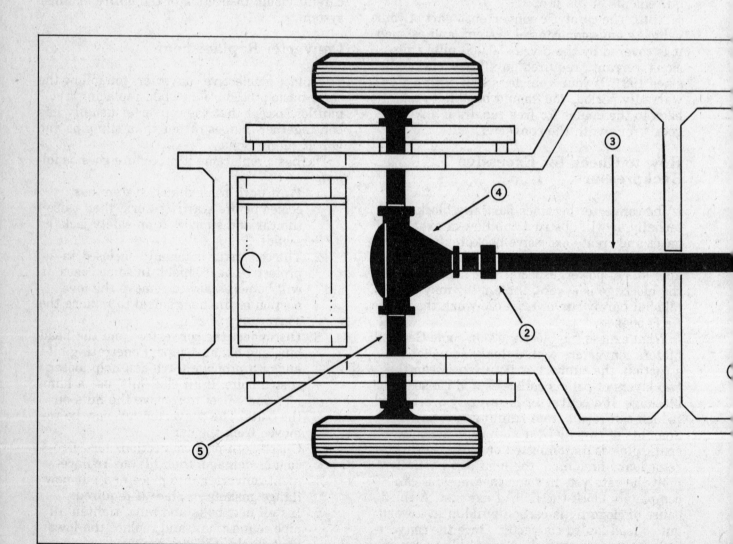

passenger cars in use today are equipped with an automatic transmission that performs all clutching and gearshifting operations with minimum assistance from the driver. However, many cars equipped with manual transmissions are sold each year. These cars must have a clutch, which is foot-pedal-operated, and a transmission that is shifted from gear to gear by hand.

A clutch is merely a link or coupling between the engine and the rest of the driveline. The clutch permits a gradual application of engine power to begin moving the car. Once the clutch is engaged, all of the engine power is applied to the transmission and the rest of the driveline. In addition to aiding in the initial motion of the car, the clutch enables the driver to disengage the engine from the driveline so that the transmission may be shifted smoothly from one gear to another, or bring the car to a stop without stalling the engine.

You will find only two pedals, the accelerator pedal and brake pedal, on the floor of a car equipped with an automatic transmission. There is no need for a separate clutch pedal assembly as the torque converter (used instead of the clutch assembly), operating with other components in the transmission, automatically transfers engine power to the driveline.

Aside from using a lever to select the mode of operation desired—"park," "reverse," "neutral," "drive," "drive 1," "drive 2"—very little is required of the driver. As long as it is in good operating condition, the automatic trans-

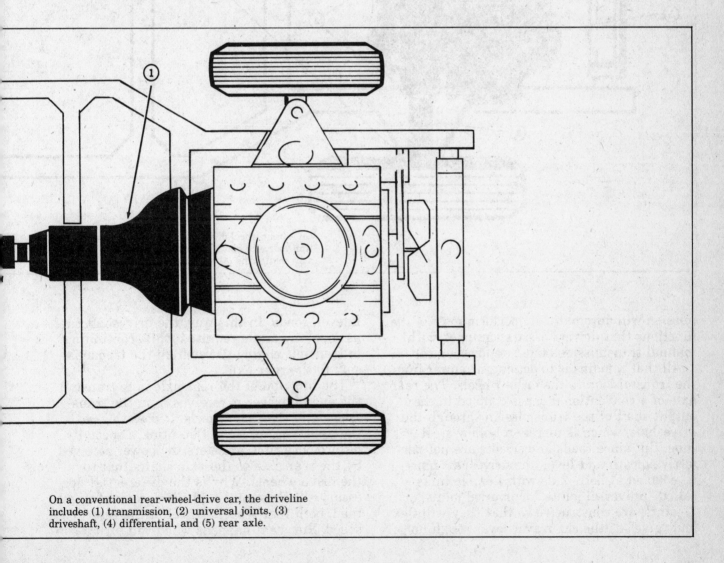

On a conventional rear-wheel-drive car, the driveline includes (1) transmission, (2) universal joints, (3) driveshaft, (4) differential, and (5) rear axle.

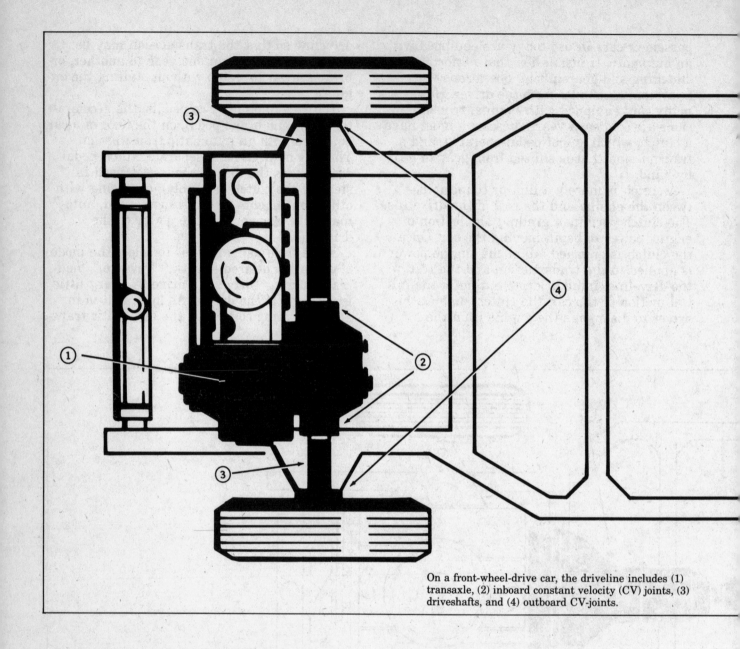

On a front-wheel-drive car, the driveline includes (1) transaxle, (2) inboard constant velocity (CV) joints, (3) driveshafts, and (4) outboard CV-joints.

mission will automatically perform most of the functions that drivers of cars equipped with manual transmissions must do for themselves.

All that remains is to get engine power from the transmission to the drive wheels. The rear axle of a conventional car is coupled to the output shaft of the transmission through the driveshaft, which is merely a hollow steel tube. But since roads and streets are not perfectly smooth and level, the driveshaft must be coupled at both ends with flexible links called "universal joints." Universal joints, or U-joints, are constructed so that they will flex and "give" as the car travels over rough and uneven roads. In this way, the driveshaft can assume any angle required while continuing to transmit engine power from the transmission to the rear axle.

The function of the rear axle is to transmit the engine power it receives from the transmission to the rear wheels. It does this with the assistance of the differential, a specially built device that transfers the power received by the rear axle to the axle shafts that turn the drive wheels. Why is the differential necessary? Well, when you drive down a straight road, both rear wheels travel at the same speed. But what happens when you turn a cor-

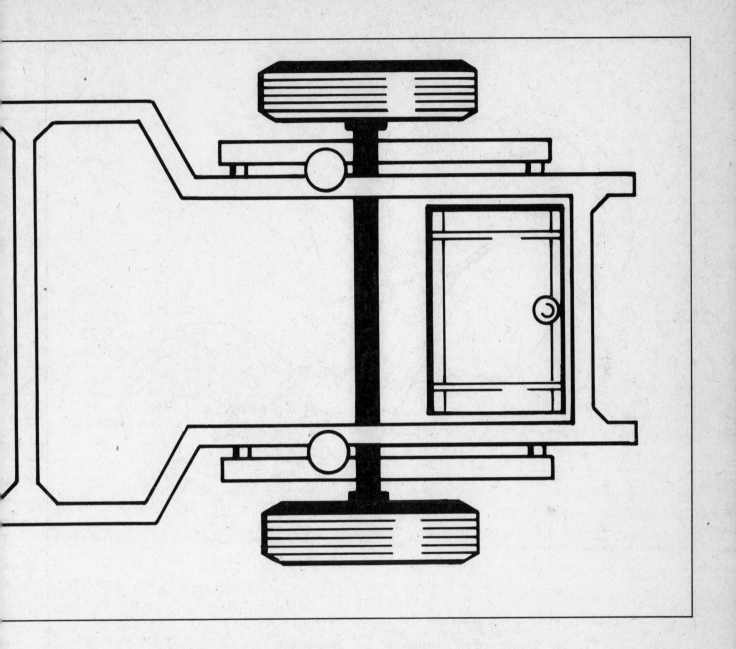

ner? If you think for a moment, you will realize that during a right turn, for example, the wheels on the left side of the car travel further than the wheels on the right side of the car. Because the left side of the car and the right side have to complete the turn together, the wheels on the left side must travel faster than the wheels on the right. This is not a problem for the front wheels because they turn independently. The rear wheels, however, are another matter and this is where the differential is important. It is constructed so that regardless of which way you turn the car, the wheels on the outside of the turn will travel faster than the inside wheels, with power from the engine still applied.

Front-Wheel-Drive Cars

Front-wheel-drive cars differ radically from conventional rear-wheel-drive cars because their drivelines do not have a single driveshaft, U-joints, or rear drivetrain. Because their drive wheels are in the front of the car where the engine is located, they have a transaxle, which consists of a clutch and manual transmission (or automatic transmission), front differential driveshafts, and bearings.

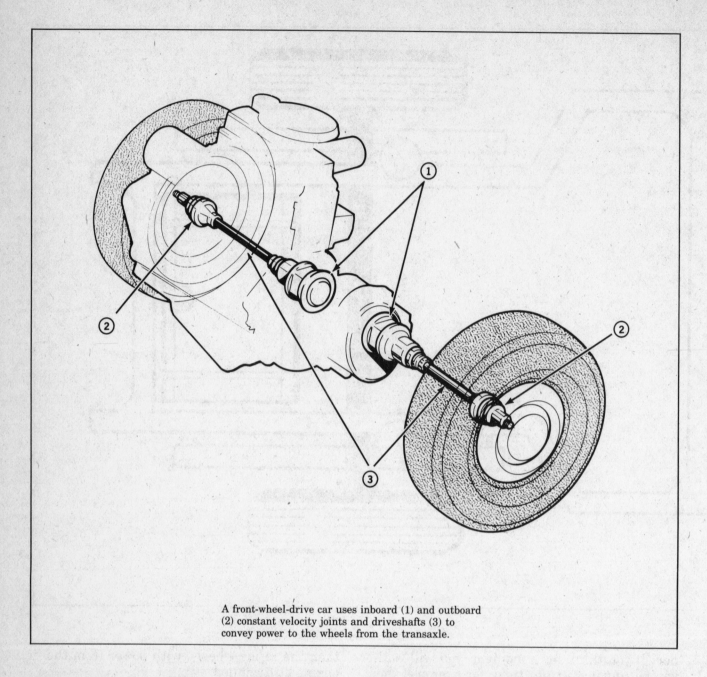

A front-wheel-drive car uses inboard (1) and outboard
(2) constant velocity joints and driveshafts (3) to
convey power to the wheels from the transaxle.

Power is transmitted to the wheels through a pair of driveshafts (also called halfshafts) equipped with inner and outer constant velocity (CV) joints rather than U-joints. Conventional U-joints can create cyclic vibrations and uneven rotational speeds if the driveshaft operates at more than 7 or 8 degrees off true center. This doesn't present any problems for most rear-wheel-drive cars, but with front-wheel drive, the front wheels also do the steering, which means the outboard driveshaft joint must be able to handle a wide range of turn-ing angles. Thus, constant velocity joints that provide uniform rotation speeds regardless of the angle of the joint are used. As for the inner joints, the same is true because the relatively short driveshafts travel up and down to follow suspension motions. An ordinary U-joint could induce vibrations under these circumstances, so CV-joints are used here too.

As you read the following sections of this chapter, you will find service tips as well as procedures for making adjustments to help you maintain the components of the driveline.

Clutches

Tools and Materials

- Hand Wrenches
- Pliers
- Open-End Wrenches
- Ruler
- Pilot Tool
- Torque Wrench
- Wheel Chocks
- Jack and Safety Jack Stands
- Penetrating Oil
- Transmission Jack, Scissors Jack,or Floor Jack

THE CLUTCH in a manual transmission is the mechanical connection between the engine and the gears that move the car. It is designed to connect or disconnect the transmission of power from one working part to another—in this case, from the engine to the transmission. The clutch, a friction-type device, is linked to a clutch pedal in the driver's compartment.

The clutch assembly is divided into four main parts: a flywheel that is bolted to the engine's crankshaft; a friction disc or clutch plate that is splined to the transmission input shaft; a pressure plate assembly that is installed over the friction disc and is bolted around its outside edge to the flywheel; and finally, the foot pedal control and mechanical or hydraulic linkage that allows the driver to engage or disengage the clutch as required.

The running engine imparts a rotary motion, or torque, to the flywheel by means of the engine crankshaft. To set the car in motion, this turning force must be transferred to the transmission input shaft. This is accomplished through the friction disc that is pressed and held against the turning flywheel until it turns with the flywheel. The turning disc, which is splined to the transmission input shaft, transfers the rotary motion (engine

torque) of the flywheel through the clutch assembly and on to the transmission.

When the driver's foot is off the clutch pedal, the clutch is engaged and the clutch disc is tightly pressed between the flywheel and the pressure plate. The clutch disc is held against the turning flywheel by spring pressure in the pressure plate assembly. When the driver's foot depresses the clutch pedal, a release, or throw-out, bearing (a part of the operating linkage) moves forward against clutch-release levers or "fingers" in the pressure plate. This movement retracts the pressure plate unit, compressing its springs. When spring pressure is removed, the clutch disc is free to turn independently of the revolving flywheel and soon coasts to a stop between the pressure plate unit and the flywheel. When the driver releases the clutch pedal, the release bearing moves back, causing the release levers to slacken their leverage on the pressure plate. The pressure plate springs once again force the pressure plate unit to sandwich the disc against the flywheel.

This system is simple but effective. With foot pressure, the driver can regulate the rate of engagement of the clutch slowly enough to apply the clutch smoothly and evenly.

Currently, there are two types of clutch pressure plate assemblies used in automobiles. They are the coil spring and the diaphragm spring types. Their basic function, however, is the same.

The pressure plate assembly is composed of one or more springs, a pressure plate unit, release fingers or levers, and a cover. The parts are assembled inside the cover, which is attached by bolts to the flywheel. The assembly rotates with the flywheel.

When the clutch is engaged, the pressure springs push the pressure plate unit forward, forcing the clutch disc firmly against the flywheel. These springs must be strong enough to hold the pressure disc against the flywheel and transmit the torque at all road speeds. The pressure plate requires more than 1000 pounds of spring pressure to hold the clutch disc against the flywheel.

Insufficient spring pressure causes loss of power, because all the engine torque will not be absorbed by the clutch disc. It would be carried to the transmission. This would cause the clutch disc to "slip." A slipping clutch disc will

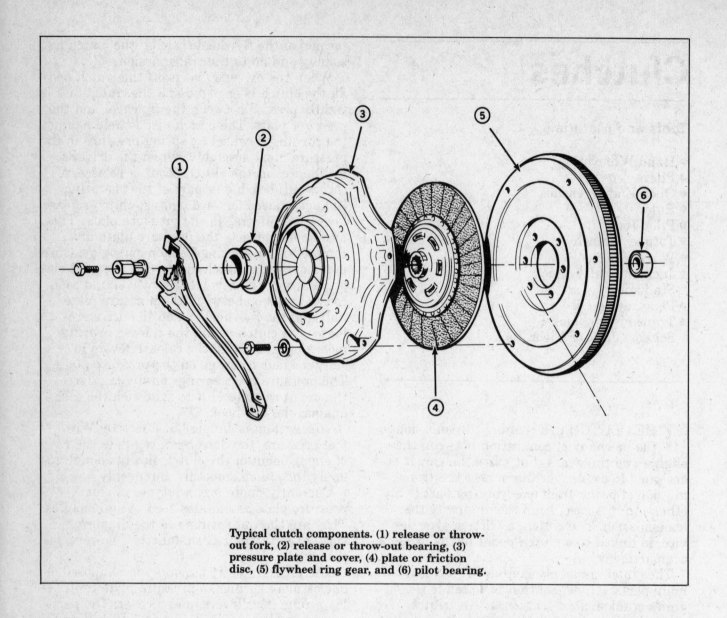

Typical clutch components. (1) release or throw-out fork, (2) release or throw-out bearing, (3) pressure plate and cover, (4) plate or friction disc, (5) flywheel ring gear, and (6) pilot bearing.

overheat and eventually cause clutch failure.

When the clutch is engaged, the clutch's friction disc is forced to revolve as a unit with the flywheel and the pressure plate assembly. All torque developed by the engine is transmitted through the clutch friction disc to the transmission input shaft. The torque is picked up by the lined faces of the clutch friction disc and transmitted through its steel hub, which is splined to the transmission input shaft. The clutch-disc facings are made from sheets of long-fiber asbestos and copper wire thread (or other semi-metallic compounds). They are as thick and durable as brake lining.

The hub to which the linings or facings are attached includes a cushioning device and a torsional vibration-dampening unit. This cushioning device between the two facings permits a smooth engagement of the clutch and eliminates clutch chatter. The torsional device, located near the center of the hub, absorbs the torsional vibrations of the crankshaft, preventing them from reaching the transmission. The center of the hub is fitted with splines to transmit engine torque to the transmission input shaft.

Clutch Adjustment

The clutch pedal is connected through linkage to a release bearing so that pedal pressure moves the bearing against the release levers to disengage the clutch. The proper clutch-pedal free-travel adjustment (at least ½ and no more than 1 inch) is necessary to compensate for wear on the clutch facings and to avoid slippage. Proper clearance must be maintained between the clutch-release bearing and the clutch-release levers. When wear of the facings has caused the release levers to move back against the release bearing, free-play is eliminated and adjustment is necessary. An adjustment of ¾-inch free-play at the pedal is recommended.

Note: On some vehicles with automatic clutch cable adjusters, the system is designed to maintain virtually no free-play. The adjuster maintains a slight tension that keeps the

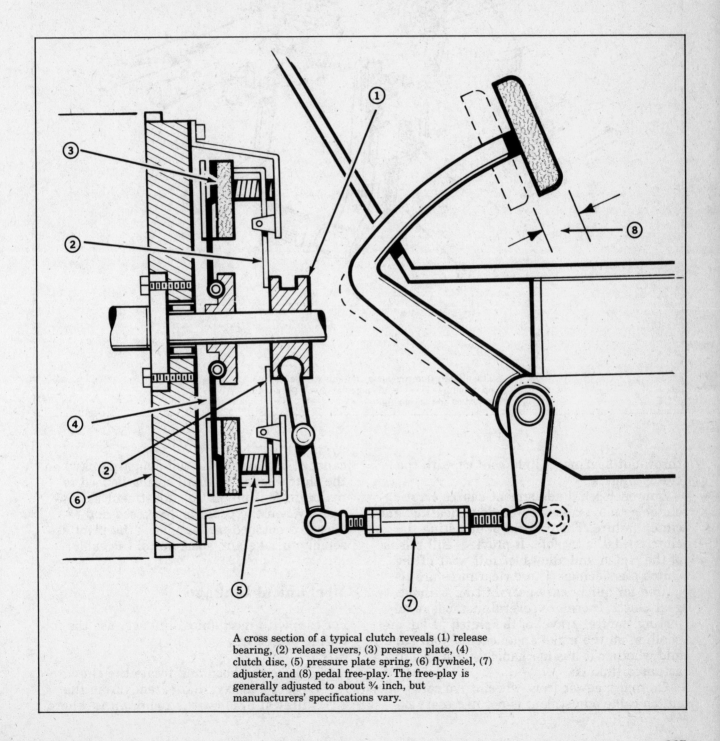

A cross section of a typical clutch reveals (1) release bearing, (2) release levers, (3) pressure plate, (4) clutch disc, (5) pressure plate spring, (6) flywheel, (7) adjuster, and (8) pedal free-play. The free-play is generally adjusted to about ¾ inch, but manufacturers' specifications vary.

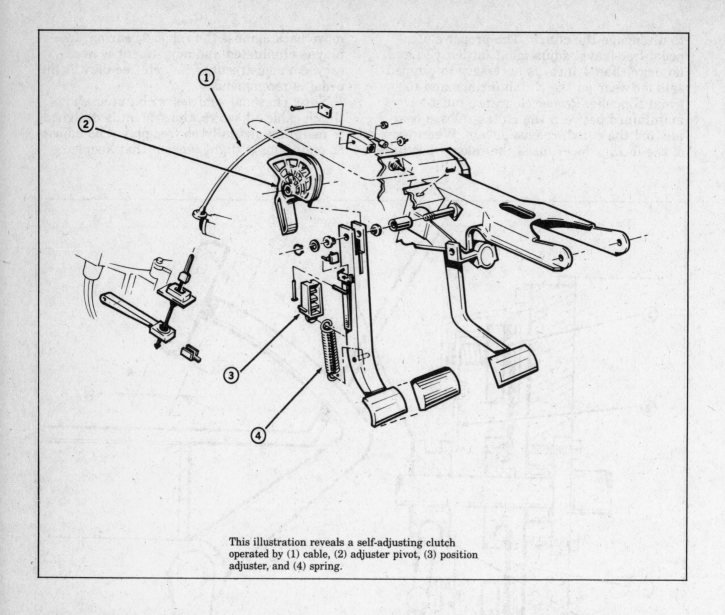

This illustration reveals a self-adjusting clutch operated by (1) cable, (2) adjuster pivot, (3) position adjuster, and (4) spring.

throw-out bearing in light contact with the clutch fingers.

Improper pedal adjustment causes erratic clutch action, excessive wear, overheating, and clutch failure. The purpose of adjusting the clutch pedal is twofold. It provides full release of the clutch and allows for full wear of the clutch-disc facings. These clearances are required for quick, easy gearshifting without gear clash. There are several methods of adjusting the free-travel of the clutch pedal, depending on the make and model of your car and whether it has mechanical- or hydraulic-actuated linkage.

On many newer front-wheel-drive cars, clutch cable adjustment is not necessary be-cause of the automatic self-adjusting pawl on the clutch pedal. A small spring is used to maintain tension on the adjustment mechanism. When the pedal is depressed and released, a notched pawl engages the pivot assembly to take any slack out of the cable.

Mechanical Linkage

For cars with mechanical linkage, use the following procedure.

1. Raise the hood and locate the clutch pedal pushrod that extends from the firewall. Follow the rod down to where

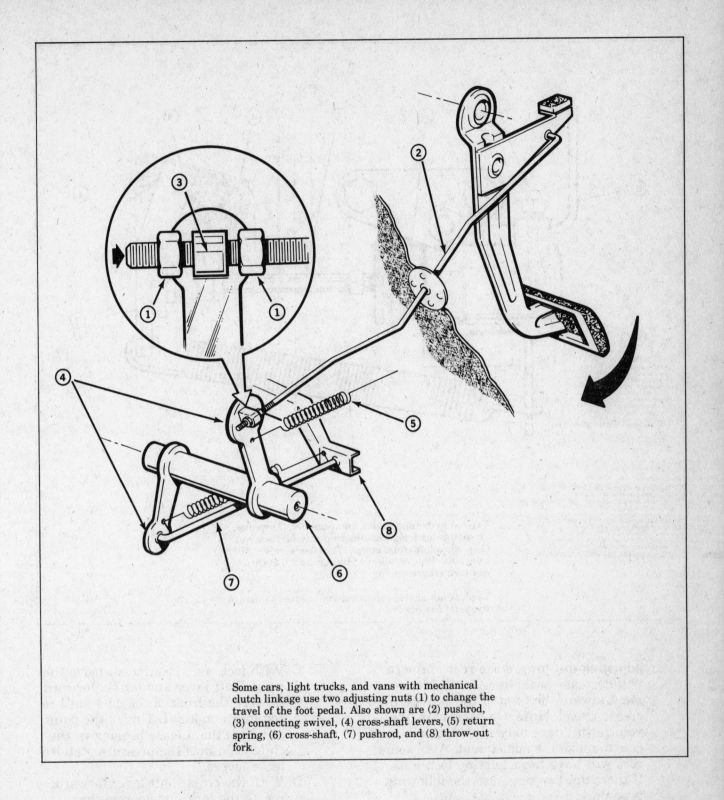

Some cars, light trucks, and vans with mechanical clutch linkage use two adjusting nuts (1) to change the travel of the foot pedal. Also shown are (2) pushrod, (3) connecting swivel, (4) cross-shaft levers, (5) return spring, (6) cross-shaft, (7) pushrod, and (8) throw-out fork.

it connects with the clutch pedal cross-shaft lever.

2. Using pliers, disconnect the clutch pedal return spring at the cross-shaft lever and the frame, or the firewall.

3. Apply penetrating oil to the adjustable linkage.

4. While holding the pushrod, rotate the single, self-locking adjusting nut with an open-end wrench. Movement of the

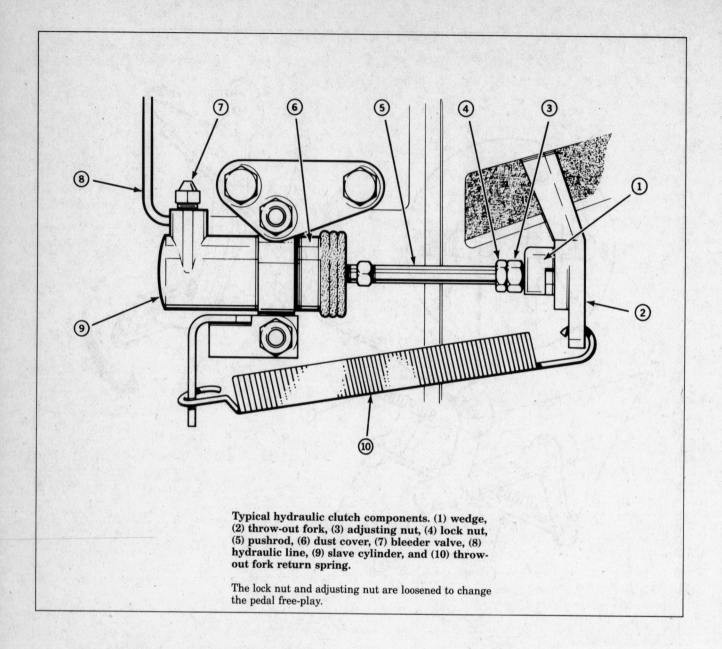

Typical hydraulic clutch components. (1) wedge, (2) throw-out fork, (3) adjusting nut, (4) lock nut, (5) pushrod, (6) dust cover, (7) bleeder valve, (8) hydraulic line, (9) slave cylinder, and (10) throw-out fork return spring.

The lock nut and adjusting nut are loosened to change the pedal free-play.

adjusting nut toward the rear of the car will decrease pedal free-travel. Movement toward the front of the car will increase travel. **Note:** On some cars, the vehicle will have to be raised to gain access to make the adjustment. Also, some cars will have two adjusting lock nuts. If there are two nuts, use the following procedure.

A. Use two open-end wrenches to loosen the lock nuts on either side of a connecting swivel.
B. Turn each lock nut at least ¼ inch away from the connecting swivel.

C. With lock nuts positioned, move the cross-shaft lever and swivel forward (toward the front of the car) until resistance is noticed. This is the point at which the release bearing in the clutch contacts the pressure plate release levers.
D. With the cross-shaft lever forward, rotate the lock nut nearest the firewall until it just contacts the swivel. This should hold the clutch pedal up completely against the pedal stop located in the car.
E. Back the lock nut off four turns.

F. With the lock nut at this point, tighten the other lock nut securely against the swivel.

5. Reconnect the pedal return spring.
6. Using finger pressure only, depress the clutch pedal while using a ruler as a gauge. There should be about ¾ inch—no less than ½ inch and no more than 1 inch—of free-travel. If it is not within this range, repeat Steps 2 through 5. *Caution: If after repeated attempts at adjustment you cannot bring free-travel within the specified range, it could indicate bent clutch linkage, a worn out disc, or other internal clutch problems. If this is the case, consult a qualified mechanic.*
7. Start the engine.
8. Place the transmission in neutral and set the parking brake.
9. Engage and disengage the clutch several times with the engine running.
10. Recheck the adjustment.
11. Road test the car and make a final check of the adjustment.

Hydraulic Linkage

For cars with hydraulic linkage, use the following procedure.

1. Place wheel chocks behind the rear wheels.
2. Jack up the front of the car and place a pair of safety jack stands in a secure position under the frame.
3. Locate the clutch pedal cross-shaft and lever, clutch throw-out fork, and clutch fork pushrod.
4. Apply penetrating oil to the adjustable linkage.
5. Loosen the lock nut with an open-end wrench and move the adjusting nut to shorten or lengthen the pushrod. To increase pedal free-travel, decrease the length of the pushrod. To decrease pedal free-travel, increase the length of the pushrod.
6. After making the adjustment, retighten the lock nut, taking care not to change the length of the pushrod.
7. Using finger pressure only, depress the clutch pedal while using a ruler as a gauge. There should be about ¾ inch—no less than ½ inch and no more than 1 inch—of free-travel. If it is not within this range, repeat Steps 5 through 7. *Caution: If after repeated attempts at adjustment, you cannot bring free-travel within the specified range, it could indicate bent clutch linkage, a worn out disc, or other internal clutch problems. If this is the case, consult a qualified mechanic.*
8. Lower the car, reversing Steps 1 and 2.
9. Start the engine.
10. With the transmission in neutral and the parking brake set, engage and disengage the clutch several times.
11. Recheck the adjustment.
12. Road test the car and make a final check of the adjustment.

Clutch Replacement

If your clutch is chattering, jerking, or slipping and adjustment of the clutch pedal doesn't help, it probably needs to be replaced. Clutch replacement is a major undertaking but it is within the abilities of a determined do-it-yourself mechanic.

On rear-wheel-drive cars, the basic procedure is to disconnect the driveshaft, support the engine, and remove the transmission and bellhousing. The pressure plate and clutch disc are then removed from the flywheel. If the clutch has been slipping because of oil contamination, a new clutch disc will be required. The old pressure plate can be reused, but a new throw-out bearing is recommended. The oil leak must be repaired before installing the new clutch, otherwise the same problem will return within a few hundred miles. Oil can leak from one of two places: the crankshaft rear main oil seal or the transmission/transaxle input shaft seal. If either is found to be leaking, it must be replaced. Resurfacing the flywheel and replacing the pilot bearing in the end of the crankshaft is also highly recommended at this time.

On front-wheel-drive cars, the job is more complex because of the layout of the drivetrain. To drop the transaxle, you first have to take off both front wheels, disconnect both driveshafts from the wheel hubs and remove the driveshafts. Then you can unbolt the

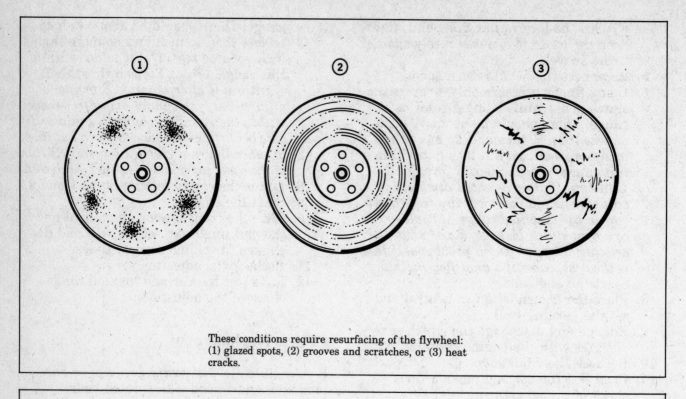

These conditions require resurfacing of the flywheel:
(1) glazed spots, (2) grooves and scratches, or (3) heat
cracks.

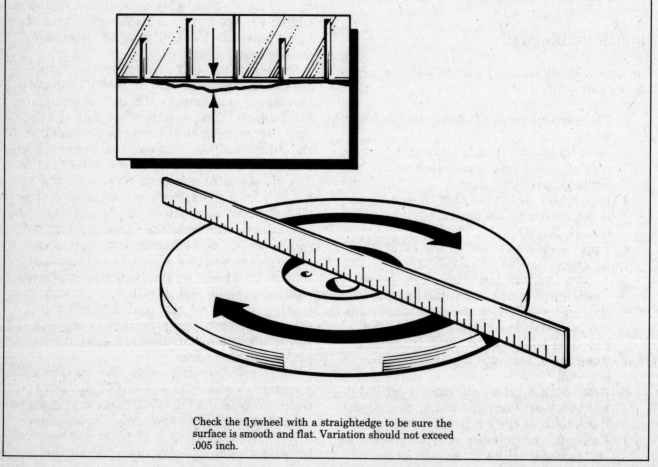

Check the flywheel with a straightedge to be sure the
surface is smooth and flat. Variation should not exceed
.005 inch.

transaxle from the engine and its mounts and drop the transaxle. On most front-wheel-drive cars, the engine must be supported from above with an engine hoist or support bar stretched between the fenders.

Because the removal and installation procedures vary greatly from vehicle to vehicle, we suggest you refer to a shop manual for specific instructions. However, we can give you some pointers on common installation errors to avoid.

● Always inspect the surface of the flywheel and the pressure plate (if it is to be reused) for nicks, scratches, wear grooves, or cracks. Minor imperfections shouldn't affect the operation of a new clutch but heavy grooves, glazed spots, or large scratches will. You should take the flywheel and/or pressure plate to an automotive machine shop to have them resurfaced. The cost usually isn't much and the results will greatly improve the operation and longevity of a replacement clutch. The one thing resurfacing can't fix is heavy cracking. If large cracks are detected in either the flywheel or pressure plate, the component should be replaced. Cracks weaken the metal and could cause it to literally explode at high rpm.

● When removing the flywheel and pressure plate, note the relative position of each component with a punch or chalk mark. Many engines are externally balanced, which means the relative position of the flywheel and sometimes even the pressure plate with respect to the crankshaft affects engine balance. If you neglect this little detail and put the flywheel back on in the wrong position, it could throw the engine out of balance and create an annoying and possibly damaging vibration. Don't forget to torque the flywheel bolts to the manufacturer's specs.

● Replacing the pilot bearing and throw-out bearing when installing a new clutch is highly recommended. Also check the torque on the flywheel bolts.

● Use a pilot tool to center the clutch disc before tightening down the pressure plate. This will make it much easier for the transmission input shaft to slip through during installation. The pressure plate should also be tightened down evenly using a cross-star pattern to avoid distorting or bending the cover.

● When installing the transmission in a

rear-wheel-drive car, don't allow it to hang unsupported once the input shaft is inside the clutch hub. Doing so will frequently bend the hub, causing a binding in the clutch that will interfere with smooth disengagement.

● After installing the transmission/transaxle back in place, check the fluid level and replace any that leaked out during removal. This step alone can often save you the cost of replacing the transmission/transaxle if it has lost much of its lubricant.

● On vehicles with hydraulic clutch linkage, now is a good time to flush and refill the system with fresh hydraulic fluid.

Manual Transmission

Tools and Materials

● Wheel Chocks
● Jack and Safety Jack Stands
● Open-End Wrenches
● Rags
● Lithium Grease
● Transmission Jack, Scissors Jack, or Floor Jack
● Wheel Puller

IN THE section on "Clutches," we explained how the powerful rotating force of the engine is transmitted through the clutch assembly to the input shaft of the transmission. This force, called torque, has the power to turn one or more shafts to accomplish useful work. In your car, this useful work is, of course, the application of engine power to turn the drive wheels. In this and remaining sections of this chapter, any reference to torque means the application of engine power through shafts and gears to turn a car's drive wheels in a forward or reverse rotation.

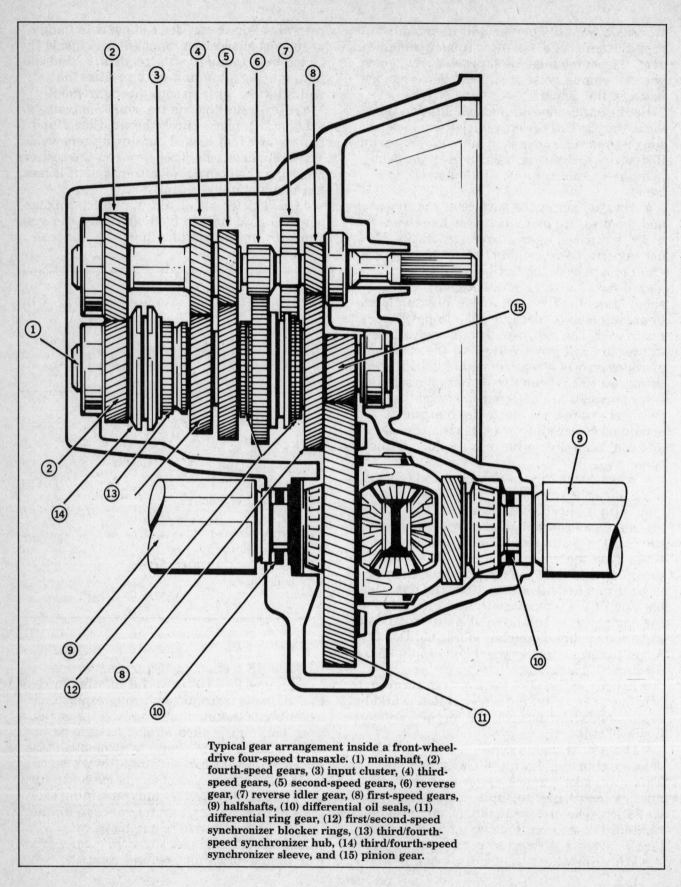

Typical gear arrangement inside a front-wheel-drive four-speed transaxle. (1) mainshaft, (2) fourth-speed gears, (3) input cluster, (4) third-speed gears, (5) second-speed gears, (6) reverse gear, (7) reverse idler gear, (8) first-speed gears, (9) halfshafts, (10) differential oil seals, (11) differential ring gear, (12) first/second-speed synchronizer blocker rings, (13) third/fourth-speed synchronizer hub, (14) third/fourth-speed synchronizer sleeve, and (15) pinion gear.

Despite the engineering marvel represented by your engine, it must have help to supply the necessary torque to meet complex variations in speed and constant changes in road and load conditions.

The car's engine is helped in one way by units or assemblies that are capable of multiplying engine torque. One such unit is the manual, or standard, transmission. By applying initial torque to a gear set or a combination of gears, the initial torque is multiplied. The driver is in control of this torque multiplication when gear ratios are activated by using the clutch and gear selector controls.

Most transmissions have at least three forward gear ratios and one reverse. Some sports or high-performance cars, as well as some with small engines, have four- or five-speed transmissions.

Transmissions are equipped with various devices to encourage longer life and quieter operation. One such device is the synchromesh, which allows all forward gears to be of constant mesh design to provide smooth gear selection without clashing or grinding.

These are the basic functions of gear selection.

NEUTRAL. The neutral gear position is the point at which the torque connection between the engaged clutch and the transmission is interrupted. This allows the engine to run with the clutch engaged and without moving the drive wheels.

LOW OR FIRST-SPEED GEAR. When low or first-speed gear is required, the engine will run at a high rpm while the car moves very slowly. The drive wheels turn at a slower speed but with increased power. The torque multiplication at this time is approximately 3 to 1. This ratio means that three engine revolutions are required for each revolution of the transmission output shaft.

INTERMEDIATE GEAR. When the operator selects an intermediate-gear position, torque multiplication is reduced to approximately 2 to 1.

HIGH GEAR. When the driver shifts to high gear, the speed of the output shaft of the transmission is the same as engine speed and there is no increase in torque. Therefore, the high-gear ratio is 1 to 1 and is called direct drive. On some cars, high gear is an "over-

drive" ratio, meaning it is slightly greater than 1 to 1. In this case, the output shaft turns faster than the engine. This reduces engine speed and improves fuel economy.

REVERSE GEAR. When the operator shifts to reverses gear, the output shaft of the transmission reverses its rotation, which causes the drive wheels to turn in reverse. The approximate reverse gear ratio is 3 to 1.

You should now see how the gears in the transmission may be used to allow the engine to turn at higher speeds than the output shafts and driveshafts and, at the same time, deliver more power. In this way, the vehicle may start smoothly and slowly without stalling the engine. Although transmissions vary in construction, most produce a gear ratio of approximately 3 to 1 for low gear and 1 to 1 for high gear.

The means of shifting manual transmissions are, for the most part, much the same. The shift pattern, however, is not always the same.

The manual transmission is very durable. If it is not mistreated, it should last as long as any other part of the drive mechanism.

Transmission Problems

The most common types of transmission problems are as follows.

● Noisy gears—May be a symptom of worn or damaged gears, worn shaft bushings, or low fluid level inside the transmission. If the fluid level is okay or if adding fluid to a low transmission doesn't quiet it down, the transmission probably needs to be rebuilt (a job for a professional) or replaced.

● Hard shifting—A clutch that fails to fully release or one that binds on the transmission input shaft can contribute to hard shifting, as can corroded, misadjusted, or bent shift linkage or cables. Hard shifting can be more of a problem on front-wheel-drive cars because most use a pair of cables to connect the shifter and transaxle. Corrosion can build up inside the cables, making them stick and bind. Any looseness or slop in the cables can also make shifting balky. The cure here is to first inspect the clutch linkage to make sure the clutch is properly adjusted, and then to check the shift cables or linkage for smooth operation by tem-

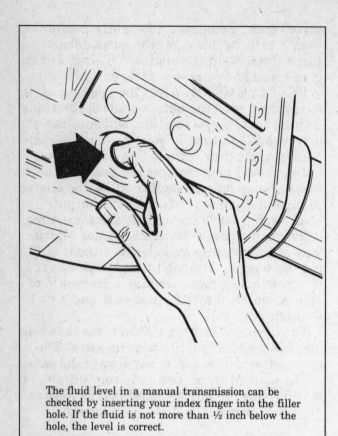

The fluid level in a manual transmission can be checked by inserting your index finger into the filler hole. If the fluid is not more than ½ inch below the hole, the level is correct.

porarily disconnecting the linkage or cables from the transmission or transaxle. Penetrating oil or graphite lubricant can sometimes restore the free operation of sticky cables, and white grease (lithium grease) works fine for lubricating mechanical linkages.

● Gears grind when shifting—If the condition only occurs when shifting a particular gear, the problem is likely the gear ring synchronizer inside the transmission. This calls for rebuilding or replacement of the transmission. If all the gears grind when shifting and/or if the transmission seems hard to shift, the most likely cause is that the clutch is binding or failing to release.

● Loss of a gear—If the transmission won't work in a particular gear, it could be a linkage problem. Check for a loose or misadjusted connection. Sometimes a small pin or grommet will work itself loose, preventing the shift linkage from shifting the transmission into the desired gear. But if the problem isn't the linkage, it indicates major internal damage in the transmission. Rebuilding or replacement

will be necessary to repair the damage.

● Transmission jumps out of gear—Sometimes this is due to a linkage adjustment problem, but it can also be caused by misalignment of the transmission and engine, worn gears or shaft bushings in the transmission, or worn or loose shift forks in the transmission. Try adjusting the linkage first before replacing the transmission or having it rebuilt.

Transmission Replacement—Rear-Wheel Drive

Although transmission rebuilding is something that requires professional skills and special tools, replacing a transmission yourself with one from a salvage yard is often the most economical means of fixing a bad transmission. This is heavy work, as a transmission usually weighs 80 to 120 pounds. Transmission jacks can be rented to make lowering and lifting the transmission a one-person job, but a floor jack can also be used.

The specifics of replacing a transmission can vary somewhat from car to car, but the basic procedure goes as follows.

1. Set the emergency brake and chock the rear wheels of the car.
2. Raise the car and support it on safety stands.
3. Disconnect the rear U-joint from the differential, and pull the driveshaft out of the transmission (it slides right out once the rear U-joint has been disconnected). On cars with a center carrier bearing, you'll have to unbolt the bearing from its support plate first.
4. Disconnect the speedometer cable, shift linkage, and any wires from the transmission.
5. Use a scissors jack, hydraulic jack, or floor jack to support the engine or bellhousing from underneath, then unbolt the transmission from its mount. Raise the engine and transmission slightly with the jack to take the weight of the transmission off its mount, then unbolt and remove the mount from the chassis.
6. Unbolt the transmission from the bellhousing.
7. Now for the hard part. Using either a transmission jack or a friend to help you

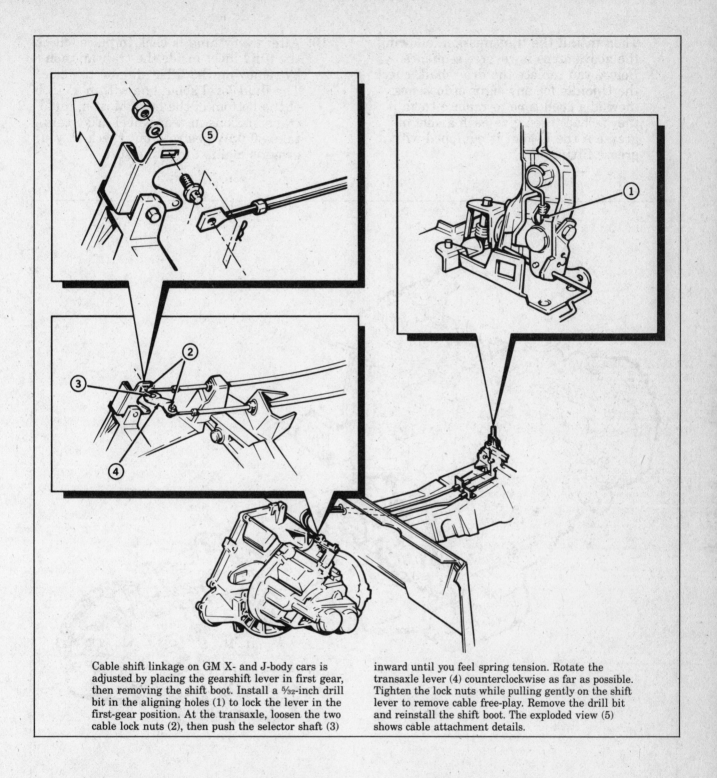

Cable shift linkage on GM X- and J-body cars is adjusted by placing the gearshift lever in first gear, then removing the shift boot. Install a 5/32-inch drill bit in the aligning holes (1) to lock the lever in the first-gear position. At the transaxle, loosen the two cable lock nuts (2), then push the selector shaft (3) inward until you feel spring tension. Rotate the transaxle lever (4) counterclockwise as far as possible. Tighten the lock nuts while pulling gently on the shift lever to remove cable free-play. Remove the drill bit and reinstall the shift boot. The exploded view (5) shows cable attachment details.

hold the transmission, carefully pull the transmission away from the bellhousing. Don't allow it to hang while the input shaft is still in the clutch hub, as doing so can bend the clutch hub. Lower the transmission and pull it out from under the car.

8. To install the replacement transmission, first make sure it matches the old transmission. Check to see that both are of equal length and that all the necessary bolt holes are in the same location.

Then install the transmission following the above steps in reverse sequence.

9. Before you replace the driveshaft, check the U-joints for any signs of looseness (now is a good time to replace them if they're bad) then give each a shot of grease if the U-joint is equipped with a grease fitting.

10. After everything is back in place, check the fluid level inside the transmission by removing the filler plug on the side. The fluid level should be within ½ inch of the bottom of the hole. Most manual transmissions in rear-wheel-drive cars take 80-90W gear oil, but check in your owner's manual to make sure.

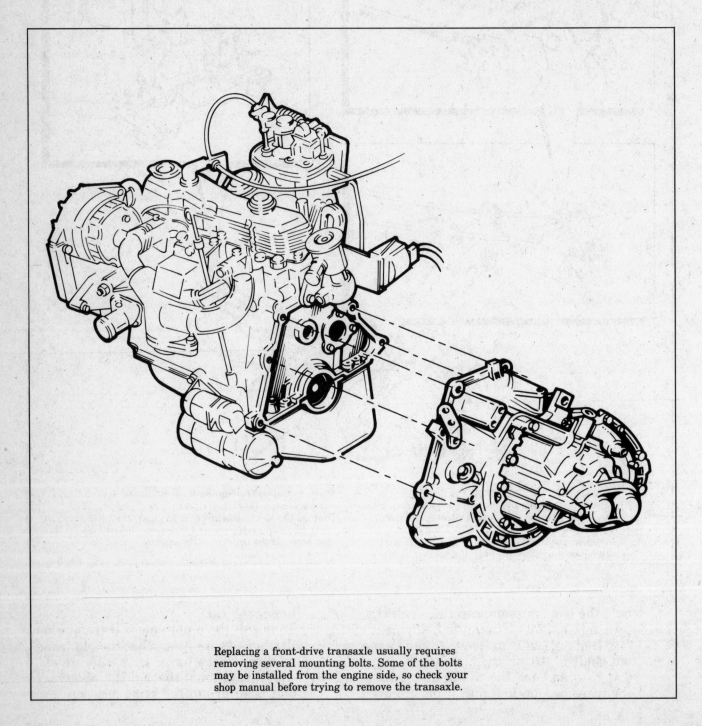

Replacing a front-drive transaxle usually requires removing several mounting bolts. Some of the bolts may be installed from the engine side, so check your shop manual before trying to remove the transaxle.

Transaxle Replacement—Front-Wheel Drive

This is a more difficult job than replacing a standard transmission on a rear-wheel-drive car, because it involves disassembling the front suspension. Again, the specifics will vary somewhat from car to car but the basics go as follows. (**Note:** See the section on "Front-Wheel-Drive Driveshaft Replacement" for more detail.)

1. Set the emergency brake and chock the rear wheels of the car. Then loosen the axle hub nuts on both front wheels, and all the lug nuts.
2. Raise the front of the car and support it on safety stands. Do not position the stands under the front suspension, transaxle, or engine cradle.
3. Remove both front wheels from the car.
4. Remove both front axle hub nuts from the car.
5. Separate the lower ball joint from the steering knuckle. On some cars a pinch bolt arrangement is used, while on others all you have to do is remove a nut on the ball joint stud. It may be necessary to use a fork or ball joint puller to separate the joint from the knuckle if prying fails to break it loose.
6. On some cars, it is also necessary to disconnect the front stabilizer bar to allow sufficient room to separate the ball joint and knuckle.
7. Separate the outer end of the halfshaft from the knuckle hub. To do this, a puller may be needed to force the stub shaft back through the wheel bearings in the hub.
8. Once the outer end of the halfshaft has been disconnected, support it with a wire or other device until the inner end of the halfshaft can be removed from the transaxle. On some cars, the inner CV-joints are not fastened (you do have to pry them, though, to get them out). Others must be unbolted. On early Chrysler front-wheel drives (through 1982) a circlip inside the transaxle must be removed before the halfshafts can be pulled out. This involves removing the

differential plate cover on the transaxle and reaching inside with needle-nose pliers to release the circlips. On some cars, the speedometer cable drive gear must also be removed. Do not pull on the halfshafts to get them out, as doing so can cause the inner CV-joint to separate.

9. After removing both halfshafts, unbolt the transaxle from its mounts. It may be necessary to support the engine prior to this step on some vehicles. An engine hoist works fine for this purpose, or a pair of 2×4 boards or metal bar stretched across the fenders and tied to the engine with a length of chain or steel cable can be used. The shift linkage or any wires should also be disconnected at this time. On some vehicles, such as General Motors front-wheel drives, the engine and transaxle sit on a cradle. Removing four bolts drops the cradle and the transaxle right along with it.
10. After rigging a support for the engine and disconnecting the transaxle from its mounts and the engine, slide the transaxle away from the engine and lower it from the chassis. On some vehicles, the cradle or chassis support must also be removed or lowered.
11. Before installing the replacement transaxle, make sure it is exactly the same as the one that came out of the car. All bolt holes, the starter location, etc., must be identical.
12. Install the transaxle following the above steps in reverse sequence.
13. Before you replace the halfshafts, inspect the condition of the CV-joint boots. Cracked or damaged boots should be replaced.
14. After everything is back together, check the fluid level inside the transaxle by removing the filler plug on the end of the transaxle. The fluid level should be within ½ inch of the bottom of the hole. Lubrication requirements vary greatly from vehicle to vehicle, some requiring 80-90W gear oil, 10W-40 engine oil, or Dexron or Type F automatic transmission fluid. Check in your owner's manual before adding any fluid.

Automatic Transmission

Tools and Materials

- Funnel
- Wheel Chocks
- Jack and Safety Jack Stands
- Socket Wrench and Short Extension
- ⅜-inch-Drive Ratchet Wrench
- Scraper
- Screwdriver
- Torque Wrench
- Lint-Free Cloth
- Transmission Fluid
- Drain Pan
- Solvent
- Transmission Filter and Gasket

A N AUTOMATIC transmission uses a hydraulic system and a torque converter to automatically transmit power from a car's engine to its drive wheels. The automatic transmission, unlike the purely mechanical manual, or standard, transmission, is driven by fluid power. The torque converter, a self-contained unit, replaces the clutch used with a manual transmission. The torque converter has the capability to multiply the torque developed by the engine, a feature not found in the conventional clutch. The torque converter couples and uncouples the force of the engine to the transmission and driveline. It does this by means of fluid or hydraulic pressure.

Because the automatic transmission reacts to accelerator pressure to increase or decrease the torque output of the engine, the need for the clutch pedal is eliminated. Once the transmission is placed in gear, the driver merely

has to increase the engine speed to transmit more power—through the operation of the converter—to the transmission. When the driver releases the accelerator pedal to slow the engine, the converter automatically will disconnect the power of the engine to the transmission.

With reasonable care, an automatic transmission will remain in sound condition for the useful life of a car. Because it is a hydraulically controlled unit, the maintenance required to keep the transmission in good working order is fairly simple. The fluid in the transmission is subject to contamination and must be changed at reasonable intervals.

Other maintenance chores include fluid level checks, the tightening of fittings that become loose due to normal vibration and road shock, and possibly a vacuum unit change due to diaphragm failure. The following procedures outline the steps for maintaining an automatic transmission.

Changing Fluid and Filter

Note: Transmission fluid should be at normal operating temperature to insure complete draining. This can be accomplished by driving the vehicle for 15 to 20 minutes after the engine has warmed up. To change the transmission fluid and filter, follow these steps.

1. Place wheel chocks behind the rear wheels and engage the parking brake.
2. Jack up the front of the car.
3. Place a pair of safety jack stands in a secure position under the frame.
4. Position a drain pan under the transmission and carefully loosen—*do not remove*—the transmission pan attaching bolts. You will need a socket wrench, a short extension, and ⅜-inch-drive ratchet wrench.

   Note: Some transmissions have drain bolts that make draining the fluid much the same as draining the engine oil. Simply remove the drain bolt with a wrench, allow the fluid to drain out, wipe the bolt and bolt hole clean, and refasten the bolt. Check a shop manual for your car to determine if your transmission has a drain bolt.

   Caution: *Be extremely careful while draining transmission fluid. Hot trans-*

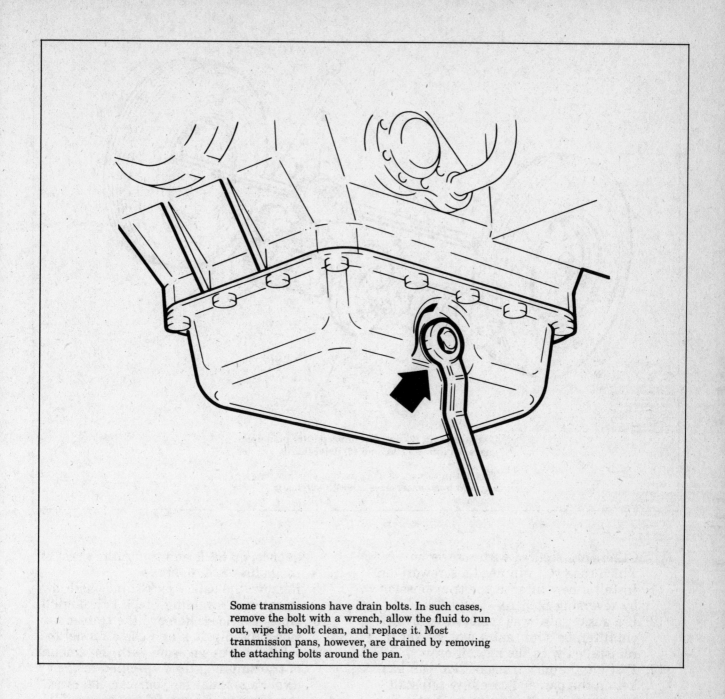

Some transmissions have drain bolts. In such cases, remove the bolt with a wrench, allow the fluid to run out, wipe the bolt clean, and replace it. Most transmission pans, however, are drained by removing the attaching bolts around the pan.

mission fluid can cause serious burns.

5. With one hand, hold up the transmission pan. With the other hand, carefully remove all of the transmission pan bolts except those holding the front of the pan to the transmission case.

6. Carefully lower the rear portion of the pan and allow the fluid to drain into the drain pan.

7. After draining, remove the remaining pan bolts and remove the pan.

8. Use a scraper to remove all old gasket material from the transmission pan and case.

9. Wash the pan with clean solvent such as kerosene or fuel oil, wipe it with a clean lint-free cloth, and allow it to air dry.

10. Remove the old filter. In some cases, a gasket between the filter and the transmission also will have to be removed. Some filters are secured with snap bails.

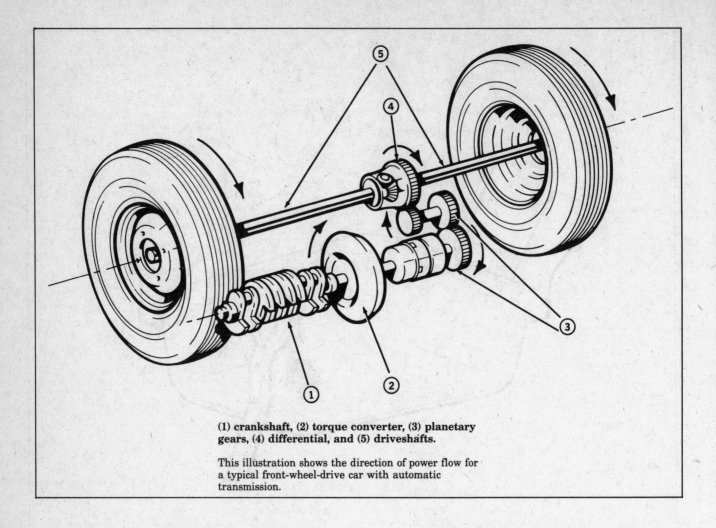

(1) crankshaft, (2) torque converter, (3) planetary gears, (4) differential, and (5) driveshafts.

This illustration shows the direction of power flow for a typical front-wheel-drive car with automatic transmission.

Others are secured with screws, in which case you will need a screwdriver.

11. Install a new filter in the transmission by reversing Step 10.

12. If a gasket also was removed with the old filter, be sure that a new gasket is reinstalled with the new filter.

13. Position the new transmission pan gasket on the pan and carefully reinstall the pan on the transmission. **Note:** The use of any type of gasket sealer is not recommended and should be avoided.

14. Using a torque wrench, tighten the transmission pan bolts to 12 to 15 foot-pounds. **Note:** To prevent damage to the transmission case and pan, always use a torque wrench and follow a tightening sequence. For example, start at a corner of the pan and tighten the bolt there. Then tighten every other bolt—1, 3, 5, etc. When you have completed this se-

quence, go back and tighten the rest of the bolts—2, 4, 6, etc.

15. Remove the safety jack stands and lower the car, reversing Steps 1 through 3.

16. Open the hood. Remove the transmission fluid dipstick and use a funnel to refill the transmission with the amount of transmission fluid specified in the owner's manual for your car. Reinsert the dipstick. Be careful not to overfill.

17. Start the engine.

18. With the engine idling and the brake applied, move the gear selector lever through all gear positions and return to park or neutral. **Note:** Refer to your owner's manual for the correct position of the selector lever for checking transmission fluid level.

19. With the engine still idling, immediately check the transmission fluid level. If necessary, add fluid to bring the level

up to the "Add One Pint" or "Low" mark on the transmission dipstick.

20. After the transmission fluid has reached normal operating temperature, recheck the fluid level. The level should now be between the "Add One Pint" or "Low" and the "Full" marks on the dipstick.

21. Road test the car. Check for leaks from the transmission pan and make a final fluid level check.

Automatic Transmission Problems

The most common types of automatic transmission problems are as follows.

● Fluid leaks—The two most likely spots where an automatic transmission will leak are the rear output shaft seal and the gasket around the pan on the bottom of the transmission. On front-wheel-drive automatic transaxles, the oil pan and both side driveshaft oil seals are the most likely leak points. A leaky pan gasket can be repaired by following the procedure just described for replacing the transmission fluid filter. To replace a leaky rear seal, the driveshaft must be removed. The old seal can then be pried out and a new one installed in its place.

● Slipping—Often due to a low fluid level, check the dipstick with the engine warm and idling. If low, add just enough fluid to bring the level up to the full mark. If the fluid level is okay, or adding fluid does not eliminate the slipping, you should take the car to a transmission specialist for further evaluation. In most cases, a rebuilt or new transmission will be required.

● Sluggish or uneven shifting—Sometimes due to a clogged or restricted transmission filter; other causes include vacuum leaks in the hose to the transmission and/or misadjusted linkage between the throttle and transmission. Unless the cause is obvious (loose hose, broken throttle to transmission linkage, dirty transmission fluid), your best advice is to take your car to a professional. If the problem is internal in nature, the transmission will have to be rebuilt or replaced.

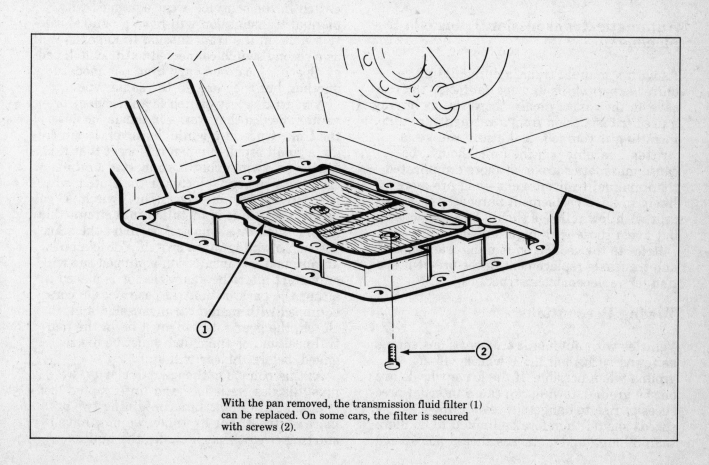

With the pan removed, the transmission fluid filter (1) can be replaced. On some cars, the filter is secured with screws (2).

• Transmission fails to downshift when the throttle is floored for passing—If the transmission fails to downshift into "passing gear", the most likely cause is faulty adjustment of the downshift cable or linkage from the throttle to the transmission. Refer to a shop manual for the correct adjustment procedure or seek the help of a professional.

• Jerky engagement or "searching" on late model transmissions with lockup torque converters—The computerized engine control system is programmed to lock up the torque converter when a predetermined speed is reached depending on throttle position and engine load. This can be a complex problem to diagnose but it usually boils down to one of several things: a faulty vehicle speed sensor, a misadjusted or faulty throttle position sensor, or a bad manifold absolute pressure (MAP) sensor. If the lockup solenoid in the transmission goes out, the transmission will never lock up and cruising fuel economy will likely be reduced a couple of miles per gallon. As with other automatic transmission problems, you should seek the help of a professional to solve the problem.

Automatic Transmission/Transaxle Replacement

As with a manual transaxle, rebuilding requires expert skills and special tools. You can save on the cost of repairs, however, by buying a used transmission from a salvage yard and installing it yourself. Make sure you get a written guarantee on the unit, though, because automatics are a lot more complicated than manual transmissions—and are more likely to have problems if purchased used. A unit with low mileage should be satisfactory, but avoid those with high mileage.

Refer to the section on manual transmission and transaxle replacement in the previous section for replacement instructions.

Towing Precautions

Vehicles with automatic transmissions should be towed with their drive wheels off the ground when possible. If the drive wheels are on the ground, towing can cause internal pressures to rise to dangerous levels. Towing speeds should therefore be limited to no more than 30 mph and distances should not exceed

10 miles. If a tow truck driver ignores these rules, he can damage your transmission.

Neutral Safety Switch

A NEUTRAL SAFETY SWITCH, which is standard equipment on all cars sold in the U.S., is designed to prevent accidental starting of a car when the transmission or the clutch is engaged.

In a car with automatic transmission and having the gear selector lever on the steering column, this switch is usually mounted at the base of the steering column in the passenger compartment. A car equipped with a console-mounted gearshift lever will have the safety switch in the console. A car equipped with manual transmission will have a neutral safety switch on the transmission linkage, as well as a second switch connected to the clutch pedal. Specific locations vary from one model to another, but they are all the same type.

A neutral safety switch is an accident prevention device that works in our favor most of the time. Once in a while, however, it can create a small problem when we forget that it is a "go/no go" switch that is connected to the transmission gear selector or the clutch, which is controlled by the driver. This switch is "go/no go" because it is installed in a circuit that is controlled by a "master" switch—the start position of the ignition switch. For example, an automatic-transmission-equipped car will only start after the gear selector is placed in either the park or neutral position. On cars equipped with manual transmission and clutch, the gear selector must be in the neutral position, or the clutch must be disengaged, before the car will start.

At this point, for the sake of clarity, we must discuss "satisfied" and "interrupted" controls that are in circuits containing two or more switches. For example, we now have a starting circuit that includes the ignition switch and the neutral safety switch. In the chapter on "The Ignition System," we discussed ignition breaker points in the primary circuit. We explained that when the points were closed, the circuit was completed (go or satisfied) and current would flow; when the breaker points were open, the circuit was broken and no current would flow.

The neutral safety switch is a contact-type switch that is installed in the starting circuit of your car. Current from the battery is supplied to the ignition switch. When the ignition switch is turned to the start position, current flows to the neutral safety switch. If the switch is closed, the circuit is satisfied (completed to go) and the starting circuit is energized, and the starter will crank the engine. If the switch is open, the circuit is interrupted (no go) at that point and current will not flow; the starter will not operate.

If your car does not start, and you have eliminated all other possible causes, the neutral safety switch "go" position is worn out and the switch should be replaced. The service manual for your car will describe the procedures to prove whether or not the switch is faulty and also how to replace it. Remember, this is a small but very important safety device. If there is any doubt regarding the proper repair procedure, you should seek help from a qualified mechanic.

Driveshafts, U-Joints, and CV-Joints

TO CONNECT the car's transmission to the differential, a driveshaft must be used in a conventional rear-wheel-drive car. (Front-wheel-drive cars have two driveshafts but no U-joints.) Most cars use a single-piece driveshaft with a universal joint (U-joint) at each

Tools and Materials

- Wheel Chocks
- Jack and Safety Jack Stands
- Hammer and Center Punch
- Box-End Wrench
- Large Screwdriver
- Drain Pan
- Masking Tape
- Solvent
- Chassis Grease and Grease Gun
- Wheel Puller

end. U-joints allow power to be transmitted through the various angles that the rear wheels create as they move up and down while traveling over a road. Working with the U-joints is a slip-yoke on the back of the transmission that allows the driveshaft to move in and out. This is necessary because the up and down movement of the rear wheels actually shortens or lengthens the distance between the rear axle housing and the transmission whenever the rear wheels go over a bump.

Ordinarily, nothing ever goes wrong with a driveshaft except for U-joint problems. Occasionally, someone may break a driveshaft or U-joint due to hard driving. Under normal driving conditions and many miles, however, U-joints do wear out. You can tell when they are worn and loose by a metallic knock when you put the car in gear. Improper differential gear lash also can make this kind of sound; that, however, is covered in the "Rear Axle Assembly" section in this chapter.

The driveshaft has a U-joint at each end and a sliding yoke, or slip-yoke, at the front. The shaft has to transmit only engine power, not take rear axle forces and twisting.

Some years ago, General Motors cars, including Chevrolet, used two-piece driveshafts with an X-type frame chassis. These cars had a support bearing in the center of the X-frame, with a short section of driveshaft in front and behind the center support bearing. Three U-joints were used. Servicing this type of drive-

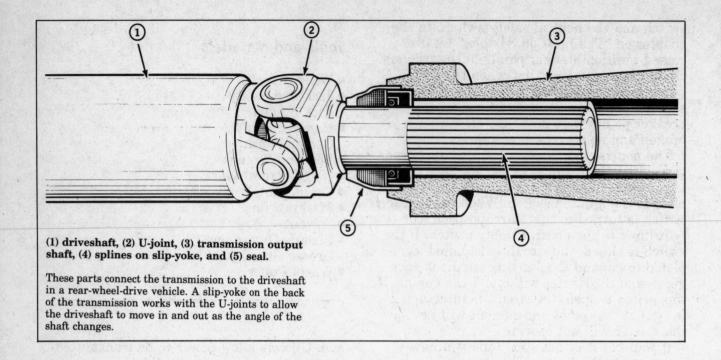

(1) driveshaft, (2) U-joint, (3) transmission output shaft, (4) splines on slip-yoke, and (5) seal.

These parts connect the transmission to the driveshaft in a rear-wheel-drive vehicle. A slip-yoke on the back of the transmission works with the U-joints to allow the driveshaft to move in and out as the angle of the shaft changes.

shaft on some older cars is a little more work, but it is essentially the same as the single-shaft, two U-joint assembly.

Before removing the driveshaft, you must mark all parts so they can be reassembled in the same position they originally held. U-joint yokes, for example, should be installed in the same rotational plane on the shaft that they occupied originally. This can be easily done by marking the shaft and the yoke before removal. Usually, there are factory index marks, but because of accumulated dirt, these marks are sometimes difficult to find. If you should forget to make the marks, or cannot find the factory marks, remember this rule of thumb. Most shafts have their U-joints indexed so yokes at the front and rear of the shaft are 90 degrees to each other. But the safest thing is to remember to mark the shaft and joint positions with a center punch before removal.

Your car probably has a plain open driveshaft with a U-joint at each end and a slip-yoke at the front, either ahead of or behind the front U-joint. When you study the U-joints on your driveshaft, you will see that there are two Y-shaped yokes with a crossarm piece that connects them. There will be bearing caps where the crossarm revolves in the yokes. The crosspiece is called the trunnion. Most cars use this type of joint. The rear U-joint on the driveshaft will be made so the bearing retainers on the rear yoke can be taken apart. The trunnion bearing caps will be secured to the yoke by simple U-bolts, perhaps some kind of small casting with cap screws, or just a strap of steel with clamps or bolts. This simplifies driveshaft removal. Just remove the rear yoke bearing retainer by removing the cap screw fasteners, and the driveshaft will be free to be lowered at the rear. Be careful that you do not drop the trunnion bearing caps. The caps should be taped to the trunnion after the driveshaft is removed. Note, too, that the rear half of the split rear or pinion yoke is attached directly to the rear axle input shaft. This is called the companion flange. You will not be doing anything with this in normal U-joint service.

After the rear U-joint is split and the back of the driveshaft is dropped, the shaft can be removed by pulling it back until the splines in the front slip-yoke come free of the transmission shaft. This distance might be as much as 4 inches.

Some driveshafts have constant-velocity joints. They resemble a double U-joint with a heavy, connecting double yoke. Driveshaft removal is the same as the single-joint type, except that there is a great deal more weight involved in handling.

Driveshaft Removal

When noise that you assume to be coming from the driveshaft prompts you to do a thorough inspection of its components, follow this procedure.

1. Park the car on a level surface.
2. Place wheel chocks in front of the front wheels.
3. Jack up the rear of the car and place a pair of safety jack stands in a secure position under the rear axle housing.
4. Place a drain pan below the transmission output shaft at the front end of the driveshaft to catch any fluid that might come out of the transmission when the slip-yoke is removed from the back of the transmission.
5. Using a hammer and center punch, mark both the driveshaft yoke and differential pinion flange yoke. This will insure correct reassembly and maintain a driveshaft index.
6. Using the proper-size box-end wrench, remove the four attaching bolts that hold the U-joint retaining straps to the pinion yoke. Then remove the hold-down straps. Some cars use two U-bolts to retain the U-joint to the flange. In this case, remove the four U-bolt nuts and lock washers, and then remove the U-bolts.
7. Use a large screwdriver to separate the driveshaft yoke and trunnion from the pinion yoke, and carefully lower the end of the driveshaft.
8. Use masking tape to secure the trunnion bearing caps to the trunnion. This will prevent the loss of bearing parts while the shaft is being removed for inspection.

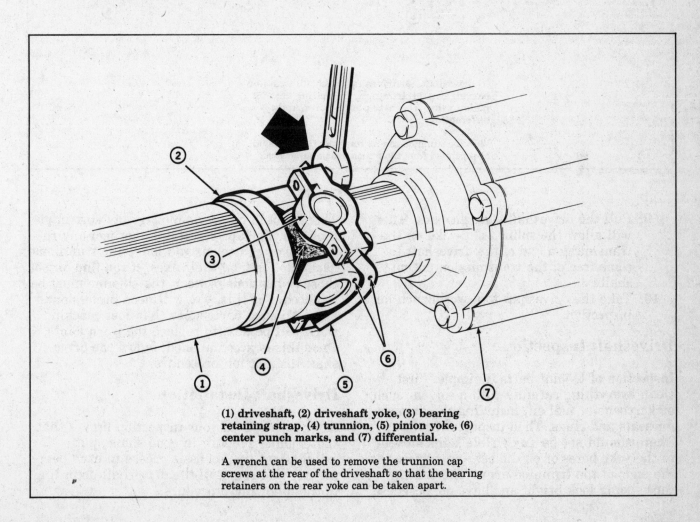

(1) driveshaft, (2) driveshaft yoke, (3) bearing retaining strap, (4) trunnion, (5) pinion yoke, (6) center punch marks, and (7) differential.

A wrench can be used to remove the trunnion cap screws at the rear of the driveshaft so that the bearing retainers on the rear yoke can be taken apart.

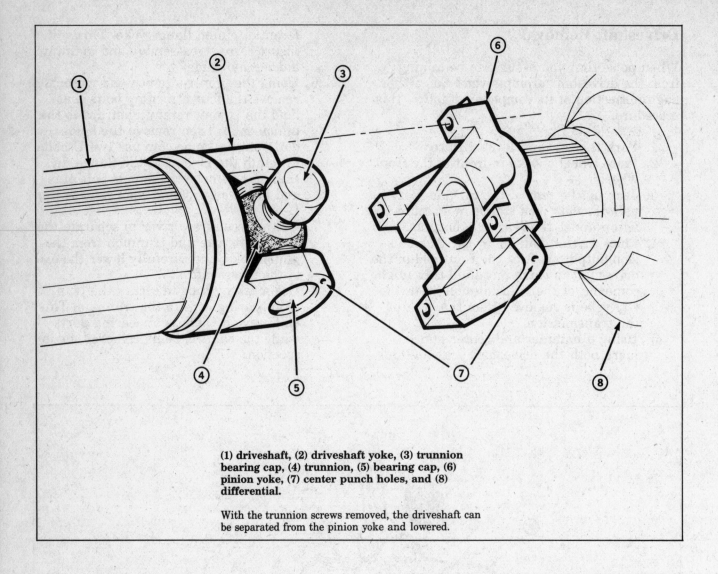

(1) driveshaft, (2) driveshaft yoke, (3) trunnion bearing cap, (4) trunnion, (5) bearing cap, (6) pinion yoke, (7) center punch holes, and (8) differential.

With the trunnion screws removed, the driveshaft can be separated from the pinion yoke and lowered.

9. Pull the driveshaft straight back. This will allow the splined slip-yoke on the transmission end of the driveshaft to come free of the transmission output shaft.

10. Take the driveshaft to a workbench for inspection.

Driveshaft Inspection

Inspection of U-joint parts is simple. First, clean everything carefuly with a solvent such as kerosene or fuel oil, including the grooves for seals and rings. Then inspect everything. There should not be any visible signs of wear in the yoke bores or on the bearing surfaces at the ends of the trunnion arms. The bearing caps should look bright and have no looseness.

There should be no visible signs of rust in either bearing cap. You should not feel any resistance or chatter as you move the trunnions back and forth on their axes. If you find any of these indications of wear, the U-joints must be replaced. For this, you will need professional help. An auto parts store that does machine work will be able to replace the worn joints. Once this is accomplished, follow the driveshaft installation procedure.

Driveshaft Installation

After repair, or if your inspection proves that the U-joints are still in good shape, put a small quantity of chassis grease in each bearing cap and reinstall the driveshaft according to the following procedure.

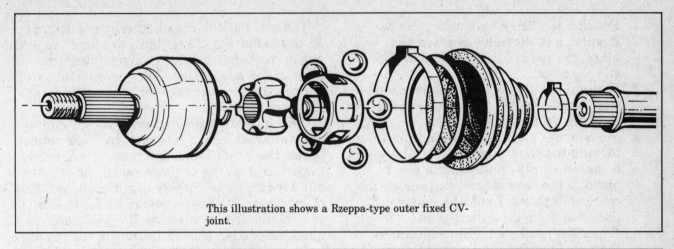

This illustration shows a Rzeppa-type outer fixed CV-joint.

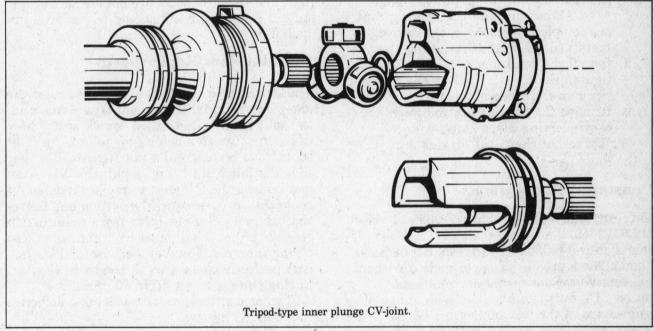

Tripod-type inner plunge CV-joint.

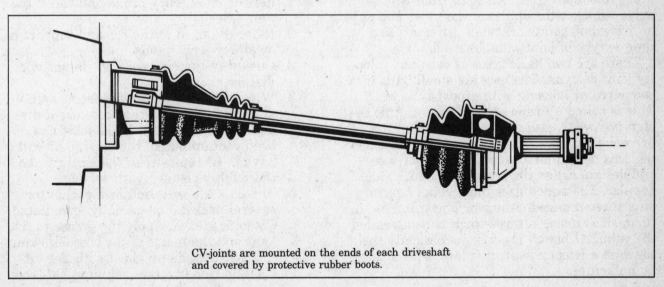

CV-joints are mounted on the ends of each driveshaft and covered by protective rubber boots.

1. Position the driveshaft under the car.
2. Assume a comfortable position that will allow you to hold the shaft up at the slip-yoke end.
3. Position the slip-yoke on the transmission output shaft splines. Turn the shaft until the splines are engaged.
4. Push forward on the shaft and continue inching the shaft forward until the yoke is seated firmly on the output shaft.
5. Move to the rear of the car. Line up the center punch marks on the pinion flange and the driveshaft yoke.
6. When the marks are aligned, connect the rear U-joint to the pinion flange yoke. Make sure that the bearing caps are completely seated in the flange.
7. Install the U-bolts or retaining straps.
8. Install the retaining nuts or bolts and tighten them securely with the proper-size box-end wrench.
9. Remove the jack stands and lower the car, reversing Steps 2 and 3 of "Driveshaft Removal" in this section.
10. Road test the car.

Constant Velocity Joints

On front-wheel-drive vehicles, constant velocity (CV) joints are used instead of ordinary U-joints on the halfshafts (driveshafts) because they allow a greater range of motion without causing vibrations or uneven rotational speeds. U-joints can handle a wide range of angles, too, if the two joints are indexed 90 degrees to one another. But with front-wheel-drive vehicles, the angles of the inner and outer driveshaft joints are often different, so a unique type of joint must be used.

There are two basic types of constant velocity joint designs. One uses six small balls in a semicircular housing with grooved tracks. This is called a Rzeppa type CV-joint. This design is always used on the outer end of the driveshafts next to the wheels. Many cars also use this design for the inner joint, but a second design, called the tripod CV-joint, is also popular. The tripod uses three roller bearings on a three-pronged trunnion. The trunnion, in turn, rides inside a three-track housing called the tulip. Although it performs basically the same as a Rzeppa joint, it is less expensive to manufacture.

The inner CV-joint, whether it is a Rzeppa or tripod design, is also built to plunge in and out to compensate for the up and down motions of the suspension. The inner or inboard joint is therefore sometimes referred to as the "plunge" joint.

CV-joints are protected against dirt and moisture and loss of lubricant by their rubber boots. The condition of the boots is extremely important because without them, the joint is quickly ruined by corrosion, abrasion, and loss of lubricant. Whenever you're under the car, you should always give the CV-joint boots a quick inspection to make sure the clamps are tight and that the boots are not cracked or damaged. Damaged boots should be replaced immediately.

CV-joint Boot Replacement

There are two kinds of replacement boots: the one-piece, original equipment style boots and the split boots (often called "quick boots" because they are so much easier to install). Split boots have become quite popular because they save the labor of having to pull the driveshaft and remove the CV-joint to replace a defective boot (this is covered in the section on "Driveshaft Removal"). Split boots use a seam that is glued together. Care must be taken when applying the glue, however, because if the seam isn't perfectly clean a weak bond will result. Curing time is about 40 to 60 minutes.

The basic procedure for replacing a defective boot goes as follows.

1. Set the emergency brake and chock the rear wheels.
2. Raise the front of the car and support it on safety jack stands.
3. Cut away the old boot and clamps and discard.
4. Wipe away the old grease from the CV-joint and check for the presence of dirt and grit in the joint. If the joint has been contaminated, the driveshaft will have to be removed so the joint can be thoroughly cleaned with solvent.
5. The boot kit will contain a packet (or several packets) of specially formulated CV-joint grease. Apply the grease to the joint and the inside of the boot following the instructions provided with the kit. Usually this involves applying half the

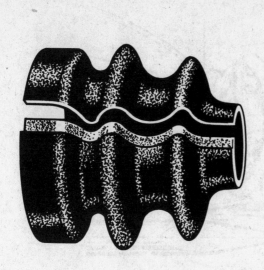

When installing a replacement CV-joint boot that uses a glue-together seam, make sure the seam is perfectly clean before applying the glue. Curing time is 40 to 60 minutes.

grease to the joint and filling the boot with the rest. Ordinary chassis grease should not be used because it may lack the high-temperature characteristics needed for the CV-joints.

6. Put the boot around the joint and glue the seam together. Fasten the support straps around the boot to hold it together while the glue dries.

7. Make sure the boot is positioned properly around the joint, then install and tighten the clamps. **Note:** Special tools may be required for this step. Consult a shop manual for your car.

8. Do not move the vehicle for an hour. Once the glue has cured, the support straps that held it together can be cut off.

CV-joint Diagnosis

A defective outer joint will usually produce a popping or clicking noise that can be heard while the car is moving. A clunk during acceleration, deceleration, or when putting an automatic transaxle into gear is another symptom of a worn inner or outer CV-joint. At high speeds, a shudder or vibration could also indicate joint trouble.

Clunks, shuddering, vibration, and sometimes rough shifting can also be caused by loose or worn engine/transaxle mounts on front-wheel-drive cars. Before condemning the CV-joints, therefore, be sure you check all the mounts.

The joints can be checked for looseness by raising the front wheels off the ground and rocking the wheels back and forth with the transmission in gear. If you can see or feel any looseness in the driveshaft, it means there is too much play in the joints and the joints should be replaced. Removing a boot clamp and sliding back the boot to watch the joint while doing this check is another good way to spot loose joints.

Dirt or water contaminated grease in the joint will quickly destroy the machined surfaces of the balls or trunnions and the tracks in which they ride. If a boot has been damaged and either dirt or water has gotten inside, the joint can be salvaged if it hasn't already been destroyed by removing the driveshaft and thoroughly cleaning the joint in solvent. The joint should not be disassembled because it is a precision assembly and intermixing balls

Loosen the hub nut with the vehicle on the floor and brakes applied.

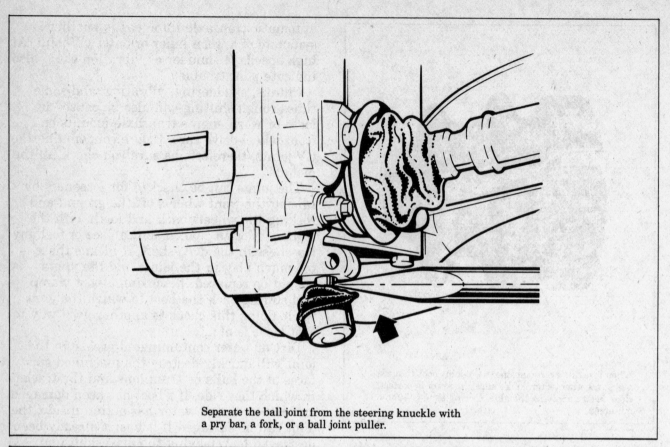

Separate the ball joint from the steering knuckle with
a pry bar, a fork, or a ball joint puller.

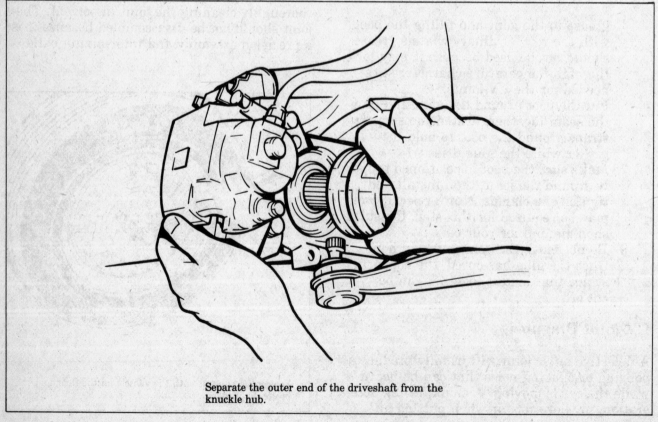

Separate the outer end of the driveshaft from the
knuckle hub.

from a Rzeppa joint with roller bearings from a tripod joint can cause binding and galling.

Front-Wheel-Drive Driveshaft Replacement

To replace both CV-joints on a driveshaft, the entire shaft assembly must be removed from the car. But if only the inner or outer CV-joint is defective, you can sometimes disconnect only that end of the shaft and leave the other in place. However, it's usually easier to pull the entire shaft and to replace the bad joint on a bench than to do it lying on your back under the car.

To remove a driveshaft (or halfshaft) from a front-wheel-drive vehicle, follow these steps.

1. With the wheels still on the ground, set the emergency brake and loosen the hub nut on the front wheel. Then loosen the lug nuts.
2. Raise the car and support it on safety stands.
3. Remove the front wheel and hub nut. **Note:** On some front-wheel-drive cars, the vehicle manufacturer recommends using a hub nut whenever the old nut is removed. The reason for doing this is because the nut distorts and loses its ability to hold torque. In plain English that means the nut might work itself loose.
4. Disconnect and separate the lower ball joint from the steering knuckle. The pinch bolt or nut on the ball joint stud must be removed to do this. If the ball joint can't be pried loose from the knuckle, a fork or ball joint puller will be necessary.
5. On some cars, it is also necessary to disconnect the front stabilizer bar from the lower control arm, and/or the tie-rod end from the steering knuckle, to allow sufficient room to push the knuckle out so the driveshaft can be pushed back through it.

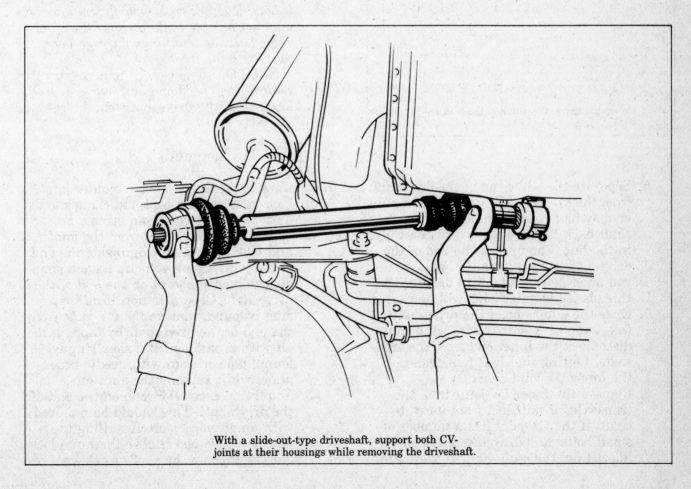

With a slide-out-type driveshaft, support both CV-joints at their housings while removing the driveshaft.

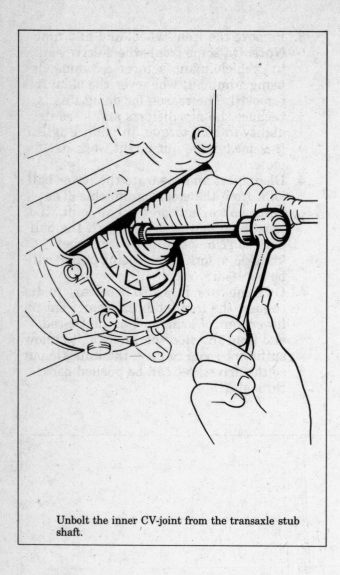

Unbolt the inner CV-joint from the transaxle stub shaft.

no bolts, it can usually be extracted by carefully prying between the joint housing and the transaxle. **Note:** On early Chrysler front-wheel drives (through 1982), a circlip inside the transaxle differential must first be removed before the inner joints will pull out. To do this, remove the differential cover and reach into the spider gears with a pair of needle-nose pliers. Release the circlip and pull the shaft out.

Caution: Do not pull on the driveshaft itself. Use the inner CV-joint housing instead, or pry between it and the transaxle. If you pull on the shaft to free the inner CV-joint, you'll probably only succeed in pulling the joint apart. The inner joint is a plunging joint, so it is free to move in and out. Yanking on it can pull it beyond its limits, causing it to fall apart. If you're going to replace the inner joint, this really doesn't make much difference. But if you're not, you'll have to remove the boot and hope you get it back together right (which you may or may not be able to do because the exact same balls or trunnions must go back into the same tracks).

Note: On some cars, it is necessary to remove the speedometer drive gear before one of the driveshafts can be removed.

CV-joint Replacement

Here's how to replace a defective outer joint.

1. Cut away the old boot and clamps and discard. Never reuse old boots.
2. Wipe the grease away from the joint and look for a snap ring inside the end of the joint. Some vehicles have a snap ring to hold the joint on the end of the driveshaft. Others do not. If no snap ring is found, remove the CV-joint from the end of the driveshaft by tapping it off with a hammer. If a snap ring is found, hold it open with needle-nose pliers while tapping the joint off.
3. You'll find a small circlip on the end of the driveshaft. This should be replaced with a new one before installing the new joint. Do not remove the large lock ring further up the shaft, as this serves

6. Separate the outer end of the driveshaft from the knuckle hub. To do this, a puller may be necessary to force the stub shaft back through the wheel bearings in the hub. Tapping on the end of the driveshaft with a hammer helps, but you must be careful not to damage the threads if the outer joint will be reused.
7. Once the outer end of the driveshaft is free, support it with a wire while you disconnect the inner end from the transaxle. Letting the shaft hang can pull the inner CV-joint apart.
8. Remove the inner CV-joint from the transaxle, or unbolt it from its stub shaft. If the CV-joint has a number of small bolts, it is disconnected by unbolting it from the stub shaft. If there are

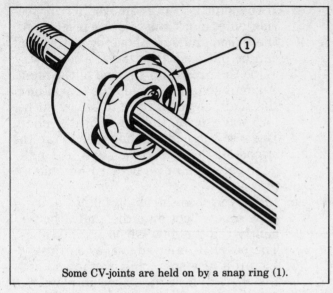

Some CV-joints are held on by a snap ring (1).

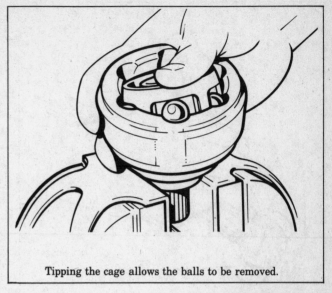

Tipping the cage allows the balls to be removed.

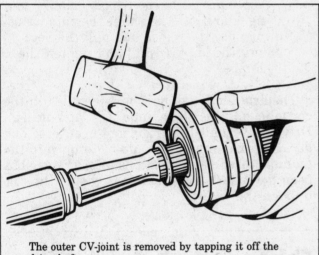

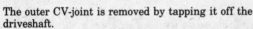

The outer CV-joint is removed by tapping it off the driveshaft.

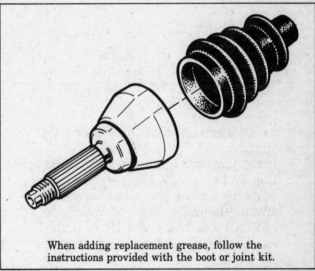

When adding replacement grease, follow the instructions provided with the boot or joint kit.

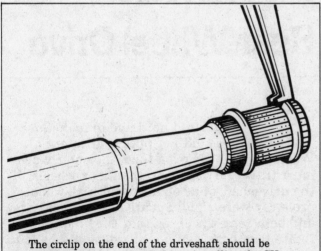

The circlip on the end of the driveshaft should be replaced with a new one before reinstalling the CV-joint.

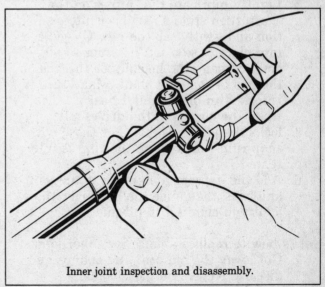

Inner joint inspection and disassembly.

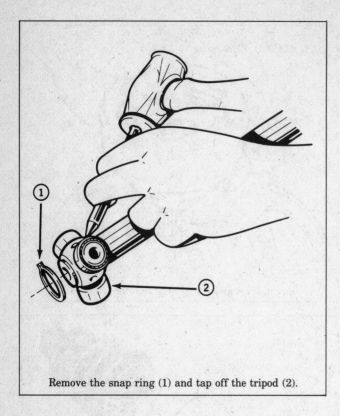

Remove the snap ring (1) and tap off the tripod (2).

as a stop to position the joint on the shaft.

4. If the joint is being removed for inspection and cleaning, you can check the balls by tipping the inner cage that positions the balls. Remove and inspect one ball and track at a time, replacing each ball before proceeding on to the next one.

5. Lightly lubricate the splines on the shaft, then slide a new boot into position and gently tap the new CV-joint into place. Use a soft hammer so you don't damage the housing or threads on the end of the joint shaft. Make sure it is locked in place. You'll hear a "click" when the circlip on the driveshaft locks the joint in place. For those with snap rings, make sure the ring is fully seated.

6. Add the appropriate grease to the joint and boot, then slide the boot over the joint and clamp it in place.

Here's how to replace a defective inner joint.
1. Cut away the old boot and clamps and discard. Never reuse old boots.

2. If the joint is being removed for inspection only, mark the relative position of the tripod and outer housing so the joint can be put back together the same way.
3. Wipe the grease off the end of the shaft. A small snap ring holds the tripod on the shaft, so you'll have to remove it before you can tap the tripod off the shaft.
4. Use a soft punch and hammer to tap the tripod off the end of the shaft. A small gear puller can also be used for this purpose.
5. Lightly grease the shaft splines and slide a new boot onto the shaft, then gently tap the new tripod into place. The beveled inner edge goes on first.
6. Install a new snap ring on the end of the shaft to lock the tripod in place.
7. Apply grease to the tripod, tulip housing, and boot. Then slide the outer housing onto the tripod and pull the boot over the joint. Install and tighten the clamps.

The driveshaft can now be reinstalled in the car following the steps under "Front-Wheel-Drive Driveshaft Replacement" in reverse order. The axle hub nut should be torqued to the manufacturer's specifications after the car has been lowered to the ground, as should the lug nuts on the wheels.

Differentials: Rear-Wheel Drive

IF YOUR car did not have to make any turns, it would not need a differential. When your car makes a turn, the outer wheels must travel farther than the inner wheels. If the driveshaft of a conventional rear-wheel-drive car were rigidly geared to a single axle and both rear wheels so that they had to rotate together, then one wheel would have to skid when the car was making a turn. To overcome this problem, the differential, a cluster of gears, is installed between the two rear axle shafts. It allows the rear wheels to rotate at different speeds during turns.

In the rear axle assembly, two small gears known as differential or side gears are splined to the inner ends of the axles. These two gears face each other and mesh with two smaller bevel gears called "spider" gears to form a square. The spider gears are mounted on a shaft that is mounted in the differential case.

Tools and Materials

- Wheel Chocks
- Jack and Safety Jack Stands
- ⅜- or ½-inch-Drive Ratchet or Adjustable Open-End Wrench

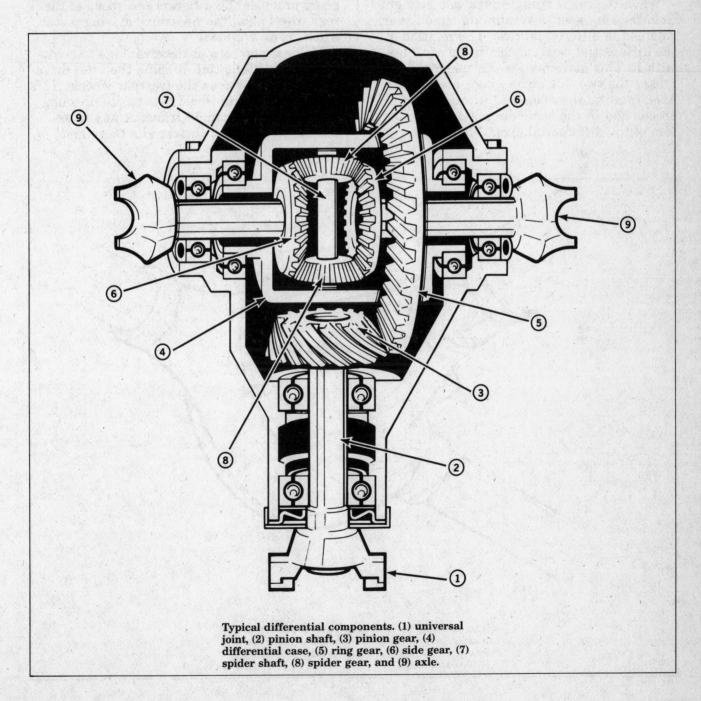

Typical differential components. (1) universal joint, (2) pinion shaft, (3) pinion gear, (4) differential case, (5) ring gear, (6) side gear, (7) spider shaft, (8) spider gear, and (9) axle.

This case surrounds the spider and side gears and keeps these four gears in constant mesh. A large gear, called the ring gear is attached to the outside of this case, which is supported in the differential housing by two bearings. These bearings permit the differential case to rotate freely inside its housing. The ring gear and differential case are driven by a pinion gear, which is connected by a universal joint to the driveshaft.

When the car is being driven in a straight line, the ring gear, driven by its pinion gear, rotates the differential case. The rotation of the differential case carries the spider shaft with it. This movement of the spider shaft makes the two side gears rotate about their axis, rotating the axles and wheels at equal speeds and in the same direction as the rotation of the differential case. When the car is being driven in a straight line, the spider gears act only as a non-rotating connection between the two rear axles.

When a car turns a corner, the outside rear wheel rotates faster than the inside one. The side gears rotate at different speeds. The spider gears no longer act as a solid connection between the two axle shafts. They start to "walk" around the slower axle side gear and rotate on their own axis. The action of the gears provides the difference in speed of the rear wheels and the necessary driving power when turns are made.

There is one serious disadvantage to a conventional differential. It splits the total drive shaft torque between the two rear wheels. This means that if one wheel gets on ice or mud, the other wheel cannot transmit any more torque. As a result, the car sits there and

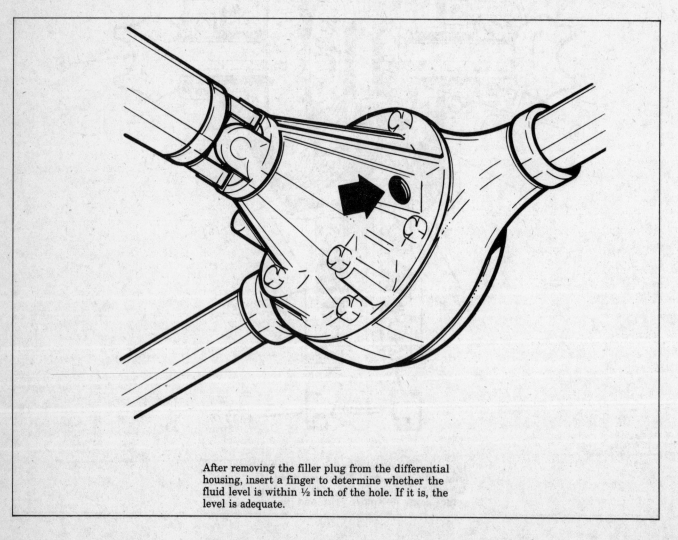

After removing the filler plug from the differential housing, insert a finger to determine whether the fluid level is within ½ inch of the hole. If it is, the level is adequate.

spins one wheel while the other is doing nothing, even though that wheel may be on a dry surface.

This problem has been somewhat overcome by certain engineering devices that have been added to the basic, hardworking differential. These include the "limited-slip," "Positraction," and "Equa-Lok" axles. These devices have special clutches that are installed between the side gears and differential case to lock up the assembly when one wheel starts to spin. Some clutches are applied by springs; others have cams that increase clutch pressure as axle torque increases. Either way, these devices are an asset when the car is being driven on ice or slick and soft terrain.

No matter what type of differential your car has, you can be sure of one important fact. It is the most durable and trouble-free assembly in your car. Other than an occasional lubricant check, the differential needs no attention from you. The lubricant check must be performed under the car. You can do it by following this procedure.

1. Park the car on a level surface.
2. Block the front wheels with wheel chocks.
3. Jack the car just high enough so that a pair of safety jack stands can be positioned under the rear axle housings.
4. Locate the filler plug. It will probably be on the driveshaft side of the differential housing and about 3 inches above the bottom.
5. Using the proper tool, remove the filler plug. If lubricant starts to dribble out, replace the plug immediately. The lubricant level is all right. **Note:** You will need one of three tools to remove the filler plug: a ⅜-inch-drive ratchet, a ½-inch-drive ratchet, or an adjustable open-end wrench.
6. If there is no evidence of dribbling fluid, insert your index finger into the filler hole.
7. If the lubricant level is within ½ inch of the filler hole, the level is sufficient. If, however, the level is lower than ½ inch, add the proper lubricant listed in your owner's manual.
8. Replace the filler plug.
9. Remove the jack stands and lower the car, reversing Steps 1 through 3.

Rear Axle Assembly

Tools and Materials

- Wheel Chocks
- Screwdriver
- Lug Wrench
- Jack and Safety Jack Stands
- Slide Hammer Axle Puller
- Ratchet Wrench, Sockets, and Extension
- Outer Grease Seal
- Chassis Grease

THE SMOOTH way in which a car moves through various road and load conditions depends largely on dependable, longlasting bearings and axles. Due to wear and sometimes loads that exceed design capability, the wheel bearings and axles cause problems. In this section, we discuss some of the ways bearing and axle troubles can be diagnosed and corrected.

Axles may be divided into two types: the dead axle, which is stationary while the wheel rotates, and the live axle in which both the axle shaft and the wheel rotate as a unit. The front wheels of most automobiles are mounted on dead axles, while the rear wheels are mounted on live axles. However, the reverse is true for cars with front-wheel drive. There are three types of live axles: semi-floating, three-quarter floating, and full-floating. Each is identified by the manner in which the outer end of the axle is supported in the axle housing. The inner ends of all axles are attached to the differential side gears by means of straight splines.

The semi-floating axle is the type used in conventional rear-wheel-drive cars. The outer or wheel end of the axle is supported in an axle housing by a single bearing mounted near the outer end of the axle. With this type of axle, the axle shaft not only transmits the driving torque, but also resists the bending movements caused by the forward motion of the car and the side thrusts imposed when the vehicle makes a turn. It also must carry its share of the weight of the vehicle. As a result, great stress is set up in the axle shaft of the semi-floating rear axle assembly.

Most rear axle trouble shows up in the form of some unusual noise from the axle, usually either gear noise in the differential or bearing noise in the outer ends of the axle housing.

Gear noise is a rather high-pitched whine that tends to get louder and quieter as road speed changes. The noise is more pronounced at one speed than at others. It also might disappear at some speeds. Gear noise is sometimes very difficult to locate.

Bearing noise is entirely different. It has a lower-pitched howl or growl that remains quite steady and tends to be louder when the car is accelerating under load than when coasting. Most often, the trouble will be in the wheel bearing at the outer end of an axle. Bearing noise can usually be pinpointed by driving the car around in a safe area such as a vacant parking lot and suddenly swerving to one side, then the other. These maneuvers throw additional side loads on the wheel bearings and the howl should get louder. Or better yet, have someone ride in the rear seat to listen on both sides for the noise while you drive.

There also is a possibility that the bad bearing could be one of the differential side bearings or the pinion bearing in the nose of the axle's center section. However, bearing trouble in the differential is much less likely than in the wheel bearings.

There are other possible axle troubles that are easy to determine. A broken axle shaft is one: the car will not move. A bad grease seal is another: there will be annoying oil spots everywhere you park the car. The grease seals are located at the wheel bearings on the outer ends of the axles. The wheel bearing seals are subjected to many stress forces under driving loads. Rear axle trouble will not be hidden for very long. It will get progressively worse and easier to locate.

With a few special tools, you can safely do some rear axle work. The simplest job is to pull an axle shaft and wheel bearing. To replace a broken shaft, however, requires some patience and expertise. But you can pull the shafts, bearings, and seals on most cars with a slide hammer axle puller and ordinary hand tools.

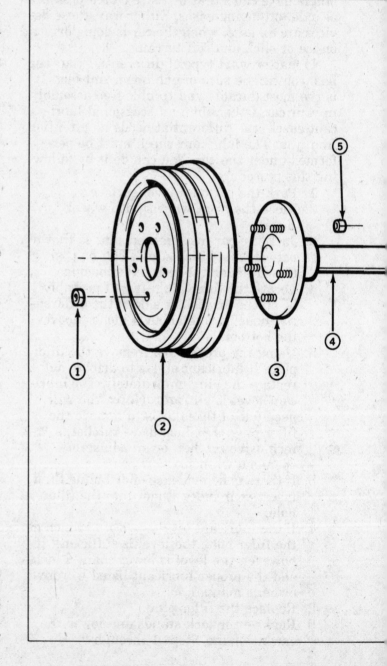

Rear Axle Removal

If you have isolated the noise or other fault and have determined that the rear axle must be removed, follow this procedure.

1. Park the car on a level surface.
2. Block the front wheels with wheel chocks to prevent the car from rolling.
3. Use a screwdriver or the pointed end of the jack handle to remove the wheel cover. Loosen the lug nuts of the wheel on the side of the axle you will be working on with a lug wrench.
4. Jack up the rear end of the car and support it under the rear axle housing with a pair of safety jack stands.
5. Remove the wheel lug nuts and the wheel.
6. Remove the brake drum. If resistance is

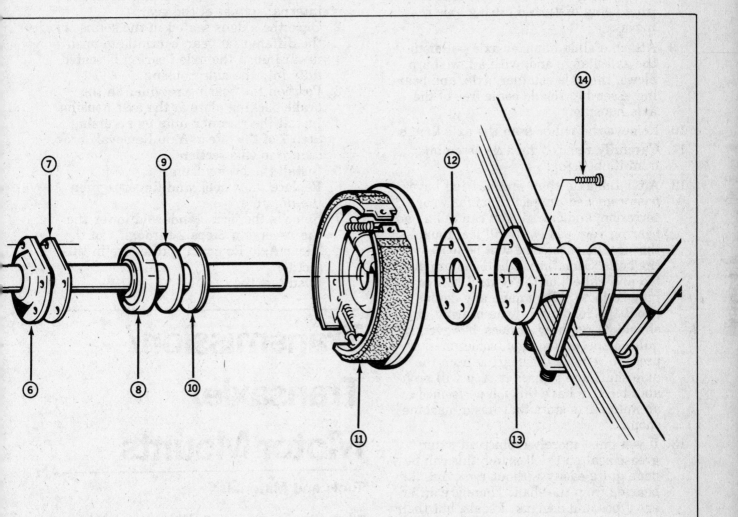

Rear axle components. (1) lug nut, (2) brake drum, (3) axle flange, (4) axle shaft, (5) nut, (6) outer retainer, (7) gasket, (8) bearing, (9) bearing retainer, (10) oil seal, (11) drum brake assembly, (12) gasket, (13) axle housing, and (14) mounting bolt.

encountered as you try to remove the drum, rotate the drum while pulling.

7. Using a ratchet, socket, and extension, remove the four or five axle retainer-to-brake-backing-plate nuts from the bearing retainer. An access hole or opening is provided in the axle flange for this purpose.

8. Separate the bearing retainer from the brake backing plate. This will prevent the backing plate and brake assembly from being disturbed during axle removal.

9. Attach a slide hammer axle puller to the axle flange and, with a few sharp blows, the axle retainer, axle, and bearing assembly should come free of the axle housing.

10. Remove the puller from the axle flange.

11. Carefully remove the axle assembly from its housing.

12. After the axle shaft and bearing have been removed, inspect them for wear, corrosion, and cracks. You can tell a bad bearing very easily. It will feel rough—that is, the outer race will be loose on the balls. Sometimes, the balls are pitted and galled, or the central ball cage may be loose. If you have any doubts about the condition of the bearing, it should be replaced. It does, however, require a special tool and, sometimes, a press to remove the bearing from the axle shaft and replace it. You will probably have to have this job performed at an auto parts store that has a machine shop.

13. If you must merely replace an outer grease seal on the bearing, this can be done quite easily without removing the bearing from the shaft. There are different types and designs of seals, but their function is the same. Usually, seals can be pried off with a screwdriver or any sharp pointed tool. Most can be installed without special tools. **Note:** Use reasonable care and always install the seal with the open edge or flange facing the lubricant.

14. Clean and lightly lubricate the axle splines with chassis grease.

Rear Axle Installation

When you are ready to replace the axle shaft, follow this procedure.

1. Carefully insert and rotate the axle shaft assembly into the axle housing until you feel the axle splines striking the differential side gear. Continue to carefully rotate and push the axle inward so that the axle splines engage the internal splines of the gear.

2. Once the axle is seated in the splines of the differential gear, continue to push inward until the axle bearing is seated fully into the axle housing.

3. Position the bearing retainer on the brake backing plate at the axle housing.

4. Install the retainer nuts by reversing Step 7 of the "Rear Axle Removal" procedure in this section.

5. Install the brake drum.

6. Replace the wheel, and finger-tighten the lug nuts.

7. Remove the jack stands and lower the car, reversing Steps 2 through 4 of the "Rear Axle Removal" procedure in this section.

8. Road test the car.

Transmission/ Transaxle/ Motor Mounts

Tools and Materials

- Pry Bar
- Hand Wrenches
- Replacement Mount
- Scissors or Floor Jack

THE ENGINE and transmission or transaxle are supported and insulated by metal and rubber mounts. The mounts hold the engine and transmission or transaxle in place, while allowing a certain amount of flex to soak up engine vibrations and to prevent those vibrations from being transmitted to the chassis.

A rear-wheel-drive in-line engine will usually have two motor mounts (one on each side of the engine) and one under the tail of the transmission. With transverse-mounted engines in front-wheel-drive cars, as many as four engine/transaxle mounts may be used to support the powertrain, with an additional "torque strap" or upper mount to limit torsional vibrations or twisting of the engine as it accelerates and decelerates.

When a mount fails, one of several things can happen. There can be a noticeable clunk or shudder when an automatic transmission is put in gear or when starting out from a stop. There can be an increase in engine noise inside the vehicle or vibration in the floor, steering wheel, or gearshift. There can be clunking and rattling as exhaust pipes come into contact with the frame or other chassis components. There can also be an accompanying exhaust system failure as the increased flexing and motion of the powertrain causes exhaust pipes, pipe connections, or gaskets to fail. Any of these symptoms could indicate a broken or collapsed mount.

On rear-wheel-drive vehicles, the mount that fails most often is the motor mount on the driver's side for engines that rotate clockwise, and the one on the passenger's side for those that rotate counterclockwise. The reason for this is because the engine's torque tends to compress one mount while stretching the other. The one that is continually stretched is the one that eventually pulls apart and allows the engine to flex whenever it's put into gear or when accelerating from a dead stop.

On front-wheel-drive vehicles, the upper mount or "torque strap" is the one most prone to failure. This mount is alternately compressed and stretched every time the engine accelerates and decelerates. Eventually, the rubber grommets wear out. The process is accelerated by high engine compartment temperatures and oil contamination. Replacement mounts that resemble a small shock absorber are available in auto parts stores and are a great improvement over the original equipment design. Called a torque strut, this type of product is also available for engines not originally equipped with an upper mount. Adding one can greatly smooth out engine vibrations while prolonging the life of the exhaust system. The head pipe on front-wheel-drive cars tends to be rather short-lived because of all the back and forth rocking the engine does during normal operation. The motion fatigues the metal and eventually causes it to crack.

Mount Replacement

To replace a mount, follow these steps.

1. Set the emergency brake and chock the rear wheels. **Note:** This step is not necessary when replacing the upper torque strap on front-wheel-drive vehicles.
2. Raise the front of the car and support it on safety stands.
3. Position a scissors or floor jack under the engine, transmission, or transaxle as required to take the weight off the mount that's being replaced.
4. Carefully raise the jack just enough to relieve pressure on the mount, then unbolt the mount and remove it.
5. Put the new mount into place, install the bolts, and lower the jack.

THE STEERING AND SUSPENSION SYSTEMS

THE DEVELOPMENT of the modern automobile embodies many engineering refinements. When the first automobile rolled out onto the road, it was little more than a horseless carriage. As speed capability increased, attention to steering and suspension became very important.

The steering characteristics of cars can be traced back to the engineering efforts of people like Rudolph Ackerman. He proved that the inside wheel of a car will always follow a sharper angle than the outside wheel in a turn, with the result that each wheel follows the circumference of a correct circle. The in-

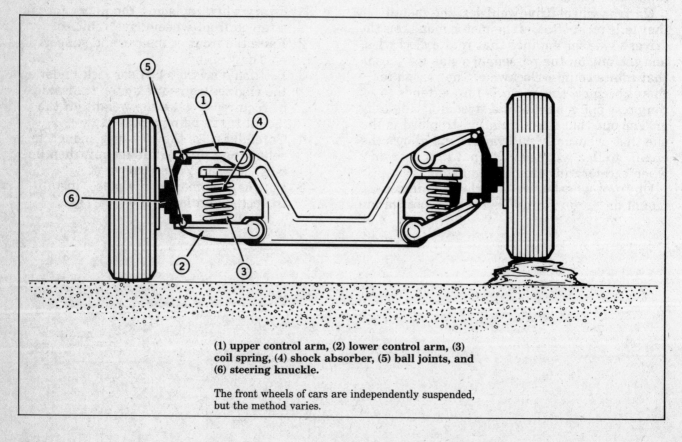

(1) upper control arm, (2) lower control arm, (3) coil spring, (4) shock absorber, (5) ball joints, and (6) steering knuckle.

The front wheels of cars are independently suspended, but the method varies.

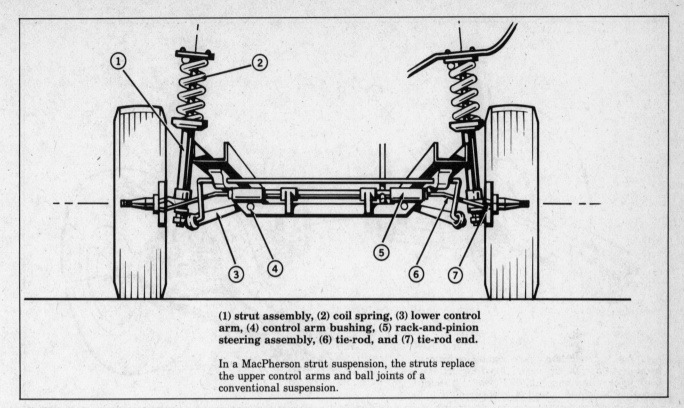

(1) strut assembly, (2) coil spring, (3) lower control arm, (4) control arm bushing, (5) rack-and-pinion steering assembly, (6) tie-rod, and (7) tie-rod end.

In a MacPherson strut suspension, the struts replace the upper control arms and ball joints of a conventional suspension.

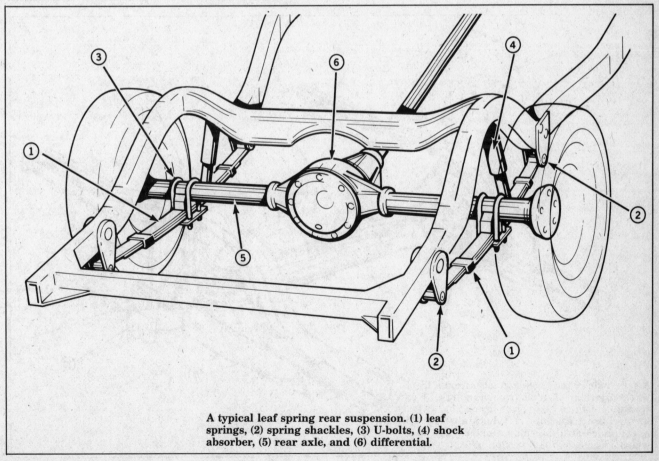

A typical leaf spring rear suspension. (1) leaf springs, (2) spring shackles, (3) U-bolts, (4) shock absorber, (5) rear axle, and (6) differential.

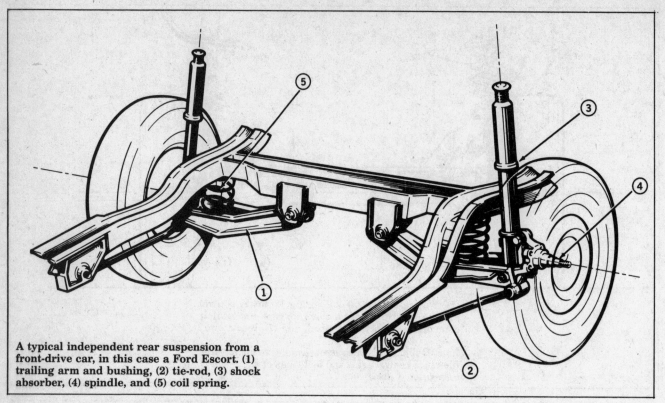

A typical independent rear suspension from a front-drive car, in this case a Ford Escort. (1) trailing arm and bushing, (2) tie-rod, (3) shock absorber, (4) spindle, and (5) coil spring.

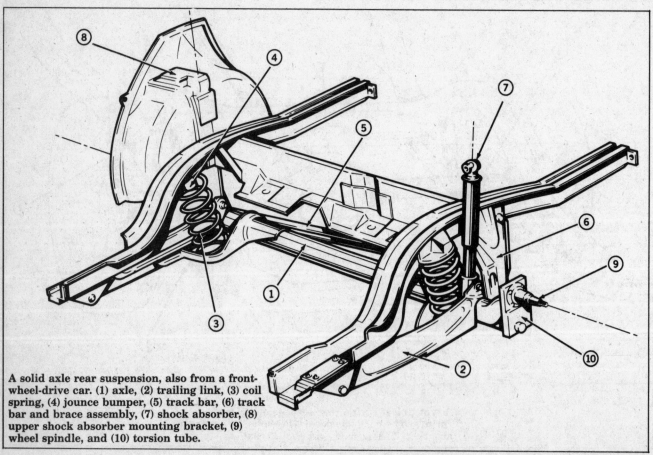

A solid axle rear suspension, also from a front-wheel-drive car. (1) axle, (2) trailing link, (3) coil spring, (4) jounce bumper, (5) track bar, (6) track bar and brace assembly, (7) shock absorber, (8) upper shock absorber mounting bracket, (9) wheel spindle, and (10) torsion tube.

side wheel, then, by necessity, will always track a smaller circle than the outside wheel. This principle describes only one of many contributions to the steering and suspension geometry of cars.

It would seem that in more than 80 years of research and development, a standard would have been set so that at least the design of suspensions would have become the same on all cars. This, however, is not the case, because there still is a difference of opinion on the best way to apply the principle.

There is a similarity in that front wheels are suspended independently of each other, but the method may involve the use of either coil springs, torsion bars, or MacPherson struts. There are, however, at least four ways in which rear wheels may be suspended, and the method may involve the use of either coil springs, leaf springs, or MacPherson struts.

These suspension differences are necessary and important in their application because they affect the ride, comfort, and ease of handling built into the car. To satisfy all the performance requirements we expect, suspension and steering must work together so that a car will handle easily, steer straight, turn corners without swaying, absorb road shock, use all the torque generated by the engine, and stand the stresses imposed by the brake system. All this must be accomplished smoothly, quietly, and without imposing on the comfort of passengers.

Front-Wheel-Drive Cars

Unlike conventional rear-wheel-drive cars, the rear suspension of most front-wheel-drive cars consists of a simple beam, or solid axle. At the front, there is a transaxle—a combined transmission and axle—which has constant velocity joints that act as steering and suspension members because they take part in all front-end movements. They convey power from the transmission to the wheels and serve as axle, suspension, and steering members.

When you suspect that your steering or suspension systems are performing at less than peak efficiency, it is time to look for telltale signs that indicate which components have become worn.

In this chapter, we will discuss methods and procedures that will allow you, in many cases, to diagnose and subsequently make repairs to

restore all the ride and handling characteristics designed into your car.

Ball Joints

Tools and Materials

- Wheel Chocks
- Screw-Type or Scissors Jack
- Wedge (bar stock steel approximately ¼ by 2 by 5½ inches)

THE STEERING knuckle at each front wheel is attached to two suspension components. The one at the top is the upper control arm. The one at the bottom is the lower control arm. Both the upper and the lower control arms are joined to the steering knuckle by ball joints.

On MacPherson strut suspensions, the strut replaces the upper control arm and ball joint. The lower ball joint on this type of suspension is identical to those on double control arm suspensions where the coil spring is mounted over the upper control arm. The lower ball joint does not carry the load.

Ball joints, which can be compared to a knee joint in a human, are often called ball-and-socket joints. The ball of the joint has a tapered shank that passes through a matching taper in the steering knuckle. The tapered shank is held firmly in the steering knuckle by a castle nut and cotter pin assembly that is threaded onto the portion of the tapered shank that sticks through the opening in the steering knuckle.

There are two basic types of ball joints. One is the load-carrying joint; the other is the follower, or helper, joint.

A load-carrying joint is a ball joint designed to support and carry more of the vehicle's

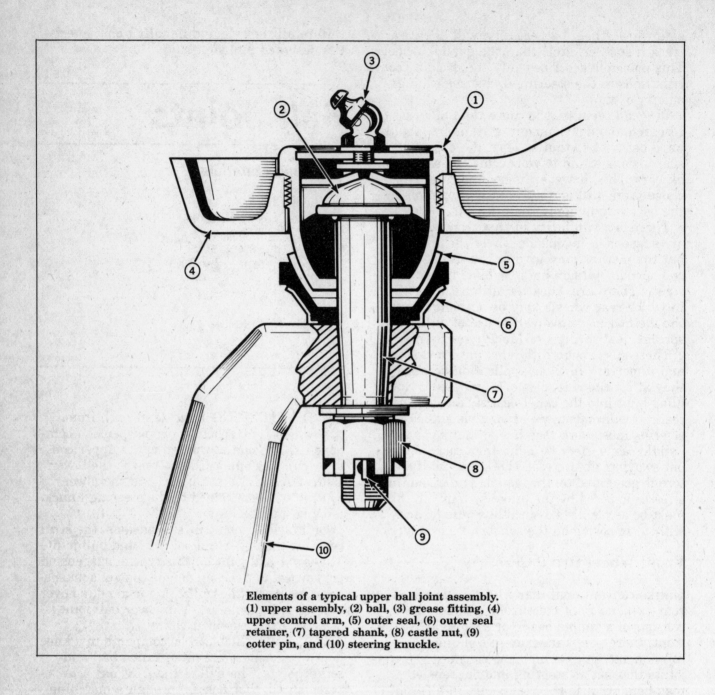

Elements of a typical upper ball joint assembly. (1) upper assembly, (2) ball, (3) grease fitting, (4) upper control arm, (5) outer seal, (6) outer seal retainer, (7) tapered shank, (8) castle nut, (9) cotter pin, and (10) steering knuckle.

weight. You can tell which is the load-carrying ball joint by examining the location of the coil spring. If the coil spring is installed between the upper and the lower control arms, the lower ball joint is the load-carrying one. If the coil spring is installed between the upper control arm and a frame member, the upper ball joint is the load-carrying ball joint. Generally, the load-carrying joint is subject to more wear than a follower ball joint.

A follower ball joint, the non-load-carrying

joint, will usually have a steel spring inside so the ball joint forms a snug connection between the steering knuckle and the control arm.

Because it bears much of the vehicle weight, the load-carrying joint is designed to have no play. The follower joint, however, does have some visible play.

While replacing ball joints is not a task for the do-it-yourselfer, it is possible for the home mechanic to inspect ball joints for wear and to determine if they need replacement. If the car

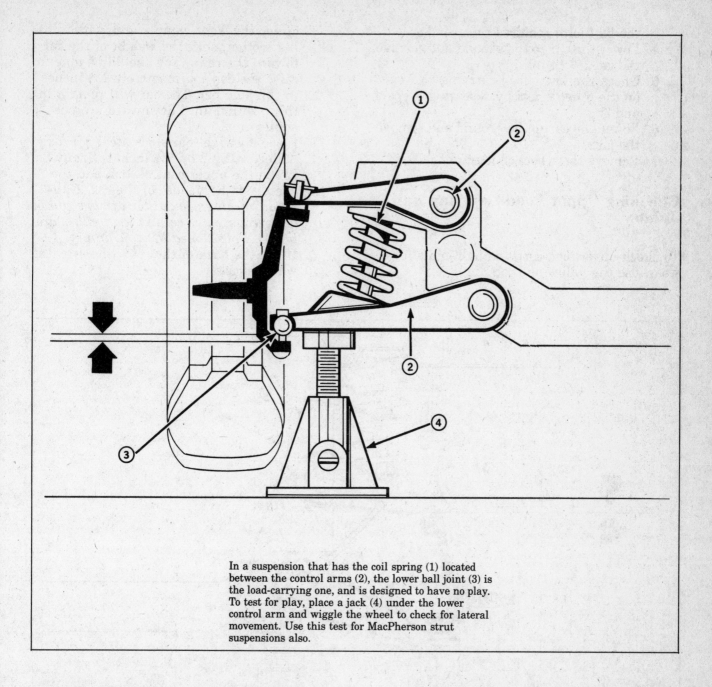

In a suspension that has the coil spring (1) located between the control arms (2), the lower ball joint (3) is the load-carrying one, and is designed to have no play. To test for play, place a jack (4) under the lower control arm and wiggle the wheel to check for lateral movement. Use this test for MacPherson strut suspensions also.

swerves badly under braking or if clunking noises are heard in the front end of the car, the ball joints may need to be replaced.

Checking Lower Load-Carrying Ball Joints

Here is how to check lower load-carrying ball joints for wear.

1. Place wheel chocks behind the rear wheels.

2. Place a screw-type or scissors jack under one of the lower control arms and jack up the car until the wheel is about 2 inches off the ground.

3. Have someone observe the lower load-carrying ball joint while you grasp the tire at the top and the bottom and wiggle it back and forth. Any side or lateral movement or play should be visible at the ball joint. If there is play in the ball joint, consult a mechanic to determine if

the ball joint requires replacement.

4. Lower the car to the ground and remove the jack.
5. Check the lower load-carrying ball joint on the other wheel by repeating Steps 2 and 3.
6. Lower the car to the ground and remove the jack.
7. Remove the wheel chocks.

Checking Upper Load-Carrying Ball Joints

To check upper load-carrying ball joints for wear, use the following procedure.

1. Grasp the front bumper and, with a lifting motion, shift the weight of the car toward the rear. (You should be able to raise the car approximately 1½ inches in this manner. The car will remain in this position until downward pressure is applied.)
2. Place a wedge (bar stock steel approximately ¼ by 2 by 5½ inches) firmly between the upper control arm and the chassis on both sides of the car. *Caution: Working around the springs can be dangerous, so be certain the wedges are properly positioned to avoid injury.*
3. Block the back of the rear wheels with wheel chocks.

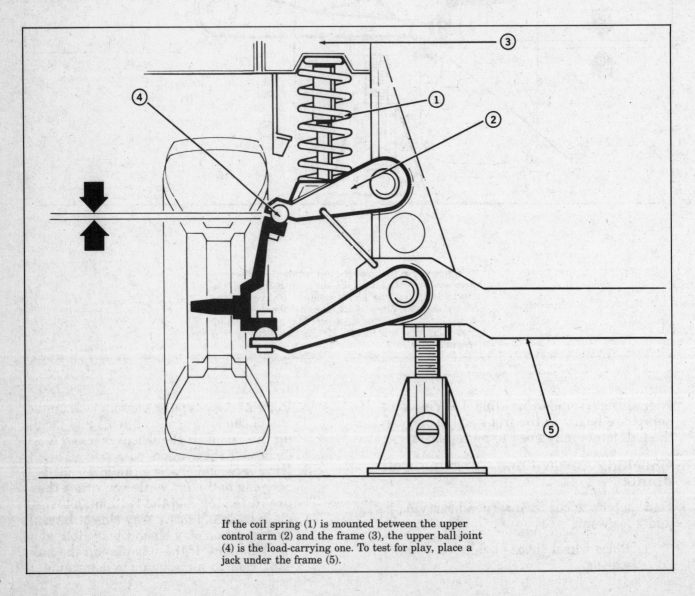

If the coil spring (1) is mounted between the upper control arm (2) and the frame (3), the upper ball joint (4) is the load-carrying one. To test for play, place a jack under the frame (5).

4. Place a screw-type or scissors jack under the chassis—not under the lower control arms—and jack up the front end of the car until the wheels are 2 inches off the ground.
5. Shake each wheel vigorously at the top only to be certain that the wedge will not come loose.
6. Check the lateral play in each ball joint using the method in Step 3 of the "Checking Lower Load-Carrying Ball Joints" procedure in this section. If there is play in the ball joint, consult a mechanic to determine if the ball joint requires replacement.
7. Lower the car to the ground and remove the jack.
8. Remove the wheel chocks.
9. To remove the wedges, repeat Step 1.

Stabilizers

Tools and Materials

- Wheel Ramps
- Wheel Chocks
- Box-End Wrench
- Socket and Ratchet Wrench
- Hacksaw
- Penetrating Oil
- Stabilizer Bar, Link Assemblies, Mounting Brackets and Bushings
- White Lubricant

MOST CARS with identical front suspensions will have a stabilizer bar, a heavy steel rod that extends across the car either in front of or behind the front lower control arm. Stabilizer bars may also be used on the rear suspension. Stabilizer bars range from ½ inch to slightly over 1 inch in diameter.

When you first look at a stabilizer, you might think that it is additional help for the main chassis springs. However, it does not help to sustain the weight of the vehicle. Rather, it is a torsion bar whose main purpose is to dampen the roll of the body and chassis of the car during turns. It accomplishes this by twisting as one side of the car leans over. The force generated helps to keep the rising side of the body level with the lowering side of the car body.

Each end of the stabilizer bar is connected to a lower control arm with a threaded fastener called a stabilizer link. The link goes through a hole in the end of the stabilizer and through a hole in the lower control arm. It is secured with a series of washers and rubber grommets.

There is a supporting bracket at each end of the stabilizer. The brackets are mounted to the frame sections of the car.

Replacing Stabilizers and Links

Stabilizers seldom break. If they do, you probably would notice that the car appears to roll much more than usual. Occasionally, the break will be visible.

What usually goes wrong with stabilizers is a loss of one or more of the rubber grommets in the links, or one of the links may break.

If your stabilizer is broken, you should replace everything that mounts or attaches to the stabilizer as well as the bar itself. **Note:** The links are likely to be rusted. Soaking the link assemblies with penetrating oil beforehand may ease removal.

Here's how to replace a stabilizer.

1. Drive the car onto wheel ramps.
2. Set the parking brake.
3. Block the rear wheels of the car with wheel chocks.
4. Get under the car and remove the links that connect the stabilizer to the lower control arms at both sides of the car. Discard all the old pieces. You will need a box-end wrench and a socket and ratchet wrench. **Note:** The links may be rusted to a point where it is not possible to remove them with the wrench. If this is the case, you can use a hacksaw to cut the stabilizer links in two in the middle

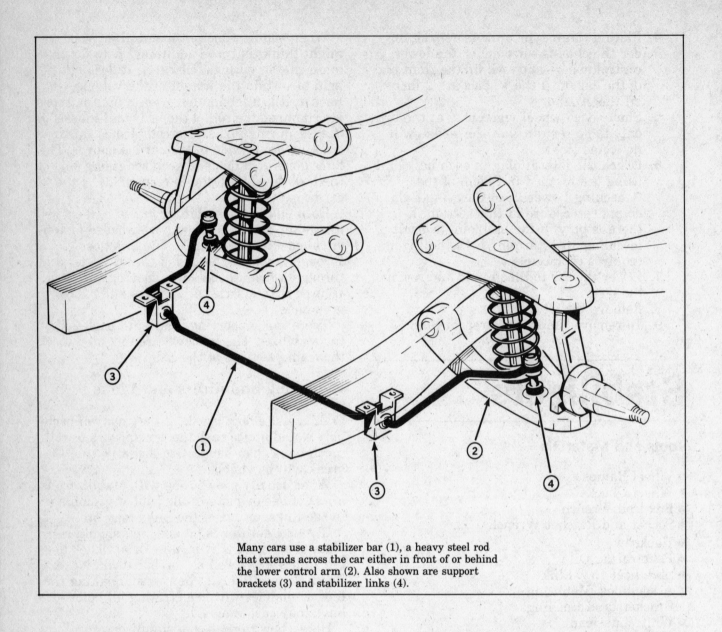

Many cars use a stabilizer bar (1), a heavy steel rod that extends across the car either in front of or behind the lower control arm (2). Also shown are support brackets (3) and stabilizer links (4).

of each link. Discard the pieces.

5. Loosen—but do not yet remove—the cap screws that hold the stabilizer support brackets to the frame sections.

6. Twist the loosened stabilizer bar so that its ends are pointing toward the ground to ease removal.

7. Remove the cap screws from one of the support brackets. Lower this end of the stabilizer bar.

8. Holding the bar with one hand, carefully remove the cap screws from the other bracket.

9. Lower the stabilizer and remove it from under the car.

10. Assemble the new mounting brackets and bushings according to instructions included with the new stabilizer. **Note:** Apply white lubricant to the surfaces of the rubber bushings before installing them around the stabilizer bar.

11. Reverse Steps 5 through 9 to install the new stabilizer.

12. Install the stabilizer link assemblies according to the manufacturer's instructions.

13. Remove the wheel chocks from the rear wheels.

14. Start the car, release the parking brake, and back the car off the ramps.

Bump Stops

Tools and Materials

- Wheel Chocks
- Jack and Safety Jack Stands
- Box-End Wrench
- Bump Stops

BUMP STOPS, or rubber bumpers, function like door stops. They are pieces of vulcanized rubber bonded to metal plates that are attached to the car's chassis or control arms. They limit the upward travel of the front or rear axle or control arms to prevent the suspension members from striking the frame.

On the front suspension, rubber bump stops are commonly mounted on the chassis below the upper control arm or below a frame section. On cars whose rear ends use leaf springs, you will find bump stops between the axle and chassis. These will be bolted to either the chassis or axle, depending on the make and model of car.

Rubber bump stops need replacement whenever they are missing or when it is apparent they are becoming unbonded from their metal plates. You can tell when the bonding is failing by pulling on the bump stop. If the rubber pulls away from the edge of the metal plate, they should be replaced.

Most bump stops are secured with a single stud on the back of the mounting plate. Some bump stops have ears on the plate and use two through-bolts.

The replacement procedure is different for front and rear bump stops.

Replacing Rear Bump Stops

For replacing rear bump stops, follow these steps.

1. Block the front of the front wheels of the car with wheel chocks.
2. Jack up the rear of the car and support it with a pair of safety jack stands under the frame.
3. Using the proper-size box-end wrench, remove the stud nut or through-bolts securing the bump stop to its mounting plate on the chassis, rear axle housing, or control arm.
4. Install the new bump stop, reversing Step 3.
5. Lower the car by reversing Step 1 and Step 2.

Replacing Front Bump Stops

To replace the front bump stops, follow these steps.

1. Block the back of the rear wheels with wheel chocks.
2. Jack up the front of the car and support it with a pair of safety jack stands under the frame.
3. Using the proper-size box-end wrench, remove the stud nut or through-bolts securing the bump stop to the chassis or a control arm.
4. Install the new bump stop, reversing Step 3.
5. Lower the car by reversing Step 1 and Step 2.

Springs and Torsion Bars

SPRINGS reduce the amount of motion transferred from a car's axle to its chassis. They are placed in a variety of ways between the axle, or other components that are designed to rise and fall independently of the chassis, and the chassis itself. Several types of

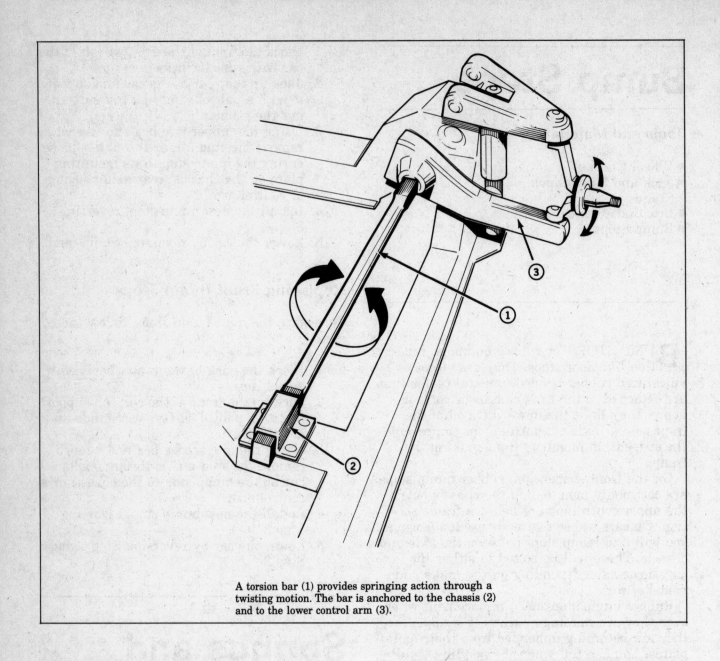

A torsion bar (1) provides springing action through a twisting motion. The bar is anchored to the chassis (2) and to the lower control arm (3).

springs are used on cars. Most are made from special types of steel, some are made of fiberglass.

Steel is used in making automotive springs because it can return to its original shape and because it is extremely durable. Properly designed, a steel spring can withstand the up-and-down motion of a wheel going over bumps for tens of thousands of miles. But, like any metal, it cannot last forever. Many cycles of use can cause it to suffer metal fatigue, or to take a set (lose some of its springiness).

The three most common types of springs are: coil springs, which are used almost uni-versally for front suspensions and in many rear suspension designs; leaf springs, which are used primarily for rear suspensions; and torsion bars, which are used in the front suspensions of most rear-drive Chrysler Corporation cars.

Torsion Bar Springs

The torsion bar springs used in most Chrysler front suspensions are simply lengths of spring steel rod whose ends are firmly fixed at one end to the car's chassis so that they cannot move. The other end is secured to the lower

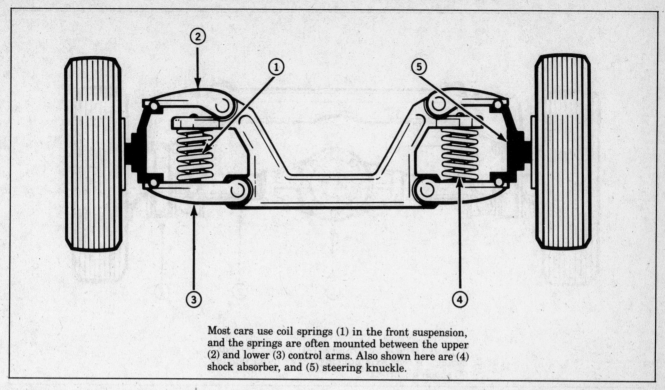

Most cars use coil springs (1) in the front suspension, and the springs are often mounted between the upper (2) and lower (3) control arms. Also shown here are (4) shock absorber, and (5) steering knuckle.

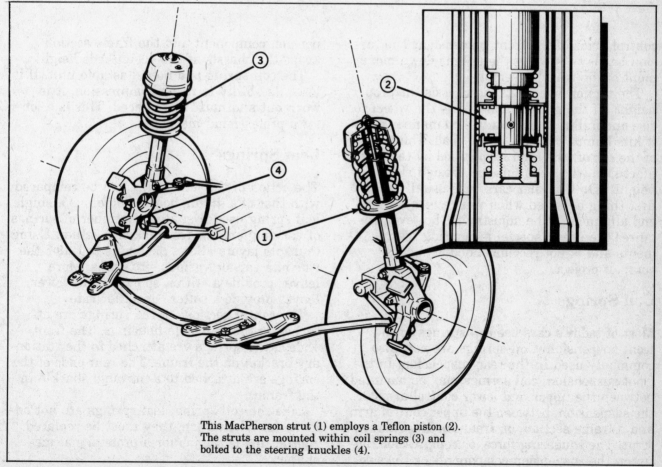

This MacPherson strut (1) employs a Teflon piston (2). The struts are mounted within coil springs (3) and bolted to the steering knuckles (4).

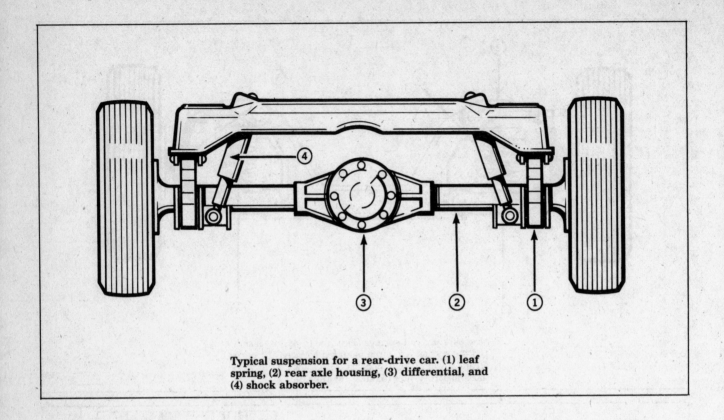

Typical suspension for a rear-drive car. (1) leaf spring, (2) rear axle housing, (3) differential, and (4) shock absorber.

control arms of the front suspension. The torsion bar is twisted by the up-and-down movement of the wheel assembly.

The torsion bar holds the chassis the proper height off the ground and allows the wheel to rise and fall in a semi-controlled manner when it hits bumps or holes in the road. The height of the car off the road is specified by the manufacturer, who calls this the "design ride height." On Chrysler cars, it is usually the first thing adjusted when you receive a front-end alignment. The adjustment, however, requires the use of special measuring instruments and is not recommended as a do-it-yourself project.

Coil Springs

Most of today's cars use coil springs in the front suspension. Coil springs are now also commonly used in the rear suspension. In the front suspension, coil springs may be mounted between the upper and lower control arms of the suspension, between the upper control arm and a frame section, or around a MacPherson strut. The squeezing force, or compression, between the suspension components or the suspension component and the frame section keeps the chassis at the design ride height.

The coil spring is a nonadjustable unit. If it loses its ability to resist compression, it is worn out and must be replaced. This is a job for a professional mechanic.

Leaf Springs

The action of the leaf spring can be compared with that of a diving board. Seldom is a single leaf spring used. Usually, a number of springs of varying lengths are stacked together. Using multiple layers allows designers to tailor the ride of a car for various situations. More leaves provide a stiffer, sportier ride; fewer leaves provide a softer, smoother ride.

The center sections of the springs are attached to the rear axle housings. The front ends of the springs are attached to the stationary bracket on the frame. The rear ends of the springs are attached to a movable shackle in the frame.

Like the coil spring, leaf springs are not adjustable. When worn, they must be replaced. Again, this is the job for a professional mechanic.

Checking Springs

If your car has sloppy handling characteristics, the problem could be sagging springs or torsion bars. Inspect the car. Is one end or side of the car lower than the other?

If you have determined that you have a sagging spring problem, the only solution is replacement of the spring. *Caution: Do not attempt to replace the spring yourself! A spring under tension is very dangerous. This is definitely a job for a professional.*

Shock Absorbers and MacPherson Struts

Tools and Materials

- Wheel Chocks
- Jack and Safety Jack Stands
- Box-End Wrenches
- Hammer and Punch
- Pipe Wrench
- Socket and Ratchet Wrench
- Adjustable Wrench
- Shock Absorbers
- Penetrating Oil
- Spring Compressor (MacPherson struts only)

THE TERM shock absorber is really a misnomer. Europeans have a more accurate word to describe the action of these devices. They call them dampers, because these components dampen the movements of the springs progressively and in a controlled manner.

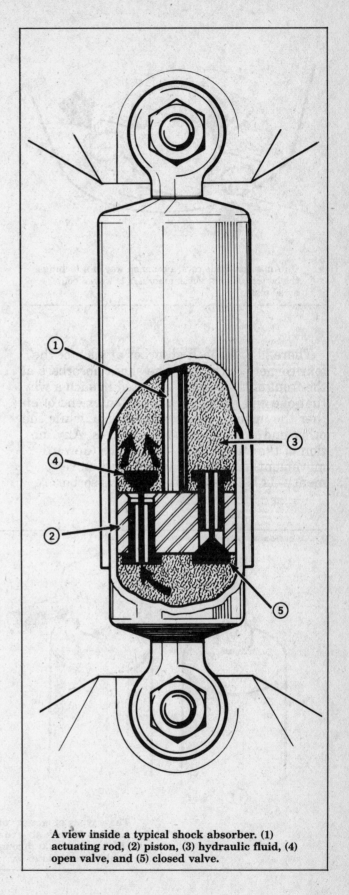

A view inside a typical shock absorber. (1) actuating rod, (2) piston, (3) hydraulic fluid, (4) open valve, and (5) closed valve.

417

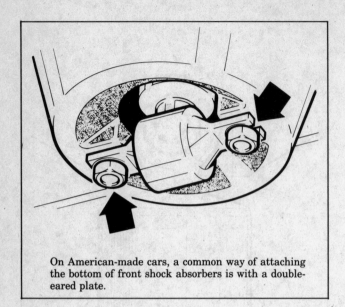

On American-made cars, a common way of attaching the bottom of front shock absorbers is with a double-eared plate.

There is one shock absorber at each of the four corners of the car. The shock absorbers at the front of the car are mounted in such a way that one end is attached to the outer end of either the upper or lower control arm, while the other end is attached to the chassis. Any motion of the suspension—the jounce (upward movement) or rebound (downward movement)—is handled by the shock absorber. A shock absorber can be located inside the spring, outside the spring, next to the spring, or on an arm not connected with the spring at all.

Each rear shock absorber is mounted in such a way that one end is connected to the rear axle and the other end is attached to the chassis or body.

Most shock absorbers are tubular and consist of a telescoping tube filled with hydraulic fluid. Inside the tube is a polished steel actuating rod or piston with valves at its foot. The fluid passes through the openings as the valves move up and down. The tube is attached to the axle or control arms, while the actuating rod will be attached to the chassis or body of the car.

There are a number of differences in shock absorbers, especially in the manner in which the valves and other features are constructed.

Basically, however, all shock absorbers work in this manner. When a wheel hits a bump, for example, the spring is compressed and the shock absorber telescopes, causing the rod and valve inside to plunge through the fluid. When the spring returns to normal position, the fluid motion in the shock absorber dampens the spring action.

In addition, a shock absorber also helps to

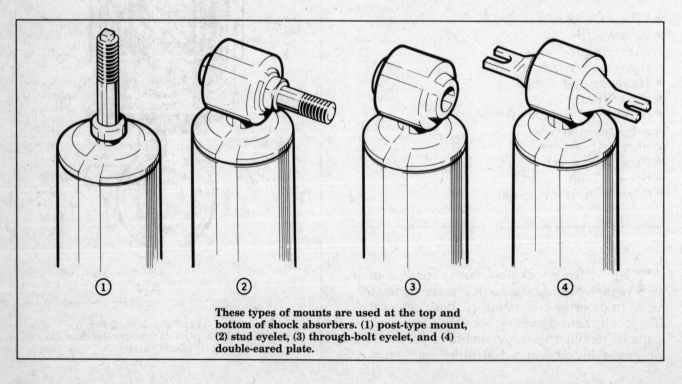

These types of mounts are used at the top and bottom of shock absorbers. (1) post-type mount, (2) stud eyelet, (3) through-bolt eyelet, and (4) double-eared plate.

limit the amount of car body sway that occurs while cornering. This helps the overall stability of the car.

The relative stiffness of a shock absorber will affect the overall ride quality of the car. The stiffer the shock, the harder the ride but the greater the ride control when cornering or when carrying heavy loads. The stiffness of a shock is determined by the size of the orifices and valves inside it.

Some replacement shock absorbers are designed to provide a smooth ride over small bumps while increasing their resistance over larger ones. These are often called "radial tuned" shocks because they also smooth out some of the harshness often associated with high-pressure radial tires.

Another innovation in shocks today is the use of nitrogen gas to pressurize the working fluid inside the shock. These "gas" shocks provide much better control, because the pressurization prevents the hydraulic fluid from foaming or cavitating under hard use.

Some shock absorbers have adjustable rates. Twisting the shock housing to the soft, normal, or firm setting when the shocks are installed positions an orifice inside the shock to allow the desired valving. Some new cars have an electrical solenoid on top of the shock that does the same thing with the flip of a switch. The driver can select the shock setting he wants to suit driving conditions. The solenoid is connected to a rod that changes the internal valving in the shock.

Shock absorbers can be mounted in a number of ways. All involve the use of rubber insulation as a cushioning device at points of attachment to other components.

One common mounting method uses a metal post coming directly off the end of the shock. The post-type mount is commonly used at either the top or the bottom of rear shocks. A post-type mount is fitted through a hole in a plate that mounts to the car chassis or body. A bottom post-type mount goes through a hole in a plate on the rear axle housing.

The post-type mount is almost universal at the top of front shock absorbers. On American-made cars, the most common arrangement for securing the bottom of the front shock absorbers to the control arm is with a double-eared plate that passes through an eyelet that is part of the bottom of the shock absorber.

Other methods of attachment include the through-bolt eyelet and the stud eyelet. In these methods of mounting, the eyelets are integral parts of the shock absorbers. In many cases, there will be an eyelet at both the top and bottom of the shock absorber.

Inspecting Shock Absorbers

Shock absorbers should be replaced when they no longer can dampen road shocks adequately. If your car continues to bounce up and down several times after the brakes have been applied, for example, one or more shock absorbers may be in poor condition. Inspect each shock for the following conditions.

1. Look for evidence of fluid leakage on the body of the shock absorber.
2. Check for worn bushings—the rubber insulation—at the top and bottom of the shock absorber mounts. Worn bushings do not affect the operation of the shock absorber, but will cause annoying squeaks or rattles.
3. Look for broken mountings at the top and bottom of the shock absorber.
4. Look for shock absorber body damage, such as dents or a bent or rusted actuating rod.

Replacing Rear Shock Absorbers

If one shock absorber obviously needs replacement, it is good practice to replace the other one on the same axle. Before beginning this task, however, be sure you have the correct replacement shocks. **Note:** You can ease the task of removing fasteners from the top and bottom mounts of shock absorbers if you apply penetrating oil to the fasteners before removal.

To replace shock absorbers on the rear axle, follow these steps.

1. Place wheel chocks in front of the front wheels.
2. Jack up the rear of the car and place a pair of safety jack stands under the rear axle housing. **Note:** On some cars access to the top rear shock mounts may be gained through the luggage compartment while the car is still on the ground. If this is the case, remove the

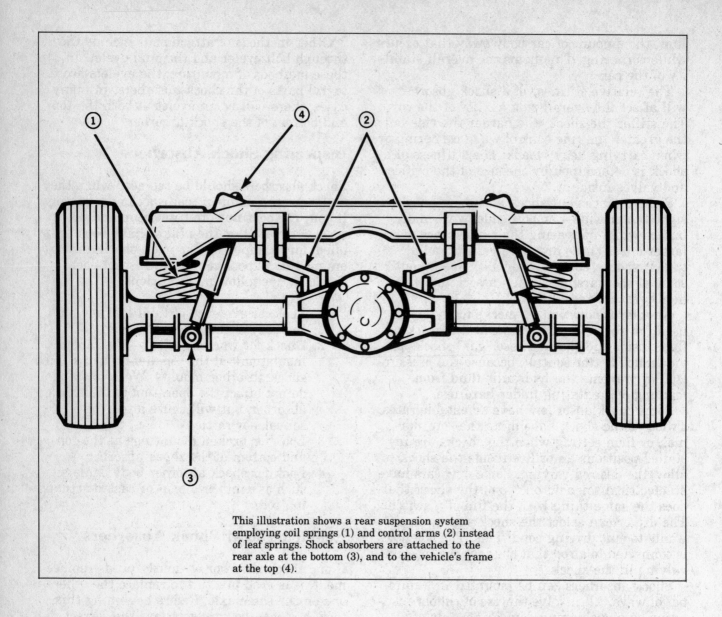

This illustration shows a rear suspension system employing coil springs (1) and control arms (2) instead of leaf springs. Shock absorbers are attached to the rear axle at the bottom (3), and to the vehicle's frame at the top (4).

fasteners from the top of both shock absorbers before jacking up the car.

3. With a box-end or socket wrench of the proper size, remove the fasteners from the top of the shock absorber. Use a hammer and punch to drift out bolts where necessary. Carefully note the order in which various washers and retainers are removed from the shock just in case the new shock absorbers do not include installation instructions.

4. Remove the fasteners from the bottom of the shock with a box-end or socket wrench of the proper size. **Note:** On some cars, it is necessary to remove the lower retaining plate from the rear axle

housing to reach the mount. Use a socket and ratchet wrench of the proper size to remove the plate, if necessary.

5. Remove the shock absorber.

6. Install the new shock by attaching the fasteners at the top mount first. Grasp the lower portion of the shock and push up or pull down slowly on the shock to align the bottom mount with the hole or plate on the rear axle housing. Once the mount is aligned, install the fasteners.

7. Replace the shock absorber on the other side of the rear axle, repeating Steps 3 through 6.

8. After installation is complete, lower the car, reversing Steps 1 and 2.

Replacing Front Shock Absorbers

If your car does not have MacPherson struts, use the following procedure to replace shock absorbers on the front axle.

1. Raise the hood and locate the shock absorber mount. **Note:** On some cars, the mount may be hidden by a flexible shield over the front fender well.
2. Apply the proper-size box-end wrench to the shock's top fastener and a small adjustable wrench to the projection on the tip of the mounting post to keep the actuating rod from turning as you remove the fastener. Remove the fastener.
3. Repeat Step 2 for the other shock absorber.
4. Place wheel chocks in back of the rear wheels.
5. Jack up the front of the car and place a pair of safety jack stands under the car.

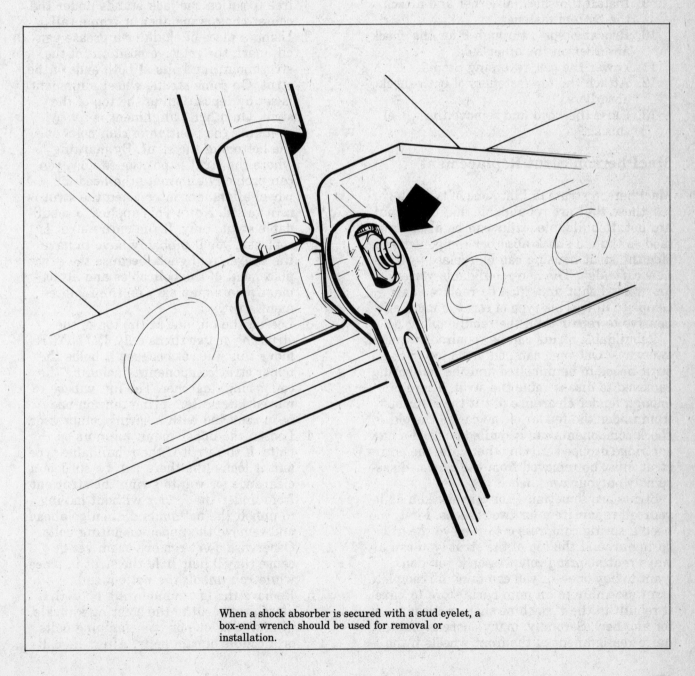

When a shock absorber is secured with a stud eyelet, a box-end wrench should be used for removal or installation.

6. Remove the fasteners from the bottom of the shock with a box-end or socket wrench of the proper size.

7. Remove the shock absorber from the bottom. **Note:** In some cases, the shock may have to be removed from the top. In this case, the top shock mounting plate will have three cap screw fasteners. Remove these fasteners. Then remove the shock from the top.

8. Fully extend the shock absorber before installing it.

9. Install the shock absorber and attach the bottom fasteners.

10. Repeat Steps 5 through 9 for the shock absorber on the other side.

11. Lower the car, reversing Step 5.

12. Attach the top fasteners of both shock absorbers.

13. Close the hood and remove the wheel chocks.

MacPherson Strut Replacement

MacPherson struts fall into one of two categories: those that are rebuildable and those that are not. Rebuildable struts can be disassembled so the old shock absorber components inside the strut housing can be replaced with a new cartridge. The non-rebuildable variety are welded shut and must be replaced as a complete unit. This type of strut is more expensive to repair than the rebuildable type.

Rebuildable struts can be repaired in one of two ways. On some cars, only the top of the strut needs to be unbolted and the coil spring removed to disassemble the strut. There is enough fender clearance to tilt the strut out from under the fender of the car so the old shock components can be pulled out and a new cartridge dropped in. On other cars, the entire strut must be removed from the car for disassembly on your workbench.

Struts are sometimes not considered a do-it-yourself repair item for two reasons. First, you need a spring compressor to remove the coil spring around the top of the strut (you can always rent a spring compressor if you don't want to buy one—or you can take the complete strut assembly to an auto parts store to have it rebuilt in their machine shop or exchange it for another). Secondly, many suspensions require realignment of the front wheels if the

struts have been removed or replaced. You can't do an accurate job of wheel alignment yourself, but you can have the wheels aligned at an alignment shop afterwards.

Because of these two "complications" you may decide it's worth the extra expense to have a professional do the job for you. But if you think you want to tackle the job yourself, follow these steps.

1. Set the emergency brake, chock the rear wheels, and raise the car. Support the vehicle so the front control arms hang free (position the jack stands under the center chassis member or frame rails).

2. Using a piece of chalk or a grease pencil, mark the relative positions of the strut mounting bolts at both ends of the strut. On some struts, wheel alignment is set by repositioning the top of the strut. On others, alignment is set by changing the position of cam bolts at the bottom of the strut. By marking where the strut is positioned now, you can probably eliminate the need for wheel alignment later when the strut is reinstalled. **Note:** This applies to rebuildable struts only. If the entire strut is replaced, you'll probably have to have the wheels realigned, because the exact placement of the bolt holes and attachment points may vary on the replacement strut.

3. Loosen the big nut at the top of the strut one or two turns only. DO NOT remove this nut yet because it holds the upper strut components (including the coil spring) together. The nut will be removed later after spring tension has been removed with a spring compressor.

4. Loosen the upper mounting nuts or bolts. If the strut is the rebuildable type and it looks like there will be sufficient clearance for you to swing the strut out from under the fender without having to unbolt the bottom end, then go ahead and remove the upper mounting bolts. Otherwise don't remove them yet because they'll help hold the strut in place while you unbolt the bottom end.

5. Remove the lower mounting bolts that attach the strut to the steering knuckle. This will be one or two clamping bolts or a couple of cam bolts. After the bolts

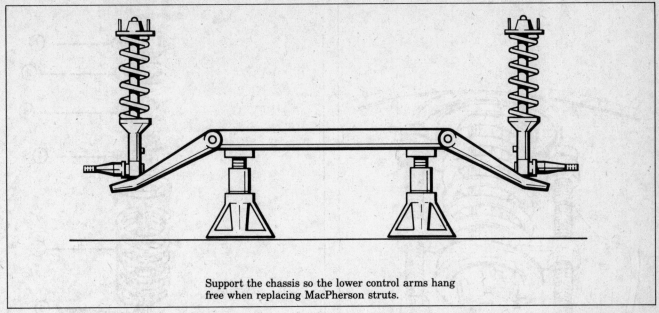

Support the chassis so the lower control arms hang free when replacing MacPherson struts.

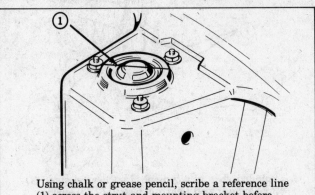

Using chalk or grease pencil, scribe a reference line (1) across the strut and mounting bracket before removing the mounting nuts at both ends of a rebuildable strut to make installation easier.

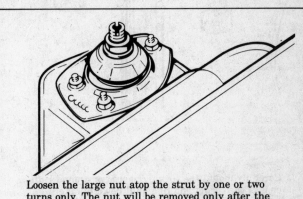

Loosen the large nut atop the strut by one or two turns only. The nut will be removed only after the strut is off the car and the spring has been compressed.

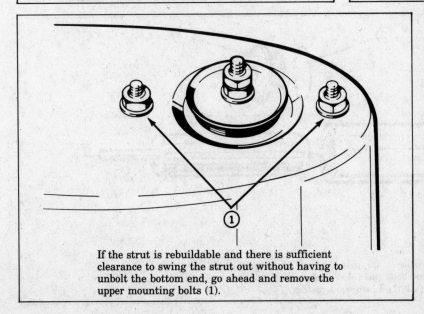
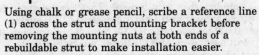

If the strut is rebuildable and there is sufficient clearance to swing the strut out without having to unbolt the bottom end, go ahead and remove the upper mounting bolts (1).

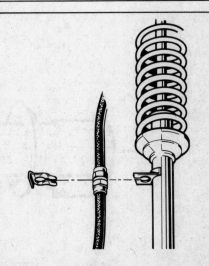

If a brake line is attached to the strut, unclip and remove it before taking out the strut.

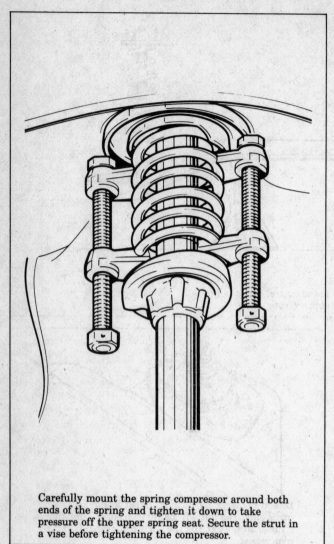

Carefully mount the spring compressor around both ends of the spring and tighten it down to take pressure off the upper spring seat. Secure the strut in a vise before tightening the compressor.

Exploded view of a typical MacPherson strut. (1) upper mount and bearing assembly, (2) spring seat, (3) jounce bumper, (4) dust cap, (5) spring, (6) strut assembly, and (7) lower mounting bolts.

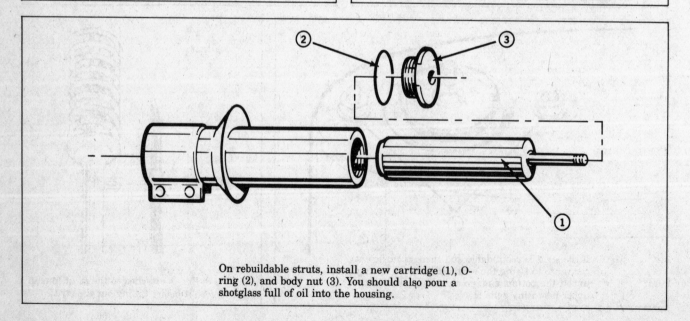

On rebuildable struts, install a new cartridge (1), O-ring (2), and body nut (3). You should also pour a shotglass full of oil into the housing.

have been removed, use a large screwdriver or pry bar to separate the strut from its mounting.

6. Before you remove the upper bolts that are still holding the strut in place (and preventing it from dropping to the floor), check to see that there aren't any brake lines attached to the strut. If there is a bracket on the strut holding a brake line, remove the clip and slip the hose out of the bracket. On a few cars, there is a hose fitting which must be opened to remove the hose. If this is the case, be sure to plug both ends of the brake hose after it's been removed, to keep dirt and moisture out.

7. Now remove the upper mounting bolts and lower the strut from the car. The strut can now be replaced or rebuilt.

8. If the strut has a coil spring around it, the spring should be removed and installed on the replacement strut. You'll also have to remove it to rebuild a rebuildable strut. Carefully position your spring compressor around the spring and tighten it down to take the pressure off the upper strut spring seat. Jaw-type compressors are the best, since they hold the spring most securely. If using two screw-clamp-type compressors, position them at opposite sides of the coil spring. Tighten them down evenly to prevent the spring from slipping. *Caution: The spring is under considerable pressure, so be extremely careful.*

9. Once the spring has been compressed, remove the single large nut at the top of the strut, lift off the upper bearing plate, mounting, and spring seat, then carefully remove the spring. Leave the spring compressor on.

10. If the strut is rebuildable, there will be a large body nut on the top of the strut housing where the strut shaft passes through the top of the housing. A large plumber's pipe wrench can be used to loosen and remove this nut—or you can rent a spanner wrench designed specifically for the struts on your car. It helps to hold the strut in a vise, but be careful not to deform or damage either the housing or the lower mount. Remove the nut and dump out the old internal components. Some struts will have cartridges inside, but most will have "wet" components (meaning you'll have a pile of parts on the floor). Save about a shotglass full of the old oil, because you'll need to pour it back into the strut when you drop in the replacement cartridge. (The oil helps with heat transfer between the strut cartridge and housing.)

11. If the strut is the non-rebuildable type, the top of the housing will be welded shut. In that case, you simply throw the old strut away and install your coil spring and upper mounting parts on the replacement unit. Put it back in the car following the above steps in reverse order. Otherwise, go on to the next step.

12. Make sure the strut housing is empty and all the old parts have been removed before you drop in the replacement cartridge. If the housing has any physical damage such as cracks or major dents, it should be replaced.

13. Drop in the replacement cartridge and pour about a shotglass full of the old oil in around it. Install a new O-ring and then the large body nut, and tighten the nut securely.

14. Put the coil spring back over the strut (if so equipped—not all struts have springs around them), and reinstall the upper mounting hardware in the same order the parts came off. Install a new nut on the top of the strut rod, and tighten it to the manufacturer's specifications. Do not attempt to hold the strut rod with locking pliers or a pipe wrench, because doing so will scratch its polished surface and damage the shaft seal in the strut. Remove the spring compressor only after the top nut is tight.

15. Now reinstall the strut back in the car following Steps 2 through 7 in reverse order. Make sure you line up your alignment marks before tightening the upper or lower mounting bolts.

16. If a brake line had to be opened to remove the strut, reassemble the hose connection and bleed the brakes (see the chapter on "The Brake System" for this procedure). The air must be removed from the system for proper brake action.

Pitman Arm Steering

Tools and Materials

- Wheel Chocks
- Jack and Safety
  Jack Stands
- Pliers
- Box-End Wrenches
- Pickle Fork
- Ball-Peen Hammer
- Wire Brush
- Locking-Jaw Pliers
- Dolly or Other Solid
  Piece of Steel
- Socket Wrench
- Penetrating Oil
- Tie-Rod Ends
- Rags
- Spray Primer or Paint
- Cotter Pins
- Relay Rod
- Idler Arm Assembly
  and Cap Screws

STEERING mechanisms can be divided into two basic categories: Pitman arm and rack and pinion. Both Pitman arm and rack-and-pinion mechanisms can be power-assisted.

If the steering column on your car goes through the firewall to a steering box that bolts to the side of the chassis in the engine compartment, you have a Pitman arm steering system. The purpose of the steering box is to translate the rotary movements of the steering column and steering wheel into a side-to-side movement that can operate the steering at the front wheels. It does this in a controlled manner and with a minimum of effort, while still preserving enough road "feel" for the driver.

The Pitman arm is a metal arm about 6 inches long located under the steering box. It attaches to a relay rod that runs across the car to relay the movement of the Pitman arm to the tie-rods. The tie-rods link the motion of the relay rod to the steering arms on the steering knuckles, which in turn relay the movement to the wheels.

The relay rod is supported at the passenger's side of the chassis by the idler arm assembly.

The idler arm assembly consists of two basic parts: the arm itself and the arm support bracket. The assembly supports the relay rod and transmits the steering motion to the passenger's side tie-rod and steering knuckle. Up-and-down motion of the steering link on the passenger side of the car is prevented by using either a bearing or a long rubber bushing in the support bracket. The support itself is attached to the passenger's side of the chassis.

Note: The system illustrated shows the tie-rods going directly from the steering arms to the relay rod. This is a common arrangement, but is not universal. Sometimes, the Pitman arm has two holes: one for the relay rod and one for the driver's side tie-rod. The idler arm also can have two holes: one for the relay rod and one for the passenger's side tie-rod. In addition, the accompanying illustration shows the steering assembly behind the front wheel axle centerline. This is also common, but not universal. Some systems have the steering system in front of the wheel centerline to clear the engine and other components.

The joints in the steering assembly must have no play in them or the wheels will shimmy and cause steering vibration.

Replacing Tie-Rod Ends

Tie-rods are connected to the relay rod at their inner ends and to the steering arms at their outer ends. The tie-rods are usually connected by a tie-rod sleeve, which is a tube with a slit in its side. It is internally threaded on both ends and works much like a turnbuckle. A mechanic can adjust the length of the tie-rod assembly simply by rotating the sleeve. Once the distances are adjusted properly, it is possible to lock the tie-rod sleeve to the tie-rod ends by tightening the tie-rod sleeve clamps.

Tie-rod ends need replacement whenever

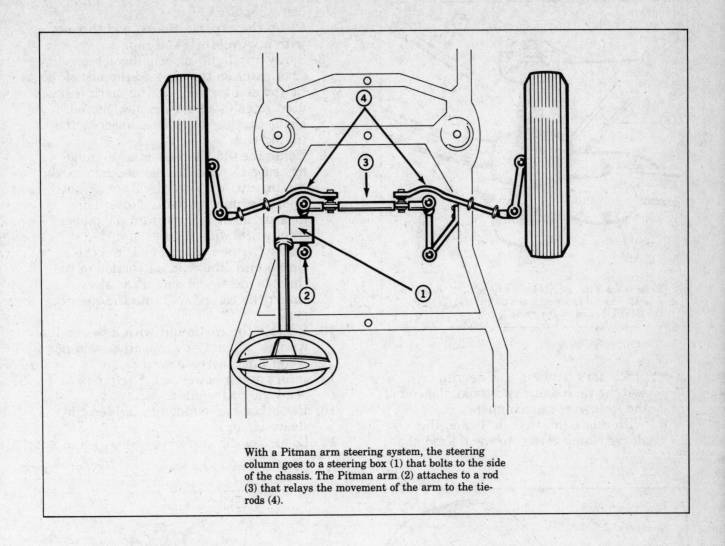

With a Pitman arm steering system, the steering column goes to a steering box (1) that bolts to the side of the chassis. The Pitman arm (2) attaches to a rod (3) that relays the movement of the arm to the tie-rods (4).

there is any vertical play in a rod end. To test tie-rod ends for play, the car must be sitting on its wheels, not jacked up.

To check tie-rod ends, grasp the tie-rod next to the rod end you want to check and try to move the tie-rod up and down to see if there is any play. Do not be fooled by rotational movement. A tie-rod assembly is supposed to have that.

If you find one or more tie-rod ends with vertical play, you should replace these tie-rod ends. Unless you are going to replace both tie-rod ends and the sleeve at the same time, you should apply penetrating oil to the threaded portions of the sleeve and tie-rod ends prior to attempting removal.

When you order tie-rods for your car, be aware that there are differences between left and right tie-rod ends, and between inner and outer tie-rod ends. Be sure to obtain the correct replacement.

To replace tie-rod ends, follow this procedure.

1. Place wheel chocks behind the rear wheels of the car.
2. Jack up the front of the car and support it with a pair of safety jack stands, preferably at the outer ball joints to keep the suspension as level as possible. **Note:** This is not absolutely necessary, but it can be helpful.
3. Using pliers, remove the cotter pin from the castle nut securing the tie-rod end. Discard the pin.
4. Using a box-end wrench, remove the castle nut.
5. Use a pickle fork and ball-peen hammer to separate the tie-rod end. Insert the

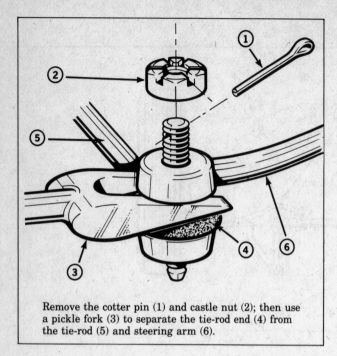

Remove the cotter pin (1) and castle nut (2); then use a pickle fork (3) to separate the tie-rod end (4) from the tie-rod (5) and steering arm (6).

being replaced.

7. Clean the exposed tie-rod end threads with a wire brush and rag.
8. Spray any light- or bright-colored primer or paint on the exposed threads of the tie-rod end to mark it. The mark will be used later to adjust the new tie-rod.
9. Using locking-jaw pliers, unscrew the tie-rod end.
10. Using the old tie-rod end as a gauge, measure the new tie-rod end and mark the threads with any light- or bright-colored primer or paint. **Note:** This measurement is important for proper front wheel alignment.
11. Screw the new tie-rod end into the sleeve until the painted portion of the threads meets the end of the sleeve.
12. Insert the tie-rod end into the steering arm.
13. Replace the castle nut with a box-end wrench, aligning the openings so a new cotter pin may be inserted.
14. Insert a new cotter pin. Use pliers to bend the cotter pin to secure it.
15. Use a box-end wrench to tighten the sleeve clamp.
16. Lower the car, reversing Steps 1 and 2.

pickle fork between the steering arm and the tie-rod end and strike the end of the fork with the hammer.
6. With a box-end wrench, loosen the sleeve clamp closest to the tie-rod end

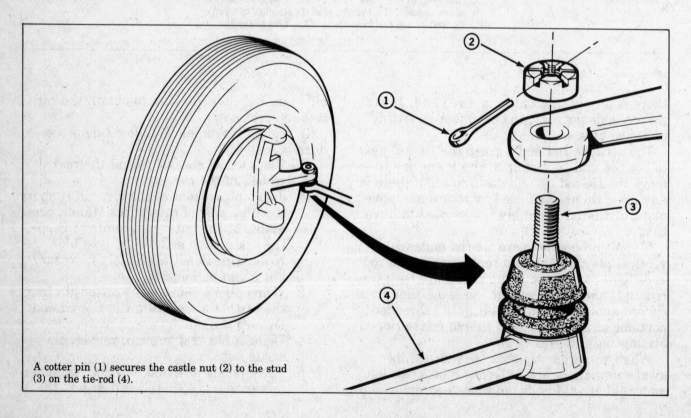

A cotter pin (1) secures the castle nut (2) to the stud (3) on the tie-rod (4).

Replacing a Relay Rod

A relay rod is a one-piece component. One end connects to the Pitman arm; the other end connects to the idler arm. In addition, there are two mounting holes in the relay rod to accept the inner ends of the tie-rods.

The relay rod ends are checked in the same manner as tie-rod ends. If there is vertical play and the relay rod must be replaced, follow this procedure.

1. Place wheel chocks behind the rear wheels of the car.
2. Jack up the front of the car and support it with a pair of safety jack stands.
3. Using pliers, remove the cotter pin from one of the inner tie-rod ends. Discard the pin.
4. Remove the castle nut with a box-end wrench.
5. Place a dolly or other solid piece of steel on top of the tie-rod end mounting hole on the relay rod. With a ball-peen hammer, strike the opposite side of the relay rod to loosen the tie-rod's stud so it can be removed. **Note:** Do not strike the tie-rod end or its stud.
6. Repeat Steps 3 through 5 at the other tie-rod connection.
7. Remove the cotter pins and castle nuts from the relay rod connection at the idler arm and the Pitman arm using the procedures outlined in Steps 3 and 4.
8. Using a pickle fork and ball-peen hammer, separate both connections using the method explained in Step 5 of the "Replacing Tie-Rod Ends" procedure in this section.
9. Remove the relay rod.
10. Install the new relay rod by connecting the idler arm and Pitman arm ends first. Reverse Steps 3 and 4, making certain to bend the cotter pins.
11. Connect the tie-rod ends to the relay rod by reversing Steps 3 and 4, making certain to bend the cotter pins.
12. Lower the car, reversing Steps 1 and 2.

Replacing an Idler Arm Assembly

The idler arm assembly supports the passenger's side of the relay rod. The support part of the assembly is bolted to the chassis with two or more cap screws. The idler arm portion is connected to one end of the relay rod. The arm and support section of the idler arm assembly are joined by a swivel.

To check the idler arm to see if it needs replacement, grasp the relay rod close to where it connects with the idler arm. Try to move the relay rod up and down. If there is an appreciable amount of play in the swivel of the idler arm assembly, the assembly must be replaced.

To remove and replace the idler arm assembly, follow this procedure.

1. Place wheel chocks behind the rear wheels of the car.
2. Jack up the front of the car and support it with a pair of safety jack stands.
3. Using pliers, remove the cotter pin from the castle nut on the relay rod end of the assembly. Discard the cotter pin.
4. Using a proper-size box-end wrench, remove the castle nut.
5. Strike the idler arm portion of the idler arm assembly with a ball-peen hammer to loosen the stud connection at the relay rod.
6. Press up on the relay rod to free the idler arm.
7. Using the proper-size socket wrench, remove the cap screws attaching the idler arm support to the chassis.
8. Remove the idler arm assembly.
9. Position the new idler arm assembly in place and fasten it to the chassis with the new cap screws. Tighten them snugly with a socket wrench.
10. Connect the idler arm portion of the new assembly to the relay rod end by reversing Steps 3 and 4, making certain to bend the new cotter pin.
11. Lower the car, reversing Steps 1 and 2.

Steering Box

Although you can diagnose steering box troubles, no service of the box, shaft, or Pitman arm should be attempted (in fact, these components will seldom need attention) by the do-it-yourself mechanic. Special pullers and other tools are needed for such operations.

Rack-and-Pinion Steering

Tools and Materials

- Wheel Chocks
- Jack and Safety Jack Stands
- Open-End Wrench
- Pliers
- Box-End Wrench
- Pickle Fork
- Ball-Peen Hammer
- Locking-Jaw Pliers
- Screwdriver
- Tie-Rod End
- Rubber Boot
- Lubricant (Lithium Grease)
- Cotter Pin

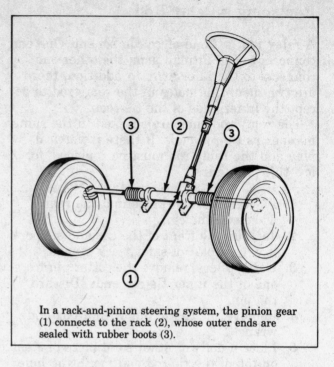

In a rack-and-pinion steering system, the pinion gear (1) connects to the rack (2), whose outer ends are sealed with rubber boots (3).

IF YOUR car has rack-and-pinion steering, the steering gearbox assembly is mounted transversely across the top of two frame members between the car's front wheels. The steering shaft is perpendicular to this assembly.

The steering gearbox assembly is contained within a tubular housing. At each end of this housing is an "accordian-type" rubber boot, a tie-rod, and a tie-rod end that connects to the steering arm. The tubular housing is firmly attached to the chassis with U-clamps and through-bolts. Inside the housing is the steering "rack"—a heavy steel bar with gear teeth cut into one surface. On the end of the steering shaft and inside the tubular housing is a pinion gear with teeth that engage with the teeth of the rack. When the steering wheel is turned, the pinion will move the rack to one side.

Each end of the rack is connected to a tie-rod, which transmits the back and forth motion of the rack to the steering arms. Flexible rubber boots fit over the ends of the tubular housing and are connected to the tie-rods. The boots, secured at both ends by clamps, protect the internal parts of the steering gearbox.

The tie-rod connection to the rack is a ball-and-socket joint that seldom needs replacement. Any problems at this connection should be handled by a professional mechanic. The tie-rod connection to the steering arm is a stud-type mount. There should be no vertical play in this tie-rod end.

Replacing Tie-Rod Ends and Boots

The tie-rod end on a rack-and-pinion steering gear is checked in exactly the same manner as a tie-rod end on a Pitman arm system. Grasp the tie-rod end and try to move it up and down. If there is any vertical play, the tie-rod end needs to be replaced.

Due to wear, it is sometimes necessary to replace the flexible rubber boot that is connected to the tubular housing and the tie-rod. To replace a tie-rod end or a flexible boot, follow this procedure.

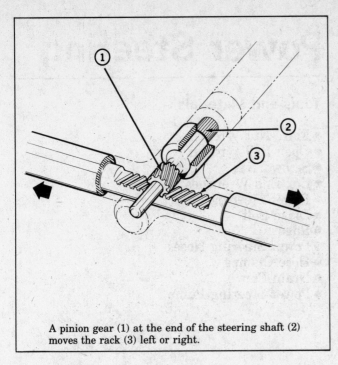

A pinion gear (1) at the end of the steering shaft (2) moves the rack (3) left or right.

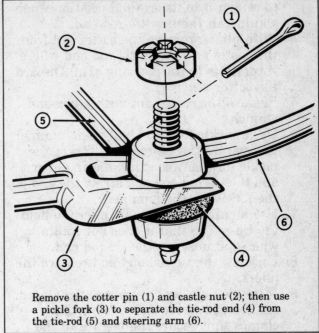

Remove the cotter pin (1) and castle nut (2); then use a pickle fork (3) to separate the tie-rod end (4) from the tie-rod (5) and steering arm (6).

1. Block the back of the rear wheels with wheel chocks.
2. Jack up the front of the car and support it under the frame with a pair of safety jack stands.

3. Using an open-end wrench of the proper size, loosen the jam nut on the rod that locks the tie-rod end in place ½ turn. **Note:** Do not turn the jam nut more than ½ turn because you must be able

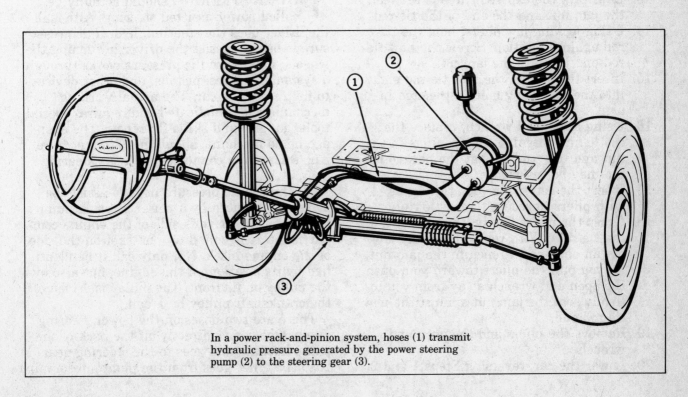

In a power rack-and-pinion system, hoses (1) transmit hydraulic pressure generated by the power steering pump (2) to the steering gear (3).

to return it to its original position when you install the new tie-rod end.

4. With pliers, remove the cotter pin from the castle nut on the tie-rod end where it connects to the steering arm. Discard the cotter pin.

5. Remove the castle nut with a box-end wrench.

6. Use a pickle fork and ball-peen hammer to separate the tie-rod end. Insert the pickle fork between the steering arm and the tie-rod end and strike the end of the fork with the hammer.

7. Use a pair of locking-jaw pliers to hold the tie-rod so that it does not rotate when you unscrew the tie-rod end.

8. Unscrew the tie-rod end and remove the pliers.

9. If the flexible boot needs to be replaced, use a screwdriver and remove the clamps that secure the boot. Pull the boot off.

10. Apply a small amount of lubricant, such as lithium grease, to the rack to replace any that may have been lost.

11. Install the new boot, carefully working the end of the boot over the jam nut.

12. Replace both clamps to the boot, reversing Step 9.

13. Lubricate the exposed threads between the jam nut and the end of the tie-rod.

14. Using locking-jaw pliers, hold the tie-rod against rotation. Screw the new tie-rod end in up to the jam nut.

15. Insert the stud of the new tie-rod end into the mounting hole in the steering arm.

16. Using a box-end wrench, replace the castle nut, aligning the openings in the nut and the stud so that the new cotter pin may be inserted.

17. Insert the cotter pin. Bend the ends with pliers to secure the castle nut.

18. Grasp the pliers firmly (they are still on the tie-rod). With your other hand, apply an open-end wrench to the jam nut. As you pull the pliers toward you, push the open-end wrench away from you to firmly seat the jam nut against the new tie-rod end.

19. Remove the pliers and the open-end wrench.

20. Lower the car, reversing Steps 1 and 2.

Power Steering

Tools and Materials

- Flare-Nut Wrench
- Open-End Wrench
- Screwdriver
- Box-End Wrenches
- Power Steering Fluid
- Drive Belt
- Rags
- Power Steering Hoses
- Hose Clamps
- Drain Pan
- Power Steering Pump

POWER STEERING should actually be called power-assisted steering. Although the driver does the steering, hydraulic pressure is used to assist the driver in turning the wheels. The hydraulic pressure works through a system of valves, pistons, and other devices to help steer the car. The actual working mechanism is complicated and requires special tools, gauges, and skills for repair. The average home mechanic should not attempt to repair some units connected with the steering gear.

The hydraulic pressure used to assist the driver is produced by a power steering pump located on the driver's side of the engine compartment. It is bolted to a bracket on the side of the engine block. Not only can it be identified by its position on the engine, but also by the pulley on its front. The pulley is driven off the crankshaft pulley by a belt.

There are two hoses on the power steering pump. One comes directly off the back of the pump housing and goes to the steering gearbox. The other goes from the pump's reservoir

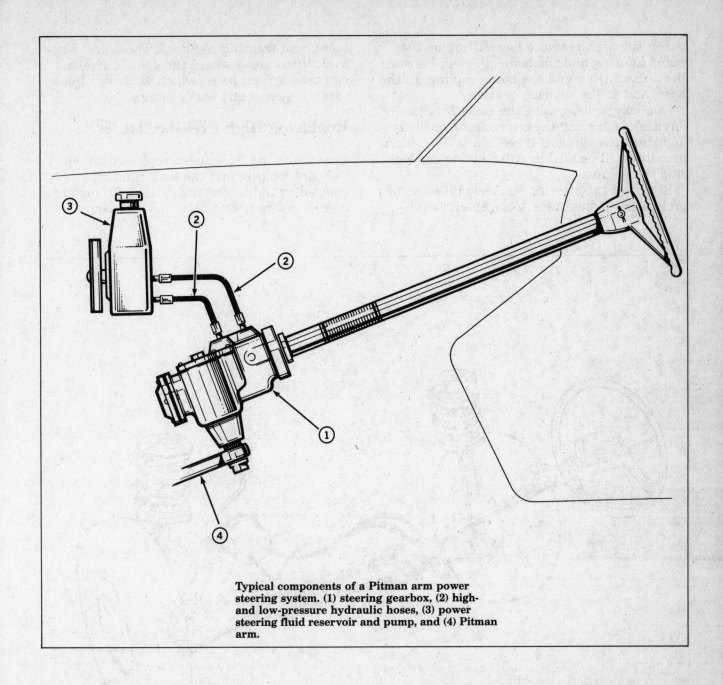

Typical components of a Pitman arm power steering system. (1) steering gearbox, (2) high- and low-pressure hydraulic hoses, (3) power steering fluid reservoir and pump, and (4) Pitman arm.

to another fitting on the gearbox. The hose on the back of the steering pump is the high-pressure hose that carries the hydraulic pressure. The other is the low-pressure return hose.

There are only three basic problems that affect the power steering system: loss of pressure and, therefore, loss of steering assist; mechanical damage that can result in noise and loss of hydraulic pressure; and leaks.

Loss of power steering pressure can be caused not only by a low fluid level, but also by a slipping drive belt. Check the drive belt on the power steering pump and, if necessary, replace it following the procedure explained in the section on "Replacing an Alternator Drive Belt" in "The Charging System" chapter.

Mechanical damage means internal damage. Evidence of internal damage can be noisy operation.

Leaks, however, are the most common power steering pump problem. They can occur almost anywhere in the system, but usually will be found behind the pump drive pulley where there is a seal for the pump mechanism, between the high-pressure hose fitting on the pump housing and the housing itself, between the pump fitting and the hose coupling, in the hose, and at the steering gearbox.

One way to determine the exact location of any leak is to clean the components with a rag and run the engine. If there is a leak, it most probably will be visible. After noting the leak, stop the engine.

Repair of the steering box should be left to professionals due to the tools, special equip-

ment, and training required. There are, however, three areas where the do-it-yourselfer can take action: belts, which we have already covered; hoses; and leaky pumps.

Replacing High-Pressure Hoses

Power steering hoses need replacement when they are leaking and the leak cannot be stopped by tightening the fittings. To replace a high-pressure hose, follow this procedure.

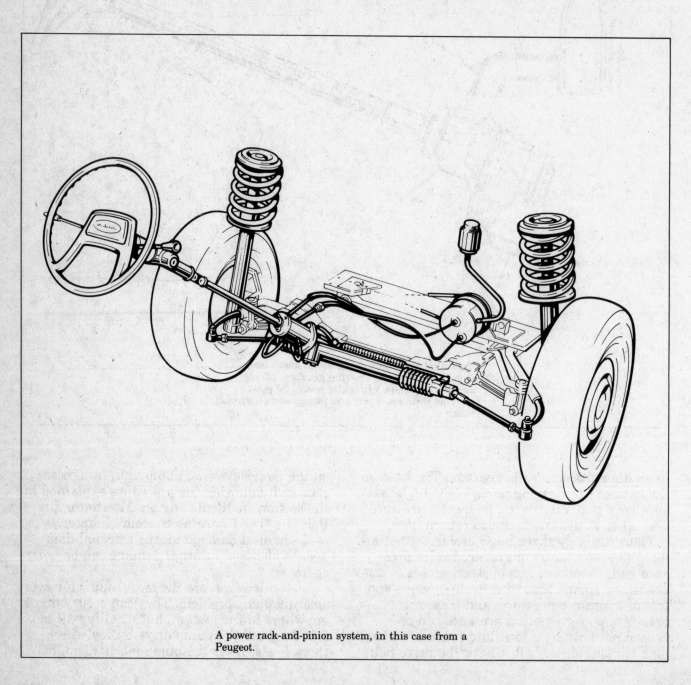

A power rack-and-pinion system, in this case from a Peugeot.

Note: This procedure is identical for many low-pressure return hoses.

1. Place rags under the hose connections.
2. Using a flare-nut wrench of the proper size, remove the fittings on the high-pressure hose beginning at the steering box. On some installations, you may also need an open-end wrench to prevent the fitting closest to the component from turning.
3. Slide the hose free, holding the ends up to prevent fluid in the hose from dripping. Discard the hose.
4. Attach the new hose, reversing Step 2.
5. Remove the rags and wipe any spills.
6. Start the engine and turn the steering wheel slowly left, then right, to remove air trapped in the system line. **Note:** An initial brief screeching sound may be heard. This is normal.

Replacing Low-Pressure Hoses

To replace the low-pressure return hose, follow this procedure.

1. Place rags under the hose connections.
2. On low-pressure return hoses without flare-nut fittings, use a screwdriver to loosen the clamps so the hose may be removed. **Note:** On some cars, there will be factory-installed clamps without screw fasteners. Use a screwdriver to pry apart the clamps.
3. Slide the hose free, holding the ends up to prevent fluid in the hose from dripping. Discard the hose and clamps.
4. Slide the new clamps on the new hose.
5. Attach the new hose, reversing Step 2.
6. Remove the rags and wipe any spilled fluid.
7. Start the engine and turn the steering wheel slowly left, then right, to remove air trapped in the system line.

Replacing a Power Steering Pump

A leak at the pulley shaft, sluggish steering response under normal driving conditions, a radical tendency to oversteer, or an obviously abnormal noise from the power steering pump are signs of problems in the system.

If you have checked or replaced your power steering drive belt and hoses and your power steering problem can be isolated to the pump, then the pump should be replaced.

The pump will be mounted on a bracket secured to the engine. One or two bolts hold the pump to the bracket. There is also an adjustng bracket that allows tension to be applied to the drive belt.

Use this procedure to replace a power steering pump.

1. Use a box-end wrench to remove the bolt in the pump's adjusting bracket.
2. Move the pump toward the engine and slip the drive belt off the pump pulley.
3. Move the pump away from the engine to gain access to the mounting bolts.
4. Use a box-end wrench to remove the bolts from the mounting bracket.
5. Remove the pump filler cap.
6. With a drain pan handy, grasp the pump—with hoses attached—and drain the fluid into the pan.
7. Rest the pump on the engine compartment and discard the fluid.
8. Remove the high- and low-pressure hoses from the pump using the procedures outlined earlier in this section.
9. Take the pump to an auto parts store for repair or replacement with a new or rebuilt unit.
10. Attach the hoses to the replacement pump, reversing Step 8.
11. Install the pump onto the mounting bracket, reversing Step 4.
12. Slip the pump drive belt onto the pump pulley.
13. Move the pump toward the engine and attach it to the adjusting bracket, reversing Step 1.
14. Adjust belt tension following the procedure outlined in the section on "Replacing an Alternator Drive Belt" in "The Charging System" chapter.
15. Remove the filler cap and fill the pump to capacity with the proper fluid.
16. Replace the filler cap.
17. Start the engine and allow it to run for at least 1 mintute.
18. Shut off the engine.
19. Remove the filler cap and recheck the fluid level. Add fluid if necessary.

THE BRAKE SYSTEM

FROM A safety standpoint, the brake system is the most important system in your car. It must be inspected and serviced on a regular basis, and any defective part—no matter how small and seemingly unimportant—must be replaced at once.

All components of the brake system do not wear out or malfunction at the same time, although it sometimes may seem that way. You may drive for many thousands of miles and never experience a bit of trouble with your brakes. Then, one day, you may make a sudden stop and discover that the brakes malfunction. If you drive at normal road speeds, you are not abusing the brake system, so it is possible to have nearly worn out brakes and not realize it.

The only way to prevent this unfortunate situation from occurring is to inspect the brakes regularly. Every 12,000 miles or each year, whichever occurs first, is a good interval for pulling at least one brake drum and examining the brake parts. Checking the entire brake system is much better. Whichever you do, you have to know what to examine.

Hydraulic principles are quite simple. They

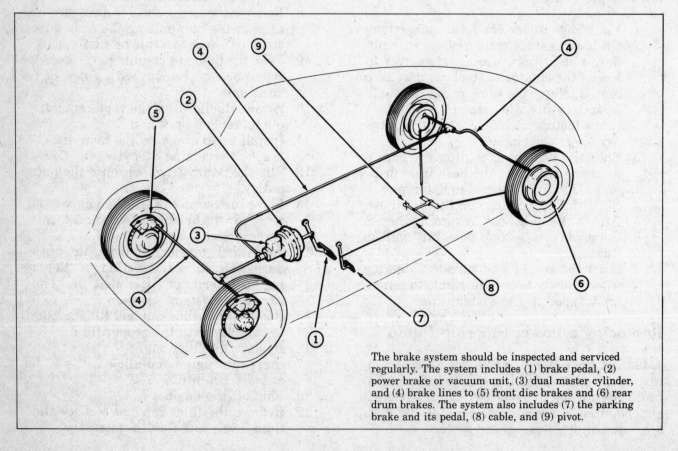

The brake system should be inspected and serviced regularly. The system includes (1) brake pedal, (2) power brake or vacuum unit, (3) dual master cylinder, and (4) brake lines to (5) front disc brakes and (6) rear drum brakes. The system also includes (7) the parking brake and its pedal, (8) cable, and (9) pivot.

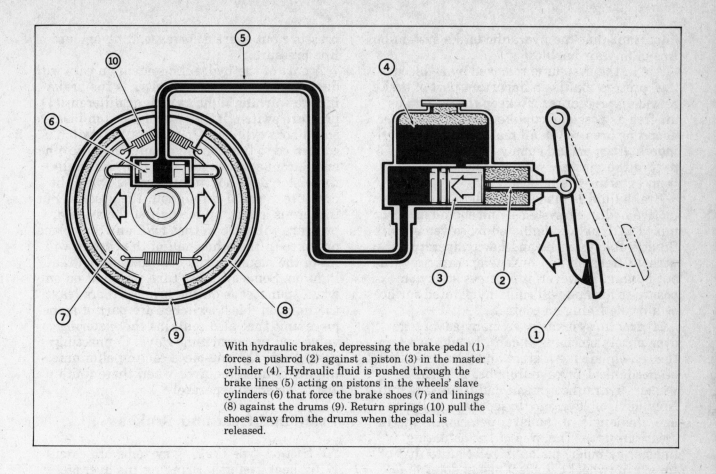

With hydraulic brakes, depressing the brake pedal (1) forces a pushrod (2) against a piston (3) in the master cylinder (4). Hydraulic fluid is pushed through the brake lines (5) acting on pistons in the wheels' slave cylinders (6) that force the brake shoes (7) and linings (8) against the drums (9). Return springs (10) pull the shoes away from the drums when the pedal is released.

are based on engineering facts. One is that fluids cannot be compressed. Therefore, it is possible to move a column of liquid (hydraulic brake fluid) from a master cylinder, through a small pipe system, to "slave" or wheel cylinders. The outward movement of wheel cylinder parts causes frictional material (brake lining) to come in contact with brake drums that rotate with the wheels and slow or stop the car.

The Master Cylinder

The master cylinder and its reservoir are filled with brake fluid. This cylinder has a piston, and a connecting rod linked to the brake pedal. Hydraulic lines connect this cylinder with the slave units at each of the wheels. These slave units are best described as a cylinder with a piston at each end. As the driver steps on the brake pedal, the master cylinder piston forces the fluid through the lines to each wheel cylinder, causing the wheel cylinder pistons to push outward, forcing the brake shoes and linings against the drum. At this

point, hydraulic pressure is equal at all wheel cylinders. Effective braking pressure cannot be applied to any one wheel until the brake shoes at all four wheels are in contact with their respective drums. This provides a self-equalizing effect on braking action.

Drum brake systems are designed to retain some hydraulic pressure even when the brakes are not being used. This system pressure is maintained by a check, or residual pressure, valve in the master cylinder.

Disc brakes do not use the check valve because the disc system has no return springs.

With a combination disc/drum system, it is necessary to have a check valve in the line to the drum brakes, but not to the disc brakes. So, in disc/drum systems, a dual master cylinder is used. In this case, the check valve is in the master cylinder outlet, where the drum brake line screws on. With a single master cylinder, the check valve is an internal part and faces the line that feeds the drum brakes.

As we said, liquids cannot be compressed, but gases such as air can be, so it is extremely important that the hydraulic brake system be free of any air bubbles.

Air in the system is removed by a "bleeding" process that is an important part of brake servicing procedures. To keep the system as air-free as possible, cuplike seals of rubber or neoprene are used in all master and wheel cylinders. Also, a fluid supply reservoir, which is part of the master cylinder, helps keep air from entering the brakes.

Brake fluid is made especially for automotive hydraulic systems, and should never be mixed with or contaminated by solvents. This fluid is able to withstand low temperatures without freezing and high temperatures without boiling. However, it becomes sticky on exposure to air and will ruin any painted surface or a brake lining on contact.

Hydraulic systems have many advantages over purely mechanical ones. In addition to the self-equalizing feature and the elimination of mechanical linkage from brake pedal to wheels, hydraulic systems can be used to multiply force or leverage. In mechanical leverage, the length of the lever determines the increase in force. The area of the actuating (master cylinder) piston in relation to that of the slave (wheel cylinder) piston determines the increase in hydraulic force.

In addition to being used to apply the necessary force to move the brake shoes or pads against the drums or discs, the brake system also is used to compensate for a change of the weight distribution during fast attempts to stop. Here, the front wheels are subjected to as much as 75 percent of the vehicle's weight and, therefore, must exert more braking force without locking the rear wheels. This is accomplished by making the front wheel cylinders slightly larger in piston diameter than rear cylinder pistons.

Tremendous hydraulic pressures are developed in the brake system. It is very important that the system be inspected for any signs of wear. A good visual examination of brake components can help eliminate the possibility that a sudden surge of pressure might cause them to break. With normal brake pedal pressure, hydraulic pressure in the system varies between 800 to 1200 pounds per square inch (psi), depending on the hydraulic leverage between master cylinder and wheel cylinder pistons. Power-assisted brakes require less foot pressure but exert a corresponding amount of line pressure.

A part of the hydraulic system on cars with dual-chamber master cylinders is the brake failure warning light switch, or differential pressure switch. It consists of a piston inside a small-bore cylinder. One end of the switch is connected to the front hydraulic line; the other end is connected to the rear line. Normally, the piston does not move because hydraulic pressure is equal throughout the system. But if there is a leak in one half of the system, pressure will drop in that half, and the normal pressure in the other half of the system will move the piston in the bore and switch the light on. Some switches turn the light on only when your foot is on the brake; others leave the light on. Most switches are part of a one-piece unit that also contains the metering valve and proportioning valve. Connecting passages in the one-piece casting eliminate the many lines required when these units were connected separately.

Frictional Heat and Brakes

All friction-type braking systems are essentially heat systems. Bringing the average-sized car to a maximum-effort stop (just short of locking the wheels) from high speed generates high heat in the linings and drums of drum brake systems. This frictional heat must be controlled and dissipated. The brake lining material is very important. It must be durable, yet compatible with the drum material; that is, it must maintain its coefficient of friction throughout the braking cycle without causing excessive wear to the brake drum. Any oil, water, or hydraulic fluid between the lining and the drum destroys its proper coefficient of friction.

Cooling the drum brake assembly is difficult. High-speed stops make it impossible for the brake cooling system to stay ahead of heat buildup. Cast-iron drums, which are most commonly used, depend on air circulation for cooling. This is difficult in the rather restricted area of the wheel recess. Air flow can be improved by ducting air into the wheel/drum cavity, finning the drums, and combining cast-iron liners with aluminum drum housings. Usually, larger cars have one or more of these cooling devices.

Brake linings also assist in transferring some of the heat, but the necessity of a backing plate makes internal cooling without ducting difficult. In addition to holding the necessary shoe assembly, the backing plate is designed to reduce the chance of water and abrasive dirt getting into the critical space between the brake shoe and drum. While moderately effective in keeping small quantities of dust and water out, any that does get through is, unfortunately, trapped by this very same shield. The adverse effect of dust and water on braking efficiency, however, has been virtually eliminated by the caliper disc brake system.

The disc brake system consists of a steel disc, or rotor, that is connected to the wheel and a caliper that can grip the disc with padded jaws. When the brake cylinder has pressure applied to it in the form of hydraulic brake fluid, the caliper closes on both sides of the disc, an action that generates friction and slows the car. Because the disc brake spreads the generated heat over a larger surface, it cools more rapidly than does the drum-type brake.

Disc brakes also have superior fade resistance and retain more stopping power than drum brakes when wet. However, disc brakes are more expensive, which is why they are used only on the front wheels on most cars.

The efficiency of a disc braking system depends on the condition of the friction surfaces of the disc and the caliper.

The efficiency of a drum braking system depends on proper lining material of adequate thickness, internally smooth and round drums, maximum contact between lining area and drum surface, and cooling. In addition to the force exerted on the brake shoes by the mechanical and hydraulic leverage, additional pressure between shoes and drum is achieved by self-energizing brake shoe action. The actual contact of the shoe with the drum helps to apply additional force to the drum. As the brakes are applied, the friction between lining and drum attempts to force the shoes around in the direction of drum rotation. This slight movement accelerates brake application. The location of the brake shoe pivot point determines whether or not the shoe is forced against the drum to create self-energizing action.

Most modern brake designs get additional braking power by linking the two brake shoes in a drum together. In this system, both shoes are self-energizing. When the brakes are applied, a primary shoe exerts pressure on the secondary shoe, pushing the secondary shoe into the drum with increased force. This is called "duo-servo action." Despite the rather long up and down travel of the brake pedal, the wheel cylinders and brake shoes do not move very far to make contact with the drum. This is due to the mechanical and hydraulic leverage advantage.

To compensate for lining and drum wear, an automatic adjustment for setting the shoes closer to the drum is incorporated into the brake assembly. This self-adjusting feature has been standardized and eliminates the frequent need for brake adjustment service. The self-adjusting linkage uses the self-energizing shoe action in reverse to operate an adjustment lever. This lever uses ratchet action to move the star wheel adjusting nut in the drum when the brakes are applied and released. This automatic brake adjustment, however, will happen only when the car moves in reverse.

Road Testing the Brakes

Before starting a brake inspection on your car, try to determine by a road test just what service might be required. Select a dry, smooth, paved section of street or road free of traffic or other obstacles where sudden stops can be made safely. At a speed of 20 miles an hour, apply the brakes firmly for a rapid stop without skidding the wheels. If the pedal depresses to within 2 inches or less of the floorboard:

- The linings may be badly worn
- Brake fluid level may be low
- The shoes may need adjusting

A spongy feeling to the pedal indicates air in the system.

With the car stopped and the ignition off, press the brake pedal as hard as possible, holding it down firmly. Note whether it continues to move slowly downward. Any such movement indicates master cylinder problems or a leak somewhere in the hydraulic system.

If the car pulls or sways to one side or the other, or if one wheel grabs when the brakes are applied, it is an indication of several possible problems:

- Improper brake adjustment

- Grease or hydraulic fluid on the linings
- Loose brake backing plate
- Reversed primary and secondary shoes
- Brake shoes not properly fitted to the drum, resulting in partial contact
- An out-of-round drum

While conducting rolling brake tests, listen for grinding or rubbing noises with the brakes off and applied. Rubbing sounds without brake application may be due to:

- Improper initial adjustment
- Faulty or broken return spring
- Binding wheel cylinder or shoe guides

Grinding or squeaks when the brakes are applied can mean:

- Brake linings are worn out
- Improper lining material
- Oil or grease on the linings
- Warped backing plates

Faulty front wheel bearings can contribute to poor braking efficiency. A bad bearing can cause a lot of unnecessary searching for a defect in the brake assembly, when it is really a bearing fault.

Do not forget to check the mechanical linkage for the parking brake every time you do a brake inspection.

Your decision to work on your brake system must include adequate time. Do not hurry—you are likely to make mistakes.

The tasks you accomplish here must be complete in every respect.

Inspecting Front Brakes

A VERY THOROUGH brake inspection should include a visual examination of the friction surfaces, lining condition, and any components contained in the brake assembly at the wheels. This inspection is necessary not only to verify the wear condition of the brake surfaces, but also to examine any parts that may have failed and cannot be detected without a visual inspection.

Tools and Materials

- Screwdrivers
- Wheel Chocks
- Jack and Safety Jack Stands
- Water-Pump Pliers
- Pliers
- 12-inch Adjustable Wrench
- Brake Spoon
- Face Mask or Respirator
- Paintbrush or Vacuum Cleaner
- Ruler
- Torque Wrench and Socket
- Rags
- Cotter Pins

The procedure for examining front drum brakes differs from that for examining rear drum brakes because there are many more components on the front drum brakes. In addition, the procedures for examining front drum brakes and front disc brakes differ.

Inspecting Front Drum Brakes

To inspect front drum brakes, proceed as follows.

1. Engage the parking brake.
2. Remove the wheel covers from the front wheels, using a large screwdriver or the pointed end of the car's jack handle.
3. Using the wrench end of the jack handle or a socket wrench of the proper size, loosen the lug nuts on both front wheels about one turn.
4. Place wheel chocks behind the rear wheels to prevent the car from rolling.
5. Using the jack, raise the front of the car until the wheels are off the ground.
6. Place safety jack stands under the

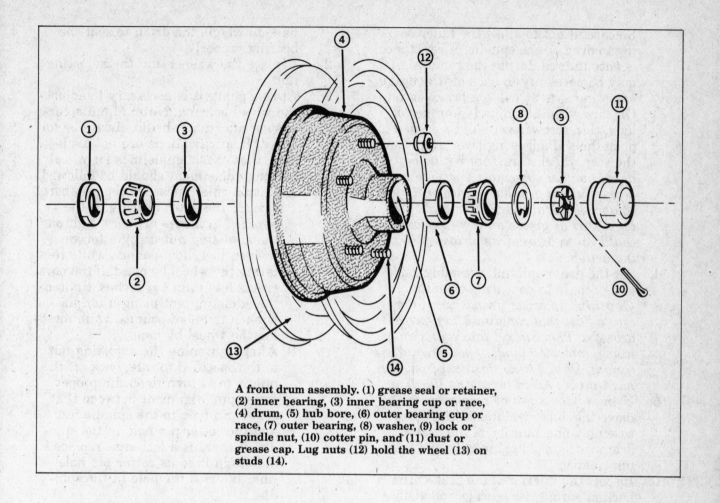

A front drum assembly. (1) grease seal or retainer, (2) inner bearing, (3) inner bearing cup or race, (4) drum, (5) hub bore, (6) outer bearing cup or race, (7) outer bearing, (8) washer, (9) lock or spindle nut, (10) cotter pin, and (11) dust or grease cap. Lug nuts (12) hold the wheel (13) on studs (14).

frame of the car to support it solidly.

7. Remove the lug nuts of the passenger's side wheel first, placing the nuts in the wheel cover for safe-keeping. Most lug nuts can be removed by turning them counterclockwise. A few cars, however, may have a left-hand thread on the lug nuts. In such a case, the lugs may be marked with the letter "L." If your car has left-hand threaded lugs, turn the nuts clockwise to remove them.

8. Remove the wheel and tire assembly from the car.

9. Remove the dust, or grease, cap. Use large water-pump pliers in combination with a screwdriver. Grip the dust cap with the pliers and pry it off with the screwdriver.

10. Remove the cotter pin with pliers.
Note: The assembly is held in place by one or two nuts. If there are two nuts, the outer nut, or lock nut, is a castel-lated nut that is held in position by a cotter pin; the inner nut is the adjusting nut. If there is only one nut, it is the adjusting nut, and it is held in place by a cotter pin.

11. Use a wrench to remove the nut, or nuts, and washer. If the nut, or nuts, cannot be removed by turning counterclockwise, try turning clockwise.

12. Rock the drum and hub assembly to work the outer bearing loose. Use care to avoid having the bearing fall out onto the floor. Have your hand ready to catch it. Place the outer bearing, washer, and adjusting nut on a clean rag.
Note: If you have not inspected or lubricated the bearings within the interval recommended in the owner's manual, refer to the section on "Repacking Wheel Bearings" in the "Maintaining Your Car" chapter.

13. Slide the drum and hub assembly off.

Be careful not to allow the inner bearing to drag on the spindle. If resistance is encountered during the removal, it may be necessary to back off the brake adjusting star by using a brake spoon. On cars with self-adjusting brakes, a long, thin screwdriver will be needed to push the self-adjusting lever away from the star wheel. *Caution: While the drum and hub assembly is off the car, be careful not to allow grease or dirt to contact the drum surface or brake linings. Dirt or grease on these surfaces could cause brake drag or loss of braking action.*

14. Set the drum and hub assembly aside and prepare to do a little cleaning. *Caution: As brake linings wear, they create dust that contains 3 to 6 percent asbestos. This can get into your skin or, worse, into your lungs if you are not careful. Do not blow this dust from the mechanism. Avoid breathing the dust!*

15. Using a face mask or respirator, remove the dusty residue on the brake assembly and interior of the brake drum with an old paintbrush or a vacuum cleaner.

16. Inspect the interior of the brake drum's friction surface for scoring and visible cracks. Make sure the surface is smooth. If the surface is worn, it should be resurfaced by an auto parts store that has a machine shop.

17. Examine the wheel cylinder on the brake assembly for evidence of leakage. If any is evident, have the brakes inspected by a professional mechanic.

18. Inspect all springs in the brake assembly to see if they are secured and not broken.

19. Inspect the brake shoe linings. If the linings are riveted, see if any rivet heads are level with the lining surface. If the linings are bonded, they should be no thinner than 1/16 inch. If shoe linings need replacement, refer to the section on "Relining Drum Brakes" in this chapter.

20. Replace the brake drum; you may have to rotate it slightly forward as you install it.

21. Replace the wheel bearing; you may have to wiggle the drum to seat the bearing properly.

22. Replace the washer and the adjusting nut.

23. At this point, it is necessary to adjust the wheel bearing. **Note:** Manufacturer's specifications should always be followed. If specifications are not available, these basic guidelines for wheel bearing adjustment should be followed.

A. With a ruler, measure the hub bore size for the outer bearing. If the bore is 1¾ inches or more, tighten the adjusting nut using a torque wrench to 17 foot-pounds while rotating the wheel by hand. If the bore size is less than 1¾ inches, tighten the adjusting nut using a torque wrench to 8 foot-pounds while rotating the wheel by hand.

B. After tightening the adjusting nut to the specified torque, back off the nut 1/6 to ¼ turn to obtain proper cotter pin alignment between the cotter pin hole in the spindle nut and the cotter pin hole in the spindle. If there is a lock nut, replace it and align it so its cotter pin hole lines up with the hole in the spindle.

Note: If the drum brake adjustment mechanism was altered during drum removal, proper brake adjustment will be necessary. This is covered in the section on "Adjusting Drum Brakes" in this chapter.

24. Install a new cotter pin through the adjusting nut or lock nut and spindle. Bend the ends of the pin around the nut with pliers so that it will not come out.

25. Reinstall the dust cap and tire and wheel assembly, reversing Steps 7 through 9. **Note:** Some cars come equipped with spring static suppressors in the dust cap. Be sure that the ends of the cotter pin do not contact the suppressor.

26. Follow Steps 7 through 25 for the drum brake on the other front wheel.

27. After the brakes have been inspected, lower the car, reversing Steps 1 through 6.

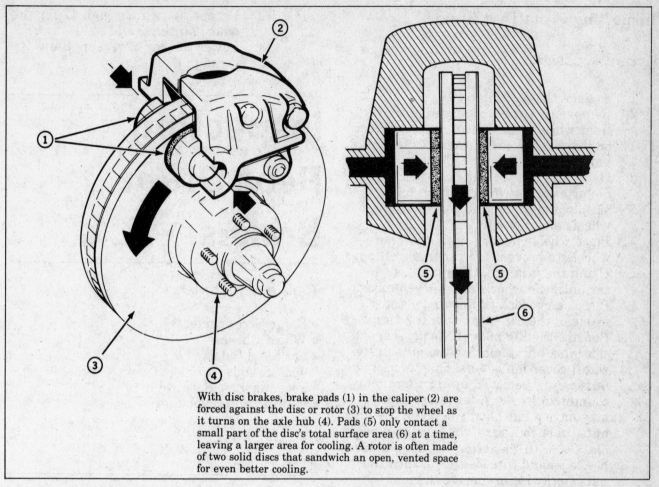

With disc brakes, brake pads (1) in the caliper (2) are forced against the disc or rotor (3) to stop the wheel as it turns on the axle hub (4). Pads (5) only contact a small part of the disc's total surface area (6) at a time, leaving a larger area for cooling. A rotor is often made of two solid discs that sandwich an open, vented space for even better cooling.

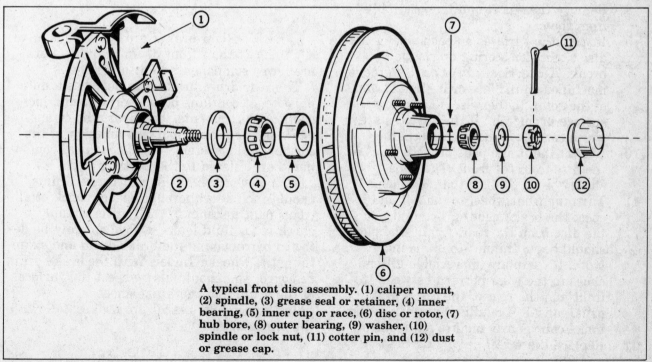

A typical front disc assembly. (1) caliper mount, (2) spindle, (3) grease seal or retainer, (4) inner bearing, (5) inner cup or race, (6) disc or rotor, (7) hub bore, (8) outer bearing, (9) washer, (10) spindle or lock nut, (11) cotter pin, and (12) dust or grease cap.

Inspecting Front Disc Brakes

Follow these steps.

1. Engage the parking brake.
2. Remove the wheel covers from the front wheels, using a large screwdriver or the pointed end of the car's jack handle.
3. Using the wrench end of the jack handle or a socket wrench of the proper size, loosen the lug nuts on both front wheels about one turn.
4. Place wheel chocks behind the rear wheels to prevent the car from rolling.
5. Using the jack, raise the front of the car until the wheels are off the ground.
6. Place safety jack stands under the frame of the car to support it solidly.
7. Remove the lug nuts of the passenger's side wheel first, placing the nuts in the wheel cover for safe-keeping. Most lug nuts can be removed by turning them counterclockwise. A few cars, however, may have a left-hand thread on the lug nuts. In such a case, the lugs may be marked with the letter "L." If your car has left-hand threaded lugs, turn the nuts clockwise to remove them.
8. Remove the wheel and tire assembly from the car.
9. Inspect the surfaces on each side of the disc (rotor) for scoring or visible breaks. **Note:** Some discs have a groove machined on the face or friction surface of the rotor. (Otherwise, make sure the surface is smooth.) If the surfaces are worn, consult a qualified mechanic.
10. Inspect the brake pads on both sides of the disc from the front. The pads should be no thinner than 1/16 inch.
11. Turn the front wheel to the left and inspect the brake pads on both sides of the disc from the rear. Again, the pads should be no thinner than 1/16 inch. **Note:** If there are appreciable differences in the wear pattern between the front and the rear of the disc's brake pads, consult a qualified mechanic; the brake caliper may require realignment.
12. Replace the wheel, reversing Steps 7 and 8.
13. Repeat Steps 7 through 12 for the wheel on the driver's side.
14. Lower the car, reversing Steps 2 through 6.

Inspecting Rear Drum Brakes

Tools and Materials

- Large Screwdriver
- Wheel Chocks
- Jack and Safety Jack Stands
- Face Mask or Respirator
- Paintbrush or Vacuum Cleaner

REAR DRUM brakes are a little easier to inspect than front drum brakes—there are fewer components to disassemble.

The rear drum brake assembly has a dual purpose. It contains both hydraulic and mechanical components. The hydraulic components perform an important function in the service brake system. The mechanical components are related to the parking brake.

Your inspection of the rear brake drums should include a thorough visual check of all component fasteners. Another important check is for fluid leaks, which can only be detected by removing the brake drum and examining the wheel cylinder. With the brake drum removed, you should also inspect the surfaces of the drum and the brake shoes.

To inspect your rear drum brakes, follow this procedure.

1. Engage the parking brake.

2. Remove the wheel covers from the rear wheels, using a large screwdriver.

3. Using the wrench end of the jack handle or a socket wrench of the proper size, loosen the lug nuts on both rear wheels about 1 turn.

4. Place wheel chocks in front of the front wheels to prevent the car from rolling.

5. Using the jack, raise the rear of the car until the wheels are off the ground.

6. Place safety jack stands under the frame of the car to support it solidly.

7. Remove the lug nuts of the passenger's side wheel first, placing the nuts in the wheel cover for safe-keeping. Most lug nuts can be removed by turning them counterclockwise. A few cars, however, may have a left-hand thread on the lug nuts.

8. Remove the wheel and tire assembly.

9. Pull the drum free of the studs as you rotate it slightly forward. **Note:** There may be a spring steel clip on one of the studs. Pry the clip free with a screwdriver and then remove the drum.

10. Using a face mask or respirator, remove the dusty residue on the brake assembly and interior of the brake drum with an old paintbrush or a vacuum cleaner. *Caution: Avoid breathing this dust! It contains asbestos.*

11. Inspect the interior of the brake drum's friction surface for scoring and visible cracks. Make sure the surface is smooth. If the surface is worn, it should be resurfaced by an auto parts store that has a machine shop.

12. Examine the wheel cylinder on the brake assembly for evidence of leakage. If any is evident, have the brakes inspected by a professional mechanic.

13. Inspect all springs in the brake drum assembly to see if they are secured and not broken.

14. Inspect the brake shoe linings. If the linings are riveted, see if any rivet heads are level with the lining surface. If the linings are bonded, they should be no thinner than $1/16$ inch. If shoe linings need replacement, refer to the section on "Relining Drum Brakes" in this chapter.

15. Replace the brake drum; you may have

to rotate it slightly forward as you install it over the studs.

16. Replace the wheel and tire assembly, reversing Steps 7 and 8.

17. Repeat Steps 7 through 16 for the wheel on the driver's side of the car.

18. Lower the car, reversing Steps 2 through 6.

Relining Disc Brakes

Tools and Materials

- Wheel Chocks
- Jack and Safety Jack Stands
- Lug Nut Wrench
- Hand Wrenches
- Hammer and Soft Drift or Punch
- Wire Brush
- Pliers
- Screwdriver
- Torque Wrench and Socket
- White Lubricant or Silicone Spray
- Disc Brake Pads
- Caliper Mounting Hardware

RELINING disc brakes is a fairly simple job for the do-it-yourselfer on most cars. In fact, you'll probably find it is easier than relining drum brakes. With the removal of a couple of bolts or pins, the caliper can be lifted off and new brake pads installed.

But don't let the apparent simplicity of the job fool you. There's more to doing a disc brake job than taking the brakes apart, installing new pads, and putting them back together again. Although it isn't absolutely necessary to rebuild or replace the calipers when relining the brakes, many professional mechanics include a caliper overhaul as part of every brake job. You can probably get by without having to do this step if neither caliper is leaking, if the dust boots on both calipers are in good condition with no cracks or tears, if there is no evidence of the piston in the caliper sticking (brake pull or rapid pad wear on one side of the car) and the vehicle doesn't have a lot of miles on it (over 50,000). In other words, if the calipers seem to be in good condition and aren't causing any problems, then there's no reason why you can't just install a new set of pads and skip overhauling or replacing the calipers.

A word about do-it-yourself caliper rebuilding: Overhaul kits are available that include replacement seals, dust boots, and pistons. If the piston bore in the caliper is not heavily scored or corroded and the caliper has not suffered any other major damage (such as cracks or heavy corrosion) a do-it-yourself overhaul will likely produce satisfactory results. But if the bore is in bad shape, has been leaking a lot of fluid—or you can't get the piston out— then your other option is to replace the caliper with a new or remanufactured unit.

The mounting hardware that holds the caliper in place should also be carefully inspected. Corrosion is the main problem here. If the hardware becomes corroded, it will prevent the caliper from "floating" or centering itself over the brake rotor. This results in uneven pad pressure against the rotor which causes the pads to wear unevenly. So if you tear apart a disc brake and discover that the outer pad is barely worn but the inner one is down to the metal (or vice versa), then the caliper is not floating as it should be, indicating the mounting hardware is corroded and should be replaced.

Another item that is often overlooked is the condition of the brake rotors. If the rotors are not badly scored, scratched, warped, or glazed, they do not have to be resurfaced. But if the surface of the rotor resembles a phonograph record with many grooves or if it is cracked or has glazed spots or heavy scratches, it will have to be resurfaced or replaced. This is something you can't do yourself, but you can take the rotors into an automotive machine shop. The shop will measure the rotors to see if they can be safely resurfaced without ex-

ceeding the minimum thickness standards for the rotor. Once a rotor has worn beyond a certain point, it must be replaced. There simply isn't enough metal left to absorb and dissipate heat properly without risk of breaking. On many rotors with a vented design, rotor collapse is another problem. Corrosion and wear can weaken the rotor and literally cause it to collapse inward. A pulsating or jerking brake pedal when the brakes are applied indicates warpage, often the result of this kind of failure. Sometimes resurfacing will cure the problem, but more often than not, the rotor will have to be replaced. Hard spots in the metal can cause a warpage problem to return after resurfacing.

The last item that is frequently neglected is the condition of the front wheel bearings. On rear-wheel-drive cars, the front wheel bearings should always be repacked when doing a brake job whether the brakes are disc or drum. This procedure is covered in the front of this book in the "Maintaining Your Car" chapter. With most front-wheel-drive vehicles, though, this step isn't necessary because the wheel bearings are factory-sealed. Unless a bearing is bad and must be replaced, they don't require any kind of maintenance. But not all front-wheel-drive cars fall into this category. Check in your owner's manual to find out if your car's front wheel bearings require periodic repacking.

To briefly summarize, the basic procedure for relining disc brakes begins with removing and inspecting the brake calipers and mounting hardware, inspecting (and resurfacing if needed) the rotors, then installing the new brake pads and putting it all back together. To finish the job, the system should be refilled with fresh brake fluid and bled.

Disc Brake Relining Procedure

Although most disc brakes are basically the same in function, mounting hardware, caliper design, and pad replacement can vary from vehicle to vehicle. We'll give you the basic procedure, but we also recommend referring to the specific replacement instructions for your vehicle in a shop repair manual.

Follow this procedure to reline the front disc brakes.

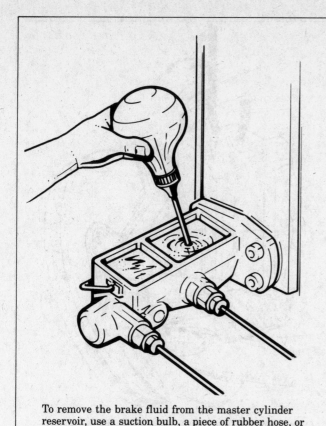

To remove the brake fluid from the master cylinder reservoir, use a suction bulb, a piece of rubber hose, or a small cup. About half of the fluid should be taken from the reservoir to allow space for brake fluid that will back up into the reservoir when working on the calipers.

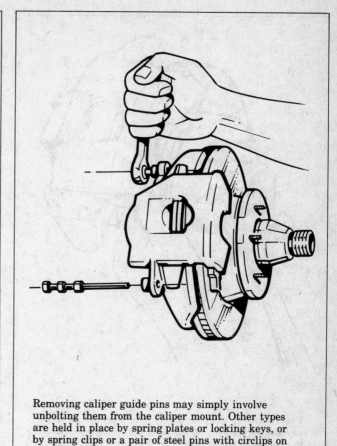

Removing caliper guide pins may simply involve unbolting them from the caliper mount. Other types are held in place by spring plates or locking keys, or by spring clips or a pair of steel pins with circlips on the ends. Taking out the pins loosens the calipers for removal.

1. With the front wheels still on the ground, remove the hubcaps and loosen the lug nuts.
2. Open the hood, locate the master cylinder, and open the fluid reservoir. Using a piece of rubber hose, a suction bulb, or a small cup, remove about half the fluid from the master brake cylinder fluid reservoir. The reason for doing this is to compensate for the fluid that will back up into the fluid reservoir when you remove the calipers.
3. Raise the front wheels and support the car on safety stands.
4. Remove the front wheels, and pry the brake pads back away from the rotors slightly, using a large screwdriver.
5. Remove the calipers. Depending on what type of disc brakes your car has, one of several mounting methods may be used. Some calipers are bolted in place. Others use a bolt to hold a spring plate or locking key, which in turn holds the caliper to its mount. Spring clips or a pair of steel pins with circlips on the ends may also be used. On calipers that have spring plates or locking clips, a hammer and punch will be needed to tap the plate to one side to free the caliper. The hammer may also come in handy to remove caliper pins.
6. Once the caliper is free, don't let it hang by the brake line. Support it with a piece of wire or rest it on the control arm or knuckle mount.
7. Inspect everything. Begin by noting the relative condition of the inner and outer brake pads. Uneven wear means the caliper is not centering itself over the rotor, so check the mounting hardware for corrosion or damage. Examine the caliper once you've popped out the

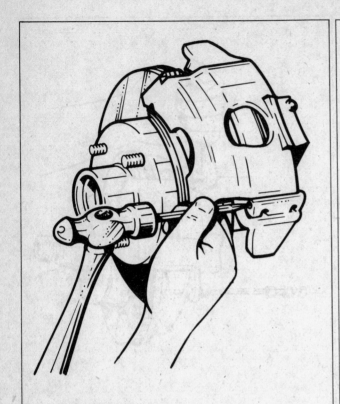

Use a hammer and punch to remove a caliper support key and spring holding the caliper in place. Removing the key and spring by tapping them to one side with the hammer and punch will free the caliper. A hammer may also be used to remove caliper pins.

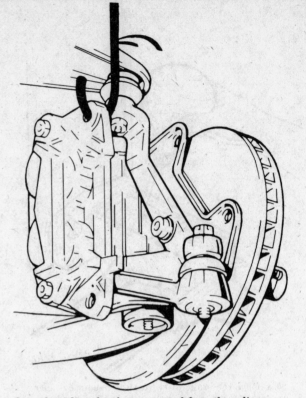

Once the caliper has been removed from the caliper mount, hang it from the car by a wire hook. Hanging the caliper by a wire keeps it from putting strain on the brake line. The caliper can also be rested on the control arm or knuckle mount.

brake pads for any signs of leakage. Check the piston dust boot for cracks or tears. If the caliper appears to be okay and there was no indication of a brake dragging, the calipers don't have to be rebuilt or replaced—unless the car has a lot of miles on it. In that case, rebuilding the calipers is recommended as a preventative maintenance item. Since you have the brakes apart, now is the time to make any repairs. Next check the condition of the rotors. Again, if they're not relatively smooth and flat, they should be resurfaced. You can hold a straightedge up against the rotors to check for warpage. More than about .005 inches variation across the surface will produce a pulsating brake pedal. High spots will normally appear glazed, shiny, and/or discolored. Finally, check the condition of the

wheel bearings by spinning the rotor by hand. On front-wheel-drive vehicles, the transmission must be in neutral. If the wheel bearings feel rough or have excessive play in them, they may require service.

8. If everything passes inspection, go ahead and install the new brake pads on the caliper. Pads are sometimes marked "inner" and "outer." If the caliper, rotor, or wheel bearings require service, make sure the needed repairs are done *before* installing the new pads. A leaky caliper will quickly ruin new pads, as will a rough rotor.

9. Before remounting the caliper on the rotor, clean the mounting points with a wire brush to remove rust and corrosion. Lightly lubricate the contact points where the caliper slides back and forth to center itself over the rotor

with white grease. Do not wire brush plated caliper mounting pins (if this is what your car has on it) because doing so will remove the protective surface plating and encourage corrosion. If the pins are corroded, replace them with new ones.

10. Lightly lubricate the mounting pins, retaining plates, or spring clips before using them to lock the caliper in place. A hammer may be needed to tap pins or plates into place.

11. Torque any fasteners or bolts to the manufacturer's recommended specifications.

12. Open the bleeder screw on the back of each caliper to flush and bleed the system. The brake bleeding procedure should begin with the farthest wheel and work towards the closest wheel with respect to the master cylinder. To do this, open a bleeder screw on a back wheel and pump the brake pedal while adding fresh brake fluid to the master cylinder. When clean fluid is observed coming from the bleeder screw, close it and move on to the other rear wheel. Then do the two front wheels, one at a time, until the entire system has been flushed and bled.

13. Put the front wheels back on.

14. Lower the car to the ground and tighten the lug nuts. Use of a torque wrench is recommended for even tightening (use a star pattern sequence to tighten the lug nuts).

15. Pump the brake pedal several times to remove the play from the relined disc brakes, then start the car and give it a test drive.

Caliper Rebuilding

To disassemble a caliper, you can use one of several procedures. The caliper can be disassembled while still attached to the hydraulic line on the car, or it can be removed and disassembled on a bench. The basic problem is how to get the pistons out of their bores. Special puller tools are available for this purpose, but few do-it-yourselfers would want to buy one for a one-time job. Nor are they readily available in the rental market. Your remaining options,

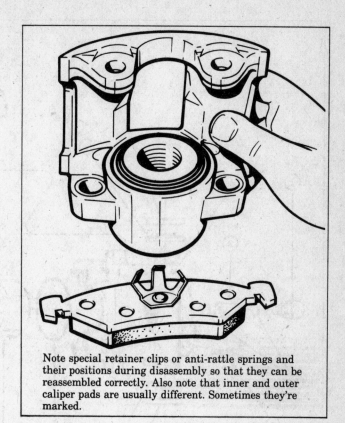

Note special retainer clips or anti-rattle springs and their positions during disassembly so that they can be reassembled correctly. Also note that inner and outer caliper pads are usually different. Sometimes they're marked.

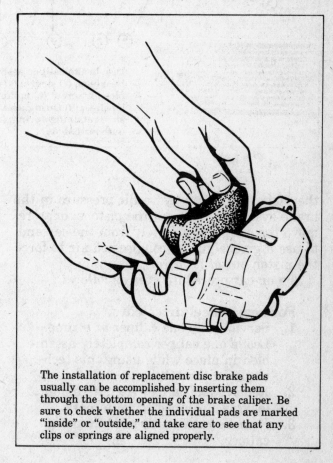

The installation of replacement disc brake pads usually can be accomplished by inserting them through the bottom opening of the brake caliper. Be sure to check whether the individual pads are marked "inside" or "outside," and take care to see that any clips or springs are aligned properly.

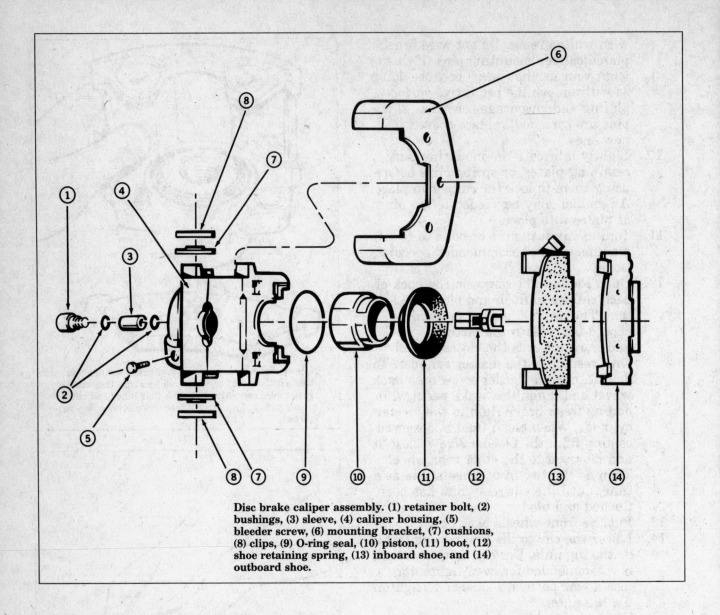

Disc brake caliper assembly. (1) retainer bolt, (2) bushings, (3) sleeve, (4) caliper housing, (5) bleeder screw, (6) mounting bracket, (7) cushions, (8) clips, (9) O-ring seal, (10) piston, (11) boot, (12) shoe retaining spring, (13) inboard shoe, and (14) outboard shoe.

therefore, are to use hydraulic pressure in the brake system to push out the pistons, or to remove the caliper completely from the car and to use a grease gun or compressed air to force the piston out of its bore.

The on-car procedure goes as follows.

For rear-wheel-drive cars.
1. Service only one caliper at a time. Leave one caliper completely assembled in place while using this technique on the other.
2. Remove one caliper from its mount, leaving it connected to its hose.
3. Remove both brake pads from the caliper.

4. Step on the brake pedal to force the piston out of its bore.
5. After the caliper has been rebuilt and reinstalled in place, repeat the same procedure for the other one.

For front-wheel-drive cars.
1. Because the hydraulic system is split diagonally, you can do both calipers at the same time.
2. Disconnect both calipers from their mounts.
3. Remove inner and outer brake pads.
4. Step on the brake pedal to force both pistons out of their bores. This doesn't work on rear-wheel-drive cars, because

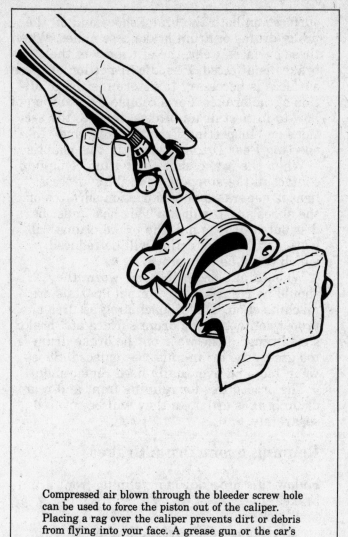

Compressed air blown through the bleeder screw hole can be used to force the piston out of the caliper. Placing a rag over the caliper prevents dirt or debris from flying into your face. A grease gun or the car's hydraulic system can force the piston out as well.

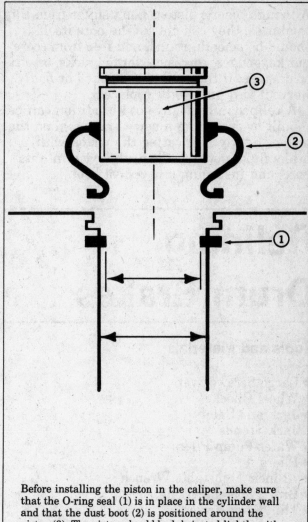

Before installing the piston in the caliper, make sure that the O-ring seal (1) is in place in the cylinder wall and that the dust boot (2) is positioned around the piston (3). The piston should be lubricated lightly with brake fluid.

the hydraulic system is split front to rear. As soon as one of the pistons pops out, pressure is lost, so the other piston remains in its bore.

The bench disassembly technique goes as follows.

1. Remove both calipers from the car, disconnecting and plugging the brake hoses to prevent dirt from getting into the system.
2. Remove inner and outer pads from the caliper.
3. Open the bleeder screw on the back of the caliper and connect a grease gun to the fitting. Pumping grease into the caliper will build up pressure, which will force the piston out of its bore.
4. An alternative technique is to remove the bleeder fitting and use compressed air to blow the piston out. *Caution: This can blow the piston out with great force so do it with the piston aiming down toward the workbench with a rag over the caliper to prevent dirt or debris from flying up into your face. Be sure to keep your fingers clear, too.*

Once the piston has been removed from the caliper using any of the above techniques, you can inspect the condition of both piston and bore. Steel pistons are very prone to corrosion.

Although plastic pistons don't suffer from this weakness, they can crack. The bore itself should be smooth, round, and free from score marks, gouges, corrosion, large cracks, or other damage. If the caliper is cracked or badly worn, it will have to be replaced.

A caliper in basically good condition can be rebuilt by installing a new O-ring seal on the piston, lightly lubricating the piston with brake fluid, pushing the piston back into its bore, and installing a new dust boot.

Relining Drum Brakes

Tools and Materials

- Large Screwdriver
- Wheel Chocks
- Jack and Safety Jack Stands
- Water-Pump Pliers
- Pliers
- 12-inch Adjustable Wrench
- Brake Spoon or Long, Thin Screwdriver
- Face Mask or Respirator
- Paintbrush or Vacuum Cleaner
- Wheel Cylinder Clamp
- Brake Shoe Spring Removal-and-Installation Tool
- Ruler
- Torque Wrench and Socket
- Rags
- Pencil and Paper
- White Lubricant
- Brake Shoes and Linings
- Cotter Pins

IN ORDER for a car's brake system to stop the wheels from turning with efficiency, the brake shoes and linings must make contact with the brake drums. There are friction surfaces on both the brake shoes and on the brake drums of drum brake assemblies. When these surfaces wear, the efficiency of the brakes is affected. Periodic inspection of these surfaces is necessary to determine the condition of the brakes. For a complete discussion of how to inspect drum brakes, refer to the sections on "Inspecting Front Brakes" and "Inspecting Rear Drum Brakes" in this chapter.

When the brake shoes and drum come into contact in the stopping or braking process, heat is generated on the friction surfaces of the shoes and the drum. This heat must be dissipated. If it is not, the brake drums will warp and braking action will be reduced, which could be dangerous.

When brake drums become worn, they should be resurfaced by an auto parts store machine shop. This remachining assures a proper contact of the drum surface and brake shoe lining. If the wear on the brake drum is too great, the drum must be replaced. Shoes wear, too, and eventually need replacement.

The procedures for relining front and rear drum brakes differ, so they will be covered separately.

Relining Front Drum Brakes

Follow this procedure for relining front drum brakes.

1. Engage the parking brake.
2. Remove the wheel covers from the front wheels, using a large screwdriver or the pointed end of the car's jack handle.
3. Using the wrench end of the jack handle, or a socket wrench of the proper size, loosen the lug nuts on both front wheels about one turn.
4. Place wheel chocks behind the rear wheels to prevent the car from rolling.
5. Using the jack, raise the front of the car until the wheels are off the ground.
6. Place safety jack stands under the frame of the car to support it solidly.
7. Remove the lug nuts of the passenger's side wheel first, placing the nuts in the wheel cover for safe-keeping. Most lug nuts can be removed by turning them counterclockwise. A few cars, however, may have a left-hand thread on the lug

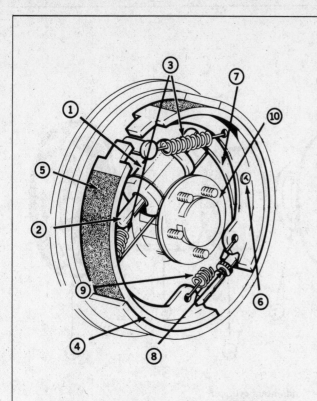

Rear drum brake components. (1) wheel cylinder, (2) pushrod, (3) return springs, (4) brake shoe, (5) brake lining, (6) hold-down spring and clip, (7) parking brake actuating lever, (8) star wheel adjusting nut, (9) adjustment retaining spring, and (10) hub.

nuts, and washer. If the nut, or nuts, cannot be removed by turning counter-clockwise, try turning clockwise.

12. Rock the drum and hub assembly to work the outer bearing loose. Use care to avoid having the bearing fall out onto the floor. Have your hand ready to catch it. Place the outer bearing, washer, and adjusting nut on a clean rag. **Note:** If you have not inspected or lubricated the bearings within the interval recommended in the owner's manual, refer to the section on "Repacking Wheel Bearings" in the "Maintaining Your Car" chapter.

13. Slide the drum and hub assembly off. Be careful not to allow the inner bearing to drag on the spindle. If resistance is encountered during the removal, it may be necessary to back off the brake adjusting star by using a brake spoon. On late model cars that are equipped with self-adjusting brakes, a long, thin screwdriver will be needed to push the self-adjusting lever away from the star wheel. *Caution: While the drum and hub assembly is off the car, be careful not to allow grease or dirt to contact the drum surface or brake linings. Dirt or grease on these surfaces could cause brake drag or loss of braking action.*

14. Using a face mask or respirator, remove the dusty residue on the brake assembly and interior of the brake drum with an old paintbrush or a vacuum cleaner. *Caution: Avoid breathing this dust! It contains asbestos.*

15. Inspect the interior of the brake drum's friction surface for scoring and visible cracks. Make sure the surface is smooth. If the surface is worn, it should be resurfaced by an auto parts store that has a machine shop.

16. Install a wheel cylinder clamp on the dust caps at each end of the wheel cylinder. This will prevent the cylinder parts from expanding out of the cylinder when the brake shoe return springs are removed.

17. Remove the two brake shoe return springs. Use a brake shoe spring removal-and-installation tool. **Note:** Make a simple sketch of the way the

nuts. In such a case, the lugs may be marked with the letter "L." If your car has left-hand threaded lugs, turn the nuts clockwise to remove them.

8. Remove the wheel and tire assembly from the car.

9. Remove the dust, or grease, cap. Use large water-pump pliers in combination with a screwdriver. Grip the dust cap with the pliers and pry it off with the screwdriver.

10. Remove the cotter pin with pliers. **Note:** The assembly is held in place by one or two nuts. If there are two nuts, the outer nut, or lock nut, is a castellated nut that is held in position by a cotter pin; the inner nut is the adjusting nut. If there is only one nut, it is the adjusting nut, and it is held in place by a cotter pin.

11. Use a wrench to remove the nut, or

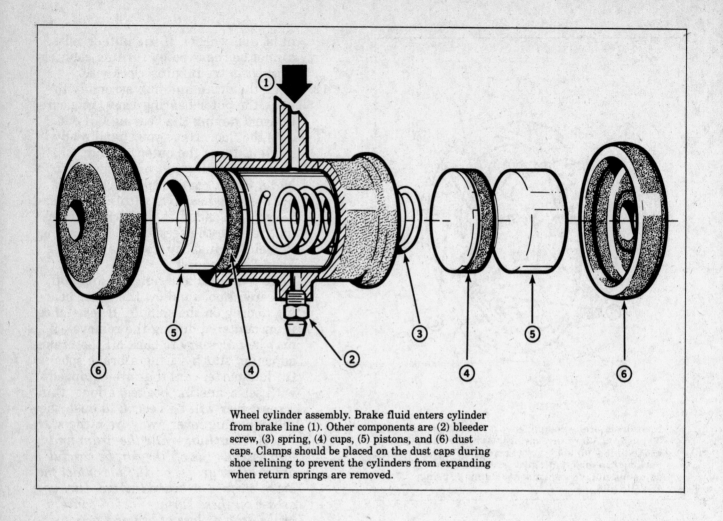

Wheel cylinder assembly. Brake fluid enters cylinder from brake line (1). Other components are (2) bleeder screw, (3) spring, (4) cups, (5) pistons, and (6) dust caps. Clamps should be placed on the dust caps during shoe relining to prevent the cylinders from expanding when return springs are removed.

springs are hooked up to ease the installation of new springs. Note the differences in coil diameter of the springs.

18. Using pliers, remove the brake shoe hold-down springs by pressing in and turning the fastener ¼ turn either clockwise or counterclockwise.

Note: If your car is equipped with a self-adjusting brake mechanism, there is another step that must be taken before the brake shoes can be removed: use pliers to remove the cable, tension spring, and the self-adjusting lever.

19. Make a simple sketch of the star wheel adjusting mechanism, noting the location of the star wheel in reference to the left or right shoe. It will be closer to one of the shoes. Remove both brake shoes as an assembly.

20. Move the brake shoes toward one another. This will release the spring and the star wheel adjusting nut.

21. Use a small amount of white lubricant to lubricate the tabs on the brake backing plate. Usually, there are six tabs.

22. Install the new brake shoes and linings, reversing Steps 16 through 21. This is where your sketches should come in handy.

23. Replace the brake drum; you may have to rotate it slightly forward as you install it.

24. Replace the wheel bearing; you may have to wiggle the drum to seat the bearing properly.

25. Replace the washer and the adjusting nut.

26. At this point, it is necessary to adjust the wheel bearing. **Note:** Manufacturer's specifications should always be followed. If specifications are not available, these basic guidelines for wheel

bearing adjustment should be followed.

A. With a ruler, measure the hub bore size for the outer bearing. If the bore size is 1¾ inches or more, tighten the adjusting nut using a torque wrench to 17 foot-pounds while rotating the wheel by hand. If the bore size is less than 1¾ inch, tighten the adjusting nut using a torque wrench to 8 foot-pounds while rotating the wheel by hand.

B. After tightening the adjusting nut to the specified torque, back off the nut ⅙ to ¼ turn to obtain proper cotter pin alignment between the cotter pin hole in the spindle nut and the cotter pin hole in the spindle. If there is a lock nut, replace it and align it so its cotter pin hole lines up with the hole in the spindle.

Note: If the drum brake adjustment mechanism was altered during drum removal, proper brake adjustment will be necessary. This is covered in the section on "Adjusting Drum Brakes" in this chapter.

27. Install a new cotter pin through the adjusting nut or lock nut and spindle. Bend the ends of the pin around the nut with pliers so it will not come out.

28. Reinstall the dust cap and tire and wheel assembly, reversing Steps 7 through 9. Note: Some cars come equipped with spring static suppressors in the dust cap. Be sure that the ends of the cotter pin do not contact the suppressor.

29. Follow Steps 7 through 28 for the drum brake on the other front wheel.

30. After the brakes have been inspected, lower the car, reversing Steps 1 through 6.

Relining Rear Drum Brakes

To reline rear drum brakes, follow these steps.

1. Engage the parking brake.
2. Remove the wheel covers from the rear wheels, using a large screwdriver or the pointed end of the car's jack handle.

3. Using the wrench end of the jack handle or a socket wrench of the proper size, loosen the lug nuts on both rear wheels about one turn.

4. Place wheel chocks in front of the front wheels to prevent the car from rolling.

5. Using the jack, raise the rear of the car until the wheels are off the ground.

6. Place safety jack stands under the frame of the car to support it solidly.

7. Remove the lug nuts of the passenger's side wheel first, placing the nuts in the wheel cover for safe-keeping. Most lug nuts can be removed by turning them counterclockwise. A few cars, however, may have a left-hand thread on the lug nuts. In such a case, the lugs may be marked with the letter "L." If your car has left-hand threaded lugs, turn the nuts clockwise to remove them.

8. Remove the wheel and tire assembly from the car.

9. Pull the drum free of the studs as you rotate it slightly forward. Note: There may be a spring steel clip on one of the studs. Pry the clip free with a screwdriver and then remove the drum.

10. Using a face mask or respirator, remove the dusty residue on the brake assembly and interior of the brake drum with an old paintbrush or a vacuum cleaner. *Caution: Avoid breathing this dust! It contains asbestos.*

11. Inspect the interior of the brake drum's friction surface for scoring and visible cracks. Make sure the surface is smooth. If the surface is worn, it should be resurfaced by an auto parts store that has a machine shop.

12. Examine the wheel cylinder on the brake assembly for evidence of leakage. If any is evident, have the brakes inspected by a mechanic.

13. Inspect all springs in the brake assembly to see if they are secured and not broken.

14. Install a wheel cylinder clamp on the dust covers at each end of the wheel cylinder. This will prevent the cylinder parts from expanding out of the brake cylinder when the brake shoe return springs are removed.

15. Remove the two brake shoe return springs. Use a brake shoe spring removal-and-installation tool. **Note:** Make a simple sketch of the way the springs are hooked up to ease the installation of new springs. Note the differences in coil diameter of the springs.

16. Using pliers, remove the brake shoe hold-down springs by pressing in and turning the fastener ¼ turn either clockwise or counterclockwise.

    Note: If your car is equipped with a self-adjusting brake mechanism, there is another step that must be taken before the brake shoes can be removed: use pliers to remove the cable, tension spring, and self-adjusting lever.

17. Remove the emergency brake cable by slipping it up and out of the lever bracket that is attached to the larger of the two brake shoes.

18. Make a simple sketch of the star wheel adjusting mechanism, noting the location of the star wheel in reference to the left or right shoe. It will be closer to one shoe. Remove both brake shoes as an assembly.

19. Move the brake shoes towards one another. This will release the spring and the star wheel adjuster.

20. Use a small amount of white lubricant to lubricate the tabs on the brake backing plate. Usually, there are six tabs.

21. Install the new brake shoes and linings, reversing Steps 14 through 19. This is where your sketches should come in handy.

22. Replace the brake drum; you may have to rotate it slightly forward as you install it over the studs.

23. Replace the wheel and tire assembly, reversing Steps 7 and 8.

24. Repeat Steps 7 through 23 for the wheel on the driver's side of the car.

25. Lower the car, reversing Steps 2 through 6.

Adjusting Drum Brakes

Tools and Materials

- Wheel Chocks
- Jack and Safety Jack Stands
- Screwdrivers
- Brake Spoon
- Pliers
- Coat Hanger

PROPER CONTACT of the brake shoe with the brake drum is necessary for maximum braking efficiency. A brake adjustment is simply a readjustment of these surfaces in relation to one another.

While drum brake systems do incorporate self-adjusting levers that "complete" the adjustment process, they are not completely self-adjusting. Part of the adjusting mechanism is a star wheel adjusting nut positioned between the two brake shoes on the brake assembly. By turning this nut, the distance between the brake shoe and the drum surface can be varied.

Most drum brake systems provide access to the star wheel adjusting nut through a hole—an adjustment access—in the brake backing plate. On such systems, it is not necessary to remove the wheels to make the adjustment. Other systems provide access to the star wheel adjusting nut through a hole—adjustment access—in the drum itself. In these systems, it is necessary to remove the wheels to make the adjustment.

If your braking action is not what it should be, your brake pedal is lower than normal, or you hear squeaking sounds when the car is stopped and the brakes are applied, your first course of action should be a brake adjustment. This could correct the problem.

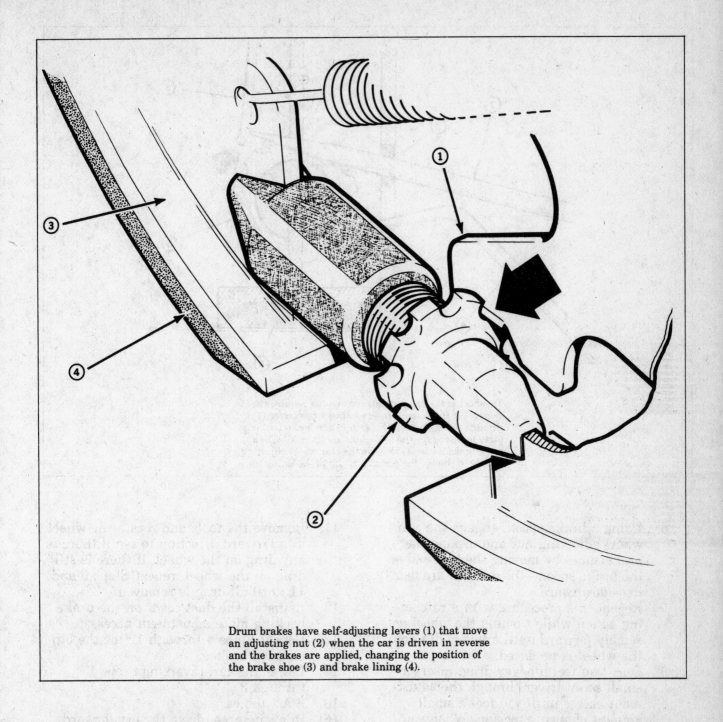

Drum brakes have self-adjusting levers (1) that move an adjusting nut (2) when the car is driven in reverse and the brakes are applied, changing the position of the brake shoe (3) and brake lining (4).

Adjustment Without Removing Wheels

Here is how to adjust brakes on systems where you do not have to remove the wheels.

1. Place wheel chocks behind the rear wheels. **Note:** The parking brake must *not* be engaged.
2. Jack up the front of the car and place a pair of jack stands under the frame.
3. Jack up the rear of the car and place a pair of safety stands under the frame. Remove the wheel chocks.
4. Locate the brake adjustment access on the brake backing plate on the inside of the wheel assembly of a front wheel.
5. Remove the dust cover from the brake adjustment access with a screwdriver.

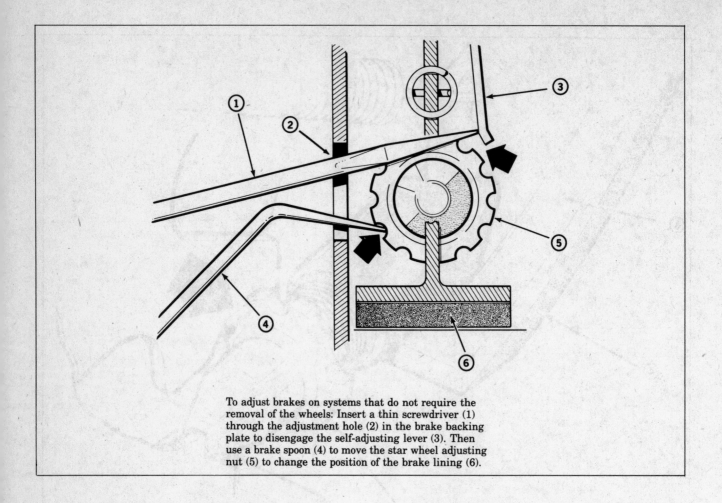

To adjust brakes on systems that do not require the removal of the wheels: Insert a thin screwdriver (1) through the adjustment hole (2) in the brake backing plate to disengage the self-adjusting lever (3). Then use a brake spoon (4) to move the star wheel adjusting nut (5) to change the position of the brake lining (6).

6. Using a brake spoon, engage the star wheel adjusting nut and expand the brake shoes by moving the free end of the brake spoon—the end you are holding—downward.

7. Repeat this procedure with a ratcheting action while turning the wheel assembly forward until a heavy drag on the wheel is produced.

8. Once you feel a heavy drag, insert a small screwdriver through the adjustment access until you feel a small amount of spring tension. When you feel this tension, you have disengaged the self-adjusting lever from the star wheel adjusting nut. The star wheel can now be turned in a counter-rotation.

9. Reverse the action of the brake spoon by engaging the star wheel adjusting nut and pushing up.

10. Repeat this three more times.

11. Remove the tools and rotate the wheel in a forward direction to see if there is any drag on the wheel. If there is still drag on the wheel, repeat Steps 9 and 11 until all drag is removed.

12. Reinstall the dust cover on the brake backing plate adjustment access.

13. Repeat Steps 4 through 12 for the other drum brakes.

14. Lower the car, reversing Steps 1 through 3.

15. Start the car.

16. In a safe area, drive the car forward and apply the brakes firmly.

17. Back up a short distance and apply the brakes firmly.

18. Repeat Steps 16 and 17 ten times to assure that proper adjustment has been made and that the self-adjusters have established proper shoe to drum clearance.

19. Road test the car.

Adjustment With Wheels Removed

On some General Motors cars, access to the star wheel adjusting nut is provided through the drum. In this case, you will have to remove the wheels to adjust the brakes. Follow this procedure.

1. Place wheel chocks behind the rear wheels. **Note:** The parking brake must *not* be engaged.
2. Remove the wheel covers from all the wheels, using a large screwdriver or the pointed end of the car's jack handle.
3. Using the wrench end of the jack handle or a socket wrench of the proper size, loosen the lug nuts on each wheel about one turn.
4. Using the jack, raise the front of the car until the wheels are off the ground.
5. Place safety jack stands under the frame of the car to support it solidly.
6. Using the jack, raise the rear of the car until the wheels are off the ground.
7. Place safety jack stands under the frame of the car to support it solidly.
8. Remove the lug nuts from a front wheel, placing the nuts in the wheel cover for safe-keeping. Most lug nuts can be removed by turning them counterclockwise. A few cars, however, may have a left-hand thread on the lug nuts.
9. Remove the wheel and tire assembly from the car.
10. Rotate the drum until the adjustment access is at the bottom. Remove the

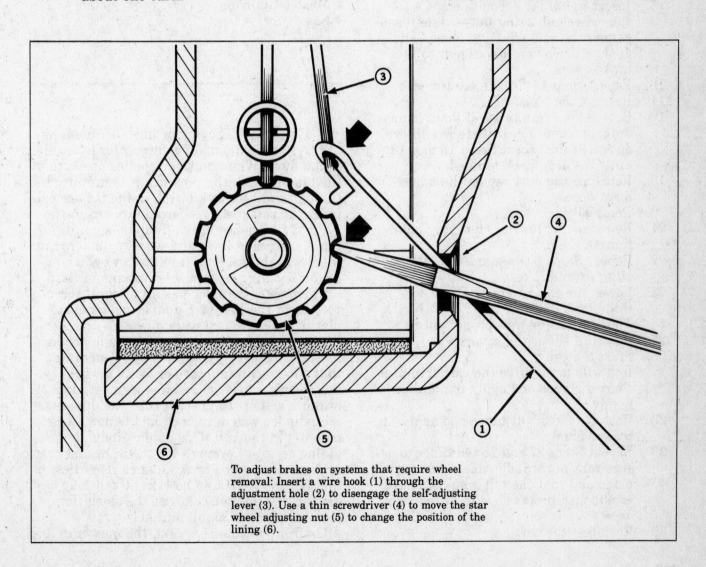

To adjust brakes on systems that require wheel removal: Insert a wire hook (1) through the adjustment hole (2) to disengage the self-adjusting lever (3). Use a thin screwdriver (4) to move the star wheel adjusting nut (5) to change the position of the lining (6).

dust cap from the access.

11. Insert a brake spoon into the adjustment access to engage the star wheel adjusting nut.

12. Move the free end of the brake spoon upward with a ratcheting action to expand the shoes. Repeat this procedure while turning the drum forward until a heavy drag is felt on the drum.

13. Use pliers to fashion a hook by bending a ½-inch section on one end of a length of stiff wire, such as a coat hanger, 90 degrees.

14. Insert the bent end of the wire through the adjustment access on an upward angle. Hook the wire onto the adjusting lever and exert a slight pull to disengage the self-adjusting lever from the star wheel adjusting nut.

15. Insert the brake spoon to engage the star wheel adjusting nut—while disengaging the self-adjusting lever—and apply a downward movement to the brake spoon.

16. Repeat Step 15 three more times.

17. Remove the tools.

18. Rotate the drum to see if there is any drag on the drum. If there is still drag on the drum, repeat Steps 15 and 18 until the drag is eliminated.

19. Reinstall the dust cap on the adjustment access.

20. Reinstall the wheel.

21. Reinstall the lug nuts but only hand-tighten them.

22. Repeat Steps 8 through 21 for the other drum brakes.

23. Lower the car, reversing Steps 4 through 7.

24. Tighten the lug nuts on all wheels.

25. Reinstall the wheel covers.

26. Start the car.

27. In a safe area, drive the car forward a short distance and apply the brakes firmly.

28. Back up a short distance and apply the brakes firmly.

29. Repeat Steps 27 and 28 ten times to assure that proper adjustment has been made and that the self-adjusters have established proper shoe to drum clearance.

30. Road test the car.

Master Cylinder Service

Tools and Materials

- Screwdriver
- Socket and Ratchet Wrench
- Box-End Wrench
- Flare-Nut Wrench
- Hydraulic Brake Fluid
- Master Cylinder
- Rag

THE MASTER cylinder in your car's brake system is the main reservoir for hydraulic brake fluid. When a driver applies pressure to the brake pedal, the pressure is transmitted through linkages to a piston in the master cylinder. As this piston is forced forward in the cylinder, it pushes brake fluid ahead of it. Since the brake lines and wheel cylinders are filled with brake fluid, the master cylinder piston is acting upon a solid column of fluid.

The master cylinder has an integral reservoir or, in the case of a dual or double-piston master cylinder, two reservoirs.

For years, one danger in the single-piston master cylinder hydraulic brake system was that a brake line rupture or leaking wheel cylinder could cause sudden and complete loss of braking action. To prevent this, the dual master cylinder was developed and is now in common use in the U.S. This dual cylinder, by providing separate systems for the front and rear brakes, offers some braking force regardless of line failure. Although both front and rear hydraulic systems could fail at the same time, such an event is highly unlikely.

On front-wheel-drive cars, the master cylinder is split diagonally. One chamber supplies pressure to the left front and right rear wheel while the other chamber operates the right front and left rear wheel. The reason for doing this is because front-wheel-drive cars rely on the front brakes to a much greater extent than rear-wheel-drive cars. If pressure was lost to both front wheels at the same time (as would be the case if the system were split front-to-rear and the front developed a leak), the rear brakes alone might not be able to stop the car safely.

Master cylinders, manufactured of cast iron, have brackets and holes for mounting on the engine compartment side of the firewall—the partition between the driver and the engine. In this location, it can be inspected and serviced easily. On power brake systems, the master cylinder is mounted on the vacuum unit, which, in turn, is mounted on the firewall.

Checking the Master Cylinder

To check the master cylinder, use the following procedure.

1. Engage the parking brake and raise the hood.
2. Locate the master cylinder and remove the cover, using a screwdriver. Be careful not to disturb any gasket. The cover is secured by a bail or a screw.
3. Check the fluid level. It should be within ¼ inch of the top. If it is low, replenish it with hydraulic brake fluid.
4. Replace the cover, reversing Step 2.
5. Close the hood.
6. Pump the brake pedal several times and maintain steady foot pressure on the pedal for 30 seconds. If, during this period, the pedal slowly recedes under foot pressure, it indicates worn or malfunctioning parts in the master cylinder, requiring replacement of the master cylinder. If pedal pressure does not cause the pedal to recede, the master cylinder is functioning properly. **Note:** If your car has power-assisted brakes, depress and release the brake pedal five times to exhaust the vacuum pressure in the power brake system before performing Step 6.

Replacing the Master Cylinder

To replace the master cylinder in your car, follow these steps.

1. Engage the parking brake and raise the hood.
2. Locate the master cylinder and *loosen* the three cap screws that secure it to the firewall about one turn with a socket and ratchet wrench. **Note:** On power-assisted systems, the master cylinder is attached to the vacuum unit with three cap screws. If this is the case, loosen the cap screws and proceed directly to Step 5.
3. Look under the dashboard and locate the linkage on the brake pedal that secures the master cylinder pushrod to the brake pedal. The linkage is secured to the pedal by a bolt below the linkage's pivot point.
4. Remove the bolt with a box-end wrench.
5. Using a flare-nut wrench, disconnect the brake line(s) from the master cylinder. **Note:** Dual-chamber cylinders will have two lines to disconnect.
6. Once the brake line(s) is disconnected, remove the cap screws holding the master cylinder in place with the socket and ratchet wrench.
7. Grasp the master cylinder and carefully move it forward, away from the firewall. **Note:** Be careful not to accidentally bend the disconnected brake line.
8. Position the new master cylinder carefully, reversing Step 7.
9. Thread the three cap screws by hand just enough to hold the master cylinder in position.
10. Attach—but do not tighten—the brake line(s) using a flare-nut wrench. **Note:** If you are working on a power-assisted system, proceed to Step 12.
11. Under the dashboard, reconnect the brake pedal linkage, reversing Step 3.
12. Under the hood, tighten the three cap screws securing the master cylinder in place.
13. Remove the master cylinder cover with a screwdriver and fill the reservoir

with fresh hydraulic brake fluid to within ½ inch of the top. Replace the cover but do not secure it.

14. Wrap a disposable rag securely around the loose brake line and brake line fitting at the master cylinder.
15. Slowly pump the brake pedal all the way down and up five times to charge the new cylinder.
16. Remove the rag from the brake line and fitting and dispose of it. *Caution: The rag will be saturated with fluid. This fluid is highly corrosive and will damage painted surfaces such as those on your car.*
17. With a flare-nut wrench, tighten the brake line to the fitting securely.
18. Remove the master cylinder cover and replenish the cylinder with fluid.
19. Refasten the cover and close the hood.
20. Release the parking brake.
21. Start the car and carefully drive the car forward a short distance and firmly apply the brakes to check their operation.

Inspecting Power Brakes

Tools and Materials

- Small Screwdriver
- Utility Knife
- Rag
- Vacuum Unit Air Filter
- Vacuum Hose

POWER BRAKES are really power-assisted brakes that help the driver in applying the brakes; they add additional force to the force that the hydraulic system exerts on the brakes.

The vacuum or power brake unit is mounted on the firewall, between the firewall and the master cylinder. The vacuum unit is a canister anywhere from 7 inches to more than 12 inches in diameter and from 3 to 10 inches thick.

A vacuum unit uses engine vacuum from the intake manifold to supply its additional braking force. Under normal circumstances, a vacuum unit cannot be repaired. If faulty, it must be replaced. However, certain maintenance checks can be made to prove whether the vacuum unit is performing adequately or not.

Testing the Vacuum System

To verify that the vacuum unit for your power brakes is operating properly, follow these steps.

1. With the engine off, slowly pump the brake pedal all the way down to exhaust the vacuum in the vacuum reserve tank.
2. Press the brake pedal down, and while maintaining pressure, start the engine. If the vacuum unit is operating, the brake pedal will move downward. If the brake pedal does not move downward, there is a vacuum leak in the vacuum unit system.

Locating a Leak

If you suspect a leak in the vacuum system, follow this procedure to locate it.

1. With the parking brake engaged and the engine running, raise the hood and disconnect the hose at the vacuum unit. Simply pull it off.
2. Block the hole on the end of the hose with your finger. If the engine speed is noticeably reduced, the hose is in good condition. If the engine speed does not change, the hose must be replaced.
3. Reconnect the good vacuum hose to the vacuum unit.
4. When the good hose is connected, the engine speed should be noticeably increased. If it does not change, there is a problem in the vacuum unit. Consult a qualified mechanic.
5. Remove the air filter on the firewall side of the vacuum unit. In most cases, it is around the valve rod and is cov-

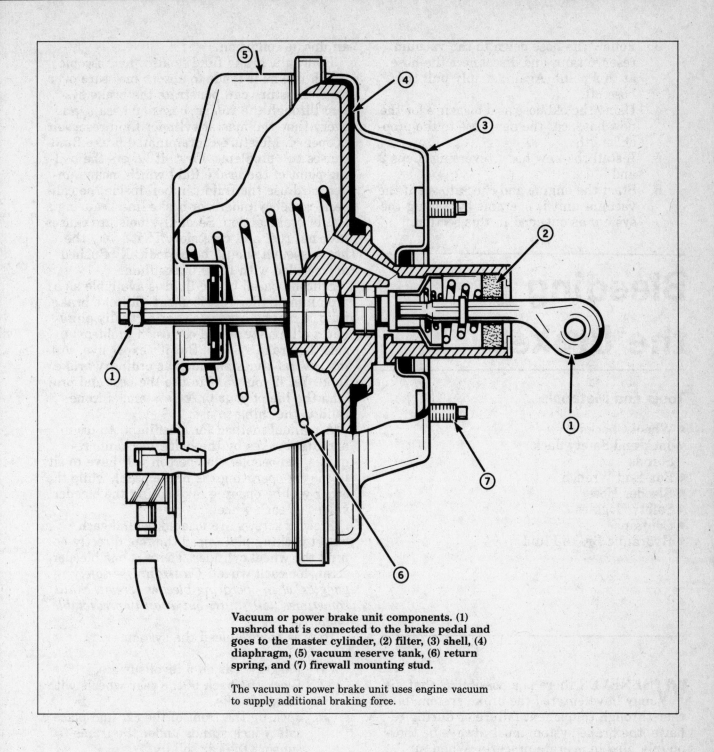

Vacuum or power brake unit components. (1) pushrod that is connected to the brake pedal and goes to the master cylinder, (2) filter, (3) shell, (4) diaphragm, (5) vacuum reserve tank, (6) return spring, and (7) firewall mounting stud.

The vacuum or power brake unit uses engine vacuum to supply additional braking force.

ered by a flexible dust cover. Use a small screwdriver to pry it free.

6. Wipe the filter clean with a soft, clean rag—an old diaper or towel is fine.

7. Blow through the filter to see if it is clear. If it is, reinstall it and the dust cover. If it is not clear, you will have to replace the filter.

Replacing a Vacuum Hose

To replace a vacuum hose, follow this procedure.

1. Engage the parking brake.
2. Raise the hood and disconnect the vacuum hose at the top of the vacuum unit. Simply pull it off.

3. Follow the hose down to the vacuum reserve tank and disconnect the hose at this point. Again, simply pull the hose off.
4. Using the old hose as a measure for the new hose, cut the new hose to the proper length.
5. Install the new hose, reversing Steps 2 and 3.
6. Start the engine and check to see if the vacuum unit is operable by testing the system as outlined in this section.

Bleeding the Brakes

Tools and Materials

- Wheel Chocks
- Jack and Safety Jack Stands
- Box-End Wrench
- Bleeder Hose
- Safety Goggles
- Container
- Hydraulic Brake Fluid

WHENEVER there is a possibility that air may have entered the brake system, either through component failure or during repairs, the brake system must always be thoroughly bled to operate properly. When air enters the brake system, the result will be a spongy or totally useless brake pedal.

Hydraulic fluid is used to operate the wheel cylinders or disc brake pistons because it does not compress when the brake pedal is pushed and pressure is formed in the brake lines. Even the slightest amount of air in the lines will cause the brakes to feel spongy, causing an unsafe condition.

Hydraulic brake fluid is also "hydroscopic," which means it tends to absorb moisture over time. Moisture can penetrate the brake system through the rubber hoses and seals, and every time the master cylinder fluid reservoir is opened. Moisture-contaminated brake fluid causes two problems. First, it lowers the boiling point of the brake fluid which means under hard use the fluid can boil inside the calipers, wheel cylinders, or brake lines, causing a loss of brake action. Secondly, moisture causes internal rust and corrosion. That's why the brake system should be periodically flushed and refilled with fresh brake fluid.

Silicone-based brake fluid is available as a premium quality replacement. Silicone brake fluid is non-hydroscopic so it virtually eliminates all moisture and corrosion problems inside the brake system. But it's expensive, costing several times as much as ordinary brake fluid. Yet if you want to use the best and prolong the life of your brake system, silicone fluid is the thing to use.

A manual method for bleeding both drum and disc brakes by the home mechanic requires two people. One person will have to sit in the car operating the brake pedal, while the other will be opening and closing the bleeder valves at each wheel.

Bleeder screws are located behind each wheel backing plate near the top, directly behind the wheel cylinder. There is one bleeder screw for each wheel. *Caution: Use safety goggles when operating bleeder screws. Fluid sometimes will squirt out at an unpredictable angle.*

Here is how to bleed the system.

1. Park the car on a level surface.
2. Block the back of the rear wheels with wheel chocks.
3. Jack up the front of the car and place safety jack stands under the frame to support the car solidly.
4. Jack up the rear of the car and place safety jack stands under the axle housing at both sides.
5. Remove the wheel chocks.
6. Using a box-end wrench, open and close each bleeder screw ½ turn. There is some pressure in the system and a small amount of fluid should ooze out.

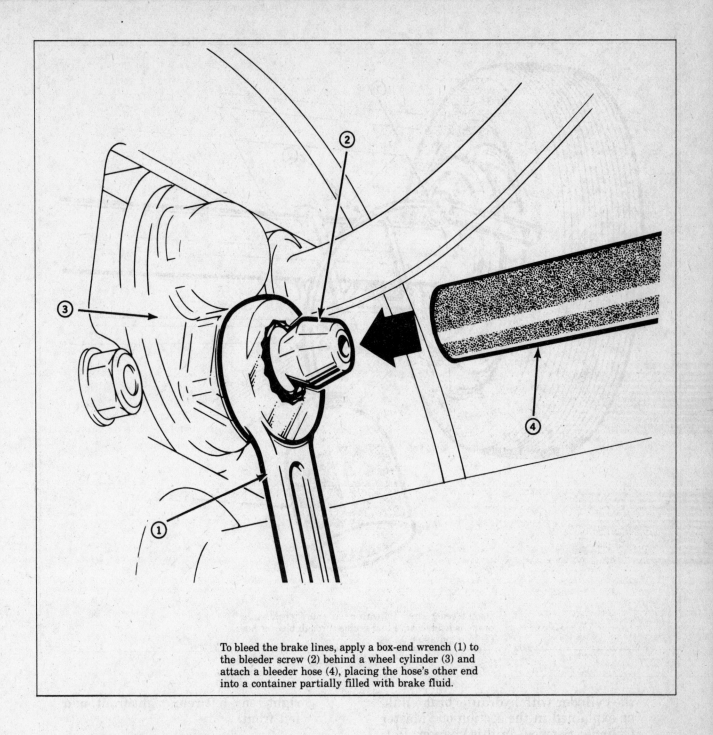

To bleed the brake lines, apply a box-end wrench (1) to the bleeder screw (2) behind a wheel cylinder (3) and attach a bleeder hose (4), placing the hose's other end into a container partially filled with brake fluid.

This will prove that the screws are free to operate.

7. Apply the box-end wrench to the screw farthest from the master cylinder. Usually, this will be the right rear wheel.

8. Attach a bleeder hose to the screw and place the other end in a container partially filled with brake fluid.

9. Have your assistant pump the brake pedal and hold continuous pedal pressure.

10. Open the bleeder screw. Fluid will escape into the container—the pedal will sink to the floor. Instruct your assistant to hold the pedal down while you tighten the screw, and then have him release the pedal.

11. Open the master cylinder cover and fill

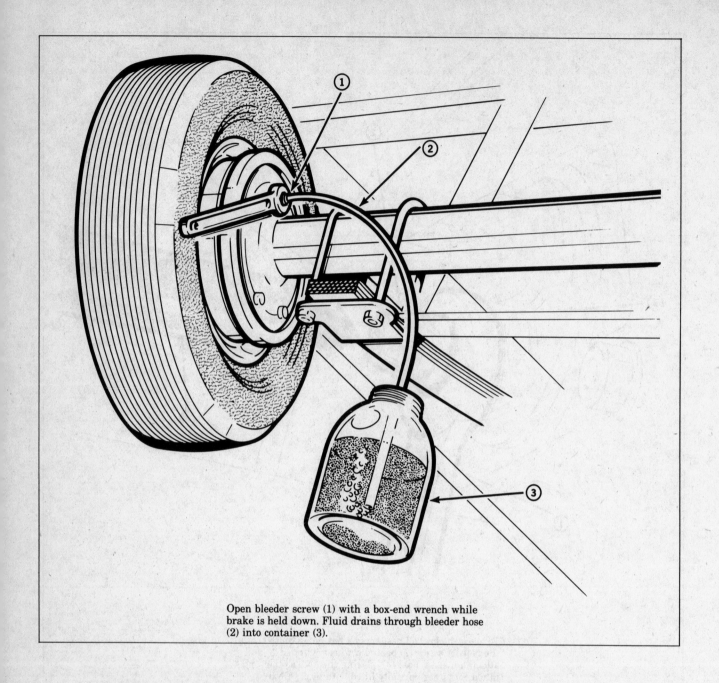

Open bleeder screw (1) with a box-end wrench while brake is held down. Fluid drains through bleeder hose (2) into container (3).

the cylinder with hydraulic brake fluid, as explained in the section on "Master Cylinder Service" in this chapter. Put the cover back on but do not tighten it, because more fluid will be required later.

12. Repeat Steps 7 through 10 for each bleeder screw. **Note:** The procedure is to start at the wheel farthest from the master cylinder and to finish with the wheel closest to the master cylinder. On most cars, the proper order will be: right rear, left rear, right front, and left front.

Caution: After pumping several times, check the master cylinder. Keep it filled with fluid. If the master cylinder runs dry while bleeding, you will have additional work because the master cylinder itself will have to be bled as explained in the section on "Master Cylinder Service" in this chapter.

13. After finishing the bleeding procedure,

fill the master cylinder with hydraulic brake fluid again. Tighten the cover.

14. Lower the car, reversing Steps 3 and 4.
15. Road test the car. The pedal action should not be spongy. If the pedal can be pushed almost to the floor, a brake adjustment may be required. See the section on "Adjusting Drum Brakes" in this chapter.

Brake Lines and Hoses

Tools and Materials

- Wheel Chocks
- Jack and Safety Jack Stands
- Open-End Wrench
- Flare-Nut Wrench
- Ball-Peen Hammer and Punch
- Brake Hoses

WHEN YOU put your foot on the brake pedal to stop your car, several things happen at once. The pressure you apply to the pedal is transmitted to the brake system master cylinder (either directly or through a booster assembly called a vacuum unit). This pressure is further transmitted by means of hydraulic brake fluid to the wheel cylinders through a series of steel lines and flexible hoses. As the pressure is applied to the wheel cylinders, it causes the cylinder pistons to move and pressure is applied to the brake drum or disc through the brake shoes or pads. The friction that then exists between the brake shoes or pads (which are lined with friction material) and the brake drum or disc is what stops the wheels from turning.

Routine maintenance of your car should include brake line and hose inspection. Check for leaks, kinks, and rust on the lines and leaks or other deterioration at the flexible hoses.

If there is any doubt as to the condition of a brake line or hose, replace it. High hydraulic pressure is built up in the brake system upon application of the brakes. Any weakness in the system will cause a failure and possible accident. Brake line replacement is *not* a task for the do-it-yourselfer. It should be handled by a professional mechanic.

There are always three brake hoses if the differential housing is of solid axle construction—two front and one rear. Cars with swing axle or transaxle installations will have four hoses—two front and two rear. If one front hose needs replacement, a good practice is to replace both. The same applies for the rear hoses—if your car is equipped with two.

Front brake hoses are connected to the wheel cylinder or brake caliper—whichever applies—at one end and to the brake line via a support bracket on a frame member near an upper control arm at the other end. Rear brake hoses are connected to a junction block on an axle housing at one end and to a brake line via a support bracket on a frame member at the rear of the car at the other end.

Replacing a Brake Hose

To replace a brake hose, follow these steps.

1. Engage the parking brake.
2. Block the back of the rear wheels with wheel chocks. **Note:** If you are working on a rear hose, the front wheels would be blocked and you would jack up the rear of the car.
3. Jack up the front of the car and place a pair of safety jack stands under the frame to support the car solidly.
4. Apply an open-end wrench to the brake hose fitting at the support bracket to keep it from twisting.
5. Apply a flare-nut wrench to the brake line fitting at the support bracket.
6. Holding the open-end wrench to the brake hose fitting, unscrew the brake line fitting and work the fitting back

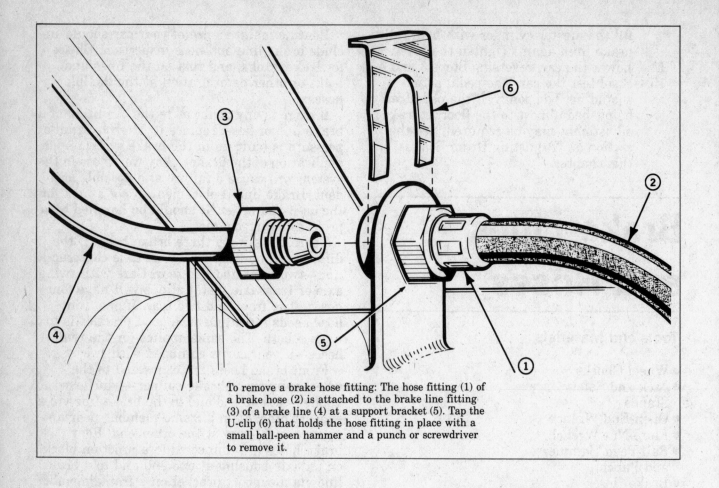

To remove a brake hose fitting: The hose fitting (1) of a brake hose (2) is attached to the brake line fitting (3) of a brake line (4) at a support bracket (5). Tap the U-clip (6) that holds the hose fitting in place with a small ball-peen hammer and a punch or screwdriver to remove it.

and forth ¼ turn several times until it can be turned freely on the brake line.

7. When the brake line fitting rotates freely, unscrew it from the brake hose. **Note:** Some fluid will ooze from the brake line. This is normal.

8. Using a small ball-peen hammer and a punch or an old screwdriver, remove the U-clip holding the brake hose fitting to the support bracket. Put the punch or screwdriver at the top of the clip's projection and strike the other end of the tool to drive the U-clip free. Save the clip.

9. Pull the brake hose free of the support bracket.

10. Using an open-end wrench, unscrew the brake hose fitting at the other end of the hose. If you are working on a front hose, this connection will be at the wheel cylinder or brake caliper— whichever applies. If you are working on a rear hose, this will be at the junc-

tion block on an axle housing.

11. Using a new brake hose, reverse Step 10.

12. Position the other end of the brake hose in the support bracket.

13. Position the U-clip and strike the top projection with a ball-peen hammer to secure it.

14. Insert the brake line fitting into the brake hose and tighten the fitting with a flare-nut wrench while holding the brake hose fitting with an open-end wrench to keep it from twisting.

15. Bleed the brake system at the wheels where hoses have been replaced. For example, if you replaced the rear hose, you must bleed the system at *both* rear wheels. Refer to the section on "Bleeding the Brakes" in this chapter.

16. Lower the car, reversing Steps 2 and 3.

17. Disengage the parking brake; start the car.

18. Road test the car.

Parking Brake

Tools and Materials

- Wheel Chocks
- Jack and Safety Jack Stands
- Creeper
- Open-End Wrenches
- Penetrating Oil

AN AUTOMOBILE'S parking brake is operated by mechanical cable linkage—either a foot pedal or a hand lever. When the car's parking brake lever is engaged, cables are pulled and a lever pivots on each rear drum brake. This lever pushes the brake shoes into the drums to hold the vehicle in place.

These cable-operated parking brakes need adjustment whenever the parking brake will not hold the car from rolling or when the rear brake shoes are worn. Here is how to adjust the parking brake.

1. Park the car on a level surface.
2. Block the front of the front wheels with wheel chocks so that the car will not roll.
3. Jack up the rear of the car so that both

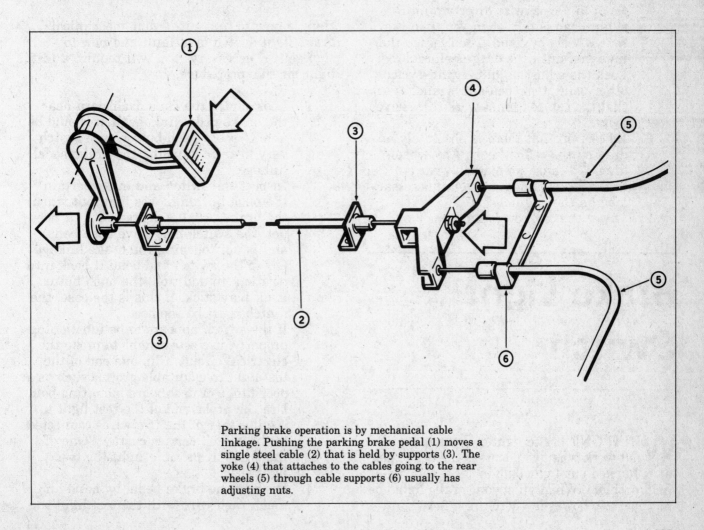

Parking brake operation is by mechanical cable linkage. Pushing the parking brake pedal (1) moves a single steel cable (2) that is held by supports (3). The yoke (4) that attaches to the cables going to the rear wheels (5) through cable supports (6) usually has adjusting nuts.

rear wheels are off the ground. Place safety jack stands under the rear axle to support the car solidly.

4. Follow the steel cables from each rear wheel to where they meet, somewhere under the middle of the car. Use a creeper to move more easily under the vehicle.

5. Where the cables meet, there will be some type of adjusting device. The most common one is a long bolt with two lock nuts. As you tighten the nuts with an open-end wrench, the cables will tighten to engage the parking brake sooner. These adjusting devices are located in a position that is extremely vulnerable to rust and dirt, so it is advisable to apply some penetrating oil on the adjusting nuts before you attempt to work on the system.

6. Tighten the adjusting nuts by turning them in a clockwise direction until a slight drag is felt when you turn the rear wheels by hand. Then loosen the nuts just until the drag is eliminated.

7. Lock the adjusting nuts against each other using two open-end wrenches so that the cables cannot work themselves loose.

8. Be certain that there is absolutely no drag on the rear wheels. Any wheel drag can cause premature wear of brake shoes and create an unnecessary load on the engine.

9. Lower the car, reversing Steps 2 and 3.

Brake Light Switch

WHEN ONE brake light on your car will not work when you depress the brake pedal, a burned out light bulb is the most common problem. When all of your brake lights do not operate, however, there are a few more

Tools and Materials

- Test Light
- Screwdriver
- Brake Light Switch
- Box-End Wrench

parts of the brake system that could be at fault. The trouble could be in the light bulbs, light sockets, wiring, the turn signal switch, or the brake light switch.

There are two types of brake light switches: mechanically and hydraulically operated switches. Check your car's service manual to determine which type your car has.

Servicing a Mechanical Switch

Here is how to find out if your mechanical brake light switch is at fault and how to change it if necessary. You will require a test light for this procedure.

1. Look under the car's dashboard near the brake pedal linkage. You should be able to see a push-button-type switch very near or touching the brake pedal linkage.

2. Inspect the switch and make certain the push button moves in or out when the brake pedal is depressed. If it does not, the switch may have been bent and is not touching the brake linkage. Grasp the switch and bend it back into position. In addition, the push button itself may stick. If this is the case, the switch must be replaced.

3. If the switch appears to be functioning properly, use a test light to probe the electrical circuit. Clip one end of the test light to a suitable ground such as a door hinge or dashboard mounting bolt. Use the probe end of the test light to see if either of the two wires connected to the switch carries current. One of the two wires should light the test light.

4. Depress the brake pedal by hand and touch each wire with the test light's

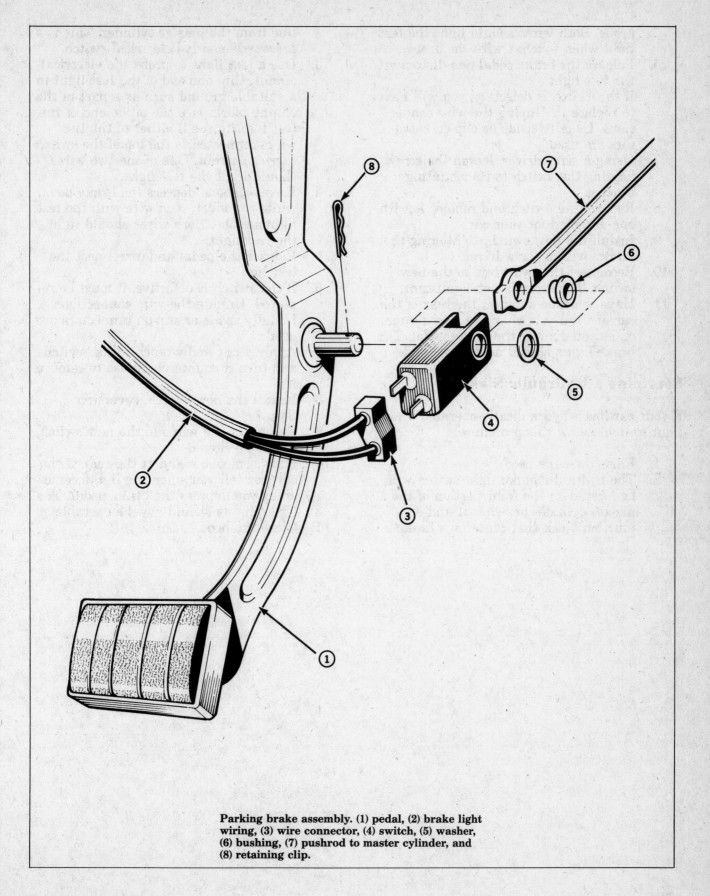

Parking brake assembly. (1) pedal, (2) brake light wiring, (3) wire connector, (4) switch, (5) washer, (6) bushing, (7) pushrod to master cylinder, and (8) retaining clip.

probe. Both wires should light the test light when touched with the probe.

5. Release the brake pedal and disconnect the test light.
6. If the switch is defective, you will have to replace it. Unplug the wire connections. Usually spade or slip-on connectors are used.
7. Using a screwdriver, loosen the screws holding the switch to its mounting bracket.
8. Remove the switch and replace it with one designed for your car.
9. Install the new switch, tightening the screws with a screwdriver.
10. Reconnect the two wires to the new switch. The order is not significant.
11. Have someone stand at the rear of the car and tell you when the lights come on as you depress the brake pedal. The brake lights should now be operable.

Servicing a Hydraulic Switch

If your car has a hydraulically operated brake light switch, follow this procedure.

1. Raise the car's hood.
2. The hydraulic brake light switch will be located on the front portion of the master cylinder or below it and on a junction block that contains a brake line from the master cylinder. This is a pressure-sensitive electrical switch.
3. Use a test light to probe the electrical circuit. Clip one end of the test light to a suitable ground such as a part of the engine block. Use the probe end of the test light to see if either of the two wires connected to the top of the switch carries current. One of the two wires should light the test light.
4. Have someone depress the brake pedal while you touch each wire with the test light's probe. Both wires should light the test light.
5. Release the pedal and disconnect the test light.
6. If the switch is defective, it must be replaced. Unplug the wire connections. Usually spade or slip-on connectors are used.
7. Apply a box-end wrench to the switch and turn it counterclockwise to remove it.
8. Install the new switch, reversing Step 7.
9. Reconnect the wires to the new switch, reversing Step 6.
10. Have someone stand at the rear of the car and tell you when the lights come on as you depress the brake pedal. The brake lights should now be operable.
11. Close the hood.

TIRES AND WHEELS

TIRES AND WHEELS

YOUR CAR'S tires affect the safety, handling characteristics, performance, comfort, and cost of operating your vehicle more than any other component. Because they are the part of the car that makes contact with the road, the tires deserve much more than casual or occasional attention. Depending on the type of driving you do and the weight of your vehicle, tires—with proper care—should last at least 35,000 miles.

Anatomy of a Tire

Before discussing selection, maintenance, and repair, you should know the various parts of a tire.

CORD BODY. The cord body consists of layers of rubber-impregnated fabric, or cords, called plies, that are bonded into a solid unit.

BEAD. The bead is the portion of the tire that helps keep the tire in contact with the

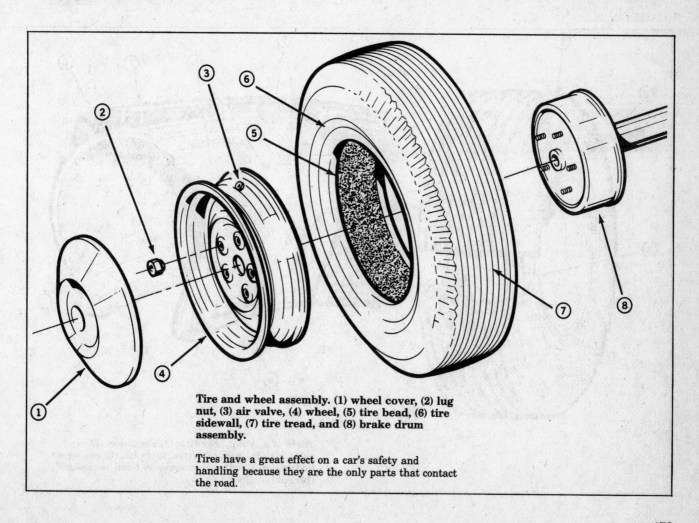

Tire and wheel assembly. (1) wheel cover, (2) lug nut, (3) air valve, (4) wheel, (5) tire bead, (6) tire sidewall, (7) tire tread, and (8) brake drum assembly.

Tires have a great effect on a car's safety and handling because they are the only parts that contact the road.

rim of the wheel and provides the air seal on tubeless tires. The bead is constructed of a heavy band of steel wire wrapped into the inner circumference of the tire's ply structure.

TREAD. The tread, or crown, is the portion of the tire that comes in contact with the road surface. It is a pattern of grooves and ribs that provides traction. The grooves are designed to drain off water, while the ribs grip the road surface. Tread thickness varies with tire quality.

SIPES. On some tires, small cuts, called sipes, are molded into the ribs of the tread. These sipes open as the tire flexes on the road, offering additional gripping action, especially on wet road surfaces.

SIDEWALLS. These are the sides of the tire body. They are constructed of thinner material than the tread to offer greater flexibility.

WEAR BARS. Tires now feature horizontal wear bars, bands or indicators in the tread pattern that become visible when the tread has worn to a level that is only 1/16-inch deep. After that level has been reached, they produce a thumping sound to remind the driver that the tire is ready for replacement.

Types of Tires

When buying tires, good judgment can save you money. It also can save your life. A tire that is not up to the task of accepting additional load during emergency handling may fail just when you need that extra margin of safety. A tire that cannot withstand the impact of a curb or pothole when you have an extra-heavy load in your car is giving you a false sense of security. Therefore, you should invest in tires that are at least as good as the original ones, or better if you think you will need them.

Basically, there are three types of tire con-

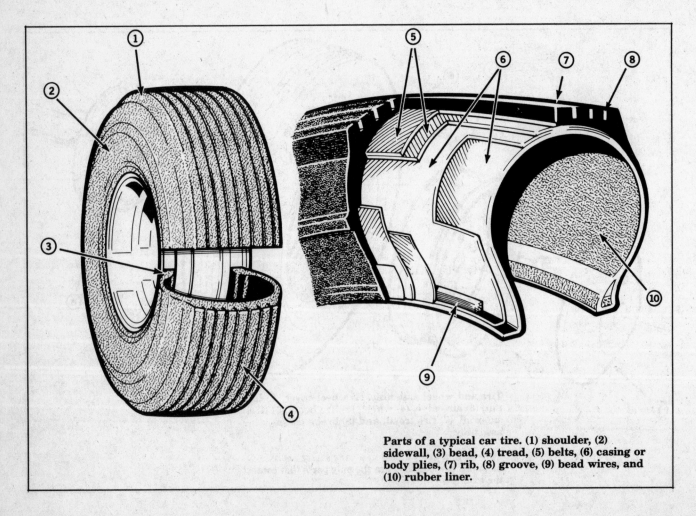

Parts of a typical car tire. (1) shoulder, (2) sidewall, (3) bead, (4) tread, (5) belts, (6) casing or body plies, (7) rib, (8) groove, (9) bead wires, and (10) rubber liner.

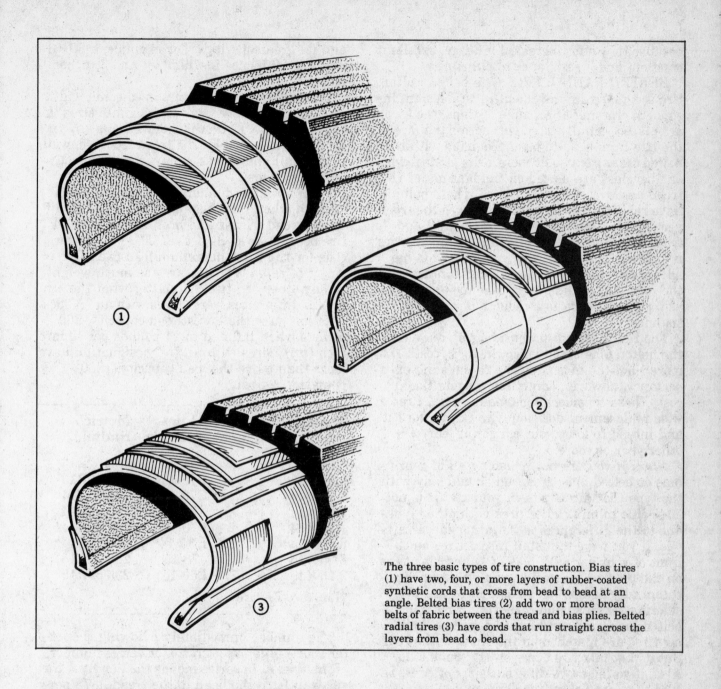

The three basic types of tire construction. Bias tires (1) have two, four, or more layers of rubber-coated synthetic cords that cross from bead to bead at an angle. Belted bias tires (2) add two or more broad belts of fabric between the tread and bias plies. Belted radial tires (3) have cords that run straight across the layers from bead to bead.

struction: bias, belted bias, and belted radial.

BIAS TIRE. Until the late 1960s, the bias tire was the standard for most cars made in the United States. It has two, four, or more plies or layers of rubber-coated synthetic cords (rayon, nylon, polyester, or other material) that cross from one bead to the other at an angle, or bias, of about 35 or 40 degrees. These plies alternate in direction with each ply to provide sidewall strength. Advantages of bias tires include low cost, good mileage, and dependability.

BELTED BIAS TIRE. The construction of the belted bias tire is similar to the bias tire but it also features two or more broad belts of fabric between the tread and the bias plies. These belts, generally made of polyester, fiberglass, or finely woven steel wire, are not connected to the tire beads as are the bias plies. They lend stability to the tire by reducing tread motion or "squirming" as the tire is rolling. And, the tread remains in better contact with the road surface. Belted bias tires are common replacement tires for most cars because they offer increased mileage, excellent traction, and a resistance to punctures.

BELTED RADIAL TIRE. The belted radial tire is a major improvement in tire design. Instead of crossing at an angle or bias, the cords are placed radially (straight) across the face of the tire from bead to bead. Then, as with the belted bias tire, two or more belts of steel wire or fiberglass are placed on the bias under the tread and over the radial plies. These belts have relatively little "give" and keep the tread very stable, improving steering control and tread life. And, because flexing within the tire is reduced, the radial tire runs cooler. Other advantages include greater tread contact with the road surface and fuel economy—as much as 6 percent—due to a reduction in rolling resistance.

The radial tire costs considerably more than the belted bias type, which, in turn, costs more than the bias tire. The radial's life expectancy, however, can offset the additional cost. These considerations make radial tires a wise replacement decision if you can afford it and intend to keep your car for at least another year or more.

Note: If you are not replacing all of your bias or belted bias tires, you should stay with the type that already is on your car. It is not advisable to mix radial tires with other types due to the differences in handling characteristics. If you were to install radial tires on the front of your car with bias or belted bias tires on the rear, or vice versa, you would have a potentially dangerous vehicle in terms of steering response and cornering. Bias and belted bias tires can be used together if similar tires are matched on the front or the rear. But do not mix tire types on the same axle. Also, if you use two different sizes of tires, be sure they are not on the same axle.

Tire Sizes

TIRE SIZE was once a fairly simple matter of numbers. In the early 1920s, the size of a tire was determined by its outside diameter

and its greatest width. For example, a 30 × 3 tire was 30 inches in diameter and 3 inches wide.

Later, tire manufacturers used tread width and wheel rim diameter to designate sizes. If you saw 7.75 × 14 on the sidewall of a tire, it was 7¾ inches across the tread from sidewall to sidewall and it was mounted on a 14-inch-diameter wheel.

Then an alpha-numeric size system was adopted when tires began to be offered in different tread widths and profiles. A 7.75 × 14 tire became an F78-14 tire. "F" is the letter code for the tire's maximum load capacity. Any tire rated "F" can carry as much weight as any other "F" tire, no matter what the other size differences were. Tires with an "A" designation have the lowest load capacity, 900 pounds when inflated to 24 pounds per square inch (psi). Tires with an "N" designation have more than twice the load capacity, 1880 pounds at 24 psi.

Tread Width × Wheel Diameter	Alpha-Numeric	Metric Radial
6.00 × 13	A78-13	165/80R13
6.50 × 13	B78-13	175/80R13
6.95 × 14	C78-14	175/80R14
7.35 × 14	E78-14	185/80R14
7.75 × 14	F70-14*	195/70R14*
8.55 × 14	H60-14*	215/60R14*
8.85 × 15	J78-15	225/75R15
9.15 × 15	L50-15*	235/50R15*

*Low profile tire

The number immediately following the letter code is the aspect ratio, or series number, of the tire. A 78 series means the height of the sidewall from the bead to the tread is 78 percent of the tread width. A 70 series tire (F70-14) means the height of the sidewall is only 70 percent of the tread width, giving it what tire manufacturers term a lower profile. Tires with an "R" in their size, such as FR70-14, are of radial-ply construction.

Most tires sold today are radials measured under the metric system. An FR70-14 tire in metric measurements is 195/70R14. "195" is the width in millimeters, "70" is still the height of the sidewall in relation to the width of the tread, "R" stands for radial, and "14" is

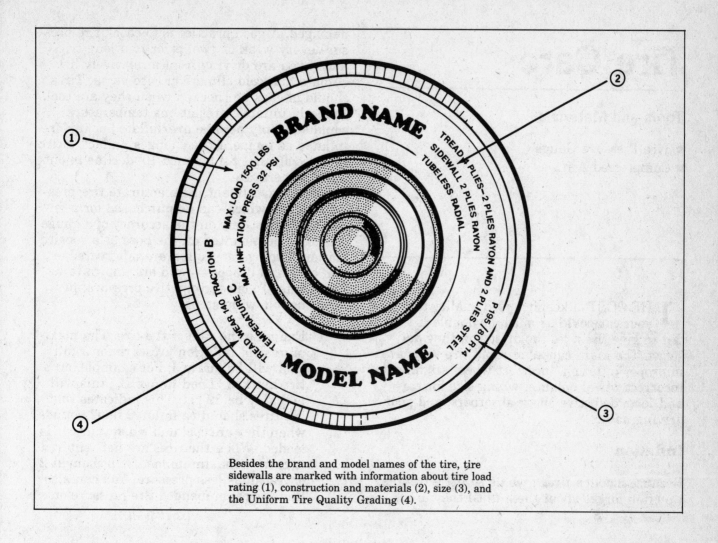

Besides the brand and model names of the tire, tire sidewalls are marked with information about tire load rating (1), construction and materials (2), size (3), and the Uniform Tire Quality Grading (4).

the wheel diameter. In addition, many radial tire sizes have the prefix "P," for passenger car tire. See the accompanying table to compare popular tire sizes under three measuring methods.

In addition to serving as "billboards" for the tire manufacturers, the sidewall contains a good deal of useful information required by the U.S. Department of Transportation. This information includes the maximum load, maximum inflation pressure, type of construction (such as tubeless, radial ply), and the materials used in the tread and sidewall and how many plies of material each has.

All tires must also have the Uniform Tire Quality Grading, which rates tires according to treadwear, wet weather traction, and temperature resistance. Treadwear is expressed in numbers divisible by 10, with 100 being the median number. A tire with a treadwear rating of 140 should last 40 percent longer than one with a rating of 100, on the average. The traction rating is expressed as either A, B, or C, with A as best and C the worst in terms of the tire's ability to stop on a wet surface. Temperature resistance is also expressed with the letter A, B, or C. An A-rated tire will run cooler at highway speeds than tires rated B or C, which means the A-rated tire is less likely to suffer a blowout or tread separation at highway speeds because of excessive heat.

Always replace tires with a size at least as large as the tires that originally came with the car, and never mix radial ply with bias ply or belted bias tires since radials have different handling, traction, and temperature resistance characteristics. If you are buying larger tires, be sure they will still allow sufficient clearance in turns, stops, and with a full load of passengers and luggage.

Tire Care

Tools and Materials

- Tire Pressure Gauge
- Compressed Air

THE COST of keeping good quality tires on your car could as much as double if you fail to give the tires the attention they deserve. The main causes of rapid tire wear are improper inflation, incorrect wheel alignment, incorrect wheel balance, wrong size for car and load, defective shock absorbers, and poor driving habits.

Inflation

Because modern tires give us so little trouble, we often forget about them until they are damaged. A good practice is to check tire pressure every week or two, prior to a long trip, and if you are driving from a relatively hot climate to a cold climate or vice versa. Tires should always be checked when they are cool. Properly inflated tires at one temperature could suddenly become overinflated or underinflated as temperature changes. In fact, a tire can lose about 1 psi for each 10° decline in outdoor temperature.

A good investment is an accurate tire pressure gauge, which can be purchased for a few dollars. Do not rely on the accuracy of a gauge that may be mounted on the hose at a service station. Such gauges often are mistreated—run over and dropped—and are known to be inaccurate. To check your tire pressure, perform the following steps.

1. Examine the side of the tire. The maximum cold inflation pressure for a full load will be marked. For example, on a tire marked "Load Range B," this will probably be 32 psi. This indicates that the tires should be inflated to 32 pounds when they are cool and when your car is loaded. When the tires are not required to carry a maximum load, run them at 2 or 3 pounds less pressure. You can also find the recommended tire pressure on a

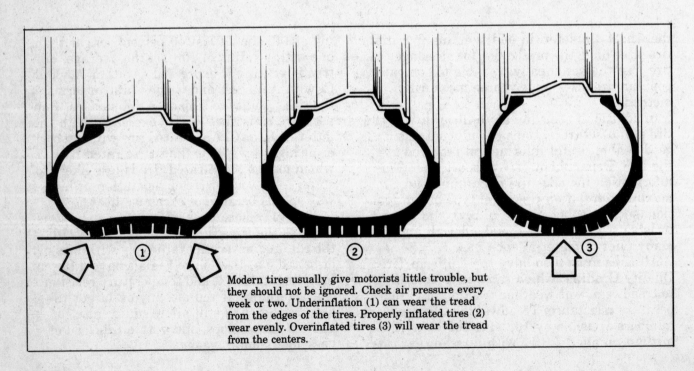

Modern tires usually give motorists little trouble, but they should not be ignored. Check air pressure every week or two. Underinflation (1) can wear the tread from the edges of the tires. Properly inflated tires (2) wear evenly. Overinflated tires (3) will wear the tread from the centers.

sticker inside the glove compartment or in your owner's manual. **Note:** Never deflate tires when they are hot just because they indicate an overinflated condition. When they cool, they will return to their normal inflation pressure.

2. Locate the tire air valve on the wheel.
3. Unscrew the cap on the air valve counterclockwise by hand.
4. Fit the end of your tire pressure gauge over the tire air valve. Press down to obtain a pressure reading in pounds per square inch (psi).
5. Read the tire air pressure indicated on the gauge.
6. If the pressure is correct, reinstall the tire air valve cap.
7. If the tire pressure is too high, depress the pin in the center of the valve to release some air. Recheck the tire pressure with your gauge. Repeat, letting out a little air at a time, until the pressure is correct.
8. If the tire is underinflated, place the end of the compressed air supply hose over the tire's air valve. If the nozzle of the air supply hose is equipped with a lever, squeeze it to release air into the tire; hoses without a lever supply air when you press the end of the nozzle down on the tire's air valve. If the air supply hose has an indicator that shows the amount of air pressure in the tire, use it only as a general guide. Check the pressure with your own gauge.

    Note: If you are carrying a heavy load or are pulling a trailer, you should put in 2 to 4 pounds more pressure than normal.
9. Once the air pressure in the tire is correct, reinstall the air valve cap.
10. Repeat Steps 1 through 9 for each tire.

Whenever checking the tire pressure, you also should take time to check as best you can for bruises, cuts, or unusual wear patterns. The best time to do this task thoroughly, however, is when your car is elevated during lubrication. Do not just examine the tread and outside sidewall. Check the inside sidewall too. Remove nails, small stones, or other objects imbedded in and between the tread. Do not forget to examine the tire air valve for dam-

age. Keep all air valves equipped with extensions, if necessary, and caps to keep out dirt and moisture.

You can identify probable inflation problems by visually checking your tires. An underinflated tire wears more rapidly on the outer edges of the tread. This is because the too-soft body of the tire tends to flex more at the center, with most of the weight of the car being supported by the sidewalls. When properly inflated, the weight of the car is evenly distributed across the tread.

An overinflated tire will show the greatest wear at the center of the tread pattern. The tire is distended at the center where the greatest concentration of weight is placed.

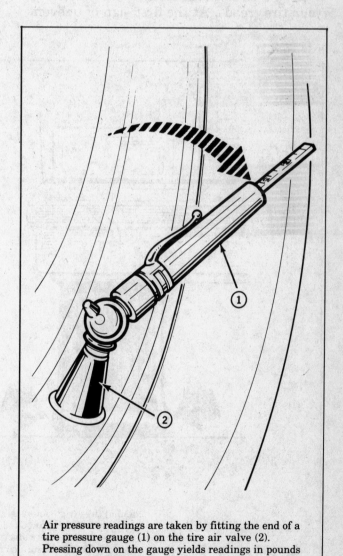

Air pressure readings are taken by fitting the end of a tire pressure gauge (1) on the tire air valve (2). Pressing down on the gauge yields readings in pounds per square inch (psi).

Wheel Alignment

When your wheels are misaligned, the tires are "bucking the system." In effect, you are trying to make the car go in one direction while the tires are pulling in another direction. Therefore, in the process of forcing them back on track, you are scrubbing rubber off the tread.

This scrubbing action generally shows up as cut or feathered areas on the tread. Eventually, such tires will begin to thump due to this unevenness. An experienced wheel alignment specialist can tell whether or not you have an alignment problem by studying the treads of your tires.

Keep a close check on the wear pattern of your tire treads. At the first sign of unevenness, check inflation and have the alignment rechecked.

Wheel Balancing

It is extremely rare when a tire comes off the production line in perfect balance. The rubber in the plies just does not go on that smoothly. There are places where the plies butt together to form a spot that is slightly heavier.

If you were to mount a new tire on a rim and drive away without having it balanced, you would soon—if not immediately—begin to feel a vibration caused by such heavy spots as they spin at high speeds. Such a wheel would lack static, or centrifugal, balance.

To correct this, wheels and tires are balanced as a unit, or assembly. This is accom-

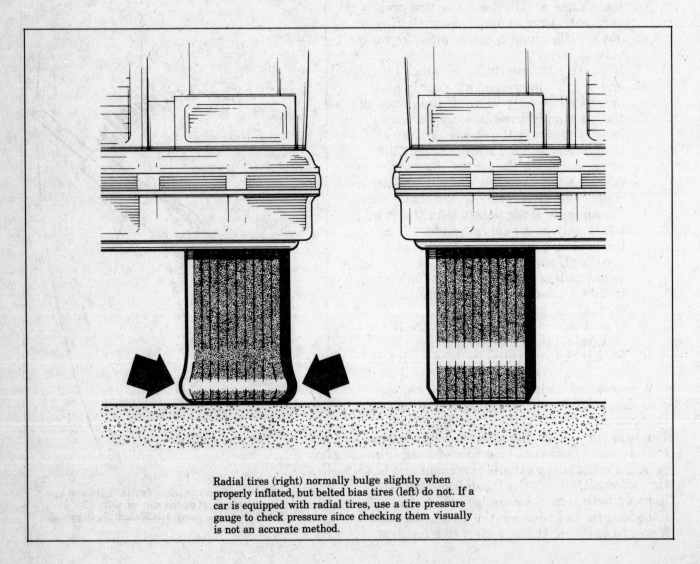

Radial tires (right) normally bulge slightly when properly inflated, but belted bias tires (left) do not. If a car is equipped with radial tires, use a tire pressure gauge to check pressure since checking them visually is not an accurate method.

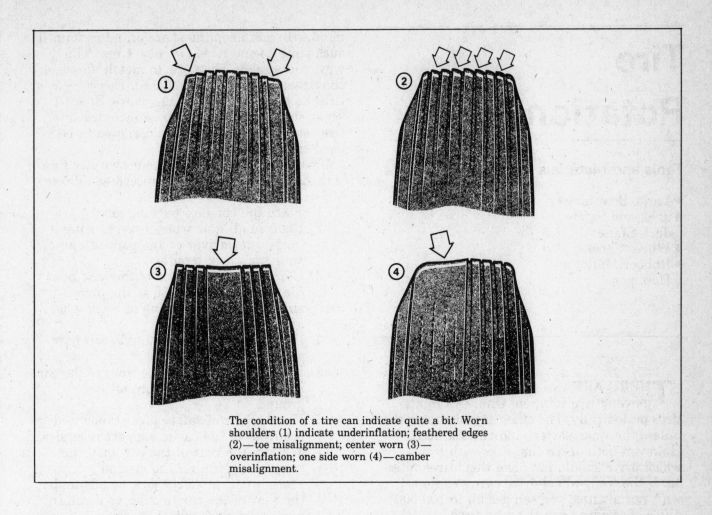

The condition of a tire can indicate quite a bit. Worn shoulders (1) indicate underinflation; feathered edges (2)—toe misalignment; center worn (3)—overinflation; one side worn (4)—camber misalignment.

plished by adding a lead weight opposite the heavy spot that is equal to the weight of the heavy spot. It is not quite as simple as it sounds, however, because weights are added at various locations for optimum balancing.

If there is a difference in weight between the inner and outer faces of the tire, the wheel will shimmy or wobble as it turns. The wheel would then lack dynamic balance. Both static and dynamic imbalances are solved by positioning small lead weights on the wheel rim opposite any heavy areas.

One method of balancing uses a "bubble" machine. The wheel and tire assembly is set horizontally on a balancing device. A bubble indicator at the center of the wheel tells the operator when the assembly is in static balance.

While some specialists say they can achieve perfect static and dynamic balance using the bubble device, we recommend having the assembly checked by the dynamic method.

Dynamic balancing is the most common and generally accepted system of wheel balancing. It means spinning the tire and wheel assembly at high speeds with the wheels either on the car or dismounted and placed on a special machine. Actually, spin-balancing covers both dynamic and static conditions, and is the surest way of knowing your wheel and tire assembly will be in balance when you are traveling at highway speeds.

Poor Driving Habits

The only one who can correct poor driving habits is the driver. Tire life can be increased—sometimes significantly—by avoiding jackrabbit starts, panic-like stops, and hard, fast cornering that scrubs off tread from tires. Other factors that contribute to shortening the lifespan of tires are impacts against curbs and potholes, and high-speed driving.

Tire Rotation

Tools and Materials

- Large Screwdriver
- Jack and Safety Jack Stands
- Wheel Chocks
- Rubber Mallet or Hammer

THERE ARE two schools of thought regarding tire rotation. One says rotate tires periodically. The other says do not bother unless the wear pattern indicates a need. However, both agree that cars with front-wheel drive should not have their tires rotated. If the front-wheel-drive car is equipped with radial tires, you can get up to 100,000 miles of service from the rear tires.

The principle of tire rotation is that tires be changed periodically from position to position on the car to level out any unevenness that may develop due to driving conditions and load factors. In most cases, rotation has the benefit of extending tire life because tread wear is more even during the life of all four (or five, including the spare) tires. The tires all tend to wear out at the same time.

A negative factor is that once your tires are balanced on a wheel, rotation could conceal alignment problems. However, you will probably get satisfactory performance by letting your tires stay where they are, providing inflation is maintained and wheels are kept in alignment. If you move a tire from left front to right rear, for example, you may have to have the tires rebalanced.

Those in favor of rotation say the spare tire should also be taken into consideration. Why have a brand new spare in the trunk while the rest of the tires wear out? But, on the other hand, why not keep the spare brand new until such time as you need two new tires? This way, you already have one to match up with the new one you just purchased. However, tires do deteriorate with age. **Note:** Space-saver spare tires are not to be included in a tire rotation; these tires are designed to be used only in emergencies.

If you should decide to do your own tire rotation, do it once a year and proceed as follows.

1. Place the car into parking gear.
2. Remove all four wheel covers, using a large screwdriver or the pointed end of your car's jack handle.
3. Using the wrench end of the jack handle or a socket wrench of the proper size, loosen the lug nuts on each wheel about one turn.
4. Place a wheel chock behind each rear wheel.
5. Using the jack, raise the front of the car until the front wheels are off the ground.
6. Place a pair of safety jack stands under the front of the car to support it solidly.
7. Jack up the rear of the car until the rear wheels are off the ground.
8. Place a pair of safety jack stands under the rear of the car to support it solidly and remove the wheel chocks.
9. Remove the lug nuts of each wheel, placing the nuts into their respective wheel covers for safe-keeping. Most lug nuts can be removed by turning them counterclockwise. Some cars, however, may have a left-hand thread on the lug nuts. In such a case, the lugs may be marked with the letter "L." If your car has left-hand threaded lugs, turn the nuts clockwise to loosen them.

Note: On some cars, it is difficult to remove the rear wheels unless the car body is jacked up above the rear wheels. If you encounter this situation, carefully jack up the rear bumper of the car while it is still on the jack stands to slide the tire off the lugs. *Caution: Be careful not to raise the car off the jack stands!*

If your car is equipped with full rear wheel fender skirts, they must be removed before you can remove the rear wheels. There is a locking bar on the in-

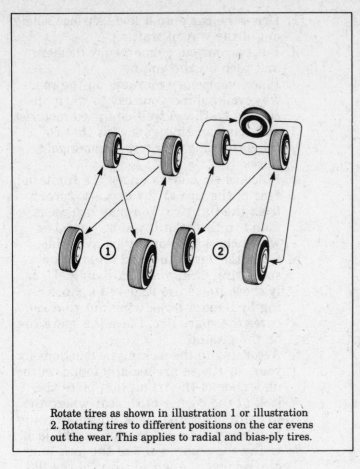

Rotate tires as shown in illustration 1 or illustration 2. Rotating tires to different positions on the car evens out the wear. This applies to radial and bias-ply tires.

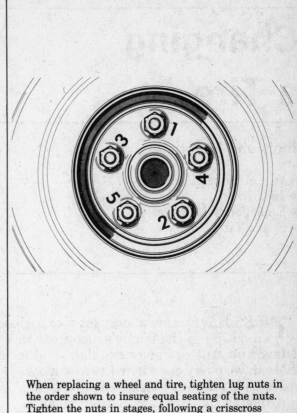

When replacing a wheel and tire, tighten lug nuts in the order shown to insure equal seating of the nuts. Tighten the nuts in stages, following a crisscross pattern.

side of the fender skirt. Lift it upward with your hand to remove the fender skirt.

10. Relocate the tires as shown in the accompanying diagram. **Note:** Tire manufacturers used to warn against rotating radial tires side to side, recommending front to rear switching only. The reason for this was that early radial tires tended to take a directional set which could result in a pull or ply separation problem if the tire was installed on the opposite side of the car. That situation is no longer true with today's radial tires, so cross rotation is acceptable.

11. Remount all the wheels into their new positions.

12. Firmly tighten the lug nuts by hand on each wheel. **Note:** Tighten the uppermost lug nut first and then tighten the opposite one on the bottom. Then continue around the tire, tightening opposing pairs. When all nuts on a wheel

have been tightened firmly but not completely, spin the wheel and check to make sure all the lug nuts have been seated properly.

13. Raise the rear of the car with the jack and remove the jack stands.

14. Lower the car until the wheels are firmly on the ground.

15. Place a wheel chock behind each rear wheel.

16. Raise the front of the car and remove the jack stands.

17. Lower the car until the wheels are firmly on the ground.

18. With the car's wheels on the ground, tighten all the lug nuts snugly with the jack wrench or socket wrench. **Note:** As you tighten the lug nuts, tighten them in the manner described in Step 12.

19. Reinstall the wheel covers. You may need a rubber mallet or hammer for this task.

20. Remove the wheel chocks.

Changing a Tire

Tools and Materials

- Wheel Chocks
- Jack
- Emergency Markers
- Spare Tire

TIRES HAVE come a long, long way. Once, an outing in the family's motor car was delayed by at least one or two flats, and in those days, every car carried two or more spare tires for such routine emergencies.

Although flat tires are nowhere near as common as they once were, everyone who drives a car should know how to change a tire. Trouble could occur when no one else is around to lend a hand.

Changing a tire is relatively simple if you follow a few directions and are aware of a few safety precautions. One thing to remember if you have tire trouble is: always drive your car well off the road and as far away from traffic as possible. If you do not, you are endangering your own life as well as the lives of others should an accident happen. If you are in a position where you cannot quickly pull off the road to a safe site, such as on an interstate highway or a bridge, it is better to risk damaging your tire than to risk lives. Drive on the flat until you can find a safe site to pull over.

If you have tire trouble, the spare tire in your car becomes part of the repair. For this reason, it is good practice to periodically check the air pressure of the spare tire. You never know when you will need it. Study your owner's manual. It contains specific information about the storage location, assembly, and proper use of the jack, and how to change a tire on your car. However, you can follow these general steps to change a flat tire.

1. Drive the car onto a level surface safely out of the way of traffic.
2. Put on your car's emergency flashers and turn off the engine.
3. Place emergency markers on the roadway well behind your car to warn oncoming traffic. A well-equipped motorist will have an emergency kit that contains warning markers or emergency flares.
4. Place wheel chocks under the front and rear of the tire at the opposite corner from the flat tire. You may use rocks found in the area if you do not have wheel chocks of some type available.
5. Open the car trunk and remove the spare tire, jack, and jack handle. Usually these items are removed by unscrewing by hand a large wing nut that secures the spare tire. Place the spare tire on the ground.
6. According to the jacking instructions for your car (these are usually found on the underside of the trunk lid), place the jack at the corner of the car where the flat tire is located. Jack up the car only high enough to put tension on the jack.
7. Using the pointed end of the jack handle, remove the wheel cover of the flat tire wheel. **Note:** If you are working on a rear wheel, there may be a fender skirt that must be removed before the tire can be removed from the wheel. There is a locking bar on the inside of the fender skirt. Lift the bar upward with your hand to remove the fender skirt.
8. Using the lug wrench end of the jack handle, loosen the wheel's lug nuts one full turn by turning them counterclockwise. **Note:** Some cars will have a left-hand thread on the lug nuts. In such a case, the lugs may be marked with the letter "L." If your car has left-hand threaded lugs, turn the nuts clockwise to loosen them.
9. With the lug nuts loosened one full turn, jack up the car until the tire is off the ground.
10. Remove the lug nuts and remove the flat tire.
11. Place the spare tire in position on the lugs and reinstall the lug nuts by hand.

Begin with the uppermost nut. Then tighten the opposite nut on the bottom. Continue to tighten opposite pairs until all nuts have been tightened firmly by hand. Spin the tire and check to see if the wheel is on properly and all nuts have been seated correctly.

12. With the jack, lower the car until the tire is touching the ground.
13. Tighten the lug nuts snugly with the lug wrench end of the jack handle.
14. Lower the car the rest of the way to the ground and remove the jack from under the car.
15. Replace the wheel cover and fender skirt if applicable.

16. Place the flat tire, jack, jack handle, warning markers, and wheel chocks in the trunk.
17. Turn off the emergency flashers.
18. Have the flat tire repaired as soon as possible.

Temporary Spares

Many cars today are equipped with "temporary" compact spare tires that save space and weight. These tires are not designed for prolonged use, but are intended only for emergency use to help you reach the nearest repair facility. Some have warnings printed on them cautioning you not to drive on them at speeds greater than 50 mph or for distances of more than 50 miles.

The temporary spare is also much smaller than the tires on your car which means it will cause your car to drive, handle and brake differently when it is installed.

Collapsible or "folding" spares are stored in a deflated condition. The tire is not inflated until it it mounted on the car. With the tire still off the ground, a Freon or carbon dioxide filled pressure canister is attached to the special valve on the spare tire which inflates it to the right pressure. If your car has one of these spares, you should check in the trunk to make sure the inflation canister is also there. Once the canister has been used, it must be replaced with a new one. When the spare tire is removed, it usually has to be deflated to fit back into its storage compartment.

Another type of temporary spare is the high-pressure spare. Smaller then the standard tires on your car, it is pressurized to about 60 psi and has a much thinner tread. You should check the pressure periodically on this type of spare to make sure it is properly inflated when you need it.

The third type of temporary spare is the "skin" spare. This tire is closer in size to the tires on your car but it is much lighter in weight because it has little tread on it. Like the high pressure spare, it is ready to use and usually has more pressure than the wheels on your car. It may be inflated to 35 to 40 psi. You should check it periodically to see that is has not lost air.

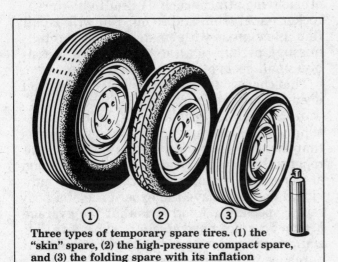

Three types of temporary spare tires. (1) the "skin" spare, (2) the high-pressure compact spare, and (3) the folding spare with its inflation canister.

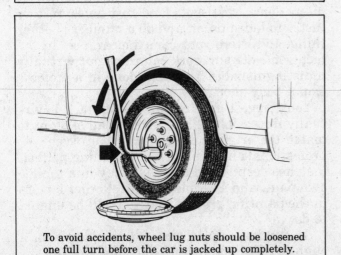

To avoid accidents, wheel lug nuts should be loosened one full turn before the car is jacked up completely. With the wheel off the ground, the loose nuts can then be removed safely.

CAR BODY REPAIR

IF YOU have owned your car for 6 months or more, chances are it already needs some body repair. In fact, most new cars need some minor body repair the minute they leave the dealer's showroom. Many unsuspecting new-car buyers drive away with chipped paint, small scratches, and other minor imperfections that can be the breeding ground for major corrosion later.

To prevent corrosion, always give any new car a meticulous inspection before you buy it. Open all the doors, the trunk, the hood, and check their metal edges (do not forget the bottom edges of the doors) for chipped paint, scratches, and beginning rust. These are areas often ignored by the new-car buyer. If left unrepaired, they can cause major problems later. Once rust starts, it just keeps spreading until it is stopped. And, it is much easier and cheaper to stop a small rust spot than to stop and repair a large one.

When purchasing a new car, you are perfectly within your rights to request the dealer to repair those minor chips and scratches before he delivers the car to you. Any reputable dealer will fix them.

If your new car is some months old and you neglected to give it a close inspection before you bought it, do it now—or even if you did, do it again. By now, you probably have some minor body repairs to make. Make them now and continue to inspect your car at least once every 6 months.

Inspection is simple. Pay particular attention to edges—any edges—including door edges and edges and folds in the metal where other items attach, such as headlight rims, rocker panel trim, and so on. You will usually find a few areas with small chips of paint missing, perhaps a scratch or two and, possibly, small spots of rust here and there.

This chapter tells you most everything you need to know about making body repairs on your car with materials available from auto supply stores. It must be pointed out, however, that the average person cannot always make repairs that look as good as quality professional work. One reason is that the average individual does not have the experience of a body repair specialist. Another is that the average person does not have access to expensive equipment, and it would not be economical to purchase it. Despite these reasons, you can still make satisfactory repairs to scratches, many dents, rust spots, and rust holes; restore luster to faded paint; and do a number of other things to restore your car's appearance. In fact, some of your work can come out virtually indistinguishable from that done in a professional body shop.

Your biggest problem will be paint. It is virtually impossible to buy a spray can of paint to match the original color of your car. Even professionals have problems obtaining perfect matches despite the fact that they mix their own paint and are able to control other factors in the painting process that you will be unable to do.

So, you have two choices—either settle for a slightly off-shade paint job, or prepare the metal to the point where it is ready for painting and let a professional apply the paint.

Using Masking Tape

Tools and Materials

- Single-Edge Razor Blade and Blade Holder
- ½-inch Masking Tape
- Newspaper

IF YOU are going to be doing any painting on your car, you will require masking tape. Masking tape is used to mask off portions of the car's body and trim so you will not get primer or paint on chrome, glass, or other parts that do not require painting.

Masking tape is made for this purpose. It adheres tightly enough, when applied properly, to keep paint from seeping into other areas, yet it is easy to remove once the painted surface is dry. And, unlike some other types of tape, it does not leave any adhesive behind when it is removed. Although it is available in a variety of widths, ½-inch masking tape is recommended for most repair purposes.

Masking Repairs

To mask off an area of the car's body for priming or painting, follow this procedure.

1. Align masking tape along one edge of a sheet of newspaper so that about ¼ inch of the ½-inch tape is left exposed. Use the tape directly from the roll rather than cutting it to length first. **Note:** Do

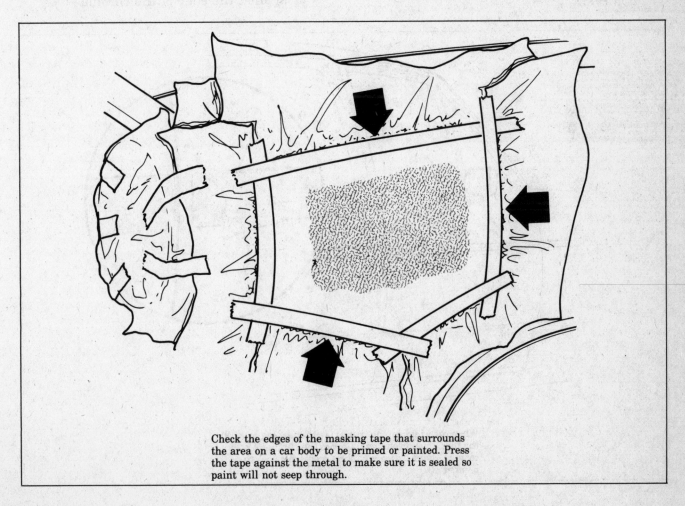

Check the edges of the masking tape that surrounds the area on a car body to be primed or painted. Press the tape against the metal to make sure it is sealed so paint will not seep through.

not mask right up to the repair—leave enough space, but no more than 5 inches, so that some spray will fall lightly around the repair.

2. The edge of the newspaper with the exposed tape should be positioned along one side of the area to be repaired. Apply the exposed tape to the metal surface of the car.

3. Repeat Step 2, completely surrounding the area to be primed or painted. Tack the other sides of the newspaper to the car with pieces of tape.

4. Double-check the masking tape seal surrounding the repair by pressing it against the metal with your fingers to make certain that it is firmly sticking to the car's metal surface and that there are no "ripples" or openings that could allow paint to seep through. **Note:** A single-edge razor blade in a blade holder is handy for cutting and butting pieces of tape.

A careful masking job is the mark of a good paint job. If you do a careless masking job, the resulting paint job will be sloppy too, so take your time.

Often, people mask too much of an area. In general, sufficient protection is provided by masking no more than 4 feet beyond the area to be painted.

Masking Chrome

For areas with chrome trimwork that cannot be removed, be particularly careful about how you apply masking tape. The tape should completely cover the chrome, but it should not come in contact with adjoining metal surfaces to be painted or you will leave a thin, often noticeable, edge between the paint and the masking tape. Use the following procedure to apply masking tape to chrome areas.

1. Place one edge of the tape carefully against the edge of the chrome—be

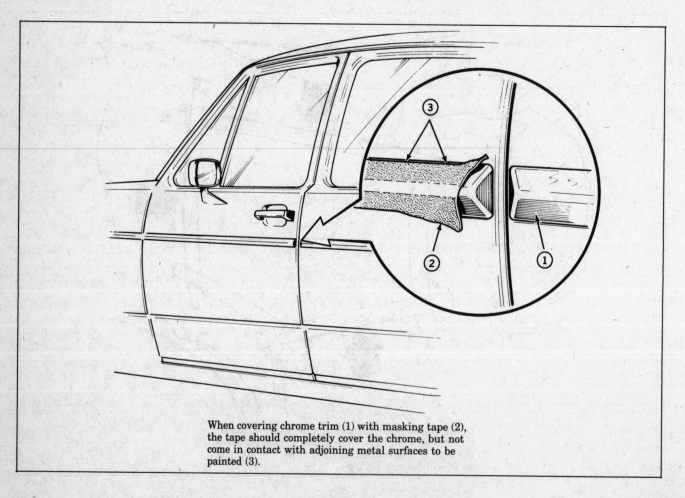

When covering chrome trim (1) with masking tape (2), the tape should completely cover the chrome, but not come in contact with adjoining metal surfaces to be painted (3).

careful not to touch the metal surface being painted with the edge of the tape. Press only the edge of the tape—not the full width—against one edge of the chrome. Do this slowly until you have masked off the length of chrome along one edge.

2. After you have the edge of tape perfectly aligned with one edge of the chrome, press the rest of the tape against the chrome to complete the masking operation.

Preparing Metal for Painting

Tools and Materials

- Sanding Block
- Safety Goggles
- Electric Drill and Sanding Disc Attachment or Electric Grinder
- #50 or #80 Sandpaper or Sanding Disc
- Spray Can of Primer
- Rags
- Rubbing (Isopropyl) Alcohol
- Masking Tape
- Newspaper
- Detergent
- Water
- Sponge
- Petroleum-Based Solvent
- #400 Wet-or-Dry Sandpaper
- Tack Cloth

ONE OF the differences between a good paint job and a poor one is the preparation of the surface to be painted. In performing minor body work on your car, you will be doing one of two types of painting—painting on a bare metal surface where all the layers of paint and primer have been removed, or painting over a surface that has layers of primer and paint on it.

Sanding to Bare Metal

If the job requires you get down to the car's bare metal surface, there are two ways to do this: hand or power sanding—or grinding as it is sometimes called. With hand sanding, you will need a sanding block, which is nothing more than a rubber or plastic block designed to hold a sheet of sandpaper. Here is how to sand an area down to bare metal.

1. Fasten a sheet of coarse #50 or #80 sandpaper to the sanding block and sand the area in a back-and-forth motion until the bare sheet metal is exposed. Hand sanding is time-consuming and requires considerable effort, especially if the area to be sanded is large. It can be much easier and faster to use an electric drill with a sanding disc attachment or an electric grinder.

   If you have an electric drill or grinder, use a #50 or #80 sandpaper disc. *Caution: Wear safety goggles when using a sanding disc.* Hold the sanding disc at a very slight angle—about 10 degrees from the flat metal surface on which you are working—and sand back and forth until the shiny metal surface is exposed. When using a disc-type sander, you must be careful not to catch the paper disc on a jagged edge of metal. This will tear the disc and you will have to replace it sooner than necessary. In addition, always keep the sander in motion at the proper angle to avoid making gouges or depressions in the repair area.

2. After the area has been sanded down to the bare, shiny metal, you must clean the surface so the primer coat will adhere well. Follow the instructions provided on the can of primer you are going to use. Most manufacturers will tell exactly how to prepare the metal surface for priming to obtain the best results with their product. However, the sanded area can be wiped clean with a clean rag saturated with rubbing (isopropyl) alcohol.

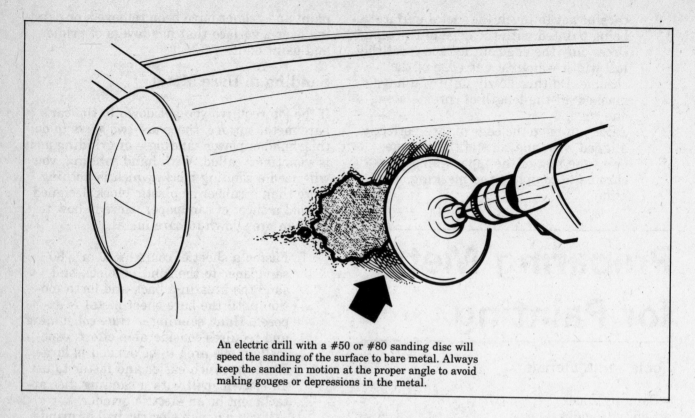

An electric drill with a #50 or #80 sanding disc will speed the sanding of the surface to bare metal. Always keep the sander in motion at the proper angle to avoid making gouges or depressions in the metal.

3. If there is a possibility of getting primer on surrounding areas that are not to be primed or painted, mask off the area to be primed before applying the primer coat according to label directions.
4. Prime the area. Refer to the "Using Primer and Paint" section in this chapter.

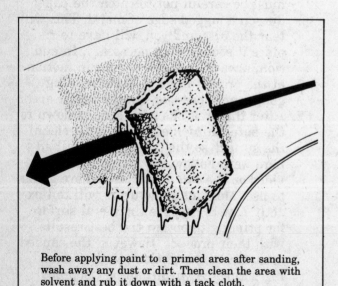

Before applying paint to a primed area after sanding, wash away any dust or dirt. Then clean the area with solvent and rub it down with a tack cloth.

Sanding Primer or Paint

When you are preparing a surface for painting but are not going down to the bare metal surface, follow these steps.

1. Wash the damaged area with detergent—not soap—and water, using a cellulose sponge. Rinse the area thoroughly, and use a clean rag to wipe the area dry.
2. Wipe the area with a petroleum-based solvent to remove any remaining grease or wax.
3. Wet-sand the damaged surface carefully. Using #400 wet-or-dry sandpaper on a sanding block, taper the surrounding paint toward the scratch or chip. Sand back and forth—do not use a circular motion. As you sand, use a cellulose sponge to flood the area with water. What you want to do is simply level or smooth down the area around the scratch and provide a "tooth" to the old paint so that the new coat of paint will adhere well to the surface.
4. After the old paint in the repair area

has been scuffed, clean the area with solvent. When preparing a surface for priming or painting, always use a clean tack cloth to rub the metal surface clean of small particles of dust and lint. A tack cloth is an inexpensive, chemically treated cloth.

5. If there is a possibility of getting paint on surrounding areas, mask off the area to be painted before applying the new paint.
6. Paint the area according to the directions found on the paint can. Refer to the "Using Primer and Paint" section in this chapter.

Using Primer and Paint

Tools and Materials

- Spray Can of Primer
- Newspaper
- Masking Tape
- Paint Thinner or Other Petroleum-Based Solvent
- #400 Sandpaper
- Tack Cloth
- Spray Can of Paint
- Rubbing Compound
- Rags

WHY IS it necessary to use a primer coat before applying paint? Why not just spray paint on the bare metal surface? The primer coat serves two purposes: it acts as a filler to help smooth out a rough metal surface and as a bonding agent. If you would apply paint directly onto bare metal, it would not adhere well. The primer coat bonds to metal much better than paint, and paint adheres well to the primer coat. Whenever you must paint a bare metal surface, it is a two-step process. You must first prime the metal and then apply paint to the primer.

Applying Primer

Here is how to apply primer to bare metal using cans of spray paint.

1. Shake the can of primer coat well. The spray can will have a metal ball inside that will mix the primer as you shake the can. Shake for about a minute after the agitator ball inside the can begins to rattle.
2. Tape a sheet of newspaper to a wall or other vertical surface with masking tape and depress the button on the spray can while aiming the nozzle at the newspaper. Hold the can approximately 12 inches away from the paper. This is to make certain that the can will emit a fine, even spray. If there is a primer buildup clogging the nozzle, pull the nozzle off the can and soak it in paint thinner or other petroleum-based solvent to clear the passage. When the nozzle is clean again, replace it.
3. If you have never applied primer before, practice on an old board or piece of metal. Hold the can about 12 inches away, depress the nozzle, and move the can in even, slightly overlapping, side-to-side strokes across the board or metal. Your stroke should always remain the same distance away from the object you are spraying. Often, people use a semicircular motion as they spray, with the middle of their stroke closer to the object than the ends. This results in an uneven amount of primer on the surface of the object being sprayed.
4. After practicing, apply the primer in smooth, even strokes across the surface of the repair area. Overlap the first side-to-side stroke with a second stroke and so on until the entire area to be primed is covered. **Note:** Do not attempt to completely cover the area with a heavy coat of primer. Best results are obtained by applying several fine, misty coats.
5. After allowing the first, thin coat of primer to dry for 2 to 5 minutes, apply a second light coat. **Note:** If the primer coat accidentally begins to run, allow it

to dry thoroughly. Then sand the run with #400 sandpaper. Wipe the area clean with a tack cloth and apply another coat of primer over the area.

6. Allow the final primer coat to dry.

When applying primer from a spray can, never hold the nozzle closer than 12 inches to the object being sprayed. If you hold it too close, you are likely to get runs. Also, after each coat has been sprayed, turn the spray can upside down and aim it at some old newspaper, depressing the nozzle for a few seconds until the primer stops coming out of the can. This will help clear the nozzle and prevent it from clogging.

Before applying paint to the primer, you must sand and clean the primer coat. Refer to the section on "Preparing Metal for Painting" in this chapter.

Applying Paint

After the primer coat has been sanded and cleaned with solvent and a tack cloth, you are ready to apply paint to the repair area. Here is the procedure.

1. Shake the can of spray paint well. The spray can will have a metal ball inside that will mix the paint as you shake the can. Shake for about a minute after the agitator ball inside the can begins to rattle. Follow the directions on the can. With paint, this is especially important. If the paint is not completely mixed, you will probably get a poor color match.

2. Tape a sheet of newspaper to a wall or other vertical surface with masking tape and depress the button on the spray can while aiming the nozzle at the newspaper. Hold the can approximately 12 inches away from the paper. This is to make certain that the can will emit a fine, even spray. If there is paint buildup clogging the nozzle, pull the nozzle off the can and soak it in paint thinner or other petroleum-based solvent to clear the passage. When the nozzle is clean again, replace it on the can.

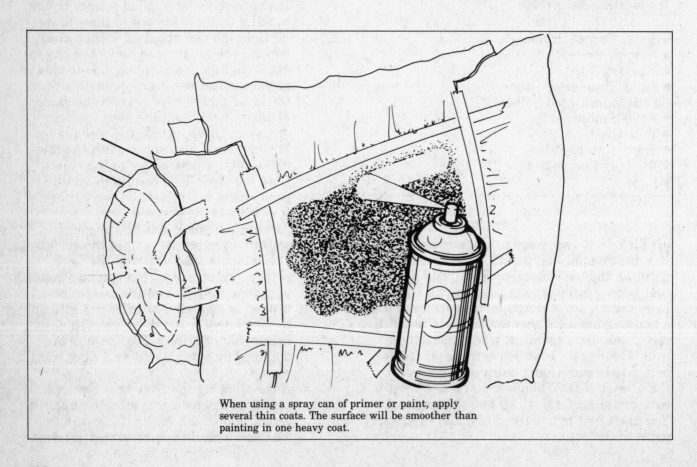

When using a spray can of primer or paint, apply several thin coats. The surface will be smoother than painting in one heavy coat.

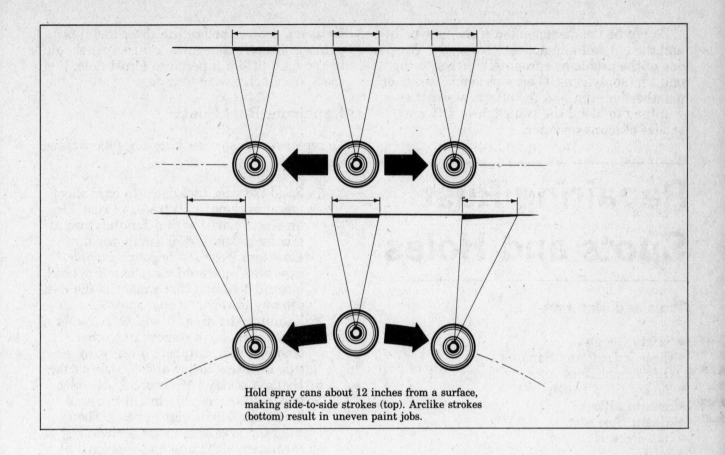

Hold spray cans about 12 inches from a surface, making side-to-side strokes (top). Arclike strokes (bottom) result in uneven paint jobs.

3. If you have never applied paint before, practice on an old board or piece of metal. Hold the can about 12 inches away, depress the nozzle, and move the can in even, slightly overlapping, side-to-side strokes across the board or metal. Your stroke should always remain the same distance away from the object you are spraying. Often, people use a semicircular motion as they spray, with the middle of their stroke closer to the object than the ends. This results in an uneven amount of paint on the surface of the object being sprayed.

4. After practicing, apply the paint in smooth, even strokes across the primed surface of the repair area. Overlap the first side-to-side stroke with a second stroke and so on until the entire area to be painted is covered. **Note:** Do not attempt to completely cover the primer with a coat of paint on the first coat. Best results are obtained by applying several fine, misty coats. In fact, after the first coat, you should still be able to see plenty of the primer through the paint.

5. After allowing the first light coat of paint to dry for 2 to 5 minutes, apply a second coat in the same manner. Applying several thin coats of paint will result in a better paint job than trying to apply one or two thick coats. The finish will be smoother and your chances of having the paint run are reduced. If the paint should accidentally run, allow it to dry thoroughly. Then sand the run with #400 sandpaper. Wipe the area clean with a tack cloth and apply another coat of paint over the area. **Note:** Allow each coat of paint to dry thoroughly before applying another coat.

6. After the paint has dried for at least 2 days, apply a little rubbing compound with a clean, soft cloth to rub the paint out. This will result in a more professional-looking job. Rubbing compound applied according to the directions on the product adds luster to the paint and helps it blend in with the older paint.

Do not be too disappointed if the new paint and the old paint do not match exactly. This is one of the problems encountered when using paint in spray cans. Over a period of weeks or months, sunlight and the effects of weather will tend to blend the two slightly different shades of paint together.

Repairing Rust Spots and Holes

Tools and Materials

- Safety Goggles
- Electric Drill and Sanding Disc Attachment
- Rotary Wire Brush
- Sanding Block
- Plastic Spreader
- Ball-Peen Hammer
- Scissors
- Utility Knife
- #50 Sandpaper Disc and Sandpaper
- Distilled White Vinegar
- Rags
- Rubbing (Isopropyl) Alcohol
- Body Filler
- #80 Sandpaper Disc and Sandpaper
- Spot Putty
- Petroleum-Based Solvent
- Tack Cloth
- Body Repair Kit
- Detergent
- Water
- Rust Treatment Chemical

RUST ON a car's body will spread if it is not stopped. All rust begins as a tiny rust spot, generally because some bare metal was exposed to moisture or other corrosive elements. This can even occur during the manu-facturing process before the sheet metal is painted. Despite the cause, a rust spot should be repaired before it becomes a rust hole. Rust spots are much easier to repair.

Repairing Rust Spots

To repair a rust spot on your car, follow these steps.

1. Sand the rust spot down to bare sheet metal to remove all traces of rust. Use an electric drill with a sanding disc attachment and a #50 sandpaper disc. *Caution: Wear safety goggles while sanding.* You could use a sanding block, but the drill and disc sander is the easiest way to repair a rust spot.
2. Examine the area. It will be pitted or pock-marked. To remove any other traces of rust, saturate a rag with distilled white vinegar and rub the surface.
3. Using a rotary wire brush in the electric drill, thoroughly brush the area. *Caution: Wear safety goggles.* Then wipe the area clean with a clean rag saturated with rubbing (isopropyl) alcohol.
4. If the surface still has small pits or indentations where rust is visible, you should apply a rust treatment chemical to convert the rust to black oxide. These chemical products are sold under a number of brand names but they can help protect the surface by turning the rust into a protective oxide coating. Allow the product to dry completely before painting or applying body filler. This is usually overnight or 24 hours.
5. Decide whether body filler is required to level any indentation in the sheet metal. If no indentation is left, proceed to Step 9; otherwise, proceed to Step 6.
6. To fill an indentation in the sheet metal, mix enough body filler material to fill the indentation. Mix the body filler according to label directions. Apply slightly more filler than is necessary. The slight excess will be removed by sanding.
7. Allow the body filler to dry thoroughly according to the directions on the product you use.

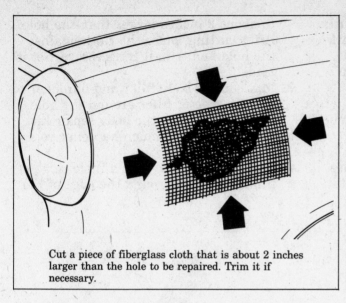

Cut a piece of fiberglass cloth that is about 2 inches larger than the hole to be repaired. Trim it if necessary.

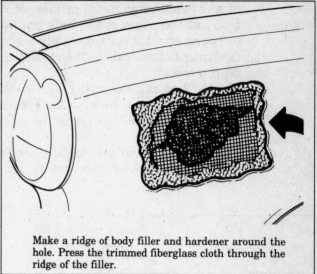

Make a ridge of body filler and hardener around the hole. Press the trimmed fiberglass cloth through the ridge of the filler.

8. Sand the repair by hand with #80 sandpaper until the area is smooth and blends in with the surrounding sheet metal.

9. If, after sanding, there are any minor imperfections in the body filler, they may be filled in with spot putty. Rub a very thin layer of spot putty over the imperfections with a plastic spreader, which is provided with many auto body repair kits.

10. Allow the spot putty to dry.

11. Sand the repair smooth by hand using #80 sandpaper. **Note:** When sanding by hand, the four fingers of your hand should apply even pressure for the best results.

12. After sanding, clean the repair with a petroleum-based solvent and a tack cloth.

Once the repaired rust spot has been cleaned, it is ready for priming and painting. Refer to the section on "Using Primer and Paint" in this chapter.

Repairing Rust Holes

If you ignore a rust spot on your car, it is likely to become a hole before too long. Assuming the rust hole is still small enough for the do-it-yourselfer to repair, purchase a body repair kit from an auto supply store. The contents of various kits vary, but most contain body filler, hardener to make the filler harden, fiberglass cloth, and a plastic scraper. Follow this procedure.

1. Wash the area to be repaired thoroughly using a detergent cleaner—not soap—and water. Add just enough detergent to the water to make light suds. Rinse the area well, and wipe it dry with a clean rag.

2. Use a rag saturated with a petroleum-based solvent to wipe the entire area to be repaired. Only thorough wiping will remove all grease, tar, and wax.

3. Sand the damaged area with coarse #50 sandpaper. An electric drill with a sanding disc attachment will save time and effort. Continue the sanding operation until at least 2 inches of bare metal is exposed all around the hole. *Caution: Wear safety goggles while sanding.*

4. Carefully beat the edges of the hole inward with a ball-peen hammer until all sharp points are crimped back about ¼ inch.

5. Use the hammer to depress the solid metal around the hole to about a 45-degree angle.

6. Use a rotary wire brush in an electric drill to brush the area. *Caution: Wear safety goggles while brushing.* Make absolutely sure that the bare metal is free

of any remaining paint, primer, or rust. Start at the edges of the hole and work outward about 2 inches. Apply a rust treatment chemical if all the rust can't be removed.

7. Use a clean rag saturated with rubbing (isopropyl) alcohol to wipe the area to be repaired. Allow about 15 minutes for the area to dry.

8. Use scissors to cut a piece of fiberglass cloth, provided with the body repair kit, to about 2 inches larger than the hole. After cutting, place the cloth against the hole and trim it if necessary. Set it aside.

9. Mix enough body filler and hardener to make a ring of filler around the hole. Instructions with the body repair kit will explain how much hardener you mix.

10. Apply the filler so that a little ridge of filler is formed around the edge of the

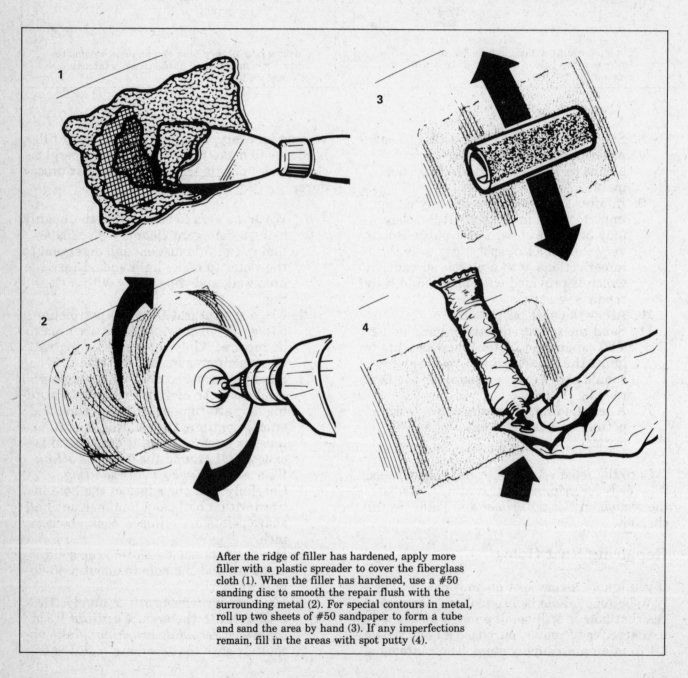

After the ridge of filler has hardened, apply more filler with a plastic spreader to cover the fiberglass cloth (1). When the filler has hardened, use a #50 sanding disc to smooth the repair flush with the surrounding metal (2). For special contours in metal, roll up two sheets of #50 sandpaper to form a tube and sand the area by hand (3). If any imperfections remain, fill in the areas with spot putty (4).

hole where you have beaten the metal inward.

11. Taking the cut piece of fiberglass cloth, position it over the hole and press its edges down through the ridge of filler.

12. After the fiberglass cloth is in position, use the plastic scraper tool or spreader to smooth out the ridge of body filler so that it is almost flush.

13. Allow the body filler to harden. Once the body filler has hardened, it should hold the fiberglass cloth.

14. Mix enough body filler and hardener to cover the fiberglass cloth.

15. Apply the body filler on the fiberglass cloth with the plastic spreader, and smooth it over the repair. Allow the body filler to harden thoroughly. **Note:** When the filler is almost hard, you can use a knife to shape the repair.

16. After the body filler has hardened, use an electric drill and a #50 sanding disc to smooth the repair until it is flush with the surrounding metal area. **Note:** If there are any folds or bends in the area being repaired, roll up two sheets of #50 sandpaper to form a tube and sand the area by hand. This round shape will fit into a fold and smooth the area better than a disc sander. Using two sheets keeps the paper from collapsing when you press it against the fold.

17. After sanding, mix some body filler and hardener and apply it to any remaining imperfections.

18. After the filler dries, sand the repair once more with a #80 sanding disc. **Note:** Use #80 sandpaper as explained in Step 16 to contour-sand any folds or bends.

19. If any tiny imperfections remain in this final layer of body filler, fill them with spot putty, following the manufacturer's directions.

20. Allow the spot putty to dry.

21. Hand sand the area with #80 sandpaper until the repair blends in with the surrounding metal. **Note:** When sanding by hand, the four fingers of your hand should apply even pressure for the best results.

22. After sanding, clean the repair with solvent and a tack cloth.

Repairing Scratches and Dents

Tools and Materials

- Artist's Brush
- Hammer and Block of Wood
- Locking-Jaw Pliers
- Blunt-Faced Hammer and Dolly
- Safety Goggles
- Electric Drill, Drill Bit, and Sanding Disc Attachment
- Plastic Spreader
- Rags
- Water
- Rubbing Compound
- Car Wax
- Sponge
- #400 Wet-or-Dry Sandpaper
- Petroleum-Based Solvent
- Tack Cloth
- Touch-Up Paint
- Cream Polish
- Sheet Metal Screw
- #80 Sanding Disc
- Body Filler
- Spot Putty

MINOR SCRATCHES and dents on cars are common, and removing most of the minor ones is not difficult provided you are willing to spend a little time to do the job right.

Basically, there are two types of scratches. A shallow, or superficial, scratch just mars the surface layer or layers of paint and does not penetrate through to the bare metal. The deep scratch does.

Repairing a Shallow Scratch

Examine the scratch to determine if it is minor. Run your fingernail across it; if your nail does not catch, the scratch is shallow and can be removed very simply. Follow these steps.

1. Fold a clean, soft rag into a pad and dampen it with a little water.
2. Add a small amount of rubbing compound to the pad.
3. Using just the tip of one finger, gently rub back and forth—never in a circular motion—along the scratch with the compound until the scratch vanishes. *Caution: Rubbing compound is an abrasive that can remove paint and primer. Check your progress often and stop as soon as the scratch disappears.*
4. Wax the car after removing the scratch.

Repairing a Deep Scratch

Repairing a deep scratch that penetrates to the bare sheet metal, is not too much more difficult than repairing a shallow one. Examine the scratch. Run your fingernail across it; if your nail catches, it is a deep scratch. Follow this procedure.

1. Sponge the scratch with water.
2. Carefully and lightly sand along the scratch with #400 wet-or-dry sandpaper. Sponge on water as you sand. Sand until the area around the scratch is smooth from surrounding paint to the bare metal of the scratch.
3. Wipe the area dry with a rag.
4. Clean the area of the scratch with a petroleum-based solvent and wipe it dry with a clean tack cloth.
5. Using a small artist's brush, apply touch-up paint that matches the car's finish to the scratch *only*; do not let the paint go beyond the edges of the scratch.
6. Let the paint dry for about 30 minutes.
7. If the touched-up scratch is still visible as a depression, apply a second coat of touch-up paint to level it and let the paint dry for about 30 minutes. If the touched-up area is higher than the surrounding paint, use a little rubbing

compound on a slightly damp rag to even it out.
8. Apply cream polish to the repaired area to help protect the new paint.
9. Wax the car.

Repairing a Minor Dent

Fixing a dent is one of the more difficult jobs for the average do-it-yourselfer. Repairing the dent is not that difficult, but making the completed repair job look as if no dent ever existed is the hard part. Sometimes the average do-it-yourselfer can accomplish it; sometimes he cannot. Actually, there are really no hard and fast rules about repairing dents. You try to knock them out the best way you can. If you decide to repair a minor dent yourself, here are the steps to follow.

1. Inspect the dent and decide whether you can fix it and whether you have enough confidence to do a good job. If the sheet metal has a sharp crease—even if the dent is small—special body repair tools and experience will be required to fix it; take the car to a professional. If the dent is in a relatively flat area, such as in the middle of a car door, however, you

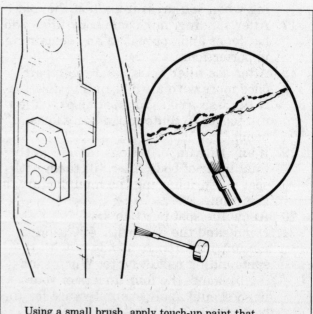

Using a small brush, apply touch-up paint that matches the car's finish to the scratch only. Do not let the paint go beyond the edges of the scratch.

may be able to remove it in one of several ways.

A. If the dent is a shallow, round depression, remove part of the inside door panel so that you can squeeze a deflated basketball connected to a bicycle air pump into the door, directly behind the dent. Carefully inflate the basketball. Sometimes, the dent will suddenly pop back out, restoring the door to its original shape.

B. An alternative for large, bulging dents is to remove the door panel completely and strike the center of the dent sharply with the heel of your hand once or twice. Or, place a block of wood against the dent and strike it with a hammer.

C. Another way is to drill a small hole into the center of the dent from the outside and twist a sheet metal screw about half or three-quarters of the way into the hole. Grip the head of the screw with locking-jaw pliers and yank the dent out. Remove the screw. The hole, of course, will have to be repaired. Refer to the section on "Repairing Rust Spots and Holes."

D. Many dents require special body repair tools. If you buy an auto body repair tool kit, it should contain a blunt-faced hammer and a mushroom dolly, a heavy piece of metal used to contour the dent out.

    Remove the inside door panel. Set the curve of the dolly against the inside of the dent, and hammer the outside surface of the sheet metal with the hammer until the approximate original contour of the sheet metal is restored. Then sand the repaired area.

2. Once the dent has been removed, it may be necessary to sand the damaged area down to bare sheet metal with an electric drill and sanding disc attachment using a #80 sanding disc. *Caution: Wear safety goggles while sanding.*

3. If required, body filler and spot putty may be used to smooth the metal surface for priming and painting. If so, refer to the section on "Repairing Rust Spots and Holes" in this chapter.

Repairing Plastic Body Parts

Tools and Materials

- Sandpaper or Drill and Sanding Discs (#80, #180, #240, and #400 grit)
- Rags
- Tack Cloth
- Special Plastic Filler
- Masking Tape
- Newspaper
- Can of Spray Paint

MANY LATE MODEL cars have soft plastic or flexible front body parts such as bumper, headlights, and grille coverings. Ordinary body filler doesn't work well on repairing gouges or holes in this type or material because it isn't flexible enough and will gradually crack and peel loose. It also lacks the structural strength to hold damaged plastic together. For this type of repair work, a special flexible body filler designed exclusively for soft plastic body parts must be used. If the repair area is small, ordinary spray paint will work, but for large areas or parts exposed to frequent rubbing or flexing, a flexible additive must be mixed into the paint for the job to last. This is something best left to a professional painter unless you have your own compressor and spray gun. Flexible additives are available but they require skill in mixing for proper color match.

Some cars have hard plastic body panels. Depending on what the body part is made from, ordinary body filler may or may not adhere to it. In most cases, conventional repair techniques still work on hard, non-flexible panels.

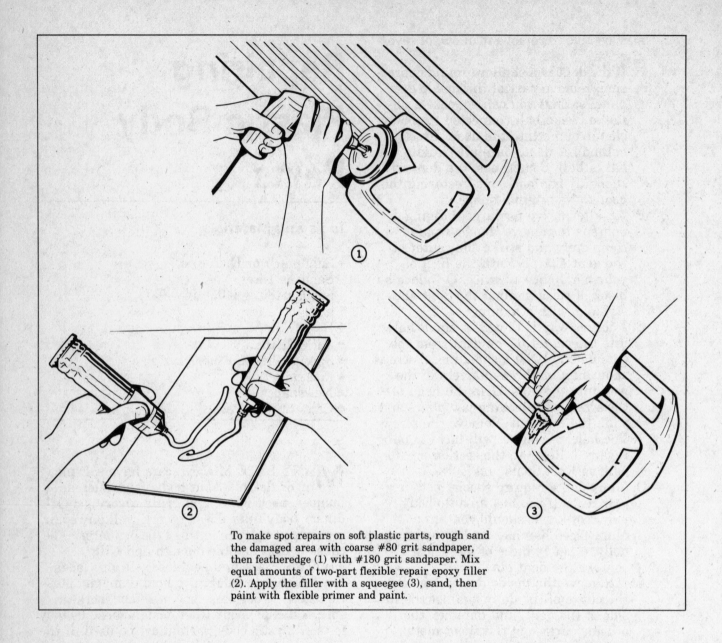

To make spot repairs on soft plastic parts, rough sand the damaged area with coarse #80 grit sandpaper, then featheredge (1) with #180 grit sandpaper. Mix equal amounts of two-part flexible repair epoxy filler (2). Apply the filler with a squeegee (3), sand, then paint with flexible primer and paint.

Soft Plastic Spot Repairs

Follow these steps to repair punctures, gouges or tears in soft body parts.

1. Rough sand the damaged area with coarse #80 grit sandpaper to remove the paint and surface damage from the repair area.
2. Featheredge the repair area by sanding with #180 grit sandpaper to blend the paint to the sanded area.
3. Wipe off the area with a clean rag.
4. If back-up reinforcing is needed to fill a hole or tear, clean the underside of the damaged area and apply tape to the underside.
5. Mix the two-part flexible repair epoxy together, using equal amounts of each. Follow the instructions provided with the product.
6. Apply the flexible filler to the damaged area with a squeegee, pressing the filler into the damaged area and smoothing it until it is roughly level with the surrounding surface.
7. Allow the filler to dry for 20 or 30 minutes, then, after it has cured, sand the

surface level with #180 followed by finer #240 grit sandpaper.

8. Fill in any imperfections or spots with more filler and finish sanding with #240 grit followed by #400 grit sandpaper.

9. The damaged area can now be painted with flexible primer followed by flexible top coat.

Repairing Chipped Paint

Tools and Materials

- Utility Knife
- #80 and #400 Sandpaper
- Petroleum-Based Solvent
- Tack Cloth
- Can of Spray Primer
- Cardboard
- Masking Tape
- Newspaper
- Can of Spray Paint
- Rags
- Rubbing Compound

CHIPPED PAINT is common on cars, even those fresh from the showroom floor. It is pretty easy to chip away small pieces of paint, particularly around the edges of doors.

If the paint is not chipped away to bare metal, rust will not be able to attack. But if the chip includes the primer coat and bare metal is visible, it is only a matter of time before rust sets in.

If you discover paint that is chipped down to the bare metal, follow this procedure.

1. Using a sheet of #80 sandpaper, hand sand the chipped area. Most likely, there will be at least a little surface rust unless the chip is very recent. Sand the chipped area until the metal is clean and shiny.

Note: When sanding, use one fingertip to press the sandpaper on the chipped spot. You can sand in back-and-forth motions or in small circles. It does not matter. Be sure to sand a little of the paint surrounding the chip. This is so that the primer and paint will adhere to the paint better.

2. After sanding, clean the repair with a petroleum-based solvent and a tack cloth.

3. Apply primer to the chipped spot. **Note:** One way to spray primer (and paint) onto a small area is to cut a small hole about twice the size of the chipped area in a piece of thin cardboard that is approximately 12 inches square or larger. Hold the cardboard's hole a few inches from the chipped area to be sprayed. This will prevent the primer from striking the surrounding area. In some cases, it might be necessary to mask the immediate area around the chipped spot. Refer to the section on "Using Masking Tape" in this chapter. You also should practice spraying through the cardboard's hole to see how much of an area is affected and exactly how far away you should hold the cardboard to obtain the best results.

4. After the primer coat dries, lightly sand the repair area with #400 sandpaper. Apply even pressure with the four fingers of your hand as you lightly sand. You are just trying to scuff the primer enough so that the paint will adhere well.

5. After sanding, clean the area with solvent and a tack cloth.

6. Apply the paint, spraying several light, thin coats through the hole in the piece of cardboard used to apply the primer coat. Allow each coat of paint to dry.

7. After several hours, remove the masking tape and newspaper.

8. Allow at least 2 days for the paint to dry thoroughly. Then, rub out the area with a soft, clean rag treated with rubbing compound. Refer to the section on "Restoring Faded Paint" in this chapter.

Restoring Faded Paint

Tools and Materials

- Rags
- Water
- Rubbing Compound
- Car Wax

IT IS UNFORTUNATE that the smooth, shiny paint job on a new car does not remain that way. Fading can be stalled by regular washing and protective waxings, and by parking the car inside a garage when it is not in use. But sooner or later, sun, wind, rain, snow, sleet, hail, road salt, and pollutants are going to take their toll on your car's paint job.

If your car is already at the stage where its paint finish has as much shine as a piece of used sandpaper, you can bring back much of the original luster. And, you can do it cheaply. All you need is rubbing compound, which essentially is an abrasive wax. It actually rubs off layers—hopefully only faded layers—of paint. *Caution: Rubbing compound should not be used on cars with a clear coat top layer of paint. The clear coat is what gives the paint its gloss. Removing it can dull the finish.*

To restore some luster to your car's faded paint, follow these steps.

1. Wash the car and dry it. Refer to the section on "Appearance" in the "Maintaining Your Car" chapter.
2. Fold a soft, clean rag into a pad and dip it in water, wringing out the excess water.
3. Dip the damp pad into a can of rubbing compound.
4. Apply the rubbing compound sparingly to the car in firm back-and-forth motions—never in a circular motion—rinsing and wringing out the pad regularly. Work by sections, rubbing until you remove enough faded paint. Then move to the next section.

    Note: Be patient. The job is not accomplished quickly, especially when rubbing out an entire car. And, since rubbing compound is abrasive, excessive rubbing can remove all the paint and primer too. So, rub only until the shine comes back and move to another section.
5. After the entire car has been treated with the rubbing compound, apply a quality paste wax to the car's finish.

In the future, wash the car and wax it just as you would normally. Do not use rubbing compound as a substitute for wax. If you do, you eventually would remove all your car's paint.

After the entire faded surface has been treated with rubbing compound, apply a quality paste wax to the car's finish.

Molding and Weatherstripping

MOLDING on your car's body plays more than just an ornamental role. Some of it is designed to protect the car from being scratched and dented.

Sometimes, molding comes loose. Often, you

Tools and Materials

- Carpenter's Level
- Pencil
- Utility Knife
- Single-Edge Razor Blade and Blade Holder
- Petroleum-Based Solvent
- Rags
- Trim or Weatherstrip Cement
- Cardboard
- #600 Sandpaper
- Rubbing Compound
- Molding
- Masking Tape
- Molding Fasteners
- Mastic Remover
- Weatherstripping
- Weatherstrip Preservative

can easily fix it yourself. Basically, there are two kinds of molding. One type is glued to the car body, another is secured by plastic or metal fasteners. You can always repair the molding that is glued. Many cars today have this type. Molding that is held by fasteners can be more difficult to repair.

Repairing Molding

To repair loose molding that is glued into place, follow these steps.

1. Clean the car body where the molding was glued with a petroleum-based solvent.
2. After cleaning, use a clean rag to dry the area completely.
3. Apply a thin line of trim or weatherstrip cement along the middle of the back of the molding to be resecured. **Note:** Be sure to use only a thin line of cement. When you press the molding firmly against the car body, the pressure will force the cement outward. Too much cement will ooze from the edges of the molding.
4. Press and hold the molding into position

against the car. Take care that it is positioned correctly. The cement hardens quickly.
5. Immediately inspect the molding to see if cement has seeped out from behind the molding. If it has, take a small piece of thin cardboard, such as a business card, and bend it into a V-shape. Run the bottom of the "V" between the car body and the molding to scrape away any excess cement. **Note:** You must do this immediately or the glue will harden and be very difficult to remove. If the cement should harden, use a piece of #600 sandpaper to sand the cement away. Then rub the area with rubbing compound applied to a soft, clean rag. *Caution: Use the sandpaper and rubbing compound only enough to remove the cement—not the finish of the car.*

Applying Adhesive Molding

If your car is lacking molding and you would like to apply some, you can purchase accessory molding. To apply new molding that has an adhesive backing, follow these steps:

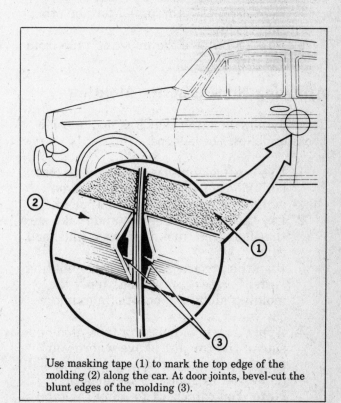

Use masking tape (1) to mark the top edge of the molding (2) along the car. At door joints, bevel-cut the blunt edges of the molding (3).

1. Use a petroleum-based solvent to clean both sides of the car along the area where the molding is to be applied.
2. Dry the area, and make sure that it is free from dust, wax, and road film.
3. Plan the precise pattern of the molding. **Note:** For best protection, apply the molding along the point of maximum car width.
4. Apply a strip of masking tape along one side of the car just above where you plan to place the molding; the tape will guide you in applying the molding. **Note:** You can check to see if the tape is horizontal by using a level. If it is not, simply lift the tape and realign it.
5. Beginning on one side of the car, measure and mark each section of molding.
6. Trim the molding to fit with a utility knife. Make sure that a section butting up to a door joint is trimmed properly; it should be beveled to about a 45-degree angle if trimmed close to the joint.
7. Begin applying sections of molding; peel off the protective backing on a section, align its top edge with the bottom edge of the masking tape, and press the molding firmly into position.
8. Repeat Steps 3 through 7 for the other side of the car.
9. Finally, remove the masking tape from the car.

Applying Non-Adhesive Molding

To apply new molding that has no adhesive backing, follow these steps.

1. Use a petroleum-based solvent to clean both sides of the car along the area where the molding is to be applied.
2. Dry the area thoroughly, and make sure that it is free from dust, wax, and road film.
3. Plan the precise position of the molding. **Note:** For best protection, apply the molding along the point of maximum car width.
4. Apply a strip of masking tape along one side of the car just above where you plan to place the molding; the tape will guide you in applying the molding. **Note:** You can check to see if the tape is

horizontal by using a level. If it is not, simply lift up the tape and realign it.
5. Beginning on one side of the car, measure and mark each section of molding.
6. Trim the molding to fit with a utility knife. Make sure that a section butting up to a door joint is trimmed properly; it should be beveled to about a 45-degree angle if trimmed close to the joint.
7. Apply a thin line of trim or weather-strip cement along the middle of the back of the molding. **Note:** Be sure to use only a thin line of cement. When you press the molding firmly against the car body, the pressure will force the cement outward. Too much cement will ooze from the edges of the molding.
8. Press and hold the molding into position against the car. Take care that it is positioned correctly. The cement hardens quickly.
9. Immediately inspect the molding to see if cement has seeped out from behind the molding. If it has, take a small piece of thin cardboard, such as a business card, and bend it into a V-shape. Run the bottom of the "V" between the car body and the molding to scrape away any excess cement. **Note:** You must do this immediately or the glue will harden and be very difficult to remove. If the cement should harden, use a piece of #600 sandpaper to sand the cement away. Then rub the area with rubbing compound applied to a soft, clean cloth. *Caution: Use the sandpaper and rubbing compound only enough to remove the cement—not the finish of the car.*

Molding Held With Fasteners

Molding that is held to a car with fasteners can be more difficult to repair. Visit the car dealer that handles the make and model of car you own, an auto supply store, or a local body shop, if necessary, to see if any carry the kind of fasteners that hold your car's molding. These fasteners may be screws, clips, nipples that slide into holes, and so on. Examining the fasteners or checking the service manual for your car will tell you what type to seek.

If you are unable to obtain new molding and fasteners, you could remove the old molding and fasteners and repair any holes in the sheet metal. Refer to the section on "Repairing Rust Spots and Holes" in this chapter. You then could glue on new accessory molding in the manner described in the procedure for "Applying Adhesive Molding" in this section.

Weatherstripping

Weatherstripping plays an important role in keeping your car dry. If it should get cracked, chipped, loose, or develop gaps, you can easily get water and wind noise inside your car. To prevent this, inspect your vehicle's weatherstripping about every 6 months. Follow this procedure.

1. Inspect the weatherstripping visually and with your fingers. Pull or push gently to make certain that it is firmly glued in place.
2. If it has come loose but generally is still in good condition, you can glue it back with weatherstrip cement. If part or all of the weatherstripping around a door or trunk area, for example, is missing or damaged, proceed to the next step.
3. If the weatherstripping is damaged, peel it off. Scrape any glue left by the old

weatherstripping. Do not use a single-edge razor blade to remove the adhesive; use a mastic remover instead.
4. Clean the area with a rag dampened with a petroleum-based solvent, and wipe it dry with a clean rag.
5. Using the old weatherstripping as a guide to measure by, or measuring the area in which new weatherstripping will be installed, cut a length of new weatherstripping that is slightly longer than the length of material you are replacing.
6. Apply adhesive to the back of the new weatherstripping and press it into place, starting at one end. When you reach the other end, trim the excess weatherstripping carefully with a single-edge razor blade in a blade holder.
7. Before closing a door or trunk, allow the adhesive to dry thoroughly, according to the manufacturer's instructions.

Weatherstripping that is cracked in a few places, but not severely, may not require replacement. Such weatherstripping may be treated with a preservative. To maintain newly installed weatherstripping, it also is a good idea to use such a preservative at least once a year.

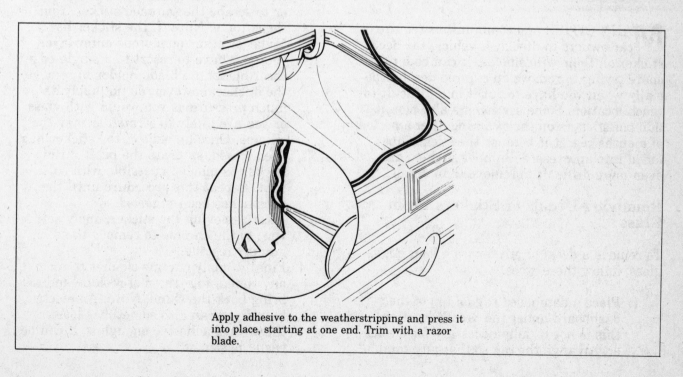

Apply adhesive to the weatherstripping and press it into place, starting at one end. Trim with a razor blade.

Removing Decals and Stickers

Tools and Materials

- Single-Edge Razor Blade and Blade Holder
- Pliers
- Plastic Ice Scraper
- Rags
- Water
- Detergent
- Glass Cleaner
- Rubbing Alcohol
- Petroleum-Based Solvent
- Chrome Cleaner
- Rubbing Compound
- Car Wax

MANY CITIES and communities require car owners to display a vehicle tax decal sticker on their windshields. It can be a real chore trying to remove an expired decal, especially when you have to put it in a difficult-to-reach location. Some car owners also mount bumper stickers on their car and after a period of months regret it because the sticker has faded into an eyesore. Bumper stickers are even more difficult to remove than decals.

Removing Decals or Stickers From Glass

To remove a decal or sticker from your car's glass, follow these steps.

1. Place a dampened rag on top of the dashboard under the decal's location; this is not usually necessary for a sticker. Arrange the rag so that any small pieces of decal will fall onto the rag and not into difficult-to-reach crevices or defroster vents.
2. Using a blade holder, place the edge of a sharp single-edge razor blade firmly against the glass above the decal or sticker and scrape down, attempting to get the blade behind the decal or sticker. In difficult-to-reach spots, you might use pliers to hold the razor blade holder as you scrape. Periodically soak the decal with warm, soapy water.
3. After removing all traces of the decal or sticker from the glass, clean the area with glass cleaner. **Note:** If a sticker was removed, soak a clean cloth with rubbing alcohol and rub the area vigorously to remove any gummy residue.

Removing Stickers From Chrome

Stickers placed on chrome require extra care and extra work. Follow this procedure.

1. Soak the sticker with a petroleum-based solvent so that it penetrates the sticker thoroughly.
2. After the sticker has been saturated with the solvent, use a plastic ice scraper to scrape the softened sticker from the chrome. **Note:** If the sticker has a Mylar or other nonporous outer layer, you may have to resort to a single-edge razor blade in a blade holder to remove the sticker; however, do not apply as much pressure as you would with glass or you are likely to scratch or mar the chrome. Once an edge of the sticker has been raised, saturate the back of the sticker as much as possible with solvent. Repeat this procedure until the sticker has been removed.
3. After removing the sticker, apply solvent to the chrome to remove the gummy residue.
4. Finally, apply chrome cleaner to remove any remaining traces of residue and to bring back the shine. **Note:** An electric hair dryer can also sometimes loosen the sticker adhesive enough so it can be easily peeled off.

ACCESSORIES

IF YOU WERE to look at the catalog of a standard-size automobile of the early 1940s, you would find that very few options or accessories were available. Equipment that we take for granted on cars today—radio, heater, even turn signals—had to be specially ordered by the customer.

Options, such as air conditioning, power steering and power brakes, automatic transmission, power windows, and automatic door locks, still must be specified by the car buyer, but they are quickly become standard equipment on most full-size cars.

Other accessories, including AM/FM radio (some with stereo), automatic speed control, and other comfort or entertainment features, also are gaining in popularity.

Whether these electrically operated options and accessories are installed by the car manufacturer as original equipment or added later by the car dealer or some independent installer, service and repair occasionally are necessary.

We will not attempt to explain all of the various services that might be performed to optional and accessory items. In this chapter, however, we will offer some of the checks, services, and repair procedures for a few useful aftermarket items.

Because many of the components discussed are built into the car and involve complex wiring, panels, and so on, you may find it more practical to have an experienced mechanic work on such things as electric window circuitry, automatic speed control and other instrument repairs. But, if you are nimble, flexible, and patient enough to work in close quarters under the instrument panel, there is plenty you can accomplish on your own.

Windshield Wipers and Washers

Tools and Materials

- Screwdriver or Wrench
- Thin Wire
- Locking-Jaw Pliers
- Wiper Blade Refills
- Wiper Blade Arms
- Windshield Washer Fluid
- Rags
- Fuse

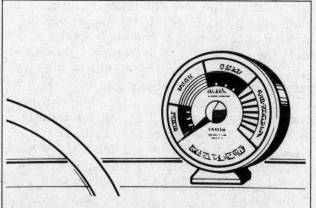

A vacuum gauge can help a driver obtain maximum efficiency from an engine, and it is relatively easy to install.

JUST AS you can count on your tires eventually wearing out and your gas tank going dry if you do not refill it, so you can count on your windshield wiper blades wearing out and your windshield washer reservoir running out of solvent if they are not maintained. Unfortunately, we often discover this during a rainstorm or after a passing truck has splashed mud on the windshield. Keeping a

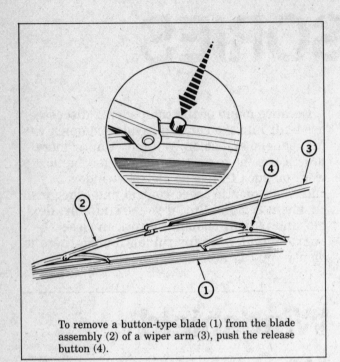

To remove a button-type blade (1) from the blade assembly (2) of a wiper arm (3), push the release button (4).

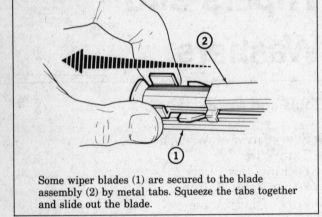

Some wiper blades (1) are secured to the blade assembly (2) by metal tabs. Squeeze the tabs together and slide out the blade.

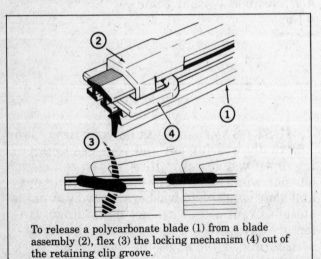

To release a polycarbonate blade (1) from a blade assembly (2), flex (3) the locking mechanism (4) out of the retaining clip groove.

close check on the wiper-washer system is as important to safety as knowing the lights are working properly.

Replacing Wiper Blades

Frequently, the only thing you will need to renew your wiper blades is a pair of refills. Wiper blades are the rubber parts that slip into the metal blade assembly. But if the metal blade frame or wiper arm has been damaged, you will have an extra investment to make. A thoughtful motorist carries at least a spare set of wiper blade refills in the car and thinks about checking and replacing the car's blades when the weather is dry.

Before buying refills, check the type and size of blade on your car. Many stores have charts to tell you which size refill is designed for your car.

There are three types of wiper blade refills, which differ somewhat on the method of replacement. One type has a black or red plastic button or pin about one third of the way up the blade frame. When you push the button down by hand, it releases a lock, allowing the rubber blade to slide out of the metal frame. A new blade refill will slide back in the same way, locking securely in place.

Another type of blade refill unlocks at the end of the rubber portion of the blade where there are two small metal tabs. By squeezing these tabs together, the rubber blade is released and can be slid out of the frame. A new refill is replaced in the same way. **Note:** Be careful to engage all frame tabs as the blade refill slips into place. When the blade is slid into position, the tabs should click, locking the blade into place. Check for proper operation, making sure no part of the blade holder contacts the windshield. This is especially important if you have metal blade holders, which can scratch your windshield glass.

The most recent type of wiper blades are made of polycarbonate. They have a locking mechanism at one end of the blade. The mechanism flexes downward out of the groove that the retaining clips on the frame fit into, allowing the blade to be released and slid out of the frame.

Note: Some types of windshield wiper assemblies feature an airfoil design. The purpose is to prevent the blade from lifting off the windshield at high speeds. An airfoil is mounted on top of the wiper blade and responds to wind pressure, pressing the blade against the glass.

If your windshield wipers are the type that are hidden below the cowl in front of the windshield, you can bring them into an accessible position for checking or replacement by turning the ignition switch to the on position, turning the wiper switch on, and turning the ignition switch off as soon as the blades have reached a covenient position on the windshield.

Replacing Wiper Arms

Wiper arms do not last forever. They are designed to press the wiper blade against the windshield at a specific tension. But when age and the elements have taken their toll of the arm spring and pivots, it may be necessary to install new arms. Your service station or auto supply store can supply you with the proper wiper arm designed for your car.

Most wiper arms are held in place on a knurled shaft by a locking device contained on the wiper arm. The arm can be removed by pulling the wiper arm end out away from the windshield to unlatch the locking device and pulling up on the end that is attached to the part that drives the wipers. In some cases, it is necessary to use a special puller tool to remove an arm. If this is the situation, go to a mechanic who has the equipment. But before tugging on the wiper arm, make sure that it is not secured at the base with a screw or nut. You may have to loosen or remove the screw or nut first, using a screwdriver or a wrench.

Another is the bayonet-type arm. This kind of arm is removed by depressing a tab on the wiper frame.

Windshield Washers

Windshield washers are standard equipment on new cars today and require very little maintenance. But, if you have ever been caught in a situation where your windshield was streaked by mud and your washers were not working properly, you know how important it is to keep the system in good condition.

The most a home mechanic need do for windshield washers is keep the fluid in the

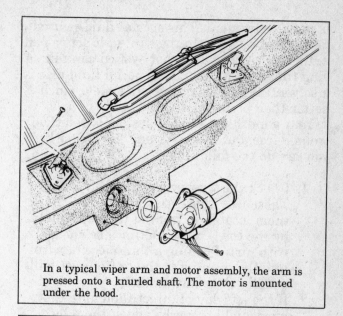

In a typical wiper arm and motor assembly, the arm is pressed onto a knurled shaft. The motor is mounted under the hood.

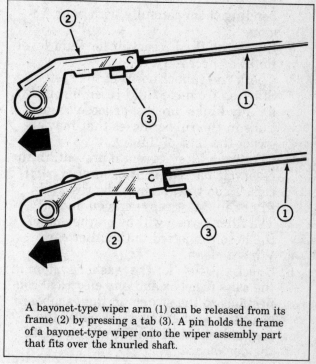

A bayonet-type wiper arm (1) can be released from its frame (2) by pressing a tab (3). A pin holds the frame of a bayonet-type wiper onto the wiper assembly part that fits over the knurled shaft.

washer reservoir filled to the proper level. Most cars have the washer fluid reservoir under the hood in the engine compartment. Usually, the reservoir bottle is plastic, with level marks indicated on the side. Simply fill the container with windshield washer fluid to the recommended level.

Windshield washer fluid either comes ready-mixed or in a concentrate form. The ready-mix is more convenient. This special fluid is used for several reasons. In the winter, it acts as an antifreeze. A frozen washer system can take a long time to thaw out. The special fluid also is a solvent. It will clean the windshield much better then plain water.

Your windshield washer system is relatively trouble-free, but if the system fails to work, you can do the following.

1. Check the washer jets for obstruction. These jets (there are usually two of them located in front of the windshield by the cowl) can sometimes be clogged with dirt. Pushing a thin piece of wire into the opening in the end of a jet will usually clear any obstacle.
2. If the jets do not direct fluid onto the windshield properly, adjust them by bending them carefully with your fingers.
3. Check the fluid reservoir for fluid level. Refill as necessary.
4. Check the rubber hoses of the system. Starting from the fluid reservoir, look for any kinks, breaks, or loose connections in the rubber hoses that may obstruct the flow of fluid.
5. Check the filter screen, if present, in the reservoir for sediment or foreign particles. To do this, remove the reservoir filler cap. Most caps snap on and off. The filler screen will be on the end of the hose connected to the filler cap. Wipe it clean.
6. Check the fuse for the washer system in the car's fuse box and any electrical connections to the switch on the dashboard or at the washer pump. Usually, the fuse is located in the fuse block under the dashboard.

If all of the checks fail to find any problem, you may need a new washer pump. Replacement pumps are available from an auto supply store, but this is a job for a professional mechanic. Have your mechanic examine your system and make the necessary repairs or parts replacements.

Windshield Wiper Problems and Cures

The following are some of the more common problems affecting windshield wipers. Their causes and cures are examined.

If the wiper blades streak or smear the windshield, this may be caused by hardened or cracked wiper blades. If so, the blades should be replaced. A dirty windshield or dirty wiper blades also may cause the problem. If this is the case, the windshield and wiper blade assembly should be cleaned with soap and water. Finally, cold weather and dirty driving conditions can streak and smear windshields. If such conditions are present, simply use plenty of windshield washer fluid from the washer system.

If your problem is a chattering wiper blade, it may be caused by an improper wiper arm tip attitude. If so, operate the wipers and then, when the wiper blades are at midstroke, shut off the ignition switch to stop the blades. Remove the offending blade or blades as explained elsewhere in this section. Check to see if the arm tip is parallel to the windshield glass. If not, use locking-jaw pliers to bend the arm parallel to the glass. If this fails to correct the problem, replace the wiper arm.

Another possible cause of chattering is a permanent set of a wiper blade lip due to cold weather or age. The cure for this condition in cold weather is to remove the blade and rinse it in warm water. If this does not solve the problem, the blade should be replaced.

High-speed driving also can cause chattering in wiper blades. One obvious solution is to slow down. Another is to install wiper blade assemblies that feature an airfoil on top to keep the blades on the windshield during high speeds.

Weak arm pressure is another reason for chattering and the answer here is to replace the wiper arm.

Finally, an improperly installed blade can chatter. This problem can be solved by removing the blade and installing it correctly.

Sometimes, a wiper blade may smear the windshield when it travels in only one direction. There are two possible causes. One is a permanent set of the wiper blade lip, which is cured by warming the blade if it occurs in cold weather. Otherwise, replace the blade. Another cause is that the wrong blade may have been installed in your car. If this is the problem, replace the wiper blade with the correct model designed for your car.

Rear Window Defrosters

Tools and Materials

- Voltmeter
- Heating Grid Repair Paint
- Jumper Wire
- Masking Tape

MANY CARS today have a heated rear window defroster as an option. Heat is created by applying voltage to the grid painted on the back window. The paint contains metallic additives that enables it to conduct electricity and provide sufficient resistance for heating. The defroster is controlled by a switch, control relay, and timer. When turned on, the timer continues to supply power to the window for a preset period of time, usually around 10 minutes.

A defective power switch, a bad timer or control solenoid, or a blown fuse can prevent the rear window defroster from working. A poor ground connection between the window grid and car body or an open circuit in the wir-ing between the grid and power supply can also render it useless.

Diagnosing Electrical Problems

If the rear window defroster doesn't work when you turn it on, first check the fuse panel for a blown fuse. Then check for voltage reaching the grid with your voltmeter. If you do get a 12 volt reading with the power switch on (but the window doesn't heat) power is reaching the grid but it isn't completing the circuit probably because of a poor ground. Check the ground for loose or broken wires, a loose screw, or a corroded mount.

If a voltmeter check shows no voltage at the rear grid when the switch is on, the problem is in either the switch, timer, relay, or wiring. You can try to isolate the faulty component by bypassing first the switch, then the timer and solenoid with your jumper wire. If the grid works when any of these items is bypassed, it means the part is faulty and should be replaced. Trial-and-error replacement of the switch, timer, or solenoid is not recommended because it's a waste of money if the part turns out not to be defective. And since few auto parts stores give refunds on electrical components, you're out the money.

Electrical troubleshooting can be a tedious process, so if you discover that voltage is not reaching the rear window perhaps you'd be better off turning the job over to a professional.

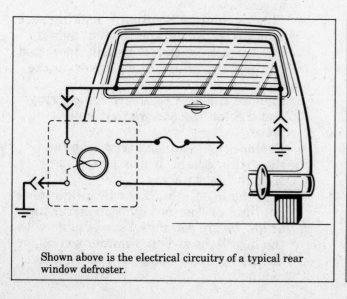

Shown above is the electrical circuitry of a typical rear window defroster.

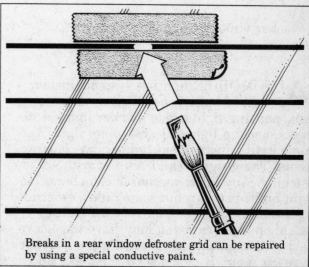

Breaks in a rear window defroster grid can be repaired by using a special conductive paint.

Defroster Grid Repairs

Sometimes you'll see a rear window defroster that fails to clear the rear window evenly. There will be strips where the grid doesn't seem to be heating. These dead spots are caused by tiny scratches that break the continuity of the conductive paint. They can be easily repaired by applying masking tape along both sides of the damaged grid line and brushing on a fresh layer of conductive paint. This paint can be purchased in most auto stores. It will be identified as rear window defroster repair paint on the packaging. Ordinary paint won't work because it isn't conductive.

Light Bulbs, Fuses, and Flashers

Tools and Materials

- Torx-Head Screwdriver
- Phillips-Head Screwdriver
- Heavy Gloves or Bulb-Base Gripper
- Flashlight
- Fuse-Puller
- Headlight or Other Bulbs
- Sandpaper, Emery Cloth, or Steel Wool
- Fuse
- Flasher Unit

AUTOMOBILE lighting systems include dozens of bulbs—headlights, turn signals, parking lights, side marker lights, taillights, backup lights, license plate lights, dome lights, instrument lights, and courtesy lights. These lights can burn out without warning. Any home mechanic can change the light bulbs in a car, but some bulbs, especially instrument lights, can be very difficult to reach; on some cars you may have to remove part of the dashboard or ventilation ductwork to reach them. It depends on the make and

model of your car.

Replacing Headlights

Replacing a burned-out headlight is not much more difficult than replacing any other bulb even though the procedure is different. Headlights are important to safe operation of your car, so replace a burned-out one immediately. Follow these steps.

1. Using a Phillips-head or Torx-head screwdriver, remove the screws that hold the headlight trim ring or molding in place. Usually trim rings are secured by one to four Phillips-head screws. **Note:** On a few cars, a grille section, also held by Phillips-head screws, may have to be removed to remove the headlight; loosen the screws and lift the grille section off.
2. Examine the visible screws around the headlight. Two larger screws are for adjusting the headlight's beam; do not touch these. Usually, there will be three other, smaller Phillips-head screws that hold an inner retaining ring in place. In some cases, it may not be necessary to completely remove these screws to remove the retaining ring, so experiment as you work. Loosen or remove the three screws and remove the retaining ring.
3. Pull the headlight out carefully and disconnect the electrical plug behind the headlight; it unplugs like most appliances.
4. Plug in the new headlight, making sure that you set it into place right side up. The correct position is usually indicated by the word "TOP" or an arrow on the light.
5. Replace the headlight's retaining ring and tighten the screws that hold it in place.
6. Replace the headlight trim ring (and the grille section, if necessary) and tighten the screws.
7. Test the headlight. If the headlight does not light or does not light on either high or low beam, you may have trouble with the headlight switch, dimmer switch, or circuit wiring. Consult a qualified mechanic.

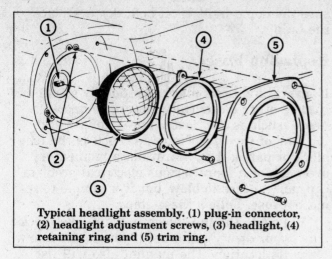

Typical headlight assembly. (1) plug-in connector, (2) headlight adjustment screws, (3) headlight, (4) retaining ring, and (5) trim ring.

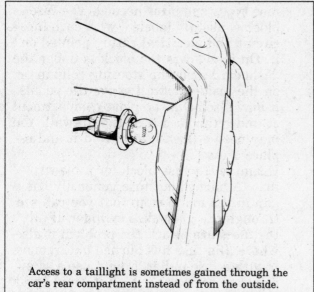

Access to a taillight is sometimes gained through the car's rear compartment instead of from the outside.

Replacing Taillights and Other Bulbs

Before you attempt to replace a bulb, check the owner's manual of your car for information about procedure. The manual will list the types and sizes of bulbs used in your car; be sure to purchase the correct bulb.

Replacement procedure depends on the bulb, but the technique for replacing a taillight, brake light, or turn signal bulb is typical. Follow these general steps.

1. Examine the light. Its plastic lens cover may be held by two or more Phillips-head screws. Remove the screws and lens cover to reach the bulb. **Note:** On some cars, access to a taillight is gained through the car's rear compartment. In such a case, remove the bulb's socket from the housing that it fits into by twisting the socket counterclockwise a ¼ or ½ turn.

2. Remove the burned-out bulb. Taillights, brake lights, and turn signal lights use bayonet-type bulbs. This kind of bulb has two knobs on its base. Grasp the bulb, push it inward slightly, and give it a ¼ turn counterclockwise. *Caution: If the bulb is difficult to remove, do not force it; it could break in your hand.* To protect yourself, wear heavy gloves. If you still cannot remove it, use a special bulb-base gripper to grasp the base of the bulb. Turn the bulb gently but firmly, and lift it out.

3. Examine the bulb socket. If there are signs of corrosion, clean the socket with fine sandpaper, emery cloth, or steel wool.

4. Install the new bulb. Align the knobs on its base with the openings in the socket, and install it by pushing it in and twisting it clockwise a ¼ turn.

5. If you removed the bulb socket from its housing to reach the bulb, replace it by inserting it in the housing and turning the socket clockwise. If you removed the lens cover, replace it, but be careful not to overtighten the retaining screws; this could crack the plastic lens.

Side marker lights are very similar to taillights. On some cars, the lens cover may be held by Phillips-head screws; remove the cover to reach the bulb. On other cars, you can reach the bulb's socket from behind the fender; turn the socket counterclockwise to remove it from its housing. Remove the old bulb and install the new one. Replace the lens cover, or resecure the socket with a clockwise twist.

On some interior lights, including many dome lights, screws may not secure the plastic lens cover. Most likely, the cover is held in place by one or more tabs. To remove this type of cover, squeeze it gently at opposite ends to release the tabs, or depress a tab with a screwdriver, or use some similar method. Some dome lights use a bayonet-type bulb similar to those used in taillights; others use cartridge-

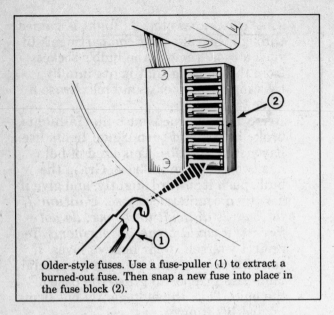

Older-style fuses. Use a fuse-puller (1) to extract a burned-out fuse. Then snap a new fuse into place in the fuse block (2).

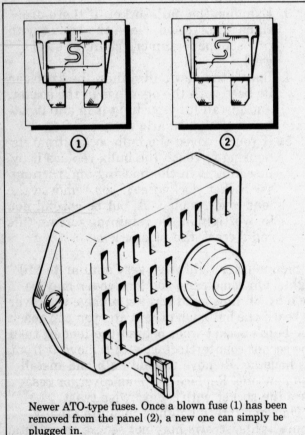

Newer ATO-type fuses. Once a blown fuse (1) has been removed from the panel (2), a new one can simply be plugged in.

sure the dome light is off before you replace the bulb.

Replacing Fuses

If several lights on your car suddenly go out or if some other electrically powered component—such as the heater fan—stops operating, one of the first things to check is the fuse block or panel. Age, vibration, a momentary overload, or a more serious electrical problem can cause a fuse to blow, but it is simple to replace a fuse. Follow these steps.

1. Locate the fuse block in your car. Check your owner's manual if you do not know its location. The manual also will list fuse types and sizes needed. The fuse block is usually labeled, with each fuse's circuit and electrical rating printed on it. On many cars the block is under the dashboard near the steering column or on the inside firewall above the pedals; it may also be in the glove compartment or under the hood near the firewall. You may need a flashlight to find it and replace a fuse.

2. Examine the fuse block for a blown fuse. A burned-out fuse generally has a gap in the metal strip that you can see through the glass fuse cylinder. If all the fuses are intact, the problem is elsewhere. If a fuse has burned out, remove it with a fuse-puller. Do not use a screwdriver or some other tool; it could break the fuse.

3. Snap a new fuse into place. The electrical rating is stamped on the end of the fuse; be sure to use the proper one. If your car uses ATO-type fuses with two prongs, plug the fuse in. *Caution: Use a fuse with the electrical rating specified in your owner's manual. Never substitute aluminum foil or other metal in place of a fuse; this can cause wiring to burn and start a fire.*

4. With the new fuse in place, the circuit it protects should operate. Energize the circuit. If the replacement fuse also burns out, consult a qualified mechanic.

Replacing Flashers

If the hazard-warning, or emergency, flashers

type bulbs, which snap in and out of retaining clips. Replace the old bulb with the type specified in the owner's manual. **Note:** To avoid blowing a fuse, close the car doors and make

on your car only work on one side of your vehicle, check for burned-out bulbs. If new bulbs do not remedy the problem, or if the hazard-warning lights do not blink on both sides of the car, you probably need a new flasher unit.

The flasher unit generally is located under the dashboard near the fuse block. This device, about the size of a large cork, plugs into a socket. If you cannot find it, check your owner's manual. Most cars have two separate units—one for turn signals and one for emergency flashers. Be sure to find the right one and take the defective flasher unit with you when you purchase a replacement.

Radio and Antenna

Tools and Materials

- Wheel Chocks
- Jack and Safety Jack Stands
- Wrenches
- Pliers
- Screwdrivers
- Allen Wrench
- Antenna and Cable With Mounting Hardware
- Fuse
- Masking Tape

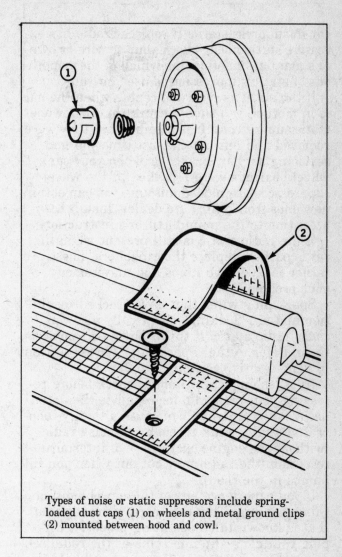

Types of noise or static suppressors include spring-loaded dust caps (1) on wheels and metal ground clips (2) mounted between hood and cowl.

MODERN AUTOMOBILE AM or AM/FM radios are fully transistorized and should only be serviced by a qualified radio technician. Although we do not recommend that you attempt to service a radio yourself, a portion of the labor charge can be saved by removing and, later, reinstalling the radio in the car yourself. Because most automakers do not manufacture their own radios, your auto dealership may not be the best place to bring a radio for service. Most likely, a dealer will send it to a specialist anyway. After you remove the radio from the car, there probably will be a label on the radio receiver identifying the manufacturer. You then can take the radio to that firm's repair center or you can take it to your local auto radio repair shop.

But before you attempt to remove the radio from your car, make certain the problem is serious enough to warrant removal.

One common problem is static noise. Cars are equipped with capacitors to suppress radio static. Normally, these devices are located in the alternator, on a coil terminal, or on the fuse block under the dashboard. Some General Motors cars use a metal radio frequency interference (RFI) shield over the ignition points in the distributor to prevent static. Many American-made cars also use springs inside the dust caps of the front wheels or metal grounding straps between the hood and the cowl of the car to suppress static. If your car radio has excessive static noise, check your service or owner's manual to determine which of these methods of static suppression is used on your car.

If the static is most noticeable when the car is in motion, you should check the front wheel static suppressors. It is possible that they were removed and left out the last time you had servicing on your brakes or when your car's wheel bearings were repacked. If the wheel suppressors are indeed missing, you can obtain new ones from your auto dealer. Install them according to the manufacturer's instructions.

If the radio static is still present when the car is parked, replace the capacitors. These are rather inexpensive items and may remedy your problem.

Spark plug wires that have cracked insulation and are "leaking" electrically also can cause radio static. If this is the case, replace them. Refer to the "Spark Plug Wires" section in "The Ignition System" chapter.

Another important item to check before removing your car radio for repair is the antenna. A faulty antenna can cause a totally inoperative radio, weak reception, a noisy radio (without the engine operating), or intermittent reception (the radio may cut out when you hit bumps in the road).

If you experience any of these problems, one thing you might try is to borrow an antenna that is known to be operating properly. Unplug your car's antenna cable at the radio receiver. Plug in the good antenna and hold it out the window of the car (the metal in the car roof will restrict reception). If radio reception improves, replace your antenna.

Replacing the Antenna

If the radio antenna must be replaced, follow these steps.

1. Locate the antenna cable behind the dashboard where it connects to the radio, and disconnect the antenna lead. Unscrew the knurled ring at the connector and pull it straight out of the radio or simply pull the cable connector straight out.
2. Examine the other end of the antenna cable to see how it is attached. Most standard AM and AM/FM aerials are

secured to a front fender with one large retaining nut. Some cars, however, have a side-cowl-mounted antenna that has two retaining nuts on a pair of mounting posts, or mounting posts fastened by Phillips-head screws and retaining nuts.

Note: Unless the antenna is mounted near the rear compartment, you will probably have to remove something to reach the base of the antenna. Although some bases are located up under a corner of the dashboard or behind an interior kick panel, most are located under a front fender.

If the antenna is mounted on a front fender, you will have to gain access up through the fender well. Because most fender wells have splash shields, you will have to remove the splash shield to reach the antenna mount.

3. Place wheel chocks behind the rear wheels.
4. Remove the wheel cover on the wheel closest to the antenna, and loosen the lug nuts on the wheel with a lug wrench.
5. Jack up the front of the car and support it with a pair of safety jack stands.
6. Remove the lug nuts and the wheel.
7. Reach up into the fender well and unbolt the splash shield with a wrench.
8. Use a wrench or pliers—whichever is necessary—to loosen the antenna retaining nut under the fender. Unscrew the nut and remove the antenna and old cable from the car; the nut and lock washer will slide along the cable as you withdraw it—set them aside if this hardware is not provided with the new antenna. Remember the route used by the old cable.
9. Insert the new antenna cable in the antenna mounting hole in the fender. From under the fender, slip the lock washer and nut onto the cable, and pull the cable through the hole. Set the new antenna into the mounting hole and adjust it so it is at the proper angle.
10. Screw the retaining nut on the base of the antenna mount under the fender and secure it tightly.
11. Replace the wheel, and hand-tighten the lug nuts.

12. Lower the car to the ground, reversing Step 5.
13. Tighten the lug nuts, replace the wheel cover, and remove the wheel chocks.
14. Route the new antenna cable to the radio, following the route of the old cable.
15. At the radio, reconnect the new cable.

Removing a Radio

If your car radio is totally inoperative, check the fuse for the radio at the fuse block under the dashboard. If it is blown, replace it with one of equal value. If you have doubts as to its rating, check the owner's manual for your car.

If all of the previously outlined conditions have been checked and determined not to be the problem with the radio or antenna, you now might consider removing the radio and taking it to a professional for servicing. Follow this procedure.

1. Most car radios are supported by two controls (on-off/volume and manual tuning) on the front of the dashboard. Carefully pull off the two control knobs. A small-bladed screwdriver may be required to pry them off gently. However, some radios have small Allen-head screws holding these knobs in place. If so, loosen these setscrews with an Allen wrench before attempting to remove the knobs.
2. After removing the knobs, remove the retaining nuts on the stems behind the knobs with the proper-size wrench.
3. On some air-conditioned cars, the air ducts under the dashboard may have to be moved before the radio can be removed. Use a wrench to remove the nuts holding the duct support brackets at the rear of the radio on cars equipped with air conditioning.
4. Remove the power, ground, and speaker wires. These wires usually pull off their respective connectors. Before pulling apart the connections, however, label each wire with a small piece of masking tape as you disconnect them so you can easily reconnect them properly later.
5. Disconnect the antenna cable from the radio.
6. Remove the radio from the dashboard and take it to a qualified radio service center.
7. After the radio has been repaired, reinstall it by reversing Steps 1 through 6.

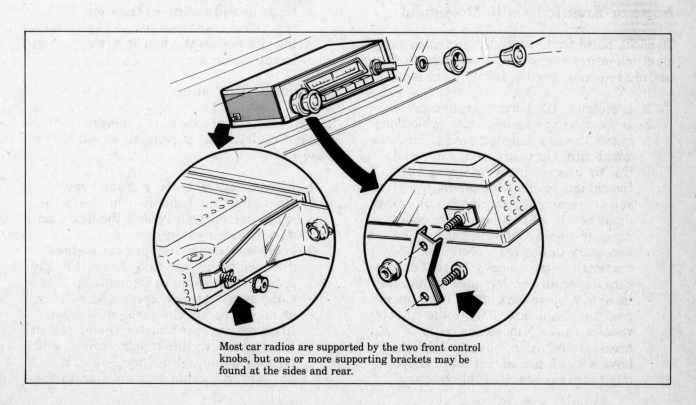

Most car radios are supported by the two front control knobs, but one or more supporting brackets may be found at the sides and rear.

Speedometers

Tools and Materials

- Screwdriver
- Pliers
- Wrench
- Speedometer Cable
- Rag
- Speedometer Cable Lube

YOUR CAR'S speedometer, by means of a cable, measures either the rotation of a wheel or the revolution of a gear in the transmission. Some common speedometer problems can be checked by a do-it-yourself mechanic to see if they can be easily repaired or whether they must be left to a qualified mechanic. These include noise from the speedometer, a jumpy or fluctuating indicator needle, or no needle movement at all.

Noise or Erratic Needle Movement

To check noise from a speedometer such as a loud tick or grating sound, or a jumpy or fluctuating indicator needle, follow these steps.

1. Disconnect the battery ground cable.
2. Disconnect the speedometer cable housing at the speedometer head behind the dashboard. On many cars, you can do this by unscrewing a retaining nut on the cable housing with pliers. Usually, you can reach this connection by going underneath the dashboard. On cars with air conditioning, however, it may be necessary to remove a section of ductwork to gain access. **Note:** On some cars, especially newer models, you may have to remove part of the instrument panel or dashboard. Also, some models require you to remove the radio to gain access. In addition, newer models may have a quick-disconnect lever or spring clip that releases the cable housing.

Be certain that you remember how to reinstall anything that you disconnect or remove. Speedometer cable servicing is not very expensive when done by a mechanic, but replacing ductwork or repairing broken parts or wiring under the dashboard can be.

3. After disconnecting the cable housing at the speedometer head, pull the cable out of the head completely.
4. Inspect the disconnected cable. Look for any kinks or broken strands of wire in the cable. If the cable is damaged in some way, it must be replaced. You can obtain the correct replacement cable for your car at an auto supply store. If the cable appears to be in good condition, wipe it thoroughly clean.
5. Sparingly, lubricate the lower two-thirds of the new cable, or the old cable if it is in good condition, with speedometer cable lube, which also is available at auto supply stores. Do not lubricate the upper third or the tip that fits into the head.
6. Install the cable in the housing, but be careful not to get dirt or other foreign matter on it.
7. Wipe any excess lubricant off the cable housing and reconnect the cable housing to the speedometer head by tightening the nut on the housing or pressing in the connector.

No Needle Movement

In the event the needle of the speedometer does not register any movement at all, follow these steps.

1. Disconnect the battery ground cable.
2. Disconnect the cable housing from the speedometer head behind the dashboard as outlined previously.
3. Have someone drive your car a short distance while you study the end of the speedometer cable in its housing. If it spins slowly at slow speed and quickly at higher speed, the problem is most likely in the speedometer head itself in the dashboard; this repair work should be done by a qualified mechanic. If, however, the cable does not spin in the

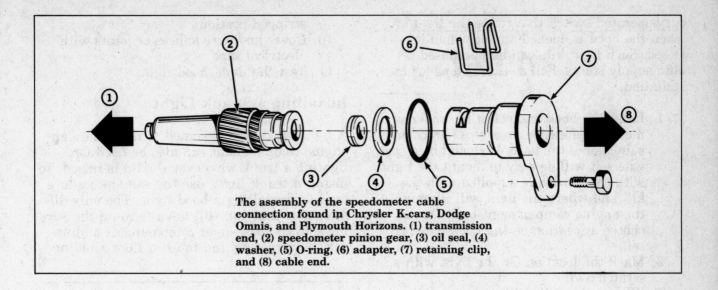

The assembly of the speedometer cable connection found in Chrysler K-cars, Dodge Omnis, and Plymouth Horizons. (1) transmission end, (2) speedometer pinion gear, (3) oil seal, (4) washer, (5) O-ring, (6) adapter, (7) retaining clip, and (8) cable end.

speedometer housing while the car is in motion, further diagnosis is required.

4. With the car stopped, withdraw the cable from its housing and check to see if the cable is broken; there should be a short, square drive section on the other end. If this section is not there, the broken cable must be replaced. If this section is on the end of the cable, the problem may be the speedometer gear at the transmission or front wheel. Proceed to the next step.

5. Disconnect the cable housing at the transmission or front wheel. **Note:** It may be necessary to raise the front of the car and support it on a pair of safety jack stands to reach this end of the cable. Check the service manual for your car to see how and where the cable is secured, or follow the route of the cable. If the cable is connected to a front wheel, it may be attached to the small inner hub of the wheel. Disconnect it by removing the cotter pin with pliers. If the cable runs to the transmission, use a wrench to loosen the connector.

6. Check for a broken cable and, if broken, withdraw the broken portion and replace the speedometer cable. If the cable is not broken, check the speedometer gear in the front wheel or in the transmission. Look for chipped, worn, or missing gear teeth. If the gear is damaged, have it repaired.

Installing a Hood or Trunk Light

Tools and Materials

- Scratch Awl
- Electric Drill and Bit
- Hood or Trunk Light Kit With Hardware
- Electrical Tape or Wiring Fasteners
- Wire Connector
- Phillips-Head Screwdriver

IN MOST CARS, an underhood or a trunk light is an optional piece of equipment. If your car lacks either or both of these items, you can have the convenience of instant light whenever you open your car's hood or trunk.

Installing a Hood Light

An underhood light contains an integral mercury-operated switch that turns the light on when the hood is opened and off when it is closed. Such light kits can be purchased at auto supply stores. Follow these steps for installation.

1. Raise the hood and select an underhood mounting location on a cross brace or subpanel of the hood. It should be a spot where it will be easy to mount the light with the hardware supplied with the kit, and where the light will illuminate the engine compartment best. Do not choose a location on the hood panel itself.
2. Mark the location for the light with a scratch awl.
3. With an electric drill and proper-size bit, drill a mounting hole for the hardware supplied with the light kit. *Caution: Apply a slight, but steady pressure to the drill, but be careful that the drill bit does not suddenly break through and damage the hood panel.*
4. Fasten the light into place with the hardware supplied, as directed by the manufacturer. Make sure the light will be level when the hood is closed. If it is not level, the light will not turn off.
5. Route the wiring from the light along the hood braces and down to the engine firewall, leaving some slack at the hood closure joint.
6. Secure the wiring in place with electric tape or wiring fasteners so it will not touch the engine or catch on any component when the hood is closed.
7. Run the end of the wiring through an existing opening for wiring in the firewall.
8. Under the dashboard, locate the wiring for accessories that are always energized.
9. Connect the wiring from the hood light to the wiring from the accessory according to the manufacturer's directions. You can use a special connector that does not require you to strip insulation from a wire. These connectors are available from auto supply stores. Or, you can connect the light's wiring by stripping insulation from the accessory's wiring and joining the light's wiring to the

stripped portion.
10. Cover any wire splices or joints with electrical tape.
11. Test the underhood light.

Installing a Trunk Light

A light kit that is designed to illuminate an engine compartment can also be used for lighting a trunk whenever the lid is raised. To install a trunk light, use the same procedure used for installing a hood light. The only difference is that you will have to route the wiring into the passenger compartment and under the carpeting and interior floor molding.

Installing a Vacuum Gauge

Tools and Materials

- Electric Drill and Bit
- Screwdriver
- Utility Knife
- Vacuum Gauge Kit
- Wire Stripper
- Electrical Tape or Hose Fasteners
- Terminal-End Connector
- Wire Connector

A VACUUM GAUGE is a popular and useful aftermarket accessory, and one of the most valuable instruments you can have permanently installed in your car. Properly used, it can tell a driver when he is obtaining the maximum efficiency from the engine and indicate poor driving habits such as jackrabbit starts. You can easily determine the most efficient driving speed by checking the gauge's indicator. Such gauges are available at auto supply stores. To install a vacuum gauge, follow these steps.

1. Mount the vacuum gauge in a conve-

nient location where it will be visible to the driver. If the gauge is a self-mounting type, peel the protective paper from the adhesive-coated mounting pad on the rear or base of the instrument, and press it firmly against a clean mounting surface on the dashboard. If the gauge is mounted on a bracket, drill mounting holes, using the bracket as a template. *Caution: Make sure that the drill bit does not damage anything behind the mounting location.* Mount the bracket, and secure the instrument in it.

2. Route the vacuum hose that comes with the gauge through an opening in the firewall into the engine compartment. **Note:** If you must drill a hole for the hose, make it large enough to insert a rubber grommet to protect the hose.

3. Connect the end of the hose in the passenger compartment to the gauge, according to the manufacturer's instructions.

4. Raise the hood and locate a vacuum hose at the intake manifold or carburetor on the engine. Instructions with the vacuum gauge kit should help you locate the proper hose.

5. Using a sharp utility knife, cut through the vacuum hose on the engine.

6. Insert and secure the T-fitting supplied with the vacuum gauge kit into the engine vacuum hose.

7. Attach the end of the vacuum hose coming from the vacuum gauge to the T-fitting.

8. Using electrical tape or hose fasteners, secure the gauge's vacuum hose to other hoses or supports.

9. Close the hood.

Note: Illuminated vacuum gauges generally have two wires to connect—a red, positive (+) wire and a black, negative (−) ground wire. Connect the ground wire to any nearby bare metal of the car under the dashboard. You can often do this by removing a fastener and scraping any paint from around the fastener to ensure contact with bare metal. Using a wire stripper, remove about ½ inch of insulation from the end of the ground wire, attach a terminal-end connector to the end of the wire, and secure the terminal-end connector under the fastener.

Connect the red, positive (+) wire to a positive (+) "hot" wire for the instrument panel lights. This can be done by using a special wire connector available in auto supply stores. It enables you to splice the two wires together easily without having to strip any insulation.

AUTOMOTIVE GLOSSARY

A

AC: Alternating current.

Accelerator: The floor pedal used by the driver to control, through linkage, the throttle valve in the carburetor.

Ackerman Principle: Bending the outer ends of the steering arms slighty inward so that when a car is making a turn, the inside wheel will turn more sharply than the outer wheel. This principle produces toe-out on turns.

Additive: Some solution, powder, or other substance that is added to gasoline, oil, grease, and other items in an effort to improve the characteristics of the product.

Advance (Ignition Timing): To set the ignition timing so that a spark occurs earlier or more degrees before Top Dead Center (TDC).

Air Filter: A device that is used to remove dust and other foreign substances from air being drawn into an engine, power brake unit, and other components.

Air/Fuel Ratio: The relative proportions of air and fuel that are mixed together by either the carburetor or fuel injection system. The ideal ratio for best economy and lowest emissions is 14.7 parts of air to every part of gasoline. A "rich" mixture is one with too much fuel and not enough air, or anything over 14.7:1. A "lean" mixture is one with too much air and not enough fuel, or anything less than 14.7:1.

Air Gap: The space between the spark plug electrodes; the space between rotating and stationary assemblies in a motor or generator; the space between contact points of a relay.

Air Horn: The top part of the air passage through a carburetor.

Air Injection: A means of forcing air into the exhaust manifold or catalytic converter to reduce exhaust emissions. The air is pumped into the exhaust system through an air pump and diverter valve.

Air Lock: A bubble of air trapped in a fluid circuit that interferes with normal circulation of the fluid.

Air Pump: A small pump for forcing air into the exhaust system to reduce exhaust emissions. The air pump is driv- en off the crankshaft pulley with a V-belt and is connected to either the exhaust manifold and/or the catalytic converter with tubing.

Alternating Current (AC): An electrical current that moves first in one direction and then in the other (positive to negative, then negative to positive).

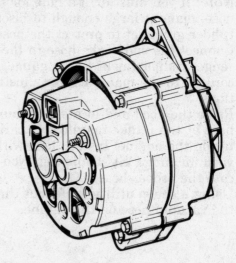

Alternator: An AC generator that produces alternating current that is internally rectified to DC current before being released.

Ammeter: An instrument used to measure the rate of current flow (in amperes).

Amperage: The total amount of current (amperes) flowing in a circuit.

Antifreeze: A chemical added to the cooling system to prevent the coolant from freezing in cold weather.

Antifriction Bearing: A bearing containing rollers or balls plus an inner and outer race. The bearing is designed to roll, thus minimizing friction.

API: American Petroleum Institute.

Arc: The flow of electricity through the air between two electrodes that produces a flash and releases a lot of heat.

Automatic Choke: A carburetor choke device that automatically positions itself in accordance with carburetor needs.

Axial: Having the same direction or being parallel to the axis of rotation.

Axle: A crossbar, supporting a vehicle, on which wheels turn.

Axle (Full-Floating): An axle used to drive the rear wheels. It does not hold the wheels on or support them.

Axle (Semi-Floating or One-Quarter Floating): An axle used to drive the wheels, hold them on, and support them.

Axle (Three-Quarter Floating): An axle used to drive the rear wheels as well as hold them on. It does not support them.

B

Back Pressure: Refers to the resistance to the flow of exhaust gases through the exhaust system.

Ball Joint: Commonly used as suspension and steering linkage connectors on independent front suspension. It has a hardened steel stud threaded on one end, is tapered in the middle, and formed into a ball on the other end.

Ball Joint Steering Knuckle: A steering knuckle that pivots on ball joints.

Ballast Resistor: A resistor that is made of a special kind of wire that tends to increase or decrease voltage in direct proportion to the heat of the wire.

Battery: A device used to store electrical energy in a chemical form.

Battery Charging: The process of renewing the battery by passing an electric current through the battery in a reverse direction.

BDC: Bottom Dead Center.

Bearing: The area or unit in which the contact surface of a revolving part rests.

Bearing Clearance: The amount of space left between a shaft and the bearing surface. This space is for lubricating oil to enter.

Belted Bias Tires: Bias tires in which several layers of plies to reinforce the tread are applied directly beneath the tread area.

Bias Tires: Tires in which the sidewall plies are applied in a crisscross, or bias, pattern.

Bleeding the Brakes: Refers to the removal of air from the hydraulic system. Bleeder screws are loosened at each wheel cylinder (one at a time), and brake fluid is forced from the master cylinder through the lines until all air is expelled.

Block: That part of the engine containing the cylinders.

Blow-By: Refers to the escape of exhaust gases past the piston rings.

Body Putty: A material that is designed to smooth out dented car body areas. Upon hardening, the putty is dressed down and the area painted.

Bonded Brake Lining: Brake lining that is attached to the brake shoe by an adhesive.

Bore Diameter: The diameter of the engine cylinders.

Brake Backing Plate: A rigid steel plate on which the brake shoes are attached. The braking force applied to the shoes is absorbed by the backing plate.

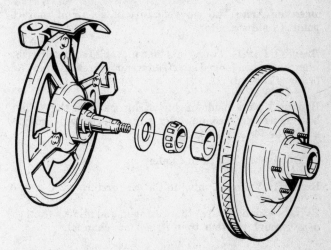

Brake—Disc-Type: A braking system that uses a steel disc with a caliper and pads. When the brakes are applied, the pad on each side of the spinning disc is forced against the disc, thus imparting a braking force. This type of brake is very resistant to brake fade.

Brake Disc or Rotor: A disc that is machined on both sides to allow for brake pads that will push or clamp against the disc to stop the car.

Brake Drum: A cast-metal cylinder attached to the wheel that is used to house the brake shoes and provide a friction surface for stopping the car.

Brake Fade: The loss of braking power due to overheating of the brake lining.

Brake Fluid: A mixture of hydraulic fluids with a high boiling point and a low freezing point plus other characteristics needed for good brake action.

Brake Lining: A molded material with a suitable coefficient of friction to stop a car. It is either riveted or bonded to the brake shoe.

Brake—Parking: A brake used to hold the car in position while parked. One type applies the rear brake shoes by mechanical means; another type applies a brake band to a brake drum installed in the drivetrain.

Brake—Power: A conventional hydraulic brake system that uses engine vacuum to operate a vacuum power piston. The power piston applies pressure to the brake pedal or, in some cases, directly to the master cylinder piston. This reduces the amount of pedal pressure that the driver must exert to stop the car.

Brake Pull: The result of a difference in friction between brakes on the two sides of a car.

Brake Shoes: That part of the brake system, located at the wheels, onto which the brake lining is attached. When the wheel cylinders are actuated by hydraulic pressure, they force the brake shoes apart and bring the lining into contact with the drum.

Brake Wheel Cylinder: A cylinder containing a movable piston that is activated by hydraulic pressure, which, in turn, pushes the brake shoes against the brake drum.

Breaker Arm: The movable part of a pair of contact points in a distributor.

Breaker Points: Two points (one movable) in the distributor that, when moved apart, interrupt current flow in the primary current.

Brush: A piece made of conducting material that when bearing against a commutator, slip ring, etc., will provide a passage for electric current.

BTDC: Before Top Dead Center.

Butterfly Valve: A valve in the carburetor.

Bypass Valve: A valve that can open and allow a fluid to pass through in other than its normal channel.

C

Cam Angle or Dwell (Ignition): The number of degrees the breaker cam in a distributor rotates from the time the breaker points close until they open again.

Camber: Tipping the top of the wheel centerline outward produces "positive" camber. Tipping the wheel centerline inward at the top produces "negative" camber. When the camber is positive, the tops of the tires are further apart than the bottoms.

Camshaft: A shaft with cam lobes (bumps) used to operate the valves.

Camshaft Gear: A gear that is used to drive the camshaft.

Capacitor (Condenser): A device used to store an electrical charge.

Carbon: Used to describe the hard or soft black deposits found in the combustion chamber, on the plugs, under the rings, and on and under the valve heads.

Carbon Monoxide: An exhaust pollutant that is formed when there is insufficient air to completely burn the fuel. Rich fuel mixtures increase carbon monoxide (CO) emissions. Carbon monoxide emissions are reduced by carefully controlling the air/fuel ratio and by afterburning in the catalytic converter.

Carburetor: A device used to mix gasoline and air in the correct proportions.

Carburetor Icing: The formation of ice on the throttle plate or valve. As the fuel nozzles feed fuel into the carburetor air horn, it turns to a vapor. This robs heat from the air, and when weather conditions are just right (fairly cold and quite humid), ice may form.

Castle or Castellated Nut: A nut having a series of slots cut into one end into which a cotter pin may be passed to secure the nut.

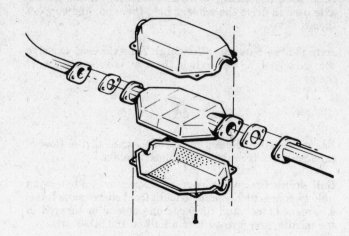

Catalytic Converter: A device that is used to convert hydrocarbons and carbon monoxide in exhaust gases into water vapor and carbon dioxide. 1981 and newer converters also remove NOx emissions from the exhaust.

C-Clip: A metal clip that fits into a recess cut in a shaft. It is used to hold things mounted on the shaft in place.

Cell, Battery: A compartment that contains one set of positive and one set of negative plates that, with electrolyte, will produce electricity when the circuit is closed.

Center Steering Linkage: A steering system utilizing two tie-rods connected to the steering arms and to a central idler arm. The idler arm is operated by a drag link that connects the idler arm to the Pitman arm.

Centrifugal Advance (Distributor): A unit designed to advance and retard the ignition timing through the action of centrifugal force.

Centrifugal Clutch: A clutch that utilizes centrifugal force to expand a friction device on the driving shaft until it is locked to a drum on the driven shaft.

Centrifugal Force: That force that tends to keep moving objects traveling in a straight line. When a moving car is forced to make a turn, centrifugal force attempts to keep it moving in a straight line. If the car is turning at too high a speed, centrifugal force will be greater than the frictional force between the tires and the road, and the car will slide off the road.

Charcoal Canister: An evaporative emission-control device located usually in the engine compartment, the charcoal canister traps and stores gasoline vapors from the fuel tank and carburetor while the engine is off. The control valve on the canister then opens after the engine starts and warms up to purge the vapors into the intake manifold so they can be burned in the engine.

Charge (Recharge): To restore the active materials in a battery cell by electrically reversing the chemical action.

Chassis: The car frame, suspension, and running gear; everything except the car body.

Choke: A butterfly valve located in the carburetor that is used to enrich the mixture for starting the engine when cold.

CID: Cubic inch displacement.

Circuit: The path of electron flow from the source through components and connections and back to the source.

Circuit (Closed): An electrical circuit in which there is no interruption of current flow.

Circuit (Open): Any break or lack of contact in an electrical circuit, either intentional (switch) or unintentional (bad connection).

Circuit (Parallel): An electrical system in which all positive terminals are joined through one wire, and all negative terminals through another wire.

Circuit (Series): An electrical system in which separate parts are connected end to end, using one wire to form a single path for current to flow.

Circuit Breaker: A device, other than a fuse, for interrupting a circuit under high load conditions.

Clearance: A given amount of space between two parts—between piston and cylinder, bearing and journal, etc.

Clockwise: Rotation to the right, as that of clock hands.

Cluster or Counter Gears: The "cluster" of gears that are all cut on one long gear blank. The cluster gears ride in the bottom of the transmission. The cluster provides a connection between the transmission input shaft and the output shaft.

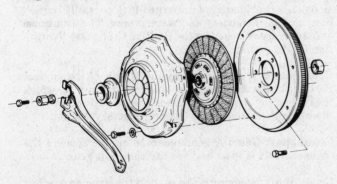

Clutch: A device that is used to connect or disconnect the flow of power from one unit to another.

Clutch Diaphragm Spring: A round dish-shaped piece of flat spring steel. It is used to force the pressure plate against the clutch disc in some clutches.

Clutch Disc: Part of a clutch assembly that is splined to the transmission clutch or input shaft. It is faced with friction material. When the clutch is engaged, the disc is squeezed between the flywheel and the pressure plate.

Clutch Housing or Bellhousing: A cast-iron or aluminum housing that surrounds the flywheel and clutch mechanism.

Clutch Pedal Free-Travel: The specified distance that the clutch pedal may be depressed before the throw-out bearing actually contacts the clutch release fingers.

Clutch Pilot Bearing: A small bronze bushing, or in some cases a ball bearing, placed in the end of the crankshaft or in the center of the flywheel, depending on the car, that is used to suppport the outboard end of the transmission input shaft.

Clutch Pressure Plate: Part of a clutch assembly that, through spring pressure, squeezes the clutch disc against the flywheel, thereby transmitting a driving force through the assembly. To disengage the clutch, the pressure plate is drawn away from the flywheel by means of linkage.

Clutch Semi-Centrifugal Release Fingers: Clutch release fingers that have a weight attached to them so at high rpm, the release fingers place additional pressure on the clutch pressure plate.

Clutch Throw-Out Bearing: The bearing that is forced against the pressure plate throw-out fingers to disengage the clutch.

Clutch Throw-Out Fork: The device or fork that straddles the throw-out bearing and is used to force the throw-out bearing against the clutch release fingers.

Coefficient of Friction: A measurement of the amount of friction developed between two objects in physical contact when one of the objects is drawn across the other.

Coil: A spiral made of wire; a device used in cars to increase the voltage to the spark plugs, or to provide the electromagnetic force in a solenoid.

Coil Spring: A section of spring steel rod wound in a spiral pattern or shape. Widely used in both front and rear suspension systems.

Combustion: The process involved during burning.

Combustion Chamber: The area above the piston with the piston on TDC. The head of the piston, the engine cylinder, and the head form the chamber.

Commutator: A device to provide a current path between the armature coil and the brushes of an electric motor or generator.

Compression: Applying pressure to a spring, or any springy substance, thus causing it to reduce its length in the direction of the compressing force.

Applying pressure to a gas, thus causing a reduction in volume.

Compression Check: Testing the compression in all the

cylinders at cranking speed. All plugs are removed, the compression gauge placed in one plug hole, the throttle opened wide, and the engine cranked until the gauge no longer climbs. The compression check is a way to determine the condition of the valves, rings, and cylinders.

Compression Gauge: A gauge that is used to test the compression in the cylinders.

Compression Ratio: Relationship between the cylinder volume (clearance volume) when the piston is on TDC and the cylinder volume when the piston is on BDC.

Compression Stroke: That part of a piston's cycle which compresses the fuel mixture in the engine's cylinder.

Computerized Engine Controls: A method of using a microprocessor and various engine sensors and solenoids to control engine performance. The sensors tell the computer what's happening so it can regulate various fuel, ignition, emissions, and transmission control functions for optimum fuel economy and reduced emissions.

Concentric: Two or more circles so placed that they share a common center.

Condensation: Moisture, from the air, deposited on a cool surface.

Condense: To turn a vapor back into a liquid.

Condenser (Ignition): A unit installed between the breaker points and coil of a distributor to prevent arcing at the breaker points. A condenser has the ability to absorb and retain surges of electricity.

Condenser (Refrigeration): The unit in an air conditioning system that cools hot compressed refrigerant and turns it from a vapor into a liquid.

Conduction: The transfer of heat from one object to another by having the objects in physical contact.

Connecting Rod: The connecting link between the piston and the crankshaft.

Constant Mesh Gears: Gears that are always in mesh with each other—driving or not.

Constant Velocity Universal Joint: A universal joint so designed that it affects a smooth transfer of torque from the driveshaft to the driving shaft without any fluctuations in the speed of the driveshaft.

Contact Points (Breaker Points): Two movable points or areas that, when pressed together, complete a circuit. These points are usually made of tungsten, platinum, or silver.

Coolant: Solution of antifreeze and water.

Coolant Recovery System: Part of a closed cooling system in which an overflow tank, or reservoir, is used to contain expanding coolant to prevent it from being lost and to promote more efficient operation by eliminating air in the cooling system.

Cotter Pin: A split metal pin. The ends are bent after insertion through a slot or hole.

Counterbalance: A weight attached to a moving part so that the part will be in balance.

Counterclockwise: Rotation to the left as opposed to that of clock hands.

Cowl: The part of a car body that is between the dashboard panel and the firewall.

Crankcase: Part of the engine that surrounds the crankshaft. This is not to be confused with the oil pan, which is a thin steel cover that is bolted to the crankcase.

Crankcase Emissions: Pollution that is created inside the engine's crankcase by combustion blow-by. The emissions consist primarily of unburned fuel, partially burned fuel, carbon monoxide, and water vapor. The crankcase emissions are removed by the Positive Crankcase Ventilation (PCV) system.

Crankshaft: A shaft running the length of the engine. Portions of the shaft are offset to form "throws" to which the connecting rods are attached. The crankshaft converts the up-down motion of the pistons to rotary motion.

Crankshaft Gear: A gear mounted on the front of the crankshaft. It is used to drive the camshaft gear.

Cross Shaft (Steering): The shaft in the steering gearbox that engages the steering shaft worm. The cross shaft is splined to the Pitman arm.

Cylinder: The hole, or holes, in the engine cylinder block that contain the pistons.

Cylinder Head: The metal section that is bolted on top of the block. It is used to cover the tops of the cylinders. In many cases, the cylinder head contains the valves. It also forms part of the combustion chamber.

D

DC: Direct current.

Dead Axle: An axle that does not rotate but merely forms a base on which to attach the wheels.

Degree (Circle): 1/360 part of a circle.

Detonation: The fuel charge firing or burning too violently, almost exploding.

Diaphragm: A flexible cloth-rubber sheet that is stretched across an area, thereby separating two different compartments.

Diesel Engine: An internal combustion engine that uses diesel oil for fuel. The true diesel does not use an ignition system but injects diesel oil into the cylinders when the piston has compressed the air so tightly that it is hot enough to ignite the diesel without a spark.

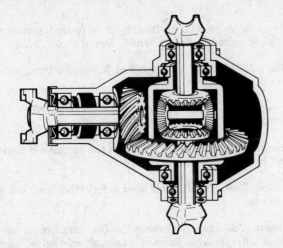

Differential: A unit that will drive both rear axles at the same time but will allow them to turn at different speeds on turns.

Differential Case: The steel unit to which the ring gear is attached. The case drives the spider gears and forms an inner bearing surface for the axle and gears.

Dipstick: The metal rod that passes into the oil sump. It is used to determine the quantity of oil in the engine.

Direct Current (DC): An electric current that flows in one direction only.

Directional Stability (Steering): The ability of a car to move forward in a straight line with a minimum of driver control. A car with good directional stability will not be unduly affected by side wind or road irregularities.

Discharge (Battery): Drawing electric current from the battery.

Displacement: The total volume of air displaced by the piston in traveling from BDC to TDC.

Distributor (Ignition): A unit designed to make and break the ignition primary circuit and to distribute the resultant high voltage to the proper cylinder at the correct time.

Distributor Cap (Ignition): An insulated cap containing a central terminal with a series (one per cylinder) of terminals that are evenly spaced in a circular pattern around the central terminal. The secondary voltage travels to the central terminal where it is then channeled to one of the outer terminals by the rotor.

Diverter Valve: Part of the air injection system, the diverter valve diverts air from the air pump to the intake manifold or vents excess pressure back into the atmosphere. On 1981 and newer cars, a second diverter valve, usually called an air diverter valve, reroutes the air to either the exhaust manifold or catalytic converter.

Draw (Amperage): The amount of current required to operate an electrical device.

Drive Belt: A V-belt usually constructed of rubber, steel wires, and fabric; it can be used to drive such components as a water pump, alternator, or air conditioning compressor.

Driveline: The propeller or driveshaft, universal joints, etc., that link the transmission output shaft to the axle pinion gear shaft.

Driveshaft: The shaft connecting the transmission output shaft to the differential pinion shaft.

Drop (Voltage): The net difference in electrical pressure when measured on both sides of a resistance.

Dual Breaker Points (Ignition): A distributor using two sets of breaker points to increase the cam angle so that at high engine speeds, sufficient spark will be produced to fire the spark plugs.

Dwell: See Cam Angle.

Dwell-Tachometer: A multi-purpose test instrument. The dwell meter measures in degrees the period in which the breaker points are closed just before each spark plug ignition. The tachometer measures engine speed in revolutions per minute (rpm).

Dynamic Balance: When the centerline of the weight mass of a revolving object is in the same plane as the centerline of the object, that object would be in dynamic balance. For example, the weight mass of the tire must be in the same plane as the centerline of the wheel.

E

Economizer Valve: A fuel flow control device within the carburetor.

Electricity: The flow of electrons from one atom to another.

Electrochemical: Chemical (battery) production of electricity.

Electrode (Spark Plug): The center rod passing through the insulator forms one electrode. The rod welded to the shell forms another. They are referred to as the center and side electrodes.

Electrolyte: A solution of sulfuric acid and water used in the cells of a battery to react chemically with the differing materials in the electrodes and produce an electrical current.

Electromagnet: A magnet produced by placing a coil of wire around a steel or iron bar. When current flows through the coil, the bar becomes magnetized and will remain so as long as the current continues to flow.

Element (Battery): A group of plates. There are six elements for a 12-volt battery. The elements are connected in series.

EMF: Electromotive force (voltage).

Engine Displacement: The volume of the space through which the head of the piston moves in the full length of its stroke, multiplied by the number of cylinders in the engine. The result is given in cubic inches, cubic centimeters, or liters.

Ethylene Glycol: A chemical solution added to the cooling system to protect against freezing.

Evaporative Emissions: Fuel vapor evaporating from the fuel tank vent or carburetor bowl. These emissions are controlled by routing them to the charcoal canister where they are trapped and stored until the engine is started. Then the canister purges its contents into the intake manifold so the fuel vapors can be burned in the engine.

Evaporator: The unit in an air conditioning system used to transform refrigerant from a liquid to a gas. It is at this point that cooling takes place.

Exhaust Gas Recirculation: The process of recirculating a small amount of exhaust gas back into the intake manifold to dilute the incoming fuel mixture so combustion temperatures remain below the point where nitrous oxide formation becomes a problem. The EGR valve regulates the flow of exhaust back into the intake manifold.

Exhaust Manifold: Connecting pipes between the exhaust ports and the exhaust pipe.

F

Fatigue: A breakdown of material through a large amount of flexing or bending. The first signs are cracks, followed shortly by breaks.

Feedback Carburetion: Used in combination with computerized engine control, a fuel mixture control solenoid inside the carburetor constantly regulates the air/fuel mixture to maintain optimum fuel economy and emissions. The feedback carburetor is controlled by the computer, which gets its input from the oxygen sensor in the exhaust manifold. When the oxygen sensor reads rich, the computer tells the carburetor to go lean. When the oxygen sensor reads lean, the computer orders the carburetor to go back to rich. In this way, the overall fuel mixture is balanced and constantly corrected.

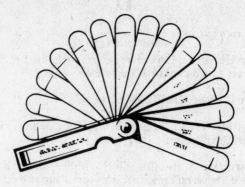

Feeler Gauge: A thin strip of hardened steel ground to an exact thickness that is used to check clearance between parts.

Field (Magnetic Field): The area in which magnetic lines of force occur.

Filament: A resistance in a light bulb that glows and produces light when a current is forced through it.

Filter: A device that is designed to remove foreign substances from oil, air, gasoline, etc.

Firewall: The metal partition between the driver's compartment and the engine compartment.

Firing Order: The order in which the engine's cylinders must be fired—1, 5, 3, 6, 2, 4, etc.

Flaring Tool: A tool that is used to form flare connections on tubing.

Flooding: A condition where the fuel mixture is overly rich or an excessive amount has reached the cylinders. Starting will be difficult and sometimes impossible until the condition is corrected.

Flywheel: A relatively large wheel that is attached to the crankshaft to smooth out the firing impulses. It provides inertia to keep the crankshaft turning smoothly during the periods when no power is being applied. It also forms a base for the starter ring gear and, in many instances, for the clutch assembly.

Flywheel Ring Gear: A gear on the outer circumference of the flywheel. The starter drive gear engages the ring gear and cranks the engine.

Foot-Pound: A measurement of the work involved in lifting 1 pound 1 foot.
   Also, a 1-pound pull 1 foot from the center of an object.

Frame: The assembly of metal structural parts and channel sections that support the engine and the body, and that is supported by the wheels and suspension system.

Free-Play: Looseness in a linkage between the start of application and the actual movement of the device, such as the movement in the steering wheel before the wheels start to turn.

Freeze Plug: Also called a casting plug, core plug, and welch plug. These plugs are inserted into openings left after an engine block is cast.

Freezing: When two parts that are rubbing together heat up and force the lubricant out of the area, they will gall and finally "freeze" or stick together.

Freon-12: A gas used as the cooling medium in air conditioning and refrigeration systems.

Friction: Resistance to slipping or skidding.

Friction Bearing: A bearing made of babbitt, bronze, etc. There are no moving parts and the shaft that rests in the bearing merely rubs against the friction material in the bearing.

Front-Wheel Drive: Refers to a car in which the front wheels are the drive wheels.

Fuel Injection: A fuel system that replaces the carburetor and sprays fuel either directly into the intake ports or into the intake manifold.

Fuel Mixture: A mixture of gasoline and air. An average mixture, by weight, would contain 14.7 parts of air to 1 part of gasoline.

Fuel Pump: A vacuum device, operated either mechanically or electrically, that is used to draw gasoline from the fuel tank and force it into the carburetor.

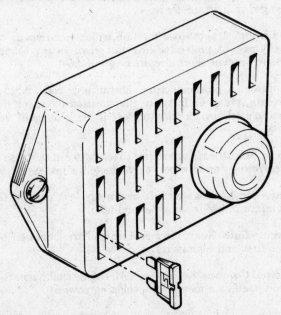

Fuse: A device consisting of a piece of wire with a low melting point inserted in a circuit. It will melt and open the circuit when the system is overloaded.

Fusion: Two metals reaching the melting point and flowing or welding together.

G

Gap: The space or "break" in the continuity of a circuit, such as between ignition contact points.

Gas: A nonsolid material. It can be compressed. When heated, it will expand and when cooled, it will contract.

Gasket: A material placed between two parts to insure proper sealing.

Gasoline: A hydrocarbon fuel used in the internal combustion engine.

Gear Ratio: The relationship between the number of turns made by a driving gear to complete one full turn of the driven gear. If the driving gear turns four times to turn the driven gear once, the gear ratio would be 4 to 1.

Generator: A device that changes mechanical energy into electrical energy.

Ground: A condition where the electrical circuit is connected to the unit frame by means of a strap or rod.

Gum (Fuel System): Oxidized portions of the fuel that form deposits in the fuel system or engine parts.

H

Heat Range (Spark Plugs): Refers to the operating temperature of a given style of plug. Plugs are made to operate at different temperatures, depending on the thickness and length of the porcelain insulator as measured from the sealing ring down to the tip.

Heated Air System: The system that routes warm air from around the exhaust manifold into the air cleaner snorkel during engine warm-up. The system uses a thermostatically controlled vacuum motor to open and close a flap in the air cleaner snorkel. As the engine warms up, warm air is not needed to help fuel vaporization, so the flap closes off the heat riser duct and admits cool air from outside the engine compartment.

Heat Riser: An area surrounding a portion of the intake manifold through which exhaust gases pass to heat the fuel mixture during warm-up.

Helical Gear: A gear that has the teeth cut at an angle to the centerline of the gear.

Hg: The chemical symbol for mercury. Vacuum is measured in inches of mercury.

High-Compression Heads: A cylinder head with a smaller combustion chamber area, thereby raising the compression. The head can be custom built or can be a stock head milled (cut) down.

High-Tension Wire: The high-voltage wire from the ignition coil.

Horsepower: A measurement of the engine's ability to

perform work. One horsepower is defined as the ability to lift 33,000 pounds 1 foot in 1 minute.

Horsepower-Weight Factor: The relationship between the total weight of the car and the horsepower available. By dividing the weight by the horsepower, the number of pounds to be moved by 1 horsepower is determined. This factor has a great effect on acceleration, gas mileage, and all-around performance.

Hot Wire: A wire connected to the battery or to some part of the electrical system in which a direct connection to the battery is present.

Hub (Wheel): The component to which the wheel is bolted.

Hydraulic: Refers to fluid in motion.

Hydraulic Brakes: Brakes that are operated by hydraulic pressure. A master cylinder provides operating pressure that is transmitted by means of steel tubing to wheel cylinders, which in turn apply the brake shoes to the brake drums, or on disc brakes, apply pads to the rotors.

Hydraulic Lifter: A valve lifter that uses hydraulic pressure from the engine's oiling system to keep it in constant contact with both the camshaft and the valve stem. They automatically adjust to any variation in valve stem length.

Hydraulics: The science of liquid in motion.

Hydrocarbon: A mixture of hydrogen and carbon. Gasoline is a hydrocarbon (HC).

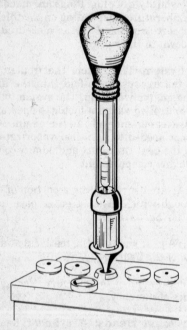

Hydrometer: An instrument with a float housed in a glass tube that measures specific gravity of a liquid.

I

Idle Speed: The normal slow speed of an engine with the throttle closed.

Ignition: The igniting of the fuel mixture by means of a spark in a gasoline engine. This is accomplished by the heat of compression in a diesel engine.

Ignition Coil: See Coil.

Impact Wrench: An air or electrically driven wrench that tightens or loosens nuts, cap screws, etc., with a series of sharp, rapid blows.

Impeller: A wheel-like device with fins. It spins to pump water, move gases, or slightly compress air, etc.

Independent Suspension: A suspension system that allows each wheel to move up and down without undue influence on the other wheels.

Induction: The imparting of electricity from one object to another not connected to it by the influence of magnetic fields.

In-Line Engine: An engine in which all the cylinders are arranged in a straight row.

Insulation: A substance through which electrons do not readily pass. A protective covering on wires or electrical parts to prevent short circuits or grounds.

Insulator: A nonconducting substance or body, such as porcelain, glass, or Bakelite, that is used for insulating wires in electrical circuits to prevent the leakage of electricity.

Intake Manifold: Connecting tubes between the base of the carburetor and the port openings to the intake valves.

Intake Stroke: That part of a piston's cycle that draws the fuel mixture into the engine's cylinder.

Intermediate Gear: Any gear in the transmission between first and high gears.

Internal Combustion Engine: An engine that burns fuel within itself as a means of developing power.

J

Jet: A small hole or orifice used to control the flow of gasoline in the various parts of the carburetor.

Jumper Cables: A pair of insulated heavy cables with

spring clamps on each end. The cables are used to jump-start a battery with a weak charge by means of a battery that is fully charged.

K

Kilometer (km): A unit of metric measurement that is equal to 0.62 mile.

Knocking (Fuel): A condition, accompanied by an audible noise, that occurs when the gasoline in the cylinders burns too quickly. This is also referred to as detonation.

Knurl: A roughened surface caused by a sharp wheel that displaces metal outward as its sharp edges push into the metal surface.

L

Laminated: Something made up of many layers.

Leaf Spring: A suspension spring made up of several pieces of flat spring steel. Varying numbers of leaves (individual pieces) or leaf thicknesses are used, depending on the intended use.

Lever: A rigid bar or beam capable of turning about one point called a fulcrum.

Limited-Slip Differential: A differential unit designed to provide superior traction by transferring driving torque, when one wheel is spinning, to the wheel that is not slipping.

Linkage: A system of links and levers connected together to transmit motion or force.

Live Axle: An axle on which the wheels are firmly affixed. The axle drives the wheels.

Live Wire: See Hot Wire.

Load Range: A system of letters on tires to indicate a specific tire load and inflation limit.

Long and Short Arm Suspension: A suspension system using an upper and lower control arm. The upper arm is shorter than the lower. This is done so as to allow the wheel to deflect in a vertical direction with a minimum change in camber.

Longitudinal Leaf Spring: A leaf spring that is mounted so that it is parallel to the length of the car.

Low Brake Pedal: A condition where the brake pedal approaches too close to the floorboard before actuating the brake.

Low Pivot Swing Axle: A rear axle arrangement that attaches the differential housing to the frame by means of a pivot mount. A conventional type of housing and axle extend from the differential to one wheel. The other side of the differential is connected to the other driving wheel by a housing and axle that is pivoted at a point in line with the differential to frame pivot point.

Lubricant: Any material, usually of a petroleum nature such as grease or oil, that is placed between two moving parts in an effort to reduce friction.

M

Magnet (Permanent): A piece of magnetized steel that will attract all ferrous material. The permanent magnet does not need electricity to function and will retain its magnetism over a period of years.

Manifold: A pipe that connects multiple cylinders to one inlet or outlet.

Manifold Heat Control Valve: A valve placed in the exhaust manifold, or in the exhaust pipe, that deflects a certain amount of hot gas around the base of the carburetor to aid in warm-up.

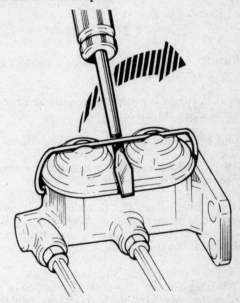

Master Cylinder: That part of the hydraulic brake system in which pressure is generated.

Mechanical Brakes: Service brakes that are actuated by a mechanical linkage connecting the brakes to the brake pedal.

Metering Rod: A movable rod used to vary the opening area through a carburetor jet.

Metric Size: Units made to metric system measurements.

Micrometer: A precision measuring tool that will give readings accurate to within a fraction of 0.0001 inch.

Millimeter: A metric measurement equivalent to 0.039370 inch.

Motor: An electromagnetic device used to convert electrical energy into mechanical energy.

MPH: Miles per hour.

Muffler: A component through which exhaust gases are passed to quiet the sounds of the operating engine.

Multiple Disc Clutch: A clutch that uses several clutch discs in its construction.

Multi-Viscosity Oils: Oils meeting SAE requirements for both the low temperature requirements of a light oil and the high temperature requirements of a heavy oil; for example, SAE 10W-30.

N

Negative Terminal: That terminal, such as that on the battery, from which the current flows on its path to the positive terminal.

Neoprene: A synthetic rubber that is highly resistant to petroleum products.

Nonferrous Metals: All metals containing no iron.

O

Octane Rating: A rating that indicates a specific gasoline's ability to resist detonation.

Odometer: A device that is used to measure and register the number of miles traveled by a car.

Ohm: A unit of measurement of electrical resistance.

Ohmmeter: An instrument used to measure the amount of resistance in a given unit or circuit.

Ohm's Law: A law of electricity that states the relationship between voltage, amperes, and resistance. It takes a pressure of 1 volt to force 1 ampere of current through 1 ohm of resistance. Equation: Volts = amperes × ohms (E = 1 × R).

Oil Bath Air Cleaner: An air cleaner that utilizes a pool of oil to insure the removal of impurities from air entering the carburetor.

Oil Filter: A device used to strain the oil in the engine, thus removing abrasive particles.

Oil—"ML" (Motor Light): Engine oil designed for light-duty service under favorable conditions.

Oil—"MM" (Motor Medium): Engine oil designed for moderate-duty service with occasional high speeds.

Oil—"MS" (Motor Severe): Engine oil designed for high-speed, heavy-duty operation. Also for a great deal of stop-and-go driving.

Oil Pump: The device used to force oil, under pressure, to various parts of the engine. It is driven by a gear on the camshaft.

Oil Pumping: A condition wherein an excessive quantity of oil passes the piston rings and is consumed in the combustion chamber.

Oil Seal: A device used to prevent oil leakage past a certain area.

Oscillation: A rapid back-and-forth movement of a gauge.

Overdrive: A unit using a planetary gear set so actuated as to turn the driveshaft about ⅓ faster than the transmission output shaft.

Overrunning Clutch: A clutch mechanism that will drive in one direction only. If driving torque is removed or reversed, the clutch slips.

Overrunning Clutch Starter Drive: A starter drive that is mechanically engaged. When the engine starts, the overrunning clutch operates until the drive is disengaged.

Oversteer: The tendency for a car, when negotiating a corner, to turn more sharply than the driver intends.

Oxides of Nitrogen (NOx): Air pollutants formed when combustion temperatures exceed 2500°, causing nitrogen and oxygen to combine. NOx emissions are reduced by the exhaust gas recirculation system, and by the catalytic converter on 1981 and newer vehicles.

Oxygen Sensor: A sensor in the exhaust manifold that reacts to changes in the oxygen content of the exhaust gases. This information is used by the engine control computer to determine the relative richness or leanness of the fuel mixture so changes can be made to maintain a balanced fuel mixture. The oxygen sensor produces a voltage that increases as the amount of oxygen in the exhaust decreases.

P

Pan: The cover that is bolted to the bottom of the crankcase to hold the engine.

Parallel Circuit: An electrical circuit with two or more more resistance units so wired as to permit current to flow through both units at the same time. Unlike the series circuit, the current in the parallel circuit does not have to pass through one unit to reach the other.

Parallelogram Steering Linkage: A steering system utilizing two short tie-rods connected to the steering arms and to a long center link. The link is supported on one end on an idler arm and the other end is attached directly to the Pitman arm. The arrangement forms a parallelogram shape.

Parking Brake: A foot- or hand-operated brake that prevents the car from moving by locking the rear wheels or the transmission output shaft.

Pawl: A stud or pin that can be moved or pivoted into engagement with teeth cut on another part; for example, the parking pawl on the automatic transmission that can be slid into contact with teeth on another part to lock the rear wheels.

PCV: Positive crankcase ventilation.

Peen: To flatten out the end of a rivet, etc., by pounding with the round end of a hammerhead.

Penetrating Oil: A special oil that is used to free rusted parts so that they can be removed.

Phillips-Head Screw: A screw having a fairly deep cross slot instead of the single slot as used in conventional screws.

Pinging: A metallic rattling sound produced by the engine during heavy acceleration when the ignition timing is too far advanced for the grade of fuel being burned.

Pinion Carrier: That part of the rear axle assembly that supports and contains the pinion gear shaft.

Piston: A round plug, open at one end, that slides up and down in an engine cylinder. It is attached to the connecting rod and when the fuel mixture is fired, the piston will transfer the force of the explosion to the connecting rod and then on to the crankshaft.

Piston Head: That portion of the piston above the top ring.

Piston Pin or Wrist Pin: A steel pin that is passed through the piston. It is used as a base upon which to fasten the upper end of the connecting rod. It is round and is usually hollow.

Piston Ring: A split ring installed in a groove in the piston. The ring contacts the sides of the ring groove and also rubs against the cylinder wall, thus sealing the space between the piston and the wall.

Also, a ring designed to seal the burning fuel charge above the piston. Generally, there are two compression rings per piston and they are located in the two top ring grooves.

Also, a piston ring designed to scrape oil from the cylinder wall. The ring is of such a design as to allow the oil to pass through the ring and then through holes or slots in the groove. In this way, the oil is returned to the pan. There are many shapes and special designs used on oil control rings.

Piston Ring Side Clearance: The space between the sides of the ring and the ring lands.

Pitman Arm: A short lever arm splined to the steering gear cross shaft. The Pitman arm transmits the steering force from the cross shaft to the steering linkage system.

Plates (Battery): Thin sections of lead peroxide or porous lead. There are two kinds of plates—positive and negative. The plates are arranged in groups called elements in an alternate fashion. They are completely submerged in the electrolyte.

Play: Movement between two parts.

Plies: The layers of rubber-impregnated fabric that make up the body of a tire.

Plug Gapping: Adjusting the side electrode on a spark plug to provide the proper air gap between it and the center electrode.

Polarity: The quality or condition inherent in a body that exhibits opposite properties or powers in opposite parts or directions.

Poles: The positive and negative terminals in a cell or battery.

Positive Terminal: The terminal at which electrons enter a battery or a generator.

Power Steering: A steering system that uses hydraulic pressure to decrease the driver's turning effort. The pressure is utilized either in the gearbox itself or in a hydraulic cylinder attached to the steering linkage.

Preheating: The application of some heat prior to the later application of more heat.

Preignition: The ignition of the fuel mixture before the spark plug fires.

Preload: The amount of load imposed on a bearing before actual loads are imposed. It is accomplished with an adjusting nut such as the spindle nut on front wheel bearings.

Pressure Bleeder: A device that forces brake fluid, under pressure, into the master cylinder so that by opening the bleeder screws at the wheel cylinders, all air will be removed from the brake system.

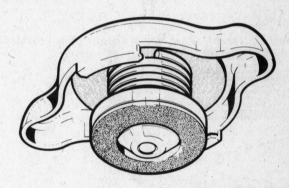

Pressure Cap: A special cap for the radiator. It holds a predetermined amount of pressure on the water in the cooling system. This enables the water to run hotter without boiling.

Pressure Relief Valve: A valve designed to open at a specific pressure. This will prevent pressures in the system from exceeding certain limits.

Primary: The inducing current to the coil windings or capacitor that is the source of the secondary high-tension voltage in an ignition system.

Primary Circuit (Ignition Switch): The low-voltage part of the ignition system.

Primary, Forward, or Leading Brake Shoe: The brake shoe that is installed facing the front of the car. It will be a self-energizing shoe.

Primary Wires: The wiring that serves the low-voltage part of the ignition system.

Progressive Linkage: Carburetor linkage that is designed to open the throttle valves of multiple carburetors. It opens one to start with and when a certain opening point is reached, it will start to open the others.

Propane Enrichment: A special technique of adding propane to the carburetor through a vacuum hose to adjust the idle mixture. This is a technique used by professional mechanics on late model cars with very lean fuel calibration.

Propeller Shaft: The shaft connecting the transmission output shaft to the differential pinion shaft.

PSI: Pounds per square inch.

Pull: The tendency of a car to pull to the right or left.

Pulsation Damper: A device used to smooth out the pulsations or surges of fuel from the fuel pump to the carburetor.

Pumping the Gas Pedal: Forcing the accelerator up and down in an effort to provide extra gasoline to the cylinders.

Pushrod: The rod that connects the valve lifter to one end of the rocker arm. Used on valve-in-head installations.

R

Race: The inner or outer ring in a bearing that provides a contact surface for balls or rollers.

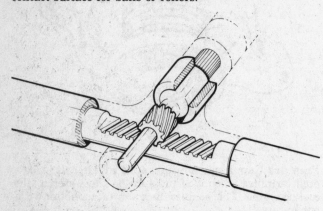

Rack-and-Pinion Gearbox (Steering): A type of steering using a pinion gear on the end of the steering shaft. The pinion engages a long rack (bar with a row of teeth cut along one edge).

Radial: Moving straight out from the center.

Radial Tires: Tires in which the sidewall plies are parallel with each other and at right angles to the centerline of the tread.

Radius: The distance from the center of rotation to the arc, or circumference, of the circle made by the rotation.

Rear Axle: The drive element or shaft between the differential side gear and the wheel.

Rebound: An expansion of a suspension spring after it has been compressed as the result of jounce.

Red Line: Top recommended engine rpm. If a tachometer is used, it will have a mark, or red line, indicating maximum rpm.

Refrigerant: The liquid that is used in refrigeration systems to remove heat from the evaporator coils and carry it to the condenser.

Regulator: A device that is used to control voltage and current output.

Relay: An electromagnetic switching device using low current to open or close a high-current circuit.

Resistance: That property of an electrical circuit that tends to prevent or reduce the flow of current.

Resistor: A device installed in an electrical circuit to permit a predetermined current to flow with a given voltage applied.

Resistor Spark Plug: A spark plug containing a resistor designed to shorten both the capacitive and inductive phases of the spark. This will suppress radio interference and lengthen electrode life.

Resonator: A mufflerlike device that is placed into the exhaust system near the end of the tailpipe. It is used to provide additional silencing of the exhaust.

Retainer: A device to hold parts together.

Retard (Ignition Timing): To set the ignition timing so that a spark occurs later or less degrees before TDC.

Reverse Flush: Cleaning the cooling system by pumping a powerful cleaning agent through the system in a direction opposite to that of normal flow.

Reverse Idler Gear: A gear used in the transmission to produce a reverse rotation of the transmission output shaft.

Riding the Clutch: Riding the clutch refers to the driver resting his foot on the clutch pedal while the car is being driven.

Ring Gear: The large gear that is attached to the differential carrier.

Ring Grooves: The grooves cut into the piston to accept the rings.

Ring Job: Reconditioning the cylinders and installing new rings.

Rivet: A metal pin that is used to hold two objects together. One end of the pin has a head and the other end must be "set" or peened over.

Rocker Arm: An arm that is used to direct the upward motion of the pushrod into a downward or opening motion of the valve stem. Used in overhead valve installations.

Rocker Arm Shaft: The shaft upon which the rocker arms are mounted.

Rocker Panel: That section of the car body between the front and rear fenders and beneath the doors.

Roller Clutch: A clutch using a series of rollers placed in ramps that will provide drive power in one direction but will slip or "free-wheel" in the other direction.

Roller Tappets or Lifters: Valve lifters that have a roller placed on the end contacting the camshaft. This is done to reduce friction between the lobe and lifter. They are generally used when special camshafts and high-tension valve springs have been installed.

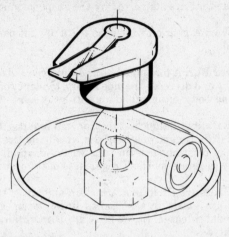

Rotor (Distributor): A caplike component placed on the end of the distributor shaft. It is in constant contact with the distributor cap central terminal and as it turns, it will conduct the secondary voltage to one of the cap's outer terminals.

RPM: Revolutions per minute.

Run-Out (Radial): Out of roundness of a wheel or other circular part.

Rustproofing: A pasty or tarlike material sprayed or injected inside body panels to prevent rust.

S

SAE: Society of Automotive Engineers.

Safety Factor: Providing strength beyond that needed, as an extra margin of insurance against part failure.

Safety Hub: A device that is installed on the rear axle to prevent the wheels leaving the car in the event of a broken axle.

Safety Valve: A valve designed to open and relieve the pressure within a container when container pressure exceeds a predetermined level.

Scale (Cooling System): The accumulation of rust and minerals within the cooling system.

Score: A scratch or groove on a finished surface.

Screw Extractor: A device used to remove broken bolts and screws from holes.

Scuffing: Sliding a tire on the road surface.

Sealed-Beam Headlight: A headlight lamp in which the

lens, reflector, and filament are fused together to form a single unit.

Sealed Bearing: A bearing that has been lubricated at the factory and then sealed. It cannot be lubricated during service.

Secondary Circuit (Ignition System): The high-voltage part of the ignition system.

Secondary, Reverse, or Trailing Brake Shoe: The brake shoe that is installed facing the rear of the car.

Self-Energizing Brake Shoe: A brake shoe (sometimes both shoes) that when applied develops a wedging action that actually assists or boosts the braking force applied by the wheel cylinder.

Series Circuit: A circuit with two or more resistance units so wired that the current must pass through one unit before reaching the other.

Servo Action: Brakes so constructed as to have one end of the primary shoe bearing against the end of the secondary shoe. When the brakes are applied, the primary shoe attempts to move in the direction of the rotating drum and in so doing applies force to the secondary shoe. This servo action makes less brake pedal pressure necessary and is widely used in brake construction.

Shackle: A swinging support by which one end of a leaf spring is attached to the car frame.

Shift Point: This refers to the point, either in engine rpm or road speed, at which the transmission should be shifted to the next gear.

Shim: A spacer to adjust and maintain the distance between two parts.

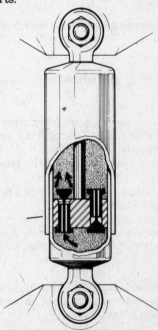

Shock Absorber: A hydraulic device to dampen or stabilize the up and down movement of the car frame by controlling the compression and rebound of the springs.

Short Circuit: A direct grounding of a circuit.

Single-Barrel, Double-Barrel, and Four-Barrel Carburetors: This refers to the number of throttle openings or barrels from the carburetor to the intake manifold.

Skid: A tire sliding on the road surface.

Slip Joint: A joint that will transfer driving torque from one shaft to another while allowing longitudinal movement between the two shafts.

Sludge: Black, mushy deposits throughout the interior of the engine. Caused by a mixture of dust, oil, and water being whipped together by the moving parts.

Solenoid: A tubular coil containing a magnetic core when the coil is energized; an electromagnetic switch.

Spark: The bridging or "jumping" of a gap between two electrodes by a current of electricity.

Spark Advance: Causing the spark plug to fire earlier by altering the position of the distributor breaker points in relation to the distributor shaft.

Spark Gap: The space between the tips of the side and center electrodes on a spark plug.

Spark Plug: A device containing two electrodes across which electricity jumps to produce a spark to fire the fuel charge.

Specific Gravity: The ratio of the weight of any volume of a liquid compared to an equal volume of water.

Speedometer: The instrument used to determine the speed of a car in miles per hour or kilometers per hour.

Spider Gears: Small gears mounted on a shaft pinned to the differential case. They mesh with and drive the axle and gears.

Spindle: A shaft or pin around which another part rotates.

Spiral Bevel Gear: A ring-and-pinion arrangement widely used in car differentials. The teeth of both the ring and the pinion are tapered and are cut on a spiral so that they are at an angle to the centerline of the pinion shaft.

Splines: Sized grooves on a shaft and in a hole that match to prevent torque slippage.

Split Manifold: An exhaust manifold that has a baffle placed near its center. An exhaust pipe leads out of each half.

Spring: An elastic device that yields under stress or pressure but returns to its original state or position when the stress or pressure is removed.

Spring Booster: A device used to strengthen up sagged springs or to increase the load capacity of standard springs.

Spring-Loaded: A device held in place or under pressure by a spring or springs.

Spring Steel: A heat-treated steel having the ability to stand a great amount of deflection and yet return to its original shape or position.

Sprung Weight: This refers to the weight of all the parts of the car that are supported by the suspension system.

Spur Gear: A gear on which the teeth are cut parallel to the shaft.

Stabilizer Bar: A torsional bar and linkage used to eliminate sway and decrease the side rolling tendency of the car frame and body, often called an anti-sway bar.

Static Balance: Balance at rest, or still balance. It is the equal distribution of weight of the wheel and tire around the axis of rotation such that the wheel assembly has no tendency to rotate by itself regardless of its position.

Static Pressure (Brakes): A certain amount of pressure that always exists in the brakes lines—even with the brake pedal released. Static pressure is maintained by a check valve.

Steering Arms: Arms that are either bolted to or forged as an integral part of the steering knuckles. They transmit the steering force from the tie-rods to the knuckles, thus causing the wheels to pivot.

Steering Gear: A device consisting of a worm and gear sector or cross shaft and roller that transmits the driver's effort with increased leverage to guide the car.

Steering Geometry: A term sometimes used to describe the various angles assumed by the components making up the front wheel turning arrangement, camber, caster, toe-in, etc.

Also used to describe the relating angles assumed by the front wheels when the car is negotiating a curve.

Steering Knuckle: The inner portion of the spindle that is affixed to and pivots on upper and lower ball joints.

Steering Linkage: That system of links, rods or tubes, and arms or levers connected together to transmit the force or motion of the steering gear to the front wheels.

Stick Shift: This refers to a transmission that is shifted manually through the use of various forms of linkage.

Stroke: The distance the piston moves when traveling from TDC to BDC.

Stud: A metal rod with threads on both ends.

Swing Axle: An independent rear suspension system in which each driving wheel can move up or down independently of the other. The differential unit is bolted to the frame and various forms of linkage are used to mount the wheels. Drive axles utilizing one or more universal joints connect the differential to the drive wheels.

Switch: A device used to open, close, or redirect the current in an electrical circuit.

Synchromesh Transmission: A manual transmission that synchronizes the speeds of gears that are being shifted together. This prevents "gear grinding." Most transmissions use synchromesh on all gears, while some older transmissions have a non-synchronized first gear.

Synchronize: To bring about a timing that will cause two or more events to occur simultaneously—for example, a plug firing when the piston is in the correct position, the speed of two shafts being the same, a valve opening when the piston is in the correct position, etc.

T

Tailpipe: The part of the exhaust system running from the muffler to the rear of a car.

Tandem: One directly in front of the other and working together.

Tap: To cut threads in a hole or the fluted tool used to cut the threads.

Tapered Roller Bearing (Antifriction): A bearing that uses a series of tapered, hardened steel rollers operating between an outer and inner hardened steel race.

TDC: Top dead center.

Terminal: A connecting point in an electric circuit. When referring to the battery, it would indicate the two battery posts.

Terminal Voltage: Voltage that is given off at the battery terminal.

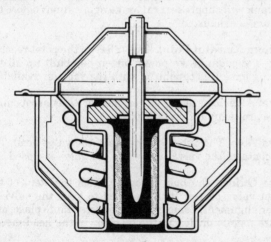

Thermostat: A temperature-sensitive device used in the cooling system to control the flow of coolant in relation to the temperature.

Throttle Body: Part of a single point fuel injection system where the fuel injector is housed. The throttle body resembles a carburetor except that it contains nothing but the injector. There is no float bowl, metering circuits, or venturi. The throttle shafts on the base of the unit give it its name.

Throttle Valve: A butterfly valve in the carburetor that is used to control the amount of fuel mixture that reaches the cylinders.

Thrust Bearing: A bearing designed to resist side pressure.

Thrust Washer: A bronze or a hardened steel washer placed between two moving parts. The washer prevents longitudinal movement and provides a bearing surface for the thrust surfaces of the parts.

Tie-Rods: In the steering system, the rods that link the center link to the steering arms.

Timing Chain: A drive chain that operates the camshaft by engaging sprockets on the camshaft and crankshaft.

Timing Gears: Both the gear attached to the camshaft and the gear on the crankshaft. They provide a means of driving the camshaft.

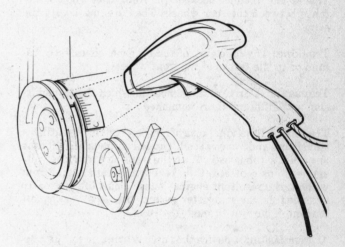

Timing Light: A stroboscope device that is connected to the secondary high-tension circuit to produce flashes of light in unison with the firing of a specific spark plug. By directing these flashes of light onto the whirling timing marks, the marks appear to stand still. By adjusting the distributor, the timing marks may be properly aligned, thus setting the timing.

Timing Marks (Ignition): Marks, usually located on the vibration damper, used to synchronize the ignition system so that the spark plugs will fire at the proper time.

Tire: The casing and tube assembled on a car wheel to provide pneumatically cushioned contact and traction with the road.

Tire Bead: That portion of the tire that bears against the rim flange. The bead has a number of turns of steel wire in it to provide strength.

Tire Casing: The main body of the tire exclusive of the tread.

Tire Rotation: Rearranging the tires on the car to equalize any wear irregularities.

Tire Sidewall: That portion of the tire between the tread and the bead.

Tire Tread: That part of the tire that contacts the road.

Toe-In: The turning in of the front wheels; wheels are closer together at the front than at the back of the wheels.

Torque: Turning or twisting effort measured in foot-pounds or inch-pounds.

Torque Wrench: A special wrench that indicates the amount of torque being applied to a nut or bolt.

Torsional Vibration: A twisting and untwisting action developed in a shaft caused by intermittent applications of power or load.

Torsion Bar Suspension: A suspension system that uses torsion bars in place of the leaf or coil springs.

Track: The distance between the front wheels or the distance between the rear wheels. They are not always the same.

Tracking: The following of the rear wheels directly behind or in the tracks of the front wheels.

Transaxle: A drive arrangement in which the transmission and differential are combined.

Transistor Ignition: Form of ignition system that utilizes transistors and a special coil. The conventional distributor and point setup is used. With the transistor unit, the voltage remains constant, thus permitting high engine rpm without the resultant engine "miss." Point life is greatly extended as the transistor system passes a very small amount of current through the points.

Transmission: A device that uses gearing or torque conversion to effect a change in the ratio between engine rpm and driving wheel rpm. When engine rpm goes up in relation to wheel rpm, more torque but less speed is produced. A reduction in engine rpm in relation to wheel rpm produces a higher road speed but delivers less torque to the driving wheels.

Transmission—Automatic: A transmission that automatically makes gear changes to meet varying road and load conditions. Gear changing is done through a series of oil-operated clutches and bands.

Transmission—Standard or Manual: A transmission that must be shifted manually to effect a change in gearing.

Transverse Leaf Spring: A leaf spring that is mounted so that it is at right angles to the length of the car.

Tune-Up: The process of checking, repairing, and adjusting the carburetor, spark plugs, points, belts, and timing to obtain the maximum performance from the engine.

Turning Radius: Difference in angles between the two front wheels and the car frame during turns. The inner wheel turns out or toes-out more.

U

Undercoating: The material sprayed on the underside of the car, under the hood, trunk lid, etc., to reduce road noise.

Understeer: The tendency of a moving car to maintain a straight-ahead line while the front wheels are being turned in either direction. Commonly known as pushing or plowing.

Unit Body: A car body in which the body itself acts as the frame.

Universal Joint: A flexible joint that will permit changes in the driving angle between the driving and the driven shaft.

V

Vacuum: An enclosed area in which the air pressure is below that of the surrounding atmospheric pressure.

Vacuum Advance (Distributor): A unit designed to advance and retard the ignition timing through the action of engine vacuum working on a diaphragm.

Vacuum Gauge: A gauge used to determine the amount of vacuum existing in a chamber. Vacuum is measured in inches of mercury (Hg).

Vacuum Reservoir: A tank in which a vacuum exists. It is generally used to provide vacuum to a power brake installation in the event engine vacuum cannot be obtained. The tank will supply several brake applications before the vacuum is exhausted.

Vacuum Run-Out Point: This refers to the point reached when a vacuum brake power piston has built up all the braking force it is capable of with the vacuum available.

Valve: A device used to either open or close an opening. There are many different types.

Valve Face: The outer lower edge of the valve head. The face contacts the valve seat when the valve is closed.

Valve Guide: The hole through which the stem of the poppet valve passes. It is designed to keep the valve in proper alignment. Some guides are pressed into place; others are merely drilled in the block or in the head metal.

Valve Lifter or Cam Follower: The unit that contacts the end of the valve stem and the camshaft. The follower rides on the camshaft and when the cam lobes move it upward, it opens the valve.

Valve Oil Seal: A neoprene rubber ring that is placed in a groove in the valve stem to prevent excess oil entering the area between the stem and the guide.

Valve Seat: The area onto which the face of the poppet seats when closed. The two common angles for this seat are 45 and 30 degrees.

Valve Seat Insert: A hardened steel valve seat that may be removed and replaced.

Valve Spring: The coil spring used to close the valves.

Valve Tappet: An adjusting screw to obtain the specified clearance at the end of the valve stem (tappet clearance). The screw may be in the top of the lifter or in the rocker arm. In the case of the ball joint rocker arm, the nut on the mounting stud acts in place of a tappet screw.

Valve Timing: Adjusting the position of the valves so they will open and close at the proper time in relation to piston position.

Valve Train: The various parts making up the valve and its operating mechanism.

Vane: A thin plate that is affixed to a rotatable unit to either throw off air or liquid, or to receive the thrust striking the vane.

Vapor: The gaseous form of a liquid.

Vaporization: Breaking gasoline into fine particles and mixing it with incoming air.

Vapor Lock: Boiling or vaporizing of the fuel in the lines from excess heat. The boiling will interfere with the movement of the fuel, and in some cases, will completely stop the flow.

Vapor Separator: A device used on cars equipped with air conditioning to prevent vapor lock by feeding vapors back to the gas tank by means of a separate line.

Venturi: That part of a tube, channel, or pipe that is tapered to form a smaller or constricted area. A liquid or a gas moving through this constricted area will speed up and as it passes the narrowest point, a partial vacuum will be formed. The taper facing the flow of air is much steeper than the taper facing away from the flow of air. The venturi principle is used in the carburetor.

Vibration Damper: A round weighted device attached to the front of the crankshaft to minimize the torsional vibration.

Viscosity: A measure of an oil's ability to pour.

Viscosity Index: A measure of an oil's ability to resist changes in viscosity when heated.

Volt: A unit of measurement of electrical pressure.

Voltage: The electrical pressure that causes current flow in a circuit.

Voltage Drop: The loss of electrical pressure that is caused by resistance in a circuit.

Voltage Regulator: See Regulator.

Voltmeter: An instrument used to measure the voltage in a given circuit in volts.

Volume: The measurement—in cubic inches, cubic feet, etc.—of the amount of space within a certain object or area.

W

Water Jacket: The area around the cylinder and valves that is left hollow so that water may be admitted for cooling.

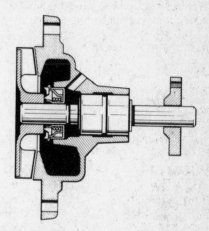

Water Pump: A centrifugal pump with an impeller that is designed to circulate coolant through a water-cooled engine.

Watt: The unit for measuring electrical power or "work." One watt is the product of 1 ampere multiplied by 1 volt (W = A x V).

Wheel Aligner: A device used to check camber, caster, and toe-in.

Wheel Alignment: The mechanics of properly adjusting all the factors of the front and rear wheels so that the car will steer a true course with the least effort, reducing tire wear to a minimum.

Wheel Balancer: A machine used to check the wheel and tire assembly for static and dynamic balance.

Wheelbase: The distance between the center of the front wheels and the center of the rear wheels.

Wheel Cylinder: That part of the hydraulic brake system that receives pressure from the master cylinder and, in turn, applies the brake shoes to the drums.

Wheel Lug or Lug Bolt: The bolts used to fasten the wheel to the hub.

Wheel Spindle: The shaft extending from the front steering knuckle about which the front wheel rotates.

Wheel Tramp: Tendency for the wheel to move up and down so it repeatedly bears hard, or tramps, on the pavement. Sometimes called high-speed shimmy.

Worm Gear: Type of gear on the lower end of the steering shaft.

INDEX

A

Accessories, 507-521
    defroster, rear window, 511-512
    flashers, 512-516
    fuses, 512-516
    hood light, 519-520
    light bulbs, 512-516
    radio, 516-517
    speedometer, 518-519
    trunk light, 519-520
    vacuum gauge, 520-521
    windshield washers, 507-510
    windshield wipers, 507-510
Air conditioning, 163-167
    compressor, 12
    compressor clutch, 165
    drive belt, 165
    recharging, 167-168
    sight glass, 165-167
Air filter
    housing, 11, 12: removing, 175
    servicing, 172-175
Air injection system, 236-241
    air pump, 240
    check valve, 240-241
    diverter valve, 240
    maintaining, 240
    problems, 239-240
    pulse air valve, 241
Alternator
    drive belt: replacing, 119-122
    location, 12
    replacing, 125-126
    testing, 122-125
American Motors
    catalytic converter, 346
    electronic ignition testing, 262-265
    ignition breaker points, 253
    ignition coil: secondary resistance, 313
    starter solenoid, 116
American Petroleum Institute, 50

B

Ball joints, 407-411
    checking, 409-411
    function, 407-409
Battery
    cables, 98-99
    capacity test, 102-103
    charging, 103-106
    clamps, 99-100
    cleaning, 97-98
    functions, 93
    hydrometer test, 100-102
    jumper cables, 106-108
    location, 11
    maintenance, 96-100
    maintenance-free, 110-112
    replacing, 109-112
    selecting, 109-112
    testing, 100-103, 262, 265, 270, 275, 277
    water level, 46-48
    winterizing, 69
Body repair, 486-506
    chipping paint, 501
    decals: removing, 506
    dents, 497-499
    faded paint, 502
    masking tape, 487-489
    molding, 502-505
    painting, 492-494
    plastic parts, 499-501
    priming, 491-492
    rusting, 494-497
    sanding, 498-501
    scratches, 497-499
    stickers: removing, 506
    weatherstripping, 502-505
    winterizing, 69, 70
Brakes, 436-472
    bleeding, 464-467
    diagnostic chart, 81
    disc: location, 12; relining, 445-452; repacking bearings, 65-66
    drum: adjusting, 456-460; relining, 452-456; repacking wheel bearings, 60-65
    fluid level, 44-45
    frictional heat, 438-439
    hoses, 467-468
    inspecting: emergency, 32; front, 440-444; pedal, 32; power, 462-464; rear drum, 444-445
    light switch, 470-472
    lines, 467-468
    master cylinder, 437-438: servicing, 460-462
    parking, 469-470
    testing, 439-440
    vacuum booster, 12: inspecting 462-464
Bump stops, 413

C

Cables
    battery, 98-99
    jumper, 106-108
Carburetor
    adjusting, 190-196
    air/fuel mixture, 195-196
    idle solenoid adjustment, 193-195
    idle speed adjustment, 192
    idle speed screw adjustment, 192-195
    location, 12
    replacing, 202-204
Catalytic converter
    checking, 241
    function, 345-346
    location, 11, 12
    replacing, 359
    servicing, 357-359
Centrifugal advance, 289-291
Charging system, 117-126
    alternator: replacing, 125-126; testing, 122-125